SECOND EDITION

Using Drupal

Angela Byron, Addison Berry, and Bruno De Bondt

O'REILLY®

Beijing · Cambridge · Farnham · Köln · Sebastopol · Tokyo

Using Drupal, Second Edition

by Angela Byron, Addison Berry, and Bruno De Bondt

Published by O'Reilly Media, Inc., 1005 Gravenstein Highway North, Sebastopol, CA 95472.

O'Reilly books may be purchased for educational, business, or sales promotional use. Online editions are also available for most titles (*http://my.safaribooksonline.com*). For more information, contact our corporate/institutional sales department: 800-998-9938 or *corporate@oreilly.com*.

Editors: Julie Steele and Meghan Blanchette	**Indexer:** John Bickelhaupt
Production Editor: Kristen Borg	**Cover Designer:** Karen Montgomery
Proofreader: Rachel Monaghan	**Interior Designer:** David Futato
	Illustrator: Robert Romano

December 2008:   First Edition.
April 2012:   Second Edition.

Revision History for the First Edition:
   2012-04-09   First release
See *http://oreilly.com/catalog/errata.csp?isbn=9781449390525* for release details.

ISBN: 978-1-449-39052-5

[LSI]

1333994938

Table of Contents

Foreword

Drupal's modular architecture and open source nature make it a popular PHP application framework and content management system for hundreds of thousands of web developers around the world. More than 900 people contributed code and ideas to the Drupal 7 release, and even more are responsible for developing and maintaining more than 15,000 contributed modules that can be used to extend Drupal's functionality.

The size, passion, and velocity of the Drupal community, combined with Drupal's strength as a platform, allow incredible things to happen. Every day, new modules are contributed and existing modules are improved upon. Whether these modules are created to catch up with the latest trends on the Web or to invent completely new paradigms, the Drupal project continues to expand in many different directions.

The beauty of all these modules is that they empower website builders to assemble rich and powerful websites quickly and easily without having to be a programmer. Millions of people are using Drupal to build personal blogs, corporate websites, intranets, online photo galleries, job posting boards, conference websites, and more.

Unfortunately, the challenge for many of these site administrators, and even seasoned Drupal developers, is to try to make sense of all these modules and the ever-expanding Drupal universe. What modules should you use to build a newspaper website? What modules should you use to build an intranet? What modules are best avoided because they are being deprecated by better ones? What modules can be used on really big websites that serve millions of pages a day? Navigating your way through the Drupal world can be daunting.

This book cuts out a lot of the research time and helps you dive headfirst into Drupal. It does an excellent job of explaining how to rapidly assemble a wide variety of websites with some of Drupal's most commonly used modules. Whether you're new to building websites or an experienced programmer, this book is full of useful information. Just as I did in the first edition, I promise that by the end of this book, you'll be much more prepared to build the Drupal site of your dreams.

—Dries Buytaert
Drupal founder and project lead
March 2012

Preface

Audience

Who is this book written for?

- If your lead developer can't seem to shut up about this weird "Drupal" thing, and you want to figure out what on earth she's talking about, this book is for you.
- If your boss has approached you and said, "We need to build a site that has X, and fast!" and "X" is a photo gallery, a product reviews section, an ecommerce store, or any of the other projects covered herein, this book is for you.
- If you know your way around Drupal, but have found yourself paralyzed by the sheer volume of contributed modules, and need help figuring out which ones are worth looking at, this book is for you.
- If you consider yourself well versed in Drupal already, but want to broaden your horizons by learning about some useful modules that you may not have encountered yet, and learn best practices for building powerful Drupal websites, this book is for you.
- If you've been building Drupal sites for a while in Drupal 6, but are new to Drupal 7 and want to find out what's new and different, this book is for you.

If you're completely new to creating websites and installing web-based scripts, this book probably *isn't* for you, yet. We assume that goofy acronyms like PHP, FTP, URL, ZIP, and HTML are in your working vocabulary. Likewise, if you're interested in hardcore, nitty-gritty details about Drupal's API functions, this book *isn't* for you: our focus here is on pointy-clicky stuff: combining *existing* modules to build out functionality, rather than creating new ones.

If you're one of the rest of us, who fall somewhere between total newbie and computer science professor, we hope that this book provides you with an invaluable reference to building practical websites with Drupal.

Assumptions This Book Makes

You'll need access to a computer or server running PHP 5.2 or higher, along with a web server (Apache preferred) and database (MySQL recommended). For local development, there are several all-in-one Apache/MySQL/PHP packages available such as WAMP for Windows (*http://www.wampserver.com*) or MAMP for Macs (*http://www.mamp.info*). Visit *http://drupal.org/hosting* for a list of Drupal-friendly web hosting companies (with referrals benefiting the Drupal Association (*https://association.drupal.org/*)), and visit *http://drupal.org/requirements* to read more about Drupal's system requirements.

You will also need to install Drupal, and the hands-on chapters assume that you're using the book's source code. Appendix A provides some basic instructions, but if you run into trouble or want to read more detailed instructions, see the Drupal installation guide (*http://drupal.org/documentation/install*). If you are not using the source code provided with the book, Appendix C contains a list of all of the modules and themes that are used for each chapter so you can re-create them.

A Note About the Modules Used in This Book

Drupal is constantly moving and its community-contributed module world is constantly shifting. The source code for the book provides the versions that the chapters were written with, and as time moves on, the versions available on Drupal.org will most likely change. Sometimes changes don't dramatically affect how things work, but other times they do. For many chapters, the hands-on sections will apply for a very long time or change so little that they will still be quite easy to follow. But even if the user interface for a module changes dramatically a year down the road, after using this book and walking through various examples, you should be equipped to explore the new functionality on your own. In addition to the specific hands-on "recipes," you will also learn tips and best practices for how to "cook" generally—that is, how to learn about modules on your own.

Also keep in mind that the Spotlight sections, which discuss module features and comparing modules, along with Appendix B, which discusses how to evaluate modules, provide a good foundation for you to make these evaluations on your own. You can do your own comparisons as newer modules come out and make the best decisions for your use. This book is intended to not only be a guide but also a springboard for your own mastery of the Drupal contributed project world.

 If you are just starting out with Drupal, we *highly recommend* sticking with the book's source code, which will always match the book's text and screenshots. Once you've made it through the book's examples, upgrading to the latest code of the day will then just be a matter of negotiating some minor differences/enhancements around what you already know.

Contents of This Book

Beyond the initial chapter that sets the stage, this book is organized as a series of recipes, each of which consists of the following structure:

Introduction

> The introduction gives an overview of what modules are covered, as well as the overall goal of the chapter.

Case study

> The case study describes the needs of a fictitious client who requires a website that can track events, have product reviews, or sell T-shirts. We describe some background information about these clients, and go into more detail about their specific requirements.

Implementation notes

> Here we discuss various solutions within Drupal to solve the client's requirements, and go into detail about which modules we've selected and why. This section compares and contrasts modules and explains when it's appropriate to use module A or why module B is a dead end.

Spotlight

> Each chapter introduces one or more major modules or Drupal concepts, and the Spotlight sections provide a "bird's-eye view" of what each specializes in and how it works. Think of this section as a miniature "product sheet" that highlights features of a given module and what it can do. If you're not interested in a pointy-clicky tutorial but instead want to get an idea of the power and flexibility of Drupal's top contributed modules, scanning the Spotlight sections should provide what you need.

Hands-on

> After describing what a module can do in the general case, the hands-on sections will show you how to configure them by providing step-by-step "recipes" to build out the precise functionality the client requires. If you're new to Drupal, following these sections will show you exactly how the concepts work in practice, and allow you to build several real Drupal sites yourself.

Taking it further

> This section of each chapter provides pointers to other helpful add-on modules that you can introduce to a particular use case to enhance its functionality and make it even more powerful. If you're extra keen, try experimenting with these modules to make the book's example projects even better!

Summary

> This section wraps up what we've learned over the course of the chapter, and provides links to the modules used, and other resources that offer more information.

Here is a list of the book's chapters and the material covered. The first three chapters are considered "required reading" if you haven't used Drupal before. The rest of the chapters will assume knowledge of these chapters, including the basics of Drupal and the Views and Field modules. If you're familiar with Drupal 6 but haven't yet used Drupal 7, you may also want to skim these chapters, as the user interface and feature set has changed significantly between versions.

Chapter 1, *Drupal Overview*
> This chapter answers the main "need to know" questions about Drupal: what's Drupal, who's using it, why are they using it, and how does it conceptually work? It also provides some historical context to Drupal, introduces essential terminology, and covers everything else you need to get up to speed.

Chapter 2, *Drupal Jumpstart*
> The first hands-on chapter hits the ground running, and will show you how to use Drupal's core functionality, as well as a few contributed modules, in order to build a basic business website. By the end of this chapter, you should feel comfortable with Drupal's core functionality and navigating the administrative section.

Chapter 3, *Job Posting Board*
> This chapter introduces the Field and Views modules by walking through the construction of a job-posting website. You will also learn to extend core's Field module with additional contributed modules. By the end of this chapter, you'll understand how to create custom content types and add form fields, as well as how to click together lists of any type of website content, which are the basis of all the other chapters in the book.

Chapter 4, *Media Management*
> This chapter helps you build a family photo gallery using core's Image module along with several contributed media modules.

Chapter 5, *Product Reviews*
> In this chapter, you will build a community product review website, with the Amazon module providing the product data, and the Voting API and Fivestar modules providing a rating widget.

Chapter 6, *Event Management*
> This chapter's all about how to do event management in Drupal, featuring the Date and Calendar modules for storing and displaying event information, and the Flag module for keeping track of who's coming.

Chapter 7, *Managing Publishing Workflows*
> This chapter talks all about implementing custom publishing workflows with the Workbench module, and uses core's Taxonomy as well as Pathauto to organize our content.

Chapter 8, *Multilingual Sites*

    This chapter describes how to build a multilingual site using the Locale and Content Translation modules and the Internationalization (i18n) suite of modules.

Chapter 9, *Online Store*

    In this chapter, you'll use the powerful Drupal Commerce package to build a T-shirt store that includes such features as a product catalog, shopping cart, and payment processing.

Appendix A, *Installing and Upgrading Drupal*

    If you're new to Drupal, this appendix will get you up to speed on how to install it, as well as how to do upgrades down the road.

Appendix B, *Choosing the Right Modules*

    Evaluating modules is often the biggest hurdle to building a Drupal site. This appendix is a breakdown of strategies and tips for figuring out which module will work for your needs.

Appendix C, *Modules and Themes Used in This Book*

    This appendix lists the modules and themes used in each chapter, for easy reference.

Appendix D, *Major Changes Between Drupal 6 and 7*

    This appendix covers the big changes that happened between Drupal 6 and 7. It lists new features, existing features that were modified, as well as a few gotchas and functionality that has been removed from core in Drupal 7.

Conventions Used in This Book

The following typographical conventions are used in this book:

Italic

    Indicates filenames, directories, new terms, URLs, and emphasized text.

`Constant width`

    Indicates parts of code, contents of files, commands, and output from commands.

    This icon signifies a tip, suggestion, or general note.

    This icon indicates a warning or caution.

Any navigation around Drupal pages is displayed as follows:

Structure→Content types (*admin/structure/types*)

This is an instruction to click the Structure link in the administrative toolbar, then click the Content types link. As a shortcut, you can also enter the path indicated in parentheses into your browser—*http://www.example.com/admin/structure/types* or *http://www.example.com/#overlay=admin/structure/types*—to view the page in the administrative overlay.

Using Code Examples

This book is here to help you get your job done. In general, you may use the code in this book in your programs and documentation.

All Drupal code, including the Drupal 7 code that you can access through the O'Reilly website (as described shortly) is subject to the GNU General Public License, version 2. Your use of Drupal code, including copying, modification, and distribution, is subject to the license. "Drupal" is a registered trademark of the founder of the Drupal project, Dries Buytaert. Information about permitted uses of the code and the trademark can be found at the Drupal website (*http://drupal.org*), where you can also find information about how the GNU General Public License affects your use of the code. More information about the license is available at *http://www.gnu.org/licenses/old-licenses/gpl-2.0 .html#SEC3*.

With respect to other code examples in this book, you do not need to contact us for permission unless you're reproducing a significant portion of the non-Drupal code. For example, writing a program that uses several chunks does not require permission. Selling or distributing a CD-ROM of examples from O'Reilly books does require permission. Answering a question by citing this book and quoting example code does not require permission. Incorporating a significant amount of example code from this book into your product's documentation does require permission.

We appreciate, but do not require, attribution. An attribution usually includes the title, author, publisher, and ISBN. For example: "*Using Drupal* by Angela Byron, Addison Berry, and Bruno De Bondt. Copyright 2012 Angela Byron, Addison Berry, and O'Reilly Media, Inc., 978-1-449-39052-5."

If you think that your use of code examples falls outside fair use or the permission given above, feel free to contact us at *permissions@oreilly.com*.

Downloading the Book's Source Code

This book's website contains a link to a downloadable copy of Drupal 7, along with all of the modules covered in the book, and the themes used in the example websites for each hands-on chapter, at *http://usingdrupal.com/source_code*.

Each hands-on chapter also has an "installation profile" (a set of starter scripts that configure default options) that bootstraps a starter site for each hands-on chapter with some basic preconfiguration. These installation profiles may be selected at the beginning of the Drupal installation process; for example, *Chapter 3: Job posting board*.

Switching between one chapter's hands-on examples and another's requires making a new site while using the same source code. You can do so with minimal fuss using the following steps:

1. Create a new database for the chapter's installation of Drupal.
2. Change the permissions on *sites/default/settings.php* so that the file is writable.
3. Copy *sites/default/default.settings.php* to *sites/default/settings.php*, overwriting the existing *settings.php* file.
4. Rerun the installation at *http://www.example.com/install.php*.

More information on how to install Drupal is available in Appendix A.

In addition to configuring some basic settings such as the site name, the theme, and so on, for each chapter, the installation profiles (with the exception of Chapter 2) also set up the following users:

username: *admin*, password: *oreilly*
> The first user, who is in the "site administrator" role; can do everything on the site

username: *editor*, password: *oreilly*
> A user in the "editor" role; used for chapters that require users with elevated permissions

username: *user*, password: *oreilly*
> A normal user in only the "authenticated user" role

It is these users the chapters refer to when the instructions reference logging in as the "editor" user, or similar. Unless otherwise specified, it is assumed that steps are completed as the "admin" user.

Safari® Books Online

Safari Books Online is an on-demand digital library that lets you easily search over 7,500 technology and creative reference books and videos to find the answers you need quickly.

With a subscription, you can read any page and watch any video from our library online. Read books on your cell phone and mobile devices. Access new titles before they are available for print, and get exclusive access to manuscripts in development and post feedback for the authors. Copy and paste code samples, organize your favorites, download chapters, bookmark key sections, create notes, print out pages, and benefit from tons of other time-saving features.

O'Reilly Media has uploaded this book to the Safari Books Online service. To have full digital access to this book and others on similar topics from O'Reilly and other publishers, sign up for free at *http://my.safaribooksonline.com*.

How to Contact Us

Please address comments and questions concerning this book to the publisher:

O'Reilly Media, Inc.
1005 Gravenstein Highway North
Sebastopol, CA 95472
800-998-9938 (in the United States or Canada)
707-829-0515 (international or local)
707-829-0104 (fax)

We have a web page for this book, where we list errata, examples, and any additional information. You can access this page at:

http://oreil.ly/using-drupal-2e

To comment or ask technical questions about this book, send email to:

bookquestions@oreilly.com

For more information about our books, courses, conferences, and news, see our website at *http://www.oreilly.com*.

Find us on Facebook: *http://facebook.com/oreilly*

Follow us on Twitter: *http://twitter.com/oreillymedia*

Watch us on YouTube: *http://www.youtube.com/oreillymedia*

Acknowledgments

First, some general kudos. We would like to thank the book's technical reviewers, Ryan LeTulle and Peter MacIntyre. Thanks to Julie Steele and Meghan Blanchette from O'Reilly, who guided us through the process of updating the book as well as being ever patient and helpful. And, of course, thanks to Dries Buytaert for inventing and opensourcing Drupal; without him, none of this would have happened.

Addison Berry would like to thank her parents, Merlin and Joan Berry, for always believing in her and supporting all of her crazy pursuits in life, and Camilla Krag Jensen for being a constant anchor, and being patient with Danish translations, both for the book and daily life. Big thanks also to Lullabot for supporting her Drupal habit.

Angela Byron would like to give tremendous, heartfelt, grovelling thanks to her awesome wife, Marci McKay, for her endless patience and support of Angie's insatiable Drupal addiction. Huge thanks also to her family, particularly Jeanne, Sara, and Keith

Byron, for all of the support both with the book and with life in general. And finally, she would also like to dedicate this book to her father, Mike Byron, who passed away very suddenly in August 2011, leaving behind a legacy of thousands of lives changed. Keep on rockin' in your big yellow Firebird in the sky, Dad.

Bruno De Bondt would like to thank his partner Ariane Khachatourians for love, patience and so many other things—"Home is wherever I'm with you." Also thank you to his parents, family and friends for inspiration and support for all he does, like moving halfway across the world. Big thanks also to the Drupal community for being amazing and building fantastic open source software.

CHAPTER 1

Drupal Overview

This book will show you how to build many different types of websites using the Drupal web publishing platform. Whether you're promoting your rock band or building your company's intranet, some of your needs will be the same. From a foundational perspective, your site will have *content*; be it audio or text or animated GIF images, a website communicates its content to the world. You will also need to *manage* this content. Although it's possible to roll your own system with enough knowledge of the underlying web technologies, Drupal makes creating your website, adding new features, and day-to-day editing of content quick and easy. And finally, your website will have *visitors*, and this book will show you many different ways in which you can engage and interact with your community using Drupal.

This chapter will begin by providing the hard facts about Drupal: what it is, who uses it, and why they chose it. It will then dive into a conceptual overview, starting with what this ambiguous term "content management" actually means, and how we arrived at building websites this way. And finally, we'll define and explain the core Drupal concepts that are necessary to understand how Drupal handles its content.

What Is Drupal?

Drupal is an open source[1] *content management system* (CMS) being used by hundreds of thousands of organizations and individuals to build engaging, content-rich websites. Building a website in Drupal is a matter of combining together various "building blocks," which are described later in this chapter, in order to customize your website's functionality to your precise needs. Once built, a Drupal website can be maintained through the use of online forms, without any code having to be changed manually. Drupal is free to use, and it has an enormous library of constantly evolving tools that you can use to make your website shine.

---

1. For more on the open source software movement, please see *http://opensource.org*—which, incidentally, is also a Drupal site.

Drupal is also a *content management framework* (CMF). In addition to providing site-building tools for webmasters, it offers ways for programmers and developers to customize Drupal using plug-in modules. Almost every aspect of Drupal's behavior can be customized with these modules, and there are thousands of them, adding features from photo galleries to shopping carts to talk-like-a-pirate translators. Many modules have been freely contributed to the Drupal community and are available for download and use on your own Drupal-based website, too. All of the functionality that we'll be discussing in this book is built using a combination of "core" Drupal and these community-created "contrib" modules.

And we would be remiss not to also acknowledge Drupal's *community*; the wetware element of Drupal is often cited as one of Drupal's biggest assets. When Drupal 7 was released in January 2011, nearly 1,000 members of the community contributed code to the core software. Additionally, more than 15,000 developers maintain contributed modules, with countless more helping with testing, documentation, usability, design, accessibility, user support, translations, and other important areas of the project. Those familiar with evaluating open source platforms will attest to the importance of a thriving community base.

Who Uses It?

Over the last few years, the popularity of Drupal has exploded, to the point where some pretty big names have taken notice. Media companies such as Sony BMG Records, Lifetime Television, and Al Jazeera are using Drupal as a means of building loyal communities around their products. Magazines such as *Spin*, *Popular Science*, and *Fast Company* use Drupal to provide interactive online content to their readers. Nonprofits such as Amnesty International, Oxfam, and the Electronic Frontier Foundation use Drupal to coordinate activism on important issues. Ubuntu Linux, Eclipse, and Java are open source projects that employ Drupal to nurture their contributor communities. Bloggers such as Tim Berners-Lee, Heather B. Armstrong (a.k.a., Dooce), and the BlogHer community use Drupal as their publishing platform. Technology companies including Twitter, Symantec, and eBay make use of Drupal to connect with their customers. Many levels of government around the world, including the White House, the United Nations, and the UK government's open data portal, are also using Drupal to provide more transparency and better connect with their citizens.

What these websites have in common is a need for powerful publishing options and rich community features.

The Drupal Showcase (*http://www.drupalshowcase.com*) website, shown in Figure 1-1, highlights some of these and other high-profile Drupal websites. Drupal's own website also has a Drupal case studies section (*http://drupal.org/cases*) containing detailed case studies and success stories. Additionally, Dries Buytaert, the Drupal project founder and project lead, maintains a list of several high-profile Drupal websites on his blog at *http://buytaert.net/tag/drupal-sites*.

Figure 1 1. The Drupal Showcase highlights high-profile sites in multiple industries, categories, and countries

What Features Does Drupal Offer?

Drupal provides a number of features, which are explained in greater detail in Chapter 2. These include:

Flexible module system
> Modules are plug-ins that can modify and add features to a Drupal site. For almost any functional need, chances are good that either an existing module fits the need exactly or can be combined with other modules to fit the need, or that whatever existing code there is can get you a good chunk of the way there.

Customizable theming system
> All output in Drupal is fully customizable, so you can bend the look and feel of your site to your will (or, more precisely, to your designer's will).

Extensible content and entity system
> You can define new types of content (blogs, events, words of the day) on the fly, and even add custom fields for the different content types. Contributed modules can extend this even further by providing new kinds of fields and different ways to manipulate them. Best of all, these fields can also be attached to anything in the system representing itself as an *entity*, such as users, comments, and taxonomy (categories).

Innate search engine optimization
> Drupal offers out-of-the-box support for human-readable system URLs, and all of Drupal's output is standards-compliant; both of these features make for search-engine-friendly websites. There are also other contributed modules that take SEO capabilities even further.

Role-based access permissions
> Custom roles and a plethora of permissions allow for fine-grained control over who can access what within the system. And existing modules can take this level of access control even further—down to the individual user level.

Social publishing and collaboration tools
> Drupal has built-in support for tools such as group blogging, comments, forums, and customized user profiles. The addition of almost any other feature you can imagine—for instance, ratings, user groups, or moderation tools—is only a download away.

A Brief History of Content Management

Before looking any closer at Drupal, let's take a brief trip back in time to the days before content management systems. To understand how Drupal and other CMS packages simplify your work, we'll take a look at how things worked when the Web was young.

A Historical Look at Website Creation

Back in the dim recesses of time (the 1990s, for those who remember zeppelins and Model T cars), web pages were nothing more than simple text files nestled comfortably into folders on a server somewhere on the Internet. With names like *index.html*, *news.html*, *about_us.html*, and so on, these files were viewable by anyone with a web browser. Using HTML (hypertext markup language), these files could link back and forth to each other, include images and other media, and generally make themselves presentable. A *website*, as the hipsters of that day would explain, was just a collection of those files in a particular folder, as pictured in Figure 1-2.

This system worked pretty well, and it made sense. Every URL that a user on the Internet could visit corresponded to a unique *.html* file on the web server. If you wanted to organize your site into sections, you made a folder and moved the files into that folder; for example, *http://www.example.com/news* would be the address to the News section of the site, and the 1997 newsletter would be located at *http://www.example.com/news/ fall_1997_products.html*. When the webmaster (or the intern) needed to fix a problem, he could look at the page in his web browser and open up the matching file on the web server to tweak it.

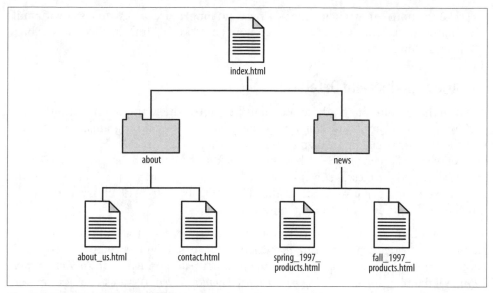

Figure 1-2. A historical look at website structure

Unfortunately, as websites grew in size, it was obvious that this approach didn't scale well. After a year or so of adding pages and shuffling directories around, many webmasters had dozens, hundreds, or sometimes even *thousands* of pages to manage. And that, friends, caused some serious problems:

Changing the site's design required an enormous amount of work
Information formatting, layout, and other site design was done individually on every single page. Cascading style sheets (CSS) hadn't yet taken the web world by storm, so tasks as simple as changing the site's default font required hand-editing (that's right) *every single file.*

The site structure resulted in massive duplication of content
Most designs for websites included a standard footer at the bottom of the page with copyright and contact information, a header image or some kind of recurring navigation menu at the top, and so on. If anything changed, every file had to be updated. If you were very, very lucky, all the webmasters before you had been conscientious about making sure that there were no layout variations, and this would be a scriptable change. Most webmasters weren't lucky, and to this day mutter darkly about sites built using FrontPage, PageMill, Dreamweaver, HotDog Professional, *and* Notepad all at once—depending on who edited the files last.

Websites were impossible to keep consistent and up-to-date
Most complex sites were already organized into directories and subdirectories to keep things reasonably tidy. Adding a news story in the *news* directory meant that you also had to update the "overview" page that listed all news stories, perhaps post a quick notice on the front page of the website, and (horror!) remember to

take the notice down when the news was no longer "fresh." A large site with multiple sections and a fair amount of content could keep a full-time webmaster busy just juggling these updates.

The Age of Scripts and Databases

The search for solutions to these problems prompted the first real revolution in web design: the use of scripts and *common gateway interface* (CGI) programs. The first step was the use of special tags called *server-side includes* (SSI) in each HTML file. These tags let web designers tell the web server to suck in the contents of another file (say, a standard copyright message or a list of the latest news stories) and include it in the current web page as if it were part of the HTML file itself. It made updating those bits much easier, as they were stored in only one place.

The second change was the use of simple databases to store pieces of similar content. All the news stories on CNN (*http://www.cnn.com*) are similar in structure, even if their content differs. The same is true of all the product pages on Apple (*http://www.apple.com*), all the blog entries on Blogger (*http://www.blogger.com*), and so on. Rather than storing each one as a separate HTML file, webmasters used a program running on the web server to look up the content of each article from the database and display it with all the HTML markup for the site's layout wrapped around it. URLs such as *http://www.example.com/news/1997/big_sale.html* were replaced by something more like *http://www.example.com/news.cgi?id=10*. Rather than looking in the *news* directory, then in the *1997* directory, and returning the *big_sale.html* file to a user's web browser, the web server would run the *news.cgi* program, let it retrieve article number 10 from the database, and send back whatever text that program printed out.

All these differences required changes in the way that designers and developers approached the building of websites. But the benefits were more than worth it: dozens or even hundreds of files could be replaced with one or more database-driven scripts, as shown in Figure 1-3.

Even with those improvements, however, there were still serious challenges:

Where do I change that setting again?
> Large sites with many different kinds of content (product information, employee bios, press releases, free downloads, and so on) were still juggling an assortment of scripts, separate databases, and other elements to keep everything running. Webmasters updating content had to figure out whether they needed to change an HTML file, an entry in a database, or the program code of the script.

Too many little pieces were cobbled together
> Dynamic content—such as discussion forums or guestbooks where visitors could interact—required their own infrastructure, and often each of these systems was designed separately. Stitching them together into a unified web experience was no simple task.

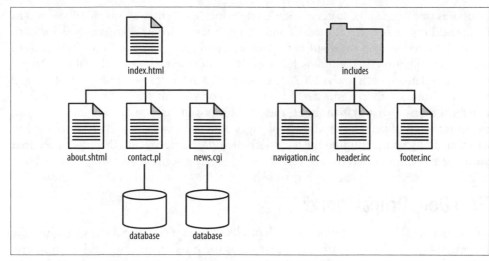

Figure 1-3. The move from individual files to database-driven scripts

The Content Revolution

Slowly but surely, programs emerged to manage these different kinds of content and features using a single, consistent user interface. The older generation of software focused on a particular task or application, but newer CMS implementations offered generalized tools for creating, editing, and organizing the information on a website. Most systems also provided mechanisms for developers to build add-ons and new features without reinventing the wheel. Figure 1-4 illustrates how a content management system uses a single database and script to integrate all of these features.

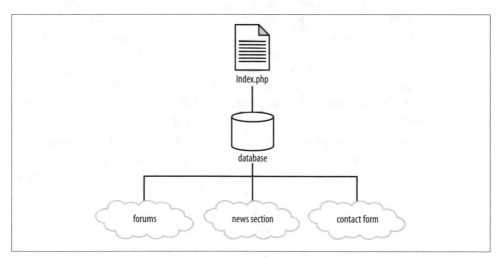

Figure 1-4. The structure of an integrated, database-driven website

Drupal is one of these next-generation content management systems. It allows you to create and organize many kinds of content, provides user management tools for both the maintainers of and the visitors to your site, and gives you access to thousands of third-party plug-ins that add new features. Dries Buytaert, the founder of the Drupal project, said in a speech to the 2007 Open Source CMS Summit that his goal for Drupal was to "eliminate the webmaster." That might sound a bit scary if you *are* the webmaster, but after that first thought, the implications are exciting. Thanks to Drupal, the grunt work of keeping thousands of pages organized and up-to-date vanishes: you can instead focus on building the features that your site needs and the experience that your users want.

How Does Drupal Work?

At a conceptual level, the *Drupal stack* looks like Figure 1-5. Drupal is a sort of middle layer between the backend (the stuff that keeps the Internet ticking) and the frontend (what visitors see in their web browsers).

In the bottom layers, things like your operating system, web server, database, and PHP are running the show. The *operating system* handles the "plumbing" that keeps your website running: low-level tasks such as handling network connections, files, and file permissions. Your *web server* enables that computer to be accessible over the Internet, and serves up the correct stuff when you go to *http://www.example.com*. A database stores, well, *data*—all of the website's content, user accounts, and configuration settings—in a central place for later retrieval. And *PHP* is a programming language that generates pages dynamically and shuffles information from the database to the web server.

Drupal itself is composed of many layers as well. At its lowest layer, it provides additional functionality on top of PHP by adding several subsystems, such as user session handling and authentication, security filtering, and template rendering. This section is built upon by a layer of customizable add-on functionality called modules, which will be discussed in the next section. Modules add features to Drupal and generate the contents of any given page. But before the page is displayed to the user, it's run through the *theme system*, which allows modification and precise tweaking for even the pickiest designers' needs.

The theme system outputs page content, usually as XHTML or HTML5, although other types of rendering are supported. CSS is used to control the layout, colors, and fonts of a given page, and JavaScript is thrown in for dynamic elements, such as collapsible fieldsets on forms and drag-and-drop table rows in Drupal's administrative interface.

We've talked about the "old" way of building websites using static HTML files, the transition to collections of scripts, and the "new" way: full-featured web applications that manage the entire website. This third way—Drupal's way—requires a new set of conceptual building blocks. Every website you build with Drupal will use them!

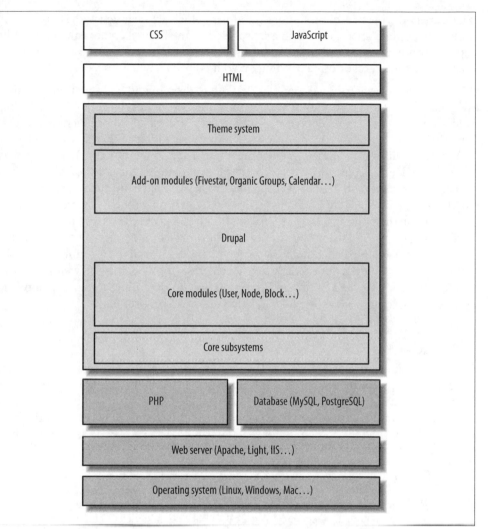

Figure 1-5. How Drupal and its conceptual layers fit with other layers of a website

Modules

Just about everything in Drupal revolves around the concept of *modules*, which are files that contain PHP code and a set of functionalities that Drupal knows how to use. All of the administrative- and end-user-facing functionality in Drupal, from fundamental features such as the ability to log in or create content to dynamic photo galleries and complex voting systems, comes from modules. Some examples of modules are the Contact module, which enables a site-wide contact form, and the User module, which handles user authentication and permission checking. In other CMS applications, modules are also referred to as *plug-ins* or *extensions*.

There are two types of modules: "core" modules, which are included with Drupal itself, and "contributed" modules, which are provided by the Drupal community and can be separately downloaded and enabled. Apart from a few required core modules, all modules can be turned on or off depending on your website's precise needs.

Though there are contributed modules that offer "drop in and go" functionality, over the years the Drupal community has generally focused on modules that do one thing well, in a way that can be combined with other modules. This approach means that you have almost limitless control over what your website looks like and how it behaves. Your image gallery isn't limited by what the original developer thought an image gallery ought to look and act like. You can drop in ratings or comments and sort the pictures by camera type rather than date if you'd like. In order to have this flexibility, however, you have to "build" the functionality in Drupal by snapping together various modules and tweaking their options, rather than just checking off a checkbox for "image gallery" and leaving it at that. Drupal's power brings with it a learning curve not encountered in many other CMS packages, and with the plethora of available modules, it can be daunting trying to determine which to use. The rest of this book—as well as Appendix B, which is dedicated to tips and tricks on how to determine module quality and suitability for your projects—is here to help you solve this problem.

Users

The next building block of a Drupal website is the concept of *users*. On a simple brochure-ware website that will be updated by a single administrator and visited only by potential customers, you might create just a single user account for the administrator. On a community discussion site, you would set up Drupal to allow all of the individuals who use the site to sign up for it and create their own user accounts as well.

 The first user you create when you build a new Drupal site—User 1—is special. Similar to the root user on a UNIX server, User 1 has permission to perform any action on the Drupal site. Because User 1 bypasses these normal safety checks, it's easy to accidentally delete content or otherwise break the site if you use this account for day-to-day editing. It's a good idea to reserve this account for special administrative tasks and configuration, and create an additional account for posting content.

Every additional user can be assigned to configurable *roles*, like "editor," "paying customer," or "VIP." Each role can be given *permissions* to do different things on the website: visiting specific URLs, viewing particular kinds of content, posting comments on existing content, filling out a user profile, even creating more users and controlling their permissions. By default, Drupal comes with two predefined locked roles: *authenticated user* and *anonymous user*. Anyone who creates a user account on the site is automatically assigned the "authenticated user" role, and any visitors who haven't yet created user accounts (or haven't yet logged in with their username and password) have the "anonymous user" role. In addition, Drupal provides a third predefined, but optional, role: *administrator*. Any user given the administrator role will automatically have access to all permissions available on the site.

Content (Nodes)

Nodes are Drupal's next building block, and one of the most important. A critical part of planning any Drupal site is looking at your plans and deciding what specific kinds of content (referred to by Drupal as *content types*) you'll be working with. In almost every case, each content type will be a different kind of node.

All nodes, regardless of the type of content they store, share a handful of basic properties:

- An author (the user on your site who created the content)
- A creation date
- A title
- Body content

Do you want to create a page containing your company's privacy policy? That's a node. Do you want users to be able to post blog entries on the site? Each entry is a node. Will users be posting links to interesting stories elsewhere on the Web? Each of those links is stored as—you guessed it—a node.

In addition to nodes' basic, common properties, all nodes can take advantage of certain built-in Drupal features, like flags that indicate whether they're published or unpublished and settings to control how each type of node is displayed. Permissions to create and edit each type of node can also be assigned to different user roles; for example, users with the "blogger" role could create "Blog entry" nodes, but only "administrator" or "editor" users could create "News" nodes.

 Nodes can also store revision information detailing each change that's been made since they were created. If you make a mistake (deleting an important paragraph of the About Us page, for example), this makes it easy to restore a previous version.

Drupal comes preconfigured with two types of nodes: "Basic page" and "Article." The only differences between those two types of nodes are their default configuration settings. "Basic page" nodes don't display any information about the author or the date on which they were posted. It's well suited to content like "About Us" and "Terms of Service," where the original author is irrelevant. Article nodes do display that information, are set to appear on the front page of the site whenever they're posted, and allow the content creator to add tags and images to the content. The result is a blog-like list of the latest news on the site.

You can use Drupal's content administration tools to create other node types yourself. Many administrators create a "press release" or "announcement" node type to post official announcements, while other contributors can post regular "article" nodes. Plug-in modules can also add new kinds of nodes to Drupal's content system that offer more features. One example (which comes with Drupal) is the Poll module. When users create new Poll nodes, they create a list of poll questions rather than the usual "body" content. Poll nodes, when they're displayed to visitors, appear as voting forms and automatically tally the number of votes for each question.

Additionally, other modules can add to nodes' properties such as comments, ratings, file upload fields, and more. From the control panel, you can specify which types of nodes receive these features. Figure 1-6 illustrates this concept.

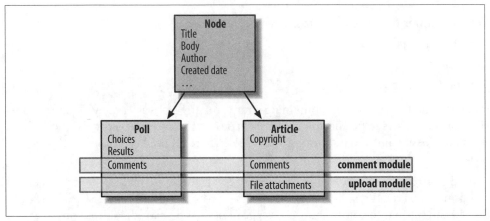

Figure 1-6. All nodes in the system share a basic set of properties; nodes may define additional, specific fields, and modules can add extra features to nodes as well

The idea that new modules add properties and build on top of the node system means that all content in Drupal is built on the same underlying framework, and therein lies one of Drupal's greatest strengths. Features like searching, rating, and comments all become plug-and-play components for any new type of node you may define, because under the hood, Drupal knows how to interface with their base elements—nodes.

Using plug-in modules to add new types of nodes—or to add extra fields to existing node types—is a common task in Drupal. Throughout the book, we'll be covering a handful of the thousands of plug-in modules, and you'll learn how to build complex content types using these basic tools.

Entities and Fields

New in Drupal 7 is the concept of *entities*, an additional layer of abstraction above nodes that spans multiple system components, including comments, users, and files. This abstraction provides the same functionality-reuse capability that nodes provide, but expand them even further because functionality can work across multiple entities, not just on nodes. Examples of entities provided by Drupal core are nodes, comments, users, files, and taxonomy. Contributed modules, such as Drupal Commerce covered in Chapter 9, can also provide their own entity types.

The most common cross-entity feature in Drupal is the *field* system. Entities provide some default data-entry fields—for example, nodes expose a Title and optional Body field; users provide a username and password field—but often sites need to capture additional data beyond the basics. Drupal provides a number of additional field types—text, number, list, image, etc.—that can be added to any entity, or even shared across entities. We'll cover fields in depth in Chapter 3, and work with them in all later chapters as well.

Figure 1-7 illustrates how entities, entity types (also known as *bundles* in programmer-speak), and fields work together to allow Drupal to be highly customized to specific data storage requirements.

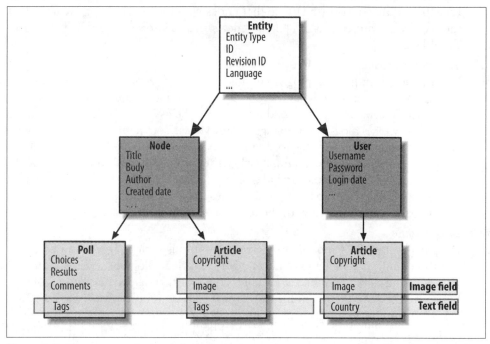

Figure 1-7. Entities are a layer of abstraction above other entity types, and allow features such as fields to be reused across multiple entity types

Ways of Organizing Content

Another important building block is really an entire toolbox of techniques for organizing the content that makes up your site. First-generation websites grouped pages using folders and directories. Second-generation sites used separate scripts to manage and display different kinds of content. Drupal, though, maintains almost everything as a node. How can you break your site up into separate topical sections, user-specific blogs, or some other organizational scheme?

First, each individual node on your site gets its own URL. By default, this URL is something like *http://www.example.com/node/1*. You can turn these URLs into user-friendly paths like *http://www.example.com/about* using Drupal's built-in Path module. For organizational purposes, all of these nodes are treated as a single "pool" of content. Drupal creates every other content page on your site—topical overviews, recent news, and so on—by pulling up lists of nodes that match certain criteria and displaying them in different ways. Here are a few examples:

The front page
> By default, the front page of a Drupal site is a bloglike overview of the 10 most recently posted articles. To build this, Drupal searches the pool of content for nodes with the "Published" flag set to true, and the "Promote to front page" flag set to true. In addition, it sorts the list so that nodes with the "Sticky" flag are always at the top; this feature is useful for hot news or announcements that every user should see.

The Taxonomy module
> We mentioned earlier that plug-in modules can add new pieces of information to nodes, and that's exactly what Taxonomy does. It allows the administrator of a site to set up categories of topics that nodes can be associated with when they're created, as well as blog-style free-tagging keywords. You might use this module to create a predefined set of "Regions" for news stories to be filed under, as well as "Tags" for bloggers to enter manually when they post. The Taxonomy module calls all of these things *terms*, and provides a page for each descriptive term that's used on the site. When a visitor views one of these pages, Drupal pulls up a list of all the nodes that were tagged with the term.

The Blog module
> Drupal's built-in Blog module implements a multiuser blogging system by doing just three things. First, it adds a new node type called "Blog post." Second, it provides a listing page at *http://www.example.com/blog* that displays any nodes of type Blog that also have their "Published" flag set to true. (If a blog post has its "Published to front page" flag set to true, it will show up on the front page as well; Drupal never hides content on one page just because it appears on another.) Third, it provides a custom page for each user on the site that displays only blog posts written by that user. *http://www.example.com/blog/1*, for example, would display all blog post nodes that are published and were written by User 1—the administrator.

Views

For anything fancier than the aforementioned cases, Drupal has an add-on module called Views, which we'll be using in nearly all of the chapters in this book. The Views module is essentially a graphical interface for creating highly customized listings, from sortable product comparison tables to sidebar blocks listing recent content to calendars of events. You'll learn more about the Views module in Chapter 3.

Drupal comes with several other modules that provide different ways of organizing nodes, and you can download hundreds of plug-in modules to organize your site in a variety of ways. The important thing to remember is that almost all "pages" in Drupal are one of two things: a specific piece of content (node), or a list of nodes that share a particular set of properties.

Types of Supporting Content

In addition to content and listings of content, there are also various ways to supplement the content on the page. Two such types of supporting content included with Drupal core are comments and blocks.

Comments are merely responses by a user to a piece of content, and exist only in relation to that content. Users may post comments to add their thoughts to the subject matter within a node, as they often do when a particularly controversial subject comes up on a blog entry or forum topic. Like nodes, comments are entities that can be expanded with fields or other contributed modules to add features such as ratings.

Blocks are content "chunks" that fit into regions on the page such as the sidebars, footers, and headers of a Drupal site. They're generally used to display helpful links or dynamic lists such as "Most popular content" or "Latest comments" and similar items. While nodes take center stage displaying content, blocks help give a single piece of content some context in the structure of your site.

Many times, blocks will display different content depending on which user is currently logged in: a "Comments by your buddies" block, for example, might display a list of posts by users that the current visitor has added to her Buddies list. Each user who logs in will see a different list. Additionally, blocks may be configured to show up only on certain pages, or to be hidden only on certain pages.

Getting Help

It's easy to focus only on the functionality you get for free with an open source application. But it would be a mistake to forget that the Drupal community itself is another vital building block for your website!

As you go through the hands-on examples in this book, you might run into some issues particular to your installation. Or, you might encounter issues as new versions of modules are released. Fortunately, the Drupal community has a wealth of resources available to help you troubleshoot even the nastiest error you might encounter:

- The Drupal Community Documentation (*http://drupal.org/documentation*) contains information on everything from community philosophies to nitty-gritty Drupal development information.

- The Getting Started Guide (*http://drupal.org/getting-started*) contains some particularly useful information to help get you through your first couple of hours with Drupal.

- The Troubleshooting FAQ (*http://drupal.org/Troubleshooting-FAQ*) has useful tips and tricks for deciphering error messages that you might encounter.

- For more one-on-one help, try the Support forums (*http://drupal.org/forum/18*) or the Drupal Answers website (*http://drupal.stackexchange.com/*) for everything from preinstallation questions to upgrade issues.

- If your question is about a specific module, you can post a "support request" issue (or a "bug report" if it's a blatant problem) to the module's issue queue (*http://drupal.org/project/issues*), which reaches the module's maintainer(s). A helpful video on how to maneuver around the Drupal.org issue queues is available from *http://drupal.org/node/273658*, and issue queues are also discussed in Appendix B.

- There's also a #drupal-support IRC channel on *irc.freenode.net* if you're more of the chatty type.

> Other IRC channels you might want to join include #drupal, for general Drupal chit-chat, and #drupal-contribute, if you're interested in participating in the community or you want to keep an eye on what's coming down the pipe (note that #drupal-contribute is *not* a support channel!). There are also numerous topical channels for everything from specific modules to general areas of Drupal like usability or design. For a list of all Drupal IRC channels, see *http://drupal.org/irc*.
>
> IRC is not only an invaluable tool for getting your problems solved, but it's also one of the best ways to get to know the people behind the project. While issue queues are normally "strictly business," IRC is not only where important stuff happens, but also where you learn about key contributors' pet cats, and their cats' video game collections.

- Finally, there are local Drupal user groups all over the world, which often hold monthly meetups and larger regional events called "camps" where you can meet real humans who understand that "Drupal" is not some kind of medical condition or a nondairy topping. It's a great way to get to know members of the community firsthand, and learn all sorts of new things about Drupal! Check *groups.drupal.org* to find a group near you.

Note that when asking for help, it's always best to do as much research as you can first, and then politely ask direct, to-the-point questions. "Foo module is giving me the error 'Invalid input' when I attempt to submit 'Steve' in the name field. I tried searching for existing solutions, and found an issue at *http://drupal.org/node/1234* filed about it, but the solution there didn't fix it for me. Could anyone give me some pointers?" will get far better, faster, and more meaningful responses than, "Why doesn't Foo module work? You developers are useless!" or "How can I build a website with Drupal?" And oftentimes, you'll find that during the process of typing out your question in enough detail for someone else to answer it, you come up with the solution yourself! For other tips on getting useful help in an open source community, see *http://catb.org/esr/faqs/smart-questions.html*.

Conclusion

In this chapter, you've learned what Drupal is. You have traced the history of websites and content management to better understand the challenges inherent in keeping a growing site healthy. We've examined the conceptual building blocks that Drupal uses when building next-generation sites, as well as how they fit together. We've also covered numerous ways to get help if you're stuck. In the following chapter, you'll put these pieces together by creating your very first Drupal website!

CHAPTER 2

Drupal Jumpstart

This chapter, intended for readers who are new to Drupal, provides a tour of its capabilities, as well as definitions for its sometimes obscure terminology. We'll demonstrate how Drupal can be used "out of the box" to build a simple website. Readers who are familiar with Drupal already may still want to skim this chapter, as later chapters will assume knowledge of all content covered here. By the end, you'll understand how to perform administrative tasks in Drupal, such as configuring modules, working with content types, and setting up site navigation.

This chapter assumes that you already have Drupal up and running. For assistance, check out Appendix A, as well as the helpful online Getting Started guide at *http:// drupal.org/getting-started*.

This chapter introduces the following modules:

Node (core)
Allows you to post content and create your own content types

Comment (core)
Allows users to create replies to node content

User (core)
Allows users to log in, and provides Drupal's robust roles and permissions systems

Block (core)
Adds dynamic sidebars and other supplementary content

Menu (core)
Handles management of a Drupal website's navigation

Path (core)
Allows entry of friendly URLs such as *http://www.example.com/about* rather than *http://www.example.com/node/1*

Module Filter (http://drupal.org/project/module_filter)
Allows administrators to quickly filter the list of modules by keyword

Contact (core)
A simple form that site visitors may use to send inquiries to website owners

The completed website will look as pictured in Figure 2-1 and at *http://jumpstart.using drupal.com.*

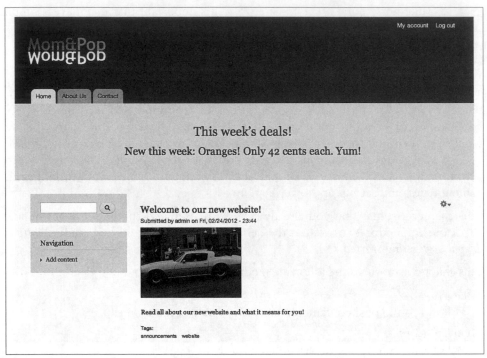

Figure 2-1. The completed Mom and Pop, Inc., website

Case Study

Mom and Pop, Inc. is a small organic grocery store in the midwestern United States run by its co-owners, Jeanne and Mike. Its current web presence is a long, endlessly scrolling, static HTML page that lists general information such as the background of the company, its hours and location, and what promotions are currently running.

Neither Mike nor Jeanne is comfortable with code, so in order to update the web page content each week they currently pay their next-door neighbor, Goldie, to hand-edit the page. Because this sort of manual labor is tedious, it usually takes a long time for Goldie to get around to doing it. As a result, the site is frequently out of date and not doing much other than costing Mike and Jeanne money to keep it online.

Mike and Jeanne would like to have a new, fresh site that they can manage themselves by filling out web forms rather than editing code. They need some static pages, such as a Home and an About page, and a contact form to receive inquiries from customers.

Mike and Jeanne also would like a place to post announcements, where they can showcase weekly deals, in-store events, or general goings-on in the community. Visitors to the site should be able to comment on these announcements, with anonymous visitors' comments going into an approval queue first.

Neither Mike nor Jeanne is very technical, so it's important that they have a simple administration panel. And finally, the site should have some basic branding—site logo and colors—so that the site "feels" like their own.

Goldie's been hearing a lot about this "Drupal" thing lately, so she decides to give it a shot for this project.

Implementation Notes

The Implementation Notes section of each chapter will discuss, compare, and contrast various options for fulfilling the client's needs in Drupal, and explain how we decided on the specific solutions chosen for each chapter.

All of the functionality required by Mom and Pop, Inc., is provided by the bundle of features that comes as part of the main Drupal software download, called "Drupal core" or just "Drupal." Drupal's Node module has the built-in ability to create various types of content on the site, including static pages, which work great for the Home and About pages. We'll use the core Path module to give these pages nice and descriptive URLs such as *http://www.example.com/about*.

Drupal also provides a robust roles and permissions system, which we can use to separate Goldie's tasks (website maintenance) from Mike and Jeanne's tasks (managing the daily website content) and from the customers on the site (who can do only things such as leave comments). There are also administrative tools, such as the Dashboard and Shortcut modules, that can help Goldie provide a specifically tailored administrative interface for Mike and Jeanne.

Drupal also comes with a module called Contact, which can be used to build a simple contact form for any website. Different categories may be set up, and each one can optionally send mail to a different email address. This feature is useful for sites with different support personnel in different departments, for example.

And finally, the announcements section, as we will see, can be handled using just the default Article content type that ships with Drupal.

Spotlight: Drupal's Administration Interface

Unlike some other content management systems, which have a totally separate back-end administration tool from the front-facing website, in Drupal the website itself and the administration tools to manage it are integrated together. In building out your site, you will frequently pop in and out of the administration section by clicking "edit" on a piece of content, or "configure" on a particular part of the page.

Figures 2-2 and 2-3 illustrate what Drupal looks like out of the box, as well as the various ways to enter the administration section and pointers on how the administrative interface works.

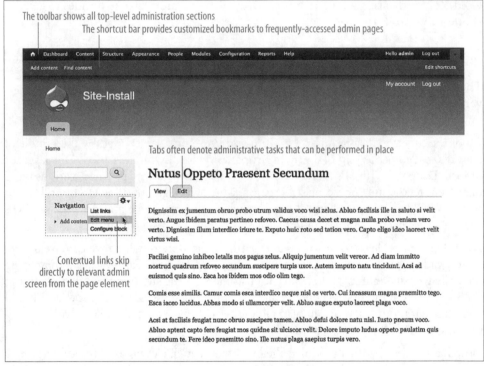

Figure 2-2. Different methods of navigating to the administration section

 If you're inheriting a Drupal site created by someone else, your administration screens may not look identical, or even very close. Everything in Drupal is very modular, flexible, and customizable, and that includes its administration tools. The screenshots here demonstrate what Drupal 7 provides out of the box through a combination of Dashboard, Toolbar, Shortcut, Overlay, and Contextual Links modules, as well as the Seven administration theme. We'll talk a lot more about modules and themes later in the chapter.

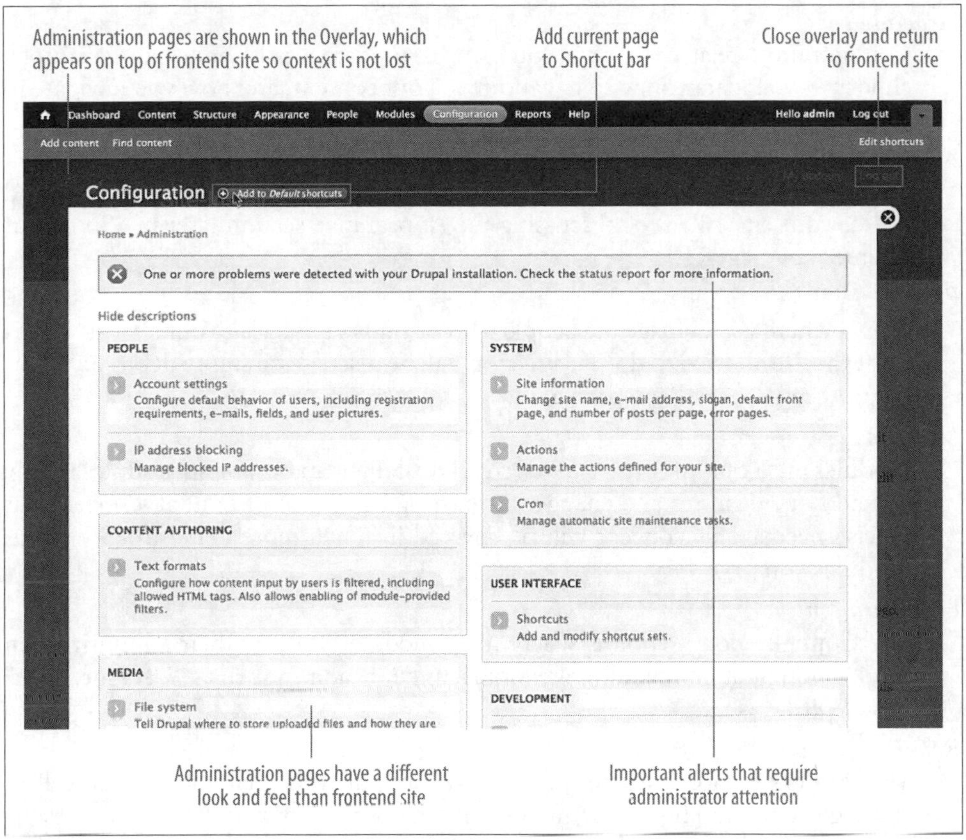

Figure 2-3. A diagram of Drupal's administration section

The administrative interface of Drupal is split into the following sections, visible in the toolbar along the top of the screen:

Dashboard

> While initially quite sparse, the Dashboard allows you to set up a custom administrative landing page for your content editors, a "one-stop shop" for all of the things they need to know, such as the recent users who've registered to the site, or comments that are awaiting approval.

Content

> Creating, editing, and deleting content and comments can be done from the Content administration link. You can also manage workflow information, such as whether or not the content is published, or whether comments awaiting moderation are approved.

Structure

Configuration related to how your site is fundamentally built—for example, choosing what data you wish to capture in your content, and how you navigate to that content—is housed in the Structure section.

Appearance

This menu allows you to choose and configure *themes*, which control the look and feel of your site. We'll be discussing the Appearance section later in "Spotlight: Themes" on page 71.

People

This is where you manage the people who administer and visit your site, as well as what they're allowed to do. This section will be discussed in more depth in "Spotlight: Access Control" on page 53.

Modules

Modules are a central construct in Drupal. Installing and enabling modules is how you add new features and change the existing behaviour of Drupal to meet your precise needs. This concept will be covered in much more detail in "Spotlight: Modules" on page 44.

Configuration

The Configuration section is where most modules will put their administration links. Configuration links are categorized under headings such as "User interface" and "Web services."

Reports

The Reports section is useful for both keeping up with maintenance as well as gaining insight into how your audience interacts with your site.

- The *Status* report offers a quick glimpse of your site's overall health and will warn you of configuration problems.

- The *Recent log entries* report allows you to monitor site activity as it happens; errors, user activity, content notifications, and more will appear here.

- The *Available updates* report will show whether your modules and themes are out of date, and also allows you to install updates from within the user interface.

- A variety of "Top" reports (e.g., *Top 'access denied' errors*, *Top search phrases*) will show you where your users are running into the most errors, what your users are searching for the most, and—if you're running the core Statistics module—the most popular content on your site.

Help

The Help section contains some basic instructions to help you get started, as well as a help page for each module you have installed. These pages provide a general overview of what the module does, as well as some specific uses and how to perform them. This is a great section to visit the first time you install something new to get a feel for how it works.

Once you know your way around Drupal a bit, the "Administration menu" (*http://drupal.org/project/admin_menu*) module can speed up your navigation through the administrative panel; it turns the top-level links into drop-downs that contain all of the subitems, so you can get to many places in just a single click.

Hands-On: Changing Administrative Settings

You'll spend a *lot* of time in Drupal's administration panel while building out your sites, so let's walk through a simple example of configuring your site: changing Drupal's "site name" in the upper-left corner to reflect the customer for whom the site is being built.

1. In the administrative toolbar, click Configuration. The Overlay will appear, indicating that you're currently in an administrative context.
2. Under System, choose the "Site information" link (*admin/config/system/site-information*). This page contains some overall settings for your site, many of which were established during installation.
3. Change the "Site name" value from whatever it currently is to "Mom and Pop, Inc."
4. Click "Save configuration" to save your settings, then click the X in the upper-right corner to close the Overlay and return to your site's frontend.
5. The site name in the upper-left corner should now read "Mom and Pop, Inc.," as pictured in Figure 2-4.

Figure 2-4. Newly customized site name

Another useful setting on this page is "Default front page," which allows you to customize which path Drupal will load when you click the Home link or site logo.

Spotlight: Content Management

Drupal's primary function is to enable users such as Mike and Jeanne to manage their own content. This section offers a tour of some of the most basic tools for content management in Drupal.

Content

As discussed in Chapter 1, each piece of content in Drupal, from a static page to a blog entry or a poll, is called a *node*. Drupal comes with two content types by default: "Basic page," intended for static content such as an About Us page, and "Article," intended for time-sensitive content such as press releases. But, like most things in Drupal, content types are fully configurable. Figure 2-5 shows the "Create content" page on a typical Drupal site with several content types available. This page is found under "Add content" (*node/add*) in either the Navigation block or the default Shortcut menu.

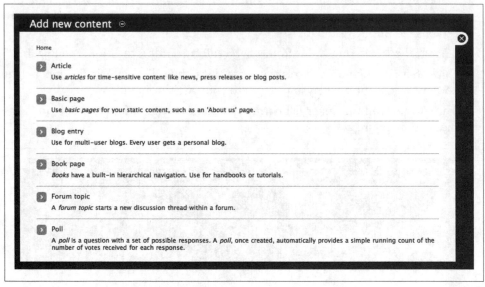

Figure 2-5. A list of available content types

Figure 2-6 shows an example of a typical node form, which is used to add or edit a piece of content. Each node has a Title field, which identifies the node in content listings and controls the title of the web page when viewed, and most nodes also have a Body field, which holds its primary content. Additional fields of varying types—for example, text, numeric, or file upload fields—may also be added to a basic node form for more granular data entry. The next chapter covers extending the fields on the node form in depth.

At the bottom of the node form fields is a set of more advanced options, enclosed in a set of vertical tabs. These tabs display the current value of each setting, and you can click them to make adjustments. Although the extensive options at the bottom of this form may seem daunting, don't worry. A general site visitor won't have permissions to change Menu settings, Authoring information, or most other settings, so the tabs simply do not show up on the form for these users.

Title *

The title shows up in lists and affects the web page title.

Summary (Hide summary)

Here is the "summary" content. This is a short blurb that appears in content listings, RSS feeds, etc. Typically, this is worded in a way that encourages the reader to click into the full body.

Leave blank to use trimmed value of full text as the summary.

Body

Here is the full body, which contains the "meat" of the content. This can be as long as you want!

Text format Filtered HTML ▾   More information about text formats ⓘ

- Web page addresses and e-mail addresses turn into links automatically.
- Allowed HTML tags: <a> <em> <strong> <cite> <blockquote> <code> <ul> <ol> <li> <dl> <dt> <dd>
- Lines and paragraphs break automatically.

Menu settings Not in menu	☑ Create new revision
Revision information New revision	**Revision log message**
URL path settings No alias	Vertical tabs show advanced settings, most of which are only visible to administrative users.
Comment settings Closed	
Authoring information By admin	Provide an explanation of the changes you are making. This will help other authors understand your motivations.
Publishing options Published	

   Save   Preview

Figure 2-6. A typical node form in Drupal

 People coming to Drupal with web development experience with a tool such as Dreamweaver often get confused by Drupal's notion of a "page." Web development tools often refer to the contents of an entire browser window from the logo in the upper-left corner down to the copyright notice in the lower-right as a "page," but in Drupal creating a new "Basic page" node affects only the *content* of a given web page: its title, its body, and any additional properties such as a byline or rating.

The Body field on a node can optionally provide a *summary*, which is a short blurb that entices people to read further. Summaries are displayed in most content listings, in RSS feeds, and in other places. When a summary is provided, the text in the Body field is displayed only when a user is looking at a piece of content directly.

The "Text format" of the Body field, and other rich-text fields, is an important setting. Text formats limit the characters that can be entered into a given field, and configuring them incorrectly can have a significant impact on the security of your site. We'll use the default (secure) settings for this chapter in the interest of brevity, but Chapter 4 has all the gory details on more permissive text format configuration.

Nodes can have a variety of options applied to them, including the ability to track and revert revisions, the ability to turn on commenting on the content type, and the ability to default to Unpublished so new nodes are not immediately visible on the site. You may set these options on a per-node basis, or specify the defaults for all nodes of this type in the administration section for content types at Structure→"Content types" (*admin/structure/types*) in the administrative toolbar and pictured in Figure 2-7.

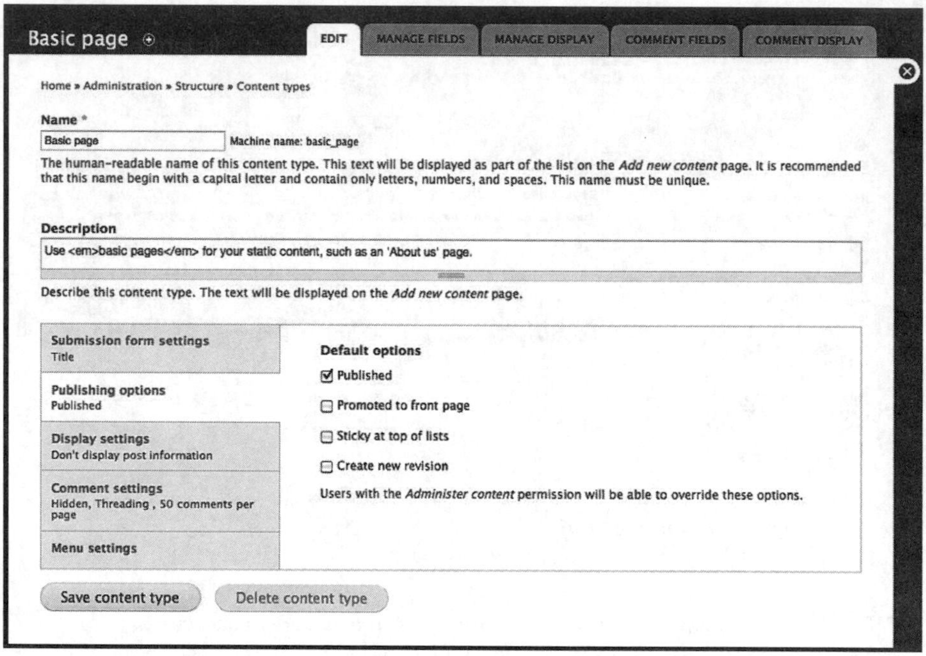

Figure 2-7. The content type administration form

 When default options for content types are switched, these settings are *not* retroactively applied to content that's already been created. It pays to spend some time thinking about what settings you'd like on each content type before you begin creating lots of content on your site.

Nodes that have the "Promoted to front page" publishing option checked appear on the default front page listing, available via the path *http://www.example.com/node*, as pictured in Figure 2-8. Nodes are displayed one after another, with "Sticky at top of lists" nodes on top, and the rest of the list ordered chronologically starting with the most recent.

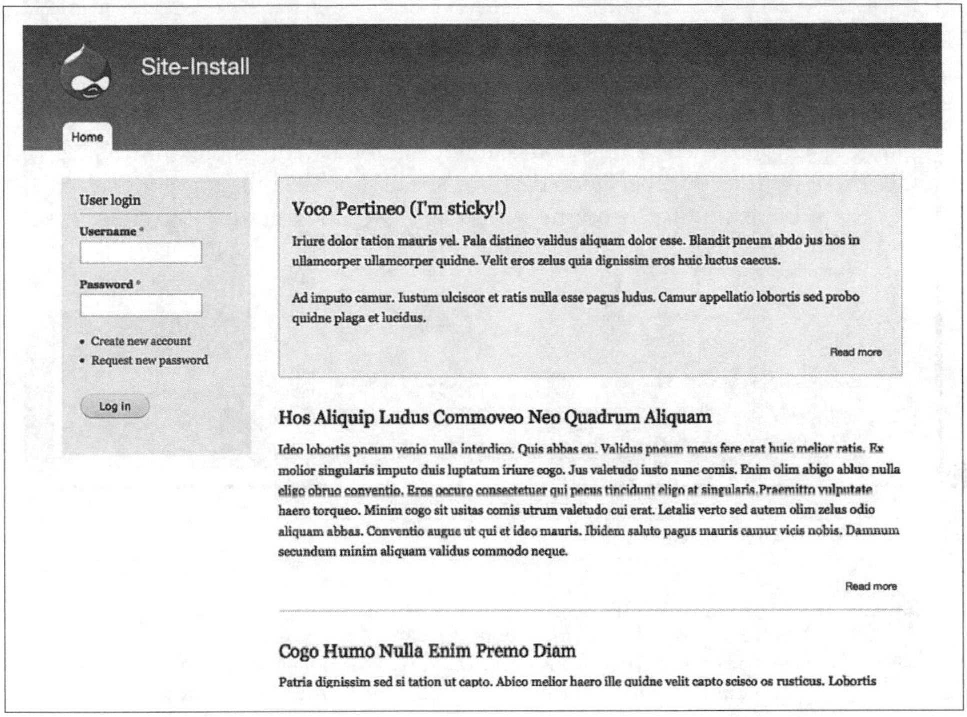

Figure 2-8. The default front page view

"Front page" is a bit of a misnomer; the listing at */node* is the front page only by default; you can change the home page to whatever page you'd like under the Configuration→System→"Site information" page (*admin/ config/system/site-information*), covered in the previous hands-on section.

Although this default view of content is very basic, you can create almost any type of content listing imaginable with the Views module (*http:// drupal.org/project/views*), discussed in depth in Chapter 3 and used extensively throughout the rest of the book.

You can make changes to content workflow once it's created on the node itself, by editing it directly, or in bulk by going to the administrative toolbar and clicking the Content (*admin/content*) link, pictured in Figure 2-9. Here, content may be deleted, published, or unpublished, or have various workflow options set.

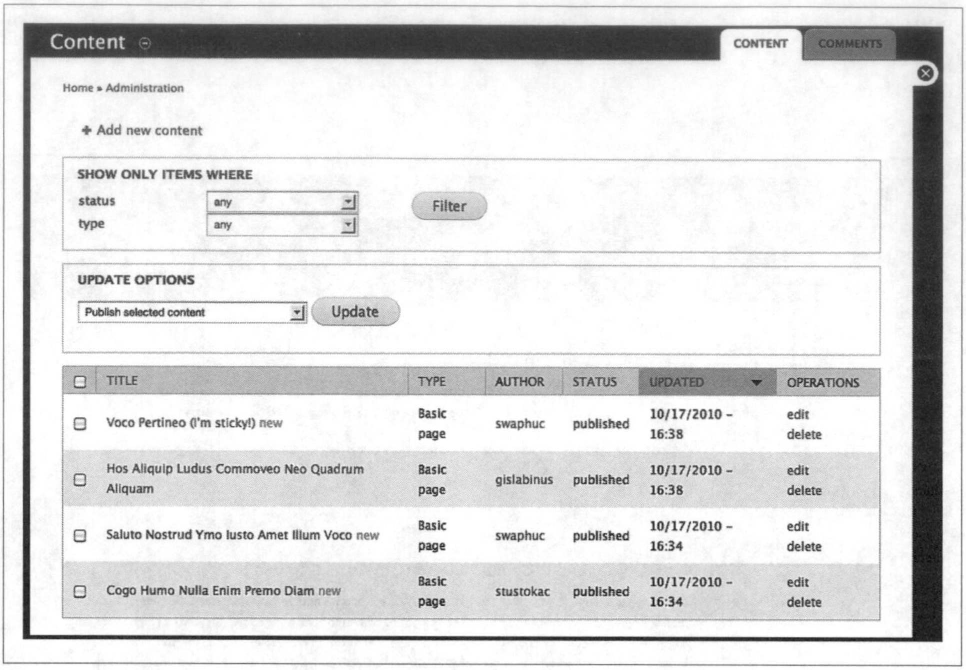

Figure 2-9. The Content administration page

If you ever "lose" a piece of content (for example, you create a node that is not promoted to the front page, and forget to add a Navigation menu item pointing to it), you can always find it again from the Content administration page. This page is sometimes colloquially referred to as the "node lost and found," and can be very helpful, since losing a piece of "missing" content is pretty easy to do when you're first starting out.

Comments

The core Comment module allows website visitors to post replies to the content within a node, enabling them to discuss the topic at hand directly with the author as well as with one another. Figure 2-10 shows commenting in action.

Most content types have comments enabled by default, although the "Basic page" type has commenting turned off initially (as it doesn't make much sense for visitors to discuss your About Us page). You may configure additional comment settings per content type from the administrative toolbar at Structure→"Content types" (*admin/structure/types*). These settings include specifying whether to require previewing of comments before posting them, as well as the number of comments to display on the page. We'll cover a few of these settings later in the chapter.

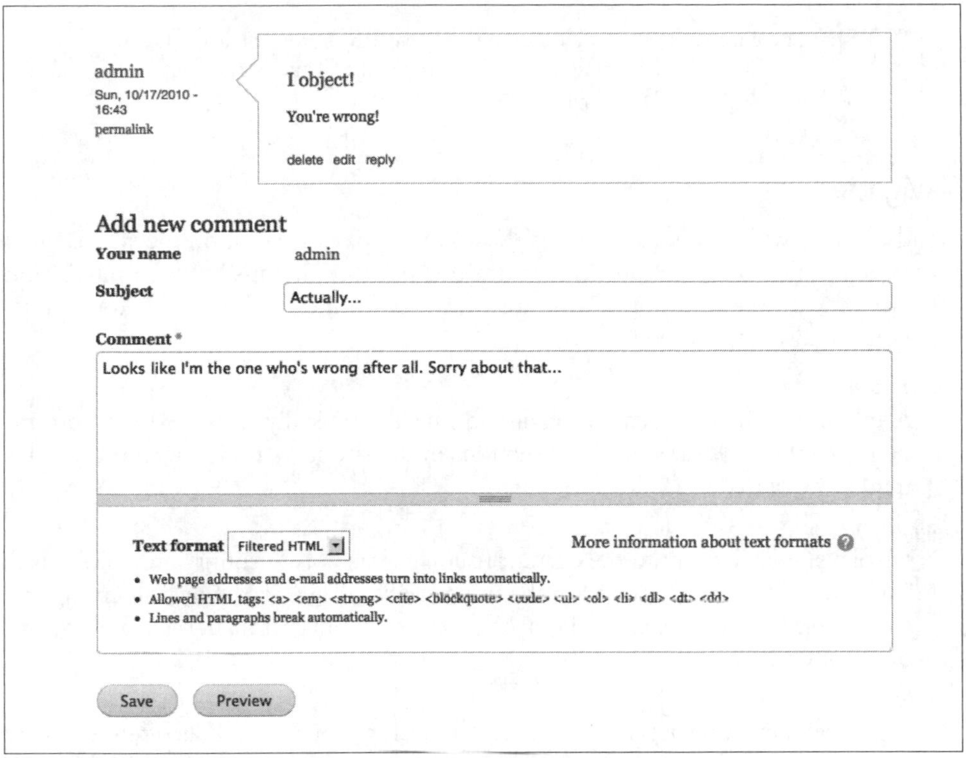

Figure 2-10. The Comment module allows visitors to discuss a piece of content

Comments may also optionally be placed in a moderation queue rather than being immediately visible on the site, which can be useful as a basic spam deterrent. Comment administration facilities are available as a subtab on the main Content screen at Content→Comments, as shown in Figure 2-11.

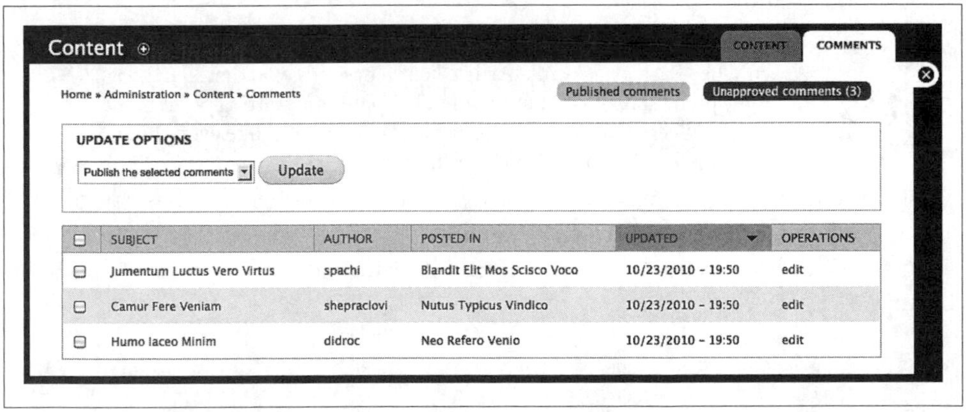

Figure 2-11. The Comment moderation queue administration page

There are a number of modules that help ease the burden of dealing with spam and abusive content. We'll discuss some of the options later in this chapter in "Spotlight: Content Moderation Tools" on page 66.

Navigation

Hand-in-hand with creating content is the ability to navigate to it on the site. Drupal provides a built-in module called Menu for this purpose. Menus hold the navigation links to various web pages on a Drupal site. Drupal comes with four default menus, and you can also add your own:

Main menu

A menu provided for custom navigation needs, typically displayed very prominently in the site's design. Major sections of the site such as Home and About Us tend to be placed in the Main menu.

User menu

Displays links relevant to the current user, such as "My account" and "Log out." This menu is generally placed in the upper-right corner. In the default configuration, these links will be printed twice: once for administrators in the Toolbar, and once for end users.

Navigation

A general menu that acts as the default "dumping ground" of links offered by new modules, when they are not strictly administrative tasks. For example, when you enable the Forum module, a "Forums" link to the forum listing page is added to the Navigation menu. Many modules offer links under the Navigation menu that are originally disabled, but can be optionally turned on.

Management

Holds links to administration tasks, essentially duplicating the administrative toolbar at the top of the page, for sites that don't use the default Toolbar module.

 As with the "Basic page" and "Article" content types, you don't *have* to use these prebuilt menus. They are merely a potential starting point that can help you get your site up and running quickly. And like everything else in Drupal, you can also make your own!

Figure 2-12 shows an example of all four menus in the default core Bartik theme. Themes will be discussed in more detail later in the section "Spotlight: Themes" on page 71.

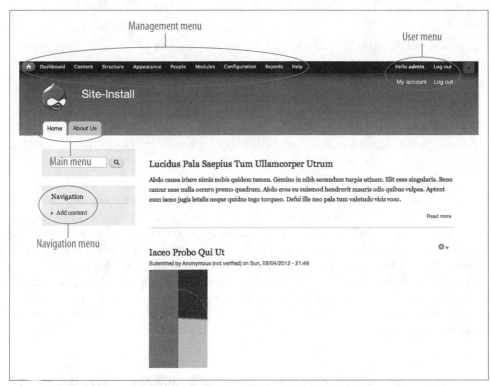

Figure 2-12. Drupal's built-in menus: Management, User, Main, and Navigation

You can configure which menu to use for "Main links" and "Secondary links" at Structure→Menus→Settings tab (*admin/structure/menu/settings*).

Under normal conditions, these two menus are different (they default to "Main menu" and "User menu," respectively). However, if you set both the Main and Secondary menus to the same value, this creates a sort of drill-down effect in which the top-level items are displayed in the "Main menu" region, and any subitems of the currently active "Main menu" link are displayed dynamically in the secondary region.

The powerful Menu Block module (*http://drupal.org/project/menu _block*) generalizes this one-off feature, allows the creation of additional "sub" menus, and provides a variety of other advanced configuration options.

Blocks

Blocks are smaller chunks of content that you can place in your pages. Examples of some default blocks provided are "Who's online," which shows a listing of users currently logged in; "User login," which displays a login form to anonymous users; and "Recent comments," which shows a list of the newest comments on the site. The Navigation bar in the sidebar, the "Powered by Drupal" text at the bottom, and even the entire content area of the page are blocks! You can also make your own custom blocks: for example, you might create a block to display an announcement about an upcoming event.

Figure 2-13 shows the Block administration page under Structure→Blocks (*admin/structure/block*). Blocks are placed within a *region* of a page. Examples of regions are "Sidebar first," "Footer," and "Content." Region names, and exactly where they appear on a page, vary depending on the *theme* (or design) of your site; some themes may define additional regions such as "Banner ad" and remove or change some of the default regions. Therefore, blocks must be configured on a per-theme basis. We'll discuss more about themes and regions later in "Spotlight: Themes" on page 71. You may use the arrow handles on the side to drag blocks to different regions. To see a visual representation of what the regions look like, as pictured in Figure 2-14, click the "Demonstrate block regions" link.

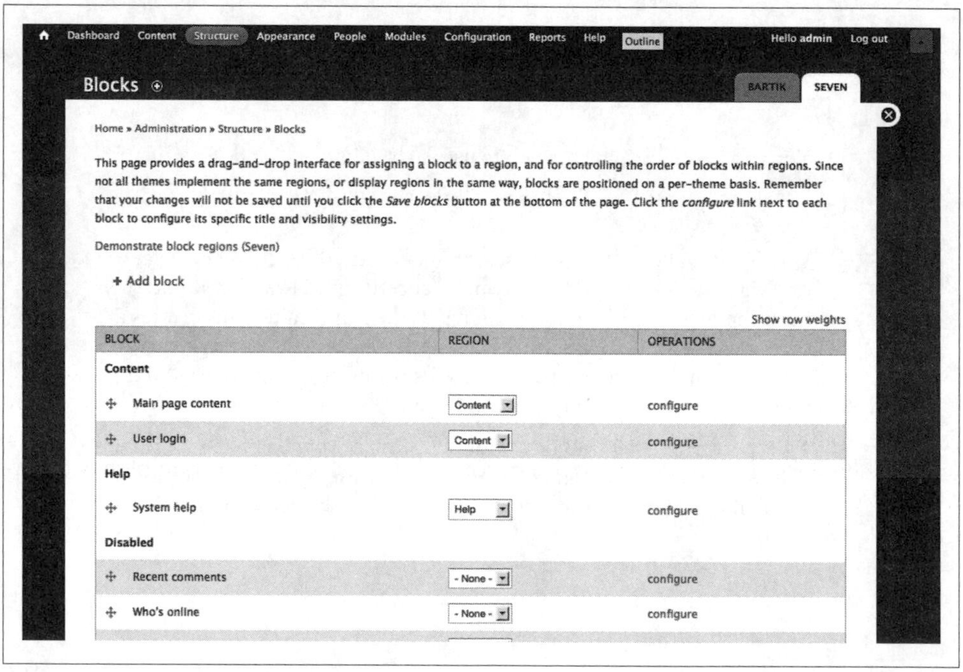

Figure 2-13. The Block administration page for the Seven administration theme

One frequently asked question is how blocks and nodes differ, as both display content. One general rule of thumb is that blocks are typically supplementary information to the actual content on the page. Block content also usually either changes often (in the case of the "Who's online" block), or consists of temporary information such as a blurb that's displayed on the front page for a few days. Block content is also not searchable, so if the content needs to be referenced permanently, a node is a much better choice.

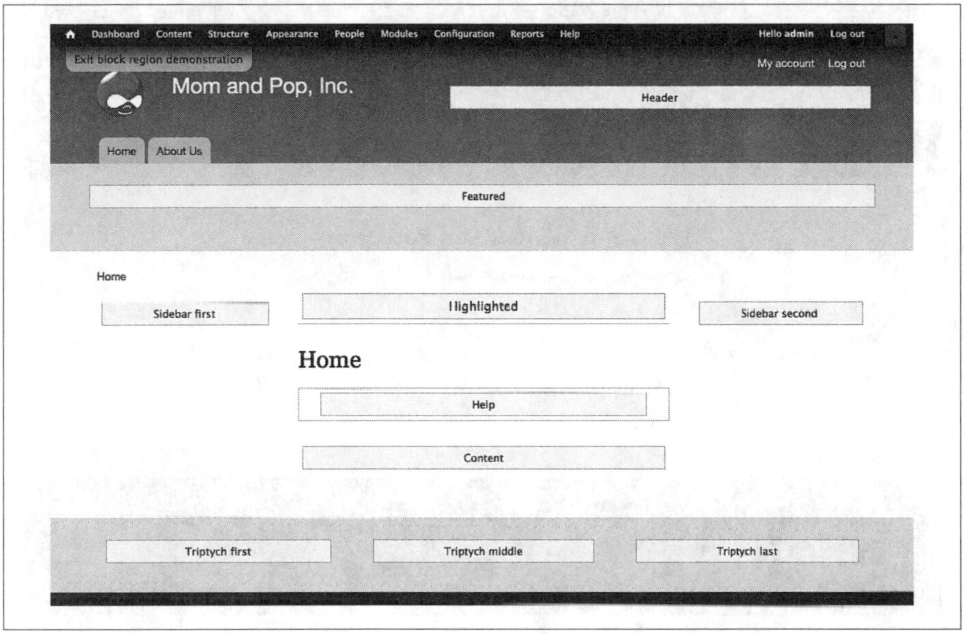

Figure 2-14. Block regions for the Bartik theme indicate visually where blocks will be displayed

You can customize the visibility of blocks, as well—for example, to show blocks on only certain pages or only to users with certain roles. If the core PHP filter module is enabled, you may also optionally use PHP to specify complex visibility settings—for example, to display a Help block to any users who have been members for less than a week. There is also an option to let users control the visibility of certain blocks themselves, so they have more control over their browsing experience.

Be careful with using and giving access to use PHP on a Drupal site. Although PHP is an extremely powerful tool, the ability to work with it within a web application like Drupal opens the door for security problems and site crashes. We'll harp on this point again in "Hands-On: Configuring Permissions" on page 62, when we talk about access permissions.

Hands-On: Content Management

Out of the box, our wonderful Drupal site (pictured in Figure 2-15) looks pretty bare. Adding some content with information about Mom and Pop, Inc., will do wonders to make this actually start looking like a website. In this section, we'll create a couple of simple pieces of content—the About Us page and a welcome announcement—and begin to build our website's navigation. We'll also add a few blocks for extra pizzazz.

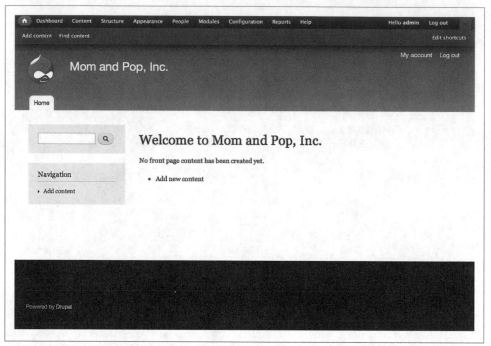

Figure 2-15. Drupal, after a fresh installation

Creating a Basic Page

First, we'll make a simple About Us page to get the hang of Drupal's content creation and editing tools.

1. Go to "Add content"→"Basic page" (*node/add/page*) in either the Navigation block or the Shortcut bar.

2. Enter the page's Title, Body, and other settings provided in Table 2-1 and pictured in Figure 2-16. Because this is a static page, we'll also place it into our site's main Navigation menu. Finally, we'll give the page a friendly path of *http://example.com/about* instead of *http://example.com/node/1* by providing a "URL path alias."

Table 2-1. About Us page values

Setting	Value
Title	About Us
Body	Our store has been providing organic food to the community since 1978. Come and see us at:
	123 Main Street
	Home Town, MN
	Store hours: 12pm–12am
Text format[a]	Filtered HTML (default)
Menu settings	
• Provide a menu link	Checked
• Menu link title	About Us (default)
• Description	Learn more about Mom and Pop, Inc.
• Parent item	\<Main menu\> (default)
• Weight	0 (default)
URL path settings	
URL alias	about

[a] We're breezing right by that "Text format" field at the moment, but this is actually an important Drupal security concept to understand, and will be covered in more detail in "Spotlight: Text Formats and Filters" on page 179. Don't miss it!

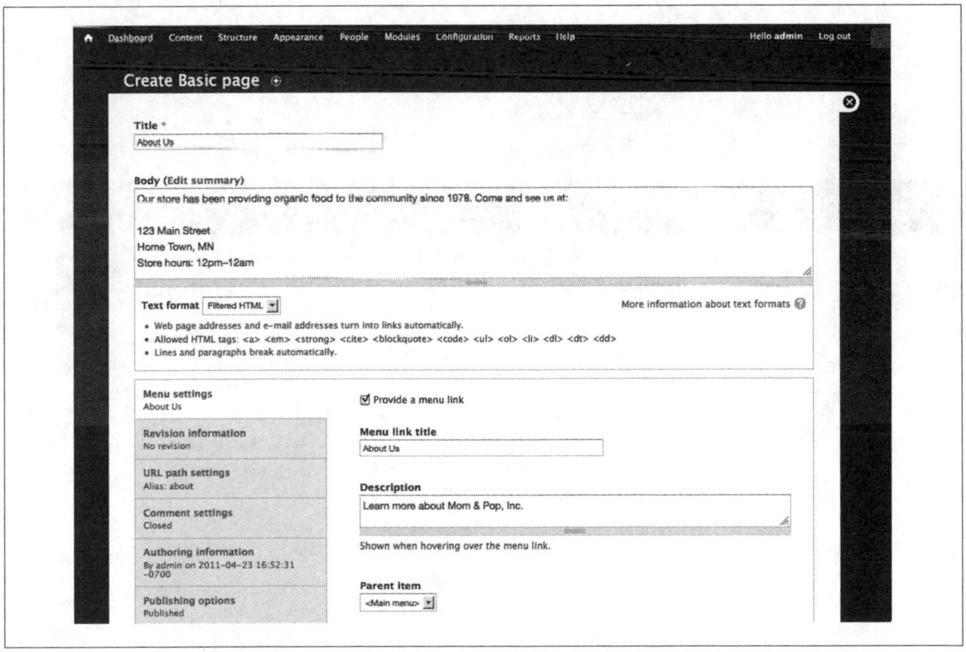

Figure 2-16. Creating the site's About Us page

Setting URL aliases by hand can be tedious. The Pathauto module (*http://drupal.org/project/pathauto*), covered in Chapter 7, allows you to set up customized rules that automatically generate friendly URLs for all of your website content (*http://example.com/content/about*), users (*http://example.com/user/admin*), and more.

3. When you've completed these steps, you should see the new page appear, and there should now be two tabs in the site's main navigation: About Us and Home, as shown in Figure 2-17.

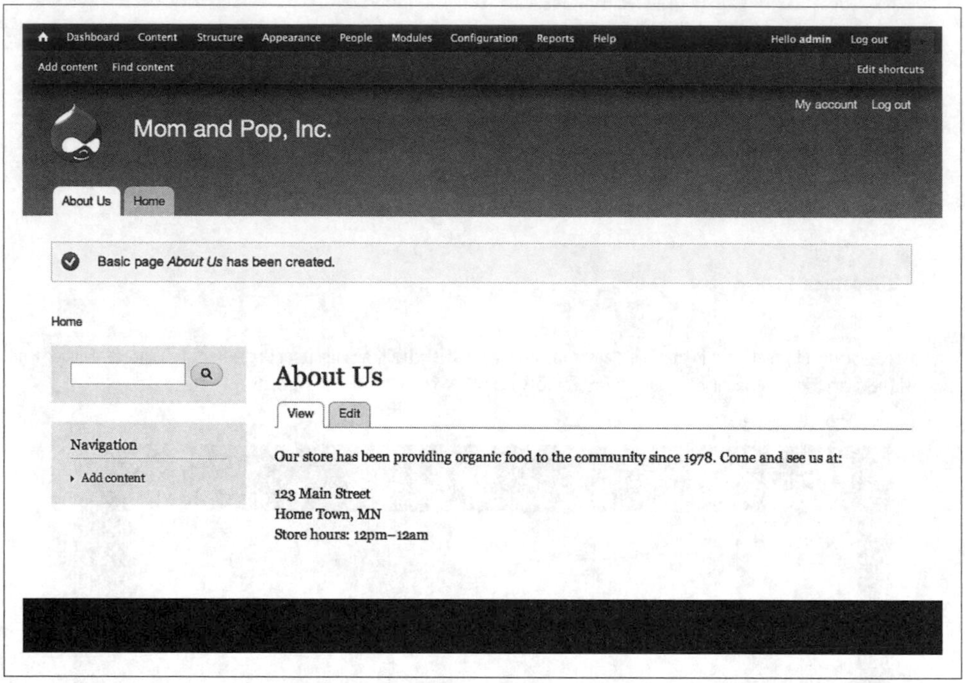

Figure 2-17. The completed About Us page

If you forgot to enter a menu item and navigate away from a page, it can be tricky to find it again without manually going to a path like *http://www.example.com/node/1*. The Content administration page under Content (*admin/content*) in the administrative toolbar can help you track down straggler pages.

Congratulations! You've just created your first of many nodes in Drupal!

Creating an Article

Next, let's experiment with creating an Article—Drupal's other default content type. Unlike "Basic page," which contains just a Title and Body field, Articles can also provide Tags (or keywords) and an Image on each post. Articles also have comments enabled, and automatically get posted to Drupal's default home page in reverse-chronological order, making them useful for things like announcements. So, let's announce the creation of our new website!

 The features described here for "Basic page" and Article are only their *default* behavior. It's possible to fully customize the capabilities of these or any other content types under the Structure→"Content types" (*admin/structure/types*) administrative page. Chapter 3 will go into much more detail about doing this sort of customization; for now, we'll stick with the defaults.

1. Go to "Add content"→Article (*node/add/article*) in either the Navigation block or the Shortcut bar.

2. Enter the article's Title, Body, and other settings provided in Table 2-1 and pictured in Figure 2-18, and click Save. This time, we're not going to supply a menu item, because this announcement will appear on our home page so we'll have a way to navigate to it. We'll also enter a Summary for this post, so that the home page shows a small bit of text but requires a user to click "Read more" to read the article's entire contents.

Table 2-2. Welcome announcement values

Setting	Value
Title	Welcome to our new website!
Tags	announcements, website
Summary (click "Edit summary" link next to the Body field to expose)	Read all about our new website and what it means for you!
Body	Welcome to our new website, powered by Drupal! Don't know what Drupal is? Don't worry; we don't either. :)
	The important thing is that we can now update our website much faster and more often than before! We'll be posting about in-store promotions, great upcoming deals, and general community events.
	Stay tuned for further announcements!
Text format	Filtered HTML (default)
Image	(upload *firebird.png* in the */assets/ch02-jumpstart* folder, or any other image you have lying around)
Alternate text (visible after uploading image)	Pa's prized 1978 Pontiac Firebird

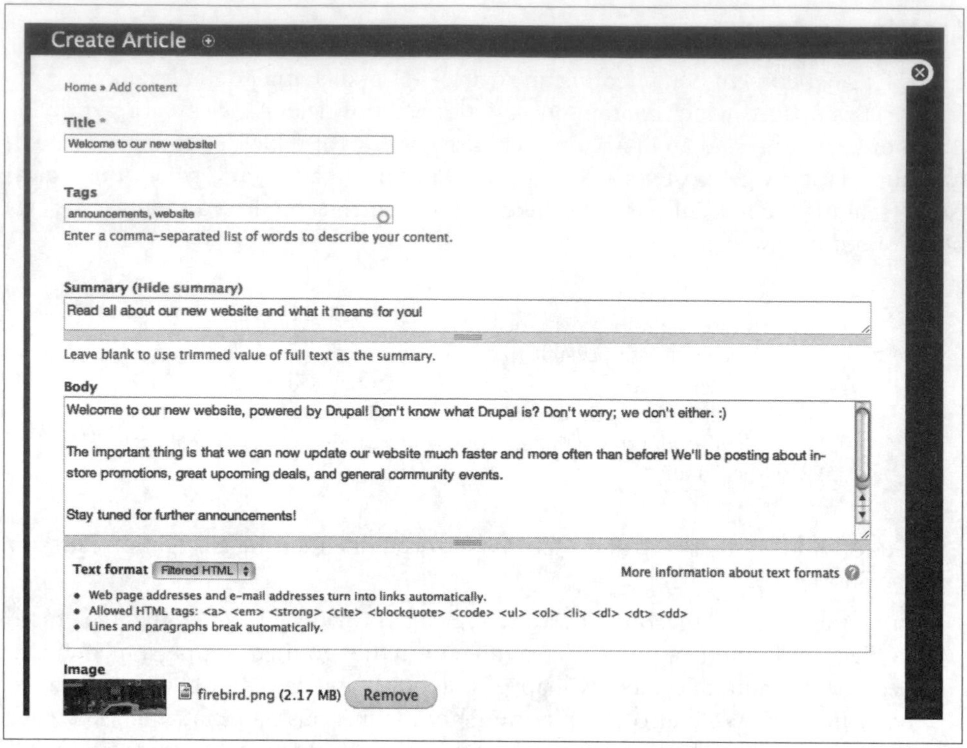

Create Article ⊕

Home » Add content

Title *
Welcome to our new website!

Tags
announcements, website
Enter a comma–separated list of words to describe your content.

Summary (Hide summary)
Read all about our new website and what it means for you!

Leave blank to use trimmed value of full text as the summary.

Body
Welcome to our new website, powered by Drupal! Don't know what Drupal is? Don't worry; we don't either. :)

The important thing is that we can now update our website much faster and more often than before! We'll be posting about in-store promotions, great upcoming deals, and general community events.

Stay tuned for further announcements!

Text format [Filtered HTML ⬍]   More information about text formats ⓘ
- Web page addresses and e-mail addresses turn into links automatically.
- Allowed HTML tags: <a> <em> <strong> <cite> <blockquote> <code> <ul> <ol> <li> <dl> <dt> <dd>
- Lines and paragraphs break automatically.

Image
📄 firebird.png (2.17 MB) (Remove)

Figure 2-18. Creating the site's first article

3. You should now be redirected to the article page, displaying your full-size image, body text, and tags, as well as a comment form. By clicking the Home link, you'll be taken to the site's home page, which will display a slightly smaller version of the image, as well as the Summary text, as shown in Figure 2-19.

> The Tags field is a built-in example of Drupal's robust categorization system, called Taxonomy. While we won't get too in depth into Taxonomy for this chapter; you can read much more about it in detail in "Spotlight: Taxonomy" on page 266.

Managing Site Navigation

Great! We now have some simple content on the site, and our Navigation menu is starting to come together. However, there's something a little funny going on: our tabs in the top-left corner are displayed in alphabetical order, which puts About Us before Home. It would make a lot more sense for Home to come first, so let's fix that by reordering the items listed in the menu:

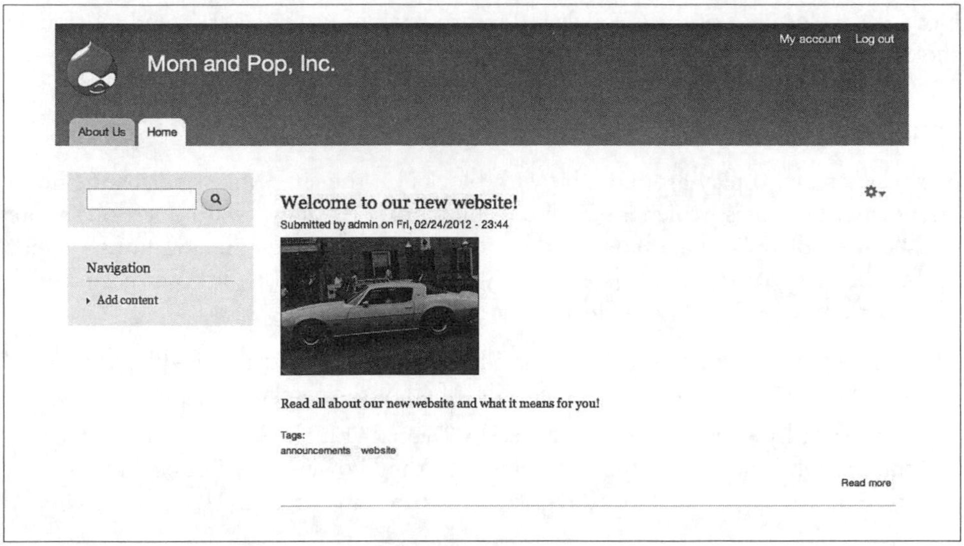

Figure 2-19. Article shown in summary view on home page

1. Go to Structure→Menus (*admin/structure/menu*) in the toolbar, and click "list links" next to "Main menu" (*admin/structure/menu/manage/main-menu*).

2. Using the handles on the left side, drag the Home item above the About Us item, as shown in Figure 2-20. You'll see a note that the changes will not be saved until the form is submitted.

3. The yellow background and asterisk indicate that the changes are not yet saved. Make sure to click "Save configuration" to save your menu settings.

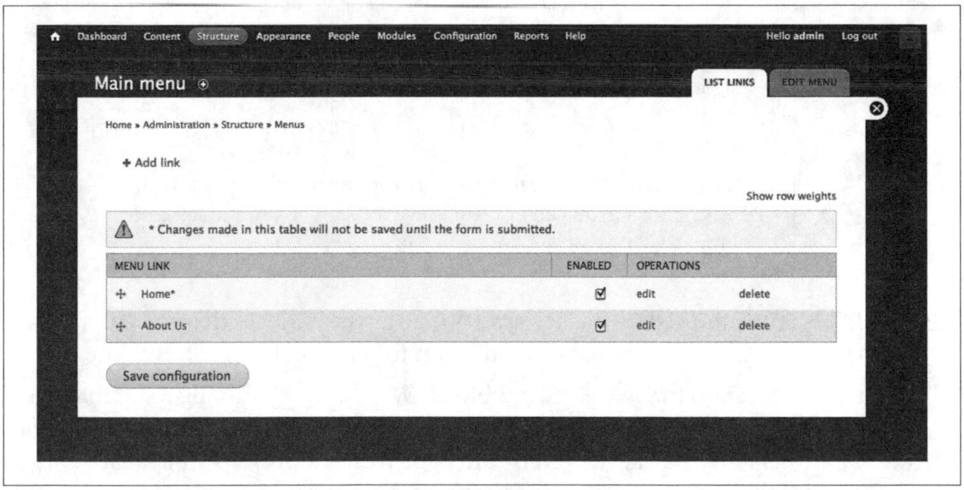

Figure 2-20. The menu administration screen allows you to reorder menu links

Now, if we close out of the Overlay and return back to our site's frontend, our menu should have Home listed first. That's more like it!

Configuring Blocks

Next, let's start to play around a bit with blocks on the site. Mike and Jeanne don't know what Drupal is, which is going to result in all sorts of awkward questions about that "Powered by Drupal" block in the footer. So let's remove it. Additionally, they want to be able to show off the latest weekly deal prominently on the home page, which is the perfect use for a custom block.

1. Begin by navigating to the Block administration page at Structure→Blocks (*admin/ structure/block*). Here, you will see a list of all of the available regions.

2. Let's start by removing the "Powered by Drupal" block. Scroll down the page to the Footer region, click the handle next to the "Powered by Drupal" block, and move it down to the Disabled region, as pictured in Figure 2-21.

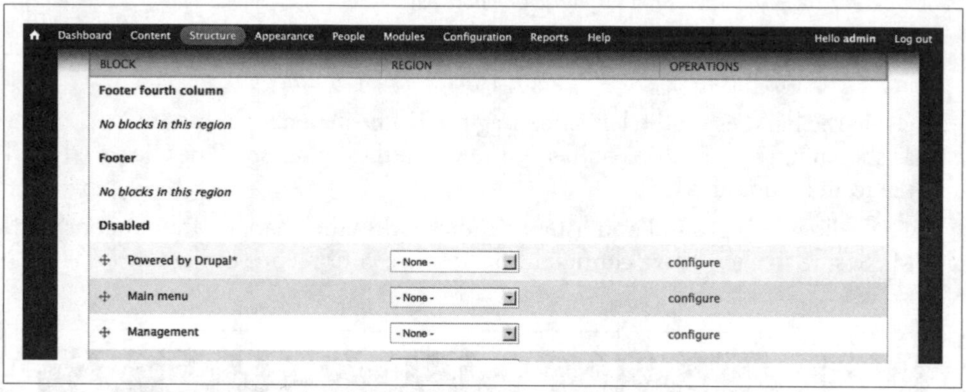

BLOCK	REGION	OPERATIONS
Footer fourth column		
No blocks in this region		
Footer		
No blocks in this region		
Disabled		
⊹ Powered by Drupal*	- None -	configure
⊹ Main menu	- None -	configure
⊹ Management	- None -	configure

Figure 2-21. Use the drag-and-drop handles to remove the "Powered by Drupal" block

 In addition to being able to drag and drop the blocks into the region of your choice, you can also use the drop-down list in the Region column to choose the region.

3. As with menus, the yellow background and asterisk indicate that the changes are not yet saved. Click the "Save blocks" button to remove the block from the footer.

4. Next, let's look into that weekly deals block. We'll start by finding a suitable place for this announcement. Click the "Demonstrate block regions" link (*admin/struc- ture/block/demo/bartik*) at the top of the page to see a preview of available block regions and their styling. Notice the Featured region displayed along the top, with a gray background. That should help it stand out from the rest of the page. Click

"Exit block region demonstration" in the upper left to return to the Block administration page.

5. Next, we need to add our own custom block. Click the "Add block" link at the top of the page (*admin/structure/block/add*).

6. Enter the settings from Table 2-3 as shown in Figure 2-22. Use the "Page-specific visibility settings" to ensure that the block shows up only on the home page. We can also add the block to the Featured region right from this form.

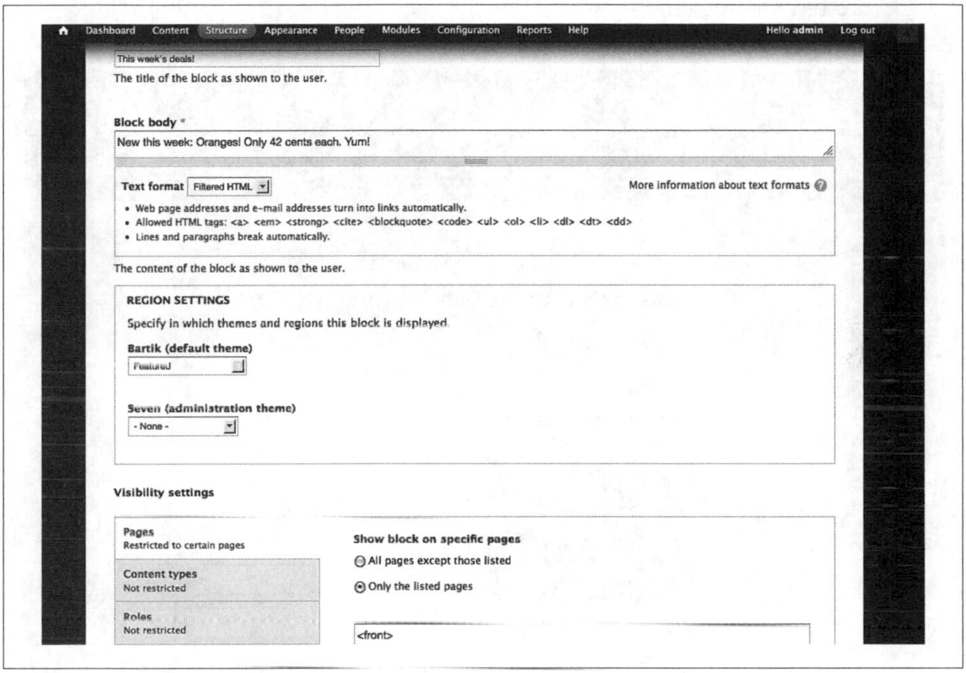

Figure 2-22. Block configuration form

Table 2-3. Settings for weekly deals block

Field	Value
Block-specific settings	
Block title	This week's deals!
Block description	Weekly deals
Block body	New this week: Oranges! Only 42 cents each. Yum!
Text format	Filtered HTML (default)
Region settings	
Bartik (default theme)	Featured
Seven (administration theme)	None (default)

Field	Value
Visibility settings: Pages	
Show block on specific pages	Only the listed pages
Pages	<front>

7. After saving this form with the "Save block" button, you'll return to the main Block administration page. Return to your site's home page, which should now look as pictured in Figure 2-23.

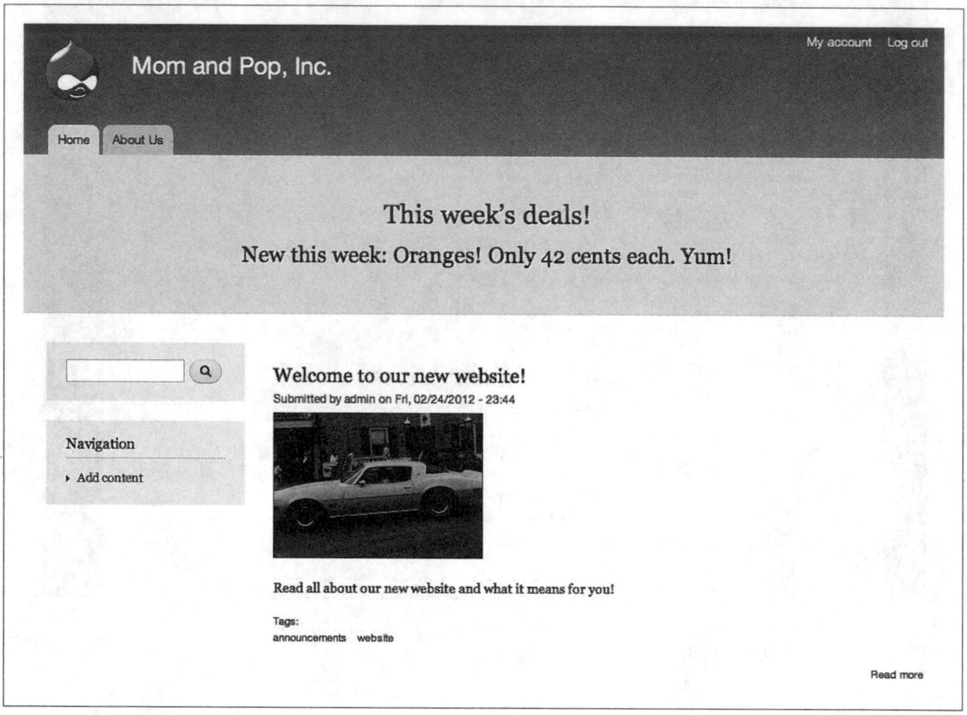

Figure 2-23. "Weekly deals" block added; "Powered by Drupal" block removed

Spotlight: Modules

As discussed in Chapter 1, modules allow you to turn on and off functionality within your Drupal website. There are two types of modules: *core* modules, which come with Drupal itself, and *contributed* modules, which are provided for free by the Drupal community and available for download from Drupal.org. This section discusses everything you need to know about modules.

Module Administration Page

The Module administration page, available in the administrative toolbar under Modules (*admin/modules*) and depicted in Figure 2-24, is where Drupal provides the ability to turn on and off your website's functionality. Related modules are grouped together within fieldsets called *packages*, and each module entry contains a description and an indication of which version is currently running on the site. This version information can be extremely useful when you're troubleshooting problems. Finally, many modules also have links to their help pages, permissions, and configuration pages. This is very handy for getting to the meat of what a module does as soon as you turn it on.

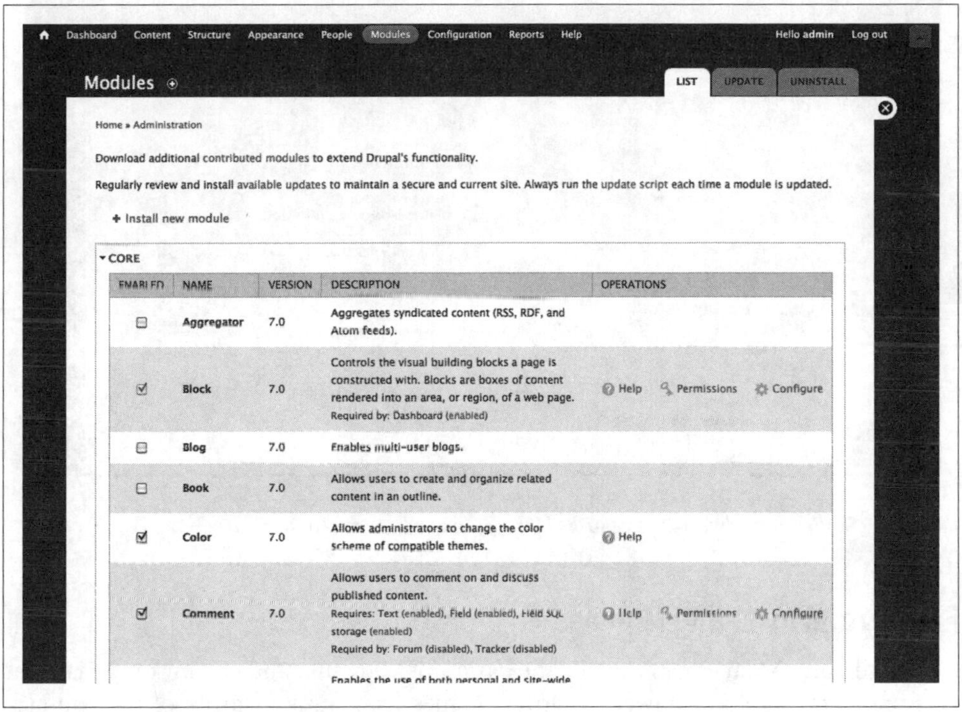

Figure 2-24. The Module administration page

You may switch modules on and off by toggling their Enabled checkboxes, which allows you to custom-tailor the functionality of any Drupal site to its unique needs, without bogging it down with needless overhead.

A module might also have *dependencies*. That is, it might require one or more other modules in order to work properly. For example, the Forum module requires both the Comment and Taxonomy modules to be enabled before it can be enabled. If you forget to do this, a confirmation screen will appear asking you whether to enable the required modules in order to proceed. Some contributed modules may also require certain *versions* of other modules in order to be enabled.

One final handy page to be aware of is the administrative Index page at *admin/index*, shown in Figure 2-25. This has a full list of administrative pages grouped by the module to which they belong.

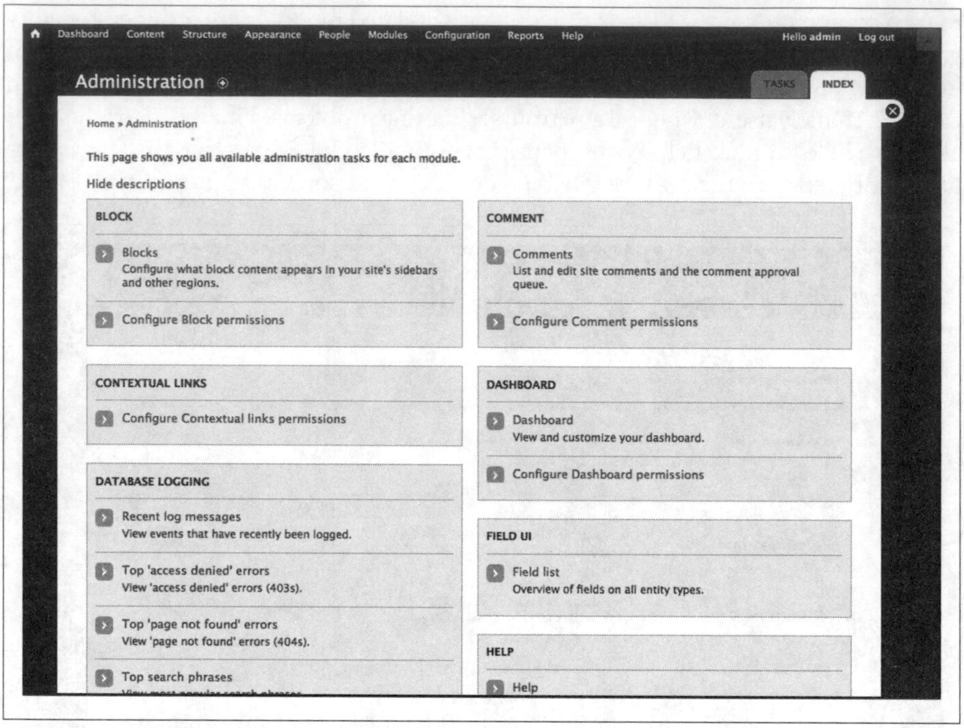

Figure 2-25. Viewing administrative tasks by module in the admin index

Finding and Installing Modules

Although core modules can provide the basics for your site, and can in some cases get you pretty far, the real power in Drupal comes from its vast array of community-contributed modules. You can browse and download all contributed modules from *http://drupal.org/project/Modules*, pictured in Figure 2-26.

> Drupal 6.x modules are not compatible with Drupal 7.x, and vice versa. It's very important to use the "Filter by compatibility" selection at the top of this screen to display modules only for the Drupal version that you are using. To display modules compatible with Drupal 7, change the drop-down to 7.x, and for Drupal 6–compatible modules, select 6.x.

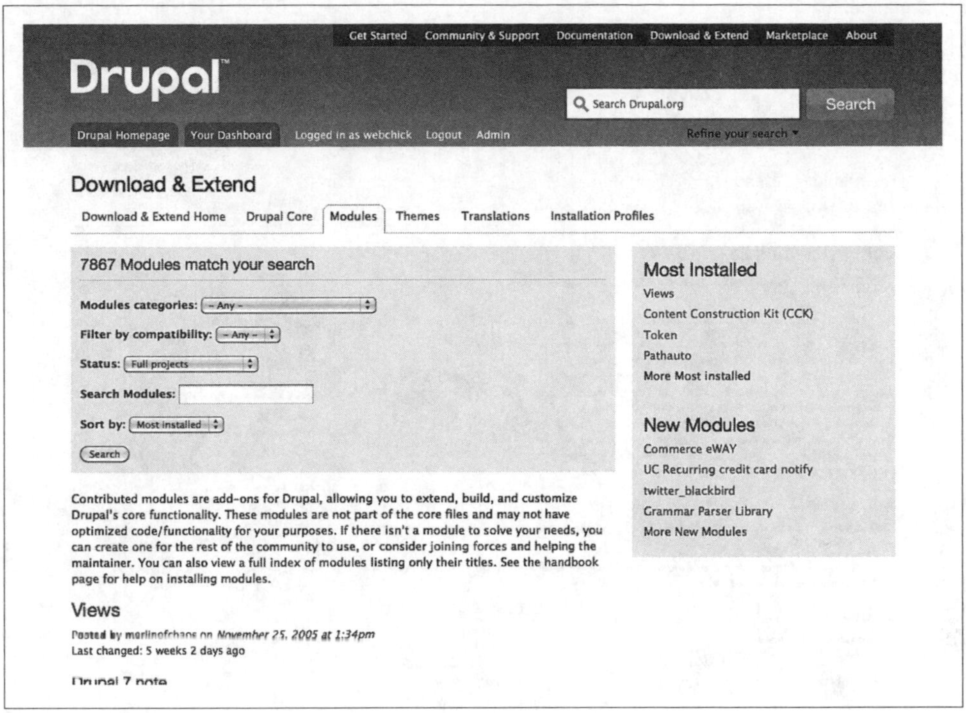

Figure 2-26. The contributed modules browsing page at Drupal.org

Each module has its own project page on Drupal.org, as indicated in Figure 2-27. Here you'll find a description and often a screenshot of the project, as well as information about its developers, what sort of bugs or features the project has, documentation links, and more. The main feature on this page is a table containing *releases* of the module that you may download. The version of the module you should download is the one in the Recommended Releases table in green, and whose version starts with "7.x-" (unless you're using Drupal 6, in which case you'd look for the release that starts with "6.x-", and so on). Visit *http://drupal.org/documentation/version-info* for much more information on Drupal's version naming conventions.

> One of the most challenging aspects of using Drupal is determining which modules to use for a given task at hand. There are many modules that appear to cover similar ground, and the quality of modules can vary greatly. Appendix B is devoted entirely to the topic of tips and tricks for selecting the right modules for your project. But it's not enough to find the modules you're looking for; you also have to keep them up-to-date. We talk more about upgrading modules in Appendix A.

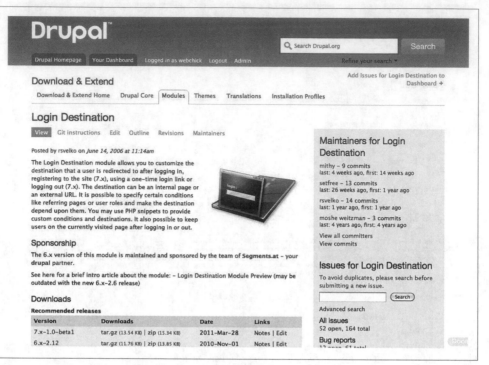

Figure 2-27. The project page for the Login Destination module

Once you've found your module, you need to get it into your Drupal site. There are two ways to do this in Drupal 7:

1. The traditional manner is to download the module to your local drive, extract it, and then move it to your Drupal site's *sites/all/modules/* directory via SFTP or similar.

2. Drupal 7 also has a feature called Update Manager that allows you to install and update modules directly from the web interface. We'll walk through using this feature in "Hands-On: Working with Modules" on page 49.

Detailed instructions on how to install modules are available in the online Installation Guide documentation at *http://drupal.org/documentation/install/modules-themes*.

Removing Modules

If you decide that you no longer want to use a module, you have two choices:

Disable
Disable a module by unchecking the Enabled checkbox and saving the form. This action switches the module off temporarily, which can be useful for troubleshooting. You can re-enable the module at any time and your website will function

exactly the same, as disabling a module does not remove the module's data from your database. You may disable a module only if no other enabled modules require it.

Uninstall

Uninstalling a module removes the module permanently. To uninstall a module, you must first disable it, and then check off from the Uninstall tab (*admin/build/modules/uninstall*). Note that many but not all modules have an uninstall function.

Uninstalling a module will delete *all data* associated with that module, possibly including content on your website. Be *very* careful when using this option, and be sure to back up your database first. Note that uninstalling a module does not remove it from the filesystem; you still have to do this manually.

Hands-On: Working with Modules

The easiest way to wrap your head around how modules work is to try installing and configuring a couple of them. This section will cover how to install, enable, and configure a contributed module called Module Filter, which can be downloaded from Drupal.org.

You've probably noticed that scrolling in the Module administration page gets a little tedious, especially if you're using the book's source code, which comes bundled with dozens of contributed modules: prepare for lots of scrolling! Wouldn't it be nice if there were a faster way to find the module you're looking for? Luckily, there is: the Module Filter module (*http://drupal.org/project/module_filter*), pictured in Figure 2-28. This module places a search box at the top of the modules page to help you quickly filter the list of modules by keyword, and optionally collapses all of the packages to vertical tabs to save screen real estate. This module does not come with core, so we will need to download it first.

1. Go to the Module Filter project page (*http://drupal.org/project/module_filter*). Look for its table of releases, pictured in Figure 2-29.

2. Look for the "Recommended release" that starts with "7.x-" (at the time of writing, the latest recommended release, as pictured in Figure 2-29, is 7.x-1.6), right-click the "tar.gz" link, and copy the link location or address, depending on what your browser calls it. In this example, it should look something like *http://ftp.drupal.org/files/projects/module_filter-7.x-1.6.tar.gz*.

3. In your Drupal site, navigate to the modules page at Modules (*admin/modules*) and click the "Install new module" link (*admin/modules/install*).

4. In the form pictured in Figure 2-30, paste in the URL to the module's *tar.gz* file copied in step 2. Click Install to proceed. You may be asked for your SFTP password if you are installing the module on a remote site.

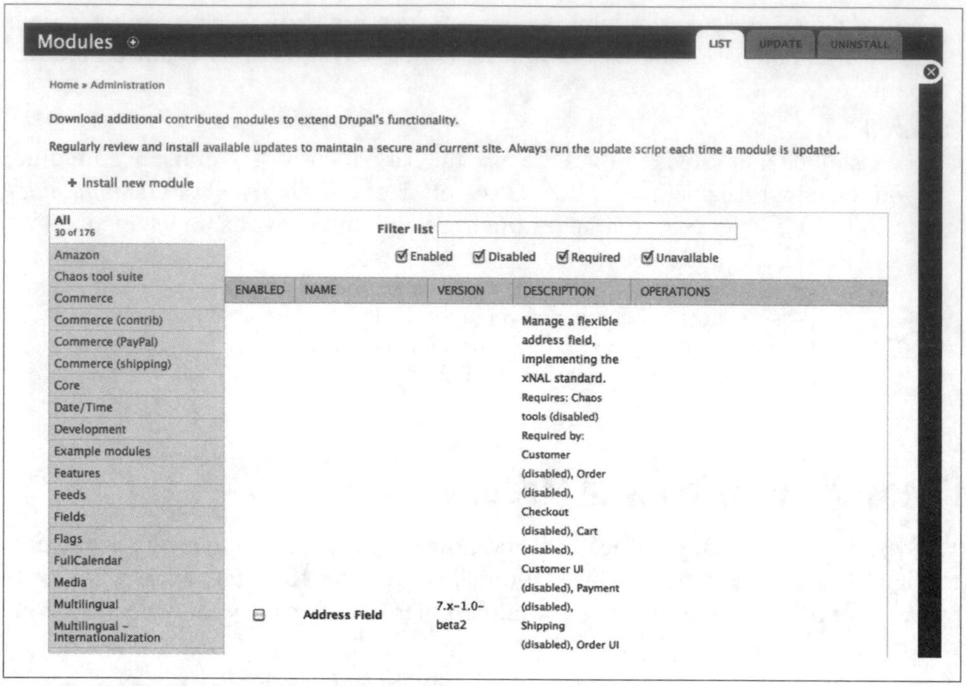

Figure 2-28. The Module Filter module adds a search box to the modules page and arranges module packages into vertical tabs

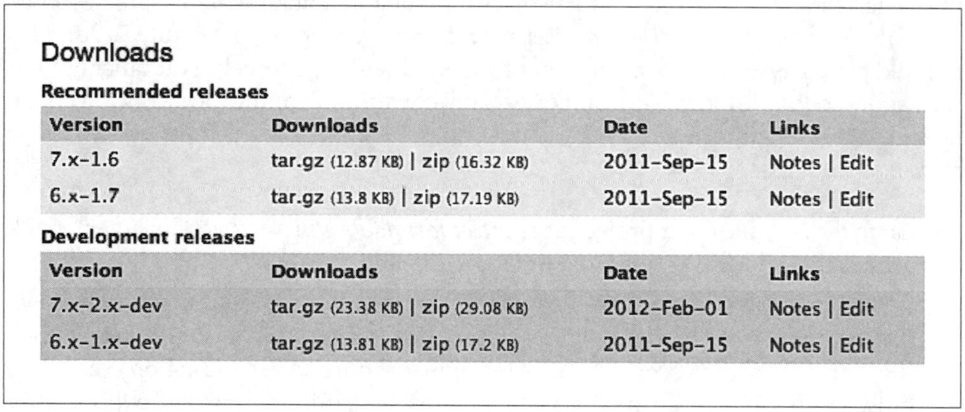

Downloads

Recommended releases

Version	Downloads	Date	Links
7.x-1.6	tar.gz (12.87 KB) | zip (16.32 KB)	2011-Sep-15	Notes | Edit
6.x-1.7	tar.gz (13.8 KB) | zip (17.19 KB)	2011-Sep-15	Notes | Edit

Development releases

Version	Downloads	Date	Links
7.x-2.x-dev	tar.gz (23.38 KB) | zip (29.08 KB)	2012-Feb-01	Notes | Edit
6.x-1.x-dev	tar.gz (13.81 KB) | zip (17.2 KB)	2011-Sep-15	Notes | Edit

Figure 2-29. The Module Filter module's release table on Drupal.org

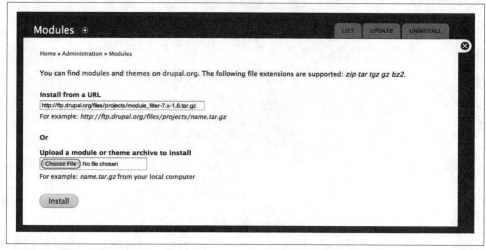

Figure 2-30. Installing a module through Drupal's update manager

5. If all goes well, a progress bar will appear and then you'll be taken to a confirmation page, as pictured in Figure 2-31. This means the module has been successfully uploaded and extracted to Drupal's *sites/all/modules* directory.

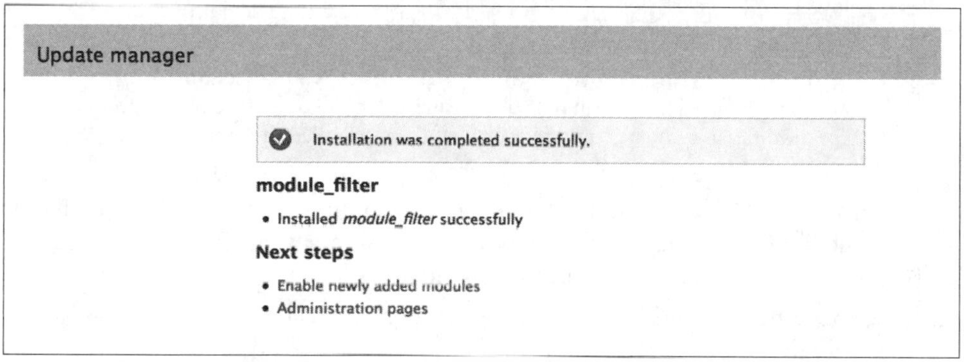

Update manager

✓ Installation was completed successfully.

module_filter

- Installed *module_filter* successfully

Next steps

- Enable newly added modules
- Administration pages

Figure 2-31. The "Update manager" screen if all is successful

6. If these steps did not complete successfully, they may also be done manually. Download and extract the module *.zip* file from the Drupal.org project page, then place the *module_filter* folder into Drupal's *sites/all/modules* folder. When you're finished, the directory should look as pictured in Figure 2-32.

With the module files in place, we can now begin the next step: enabling the module and configuring its settings.

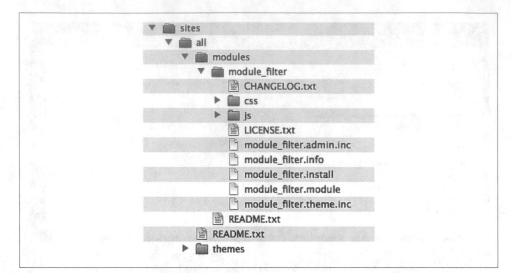

Figure 2-32. Module Filter module files in the sites directory

 From here on out, any hands-on sections that require contributed modules will assume that you've taken these steps, and that the module files are already in place in Drupal's *sites/all/modules* directory. The book's source code comes with all of the modules necessary to build the websites in future chapters already in place. If you want to follow along with the other chapters on your own Drupal website, you'll need to install each required module in this same fashion. A quick reference list of the modules and themes used in each chapter is supplied in Appendix C.

1. Return to the Module administration page at Modules (*admin/modules*) either by clicking the "Enable newly added modules" link or by navigating there by clicking the Modules link in the administrative toolbar.

2. Find the Other package fieldset and check the Enabled checkbox next to the Module Filter module.

3. Click the "Save configuration" button at the bottom of the form.

4. Immediately, you'll see the effects of this module, as pictured in Figure 2-28. The modules page is transformed, with a search box added and fieldsets turned into vertical tabs. As you type letters into the search box, you'll see the list of modules below narrow to only those that match. Handy!

5. Most modules offer additional configuration settings to allow for further customization, and Module Filter is no different. In the new search box, enter the text "modu" to reduce the list so that only Module Filter appears, and click the Configure link under the Operations column to discover the settings the module provides. Experiment with the settings (for example, uncheck the Tabs option) and observe how the Module page changes.

Now that we've seen how to install, enable, and configure modules, let's delve into detail about how to control who has access to use them.

Drush

If you are command-line-inclined, check out the Drush (*http://drupal.org/project/drush*) project. Short for DRUpal SHell, Drush is a command-line shell and scripting interface for Drupal. With it, you can use handy commands such as:

```
drush dl module_filter
```

```
drush en module_filter
```

As the command-line version of the preceding steps, this will download the latest 7.x version of the Module Filter module, place it into the correct directory, and enable it on your site, quickly and painlessly. There are a bevy of other handy tasks Drush can do as well, from clearing the site cache (important while debugging) to performing site upgrades to executing PHP and SQL commands on your Drupal website.

Even if you're not command-line-savvy, definitely check it out. Drush is a huge time-saving tool for many common (and not so common) site building tasks.

Spotlight: Access Control

One of the most powerful features of Drupal is its rich, fine-grained access control system, based around the concept of users, roles, and permissions.

User
> A visitor to the website. A user can be anyone: a casual visitor to the website, your company's president who's blogging on the site every day, your system administrator, or someone who doesn't work for your company at all but is still adding content (as with a social networking site).

Role
> A group to which users can be assigned. A role can be something like "administrator" or "sales team member." Drupal comes with three roles by default—"anonymous user" (for all users who have not logged in), "authenticated user" (for all logged-in users), and "administrator" (which gets *all* permissions)—but you can create as many different roles as you want.

Permissions
> Something that users within a role can (or can't!) do on the website. Each module can specify its own list of permissions that may be assigned. Examples of permissions are "Administer modules" and "Post comments." If a user does not have proper permissions to do something on the website, she'll receive an "Access denied" error page when trying to access the given functionality.

You can customize the "Access denied" and "Page not found" error pages by going to Configuration→System→"Site information" (*admin/config/system/site-information*).

It's worth sitting down at the beginning of each project and really thinking through what types of users will visit the site and what they're going to want to do. Different access levels will correspond to roles and permissions in the system. For example, "content editor," "forum moderator," "customer," and so on.

Configuring User Access

Controlling user access consists of three parts: (optionally) creating one or more roles to match the types of visitors your website needs to support, assigning permissions to those roles, and associating user accounts with those roles.

Under People→Permissions→Roles (*admin/people/permissions/roles*), pictured in Figure 2-33, you may create, edit, or remove roles, as well as reorder them with the drag-and-drop handles in order of escalated privileges. At this stage, there's nothing more to a role than a name. Individual users may be assigned to roles either via their user edit page or from the administration page at People (*admin/people*). Both creating and assigning roles requires the "Administer permissions" permission, which is separate from the "Administer users" permission that gives access to the main People administration page.

 Clicking the "edit permissions" link next to a role on this screen will display the matrix of permissions for only that role. This feature can be useful if you need to set several permissions for only a single role.

At People→Permissions (*admin/people/permissions*), individual permissions may be assigned to roles, as shown in Figure 2-34. Access to this screen is controlled by the "Administer permissions" permission, so different users can take care of day-to-day user-related administrative tasks without requiring an escalation of their privileges in the system.

 When you first create a role, it won't be assigned any permissions beyond what all authenticated users receive. Administrators are initially responsible for defining permissions and assigning users to the new role. If you get bug reports about people not being able to do things you think that they should be able to do, always check the permissions page!

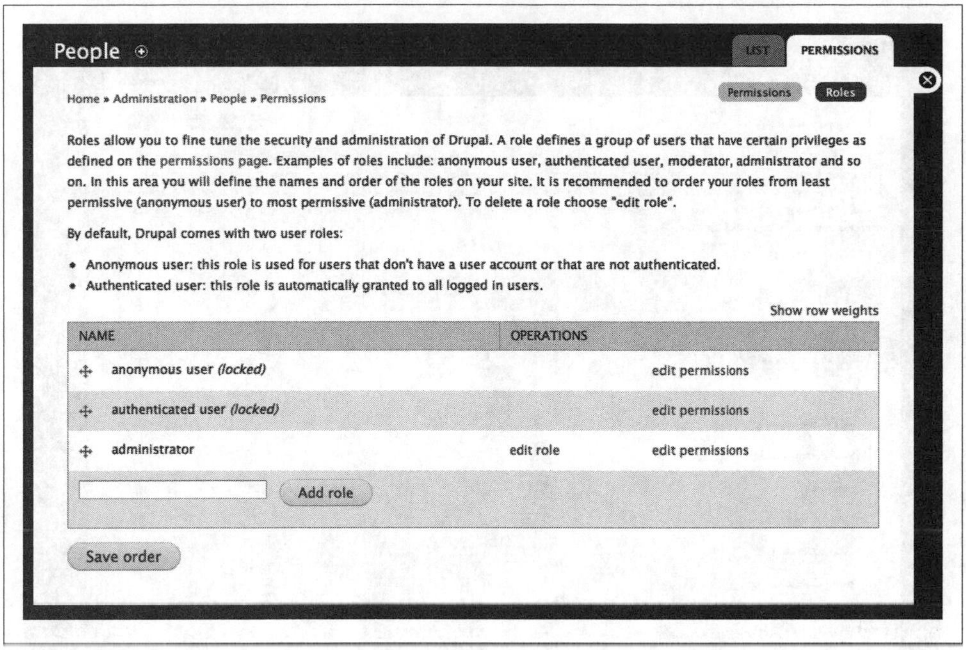

Figure 2-33. The Roles administration page

Often, permissions will have descriptions underneath them to provide more information about what they do. Additionally, modules that can impact website security will
be labeled with "Warning: Give to trusted roles only; this permission has security implications." This means that this permission should only be given to an administrator
level user, unless the full ramifications for that permission are fully understood.

Whenever you see "PHP" in a permission name, think *very* carefully
about whether you trust each and every one of the people within a given
role before you select it. A malicious user with PHP access can wreak all
sorts of havoc, from deleting all of the content on your website to spam-
ming all of your users, or potentially interfering with other applications
outside of Drupal. Beware.

All roles apart from "anonymous user" receive the permissions of "authenticated user" plus any other roles they're assigned. In Figure 2-34,
editors and administrators inherit the "View comments" permission
because they are by nature logged in (authenticated users) in order to
use the site. However, because "Administer comments and comment
settings" is an elevated permission not given to authenticated users, it
needs to be checked for both editors and administrators so that both
roles receive the permission.

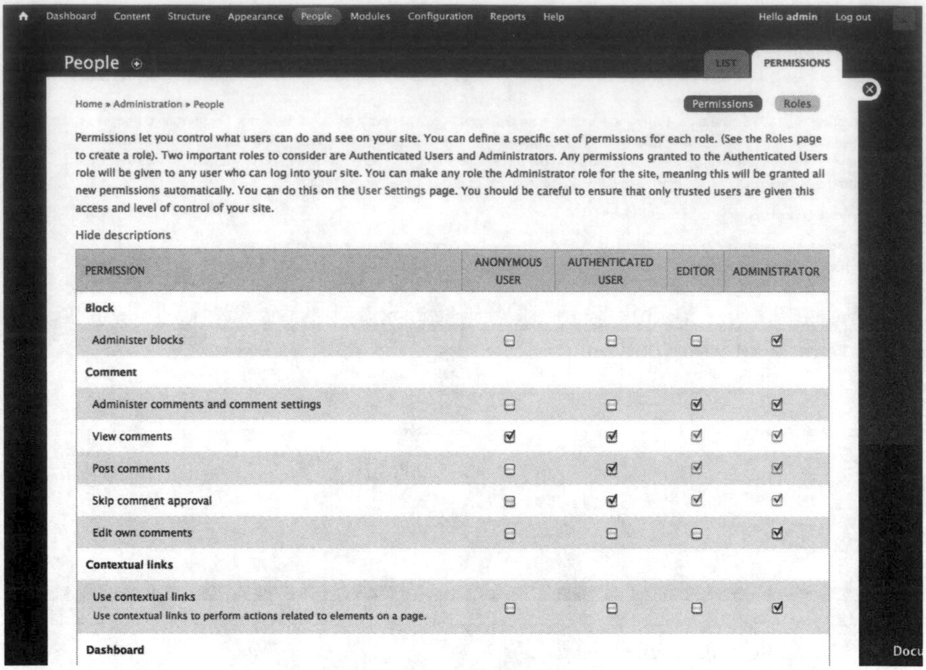

Figure 2-34. The Permissions administration page

The Importance of Testing Access Control

Make sure that you create at least one "test" user for each role that you've defined and click through the site as those users as you complete sections of it. The account created during installation, known as User 1, bypasses all permission checks in the system. Though this feature is very handy when you're initially building the site, testing as User 1 masks situations that will yield "Access denied" errors for your "mere mortal" visitors.

To test as a new user, log out and log back in as a different user with the role you wish to test. You can also keep multiple browsers open, logged in as a different test user in each. To switch between several accounts without having to log out between, the Devel module's "Switch user" block is very helpful (*http://drupal.org/project/devel*). You want to make sure that someone doesn't have more permissions than he should!

Also note that each time you enable or disable a module, the available user permissions will most likely change, so always revisit the permissions page after installing or updating a module.

User Profiles

Each user has a special page in Drupal called the *user profile*. This is the page that you see when clicking the "My account" link after you have logged in. Other users might visit your user profile page by clicking your name next to a blog entry or comment you have authored on the site. By default, the user profile page lists some simple information about the account, such as the username and the length of time that the user has been registered on the site. However, additional fields may be added to a user profile and contributed modules may provide more information here, as shown in Figure 2-35. Users may change basic settings in their user profile, such as their password and their time zone, and other modules can add extra features here as well, such as a language selection or a field to upload a picture to be displayed alongside the user's posts.

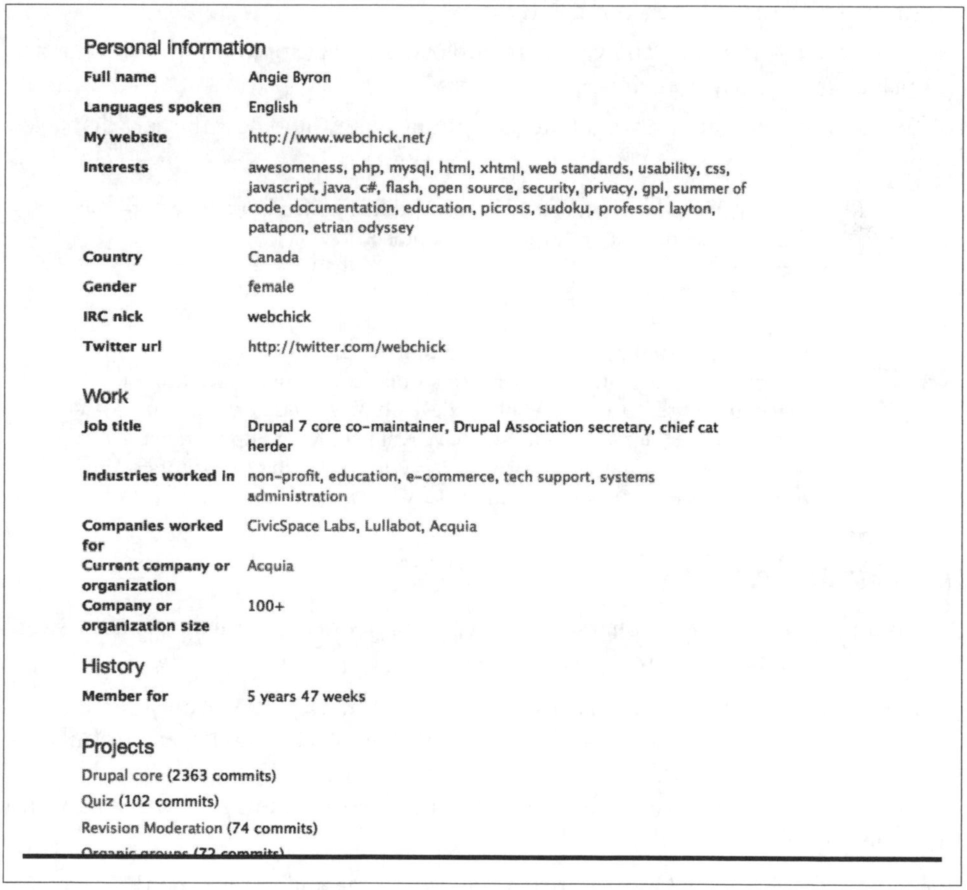

Personal information	
Full name	Angie Byron
Languages spoken	English
My website	http://www.webchick.net/
Interests	awesomeness, php, mysql, html, xhtml, web standards, usability, css, javascript, java, c#, flash, open source, security, privacy, gpl, summer of code, documentation, education, picross, sudoku, professor layton, patapon, etrian odyssey
Country	Canada
Gender	female
IRC nick	webchick
Twitter url	http://twitter.com/webchick

Work	
Job title	Drupal 7 core co-maintainer, Drupal Association secretary, chief cat herder
Industries worked in	non-profit, education, e-commerce, tech support, systems administration
Companies worked for	CivicSpace Labs, Lullabot, Acquia
Current company or organization	Acquia
Company or organization size	100+

History	
Member for	5 years 47 weeks

Projects

Drupal core (2363 commits)

Quiz (102 commits)

Revision Moderation (74 commits)

Organic groups (72 commits)

Figure 2-35. A user profile page on Drupal.org, with additional information provided by add-on modules

Account Settings

Under Configuration→People→"Account settings" (*admin/config/people/accounts*), there are many customizable user options, including:

- Various registration options, including whether users may create accounts themselves or this function is restricted to administrators only

- The exact text of various system emails sent from Drupal when, for example, a user registers, or when a user account is blocked

- How to handle the data of a user if her account is canceled

- Which role to use as the "administrator" role

- Signature support, which allows users to enter in a small bit of text to be included at the end of any of their comments

- Picture support, which allows users to upload an image or avatar that will be displayed next to any of their posts and comments

- What extra fields are shown on the user profile, if any, and how they are displayed

 The ability to add arbitrary fields to user profiles is an important feature of Drupal 7, and will be covered in Chapter 3.

By default, registration to the site requires administrative approval, which is a basic protection measure so that test Drupal sites do not attract unwanted attention while in development mode. When you're ready to make your site public and have real people sign up to it, make sure to toggle the "Who can register accounts?" setting to Visitors so your throngs of eager visitors can actually register accounts.

Handling Abusive Users

A community site of any reasonable size and popularity may eventually attract visitors with less-than-honorable intentions.

Administrators with the "Administer users" permission may change a user's status to Blocked, which will prevent him from logging in. The blocked user then has only the rights of an anonymous user. User accounts may also be canceled, and you'll be presented with a variety of options about how to handle the accounts and what to do with their content.

For more automated blocking, Drupal also provides the ability to block IP addresses, available at Configuration→People→"IP address blocking" (*admin/config/people/ip-blocking*), to help keep out repeat trolls, spammers, and the like. If you have the ability to block nefarious users from a firewall or web server level, however, that's a much more scalable approach and keeps them out of other web applications you might have on the same server.

We talk more about people with nefarious intent in "Spotlight: Content Moderation Tools" on page 66.

Hands-On: Creating Roles and Users

Earlier, we talked about Drupal's access control system, and how it's composed of users, roles, and permissions that map to who is going to use the site and what they're going to want to do on it. Let's spend a moment brainstorming about Mom and Pop, Inc.'s needs in this area.

This site will have four types of users:

- *Passing visitors*, who will basically only be able to read and search content, comment on news items once their content has been approved, and send mail with the contact form. This will map to the built-in "anonymous user" role in Drupal.

- *Customers*, who will log into the site and can freely comment on content, but aren't able to actually post news items themselves. Because they will be logged in, we'll use the built-in "authenticated user" role for customers.

- The *store owners* Mike and Jeanne themselves, who will handle writing content and some of the smaller day-to-day administration of the website. They'll need to be able to create and manage content, view logs and statistics, and change certain website settings when required. However, because they're not extremely technically savvy, the more advanced options should be hidden. We're going to call this role "editor," as they will be largely adding and editing content on the site.

- Finally, Goldie is the *webmaster*, who will actually build the site, as well as look after the more technical details for Jeanne and Mike. This will entail things like installing and upgrading modules, and configuring advanced website settings. Although she could just do everything as User 1, at some point she might want to bring on another family member to take over her duties, so it pays to be forward-thinking and make a role for this purpose. Luckily, Drupal comes with an "administrator" role by default that does just the trick.

 These standard four roles are the same ones we'll use in all future chapters. On your own Drupal site, you can have as many or as few roles as you'd like.

With that, we can begin setting up our access control:

1. Begin by creating an additional role for Mike and Jeanne. In the administrative toolbar, click on People→Permissions→Roles (*admin/people/permissions/roles*).

2. Enter **editor** as a role name and click "Add role."

3. Because *e* is alphabetically after *a*, the "editor" role ends up at the end of the role list. However, the role's level of permissions is actually between that of an "authenticated user" and an "administrator"; it will have more permissions than the former but less than the latter. Use the drag-and-drop arrows to move the "editor" role up one row so that it's placed between "authenticated user" and "administrator" and click "Save order." This will place the roles in the same order from left to right on the permission page, which will make things more intuitive.

4. After you've set up roles, it's always a good idea to set up some test users as well. Go back to People (*admin/people*) and click the "Add user" link (*admin/people/create*).

5. Enter in the settings from Table 2-4 and Figure 2-36 and click "Create new account."

Table 2-4. Values for initial website users

Setting	Value
Username	jeanne
Email address	*jeanne@example.com*
Password	Your choice, but try to pick something secure; perhaps "Mom-O-Rama"
Status	Active (default)
Roles	Check:
	• authenticated user (default)
	• editor
Notify user of new account	Unchecked (default)

> "Notify user of new account" is a handy feature on "real" Drupal sites, as it sends a quick email to the person to let him know his account was created, and provides instructions on how to log in. The exact email template used to do this, like all other user-related email templates, is configurable from Configuration→People →"Account settings" (*admin/config/people/accounts*).

6. Repeat the previous step for Mike, and repeat it again for Goldie, but add her to both the "editor" and "administrator" roles.

7. Also create a user called "customer," but do not assign any special roles.

8. When finished, your People administration screen should look like Figure 2-37.

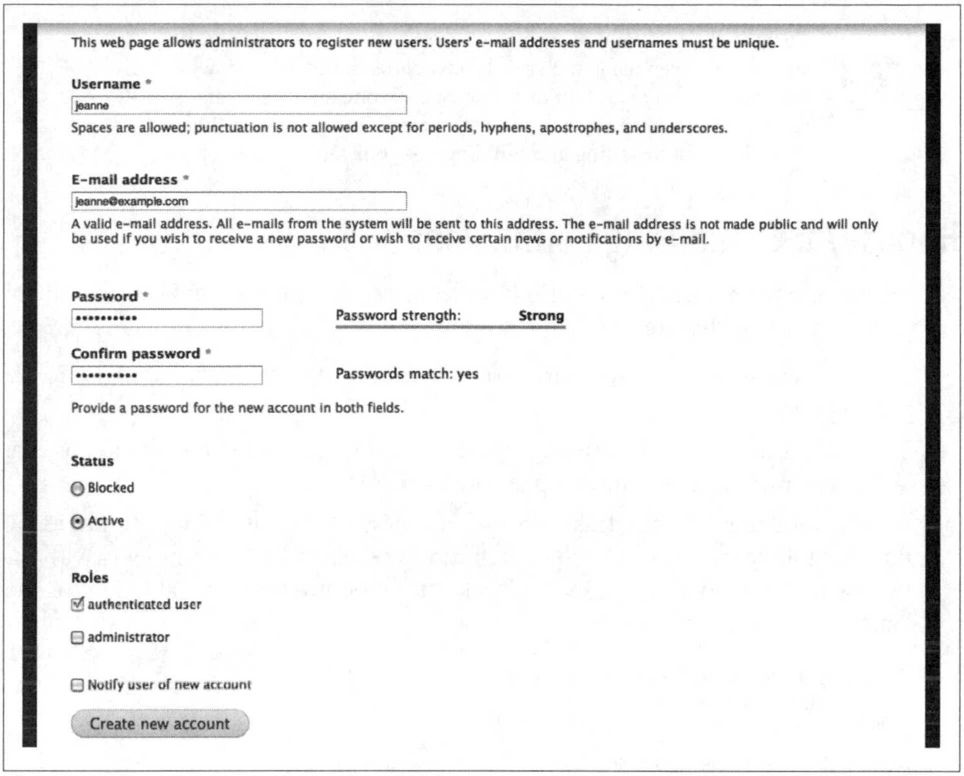

This web page allows administrators to register new users. Users' e-mail addresses and usernames must be unique.

Username *

```
jeanne
```

Spaces are allowed; punctuation is not allowed except for periods, hyphens, apostrophes, and underscores.

E-mail address *

```
jeanne@example.com
```

A valid e-mail address. All e-mails from the system will be sent to this address. The e-mail address is not made public and will only be used if you wish to receive a new password or wish to receive certain news or notifications by e-mail.

Password *

```
••••••••••
```

Password strength: **Strong**

Confirm password *

```
••••••••••
```

Passwords match: yes

Provide a password for the new account in both fields.

Status

◯ Blocked

◉ Active

Roles

☑ authenticated user

☐ administrator

☐ Notify user of new account

(Create new account)

Figure 2-36. New user account form

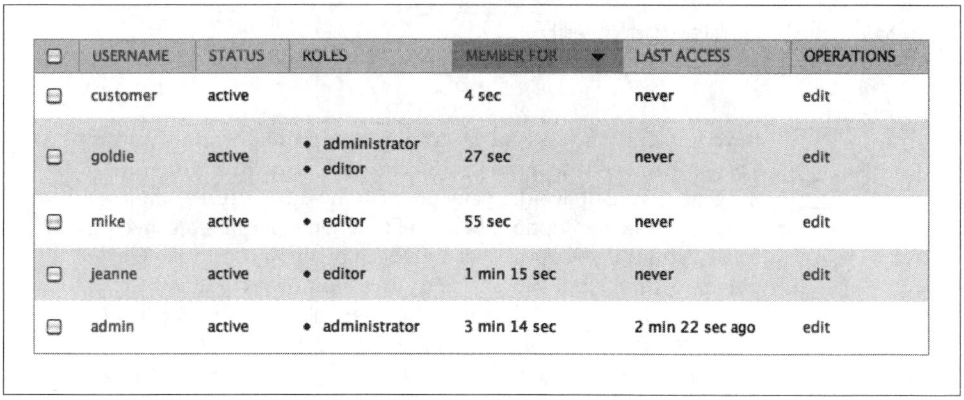

	USERNAME	STATUS	ROLES	MEMBER FOR ▼	LAST ACCESS	OPERATIONS
☐	customer	active		4 sec	never	edit
☐	goldie	active	• administrator • editor	27 sec	never	edit
☐	mike	active	• editor	55 sec	never	edit
☐	jeanne	active	• editor	1 min 15 sec	never	edit
☐	admin	active	• administrator	3 min 14 sec	2 min 22 sec ago	edit

Figure 2-37. A listing of site users

Technically, Goldie doesn't need a user account of her own, because she can just keep using the User 1, or superuser, account. However, it's best practice to create a unique user for everyone on the site, and to only use User 1 when the hugely elevated permissions are actually needed, like when first installing and building out your Drupal site.

Hands-On: Configuring Permissions

Now that we have roles and users in place, let's assign some permissions to control who can do what on the site:

1. In the administrative toolbar, go to People→Permissions (*admin/people/permissions*).

2. This screen, as shown earlier in Figure 2-34, is massive, and there's a lot to do here. We'll cover this rather daunting page on a per-role basis.

3. Anonymous users get the least amount of access on the site. They should really only be able to view and search content on the site, and post comments without bypassing the moderation queue. Check off the permissions in Table 2-5 for the "anonymous user" role.

Table 2-5. Permissions for the anonymous user role

Module	Permission
Comment	View comments (default)
Comment	Post comments
Filter	Use the Filtered HTML text format (default)
Node	View published content (default)
Search	Use search

Be **very** careful when assigning permissions to the anonymous user. These are the very definition of "untrusted" users. In addition to the general rule of avoiding any permission with "security implications" in the description, be aware that some permissions may behave erratically when assigned to the anonymous user role. For example, if the Node module's "*Article* : Edit own content" permission is applied to the anonymous user role, this will actually allow *all* anonymous users to edit articles created by *any* other anonymous user! This occurs because all logged-out users share the same user ID (0). Once again, always make sure to test your access control to ensure that it's working as you intended!

4. Authenticated users should get all the permissions of anonymous users, plus a few others. For example, their comments should appear instantly on the site, rather than having to wait to be approved. We'll also allow them to view the user profiles

of other users on the site. Choose permissions for authenticated users according to Table 2-6.

Table 2-6. Permissions for the authenticated user role

Module	Permission
Comment	View comments (default)
Comment	Post comments (default)
Comment	Skip comment approval (default)
Filter	Use the Filtered HTML text format (default)
Node	View published content (default)
Search	Use search
User	View user profiles

 Remember that choosing a permission for authenticated users selects that permission for *all* logged-in users, regardless of other roles they might have. Always give authenticated users the lowest subset of permissions you're comfortable giving all active users on the site.

5. Next, we get to the real meat of our site's access control: the "editor" role for Mike and Jeanne, our site's primary users. We'll want to give them some administrative control over the site, particularly as it relates to content management. This means providing permissions such as "Administer blocks" and "Administer comments and comment settings." However, we'll also want to hide the more advanced configuration settings from them, so as not to overwhelm them with settings, particularly if they could break the site by misconfiguring something. This means *not* granting access to permissions such as "Administer text formats and filters" or "Administer software updates." Typically, avoid granting access to permissions with "security implications" in the description to inexperienced content editors, although there are some notable exceptions.

One such exception is the Node module, which exposes two such permissions: "Bypass access control" and "Administer content." "Administer content" is a handy shortcut permission, as it provides create, edit, and delete permissions to all content types in the system. In a case like Mom and Pop, Inc. where there are only two, well-known content creators, we can trust them with this level of permissions. We can also trust them with "Bypass access control," a permission that allows the user to view all content on the site, even if it would normally be marked private. While this doesn't apply in the case of Mom and Pop, Inc., other sites may be using a module such as Content Access (*http://drupal.org/project/content_ac cess*) or Organic Groups (*http://drupal.org/project/og*) to hide content from certain users, and more caution may need to be exercised with this permission in that case.

Finally, there are also a host of permissions around using Drupal's administrative tools, such as "Use contextual links" and "Use the administration toolbar." We'll grant these to the "editor" role as well so that Mike and Jeanne can successfully administer the site going forward. One important permission to grant any editors on the site is the "Use the administration pages and help" permission from the System module. Without it, users will be unable to reach several sections of the administration panel, such as Structure, which holds block and menu configuration pages.

Configure the permissions for the editor role as outlined in Table 2-7. Note that this list excludes the permissions assigned earlier for the "authenticated user" role, because those are already provided to those in the "editor" role.

Table 2-7. Permissions for the editor role

Module	Permission
Block	Administer blocks
Comment	Administer comments and comment settings
Comment	Edit own comments
Contextual links	Use contextual links
Dashboard	View the administrative dashboard
Menu	Administer menus and menu items
Node	Bypass content access control
Node	Administer content; this obviates the need for any of the individual content type permissions
Node	Access the content overview page
Node	View own unpublished content
Node	View content revisions
Node	Revert content revisions
Node	Delete content revisions
Overlay	Access the administrative overlay
Path	Create and edit URL aliases
Search	Use advanced search
System	Use the administration pages and help
System	Use the site in maintenance mode
System	View the administration theme
System	View site reports
Toolbar	Use the administration toolbar
Users	Administer users

6. We don't need to provide a table for the administrator role; it automatically inherits all site permissions, which is as intended. However, it's worth talking about a few permissions that we've deliberately kept restricted to administrators rather than editors.

   Filter module is one of the big places in Drupal with security implications, as the filters used in text formats determine what user input gets stripped out in content, comments, and similar. While Filtered HTML in its default configuration is safe, Full HTML access is extremely dangerous! In addition to the more benign, accidental things users might do with this permission—like leave off a closing `</div>` tag that completely destroys your site's layout—more malicious and savvy users can embed cookie-stealing JavaScript and Flash code to gain control of an administrator account (or worse). Keep untrusted users to Filtered HTML only, and expand the list of allowed tags only after careful consideration of their effects.

   From both a security and site stability standpoint, it's a good idea to restrict the "Administer modules," "Administer software updates," and "Administer permissions" permissions to only users who are tech-savvy enough to maintain the site themselves. These deal with code changes and privilege escalation, which are best left to someone familiar with Drupal and its modules.

   Finally, any permission with "PHP" in its name should always be restricted to the fewest number of users possible because such permissions are incredibly dangerous. In fact, you might even want to *deselect* these permissions from the "administrator" role in order to restrict it to User 1 only (of course, you'd also have to restrict "Administer permissions" to User 1 in that case so another administrator couldn't just turn it on for herself).

7. After double-checking the permissions one more time, click the "Save permissions" button to save your work.

Now it's time for the final step: testing! Click "Log out" and notice that the toolbar disappears, there is no Navigation menu in the sidebar at all, and while you can view the contents of the site, if you try to go to a URL like */admin*, you'll receive an "Access denied" error.

8. Log in as "jeanne." You should have the ability to create content or administer the site.

9. Log out and then log in as "customer." You should be able to see the "My account" and "Log out" links in the upper-right corner, but that's about it. Click on the article we created before, and leave a comment. Note that it shows up instantly.

10. Now, log out and leave a comment as an anonymous user. You should receive the message, "Your comment has been queued for review by site administrators and will be published after approval."

11. When you've finished experimenting, log back in as the *admin* user account you created when you installed Drupal.

12. If you'd like, approve the anonymous comment by going to the administrative toolbar and clicking Content→Comments→"Unapproved comments" (*admin/content/comment/approval*). Edit the comment, and read its contents. If it's acceptable, expand the Administration fieldset at the top, change Status to Published, and save the form.

 Future chapters (and the book's source code) will name the test users for each role "user," "editor," and "admin," respectively, and give each account the password "oreilly."

Spotlight: Content Moderation Tools

When you open the floodgates for your users to become active participants in content creation, one of the inevitable things that comes up is the issue of content *moderation*—that is, ensuring that abusive, vulgar content and unsolicited advertising or spam is kept off the site and stays off.

You can help prevent this type of content using a two-tiered approach: automated spam detection and manual spam prevention.

Automated Spam Detection

Mollom (*http://mollom.com*) is a service started by Benjamin Schrauwen and Dries Buytaert, creator and project lead of Drupal. It automatically scans the content of your site comments (as well as nodes, the contact form, and multiple other places where user-generated content comes in) and, based on its analysis of millions of other blogs' content, prevents obvious spam from even being posted to the website. Your website benefits from the collective intelligence of every other website that has a Mollom plug-in installed, and Mollom is compatible with many different content management systems and programming languages.

Mollom attempts to overcome shortcomings of traditional spam-trapping tools in the following ways:

- Supports blocking not just comment spam, but also spam from the contact form, node forms (blog entries, forum topics, and so on), user registration and password request form, and others. This feature is not found in competing solutions, wherein you have to use one tool for handling comments and another for handling registration forms, which makes Mollom a one-stop solution.

- Discerns between "spam" and "ham" and for those posts that are borderline, displays what's known to web developers as a CAPTCHA (Completely Automated Public Turing test to tell Computers and Humans Apart), and is known to people like Mike and Jeanne as "those squiggly, hard-to-read characters you have to type in to get the darn form to go." This test allows humans to proceed while blocking spam robots. CAPTCHAs are displayed as both an image and an audio file for maximum accessibility. Mollom thus helps to remove the need for moderation queues and eases moderation burden for administrators; spam is blocked before it hits the site at all.

- Allows deletion not only of spam, but also of low-quality and off-topic content or violent and abusive content. Mollom also returns a quality score for each post, based on spelling, language, and punctuation, which you can use to maintain a certain level of professionalism on your site.

- Leverages the power of OpenID by assigning a "reputation score" to OpenID accounts across all websites. This ensures that humans' posts are let through instantly, while spammers' posts are blocked across any site they attempt to post to via an OpenID account.

- Generates graphs showing overall spam content, as pictured in Figure 2-38.

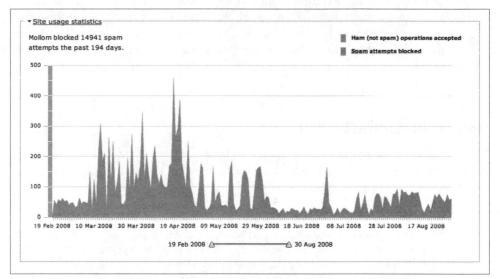

Figure 2-38. Example spam reporting from the Mollom module

Mollom's goal is to eliminate the need to do any manual intervention of content moderation, by passing the "gray area" validation to the posters themselves via the conditional CAPTCHA. And, unlike the CAPTCHA provided by most websites, users are only confronted by the scrambled character challenge if their post is "borderline"—not for every single form submission, unlike other solutions such as the CAPTCHA module (*http://drupal.org/project/captcha*).

The Mollom module is available from *http://drupal.org/project/mollom*, and you can obtain an API key by creating an account on *http://mollom.com*.

If you prefer to use other automated antispam tools such as Akismet (*http://akismet .com/*) or Defensio (*http://www.defensio.com/*), another option is the AntiSpam module (*http://drupal.org/project/antispam*). While the AntiSpam module is not as popular in the Drupal world as Mollom, its ability to evaluate multiple external services to see which provides the best protection is a nice feature.

Manual Spam Prevention Tools

Automated tools are perfect for blocking obvious spam and robots, but what do you do to prevent trolls on your site from posting pornography or other offensive content? Some websites prefer a more hands-on approach, particularly if there are legal ramifications to offensive content appearing on the website even for a second.

Drupal core includes some basic content moderation tools, such as the ability to set any content type as "unpublished" by default (hiding it entirely from everyone but the original author and administrators), and revision control so that further edits can be "rolled back" to a version that was approved. But many Drupal sites set up their own custom moderation screens with tools like the Views and Flag modules, as well as the Revisioning module (*http://drupal.org/project/revisioning*), a simple utility module that ensures that the approved version of a node stays published when subsequent edits are made.

Hands-On: Contact Form

Let's tie together everything we've learned so far and get the contact form set up, as pictured in Figure 2-39. This will involve enabling the core Contact module, configuring its settings, and adding permissions.

 In addition to a site-wide contact form, the Contact module also optionally provides each user on the site with her own private contact form, which is accessible from her user profile. This is a useful means of allowing users to talk to one another without exposing their email addresses.

1. First, enable the Contact module. In the administrative toolbar, go to Modules (*admin/modules*), and type **con** in the Module Filter search to quickly access the module's row in the modules table. Enable it and click "Save configuration."
2. Next, we need to set up the contact form's settings. Click the Configure link in the Contact module's table row; or in the administrative toolbar, go to Structure→"Contact form" (*admin/structure/contact*).
3. Click the "Add category" (*admin/structure/contact/add*) link at the top. This screen shows a list of categories that users can choose from when using the contact form.

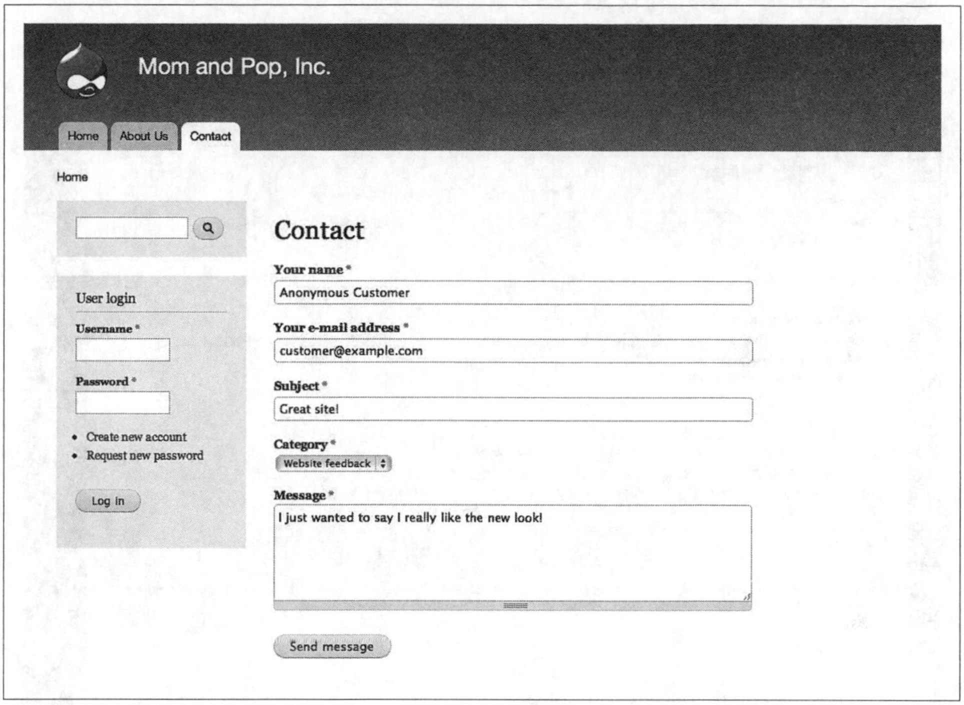

Figure 2-39. A contact form for the website

On each category, you can choose which email address(es) will receive a copy of the mail, as well as whether an autoreply message should be sent to the user. By default, the Contact module has a category called "Website feedback," which gets sent to the administrator email address.

Let's also add a new category for sales inquiries, so that customers can send in questions about Mom and Pop, Inc.'s products. We'll also make this category selected by default, to help minimize the strain on Goldie's inbox.

Enter the category settings from Table 2-8, as pictured in Figure 2-40, and click Save.

Table 2-8. Contact category settings

Setting	Value
Category	Sales inquiries
Recipients	(enter your email address)
Auto-reply	Thanks for sending us a sales inquiry! We will respond to you shortly.
Weight	0 (default)
Selected	Yes

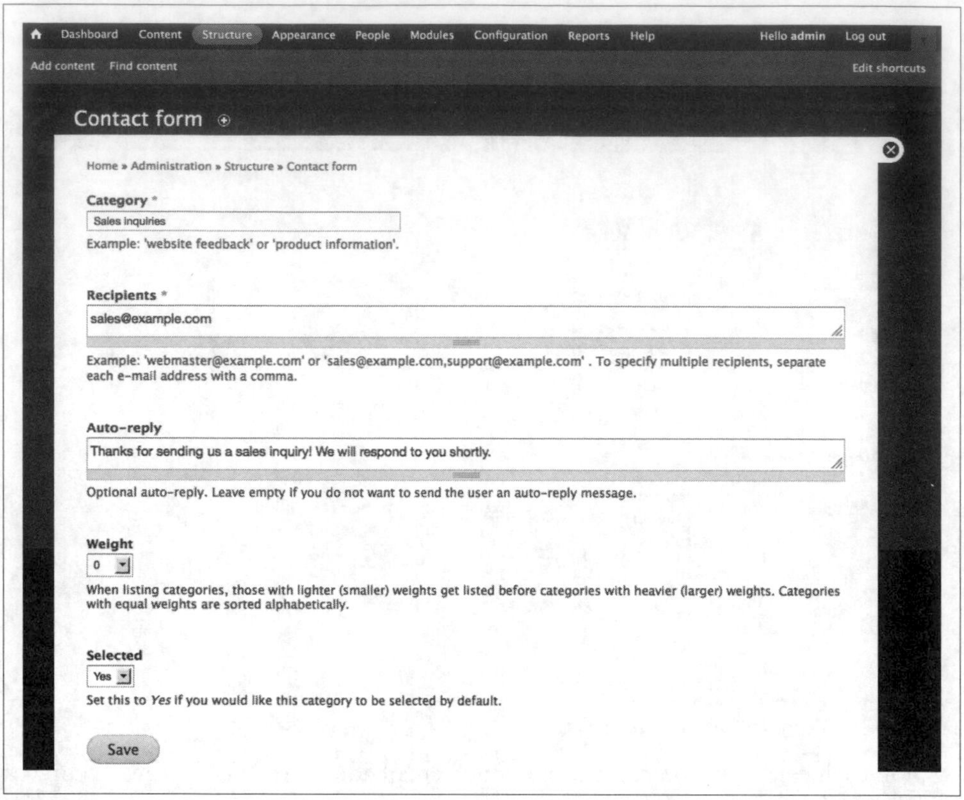

Figure 2-40. Settings for the website feedback contact form category

4. Next, we'll want to add a link in the website navigation to the contact form for visitors.

   Some modules, such as the Contact module, conveniently provide us with a menu item all ready to use, though in the Contact module's case it is not enabled by default. Anytime a module provides a menu item for you, it will always appear in the Navigation menu by default. We can easily move it to wherever we want, though.

   In the administrative toolbar, go to Administer→Structure→Menus→Navigation→"List links" (*admin/structure/menu/manage/navigation*).

5. Find the "Contact (disabled)" menu item in the list. Click its "edit" link.

6. Enter the settings from Table 2-9 and click Save. This will enable the Contact link and move it from the Navigation sidebar up to the "Main menu" tabs, just after the Home and About Us links.

Table 2-9. Contact menu item settings

Setting	Value
Menu link title	Contact
Description	Get in touch with us
Enabled	Checked
Show as expanded	Unchecked (default)
Parent link	<Main menu> (the very top selection)
Weight	10

7. Finally, we need to configure permissions on the contact form so that visitors may use it. In the administrative toolbar, head to People→Permissions (*admin/people/permissions*) and enable the permissions listed in Table 2-10. We'll give all users the ability to use the site-wide contact form, only authenticated users the ability to use each other's personal contact forms, and Mike and Jeanne the ability to tweak the contact form categories. Click "Save permissions" when finished.

Table 2-10. Permissions for the Contact module

Permission: Contact	anonymous user	authenticated user	editor	administrator
Administer contact forms and contact form settings			Checked	Checked
Use the site-wide contact form	Checked	Checked	Checked	Checked
Use users' personal contact forms		Checked	Checked	Checked

8. Finally, click the Contact link in your menu to view your shiny new contact form, as pictured in Figure 2-39!

Spotlight: Themes

Drupal gives you a lot of tools to move things around and arrange the *functionality* of your site, but often the main difference between most websites comes down to presentation.

When you think about it, there's really not much difference between the functionality of YouTube and Flickr. Certainly, one manages video content and the other focuses on photos. But these sites have more similarities than differences. Both manage media content and allow users to share their uploads. Both allow users to create a network of contacts. Users can create their own profiles, comment on others' content, and mark content as a "favorite" for later reference.

Functionally, these sites are very similar, but their presentation is completely different. The layout of the sites is different, their backgrounds are different, their entire look and feel is different—each has a different *presentation* of its elements.

Themes are the Drupal method for controlling your site's presentation. It's not enough to get a site functionally working—it also has to *feel* like your own, and has to be distinguished from other sites out there.

Drupal comes with four themes to get you started:

- Bartik
- Seven
- Garland
- Stark

Finding a Theme

Most sites won't be satisfied with the meager selection of themes that comes with Drupal core. Luckily, Drupal.org has a large repository of free themes that have been uploaded by contributors. You can find a listing of these themes at *http://drupal.org/ project/Themes*, as pictured in Figure 2-41.

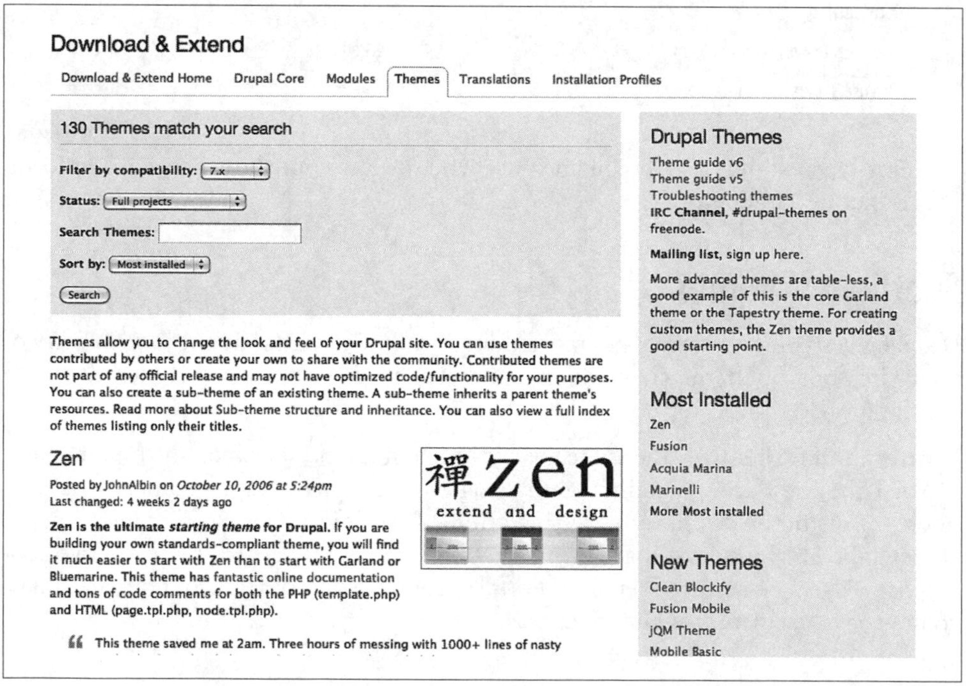

Figure 2-41. Drupal.org's themes listing, filtered by 7.x-compatible themes

Many of the themes at the top of the "Most installed" list, including themes such as Zen (*http://drupal.org/project/zen*) and Fusion (*http://drupal.org/project/fusion*), are "base" themes. These themes intentionally provide very minimal styling, or even none at all, so that they can be used as a starting point for highly customized themes by those with CSS and PHP coding skills.

Unfortunately, detailing how to write a custom theme is outside the scope of this book, but if this is a topic that interests you, you can find more about it in the Drupal.org Theming Guide (*http://drupal.org/documentation/theme*).

The quality of the themes in the Drupal.org repository varies greatly. These themes have been created for a wide variety of purposes and needs by contributors with a broad range of programming and design skills. Download several themes and be sure to read their *README.txt* files to determine how to best use them.

Several companies, such as Top Notch Themes (*http://www.topnotchthemes.com/*), offer premium, paid themes. These themes tend to be higher quality, are a bit more "bullet-proof," and may allow for easier customization by administrators.

Theme Installation

Installing a theme requires almost exactly the same process as installing a module, as we saw in "Hands-On: Working with Modules" on page 49. You can either click the "Install new theme" link at the top of the Appearance page and walk through the installation wizard, or download the theme's *.zip* or *.tar.gz* file from its Drupal.org project page and extract it into the *sites/all/themes* directory. Your new theme should appear on the Appearance (*admin/appearance*) administration page in your Drupal installation, as shown in Figure 2-42.

As with modules, themes written for Drupal 6 are not compatible with Drupal 7 and vice versa.

Theme Configuration

Themes can be enabled and disabled from the Appearance page (*admin/appearance*) in the administrative toolbar, shown in Figure 2-42.

The Appearance page is divided into Enabled and Disabled themes. Enabled themes are exposed as options in interfaces such as the Block administration page, and other contributed modules can use enabled themes to make different parts of the site look unique. The theme marked "Default theme" (in this case, Bartik) is the one displayed

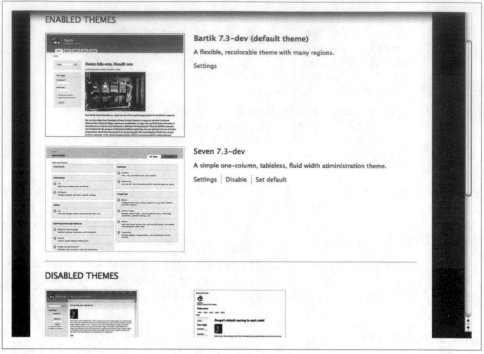

Figure 2-42. The Appearance administration page

on the frontend of the site. To set a different theme (such as Stark) as the frontend theme, click "Enable and set default" or "Set default," as appropriate.

 Stark isn't a pretty theme. It gets its name because it exposes Drupal's "stark naked" markup with only the bare minimum of styling required to make sidebars show up in the right place. If you're looking to make your own custom theme from scratch, Stark can be a useful starting point to determine what tags and styling you have to work with by default.

Drupal offers a number of configuration features that themes can take advantage of. There are two ways to configure themes. For global options (ones that you want to apply across all themes), select the Settings tab at Appearance (*admin/appearance/settings*). For settings specific to a single theme, or to configure settings that are only offered on a per-theme basis, select the Settings link next to any enabled theme (*admin/appearance/settings/<theme_name>*). The settings shown on this form will vary from theme to theme.

On these settings pages, you can toggle the display of many page elements, including the site logo, site name, site slogan, user pictures, and others, as shown in Figure 2-43. Sometimes, one or more of these checkboxes may be disabled by settings elsewhere in your installation. For example, if the Comment module is turned off, Drupal no longer lets you toggle the "User pictures in comments" and "User verification status in comments" settings.

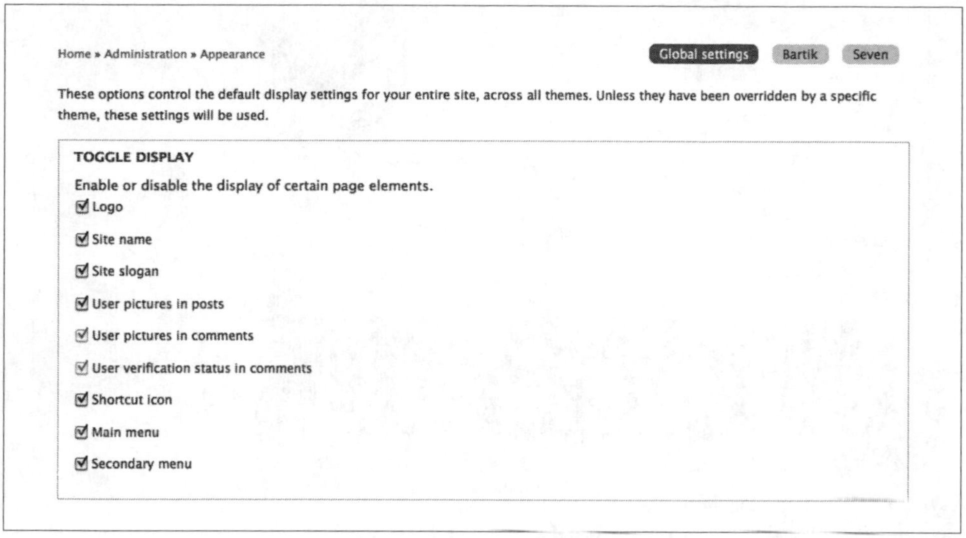

Figure 2-43. *The theme configuration page allows customization of which page elements are displayed*

> You can configure settings such as site name and site slogan at Configuration→System→"Site information" (*admin/config/system/site-information*).

The theme configuration page also allows administrators to upload their own site logo image and shortcut icon (also known as the favicon or bookmark icon, which appears in the browser's address bar) or simply point to one elsewhere on their server. Note that in order to see these settings, you must first uncheck "Use the default."

Some themes, such as the core Bartik and Garland themes, also take advantage of the Color module, which allows administrators to configure a theme's color scheme using a handy JavaScript-based color picker. Figure 2-44 shows the Color module in action.

Blocks and Regions

It's important to remember that block regions are defined by the theme, and different themes may offer different regions. If you have blocks assigned to a region in one theme and you switch to another theme that does not offer a region with the same name, these blocks could disappear from your site. After enabling a new theme, visit the Block administration page at Structure→Blocks (*admin/structure/block*) and see what regions

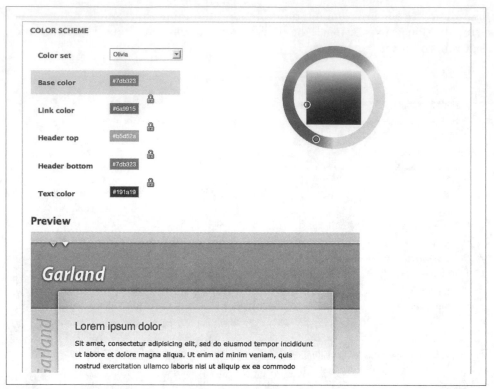

Figure 2-44. The Color module, supported in some themes, offers customization of the site's colors

are available in your theme. You may need to reassign blocks to another region to take full advantage of the new theme.

Administration Theme Setting

By default, Drupal ships with the Seven theme—which sports a neutral, no-nonsense design—for use on administrative pages. This is to help you understand when you're viewing the public frontend that your users will see and when you are in a backend, administrative context. It's also possible to use a different theme as the administrative theme, or even to use the same theme for both the front- and backends of the site. You can choose an administrative theme at the bottom of the Appearance (*admin/appearance*) page. This theme will be used for all administration pages (those starting with "admin" in the URL path and also maintenance pages such as *update.php*), and optionally for content creation and editing pages as well. Figure 2-45 shows the Administration theme settings page.

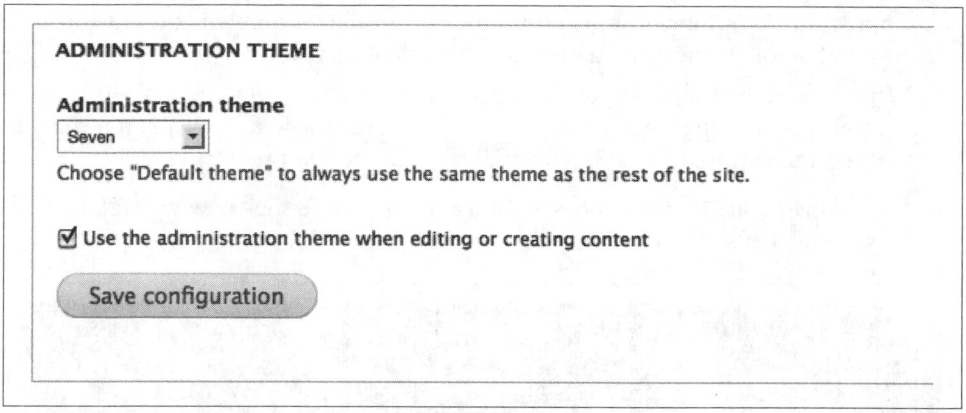

Figure 2-45. The Administration theme settings page

Hands-On: Branding the Site

Now it's time to make the site look less like Drupal and more like Mom and Pop, Inc. This section will walk through configuring a theme in order to customize the look and feel of a site:

1. In the administrative toolbar, head to the Appearance section (*admin/appearance*), and check that the first theme listed is Bartik and it's denoted as "(default theme)" in the interface. If not, click the "Set default" link next to Bartik in order to make it the default theme. This change won't appear to take effect until you exit the administrative interface and return to your public-facing website.

2. Click the Settings tab (*admin/appearance/settings*) at the top of the page to configure the global settings, which apply to all themes.

3. Under "Logo image settings," uncheck "Use the default logo" to allow customization of the site logo.

4. Upload the *mom_and_pop_logo.png* image in the *assets/ch02-jumpstart* folder in the book's source code, and click "Save configuration."

5. Close out of the Overlay or click on the Home button in the administrative toolbar to return to your site's frontend. You should now see the new logo appear in the upper-left corner, although—egad!—it looks absolutely horrendous on that blue background! Additionally, having both the text logo and the "Mom and Pop, Inc." site name text feels pretty redundant. Let's clean things up a bit.

6. Return to the Appearance settings page by going to the administrative toolbar and clicking Appearance→Settings, and click the Settings link next to the Bartik theme (*admin/appearance/settings/bartik*). This allows you to access the Bartik-specific theme settings, which include an integrated color-picker from the Color module.

7. Choose a color scheme that is pleasing to the eye and complements the logo. Be creative! Scroll down to see a preview of your colors while you work.

8. When you're happy with your color scheme results, under the Toggle Display fieldset, uncheck the "Site name" value so that only the logo appears, not the textual representation. Click "Save configuration" once you're finished.

You should have a site that now boasts Mom and Pop, Inc.'s slick new logo, along with a color scheme that's all their own, as shown in Figure 2-46.

Figure 2-46. Website bearing new logo and colors

 Interested in taking theme customization even further? Check out the Sweaver module (*http://drupal.org/project/sweaver*), which provides a visual interface for styling themes. Sweaver will let you select page elements and change not only their colors, but also their background images, spacing, font styling, and more, all without writing a single line of code. And if you *are* code-savvy, there's even a plug-in to allow you to enter custom CSS for page elements right from the browser.

Summary

This chapter provided an overview of Drupal's major functionality by walking you through building a small website. We created some simple content and content types, we set up a contact form, and we worked on how to configure Drupal's theme settings to customize a site to a particular look and feel. While this site is great for a start, we can add much more by expanding Drupal core with contributed modules, as we'll show you throughout the rest of this book.

Here is a list of contributed modules we referenced in this chapter:

- AntiSpam module (*http://drupal.org/project/antispam*)
- CAPTCHA module (*http://drupal.org/project/captcha*)
- Content Access (*http://drupal.org/project/content_access*)
- Devel (*http://drupal.org/project/devel*)
- Drush (*http://drupal.org/project/drush*)
- Mollom (*http://mollom.com*)
- Module Filter (*http://drupal.org/project/module_filter*)
- Organic Groups (*http://drupal.org/project/og*)
- Revisioning (*http://drupal.org/project/revisioning*)
- Sweaver (*http://drupal.org/project/sweaver*)

Here is a list of links that we referenced in this chapter:

- Drupal core download (*http://drupal.org/download*)
- Module downloads (*http://drupal.org/project/Modules*)
- Theme downloads (*http://drupal.org/project/Themes*)
- Akismet antispam (*http://akismet.com/*)
- Defensio antispam (*http://www.defensio.com/*)
- Drupal system requirements (*http://drupal.org/node/270*)
- Drupal version information (*http://drupal.org/handbook/version-info*)
- Drupal.org handbooks (*http://drupal.org/handbooks*)
- Drupal.org Theming Guide (*http://drupal.org/documentation/theme*)
- Getting Started guide (*http://drupal.org/node/258*)
- Support forum (*http://drupal.org/forum/18*)
- Troubleshooting FAQ (*http://drupal.org/Troubleshooting-FAQ*)

CHAPTER 3

Job Posting Board

This chapter outlines the two most powerful features in Drupal. Yes, we're saying outright that the two most powerful features are fields and views. The Field module (and its corresponding Field UI module, which provides an administrative interface) comes with core and allows you to customize existing entity forms in Drupal by adding a variety of fields—such as checkboxes, select lists, file uploads, and several others—all without writing a line of code. The Views module is the natural counterpart to Field, letting you get data out of your site rather than into it. Views allow you to create pages and blocks that pull data back out and display it to your visitors. Want a paged table showing product details that can be sorted by price or manufacturer? You can build it with Field and Views. Want to display a block that lists the fans of a particular artist in a grid as a set of user photo thumbnails? You can build it with Field and Views. Anywhere there's a list of content on your website (and most websites are almost *all* just lists of content in one form or another), Field and Views are the two key modules you need.

The Field and Views modules form the foundation of nearly every other project in this book and most of the Drupal-powered websites on the Internet. We'll cover how to set up a new content type and customize the node form so that you can add any type of field for inputting data. We'll configure a site that allows the creation of job openings, and then we'll build an interface for browsing though available jobs.

This chapter introduces the following modules:

Field (core)
    Provides infrastructure to add fields to entities

Field UI (core)
    Provides the user interface to add fields to entity forms

File (core)
    Provides file upload fields

References (http://drupal.org/project/references)
    Provides User and Node reference fields

Views (http://drupal.org/project/views)
    Creates lists of entities, like content and users

If you would like to participate in the hands-on exercises in this chapter, you should install Drupal using the *Chapter 3: Job posting board* installation profile from the book's sample code. Doing this will create the starter website on your web server, with some basic configuration. The completed website will look as pictured in Figure 3-1 and at *http://jobs.usingdrupal.com*. For more information on using the book's sample code, see the Preface.

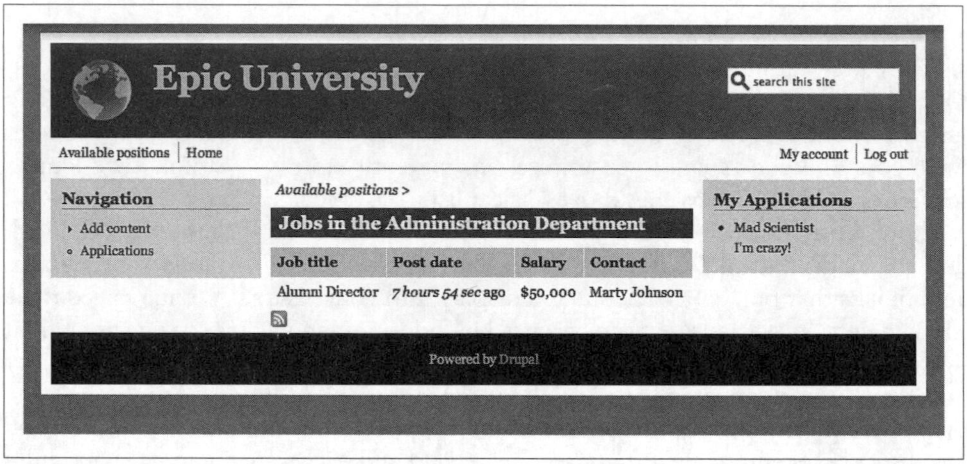

Figure 3-1. The completed Epic University site

Case Study

Several students on work-study at Epic University have been tasked with building a job posting website for their school. The university needs to have the site built in a short amount of time (not to mention cheaply) on its internal servers. Because of its flexible entity and field system, user management, and low cost, the students chose to download Drupal and get started building a site.

The Human Resources department requires that university faculty be able to post job openings, which include a description, department, contact person, and salary information. Users should be able to sign into the site and view both a list of all available openings and lists of openings within a single, specific department. Additionally, users should be able to apply for a specific position, and to view a record of all positions to which they've applied.

Implementation Notes

Drupal core provides this site with a good starting point. It provides the user access requirements and allows the creation of several different types of content, such as "job" and "application" types. Drupal's default settings give each one of these new types only a Title and Body field. We'll need quite a few more fields so that users can enter more data, and so that we can pull out information from certain fields to make listings of content.

Custom input forms

At the heart of the requirements for this website, textual data will need to be inserted through a variety of forms. The Field module will provide the means for users to enter data into the site. Drupal core provides several different kinds of fields needed, like a drop-down select list for the university department, or simple text fields for phone numbers and addresses. Contributed modules, like References (*http://drupal.org/ project/references*) or "Address field" (*http://drupal.org/project/addressfield*), give us additional fields that let us link content and users throughout the site.

File uploads

One thing we will need is the ability to upload files to the site so that applicants can include a résumé without having to type it all into a form. Drupal core's File module exposes a field that can provide this functionality.

Listings

Besides entering data into the website, job applicants and employers will want to view lists of potential jobs and applicants. For nearly any purpose of displaying content, the Views module can provide a listing of content in a variety of ways: a table, a list of full nodes or teasers, an RSS feed, a list of individual fields, and more. We'll build all the necessary lists for this chapter as views, including special views that can take a user ID or department and filter down to include only relevant content.

Spotlight: Field and Field UI

The Field module provides an extremely flexible framework for creating forms to enter content. The ability to add custom fields to forms is a new feature in core for Drupal 7. In Drupal 6, all of this functionality was provided by the Content Construction Kit (CCK) module (*http://drupal.org/project/cck*). Most of CCK is now integrated into core, but there is still a contributed CCK module in Drupal 7. The main reason for this is to provide an upgrade path for Drupal 6's CCK fields to Drupal 7's core fields. Since we are not upgrading, but instead building a new Drupal 7 site, we won't need CCK for this project.

Upon installing a new copy of Drupal, you'll see two content types provided: "Article" and "Basic page." They both have a Title and Body, which are the basic fields provided when you create a content type. Any additional content types that are created will also contain a Title field and (optionally) a Body field.

Using the Field and Field UI modules, pictured in Figure 3-2, you may add any number of custom fields to any content type. Combined with the ability to create custom content types, core lets you create completely customized forms for adding content. Figure 3-3 shows the "Basic page" form after we've added a few custom fields, such as an additional text field, an image field, and a set of radio buttons.

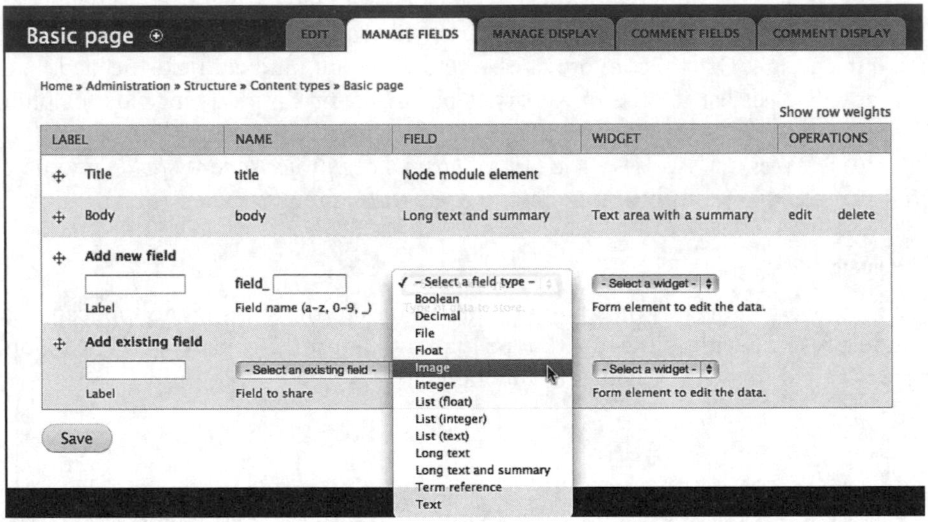

Figure 3-2. The Field UI module provides the ability to add fields to entities, including nodes, comments, and users

Another new feature in Drupal 7 is the ability to add fields to any *entity* in the system: users, comments, and taxonomy terms, with more options offered in contrib through the means of modules such as File Entity (*http://drupal.org/project/file_entity*) or Drupal Commerce (*http://drupal.org/project/drupal_commerce*). For example, it's now possible to add tags to users, or attach an upload field to comments.

When it comes to actually using fields, it is important to understand the various pieces involved. There are three main concepts to cover: field types, widgets, and displays.

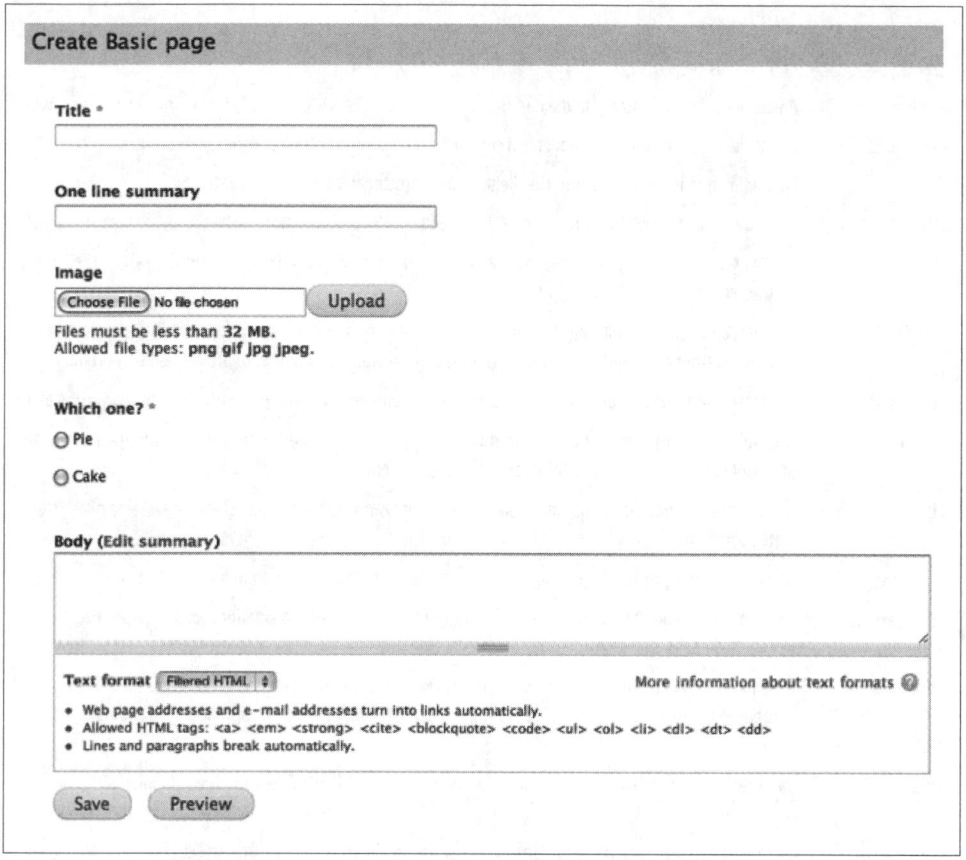

Create Basic page

Title *

One line summary

Image

Choose File   No file chosen   Upload

Files must be less than 32 MB.
Allowed file types: png gif jpg jpeg.

Which one? *

○ Pie

○ Cake

Body (Edit summary)

Text format Filtered HTML ⬍   More information about text formats ⓘ

- Web page addresses and e-mail addresses turn into links automatically.
- Allowed HTML tags: <a> <em> <strong> <cite> <blockquote> <code> <ul> <ol> <li> <dl> <dt> <dd>
- Lines and paragraphs break automatically.

Save   Preview

Figure 3-3. The "Basic page" content type form, after adding custom fields

Field Types

The type of field you choose will determine how a user will save data into your site. The field type represents the type of data that needs to be saved, such as integer, decimal, or text. It is completely decoupled from what the user will ultimately fill out and be presented with. When you're choosing a field to add to an entity, the first decision you need to make is what kind of data is being stored "behind the scenes" in the form. Will the information entered into the form be something basic like text or numbers, or something more special like a relationship to another node or user? The field types included in core are displayed in Table 3-1, along with how those fields are represented in the database. Other modules, such as Fivestar (*http://drupal.org/project/fivestar*) and Date (*http://drupal.org/project/date*), add more field types to use. Those modules are covered later in the book, in Chapters 5 and 6, respectively. You can find a full list of available field types in the Fields category from the Drupal.org module search page (*http://drupal.org/project/modules?filters=tid%3A20224*).

Table 3-1. Core field types

Field type	Common uses
Boolean	A basic on/off switch, stored in the database as either 0 or 1. This is often used for yes/no or true/false data.
Decimal	An efficient way of storing numbers to a certain decimal point. Useful for currency amounts.
File	For nonimage file uploads. Stores the filename and directory location of associated files.
Float	The most accurate way of storing numbers that need a high level of precision, such as scientific measurements.
Image	For image file uploads. Stores the relationship to the file information and metainformation about the image, such as alt text.
Integer	The most efficient way of storing a number. Use for product numbers and identifiers, or whenever you'll have an exact number of something, like track numbers on an album or number of attendees at an event.
List (float)	Used for presenting a list of options, stored as floating numbers. For example, a user's preferred version of π.
List (integer)	Used for presenting a list of options, stored as integers. Many lists, whether they're presenting a list of colors or favorite animals, can choose this type for lookup efficiency.
List (text)	Used for presenting a list of options, stored as text. For example, a list of U.S. states that stores two-letter state abbreviations.
Long text	Used to store long strings of text, such as biographies, that require more than a sentence or so.
Long text and summary	Very similar to "Long text," this stores long strings of text, along with a smaller version of that text. The default Body field on core content types uses this field type.
Term reference	Used for adding categories to entities. Stores the relationship to term entities and is used to associate vocabulary terms with content. This field will be covered in more detail in "Spotlight: Taxonomy" on page 266.
Text	Can store a string of text. This is intended for short bits of text, like names and descriptions.

 Unlike other elements of a field, its field type *cannot* be changed. If you need to change the type of field from text to integer (or any other conversion), you'll need to delete the field (along with its data!) and replace it with a new field with the desired type. Therefore, it pays to think about your choice up front.

Input Widgets

Once the type of data is determined, then it's time to think about how it should look in the form. How will people enter the data you want? In Drupal lingo, form elements are called *widgets*. Do you want a drop-down select list, or a group of radio buttons? Checkboxes or an autocomplete text field? Choose the widget that makes the most sense for the user entering the data. Note that the widgets available will vary based on the field type chosen.

The widget types included in core, and to which field types they belong, are displayed in Table 3-2. Many of these widgets, such as "Select list" and "Text field," will also apply to field types added by contributed modules, and contributed modules often expose additional widget choices as well.

Table 3-2. Core widget types

Widget type	Core field type(s)	Common uses
Autocomplete term widget (tagging)	Term reference	This provides a blank text field that will search for existing matching terms as the user types letters. A user can then select one of the existing terms, or he can enter a new term, which will then be added to the taxonomy vocabulary once the form is saved.
Checkboxes/ Radio buttons	Boolean, List, Term reference	Use when there are multiple options to select from; checkboxes will be used for fields that support selecting multiple values, radios for a single value only. A "T-shirt size" field makes sense as a radio button selection, whereas a "Favorite colors" field makes sense as a collection of checkboxes.
File	File	This provides an upload button that allows you to browse for a file and upload it to the Drupal site.
Image	Image	This widget is the same as the File widget with the additional feature that once an image is uploaded, a small thumbnail will appear next to the upload field. It also optionally allows for entry of "alt" and "title" attributes for a textual description of the image so screen readers and search engines can "see" it.
Text field	Decimal, Float, Integer, Text	This widget allows a single line of text to be entered, such as a name or phone number. Either plain text or formatted text entry (to support bold and italics or links, for example) is supported.
Text area (multiple rows)	Long text	Use this widget for entering a larger paragraph of text, such as a biography or a product description. Either plain text or formatted text entry is supported.
Single on/off checkbox	Boolean	Use when something can only be answered "yes" or "no"; for example, a field that asks whether a user would like to be added to a mailing list.
Text area with a summary	Long text and summary	This is similar to the "Text area (multiple rows)" widget in that it provides a large text box, but it also provides an (Edit summary) link at the top, which will open a new summary box when clicked. This allows you to enter a summary of the longer text, which is typically displayed in listing pages such as the default front page.
Select list	List, Term reference	An alternative to checkboxes and radio buttons is a drop-down select list. This widget type is useful when there are many different options to choose from and it would be cumbersome to display each one inline as a separate choice, such as a list of countries.

Displays, View Modes, and Formatters

Complementing the configuration of how field data is input, you can also determine how field data is output and displayed to end users. There are two aspects to configuring fields' display: configuring the output of the individual field (such as where its field label is displayed and how its value should be shown), and configuring the overall way in which fields are shown when viewed in certain contexts.

Each type of entity presents one or more *view modes* (e.g., RSS feed, search results, teaser, or full view) and can be configured to show or hide certain fields or change their output depending on the context in which the entity is being viewed. You can either configure default settings applicable to all view modes, or override the defaults by providing a custom display setting for one or more specific view modes. By default, Drupal provides a custom display override for node teasers to change how your fields are displayed on full content (and RSS and search results pages) versus on the teaser view on the default home page. This also means, however, that if you want the fields to look the same in both view modes, you have to update both the Default settings and the Teaser settings—custom display settings do not inherit the default display settings.

In Figure 3-4, you can see the Manage Display tab for the core "Basic page" content type, which shows the Teaser custom display settings enabled. Once a custom display is enabled, a new subtab will appear in the upper-right corner of the settings page.

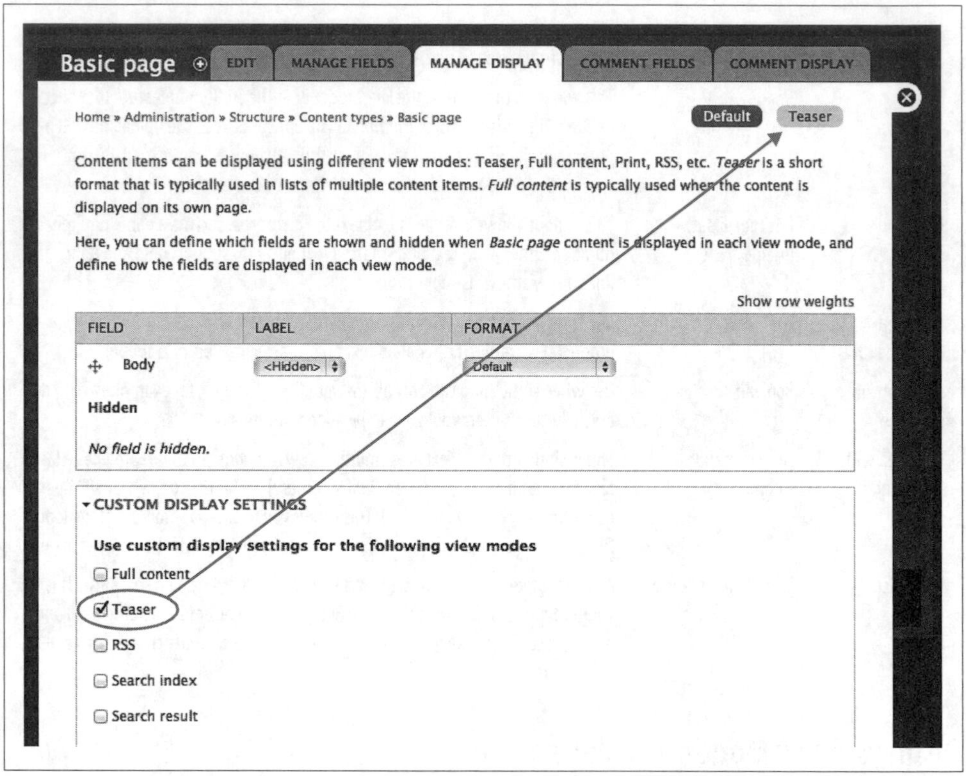

Figure 3-4. Manage Display settings with custom Teaser tab

Table 3-3 contains a list of default view modes provided by Drupal core's entities, and like everything else in Drupal, contributed modules can provide additional view modes. There are two subtabs on this page, Default and Teaser. The Default settings will control the look of the content for all view modes, except those that are checked off in the Custom Display Settings fieldset at the bottom of the page. By default, core enables one custom display: the Teaser. So with the default core settings, the changing settings on the Default tab will control how the fields look on the Full content, RSS, Search index, and Search results displays.

Content types on your site have a settings page to manage its display settings, which you can access by going to the administrative toolbar and clicking Structure→"Content types" and then clicking the "Manage display" link for your desired content type (*admin/structure/types/manage/<content type name>/display*). Other entities expose this same screen closer to their own configuration pages. For example, the field display management screen for user accounts is at Configuration→People→"Account settings"→"Manage display" (*admin/config/people/accounts/display*).

Table 3-3. Default view modes provided by Drupal core, and the entities to which they can apply

View mode	Entities	Description
Default	All	This type of display is the fallback, and will be used if no better matching view mode is found. In general, it's best to stick to the defaults if you can, because once you've customized another view mode, keeping things in sync means changing the display configuration in multiple places.
Full content	Node	This view mode is used when a node is being displayed with all of its associated data, like on the *http://example.com/node/1* page.
Teaser	Node	This view mode is used when a node is being displayed in the trimmed or summary view, like on the default home page at *http://example.com/node*.
RSS	Node	This view mode is used with a piece of content in an RSS feed like the home page's *http://example.com/rss.xml*.
Search index	Node	This view mode controls which fields are searchable. It can be useful to hide fields from the search index view mode in order to provide better search results.
Search result	Node	This view mode controls which fields will display on a search result page.
Full comment	Comment	Comments do not have teasers. This view mode represents when the entire comment is being viewed, such as on a *http://example.com/node/1* page.
Taxonomy term page	Taxonomy	For taxonomy terms, this view mode dictates which vocabulary fields will appear on a taxonomy listing page such as *http://example.com/taxonomy/term/1*.
User account	User	For users, this view mode shows fields on the user profile, on pages such as *http://example.com/user/1*.

Within each display settings page, you control the output of the fields using *formatters*. For example, long text with summary fields can be displayed as the full text or the summary, or hidden altogether, as seen in Figure 3-5. A full list of fields and the formatting options they provide can be found in Table 3-4.

Other modules may add other formatters, giving you a plethora of ways to display information. The core "Image styles" feature, covered in Chapter 4, is an example; it allows the display of thumbnail or full images, and provides those display options as formatters for Image fields.

Keep in mind that the formatters available depend on the type of data, once again making it very important to choose your field type wisely. For example, set up a field as an integer, decimal, or float if you'll be displaying numbers.

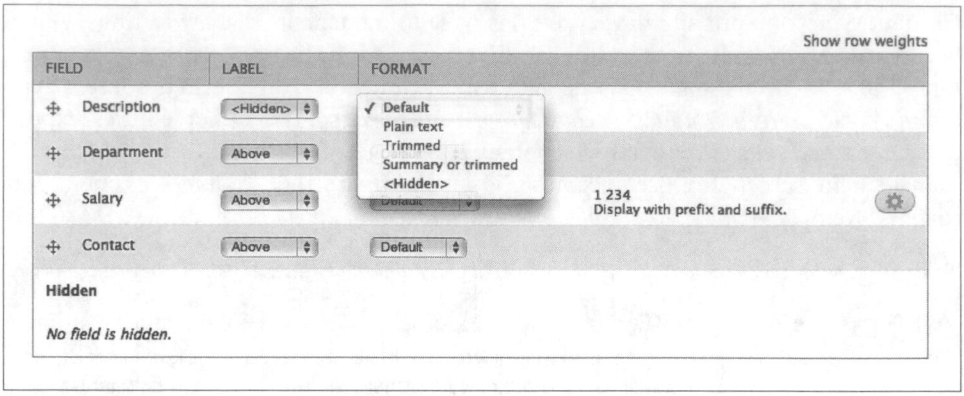

Figure 3-5. Configuring the display of a field formatter

Table 3-4. Fields and the field formatters they have available

Field type(s)	Formatters available
Boolean, List (float), List (integer), List (text)	Either display the label on the field selection (default), or the actual key stored in the database, such as 0 or 1 (key).
Decimal, Float, Integer	Specify how to show the thousands separator (decimal point, comma, space) and specify whether to show the field prefix/suffix (such as $). For float and decimal fields, specify the decimal marker (decimal point, comma) and scale (digits after the decimal point). Can also display the raw, unformatted value.
File	Files can be shown as a filename linked to the file, a table containing the file link as well as the file size, or simply the raw URL to download the file.
Image	Specify the image style (original, thumbnail, medium, large) and whether to link the image to the uploaded file or the piece of content to which it's attached.
Text, Long text, Long text and Summary	Display the field contents as formatted text (default), plain text, or text trimmed to a certain character length.

Reusing Existing Fields

Once you have created a field to add to an entity, you can reuse that field in other entities. This can be a useful time saver, and also allows you to create listing pages of multiple content types that share the same field, once we start talking about Views.

There are two "classes" of configuration on fields:

- Field-specific settings, which specify the field type and other options that dictate its database storage, such as the field length and the number of values it can store.
- Instance-specific settings, which dictate options used only on this field in the context of a particular entity or content type. Examples are its field label, the type of widget to present to admins, and whether or not the field is required.

Reusing a field on a different entity requires you to keep the same field type and name, as well as anything else under "[field] settings," but you can customize the field for each different instance by using the "[entity type] settings" for the field. You can see how this looks on a Department field on a Job content type in the configuration screens shown in Figures 3-6 and 3-7.

The Job Settings section indicates how this field will look and behave only on the Job content type. The Department Field Settings section determines the *global* settings for this field, no matter which content type it is used in. In this example, we have a Job content type with a Department select list field. We can reuse the Department field as many times as we like, but the Department field settings, which in this example determine the list of departments to choose from, will be the same across all *instances* of the field. However, we can change, per instance, settings such as the label, and whether it is required, the help text, and the default value.

Reusing fields can be very helpful if you need to use the same information across multiple entities. However, it can also be restrictive if you're trying to customize elements such as the allowed values for the field per instance. Make sure you only reuse fields when the instances are really identical.

JOB SETTINGS

These settings apply only to the *Department* field when used in the *Job* type.

Label *

```
Department
```

☐ Required field

Help text

```
Select the department in which job this belongs.
```

Instructions to present to the user below this field on the editing form.
Allowed HTML tags: <a> <b> <big> <code> <del> <em> <i> <ins> <pre> <q> <small> <span> <strong> <sub> <sup> <tt> <ol> <ul> <li> <p>
 <img>

> **DEFAULT VALUE**
>
> The default value for this field, used when creating new content.
>
> **Department**
>
> ```
> - None - ▼
> ```

Figure 3-6. Field settings that are specific to the content type

---

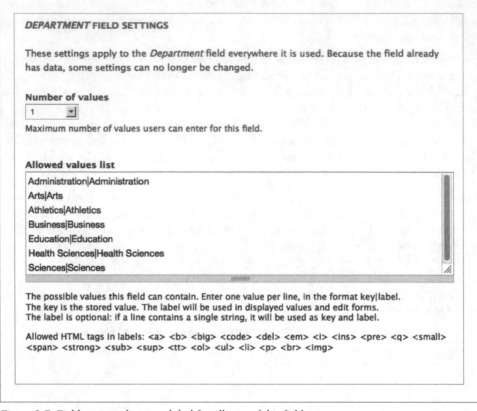

Figure 3-7. Field settings that are global for all uses of this field

Hands-On: Job Content Type

To get started with our job posting website, let's think about the different content types needed to build all the functionality that we require. The site requires two different types:

Job
    Description and details of a particular job opening.

Job application
    An application for a particular job that provides details about the applicant.

We will need to relate job applications back to the appropriate job openings, as well as relate jobs back to the appropriate contact person. The node reference and user reference fields provided by the contributed References (*http://drupal.org/project/refer ences*) module, mentioned earlier in the chapter, will be an essential tool.

To build this site, we'll need to go beyond the default "Basic page" and "Article" content types offered by Drupal core. When you're building out content types in Drupal, it's best to start with a mental picture of what the form looks like that you're trying to build. Figure 3-8 shows a sketch of both the job and job application forms that we're shooting for.

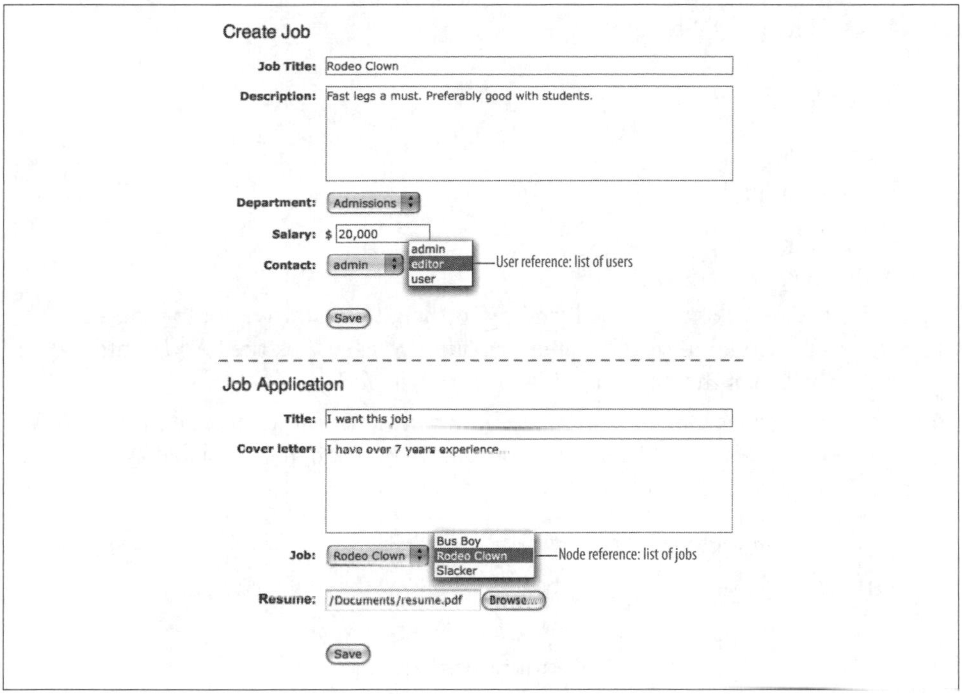

Figure 3-8. A mockup of the forms required for the job website

The Job content type will contain all the information we need to store about a particular position that's available at Epic University. It will need the following core fields:

- Job Title (the core node title field)
- Description (the core node body field)
- Department (a text list field)
- Salary (an integer text field)

Let's walk through the steps to create this new content type with the core fields we have available. We'll get to noncore fields later in the chapter.

1. If you haven't already, install Drupal using the *Chapter 3: Job posting board* installation profile from the book's sample code. See "Downloading the Book's Source Code" on page xviii for more details.

2. All core field-related modules are enabled by default in the standard installation of Drupal, so all of the modules we need should be enabled already. Double-check by going to Modules (*admin/modules*) from the administrative toolbar. Confirm that the following modules are enabled, and click "Save configuration":

- Core package:
  - Field
  - Field SQL Storage
  - Field UI
  - File
  - List
  - Number
  - Options
  - Text

3. Create the new content type by going to the administrative toolbar and clicking Structure→"Content types" (*admin/structure/types*). Click the "Add content type" link at the top of the page (*admin/structure/types/add*).

4. Using the settings indicated in Table 3-5, create a new content type called Job. We repurpose the Title field for Job Title simply by changing the label. When completed, your screen should look similar to Figure 3-9.

Table 3-5. Settings for the Job content type

Field	Value
Name	Job
Description	A currently available position.
Submission form settings	
Title field label	Job title
Comment settings	
Default comment setting for new content	Closed

5. Click the "Save and add fields" button to save your work. After submitting the form, the new content type will be created, and you will be taken to a page to begin adding your custom fields.

 If you save the content type by clicking the "Save content type" button instead of the "Save and add fields" button, you will be taken back to the main content types screen (*admin/structure/types*). You can begin editing the fields by clicking the "manage fields" link (*admin/structure/types/manage/<content type>/fields*) for the content type you wish to work with. That will take you to the same location as the "Save and add fields" button would.

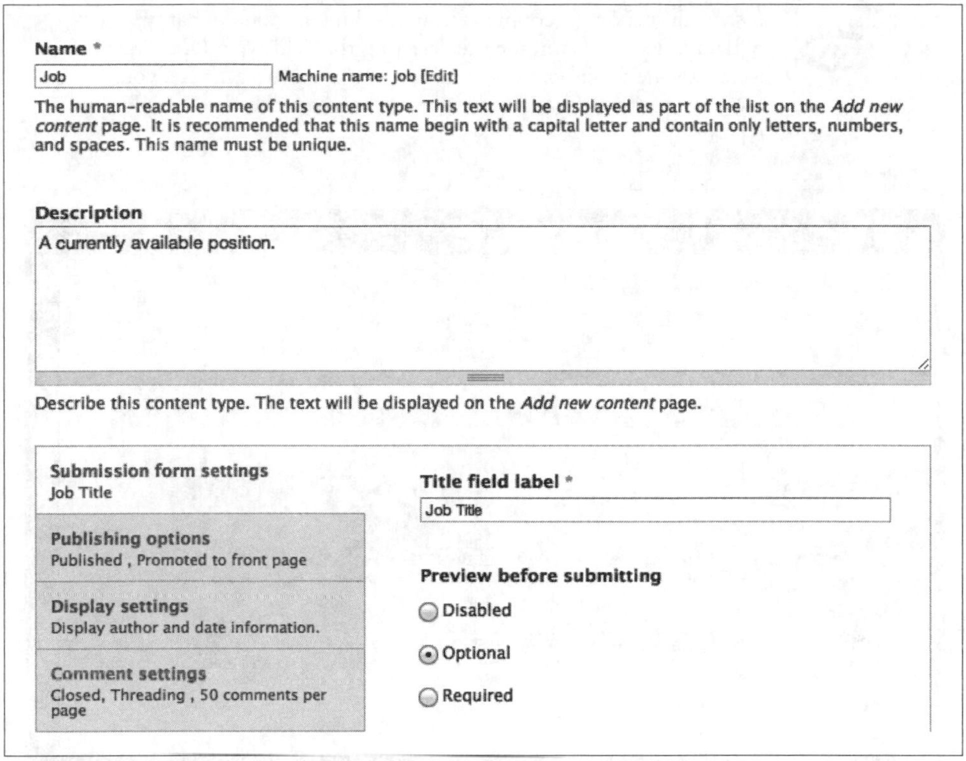

Name *

Job   Machine name: job [Edit]

The human-readable name of this content type. This text will be displayed as part of the list on the *Add new content* page. It is recommended that this name begin with a capital letter and contain only letters, numbers, and spaces. This name must be unique.

Description

A currently available position.

Describe this content type. The text will be displayed on the *Add new content* page.

Submission form settings	Title field label *
Job Title	Job Title
Publishing options	
Published , Promoted to front page	**Preview before submitting**
Display settings	◯ Disabled
Display author and date information.	◉ Optional
Comment settings	◯ Required
Closed, Threading , 50 comments per page	

Figure 3-9. Adding a new Job content type

6. Before we add our first field, let's change the label for the Body field so it makes more sense for our use case. Click the "edit" link in the Operations column for the Body field. Change the Label to say "Description" instead and click the "Save settings" button, and you will be returned to the "Manage fields" screen (*admin/structure/types/manage/job/fields*).

7. Use the settings from Table 3-6 and pictured in Figure 3-10 to complete the "Add new field" form to add a new select list for the Department field. You need to select the field type before you can select the widget type. Once you have selected the field type, the widget type drop-down will populate with the options you have available for that specific field type.

Table 3-6. "New field" settings for the Department option

Field	Value
Label	Department
Field name	department
Select a field type	List (text)
Select a widget	Select list

It's worth spending a couple of minutes thinking about what type of data a field will store before selecting the field type. Once selected, the field type can't be changed. If you make a mistake, you must delete the field and create a new one with the correct field type.

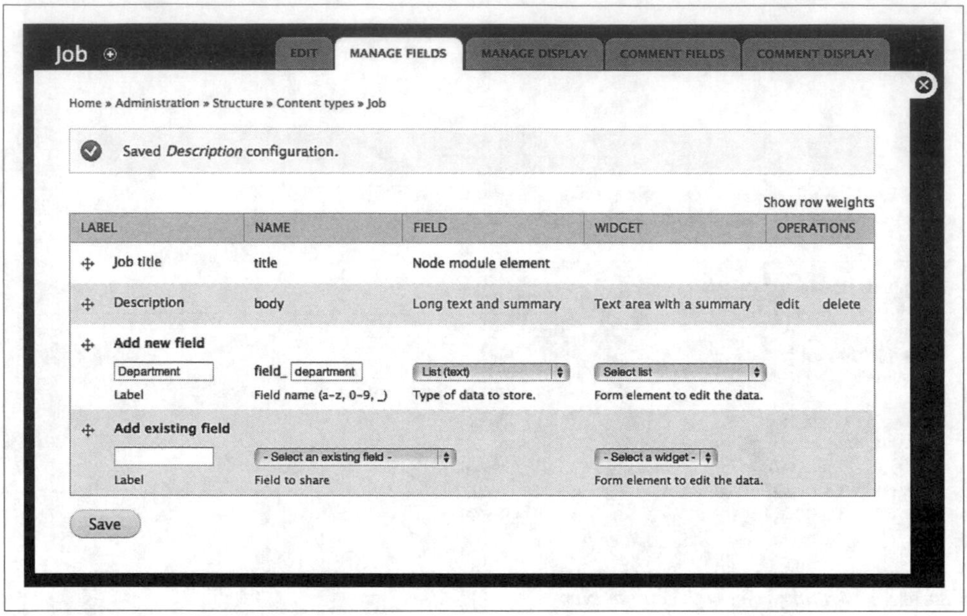

Figure 3-10. The "Add new field" form for the Department field

8. After clicking the Save button, on the next page, you'll be able to edit the global field settings. In the case of list fields, this means adding items to the select list. Use the values from Table 3-7 and pictured in Figure 3-11 to populate the options a user may select. Click the "Save field settings" button to proceed.

Table 3-7. Configuration for the Department field

Field	Value
Allowed values list	Administration
	Arts
	Athletics
	Business
	Education
	Health Sciences
	Sciences

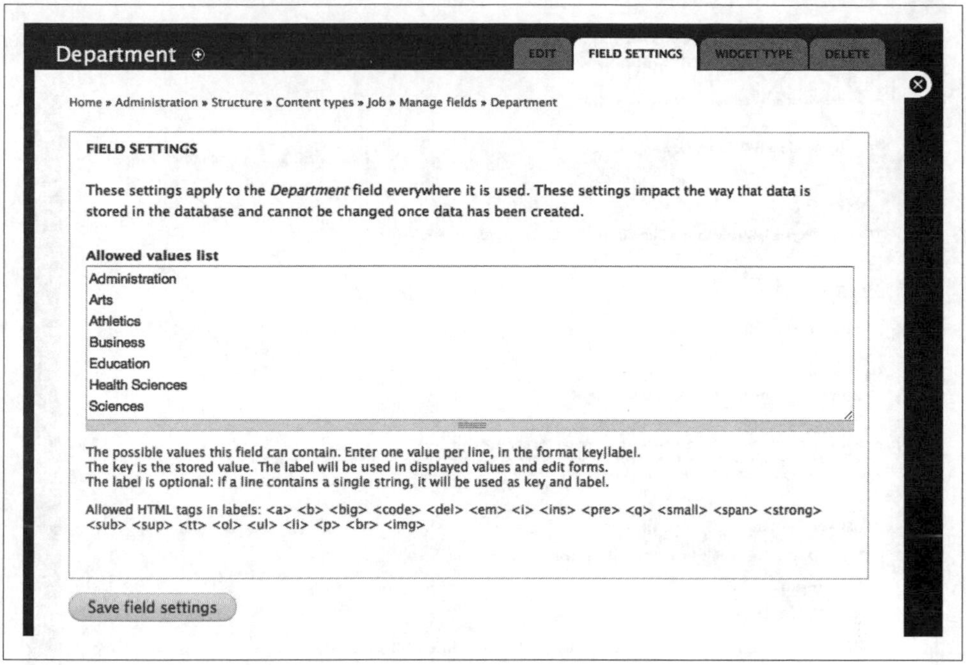

Home » Administration » Structure » Content types » Job » Manage fields » Department

FIELD SETTINGS

These settings apply to the *Department* field everywhere it is used. These settings impact the way that data is stored in the database and cannot be changed once data has been created.

Allowed values list

Administration
Arts
Athletics
Business
Education
Health Sciences
Sciences

The possible values this field can contain. Enter one value per line, in the format key|label.
The key is the stored value. The label will be used in displayed values and edit forms.
The label is optional: If a line contains a single string, it will be used as key and label.

Allowed HTML tags in labels: <a> <b> <big> <code> <del> <em> <i> <ins> <pre> <q> <small> <span> <strong>
<sub> <sup> <tt> <ol> <ul> <li> <p>
 <img>

[Save field settings]

Figure 3-11. The field settings configuration form for the Department field

Notice in the help text for the allowed values list, it mentions entering fields in the format of "key|label." This format—e.g., "edu|Education"—is useful if the department has a standard abbreviation or code that you'd like to store. Specifying a key will also ensure that the label (Education) can be changed independently and will not affect any of the existing field data pointing to that field. To ensure this safeguard, if keys are not specified for list values, the Field module will automatically generate them for you. If you go back to edit this field value later, you'll notice the options have all been changed to "Education|Education" (and the like) on your behalf. The key of a list also determines the field type of list field you want; "1234|Education" would be better as a "List (integer)" field.

9. Now we can finish up our configuration by adding some help text for our users. In the Help text field, add "Select the department in which this job belongs," as shown in Figure 3-12.

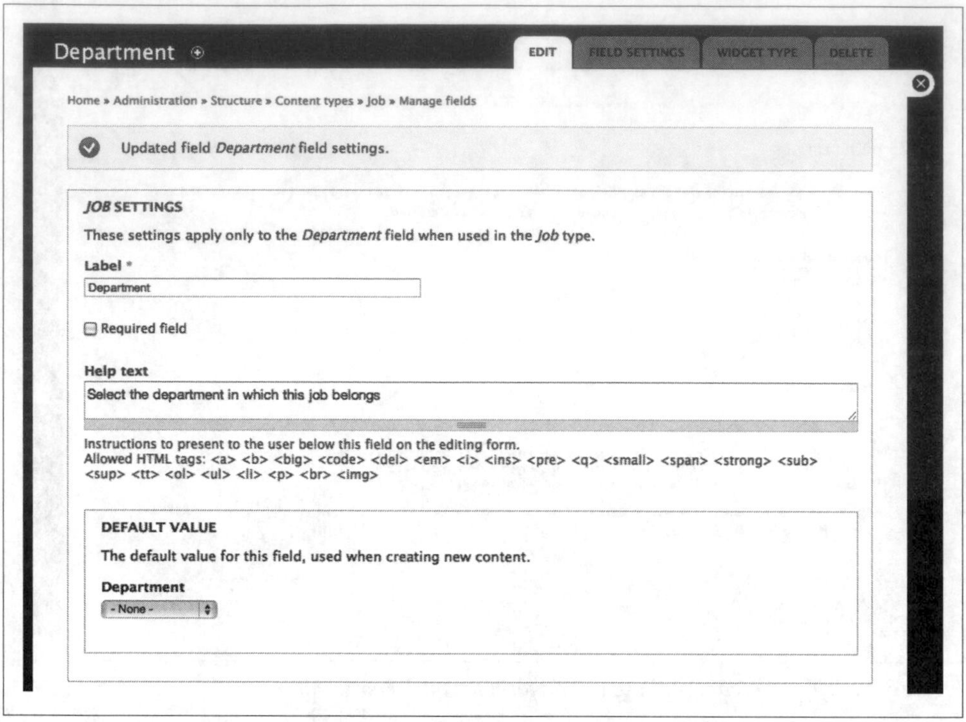

Figure 3-12. *Job settings for the Department field*

 You will notice that the settings you just added on the previous Field Settings screen are also at the bottom of this Job Settings screen. The job settings that you enter, like the help text, will apply only to the Department field in the Job content type. The field settings that are entered will be applied everywhere that you use this Department field, even in other entities. If you are using the same field in multiple entities, you should pay close attention to these settings and understand that changing field settings will make changes across all of your content types.

10. After saving the new field by clicking the "Save settings" button, you should be returned to the "manage fields" tab (*admin/structure/types/manage/job/fields*). We can now add the Salary field. Fill in the settings for the new field from Table 3-8. We'll add the salary as an integer, but if you want to include cents in the salary, you can use a decimal field instead.

Table 3-8. Settings to create the Salary field

Field	Value
Label	Salary
Field name	salary
Select a field type	Integer
Select a widget	Text field

11. Click Save to create the Salary field. There are no field settings for an Integer field, so click the "Save field settings" button to proceed at the next screen. Finish setting up the field with the options from Table 3-9 to provide some help text, make the field required, and prefix the salary with a $ (dollar sign) so it looks like a dollar amount. Click "Save settings" when finished.

Table 3-9. Configuration for the Salary field

Field	Value
Job settings	
Required	Checked
Help text	Enter a yearly salary for this position.
Minimum	0
Prefix	$

12. Finally, before any users can actually create pieces of job content, they'll need to have permission to create and edit jobs. Add permissions for the new content type by going to the administrative toolbar and clicking People→Permissions (*admin/ user/permissions*). Check the options shown in Table 3-10 and click the "Save permissions" button.

Table 3-10. Permissions for the Job content type

Permission: node module	anonymous user	authenticated user	editor	administrator
Node				
Job: Create new content			Checked	Checked
Job: Edit own content			Checked	Checked
Job: Edit any content				Checked
Job: Delete own content			Checked	Checked
Job: Delete any content				Checked

Spotlight: References

The References module is a contributed module that allows you to create relationships between nodes and/or users. When you download References, you will see that you actually have a package of several modules: References, Node Reference, and User Reference. References is the central module and is required by the other two. The Node and User Reference modules provide the actual fields that you can use to add to your site. In Drupal 6, these modules were included as part of the main CCK package.

Creating a reference field comes in very handy when you have content that has a relationship to another piece of content. A classic example of this would be a music site. You can have three content types: Artist, Album, and Song, which are obviously related to each other, but each is a unique kind of content that has different fields. If we use a Node Reference field in these content types, we can identify which Album node a Song node "belongs" to, and likewise we can identify which Artist node an Album "belongs" to. Using References, we can reuse the information we already have (Artist and Album nodes) instead of having to re-enter those values each time we create a new song. Once we create these references, we can easily display that information on the content type itself, and we can use that relationship within Views to create custom lists of related content. So we can have an Artist node that displays all of the albums for that artist, and the Album nodes can display all of the songs, or we can use Views to list all of the songs by a particular artist. You can do the same thing with users on your site using the User Reference module.

 While it's not 100% feature-compatible at the time of this writing, keep an eye on the Entity Reference (*http://drupal.org/project/entityreference*) module in the future. This module goes one better than References and creates a generic field that can form references between any two entity types. Or, if your needs call for even more complex relationships, check out the Relation (*http://drupal.org/project/relation*) module, which makes relationships entities so you can add relationships to the relationship itself. Whoa.

Hands-On: Adding a Reference Field

Now we need to add a primary contact for this job position. This will usually be the person creating the entry, but we'll allow the user to enter any of the possible faculty members on the site. This will be done as a "User reference" field, provided by the contributed References module (*http://drupal.org/project/references*). References is included in the source code that accompanies this book, so if you are using the source code, you can just enable the modules. If you are not using the source code, you should get a copy of the References module and add it to your site, as explained in Chapter 2.

1. First we will need to enable the modules we need. In the administrative toolbar, click Modules (*admin/modules*) and enable the following modules:
   - Field package:
     —Node Reference
     —References
     —User Reference

2. Navigate back to Structure→"Content types," and click the "managed fields" link next to the Job content type (*admin/structure/types/manage/job/fields*). Enter the values from Table 3-11 into the "Add new field" form, and then click Save. Note that if the site grew to include hundreds of faculty members, switching the widget type from a select list to an autocomplete text field might be a good idea, but for now, with our small site, a select list will work fine.

Table 3-11. Settings to create the Contact field

Field	Value
Label	Contact
Field name	contact
Select a field type	User reference
Select a widget	Select list

3. Configure the field settings so that only users of the "editor" role (to which faculty members are assigned) and Active status can be referenced. This narrows down the list of potential users that can be selected. Click the "Save field settings" button.

 If you're using the book's source code, this "editor" user role was already set up for you during installation, along with the "editor" user and several other sample faculty members. You can assign the "editor" role to additional users via the People (*admin/people*) menu.

4. In the Job Settings section, set the help text to "Select the faculty member who is the primary contact responsible for hiring this position." Click "Save settings" when you are done.

When finished, your completed Job content type should look as pictured in Figure 3-13.

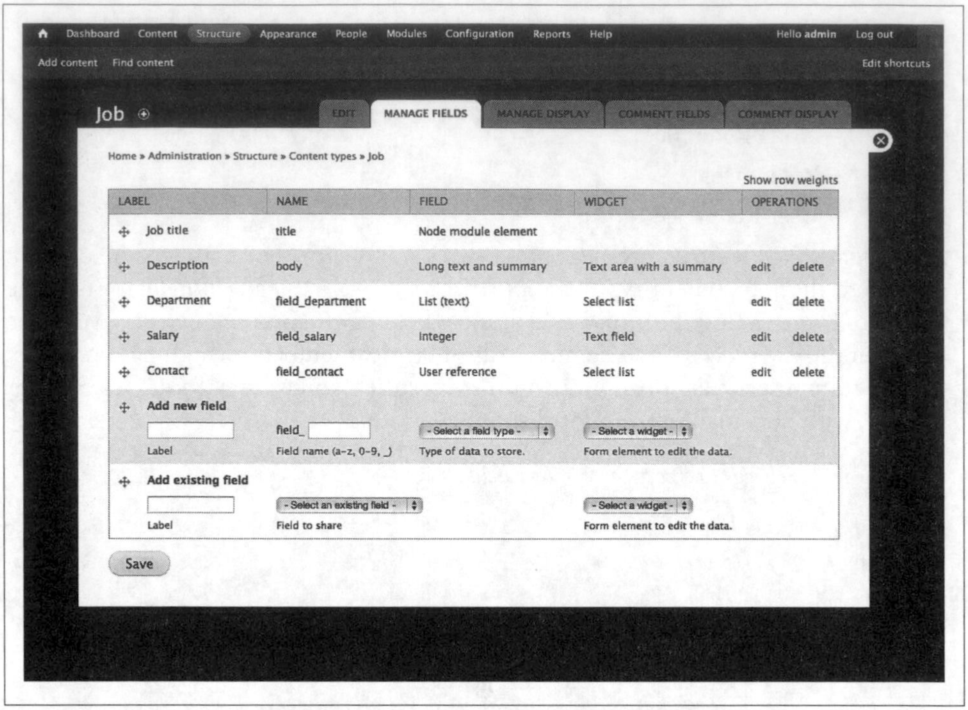

Figure 3-13. Job content type with Department, Salary, and Contact fields

Hands-On: Customizing Field Display

For usability, it's often important to display forms and page contents in a specific order, and to add formatting so that it's more clear what data is being presented. The following steps will take you through some minor customizations to the way fields are displayed.

Let's take a look at what all of our hard work has accomplished so far. Navigate to "Add content"→Job (*node/add/job*), from either the Shortcut bar or the Navigation menu. It should look as pictured in Figure 3-14.

This works for basic data entry, but there are a few things that we could do to make our job posting board more intuitive for our faculty members:

- Reorder the fields on the data entry form so that the department is selected before the job description is filled out.
- Make minor adjustments to where field labels appear and how their values are output on job postings.
- Hide certain fields—such as Contact—on the Teaser view of the job post so that readers must read the entire description in order to obtain more information.

This section will cover how to make these sorts of cosmetic changes to fields.

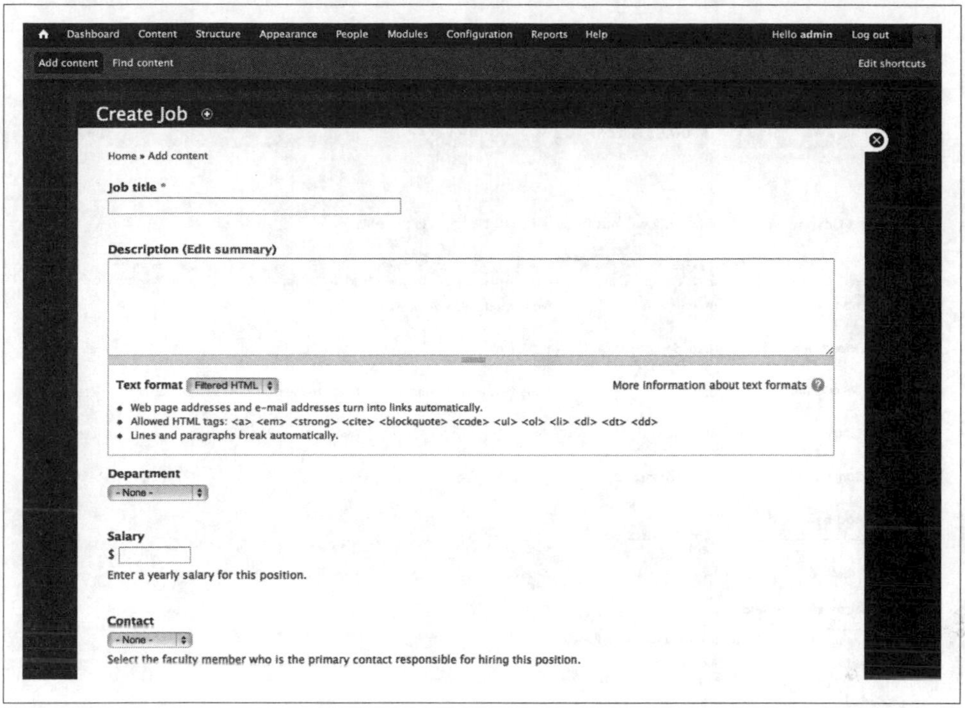

Figure 3-14. The Create Job form with no display customization

1. First, let's reorder the fields on the form so that they make more logical sense. In the administrative toolbar, go to Structure→"Content types" and click "manage fields" next to the Job type (*admin/structure/types/manage/job/fields*). Drag the handle on the left side of each row and arrange the table so that it is in the following order (shown in Figure 3-15), and then click the Save button when finished:

   - Job title
   - Department
   - Description
   - Salary
   - Contact

2. The Job content type is now nearly complete. Let's see what our form currently looks like. Log in as *editor*, enter the password *oreilly*, and create a new Job piece of content by clicking "Add content"→Job (*node/add/job*) in either the Navigation block or the Shortcut bar.

3. Fill out the values in Table 3-12, or feel free to make up your own. Now that we've reordered the fields, the form should look similar to Figure 3-16 (if you are logged in as the "admin" user, you'll see several more options that are hidden from other users). Click Save when you're finished filling in the fields.

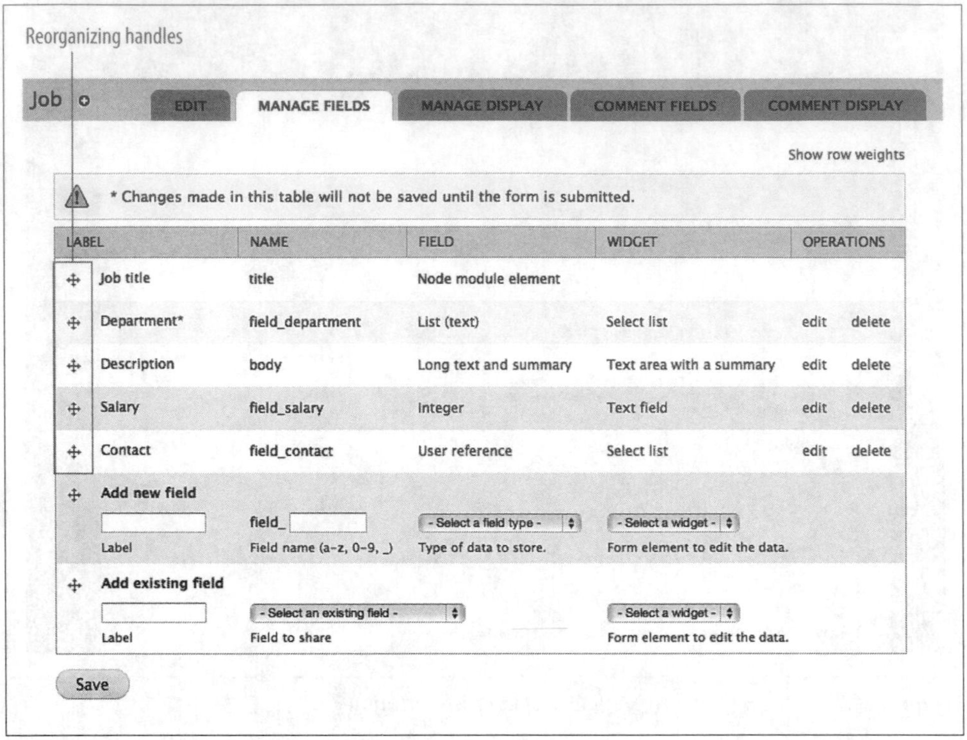

Figure 3-15. Field order for the Job content type

Table 3-12. Settings to create the Contact field

Field	Value
Job Title	Alumni Director
Department	Administration
Description	Epic University is looking for an Alumni Director. The position will require keeping track of graduate contact information as well as organizing alumni social events.
Salary	50000
Contact	Marty Johnson

Taking a look at the content after it's created, we'll see that it's not entirely pretty. Figure 3-17 shows the default output of our Job type when we view the content. The department is still listed underneath our description; the labels are included above each field, making the page longer than it needs to be; and the salary could really use a comma. Fortunately, we can use Field Formatters to change the display of the job content a bit more to our liking.

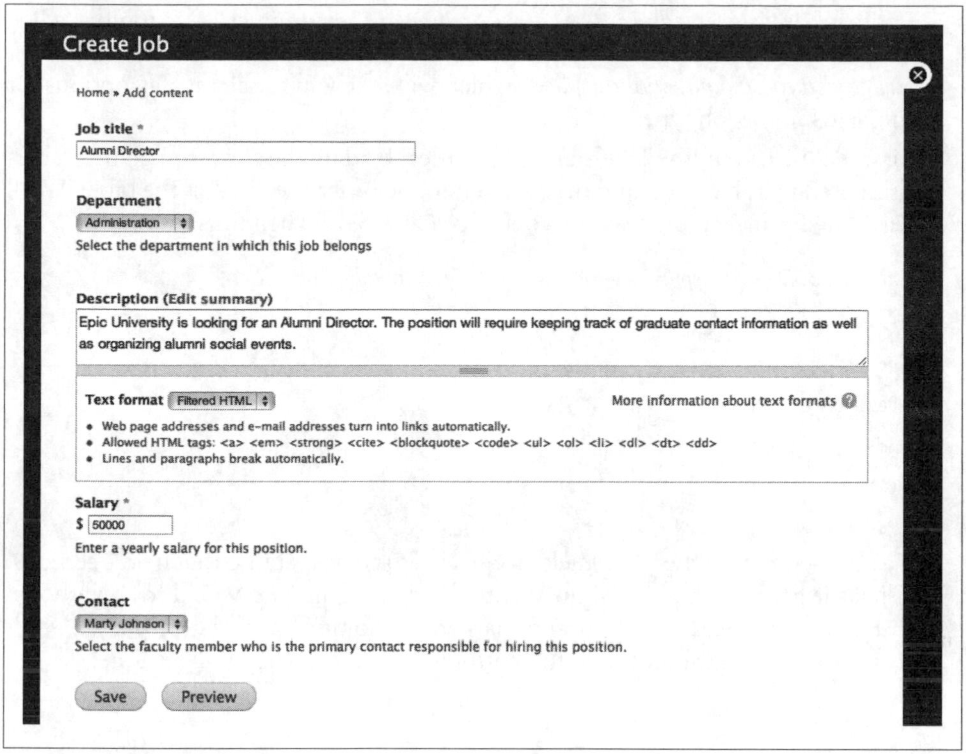

Figure 3-16. The Job form as seen by a user in the "editor" role

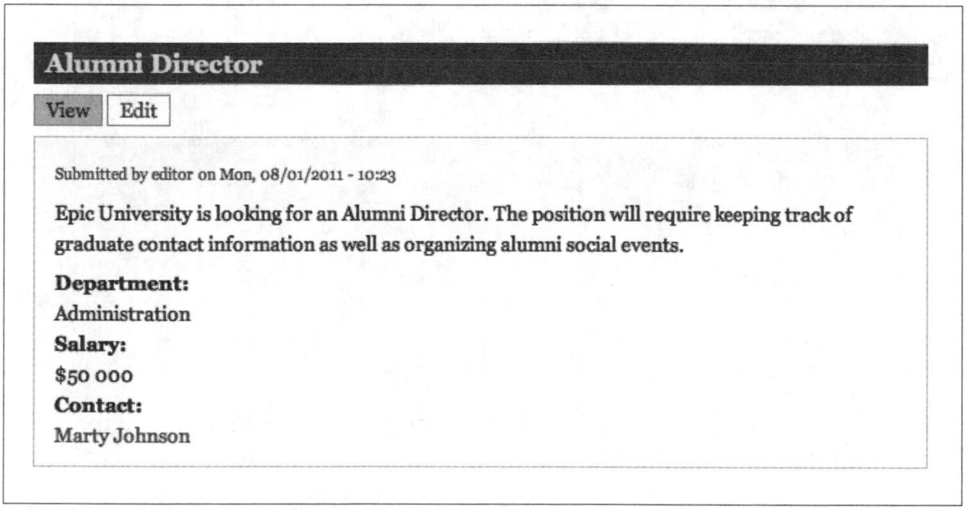

Figure 3-17. Default output of the Job content type

1. Log back in as user *admin*, password *oreilly*. In the administrative toolbar, click Structure→"Content types" and click the "manage display" link next to Job (*admin/ structure/types/manage/job/display*), which will take you to the display options for the fields in the Job type.

2. First we'll clean up the labels and field order. Update the form to use the values presented in Table 3-13, and drag them into the order specified in the table. We'll leave the Format column with its defaults. Click Save when finished.

Table 3-13. Default display field settings for the Job content type

Field	Label
Department	Inline
Description	<Hidden>
Salary	Inline
Contact	Inline

3. To add a comma to the Salary field, we'll need to go deeper into that field's settings. Click the gear icon button all the way to the right of the Salary field row, as shown in Figure 3-18. Set the "Thousand marker" to Comma, and click Update. Don't forget to hit the Save button at the bottom of the form when you're done!

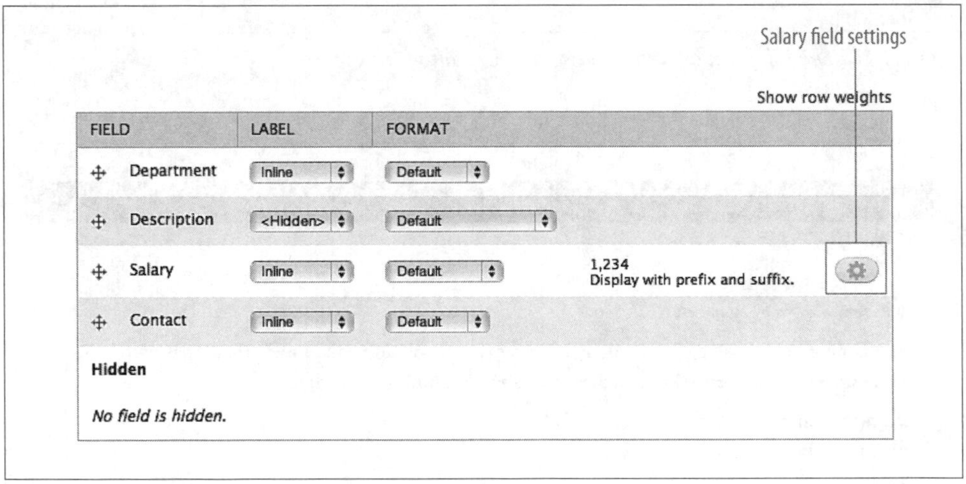

Figure 3-18. Display field settings for the Job content type

4. After saving the changes, take a look at the Job piece of content a second time. The new, cleaner look is shown in Figure 3-19.

Now you can see that our labels are displayed next to the values, rather than on a separate line. A comma is automatically placed in the correct location for the Salary field. Nice!

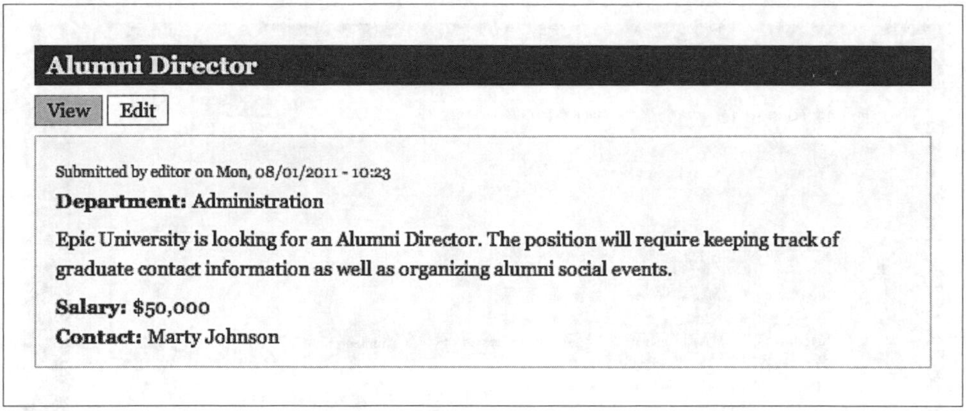

Alumni Director

View | Edit

Submitted by editor on Mon, 08/01/2011 - 10:23

Department: Administration

Epic University is looking for an Alumni Director. The position will require keeping track of graduate contact information as well as organizing alumni social events.

Salary: $50,000
Contact: Marty Johnson

Figure 3-19. Job content after configuring the field display

The last step is to fix up our Teaser display as well, since that has its own custom settings and won't automatically inherit the defaults we just set. We can also make some subtle changes in the display for that view mode.

1. Let's go back to our display settings. In the administrative toolbar, click Structure→"Content types," click the "manage display" link, and this time click the Teaser subtab (*admin/structure/types/manage/job/display/teaser*).

2. Currently, the Description field is the only one visible, and the rest of the fields are listed as Hidden. Let's move the Department field to the top of the list, with Salary below Description. Ensure that the Contact field is moved down in the Hidden section at the bottom of the page to prevent the field value from displaying altogether. Make people read the full job description before they see who to contact!

3. Now change the Salary field to use a comma, just like we did before, by clicking the gear icon for the field, changing the "Thousand marker" field to Comma, and clicking Update.

4. Finally, we should make our labels behave just as we did for the default display. Change the Label setting to Inline for the Department and Salary fields.

5. Once you've made all of your changes, make sure you save the form. It should look like Figure 3-20. If you return to the site's home page, the Alumni Director position should now show Department and Salary information.

 If you want even more flexibility over your content layout, check out the Display Suite module (*http://drupal.org/project/ds*). With Display Suite, you can divide the content area into regions such as left, right, header, and footer, and have full control over exactly where and how your fields appear. See an introduction at *http://tutr.tv/t5821*.

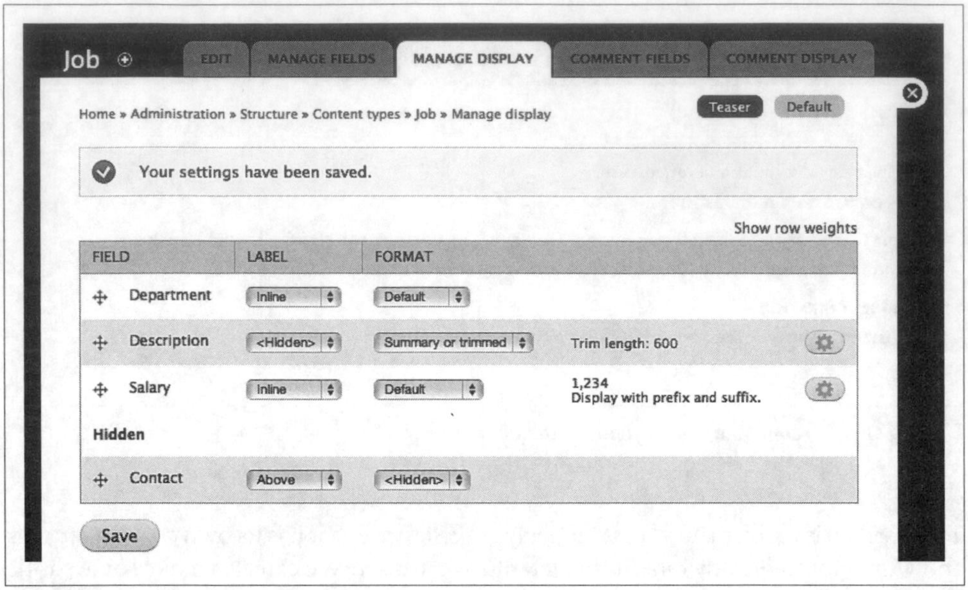

Figure 3-20. Teaser display settings for the Job content type

Hands-On: Job Application Type

Now that the university is able to create job positions, it would be helpful if prospective employees could submit résumés to the positions in which they're interested. We'll create another content type for this purpose, called Job Application.

1. Return to the main content type settings page by heading to the administrative toolbar and clicking Structure→"Content types" (*admin/structure/types*). Add another content type by clicking on the "Add content type" tab at the top of the page.

2. On the "Add content type" page, fill in the form with the values from Table 3-14. Again, we'll easily create the first two fields ("Title" and "Introductory message") by reusing the Title and Body fields provided by Drupal core.

Table 3-14. Settings for the Job content type

Field	Value
Name	Job Application
Description	An application for a job position
Submission form settings	
Title field label	Title
Publishing options	
Promoted to front page	Unchecked

3. After you submit the form with the "Save and add fields" button, the new content type will be created. Click "edit" next to the Body field and change its label to "Introductory message." Save when finished.

4. Use the settings from Table 3-15 to add a new node reference field for the job type. This will connect a particular "Job application" node with the Job node.

Table 3-15. Add field settings for Job node reference

Field	Value
Label	Job
Field name	job
Select a field type	Node reference
Select a widget	Select list

5. Click Save and select the Job content type on the "Content types that can be referenced" field at the field settings screen, to limit the select list only to job content. Click "Save field settings" to continue.

6. On the Job Application settings screen, check the Required field checkbox so that all applications are associated with a job posting. Click the "Save settings" button to complete adding the field.

7. The last thing required for our job application type is to allow users to upload a résumé or some other file with their application. We'll use a file field, which is provided by core with the File module. Add the Résumé file field using the settings from Table 3-16 and then click Save.

Table 3-16. Add field settings for the Résumé file field

Field	Value
Label	Résumé
Field name	resume
Select a field type	File
Select a widget type	File

8. On the next screen, leave the default settings and click the "Save field settings" button.

 The upload destination defaults to Public, but other contributed modules can provide additional "upload destinations" for file fields. For example, the AmazonS3 (*http://drupal.org/project/AmazonS3*) module provides a way to upload files to the Amazon Simple Storage Service rather than to Drupal itself. Handy for large files!

9. Fill out the Job Application settings with the values in Table 3-17 and click "Save settings." We want to restrict the types of file extensions that may be uploaded to just document files, and also specify that all files uploaded through the widget reside in a *resumes* subdirectory of the main Drupal *files* directory for better organization. The File module also allows control over the visibility of the file on the application itself. The provided settings will force the file to always be listed, without the possibility of being overridden. However, there are options that allow for use cases that require that sort of flexibility.

Table 3-17. Field settings for the Résumé file field

Field	Value
Job Application settings	
Required field	Checked
Allowed file extensions	pdf doc docx txt rtf pages odf
File directory	resumes
Résumé field settings	
File displayed by default	Checked

 The list of supported file extensions is included automatically below the file field when it is displayed, so there's no need to duplicate that information in the field help text.

10. Now we've added all the fields needed. Order the fields on the "Manage fields" tab as follows and click the Save button:
    - Title
    - Job
    - Introductory message
    - Résumé

    When finished, your content type should look as pictured in Figure 3-21.

11. Finally, add permissions for the new content type by going to the administrative toolbar and clicking People, then the Permissions tab (*admin/people/permissions*). We want logged-in users to be able to manage their own job applications, and for editors to be able to manage any of the applications. Check the options shown in Table 3-18 and then click "Save permissions."

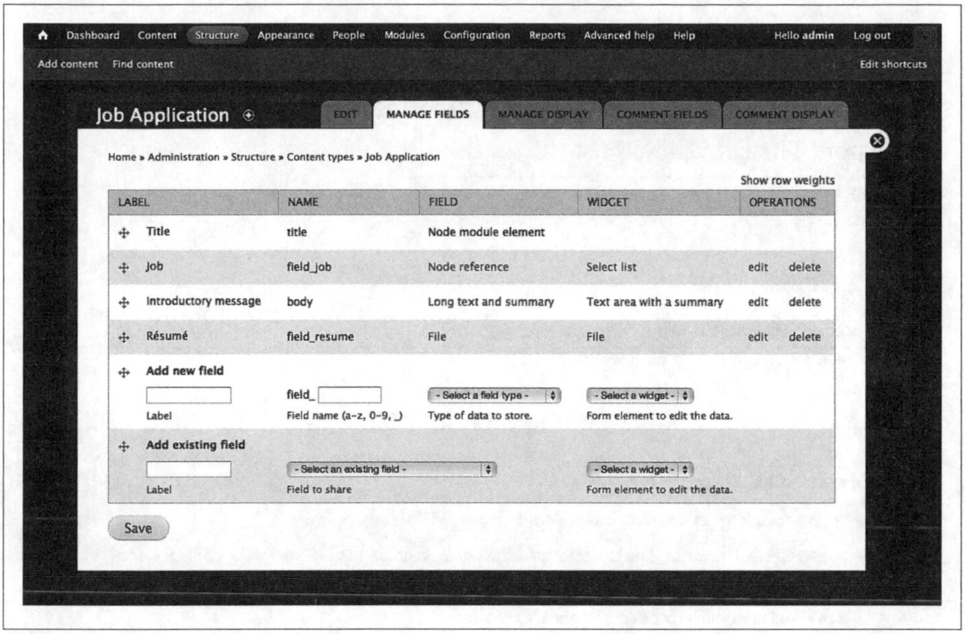

Figure 3-21. Completed job application type

Table 3-18. Permissions for the Job Application content type

Permission: Node	anonymous user	authenticated user	editor	administrator
Job application: Create new content		Checked	Checked	Checked
Job application: Edit own content		Checked	Checked	Checked
Job application: Edit any content			Checked	Checked
Job application: Delete own content		Checked	Checked	Checked
Job application: Delete any content			Checked	Checked

That finishes the configuration of the form for the Job Application content type. Let's take a look at the finished form as a user in the "authenticated user" role. After logging in with the username *user* and password *oreilly*, create a new application by clicking "Add content"→Job Application (*node/add/job-application*) in the sidebar. The form should look as shown in Figure 3-22.

The *user* user was created for you automatically when you installed Drupal from the book's source code. If you installed a different way, create a normal user with only the "authenticated user" role assigned.

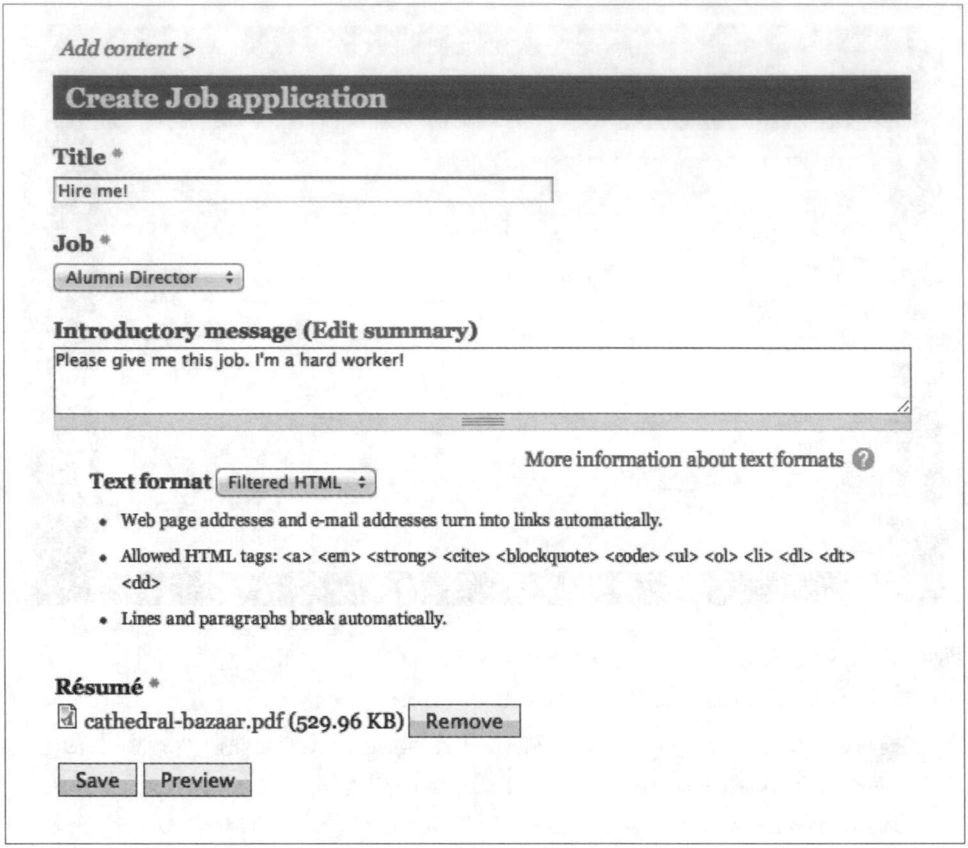

Figure 3-22. The job application form, as seen by any authenticated user

Because job applications won't be as visually important as job listings, we'll skip configuring the display options for this content type. But if you're feeling sparky, you can still make these changes by logging back in as the administrator, going to the administrative toolbar and clicking Structure→"Content types," and then clicking the "Manage display" link for the Job Application content type (*admin/structure/types/manage/job-application/display*). After a user creates a new job application, it should look something like Figure 3-23.

An important thing to note in Figure 3-23 is how our node reference field (Job) appears when given a value. The default behavior is a link to the original piece of content that is referenced. Clicking on the Alumni Director link from this application will take us back to the Alumni Director job. There are other ways to display node reference fields as well, which can be explored in the "Manage display" tab on the Job Application type (*admin/structure/types/manage/job-application/display*).

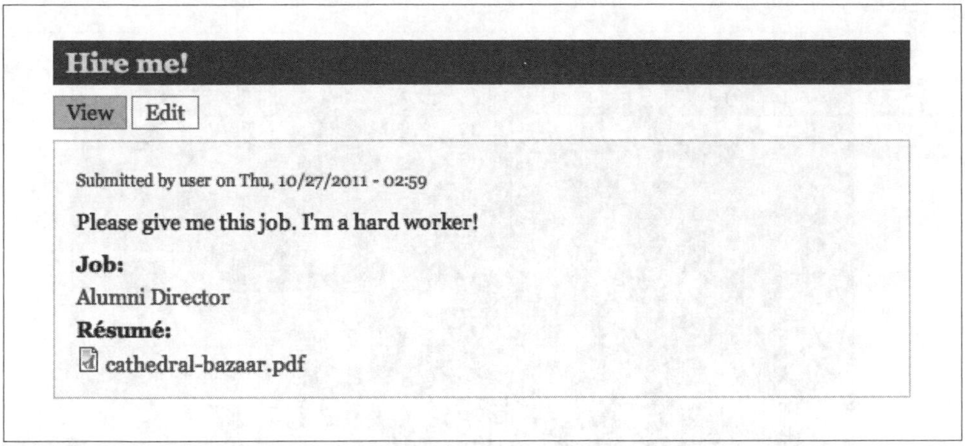

Hire me!

View   Edit

Submitted by user on Thu, 10/27/2011 - 02:59

Please give me this job. I'm a hard worker!

Job:
Alumni Director
Résumé:
cathedral-bazaar.pdf

Figure 3-23. A job application piece of content

At this point, it'd be a good idea to populate your site with some content. Log in as either *admin* or *editor* with the password *oreilly* and create several pieces of job content at "Create content"→Job (*node/add/job*). It's also a good idea to create a few applications as *user*, applying for a few different job positions. Having several pieces of content will help with the next section.

Spotlight: Views Module

The Views module provides listings of data on your site: users, comments, nodes, and more. Any listing of data provided by the Views module is called a *view*, which we'll always refer to in all lowercase to distinguish it from the Views module, which is capitalized. Figure 3-24 shows examples of some of the listings that can be built with the Views module.

Creating a basic view entails selecting the *fields* you would like displayed (node title, author name, image, etc.), how you would like that list to be *filtered* (only display "story" node types that are published), how you would like the listing to be *sorted* (newest stories on top), and what you would like the list to look like when it's *displayed* (a block showing a bulleted list of headlines).

In more technical terms, Views is a visual SQL query builder. When you build a view, you are essentially constructing a query that Views will pull from your site database. However, the Views module has significant advantages over a handcoded query. Some examples:

- Views handles not only generating the query logic, but also the wrapping display logic. Flipping a display from a simple bulleted list to a table with sortable columns to even an events calendar is a matter of a few clicks.

Figure 3-24. Several types of views created by the Views module are visible on Grammy.com

- You don't have to write any code just to make content listings, nor do you have to update code to make subsequent minor visual tweaks to it.

- Modules will tell Views about their fields; you don't need to know anything about the underlying database structure, and you are insulated in case this structure should change behind the scenes between module updates.

- The same view can be used in several places on the site, as blocks, pages, feeds, and other types of listings.

- Results can be split into multiple-page listings or use sortable table columns, AJAX pagers, or filtering drop-downs to allow visitors to "drill down" to the content they want.

- All views have support for caching results, for a performance boost.

More than anything else, Views can significantly speed up the development of your site, without your having to learn module development or a single line of PHP. Views can form the backbone of outputting content on your site.

SQL and Views

SQL is a computer database language that allows for retrieval of data from a database. SQL is made up of simple commands such as:

```
SELECT title FROM node WHERE nid = 10
```

Each of these commands is called a *query*. These queries can get quite a bit longer in order to retrieve the necessary information from the database, but that's one of the reasons Views is so helpful: it can build the queries for you.

Because a view is based upon a SQL query, many of the concepts in Views map directly to SQL. Consider the basic parts of a query: the `select` statement, `where` clause, and `order by` clause. These map directly to fields, filters, sort criteria, and other components of views covered later in this chapter.

```
SELECT [fields]
FROM [base data type and any relationships]
WHERE [filters or contextual filters]
ORDER BY [sort criteria]
```

Although you don't need to know SQL to use Views, the correlation is very strong, and it might help you to understand Views more easily if you're familiar with SQL or are converting existing code to views.

The typical way to create a new view is to go through a one-page wizard that sets up the most common settings used in views. You can either stop there and use the results of the wizard, or you can continue with a more advanced configuration of the basic view that has been created so far. Figure 3-25 shows the wizard interface. The full Views interface is pictured in Figure 3-26.

 If you install the "Advanced help" module (*http://drupal.org/project/advanced_help*), you will get access to the built-in documentation for Views (and other modules that use it to display documentation). In the Views interface, you will notice this as small gray circles with a question mark next to various elements on the page. If you click these question marks, a help page will pop up with more information.

Data Types

When building a view, the first thing that you will need to determine is exactly what sort of "stuff" is going to compose your list. In the background, Views is building database queries and, just as if you were writing some SQL by hand, you need to start with an idea of what the central data in your query is going to be. You have a lot of different kinds of data in your Drupal site. Content and users are probably the two most easily recognized and most often used, but you can also build lists of taxonomy terms, files, comments, and more. You need to select your data type when you start building

View name *

☐ Description

Show [Content ▾] **of type** [All ▾] **tagged with**

[○] **sorted by** [Newest first ▾]

☑ Create a page

Page title

Path
http://localhost/book/events/ [   ]

Display format
[Unformatted list ▾] **of** [teasers ▾] [with links (allow users to add comments, etc.) ▾]
[without comments ▾]

Items to display
[10]

☑ Use a pager

☐ Create a menu link

☐ Include an RSS feed

☐ Create a block

(Save & exit) (Continue & edit) (Cancel)

Figure 3-25. The wizard interface for building a basic view

your view, which you do in the wizard, where it states Show and provides a select list
of data types you can list, as shown in Figure 3-27.

You will notice that once you select a data type, you can't change it in
the main Views interface, as you can for the other settings you select on
the wizard page. The view name and data type are key information, and
the only way to change those settings is to build the view over again
from the start.

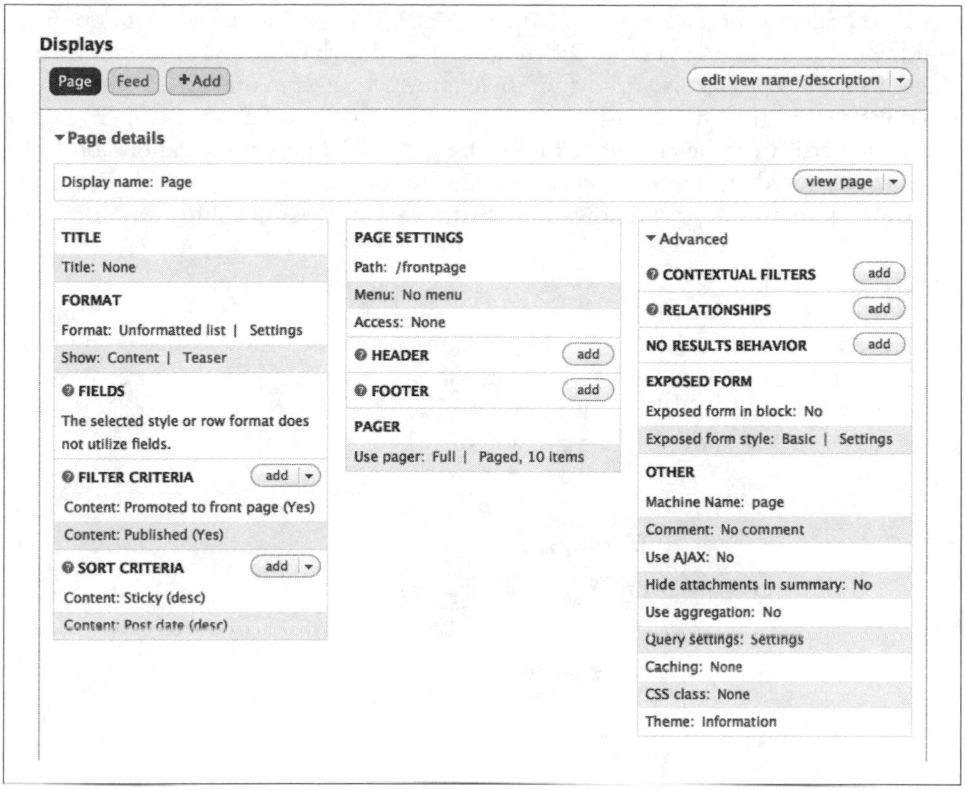

Figure 3-26. The full Views setting interface

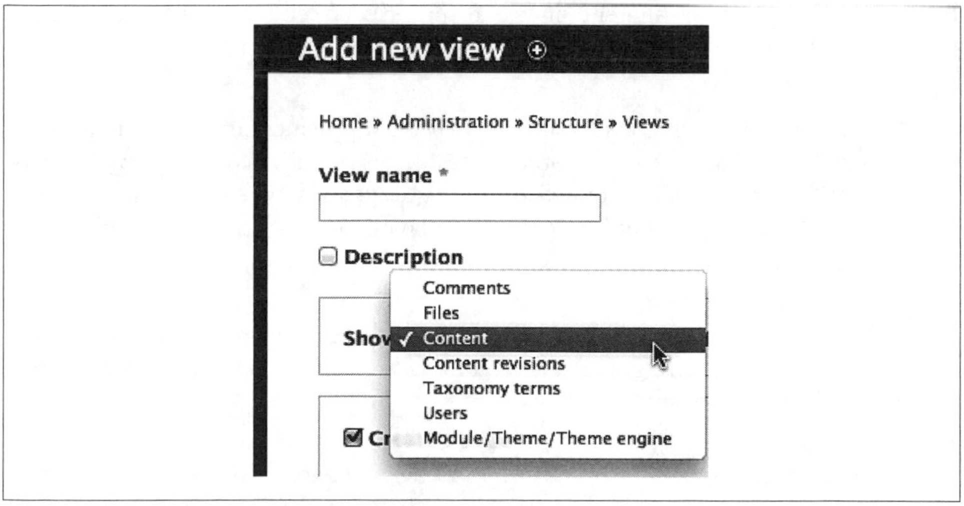

Figure 3-27. Selecting a data type for building a view

Once you select your base data type, the interface will provide the correct options to build your list for that data type. Different kinds of data have different properties that Views can use. You can also tie in additional information from other data types as you build your view, using relationships. For example, I may want a list of content on the site, but that list can be enhanced further by gathering more information about the users who created the content and adding the user data to the view as well. We'll talk more about relationships and how to use them later, in "Relationships" on page 124.

Displays

A *display* determines how a view will be presented to the user. A view can have multiple displays, and can even create several pages listing the same content in different ways. The upper-left corner of the Views interface lets you choose which display you are editing. Figure 3-28 shows adding a new display to a view.

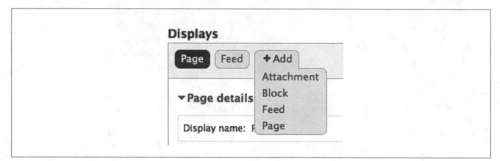

Figure 3-28. Adding a new display

By default, there are four different kinds of displays, each serving a particular purpose. Other modules may also add extra display types:

Attachment
> Think of attachments as essentially subviews: a supplementary display that can be attached above and/or below other types of displays. This display type can be helpful for giving a view context or adding a glossary when your view is being filtered. An example could be a view displaying a list of tracks beneath a view displaying albums.

Block
> You can position views exposed as blocks in sidebars or any region from the Blocks configuration page by going to the administration toolbar and clicking Structure→Blocks (*admin/structure/block*).

Feed
> The Feed display type creates a customizable RSS feed to which users may subscribe using an RSS reader. Feeds can both receive their own URL and be attached to any block or page display.

Page

   Makes a page with its own URL in which the view occupies the main content.

The Views module provides many exciting options to easily configure the display of your content. The settings for the first display you create will also be the *default* settings for any future displays; however, each display can have its own settings that override the view defaults. To change any value within the Views interface, click the option represented as a link, and the configuration for that option will appear in a pop-up modal screen. Figure 3-29 depicts the settings for all displays versus an override for a specific display, along with an example of italicized text being used to indicate an overridden value.

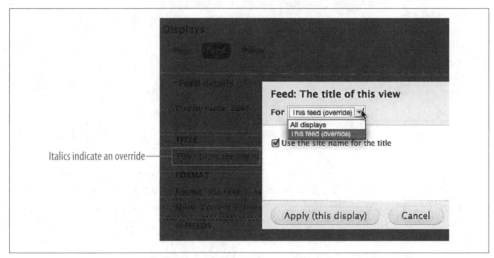

Figure 3-29. Configuration when overriding a default value

 Pay *very* close attention to whether the font for an option in the Views administration screen is italicized. Italics indicate that a setting is being overridden for that particular display, meaning that changes to it will only affect the given Page or Block. You must specifically override settings on displays; otherwise, they will affect the defaults—and thus all other non-overridden displays—regardless of which display is currently selected.

It's also important to pay attention to the particular display you are editing, as the settings change slightly between display types. Some of the most important configuration options for a view are available only when you are configuring a particular display. For example, to set a URL for a Page view, you have to be configuring a view's Page display. The URL is presented as an option within the Page settings, displayed in the middle column of the interface. The display-specific section for a Page view is shown in Figure 3-30.

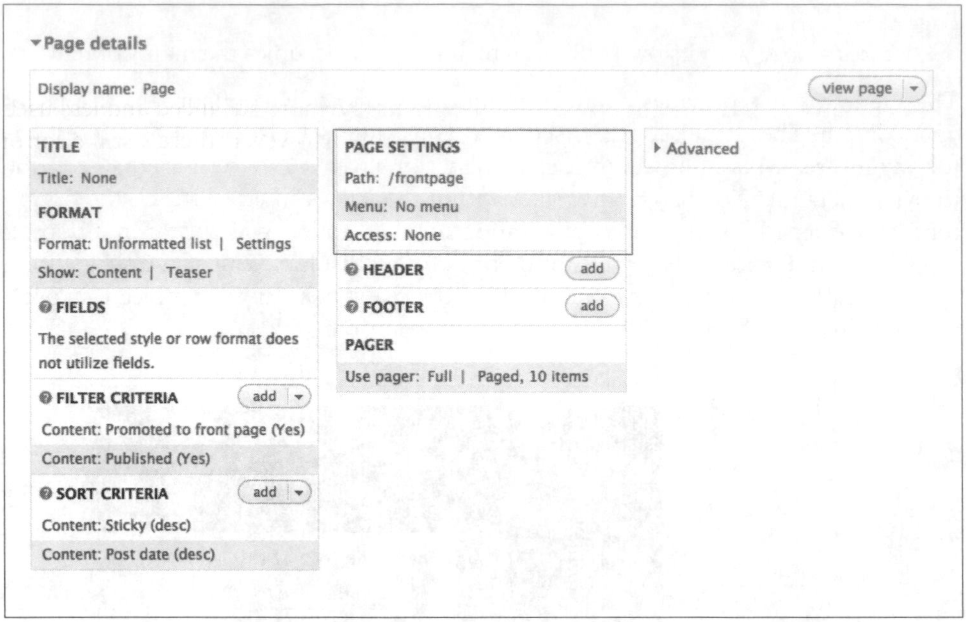

Figure 3-30. The available settings may change, depending on the display type that is being edited

One other thing to be aware of in the Views interface is how you add and rearrange the data settings. There is an "add" button on some sections for adding items. You will also notice that the "add" button sometimes has a small down arrow next to it. If you click the arrow instead of the word "add," you will see more options, like "rearrange" for the ordering of fields, or "and/or" for determining the logic of your filters. You can see an example of this interface in Figure 3-31.

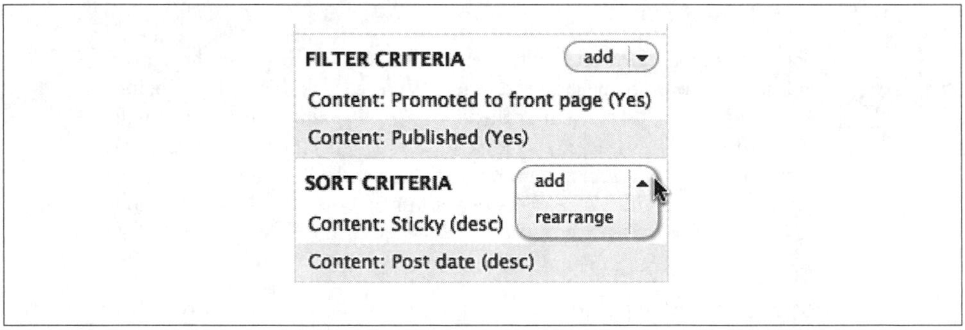

Figure 3-31. Adding data items and accessing additional actions

Pieces of a View

The main Views interface has a lot of settings, and it has been designed to provide the most often used settings right up front, while hiding the more advanced and less used settings to keep the interface as organized as possible. However, there's still a lot of information to fit in there! The interface has three main columns. The first column, on the left, contains basic information and the most commonly used criteria to build the view's query. The second column, as pointed out earlier, contains display-specific settings, in addition to a few other elements surrounding the view. The third column contains a collapsed fieldset where all of the advanced settings are kept.

Here is a rundown of each section on the Views administration page, pictured previously in Figure 3-26.

Title

The Title setting will set the title above the view when it is displayed. It is most commonly used to add a header and a page title element to a page display. So you would, for instance, get an h1 header element at the top of the view, and see the same title in the browser's title bar when on that view page.

Format

A format is how Views knows what markup to produce when displaying your view. By default, you will have several options—Grid, HTML list, Jump menu, Table, and Unformatted list—which are printed as HTML. However, other contributed modules can add to this list and provide non-HTML options, like XML or CSV, for example. The default HTML will be "Unformatted list," which will output each row of the view result in an HTML `<div>`. You can easily change to one of the other formats, which will change the overall HTML structure. Each of the formats has additional settings where you can further tweak the HTML, by clicking the Settings link next to the format name.

Under the Format setting, there is a Show link, which dictates how each row returned in the view is styled. This is where you will determine if you want to just have the full Drupal content rendered, or if you would like to control things more by having it output individual fields that you hand-select. The default for the Content data type is Content, which by default will display the view's selected nodes in a listing much like Drupal's default home page. But the most commonly used setting for most views is Fields, for more granularity over what exactly shows up in the view.

Row styles also provide additional configuration options, such as what view mode to show the content in and whether to show links and comments, in the case of a Content row style. For Fields row styles, you can specify the wrapping HTML elements to use around the values, whether certain fields should be displayed inline (next to each other) or on top of each other, and what separator characters (if any) should be placed between field values.

Fields

A field represents a piece of data to display in your view. Some examples of fields are the node title, a user's email address, the image attached to an article, a taxonomy term, or pretty much any piece of data within Drupal.

Each field provides a number of configuration options, including the ability to customize or hide the field's label, specify what Formatter it should use to output its value, use custom HTML and CSS around the field, and rewrite the field value so that, for example, it links to a different page.

Building Efficient Views

A view that uses the Content row style is usually less efficient than a view that uses Field. This is because Views is able to collect all the needed data directly when using fields, but a node listing loads every field for every node that is displayed. For example, a view that needs to display only the title and author of a node should be displayed using Field, preventing the unnecessary loading of taxonomy terms, other fields, or any other data added by other modules.

Even when you're loading a large number of fields, using the Field display type will often be more efficient, because Views can pull in all the data at once in a single query, rather than individually loading nodes (loading a single node will usually take at least 10 queries, or more depending on how many modules you have enabled).

The Views module includes some handy developer information to help with further optimizations. In the Views settings page at Structure→Views→Settings, you can turn on display of the SQL query that the view is generating as well as how long the view takes to generate. You can use this information to make adjustments and see how they affect performance.

Filter criteria

By default, the Views module will show *all* of the data—users, comments, or nodes, depending on the base view data type—available on your website. Filter criteria is used to further restrict the list of records being returned in a view. Some common filter criteria includes showing only nodes that have their Published flag turned on, only users within a specified role, or only nodes of a particular type, such as our Job or Job Application nodes.

You also have the option of *exposing* filter criteria to site visitors, which provides a user interface to let users choose what content should appear in listings. An exposed filter for node title, for example, would provide a text box that allows users to search for content containing a certain word, and an exposed filter for Department would provide a select box for users to see jobs only from the Arts department. You can also expose filter forms in a block under the "Exposed form" section under advanced settings.

Sort criteria

Once you've narrowed down results from your database and have the fields you want to display, you can use sort criteria to determine the order in which those results show up. Some examples are sorting by the created date, node title, or author username. On each sort criteria, you can choose whether it should sort ascending (A–Z) or descending (Z–A).

As of Drupal 7, sort criteria (like filter criteria) can also be exposed, to allow site visitors to fiddle with the ordering of results.

Contextual filters

Filter criteria will always filter the view in exactly the same way each time it's viewed. For example, a filter criteria of "Content: Promoted to front page (Yes)" will only ever show content that's been promoted to the front page.

However, sometimes you don't know exactly how you want to filter the results coming back from a view until the time that it's displayed. For example, in a scenario where you want to make a listing of content that appears on users' profiles, you wouldn't want to have to make a separate view for each user on your site: one filtered by user ID 1, one filtered by user ID 2, and so on.

Contextual filters are the dynamic version of filter criteria. They allow you to create a single view, and filter the results based on the context coming in from outside—for example, the user ID from the page URL.

The "context" part of contextual filters usually comes from the page URL. If your view is displayed at the URL *http://example.com/my_view*, URL parts after *my_view* would be taken as context values. For example, in the URL *http://example.com/my_view/10*, the number *10* would be the first context value. You can have as many context values as you want in your view; just keep adding more URL parts.

In addition to context values that are at the end of the URL, you can also place context values in the middle of a URL by using the % symbol in the view's Path configuration. This feature can be helpful when you want to utilize some of the existing paths in Drupal, such as user paths, which might look like *http://example.com/user/10/ my_view*. We still want 10 to be the first argument, but it's now in the middle of the URL. By specifying a URL path for the view as *user/%/my_view*, the symbol is swapped with the contents of the URL and passed into the view as the first piece of context. If this is over your head right now, don't worry—we're going to walk you through an example of this kind of argument in the section "Hands-On: The Views Module" on page 124.

Relationships

When you need to include data from an object that's not directly available (like a user's information) inside a listing of content (which is based on nodes), a relationship lets you retrieve the object information that is related to the listed content. In relational databases, a view relationship could be considered the equivalent of doing a JOIN in SQL. If the "Require this relationship" field is checked, the query will change from a LEFT JOIN to an INNER JOIN, resulting in better performance. However, you can only do this if you're sure all of the records you're showing have a correlating record in the data being related.

We'll set up an example of a relationship where a job application is related to a particular piece of job content. The user creates a piece of content (an application) that is related to another piece of content (the job). Using a Views relationship, we can create a listing of content that includes information from both the application and the job itself.

Header, footer, and no results behavior

Views also lets you customize the view's header and footer (what appears above and below its results), as well as what should happen if the view returns an empty set of results. You can either put straight-up text in these areas (like "Welcome to our job listings page" or "No jobs found. Please try again later!") or embed another view in these areas.

Hands-On: The Views Module

OK! Enough conceptual mumbo-jumbo; let's start getting our hands dirty with Views!

The requirements of our site include two particular views. One view is frontend-facing, showing all the available jobs to users of the site. Faculty users (more specifically, users in the "editor" role) will use the second view to review the list of applicants who have applied to various jobs.

The first step to using the Views module is to enable it. The Views module has two parts: the Views module itself, which handles the low-level "plumbing," and the Views UI module, which presents the screens used to configure the views. Additionally, "Advanced help" is an optional module that provides useful inline help for modules such as Views.

1. In the administrative toolbar, click "Site building"→Modules (*admin/build/modules*) and enable the following modules:
   - Chaos Tool Suite package
     — Chaos Tools

- Other package
  - —Advanced help
- Views package
  - —Views
  - —Views UI

Jobs View

The "jobs" view will provide a listing of jobs at Epic University, categorized by department. The completed view will be similar to the one pictured in Figure 3-32.

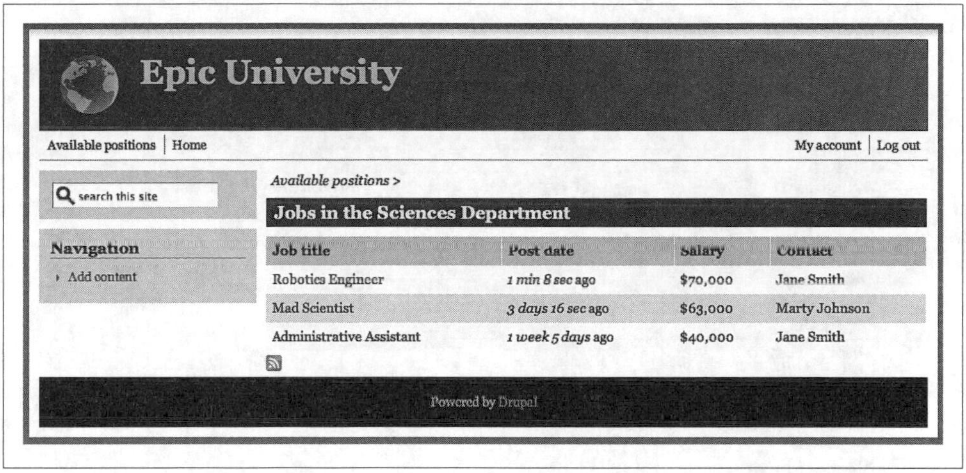

Figure 3-32. A sample page from the jobs view, listing jobs in the Sciences department

1. Get started by visiting the Views configuration page by going to the administrative toolbar and clicking Structure→Views (*admin/structure/views*).

2. Click the "Add new view" link at the top of the page, as shown in Figure 3-33, and populate the form with the values from Table 3-19. This screen is designed to set up the most common things used in a view. Your screen should look as pictured in Figure 3-34. These initial settings will provide us with a view that shows a listing of jobs, with its information displayed in a table, and a pager to move from one page of results to another if there are more than 10 items. It will also have a menu item in the Main Menu, which leads to a page showing the view. Lastly, we are adding an RSS feed so people can follow the latest job postings with an RSS feed reader.

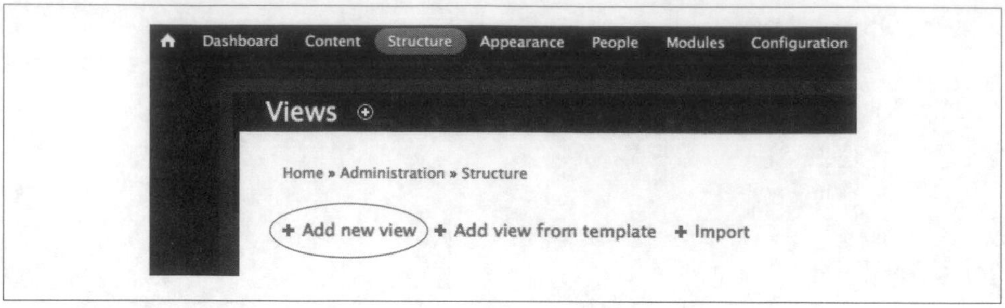

Figure 3-33. Add a new view

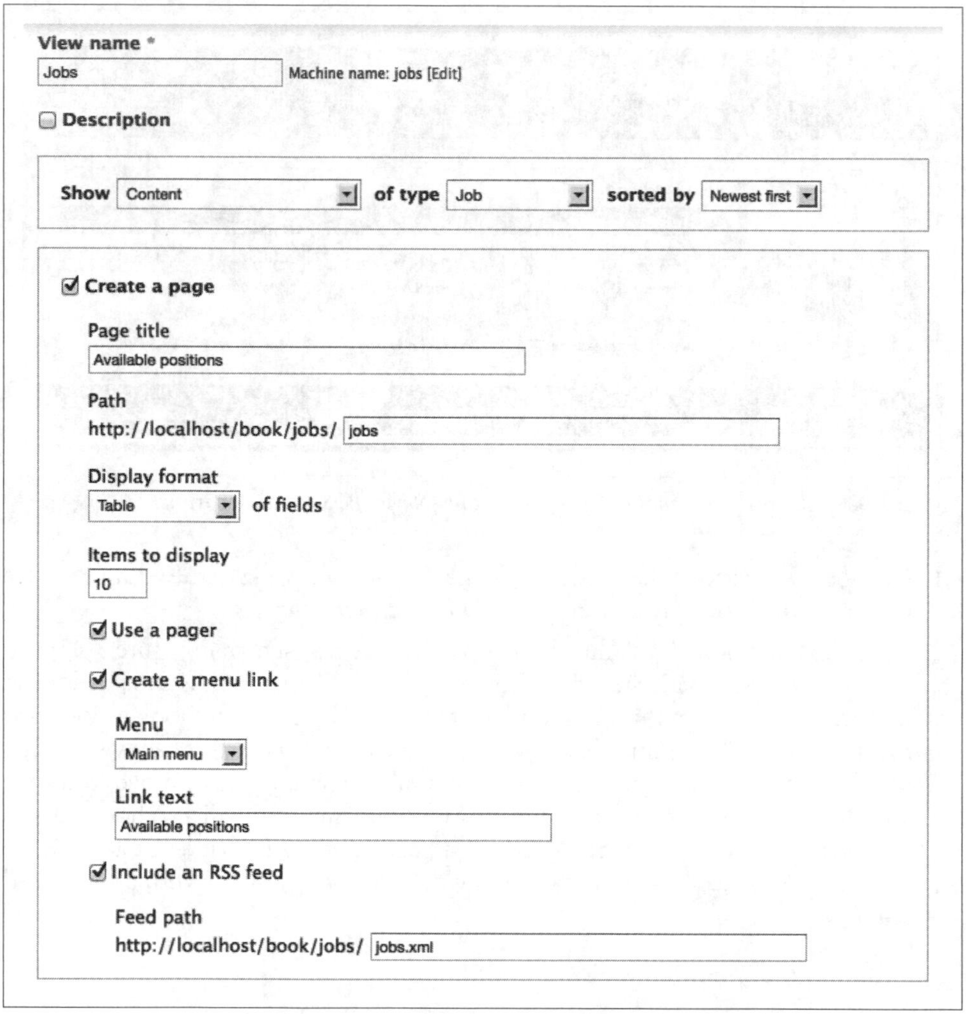

Figure 3-34. Initial view information

Table 3-19. The Jobs view configuration values

View setting	Value
View name	Jobs
Description	Checked; "A list of available positions at Epic University"
Show	*Content* of type *Job* sorted by *Newest first*
Create a page	Checked (default)
Create a block	Unchecked (default)
Page settings	
Page title	Available positions
Path	jobs (default)
Display format	*Table* of fields
Items to display	10 (default)
Use a pager	Checked (default)
Create a menu link	Checked; Menu: *Main menu*; Link text: Available positions
Include an RSS feed	Checked; Feed path: jobs.xml (default)

3. After clicking the "Continue & edit" button, Views takes you to the main view building interface, where we will tweak some of our settings to refine the view. Scroll down to the bottom of the page, and you'll see a live preview of what your view shows so far. Excellent!

4. When we created the view, we selected the Table display format, and the wizard automatically filled in that we would use fields. It didn't let us choose which fields, though, and by default it only provides the Title field in the view. However, we definitely want more information than that. Let's correct this problem by adding a few fields to the view. We want to display the Title, Post date, Salary, and Contact for each job.

5. Click the "add" button in the Fields area to start adding new fields. Include the fields from Table 3-20, as pictured in Figure 3-35. To speed up entry, you can select Content from the Filter selection to filter the list of available fields by only those pertaining to that group, or start entering characters in the Search field to limit the results. Note that we already have our Title field, so we just need to add the other three.

Table 3-20. Fields for the Jobs view

Fields: Add Fields	Value
Content: Contact	Checked
Content: Post date	Checked
Content: Salary	Checked

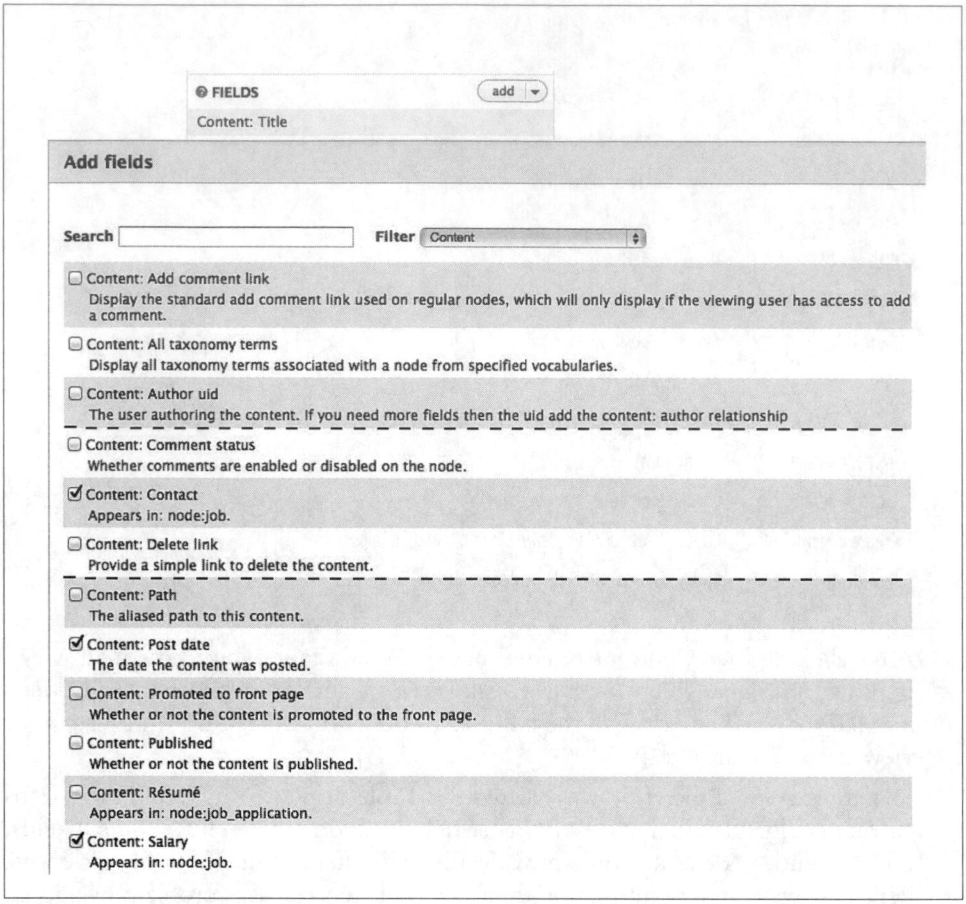

Figure 3-35. Fields for the Jobs view

6. After you click the "Apply (all displays)" button, Views will display the configuration forms for each field, one by one, to allow you to configure each field's options. When you're finished entering each of the values from Table 3-21 and pictured in Figure 3-36, click the "Apply (all displays)" button to proceed to the next field's settings. The values listed in Table 3-21 assume you will leave the rest of the fields' default settings in place and only make the modifications indicated in the table.

Table 3-21. Individual field configuration for the Jobs view

Defaults: Configure field setting	Value
Content: Contact	(Leave the defaults)
Content: Post date	Date format: Time ago (with "ago" appended)
Content: Salary	Thousand marker: Comma

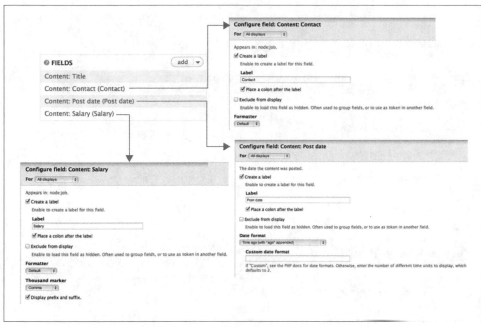

Figure 3-36. Field configuration for the Jobs view

7. Click the drop-down arrow next to the "add" button in the Fields section, select the "rearrange" item, and drag the fields in the following order, as pictured in Figure 3-37:

   - Content: Title
   - Content: Post date
   - Content: Salary
   - Content: Contact

   Once you have rearranged the fields, click the "Apply (all displays)" button to save your changes.

8. Now that our view has fields, you should save the view by clicking the Save button. If this button is grayed out, be sure to finish editing whatever field you're editing; then the button will be activated again.

9. At this point, we can pause and take a look at our view so far. If you scroll down the view edit screen, at the bottom, you will see a preview area. It automatically updates as we change the settings for the view. Our view currently looks a lot more table-like, as pictured in Figure 3-38 (with some sample content in it).

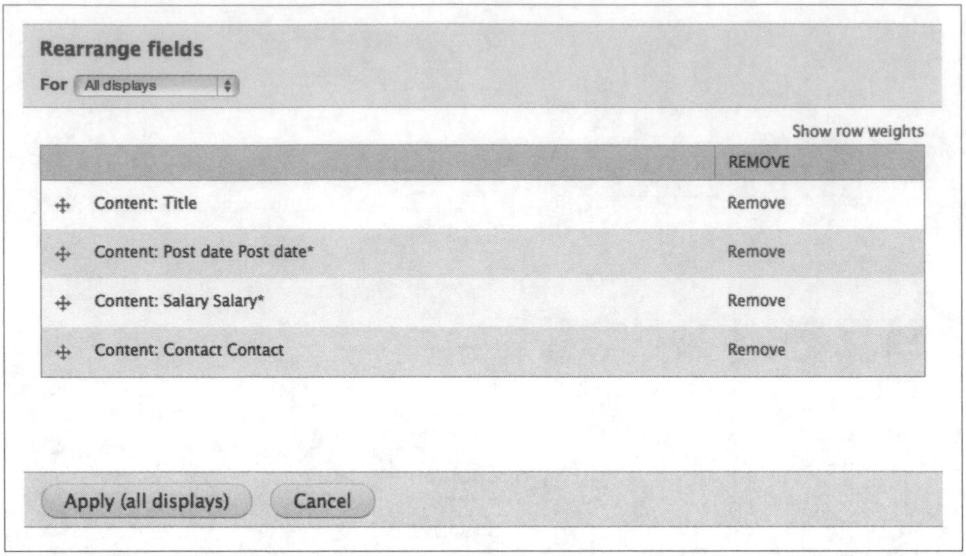

Figure 3-37. Rearrange fields for the Jobs view

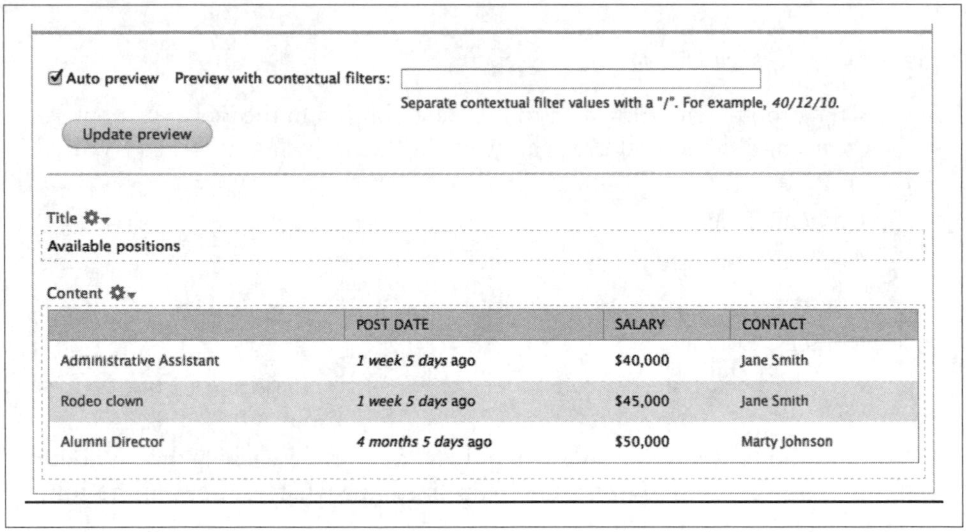

Figure 3-38. The Jobs view preview

10. Our view is coming along nicely. One thing that we did not include was a Department field in this listing, because our requirements actually call for a directory-type listing. That is, the first page of our Jobs view should display a list of departments, and then clicking on the department should provide a list of jobs inside. Because it would be tedious to create a view like this for each department, we'll accomplish this requirement with a *contextual filter*, a very powerful Views feature.

To get started implementing this directory-type listing, we're going to go into the Advanced section of the Views editor. Click on the Advanced fieldset to open the settings, and then click the "add" button next to Contextual Filters. As before with fields, you can search or filter to narrow the list of items. Select "Content: Department (field_department)" from the list and click the "Apply (all displays)" button. Then enter the settings from Table 3-22, as shown in Figure 3-39.

These settings will look like total gobbledygook at the moment, so let's step through them. What we're after is a directory at *http://www.example.com/jobs/ <department>* which, if no department is specified, will show a list of departments along with the total number of jobs they offer.

The "When the filter value is *not* in the URL" section indicates what the view should do when the URL *http://www.example.com/jobs* is accessed, rather than *http:// www.example.com/jobs/athletics*. Here, we are asking it to display a list of department names in ascending order. The Summary style will display the titles of the various departments, along with the number of jobs within that department next to it. This type of view can be very useful for directory listings. The Views module also allows you to control how the dynamic URL and title are displayed. The "%1" in the Title looks a bit funny; this will be replaced by the department name dynamically when the page is viewed (%1 means "the first context value for this view").

Finally, we do some path transformations to keep URLs consistently lowercase and dash-ified, even if the "real" department name contains capital letters and spaces.

Table 3-22. Contextual filters for the Jobs view

Setting	Values
When the filter value is *not* in the URL	Display a summary (checking this will expose a bunch of other settings, but they can be safely ignored)
When the filter value *is* in the URL or a default is provided	Override title: Checked (in the text field that appears, enter "Jobs in the %1 Department")
More	Case: Capitalize each word
	Case in path: Lower case
	Transform spaces to dashes in URL: checked

Be sure to save the view when you're done.

 We added only one contextual filter in our Jobs view. But you can add as many contextual filters as you like. They don't even have to be the same type. This way, you can get multipage structures, each drilling down additionally on the items that should appear in a list.

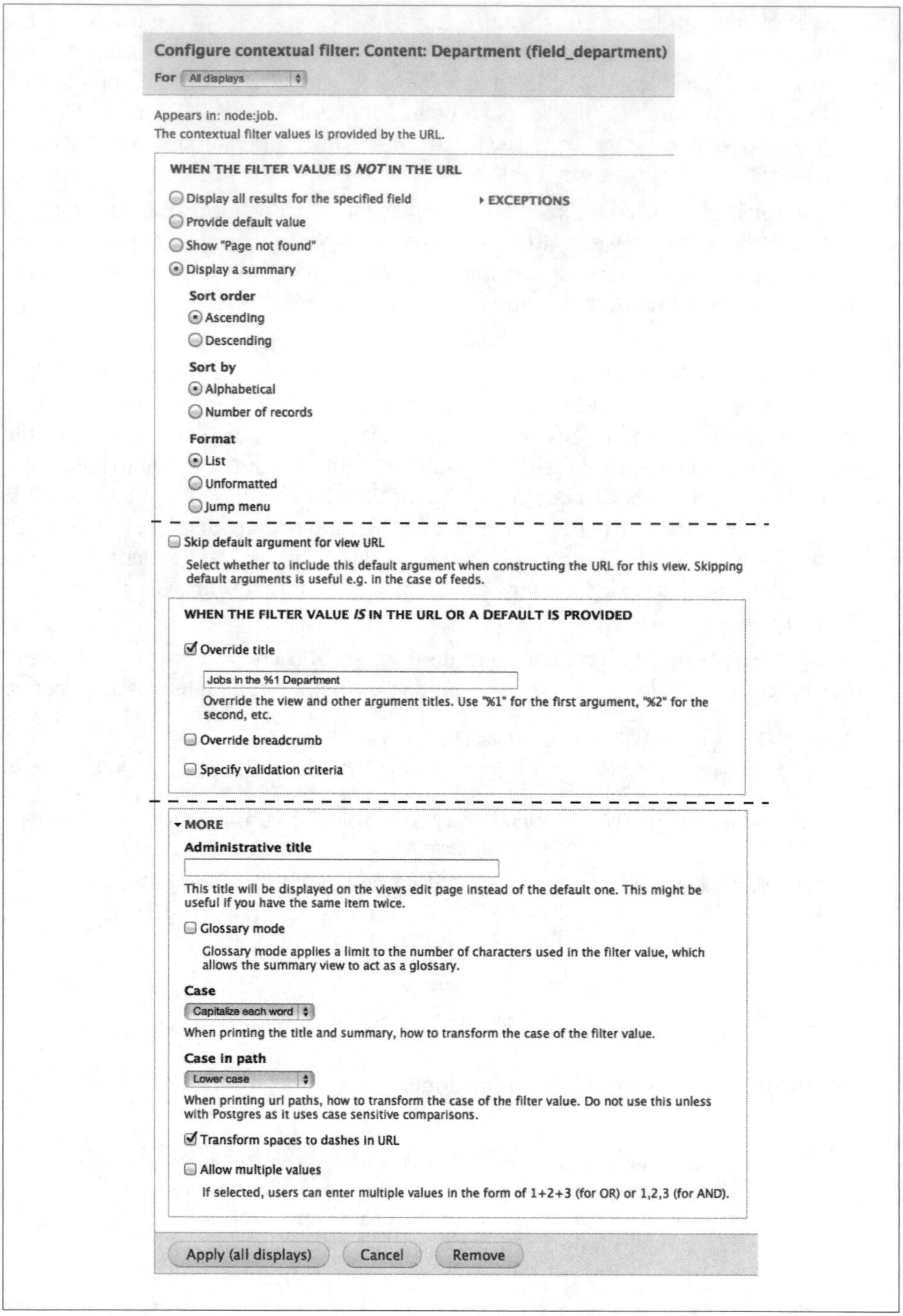

Configure contextual filter: Content: Department (field_department)

For [All displays ⇅]

Appears in: node:job.
The contextual filter values is provided by the URL.

WHEN THE FILTER VALUE IS *NOT* IN THE URL

◯ Display all results for the specified field   ▸ **EXCEPTIONS**

◯ Provide default value

◯ Show "Page not found"

◉ Display a summary

   Sort order
   ◉ Ascending
   ◯ Descending

   Sort by
   ◉ Alphabetical
   ◯ Number of records

   Format
   ◉ List
   ◯ Unformatted
   ◯ Jump menu

☐ Skip default argument for view URL

Select whether to include this default argument when constructing the URL for this view. Skipping default arguments is useful e.g. in the case of feeds.

WHEN THE FILTER VALUE *IS* IN THE URL OR A DEFAULT IS PROVIDED

☑ Override title

[Jobs in the %1 Department]

Override the view and other argument titles. Use "%1" for the first argument, "%2" for the second, etc.

☐ Override breadcrumb

☐ Specify validation criteria

▾ **MORE**

Administrative title

[   ]

This title will be displayed on the views edit page instead of the default one. This might be useful if you have the same item twice.

☐ Glossary mode

   Glossary mode applies a limit to the number of characters used in the filter value, which allows the summary view to act as a glossary.

Case

[Capitalize each word ⇅]

When printing the title and summary, how to transform the case of the filter value.

Case in path

[Lower case ⇅]

When printing url paths, how to transform the case of the filter value. Do not use this unless with Postgres as it uses case sensitive comparisons.

☑ Transform spaces to dashes in URL

☐ Allow multiple values

   If selected, users can enter multiple values in the form of 1+2+3 (for OR) or 1,2,3 (for AND).

(Apply (all displays))   (Cancel)   (Remove)

Figure 3-39. Contextual filters configuration for the Jobs view

We're now finished with the Jobs view! The final view screen should look as pictured in Figure 3-40. Take a look at our view by closing the overlay and clicking the new "Available positions" link in the Main menu. After we add this contextual filter, our view contains a nice hierarchical structure! It should be similar to Figure 3-41.

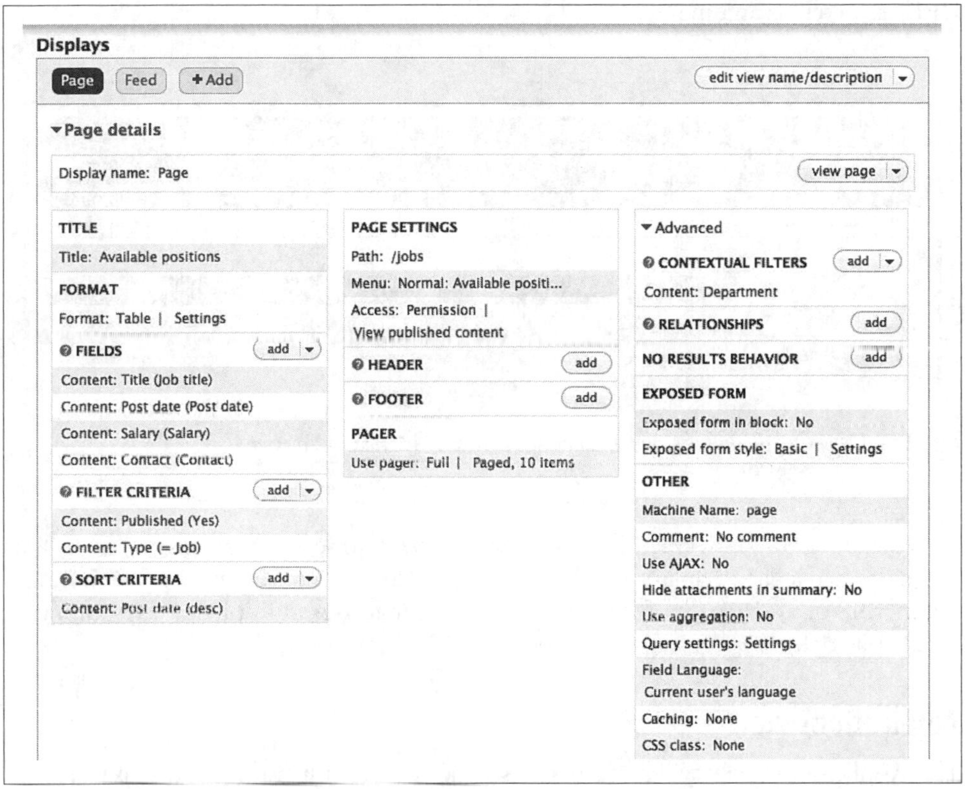

Figure 3-40. Completed Jobs view configuration

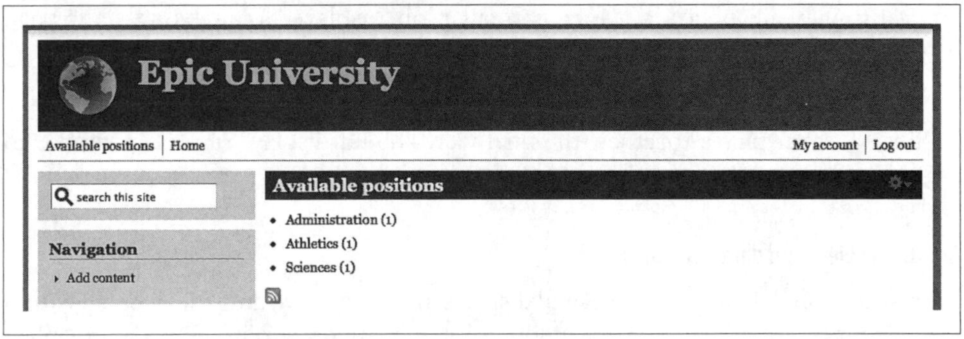

Figure 3-41. The root level of the Jobs view, with a summary display contextual filter

Clicking on any of the options will take you to a filtered listing within that category, such as in Figure 3-42. Pay attention to the URL also as you move between pages. It should be similar to *http://www.example.com/jobs/administration* or *http://www.example.com/jobs/athletics*. This is the way arguments work in Views: the path we specify displays the summary view, then any "directories" (such as *administration*) under that URL are taken as arguments.

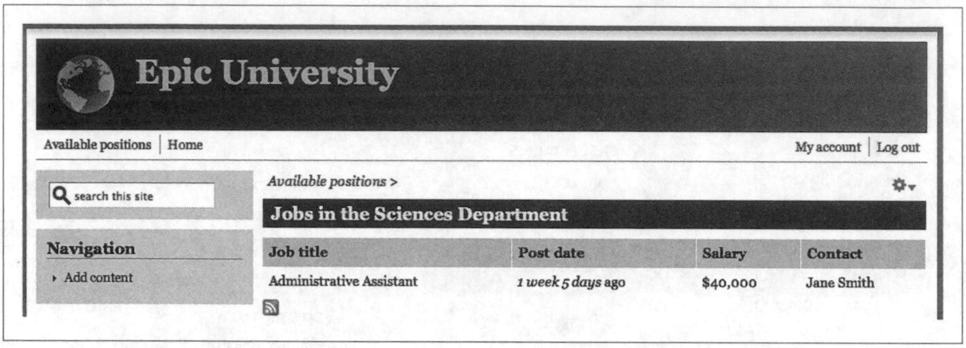

Figure 3-42. Inside the Filtered view, when the context "sciences" is passed in

This concludes our introductory view, where we've used several features of Views. This example used a Page display, added some fields, and used contextual filters in a simple manner. In our next example, we'll create a view that uses multiple displays, and gets a little bit trickier.

Applications View

The Applications view will serve both as a tool for administrators and as a reference for users. It will provide the following displays:

- A listing of all job applications in the entire system as a single page
- A listing of all applications for a particular job, displayed as a tab on the job page
- A listing of applications filled out by the currently logged-in user, displayed as a block in the sidebar

Taking all these pieces together, the final view should display something similar to Figure 3-43.

Create the view and default display

In this view, we'll be setting up several displays and then overriding the defaults within each display. By setting up a large amount of the configuration in the default display, we'll save work when we need to change properties that are common to all displays.

 contains:

Epic University

Available positions | Home

My account | Log out

search this site

Alumni Director > Applications >

Job Applications for Alumni Director

My Applications
- Mad Scientist
  I'm crazy!

Navigation
- ▸ Add content
- ○ Applications

View | Applications | Edit

Application date	Application title	Applicant name
10/27/2011 - 02:59	Hire me!	user

A link for administrators to view all applications

An administrator tab on jobs, which lists applications for this job only

A block for users, listing all of their applications

Figure 3-43. The multiple displays of the Applications view

1. Start by getting to the Views administration area by going to the administrative toolbar and Structure→Views (*admin/structure/views*). Click the "Add new view" link, and enter the settings from Table 3-23 into the wizard, then click "Continue & edit"

Table 3-23. Add view settings for the Applications view

View setting	Value
View name	Applications
Description	Checked; "A list of submitted applications, by job or user"
Show	*Content* of type *Job application* sorted by *Newest first*
Create a page	Checked
Create a block	Unchecked
Page settings	
Page title	Applications (default)
Path	applications (default)
Display format	*Table* of fields
Items to display	10 (default)
Use a pager	Checked (default)
Create a menu link	Checked; Menu: *Navigation menu*; Link text: Applications (default)
Include an RSS feed	Unchecked (default)

2. Now we'll set up some default fields. Click the "add" button in the Fields area. Check off the fields described in Table 3-24 and click "Apply (all displays)." Then configure each field's settings, clicking "Apply (all displays)" once again after each screen.

Table 3-24. Default fields for the Applications view

Defaults: Field	Values
Content: Job	(leave the defaults)
Content: Post date	Label: Application date
	Date format: Short format: 12/04/2011 - 9:30

There is one more field that would be very useful in this view: the name of the user who submitted the application. If we look for the username in the list of fields we can use, though, we won't find it. The closest field in the list is "Content: Author uid," and the help text underneath it states "The user authoring the content. If you need more fields then the uid add the content: author relationship." The uid is only a number, like 4 or 206, and isn't really that helpful. We do want more fields than the user ID number—we want the name—so we will need a new Views module trick that we haven't used yet: Relationships. Figure 3-44 shows a diagram of how relationships work. All of our Job Application nodes have an author uid associated with them. We can use that ID to connect with the rest of the user information in the database, and then pull out the bits we want once we've created the connection.

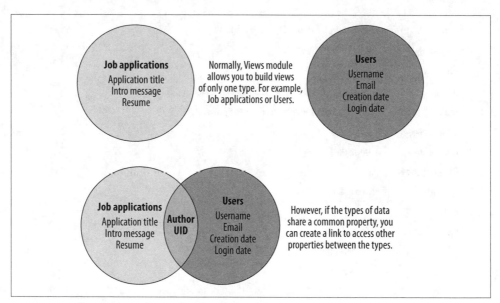

Figure 3-44. If two objects share a bond, Relationships can pull in data from one to another

1. Using relationships is a two-part process.

   First, you must identify the relationship—that is, tell Views what your connector piece is, and second, you will need to use that relationship to add the fields or other data that you want to the view. Let's create a new relationship we can use. Open the Advanced fieldset to expose more settings, and click the "add" button next to Relationships. "Select Content: Author" and click the "Apply (all displays)" button. Since all content will have an author, we can make the resulting query more efficient by checking the "Require this relationship" checkbox. Click "Apply (all displays)" once more, and that's all there is to it. We have added in the relationship, and now we can start using it.

2. Click the "add" button in the Fields section once again, and this time you will see more options than before. There is now a whole group of fields available in the User group. Select the User: Name field and click "Apply (all displays)." You will see that it is using the relationship we just created. Change the field's Label to Applicant Name and click "Apply (all displays)" again.

3. We now have all of the fields that we want for our view. Click the down arrow next to the "add" button and select "rearrange." Put the fields in the following order and click "Apply (all displays)":

   • Content: Post date
   • Content: Title
   • (author) User: Name
   • Content: Job

4. Now we need to change one last, very important setting. The default access to this view is set to allow anyone with the "View published content" permission to see the view, but we want to allow only "editor" members on the site to have access to review all the applications. This is also why we put the menu item for this view in the Navigation menu and not the Main menu, meant for all users. In the Page settings section, click the "Access: Permission" link. Use the settings from Table 3-25 to restrict access to this display and click "Apply (all displays)." When you've finished, the settings should look as pictured in Figure 3-45.

Table 3-25. Page display access restrictions for the Applications view

Settings	Values
Access restrictions	Role
Role	editor

 Restricting access to the view only prevents unprivileged users from accessing the view display at *http://www.example.com/applications*; it does *not* prevent an unprivileged user from typing in *http://www.example.com/node/4*, where node 4 is a job application that is not hers. Protecting this kind of node-level access control requires the use of a *node access* module. See "Taking It Further" on page 146 for some suggestions on resolving access concerns.

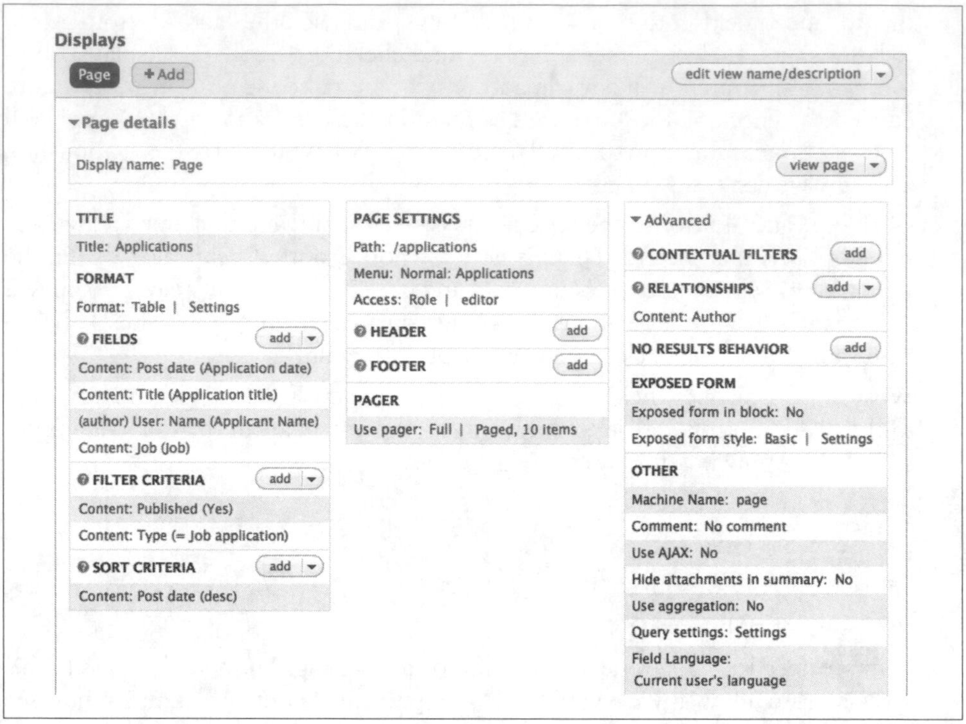

Figure 3-45. The Applications view so far

5. Save the progress on the Applications view by clicking the Save button.

This concludes the default configuration of the Applications view. We have a basic view of applications on the site, which are displayed in a page, with a menu item in the Main menu, as pictured in Figure 3-46.

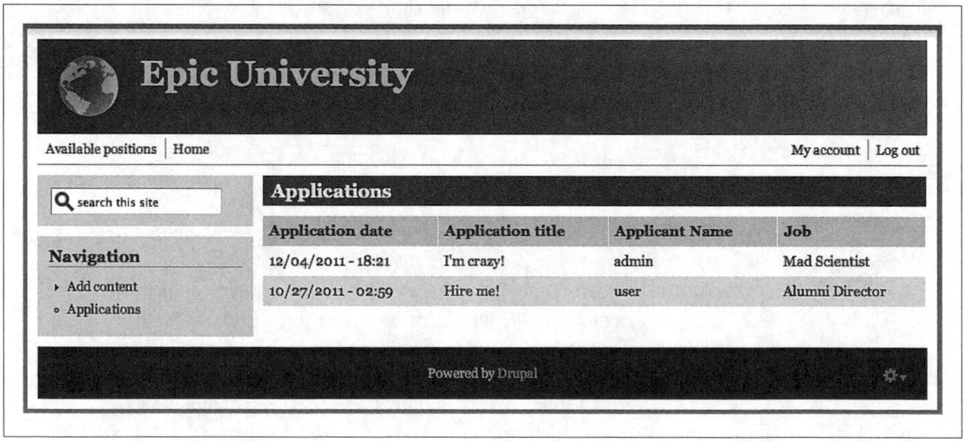

Figure 3-46. The Applications view page display in action

Create the Job Tab display

We've created a page containing all the applications on the entire site. Although this might be helpful for watching incoming applications, it's not entirely helpful for our jobs' contact people, who will be primarily interested in only the applications posted to one job. To fill this need, we'll make a display that limits the applications to just one job, using a contextual filter. We'll also need to create a new relationship to connect the application to the job being applied for so the contextual filter has something to work with. To make this page easy to find, we'll add it as a tab on the job node pages (see Figure 3-47).

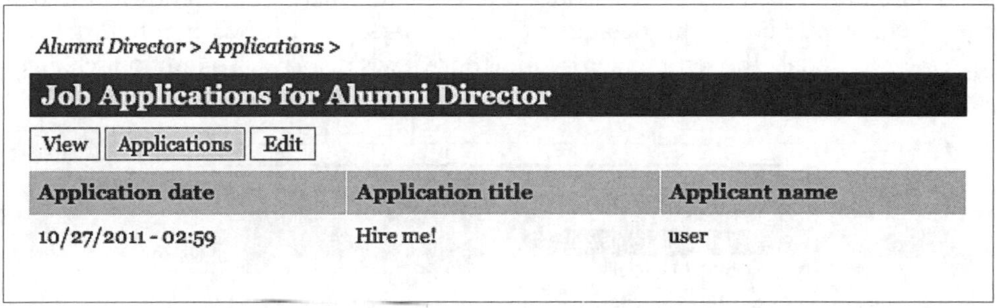

Figure 3-47. The Applications view displayed as a tab on a job node

If you've left the Views administration area, return to it by going to the administrative toolbar and clicking Administer→Structure→Views→Applications→Edit (*admin/structure/views/view/applications/edit*).

1. Click the "+ Add" link in the Displays bar, as shown in Figure 3-48, and select Page.

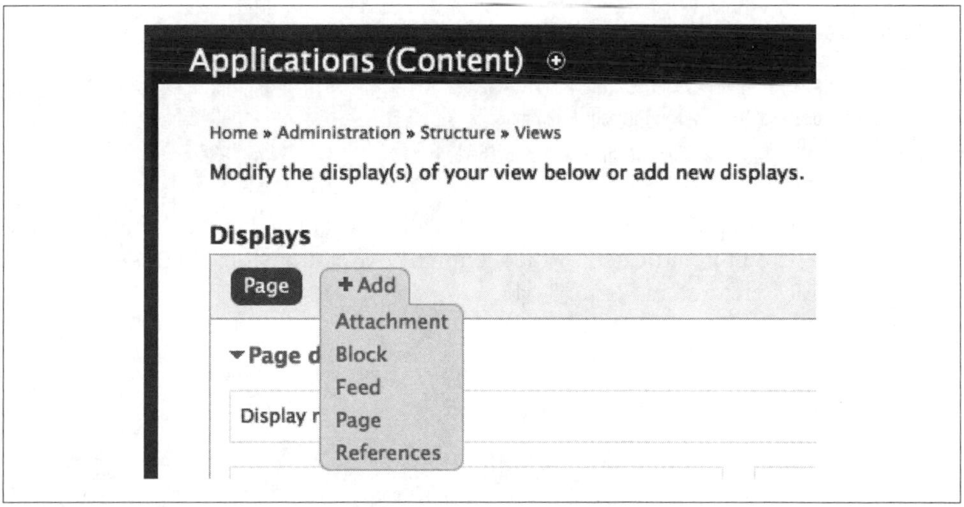

Figure 3-48. Adding a new Page display to the Applications view

2. The new display gets the name Page by default. To help distinguish it from the original Page display we created, we'll rename it to Job Tab, because this page will be displayed as a tab on job nodes. Click the Page link next to "Display name" just below, change it to Job Tab, and then click Apply.

3. To display the information required on this tab, we will need to override our default settings. We need to have a relationship to the job to which the applicant is applying, and a contextual filter to bring in the job ID. However, these settings are specific to this one display, and should not affect the default page we already set up.

   Fortunately, Views solves this with its display overrides concept. At the top of the configuration screen for each of our Views elements, there is a drop-down preceded by the word "For." This defaults to "All displays" with the assumption that we want to update the settings across all of our view's displays. To limit our changes to just *this* display, we need to select the override option, as pictured in Figure 3-49.

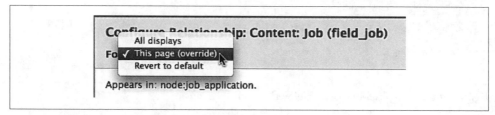

Figure 3-49. Override settings for a View

4. First, let's add a relationship to the application's job so we can pull the job's elements into our view. Open the Advanced fieldset, click the "add" button for Relationships, add the settings from Table 3-26 (shown in Figure 3-50), and click "Apply (this display)."

Table 3-26. Default relationships for the Applications view

Defaults: Relationships	Values
Content: Job (field_job)	For: This page (override)
	Require this relationship: Checked

Once you have applied your changes, you will see that you have an active override in the Views editor, indicated by the section title (Relationships, in this case) being italicized, as pictured in Figure 3-51.

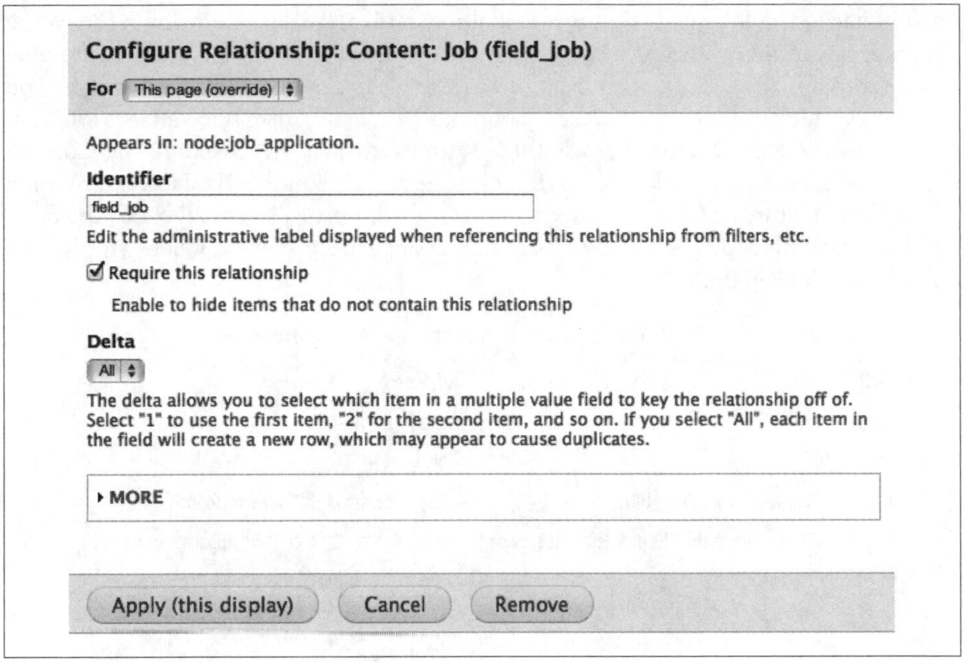

Figure 3-50. Relationship configuration for the Job Tab

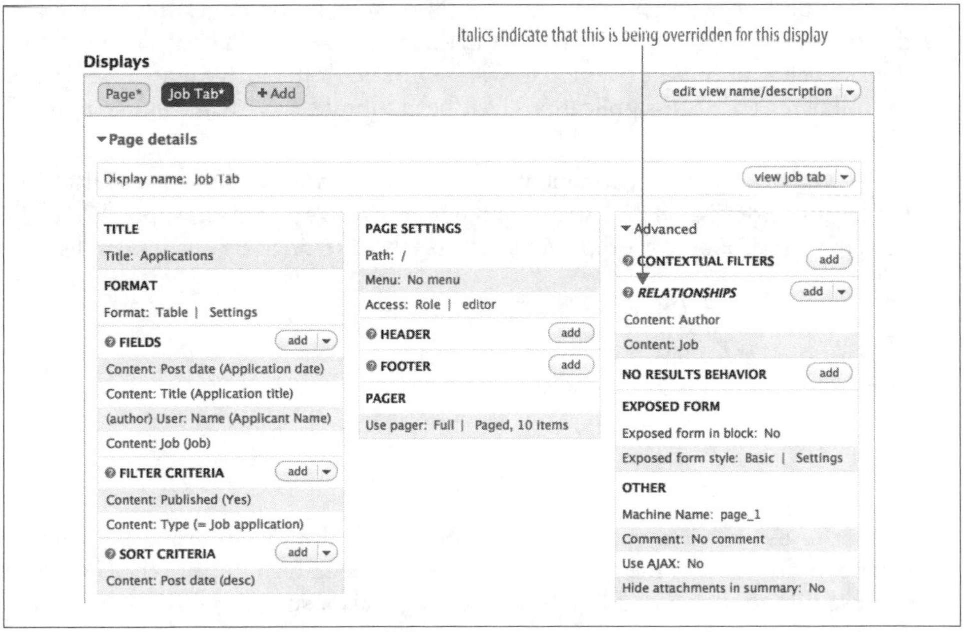

Figure 3-51. Overriding the Relationships portion of a view

5. Similar to the Jobs view that we configured earlier, we can filter down the listing of applications by adding a contextual filter to the display. We'll add a contextual filter that filters the list of applications to a single job node. Click the "add" button for "Contextual filters," select "Content: Nid," and use the values from Table 3-27. Remember to override these settings for just this display. The Content Nid contextual filter allows us to filter by one particular job's ID. Here we're using another feature of Views' contextual filters: a *validator*. Views will check the node ID passed in to the URL and verify that it belongs to a job node. Click "Apply (this display)" when done.

Table 3-27. The Job Tab "Content: Nid" settings for the Applications view

Settings	Values
For	This page (override)
Relationship	field_job
When the filter value is *not* in the URL	Display contents of "No results found"
When the filter value *is* in the URL or a default is provided	Override title: Checked; "Job Applications for %1"
	Specify validation criteria: Checked
	Validator: Content
	Content Types: Job
	Validate user has access to the content: Checked

6. We set our view to "Display contents of 'No results found'," but this is blank by default. Let's add something more useful there. Click the "add" button next to No Results Behavior (right under Relationships). Select "Global: Text area" and enter the following text: "No applications have been submitted." Then, click "Apply (all displays)."

7. Now that we've set up an argument for this display, we need to give it a URL. Use the settings from Table 3-28 to set up the Page settings and click Apply. We don't need to worry about overriding here, because these settings are always per display.

Table 3-28. Job Tab display page settings

Job Tab: Page settings	Values
Path	node/%/applications
Menu	Type: Menu tab
	Title: Applications

Similar to using %1 in the title of the contextual filter, we're using the percent symbol to specify that the first context value will be in the middle of the URL. You can use this approach to add tabs to user pages also, such as *user/%/my_display*, or any other page in Drupal with a dynamic path.

---

8. And finally, we no longer need the Job listed on this display; it would be redundant, as we'll be looking at the job directly. Click the drop-down arrow next to the "add" button in the Fields section, and select "rearrange." Override this section for this display by changing the For field to "This page (override)." Then click the "remove" link for the Content: Job Job field, and click "Apply (this display)" to save your changes.

 If you want behavior specific to one display and not others, be sure to change the For setting to "For: This page (override)." The Views module's settings default to affecting *all* displays within that view. You can end up accidentally deleting this field from more than one display if you're not in override mode. If that happens, you will need to add the field back to the main Page display, and then remove it again from the Job Tab display.

9. Click the Save button to save the view, which should now look like Figure 3-52.

Displays

| Page | Job Tab | + Add | edit view name/description ▼

▼ **Job Tab details**

Display name: Job Tab   clone job tab ▼

TITLE
Title: Applications

FORMAT
Format: Table | Settings

🔗 **FIELDS**   add ▼
Content: Post date (Application date)
Content: Title (Application title)
(author) User: Name (Applicant Name)

🔗 **FILTER CRITERIA**   add ▼
Content: Published (Yes)
Content: Type (= Job application)

🔗 **SORT CRITERIA**   add ▼
Content: Post date (desc)

PAGE SETTINGS
Path: /node/%/applications
Menu: Tab: Applications
Access: Role | editor

🔗 **HEADER**   add
🔗 **FOOTER**   add

PAGER
Use pager: Full | Paged, 10 items

▼ Advanced

🔗 **CONTEXTUAL FILTERS**   add ▼
(field_job) Content: Nid

🔗 **RELATIONSHIPS**   add ▼
Content: Author
Content: Job

NO RESULTS BEHAVIOR   add ▼
Global: Text area

EXPOSED FORM
Exposed form in block: No
Exposed form style: Basic | Settings

OTHER
Machine Name: page_1
Comment: No comment
Use AJAX: No
Hide attachments in summary: No
Use aggregation: No

Figure 3-52. Applications view with new Job tab

We've now added a tab to all job nodes (for users in the "editor" role). Visiting a node that has applications should look similar to Figure 3-47, shown earlier.

Create the Applications block display

The last display that we're going to assemble will be available to all users of the site. It will be a block that will show all the job applications that the currently logged-in user has submitted on the site. We'll also change the style of this display from a table to a list layout, because it will need to be displayed in the narrower sidebar column. The final display will look similar to Figure 3-53.

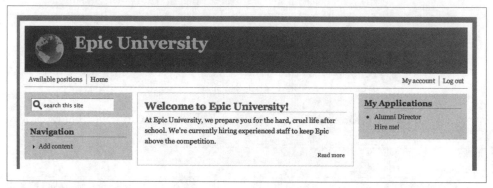

Figure 3-53. The front page with the User Applications display as a block in the right sidebar

If you have left the Views configuration screen, return to the Applications view by going to the administrative toolbar and clicking Structure→Views→Applications→Edit (*admin/structure/views/view/applications/edit*). We'll start by adding a new display to this view:

1. Click the "+ Add" link in the Displays bar and select Block from the display list.

2. Now we'll need to override some settings. Click the Title link to see the configuration screen, change For to "This block (override)," and change the title to My Applications. Click "Apply (this display)."

3. Change the Format to an unordered list by clicking the Table link in the Format section, and once again changing For to "This block (override)," and selecting "HTML list" as the format. Click "Apply (this display)." We can keep the default configuration, so just click "Apply (this display)" again to complete the change.

4. Now configure a description on the block that will show up in the block administration area. Under "Block settings," enter a block name of User Applications and click Apply.

We've now set essentially three names or titles for this block. Here's a rundown of where each title will be displayed:

Display Name
    Used within the Views interface as the name of the display. Shown in the Displays bar at the top of the Views editing screen.

Title: Title

Used as the block title when it is displayed to the end user.

Block settings: Block name

Used to refer to the block when arranging blocks by going to the administrative toolbar and clicking Structure→Blocks (*admin/build/block*).

Because this is a block that will live in the sidebar, we'll want to display far fewer fields so that it fits nicely in the narrower region of the page. To do this, we'll need to override the Fields area of this view.

1. Click on the down arrow next to the "add" button in the Fields section and select "rearrange." Select "This block (override)" and then click the "remove" link for the "Content: Post date Application date" and "(author) User: Name Applicant Name" fields. Click "Apply (this display)" to save your changes.

2. Configure the remaining fields as indicated in Table 3-29. Since we already did an override in the Fields section, by removing a few fields in the previous step, you will notice that the configuration for these fields defaults now to "This block (override)." Once you override any part of a section, everything in that section is considered to be in override mode.

Table 3-29. Block fields in the Applications view

Block: Field	Values
Content: Title (Application title)	Create a label: unchecked
Content: Job (Job)	Create a label: unchecked
	Formatter: Title (no link)

3. Reorder the fields by clicking the down arrow next to the "add" button and selecting "rearrange," so that the job comes first, then the title of the application.

4. Because we need to limit this display to job applications by the current user, we need to add a filter to the display. We'll leave the two existing filters in place— "(Content: Published (Yes)" and "Content: Type (= Job application)"—and add a single new filter for User: Current. Make sure we are using an override by selecting "This block (override)" then check off the User: Current filter and click "Apply (this display)." Select Yes for "Is the logged-in user" and click "Apply (this display)." This step will allow the block's contents to change dynamically depending on who the currently logged-in user is.

5. One last item, which is easy to overlook, is that our poor regular users on the site will not be able to see the view. We have the permissions set up to only allow access for editors on the site. In the Block Settings section, click the Role link next to Access, select "This block (override)," then change the selection to Permission. The permission defaults to "View published content," which is fine, so click "Apply (this display)" once again to finish.

6. Save the view, which should now look like Figure 3-54. Your configuration for the User Applications block display is now complete.

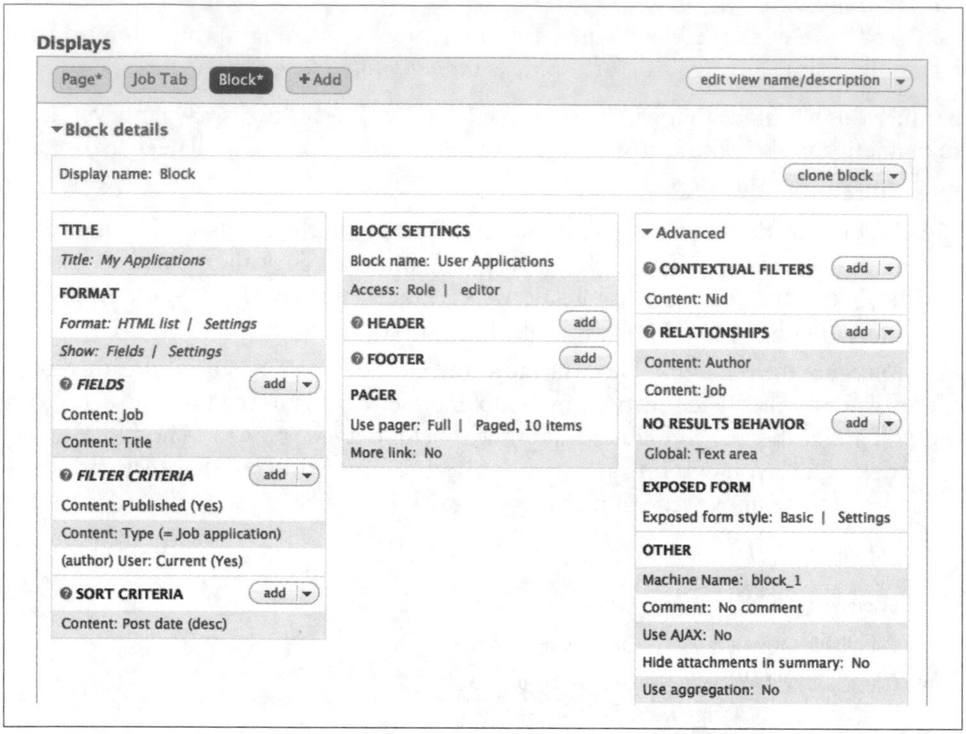

Figure 3-54. The completed Block display for the Applications view

7. By adding a new Block display, we've added a block to the Drupal site. Before it is visible anywhere, though, we need to enable the block. In the administrative tool-bar, click Structure→Blocks (*admin/structure/block*) and scroll down to the Disabled section to find your new block, User Applications. Place it in the Sidebar Second region and save your changes.

Whew! After that whirlwind tour of views, you should now see a sidebar block showing any jobs you've applied for.

Taking It Further

The basic job website that we've built only touches on the surface of the capability of Field and Views. There are a lot of possibilities for extending the functionality of this job site by adding more fields to both the Job and Job Application content types. Here are a few modules that could be used to take things a bit further with our job board:

Automatic Node Titles (http://drupal.org/project/auto_nodetitle)
> This module provides support for creating title templates for nodes. For example, rather than having users manually enter a title for their applications (which may result in nonsensical things such as "Hire me!"), this module could ensure that all application titles follow a standard format automatically, such as [author-name] – [job-title].

Node Reference URL Widget (http://drupal.org/project/nodereference_url)
> This module adds a new field widget for node references. With this, we could display a link on our Job content that says "Apply for this job," and the link would take people to the application form with the correct job already selected so they don't have to figure out which one to select from the list.

Content Access (http://drupal.org/project/content_access) and private files
> Right now, all job applications submitted to the site are public and searchable even by anonymous users. That's no good, since résumés are bound to contain sensitive information. Content Access is one example of a node access module, and can limit viewing of job applications only to site editors. When coupled with Drupal core's private files feature, configurable at Configuration→Media→"File system" (*admin/config/media/file-system*), you can specify that file fields are able to save uploaded files to the private files directory instead.

Field Permissions (http://drupal.org/project/field_permissions)
> Another way to protect certain private application information from displaying to unprivileged users, the Field Permissions module can selectively block fields from being edited or viewed, depending on the visitor's role.

Summary

This chapter taught you how to use two of Drupal's fundamental "building block" modules: Field and Views. These modules constitute the cornerstone of Drupal's power and are used extensively throughout the rest of the book. Field is used to model your website's content by adding extra fields to hold different properties, and Views is used to display lists of your website's data.

Besides the basic features of these modules, this chapter also introduced you to the methodology for Drupal site building. Rather than installing monolithic packages, in Drupal each module provides specific functionality, and works together with other modules to enhance their functionality. As we created fields for our different content types, References was working together with the core Field module. While making listings of content, Views retrieved information provided by both core modules and References. This sort of cooperation between modules serves as the foundation for the rest of the book, as more modules join the party and give new shape to our sites.

Here are the contributed modules that we referenced in this chapter:

- Automatic Nodetitle (*http://drupal.org/project/auto_nodetitle*)
- Display Suite (*http://drupal.org/project/ds*)
- Entity Reference (*http://drupal.org/project/entityreference*)
- Field Permissions (*http://drupal.org/project/field_permissions*)
- Node Reference URL Widget (*http://drupal.org/project/nodereference_url*)
- References (*http://drupal.org/project/references*)
- Relation (*http://drupal.org/project/relation*)
- Token (*http://drupal.org/project/token*)
- Views (*http://drupal.org/project/views*)

These are some other resources that we referenced and community resources for learning more about the new concepts introduced in this chapter:

- Field modules (*http://drupal.org/project/modules?filters=tid%3A20224%20drupal_core%3A103%20bs*)
- Views Developers Drupal group (*http://groups.drupal.org/views-developers*)

CHAPTER 4

Media Management

Almost every website needs some kind of media management support, ranging from allowing users to upload photos to handling automatic media encoding in different file formats. Drupal's flexibility allows for managing media in a variety of ways, and for scaling from a one-person portfolio to millions of users uploading photos on a fan site.

This chapter introduces the following modules:

Image (core)
> Provides a field for uploading images, as well as the ability to establish "styles" of images such as thumbnails

Media (http://drupal.org/project/media)
> Provides media management for Drupal: comes with a media browser and various tools that other modules can leverage and extend

Media: YouTube (http://drupal.org/project/media_youtube)
> Extends the Media module to allow users to easily embed videos from YouTube

WYSIWYG (http://drupal.org/project/wysiwyg)
> Provides support for WYSIWYG ("What You See Is What You Get") editors

If you would like to participate in the hands-on exercises in this chapter, install Drupal using the *Chapter 4: Media* installation profile from the book's sample code. This will create the example website on your web server. The completed website will look as pictured in Figure 4-1 and at *//media.usingdrupal.com*. For more information on using the book's sample code, see the Preface.

> To complete this chapter, you must have the Clean URLs feature working, and your version of PHP must have the GD library installed. See "Troubleshooting Image Styles" on page 158 for more information.

Figure 4-1. Band Wagon website

Case Study

John and Lisa are both music lovers. They love listening to records, going to shows, and talking about music with their friends. They've been thinking for a while about setting up a website where they could write reviews of new records and shows, and share their concert photos and YouTube videos of their favorite bands. Since many of their friends are also into music, John and Lisa want to do this in a way that will allow their friends to sign up and join in the fun. Lisa has heard about Drupal from her coworker, and decides that it seems like a perfect match for their project.

After a few evenings of brainstorming, John and Lisa have come up with a list of things they want the website to do. When photos are uploaded, they should be automatically resized for use on different pages: a thumbnail to use on overview pages, and a proportionally scaled version for review pages. John and Lisa also want to be able to group reviews of the same band together in overview pages, using a simple tagging system.

Since they want their friends (many of whom don't know anything about websites, let alone HTML) to be able to use the website, the process of uploading photos, posting videos, and creating attractive review pages needs to be really easy. Users should be able to easily enrich their posts by changing text styles (bold, italic, lists, etc.) and mixing and matching photos and videos with their text. When a user writes a review, it should be possible to use another user's photo or video by selecting it from a media archive.

Implementation Notes

Even though there is a wide array of options to choose from when it comes to handling multimedia in Drupal, recent developments in the Drupal community have simplified this area of Drupal a lot. The Media (*http://drupal.org/project/media*) module, together with Drupal core's tools and other contributed modules, provides solid support for multimedia, while leaving all the room you need to build a unique project.

Photo Uploads

Image handling in Drupal has long been a distributed effort between several cooperating (or competing) modules. In Drupal 7, you can still choose between several options, with Drupal core's Image module and the Media module being the main ones.

The Image module, which we encountered in "Creating an Article" on page 39, provides an image upload field that you can add to content types, taxonomy terms, users, and every other Drupal entity that you can imagine.

The Media module, which is a contributed module, is the go-to option if you want broader multimedia support. As we will see later in this chapter, it was developed specifically to solve the long-standing problem of media management in Drupal. It supports media file uploads (image, video, and audio file types are supported out of the box), management and reuse of media assets, and much more.

In this chapter, we'll use the Media module's Media field instead of the Image module's Image field. Media's solution offers not only a way of uploading photos, but also of adding other media types such as videos. It even comes with an easy-to-use media browser to add existing media assets to content.

Posting Videos

The Media module not only allows uploading and managing local media assets, but it also provides a centralized way to access media on various third-party content sources. For example, there are modules available to help you post photos from Flickr and videos from YouTube on your Drupal website by simply copy/pasting the photo's or video's URL, or its *embed code*, a string of code that allows you to show a video or photo from somewhere else on the Web on your own site.

Thumbnail Generation

Drupal core's Image module comes with a very powerful feature called "Image styles," which takes care of all sorts of image manipulation. It can not only be used to create thumbnails, but also to chain together several image effects such as crop, rotate, scale, desaturate, and sharpen to create completely customized displays of images. The Media module uses the "Image styles" functionality to take care of image manipulation.

WYSIWYG Editor

WYSIWYG editors allow nontechnical website users to use **bold** or *italic* text, create bulleted lists, or add links to other web pages (and much more than that) by using an interface that heavily resembles that of word processing software. The Media module comes with a plug-in for WYSIWYG editors, so users can easily embed media assets in their posts. Instead of choosing one of the many available standalone editor modules, we'll use the WYSIWYG module (*http://drupal.org/project/wysiwyg*) to add an editor to our site, since more Drupal 7 sites use it and the developers are much more active in maintaining it.

The next step is choosing a WYSIWYG editor to plug in to the WYSIWYG module. The WYSIWYG module is an incredibly flexible framework, and actually supports multiple WYSIWYG editors. We'll use the CKEditor (*http://ckeditor.com/*) WYSIWYG editor, as it won top billing in an extremely comprehensive review (*http://www.f3inter net.com/articles/2010/08/09/review-of-drupal-rich-text-editors/*) of all available editors for the WYSIWYG module.

Spotlight: Image Styles

When you're uploading photos to a website, it's important to ensure that they are displayed at the right size. Otherwise, when you upload an exceptionally large image, chances are good that it will break your site's layout. To prevent this, you'll want to scale these images so that they're a consistent size, and create thumbnails for use in listing pages. "Image styles," a feature that's part of Drupal core's Image module, will provide these options and many more for displaying images.

 We tackle image manipulation before going into detail on how to set up media handling for Drupal in general, since some of the concepts explained here will come in handy later.

The automatic image manipulation provided by "Image styles" allows you to combine a series of effects such as cropping, scaling, or resizing into what is called an *image style*. By combining effects, you can create a customized display of your images. Figure 4-2 shows the result of a style that combines a crop effect with rotate to make a square image that is rotated 90 degrees.

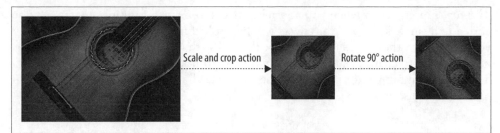

Figure 4-2. An image style combining two effects: scale and crop, then rotate

The image is generated on the fly, then saved (or "cached") in a directory with the same name as the image style. This way, the expensive part of manipulating images only happens once, and subsequent requests are read directly from disk.

Styles and Effects

The main "Image styles" page, which you can reach by clicking Configuration→ Media→"Image styles" (*admin/config/media/image-styles*), displays a list of the styles available on the site, as shown in Figure 4-3. You can add new styles and edit existing styles.

Image styles ⊕

Home » Administration » Configuration » Media

Image styles commonly provide thumbnail sizes by scaling and cropping images, but can also add various effects before an image is displayed. When an image is displayed with a style, a new file is created and the original image is left unchanged.

✚ Add style

STYLE NAME	SETTINGS	OPERATIONS
thumbnail	Default	edit
medium	Default	edit
large	Default	edit

Figure 4-3. The "Image styles" administration screen

 The style name will be part of the URL of all generated images, so it's good to keep it short, make it all lowercase, and use only alphanumeric characters, underscores, and dashes. If you're building a site where standard image sizes will be used in a variety of places, a name that describes the final output is also a good idea, such as "160_square," "200_width," or "300x200_resize." For our examples, we'll use default names like "thumbnail" and "large," which are semantic in their use.

The real fun comes in when you add new effects to a style. Multiple effects may be added to a single style, and the effects will be applied from top to bottom. Whenever you edit a style, the cached files will all be flushed so that they can be regenerated. This makes it easy to change all the images on the site from using a 100-pixel thumbnail to a 120-pixel thumbnail (or make any other possible changes). The configuration form for adding a new effect to a style is shown in Figure 4-4.

Edit *thumbnail* style ○

Preview

original (view actual size)

600px

800px

thumbnail (view actual size)

100px

100px

Image style name
thumbnail
This image style is being provided by *image* module and may not be renamed.

Show row weights

EFFECT		OPERATIONS	
⊹ Scale and crop 100x100		edit	delete
⊹ Rotate 90°		edit	delete
⊹ Select a new effect ▾ Add			

Update style

Figure 4-4. Effects on an image style

Crop

Crop allows you to trim off edges of the image that are not wanted. Crop takes pixel values, and allows you to define which part of the image is retained by choosing an anchor point. The end result of a cropping effect will be similar to Figure 4-5.

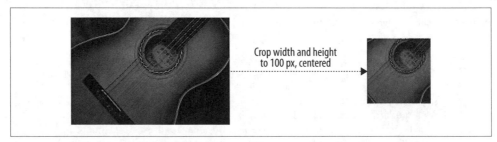

Crop width and height
to 100 px, centered

Figure 4-5. Cropping will trim off edges of an image

Desaturate

Desaturate allows you to convert a color image into a black and white image. This effect, shown in Figure 4-6, doesn't have any settings.

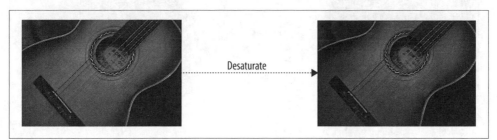

Figure 4-6. Desaturating converts a color image to black and white

Resize

Resize can be used to force an image to a particular dimension. You can enter width and height values to scale to a specific pixel size.

Usually, you'll want to use the scale action instead of resize, as resizing might make your image look squished or stretched. Rather than maintain proportions, resize forces an image to be exactly those dimensions, as shown in Figure 4-7.

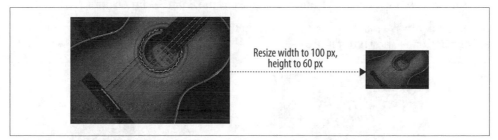

Figure 4-7. Resizing can change the aspect ratio of an image

Rotate

Rotate allows you to rotate images according to a given amount of a degrees, as shown in Figure 4-8. A positive number of degrees rotates the image clockwise; a negative number rotates it counterclockwise. You can also define a background color to fill areas of the image that are exposed after the rotation. If you want to get funky, you can even randomize the rotation angle for each image.

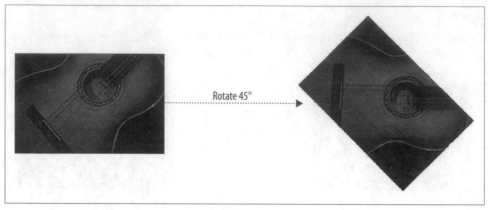

Figure 4-8. Rotate can change the rotation angle of an image

Scale

Scale is used to size images proportionally. Unlike resize, you need to enter *either* a width or height. The dimension without a value will be automatically determined when the image is scaled to the given dimension. If both dimensions are entered, the image will be scaled to fit within both values.

If your site absolutely needs images to be no smaller than a certain size, you can use the Allow Upscaling option to enlarge images to the entered dimensions.

Scaling will always maintain the aspect ratio of the original image. The end result of a scaling action is shown in Figure 4-9.

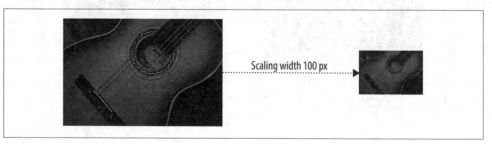

Figure 4-9. Scaling an image maintains the aspect ratio

Scale and crop

As the name implies, the scale and crop action is a single-action combination of the scale and crop functions. In this action, the image is scaled until one dimension fits within the given size, then the larger dimension is cropped off (also called a *zoom crop*). This action is most helpful for making square thumbnails while maintaining the aspect ratio of the original image. An example of the result of the scale and crop action is shown in Figure 4-10.

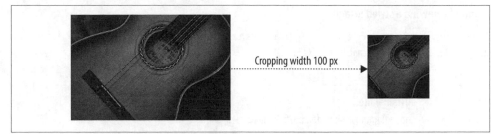

Cropping width 100 px

Figure 4-10. The scale and crop effect trims off the larger side while maintaining the aspect ratio

The effects just described are the ones that are available in Drupal core's "Image styles." For an expanded set of actions (including watermark, border, text placement, brightness, and transparency), you can install the ImageCache Actions module, available at *http://drupal.org/ project/imagecache_actions* (the name comes from the contributed ImageCache module, which was the image manipulation toolkit in previous versions of Drupal).

Using an Image Style

After setting up styles in the "Image styles" administration area, you need to tell Drupal where these styles should be used. The field that comes with Drupal core's Image module provides options to display the image in either the original size or in one of the styles you configured.

Field formatters

The typical display of images is configured with field formatters, as shown in Figure 4-11. For every style setup on your site, "Image styles" adds a field formatter. It also allows you to link the image either to the content (the node where the image is used), to the image file, or not at all.

Figure 4-11. Configuring an image field to use an image style

Manually viewing a styled image

You may view an image style at any time by manually assembling the URL to the image and style. Assembling such a URL is illustrated in Figure 4-12.

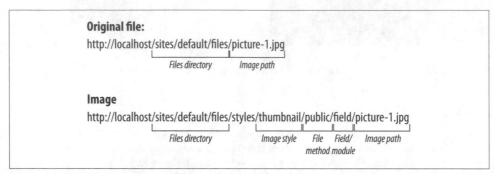

Figure 4-12. Assembling a URL to an image style

After configuring an image style, it's easy to test what an image will look like by visiting the URL of an image.

Troubleshooting Image Styles

"Image styles" makes use of several advanced PHP and Apache features, such as URL rewriting and the GD image library. Because its software requirements are steep, any misconfiguration in your server or Drupal setup may cause "Image styles" to break. The following sections describe common problems with getting "Image styles" to work. If you are able to successfully upload images to your articles, you can safely skip this section.

Check Clean URLs

The most common problem is that Clean URLs (a core feature that provides URLs like *http://example.com/node/1* instead of *http://example.com/?q=node/1*, which is the default) are not enabled, or not supported by the software on the web server. Visit the Clean URLs configuration page, as shown in Figure 4-13, by clicking Configuration in the administrative toolbar, then Clean URLs in the "Search and metadata" section on that page (*admin/config/search/clean-urls*). If you receive an error on the configuration form, see the handbook page for setting up Clean URLs (*http://drupal.org/getting -started/clean-urls*) for help configuring your server.

 Drupal's Clean URLs feature requires the Apache extension mod_rewrite, or its equivalent for your web server. See *http://drupal.org/node/717772* for instructions on setting up Clean URLs on almost every possible web server platform.

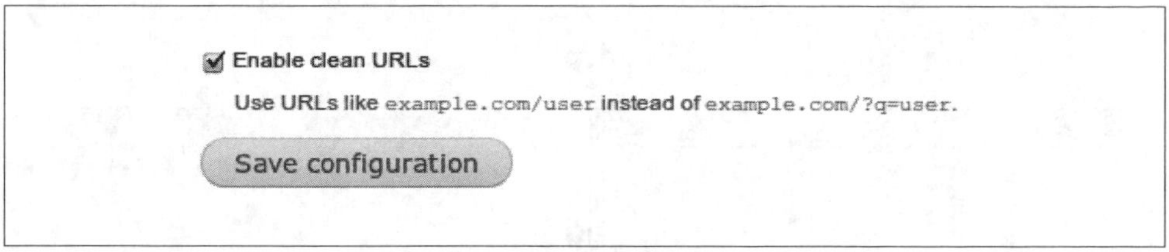

☑ **Enable clean URLs**

Use URLs like `example.com/user` **instead of** `example.com/?q=user`.

Save configuration

Figure 4-13. If the Clean URL test has successfully run, Clean URLs will be enabled when Drupal is installed

Check GD library

Another common problem is a lack of the GD image library on the server. This could be the problem if no image is being generated at all when you visit an "Image styles" URL. GD is a software package that is enabled by default with installations of PHP, but sometimes it is missing from the installation when you're doing custom installs of PHP. You can check the status of GD in your installation by clicking Reports in the administrative toolbar, then Status report (*admin/reports/status*). Halfway down the page, you should see a message similar to Figure 4-14, confirming that GD is enabled.

GD library PNG support	2.0
GD library rotate and desaturate effects	2.0

Figure 4-14. The message you should see for GD on the Status report

If GD looks OK but you're still not having images generated, try checking the configuration of your PHP installation by clicking the "more information" link next to PHP on the status report page (*admin/reports/status/php*).

Check for the "GD settings" section, which should be similar to Figure 4-15. Check that all the needed libraries are available for the kinds of images being uploaded. If the entire section is missing from this page, then GD is not installed at all.

 If you prefer to use ImageMagick instead of GD, you can download the ImageMagick module (*http://drupal.org/project/imagemagick*).

Hands-On: Image Styles

Before we can nicely publish our favorite bands' photos on our website, we need to make sure to set up image styles, in order to create scaled-down versions of the images while leaving the original images intact. Otherwise, full-resolution photos and images in different sizes will appear all over the place, which is not what we want.

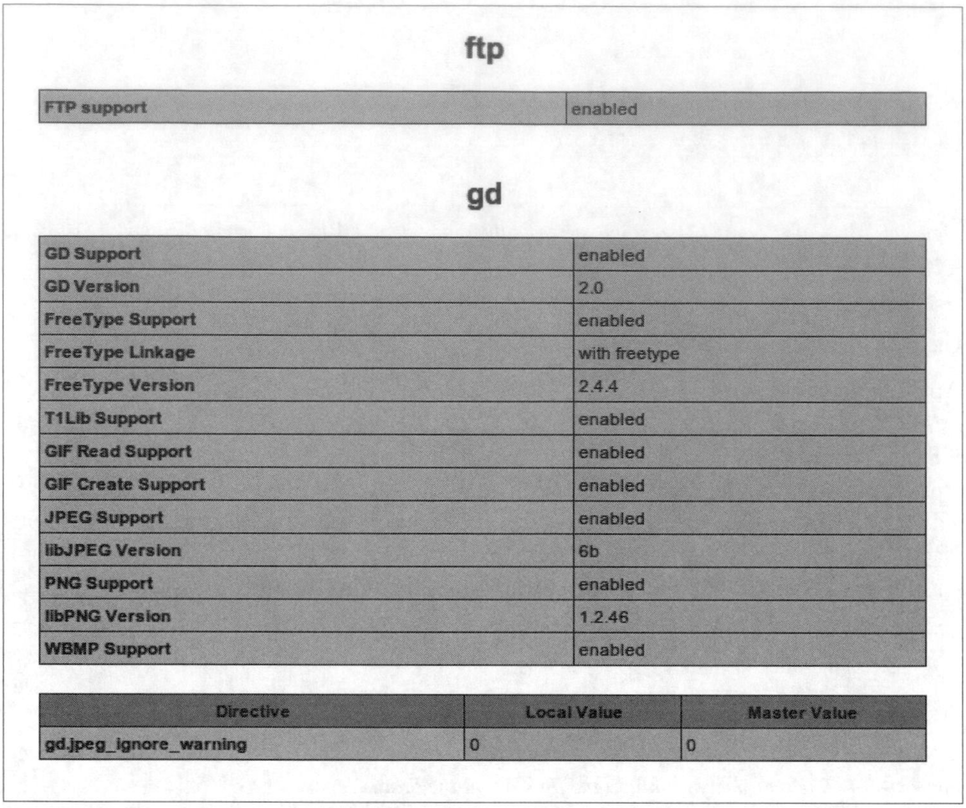

ftp	
FTP support	enabled

gd	
GD Support	enabled
GD Version	2.0
FreeType Support	enabled
FreeType Linkage	with freetype
FreeType Version	2.4.4
T1Lib Support	enabled
GIF Read Support	enabled
GIF Create Support	enabled
JPEG Support	enabled
libJPEG Version	6b
PNG Support	enabled
libPNG Version	1.2.46
WBMP Support	enabled

Directive	Local Value	Master Value
gd.jpeg_ignore_warning	0	0

Figure 4-15. Checking for GD in a PHP install

We'll set up image styles to provide us with thumbnails for listing pages and a scaled-down version to use on review pages. Later in this chapter, we'll learn how to use these image styles in various places across the site.

Create Image Styles

Drupal core's Image module, which is enabled by the book's source code, provides three image styles out of the box. It is possible to override these default styles for your own needs, or you can create new styles from scratch. In this section, we'll override existing image styles. We'll also briefly explain how to create your own custom style from scratch, which is very similar.

1. Go to the "Image styles" settings page by clicking Configuration→Media→"Image styles" (*admin/config/media/image-styles*). You'll see a list of the image styles that exist on your site (the ones that the Image module provides by default).

2. Next to the "thumbnail" style, click "edit" (*admin/config/media/image-styles/edit/thumbnail*). This will take you to the style's configuration page, pictured in Figure 4-16.

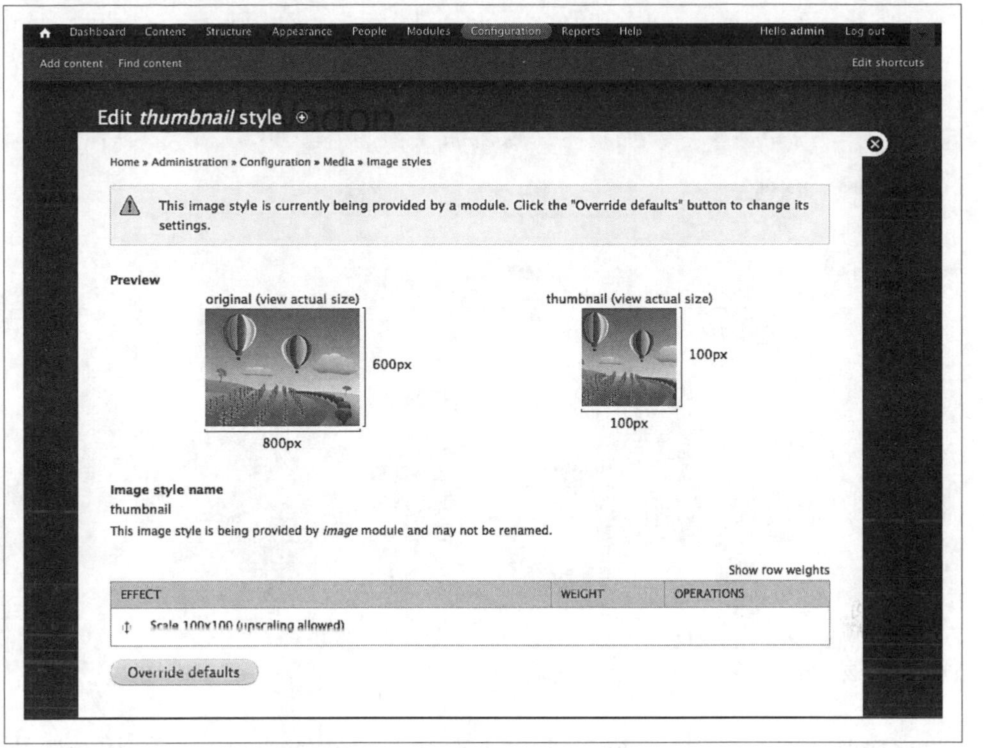

![Screenshot of the Edit thumbnail style configuration screen showing navigation bar, preview of original (800px × 600px) and thumbnail (100px × 100px) images of hot air balloons, image style name "thumbnail", effect list with "Scale 100x100 (upscaling allowed)", and an "Override defaults" button.]

Figure 4-16. The thumbnail image style configuration screen

 On the configuration page, you'll see a message that the style you're currently editing is being provided by a module. This means you can override the style, but you can also revert to the default style provided by the module later (i.e., delete whatever changes you made to the style), since the style is defined by the module's code. The ability to store site configuration to code is useful in deployments from one server to another. For information about this concept, see *http://drupal.org/node/580026*.

3. At the bottom of the configuration page, click "Override defaults." Once you've clicked that button, the form is unlocked and you can begin making changes.

4. We want to change the existing thumbnail from a rectangle into a square. To accomplish this, rather than using just the Scale effect, we'll use the "Scale and crop" effect to round off the rough edges. So first, go ahead and delete the "Scale 100×100" effect from the style by clicking "delete" next to that effect. Watch how the preview image changes in response.

5. Next, select "Scale and crop" from the effect drop-down menu and click Add.

6. On the next page, configure the "Scale and crop" effect. Enter the values from Table 4-1 and as shown on Figure 4-17 for the scale and crop effect, to create image thumbnails as 100-pixel-wide squares. Click "Add effect" when finished.

Table 4-1. Settings for the "thumbnail" scale and crop effect

Setting	Value
Width	100
Height	100

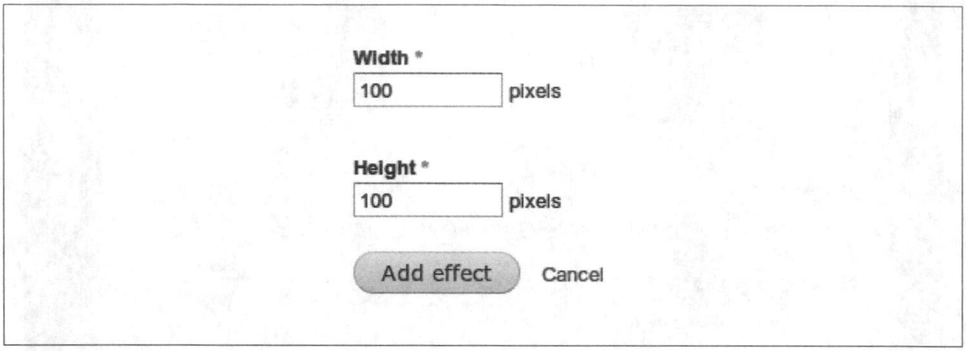

Figure 4-17. Settings for the image style effects

That completes the configuration of the thumbnail style. When you return to the style's configuration page after adding the "Scale and crop" effect, you'll see that the preview image displays a thumbnail of the correct size, as shown in Figure 4-18.

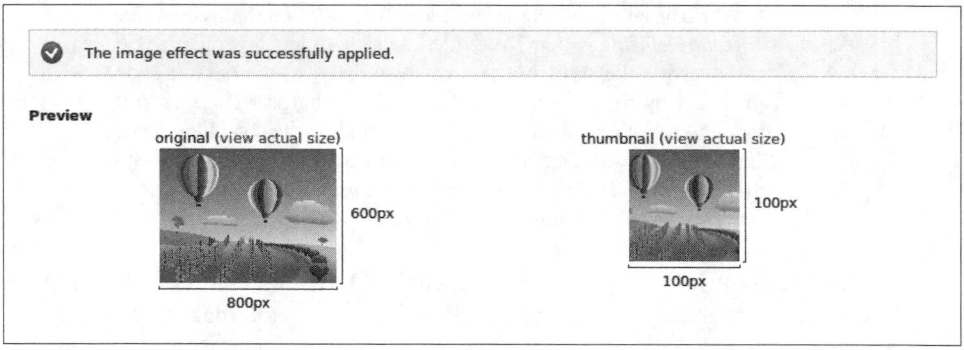

Figure 4-18. Preview for the thumbnail image style

The other two styles that come out of the box with "Image styles" are also scaling styles—just like the thumbnail style we've just overridden. This is fine, since we'll want to display scaled-down photos on the review pages. The existing "large" style, which we'll use on review node pages, needs a little tweaking, though: we want to display our photos a little bigger than these styles allow.

Changing this is easy: the only things we need to change are the width and height values for the styles:

1. Return to the main "Image styles" page either via the breadcrumb, or by navigating back to Configuration→Media→"Image styles" (*admin/config/media/image-styles*). Next to the "medium" style, click "edit."

2. Once again, override the default style, as we've just learned with the thumbnail style. Afterward, tweak the existing "Scale 480×480" effect by clicking "edit" next to it and using the values in Table 4-2 for the scale action to limit medium images to a maximum of 500 pixels wide. Uncheck the Allow Upscaling checkbox. Click "Add effect" to save the changes you've made.

Table 4-2. Settings for the "medium" scale effect

Setting	Value
Width	500
Height	500
Allow Upscaling	Unchecked

 In this section, we've overridden default styles provided by "Image styles." If you want to create your own custom image style from scratch, click "Add style" when on the main "Image styles" page (*admin/config/media/image-styles*), provide a name for your style, and click "Create new style." From there, the configuration is very similar as we've seen in this section: add effects and tweak them to your heart's content.

All our image styles are complete! We've set up two styles: a "thumbnail" style for use in listings of many images, and a "large" style to use on review node pages. We'll use these styles later in the chapter to configure how image files will be displayed on the site.

Improve Image Quality

If you were to look at a sample thumbnail generated by "Image styles" at this point, you might notice the quality of the image is a bit low and overcompressed. "Image styles" uses Drupal core's setting for image quality when processing JPEG images, which defaults to 75%. Increasing this level will generate much higher-quality images.

The steps are:

1. Go to the Image toolkit configuration for Drupal by clicking Configuration→Media→"Image toolkit" (*admin/config/media/image-toolkit*).

2. Set the JPEG quality to 90% or higher and click "Save configuration."

3. To see this effect on existing thumbnails, return to the "Image styles" administration page by going back to Configuration→Media→"Image styles" (*admin/config/media/image-styles*).

4. Next to the "large" style, for example, click "edit" to see the newly created preview images, which should appear slightly sharper.

Spotlight: Media

The Media module for Drupal 7 solves a number of long-standing media-related problems in Drupal (see "Media in Drupal: A Historical Perspective" below). At its core, Media provides a framework to manage media assets on a Drupal site, regardless of whether those assets exist on the site's server or somewhere else on the Internet; the Media Internet module, which is part of the Media module and is covered in "Spotlight: Media Internet Sources" on page 189, makes it possible to use remote files the same way as files on your server.

Media is built to be extended—a number of modules that build upon Media already exist, with a lot more to come. For example, Workbench Media (*http://drupal.org/project/workbench_media*) integrates the Media module with Workbench (covered in Chapter 7) to improve media management for editors. You'll find a full list of modules that integrate with Media and extend it at *http://groups.drupal.org/node/168009*.

Media in Drupal: A Historical Perspective

Previously, in Drupal 4.6/4.7, media assets (images, video and audio files) were treated as individual nodes in Drupal, which led to various limitations on using media on a site. Because every single media file had all the overhead of being a full node (and not simply a field like in Drupal 7), it was pretty hard to build a user-friendly interface to integrate text and multimedia—not to mention how hard it was to use the same media assets in different nodes. More often that not, users had to upload the same picture multiple times to use it in different places on their website. Or they had to battle with complex forms if they wanted to add a video to their article.

There were several modules that tried very hard to get around those limitations, and some of them worked well. But because you had to bend Drupal so hard to get decent multimedia support, it wasn't easy to migrate to a new module when one came along, or when wider developments in Drupal gave way to new approaches to handle multimedia.

With the advent of fields and CCK, several modules appeared that leveraged this new, more flexible system. In Drupal 5 and 6, the Drupal community's development trends headed toward websites built around CCK and Views. This meant that it became common to upload a media file through a field, instead of through its own separate node form. This made it easier to build usable interfaces for users, although uploading and actually using media assets on a Drupal site was still often a hairy user experience.

Because the weight shifted from nodes to fields, a number of modules succeeded fairly well in allowing the reuse of media assets across a website. However, the lack of a centralized way to manage files in Drupal core still made it very hard to do this consistently and to switch modules if you wanted to: it was either one way or the other.

Several improvements in Drupal 7, together with the high number of developers who wanted to solve "Drupal's Media problem" (instead of reinventing the wheel again and again), gave rise to the Media module. It is a solution that leverages Drupal 7's Field module and its file handling capabilities, and takes advantage of the usability improvements that were introduced in Drupal 7.

Drupal 7's new file handling system enables developers to work with files as "first-class citizens" in Drupal; they are entities, just like nodes or users. Files aren't just attachments to a node anymore, or a field in a node form: they are an independent object in Drupal, which means they can be used in different nodes, have fields of their own, and much more. The Media module uses this new approach to bring top-notch multimedia support to Drupal.

Media Files

Remember the file field that Drupal uses, which we learned about in Chapter 3? The Media module extends this field by allowing you to use it to upload and reuse media files through a media browser, as shown in Figure 4-19. Like other fields, you can configure file fields to allow multiple values, so any number of media assets can be uploaded to a single node. You can even add multiple fields to a single content type, in case you want to use a separate field for an audio file, and another for an album cover. Since we're dealing with a normal file field, it can take any type of media file you throw at it, as long as you allow the file types in your field's settings.

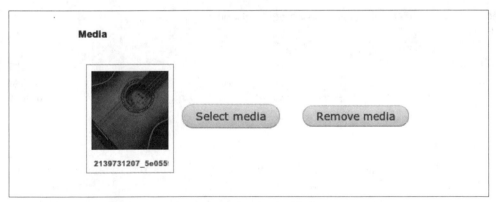

Figure 4-19. The Media module extends Drupal core's file field

Using a predefined field to handle media is a good solution for a lot of use cases, but sometimes the user needs more control over the final display of media assets in content.

To cater to this need, the Media module provides integration with WYSIWYG editors. This makes it possible to insert media assets directly into a text area and to place them where you wish in your content, instead of having your images and videos appear in a spot predefined by your site's theme. If you're not sure what a WYSIWYG editor is, don't worry: we'll learn all about it (and its integration with the Media module) later in this chapter.

 When you're starting a new site, it is often handy to be able to import a whole bunch of files at once, instead of having to upload them all one by one—for example, when you have files on your computer that you want to upload, or a previous website that hosted media files. The Media module provides a way to do this. If you navigate to Content→Files, and then click the "Import media" link (*admin/content/file/import*), you'll see a field where you can enter a directory from which to import files, as shown on Figure 4-20 (you can also use a file matching pattern to limit the files that will be uploaded). Enter the name of the directory (for example, *sites/default/files/my_pictures*) where your files are, click Preview, and then click Confirm to pull all those files into Drupal. The files will immediately be ready for use in the media browser. Note that you need the "Import media files from the local filesystem" permission to be able to import media files this way.

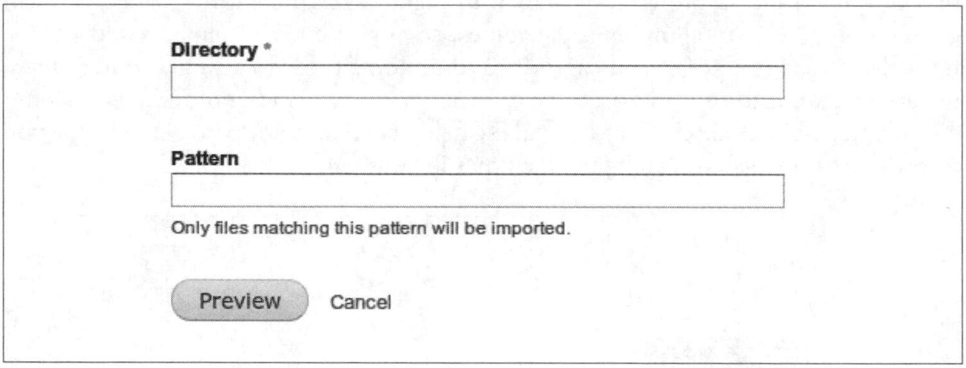

Directory *

Pattern

Only files matching this pattern will be imported.

Preview   Cancel

Figure 4-20. The Media module can import an entire directory of files at once to save time on data entry

Media Browser

The Media module not only provides a way to add media assets to a Drupal site, but an easy means to manage them. Centralized media management and reuse of media assets outside the context of a given node has always been a pain point within Drupal. The media browser, as shown in Figure 4-21, is a solution for this problem.

The media browser allows users to browse through existing media items on a site and reuse them in their own posts. By clicking the View Library tab in the pop-up window that appears when you click "Select media," you can look through media assets that users have previously added to the site. Using an existing media asset in a post is as simple as selecting it and clicking Submit.

Note that the media browser is powered entirely by the Views module, which we covered in Chapter 3. That means you can change the media browser in a number of ways. For example, you could change the filters that are displayed on the media browser. With Views' exposed filters settings, it's fairly easy to add filters for file size, or add a filter for the date a file was uploaded.

Another really interesting feature that comes with Media's Views integration is the ability to add your own tabs to the media browser. For example, a site might want to use a separate tab for video files, or a tab specifically to display newer media files. Just add a "Media browser tab" to the media browser view and tweak its filters.

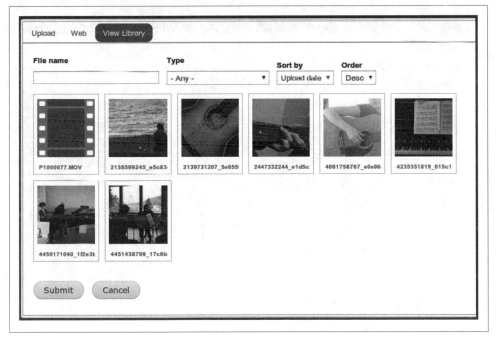

Figure 4-21. The media browser allows users to manage and reuse media assets throughout a site

File Entity, or Adding Different File Types to Drupal

If you allow users to add different types of files (for example, photos and videos) to your site, it's important that each of those file types can be used in an appropriate way. A photo might need a caption field, while a video may need a field where a user can indicate its duration. Photos may need to be cropped in various ways, while videos need a player to be watched directly on a website.

This is where the *File Entity* module, a required module for the Media module, comes in. It extends Drupal core's basic file entity, so that it becomes possible to define different *file types*. The Media module uses this functionality to provide several media file types, like *image*, *audio*, and *video*, as shown in Figure 4-22.

Like content types, it is possible to add fields to a file type, and to configure how it will be displayed in various places on your site. We'll see this in action in "Displaying Media Files" on page 173.

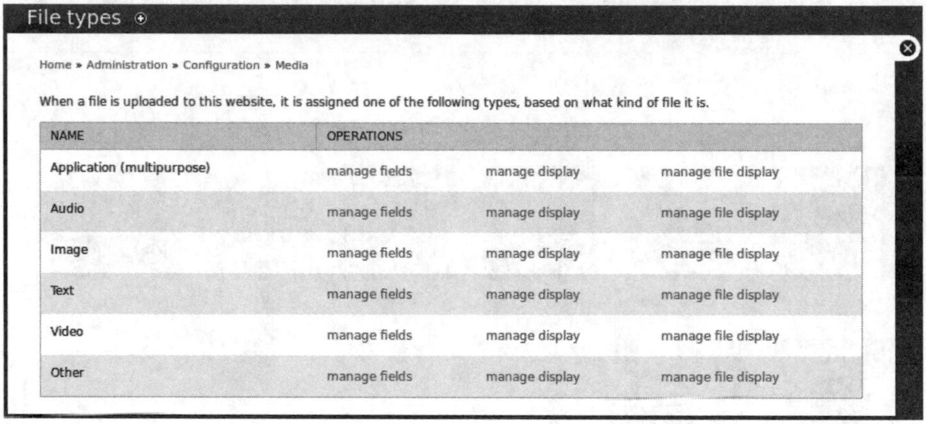

Figure 4-22. The File Entity module provides several media file types

Hands-On: Music Reviews

To begin, we need to handle some basics: creating a form with which to create reviews, and a way to tag reviews of the same band.

Review Content Type

The first thing that we'll need for our music review site is a new content type. This content type will let users enter reviews and add media assets to them. A file field will allow users to add a photo that is used as a thumbnail in teasers, and shown on the full node page in a cropped version. Later in this chapter, we will configure the content type's Body field in a way that allows users to insert media assets directly into the text area.

To help you get started, this chapter's source code provides a basic Review content type, with nothing but a Title and a Body field (if you're not using the book's source code, go ahead and create a new content type now, using the skills you learned in Chapter 3). In this section, we'll enrich our basic Review type with a file field that allows you to upload and use several types of media files through the media browser.

1. In the administrative toolbar, click Modules (*admin/modules*) and enable the following modules:

   - Chaos tool suite
     — Chaos tools
   - Media
     — File entity
     — Media
   - Views
     — Views

2. Go to the content type configuration page at Structure→"Content types" (*admin/structure/types*). Click the "manage fields" link next to the Review content type and add a file field, using the settings indicated in Table 4-3. Note that we'll use the "Media file selector" as the widget, which allows a user to upload and reuse files using the media browser.

Table 4-3. Basic settings for the file field on the Review content type

Field	Value
Add new field	
Label	Intro photo
Name	intro_photo
Field	File
Widget	Media file selector

3. After clicking Save to add the new field, you'll end up on the field's settings page, where you can configure the upload destination for this file field. Since we're using Drupal's default public filesystem (which we learned about in Chapter 3), there is nothing we need to do here. Click the "Save field settings" button to further configure the file field, and enter the values shown in Table 4-4.

   The settings form allows you to enable several media browser plug-ins: these are the tabs that will show up on the media browser, which you can configure for each field. Also important is the configuration of the allowed file extensions used for this field: this will make sure users can only upload photos to this field.

Table 4-4. Configuration for the file field on the Review content type

Field	Value
Review settings	
Label	Intro photo (default)
Required field	Unchecked (default)
Help text	Add or select a photo to be used as thumbnail and displayed on the node page (cropped).
Enabled browser plugins	Upload, Library, View Library
Allowed file extensions for uploaded files	jpg, jpeg, png
Allowed URI schemes	public:// (Public files) (default)
File directory	Leave empty (default)
Maximum upload size	500 KB
Intro photo field settings	
Number of values	1 (default)

4. After submitting the form, you'll be returned to the list of all the fields in the Review content type. Let's add a tagging field to our content type now, so users can tag reviews of the same bands in order to display them together on overview pages. If you're using the source code for this chapter, there is already a Tags field that you can use here. Under "Add existing field," add the Tags field, using the settings indicated in Table 4-5. Note: make sure to select the existing field first in the Name column, before you add a label.

Table 4-5. Basic settings for the Tags field on the Review content type

Field	Value
Add existing field	
Label	Tags
Name	Term reference: field_tags (Tags)
Widget	Autocomplete term widget (tagging)

5. After clicking Save to add the Tags field, you can configure the field using the settings in Table 4-6. Since we are sharing this field with other content types (the Article content type, which is also created by the book's source code, uses this field as well), some settings apply to all content types using this field, and some settings are specific to the Review content type. We only want to touch the latter; we'll leave the settings applying to all content types alone.

Table 4-6. Configuration for the Tags field on the Review content type

Field	Value
Review settings	
Label	Tags (default)
Required field	Unchecked (default)
Help text	The band name(s) this review is about.
Default value	Leave empty (default)

6. After submitting the form, you'll be returned to the list of all the fields in the Review content type again. Order the fields as follows by dragging them in the correct position, and click Save:

   - Title
   - Tags
   - Intro photo
   - Body

   When finished, your screen should match Figure 4-23.

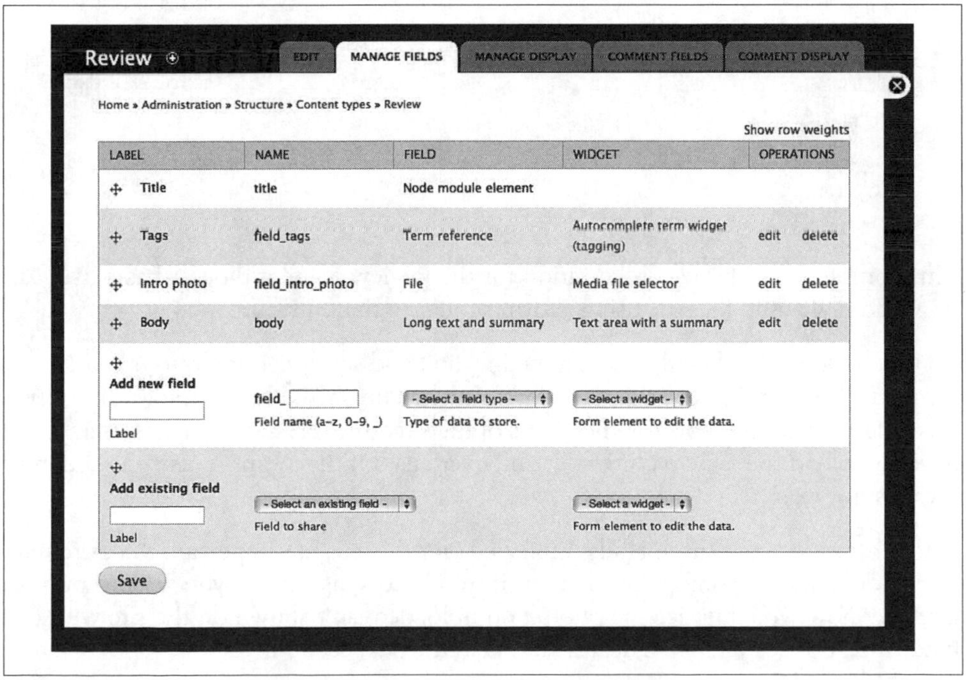

Figure 4-23. The completed Review content type with photo and tags fields

7. We're almost there. We still need to make it so that users can publish a review on the site, though. Go to People→Permissions (*admin/people/permissions*), and give each role the permissions indicated in Table 4-7.

Table 4-7. User permissions for the new Review content type

Permission	anonymous user	authenticated user	editor	administrator
Node				
Review: Create new content		Checked		
Review: Edit own content		Checked		
Review: Edit any content			Checked	Checked
Review: Delete own content		Checked		
Review: Delete any content			Checked	Checked

While we're on the Permissions page, we'll also make sure users can add media to the site. Assign each role the permissions indicated in Table 4-8.

Table 4-8. User permissions for the Media module

Permission	anonymous user	authenticated user	editor	administrator
File entity				
Administer files			Checked	Checked
View file	Checked	Checked	Checked	Checked
Edit file		Checked	Checked	Checked
Media				
Import media files from the local filesystem			Checked	Checked

This completes the basic configuration for the Review content type. A basic user can now add reviews to the site, using a form similar to that in Figure 4-24.

To upload a photo, click the "Select media" link and select the photo to upload using the form shown in Figure 4-25. Click Submit when finished. Photos uploaded through this field are also available to other users of the site; this is really handy, as users don't have to upload the same picture over and over again if they want to use it in different reviews, for example.

Before reviews can be successfully published on the site, a few important things remain to be done, like the configuration of our intro photo's display—if you were to publish a review now, you'll notice the photo you uploaded isn't shown on the site with our fancy image styles yet! We'll deal with this in the next section.

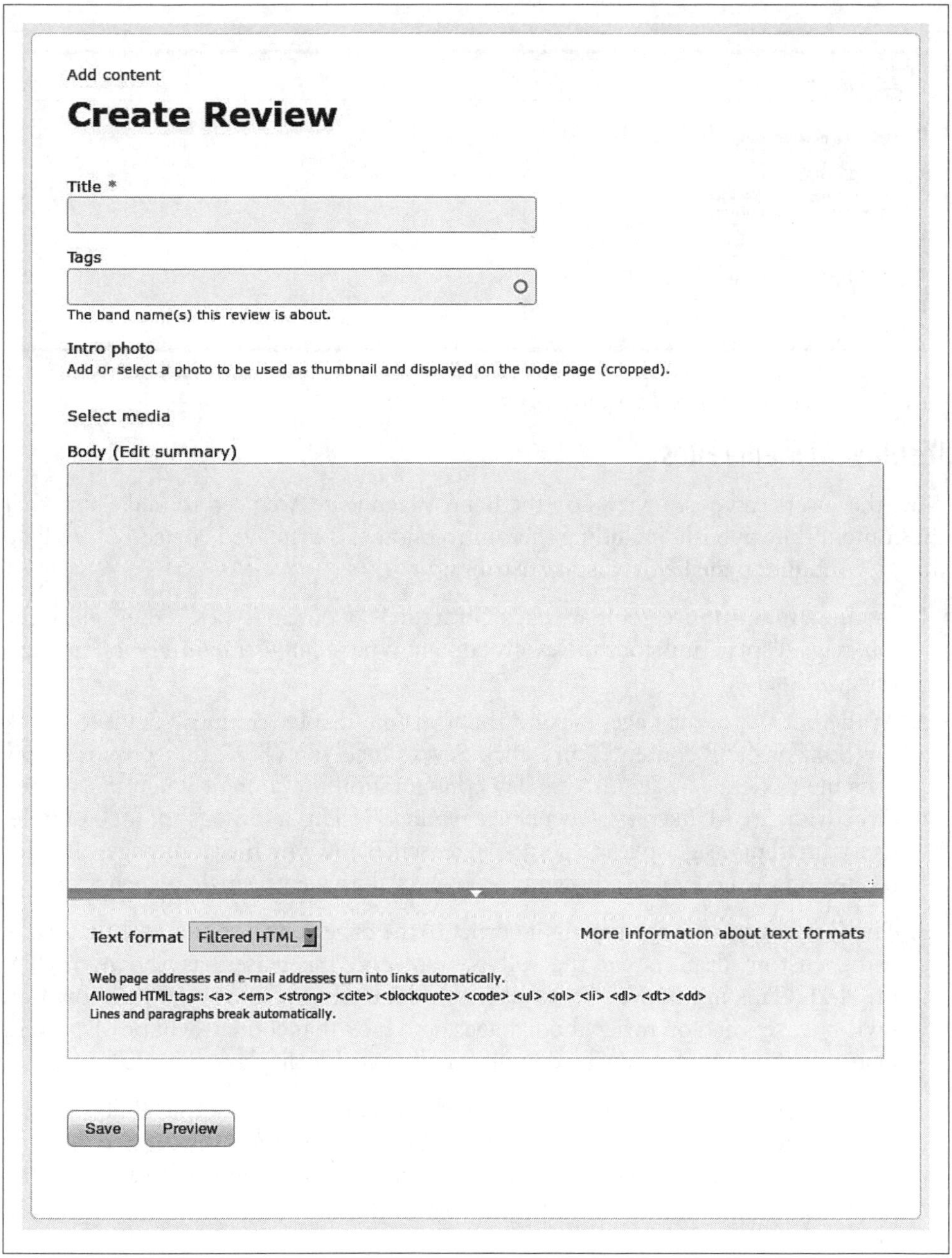

Add content

Create Review

Title *

Tags

The band name(s) this review is about.

Intro photo
Add or select a photo to be used as thumbnail and displayed on the node page (cropped).

Select media

Body (Edit summary)

Text format Filtered HTML ▾   More information about text formats

Web page addresses and e-mail addresses turn into links automatically.
Allowed HTML tags: <a> <em> <strong> <cite> <blockquote> <code> <ul> <ol> <li> <dl> <dt> <dd>
Lines and paragraphs break automatically.

Save   Preview

Figure 4-24. How our new review submission form appears when we're logged in as an authenticated user

Figure 4-25. A user can upload a photo using the new file field

Displaying Media Files

Now that users can post reviews on the Band Wagon site, we need to make sure that the content they publish, including their intro photos, is displayed correctly. We'll do this by configuring the fields' display settings.

1. In the administrative toolbar, click Structure→"Content types," then click the "manage display" link for the Review content type (*admin/structure/types/manage/review/display*).

2. At the bottom of the page, expand the "Custom display settings" fieldset, check the box for "Full content," and click Save. Once you check that box, it's now possible to define a separate display configuration for content when it's viewed directly, at a URL like *http://example.com/node/1*. This allows us to, for example, use a different image style for photos in teasers (shown on the front page) than for photos on the node page (shown when you click to view a single review).

3. The small buttons in the top-right corner of the page you're on indicate that we're using custom displays for the full content and the teaser, as shown in Figure 4-26. This means we're now able to define what content will be shown on review teasers and on review node pages, and how that content will be displayed. Leave the Body field as it is by default for all available displays.

4. To configure how photos will be displayed on node pages, click the "Full content" link in the secondary navigation (*admin/structure/types/manage/review/display/full*). Hide the intro photo's field label by setting it to Hidden, and set its format to "Rendered file" as indicated in Table 4-9. This will output the image as HTML tags.

5. After you've changed the format setting for the "Intro photo" field, you'll see an extra option appear, called "View mode": this determines how the photo will be displayed on the review node page. Change the view mode by clicking on the gear

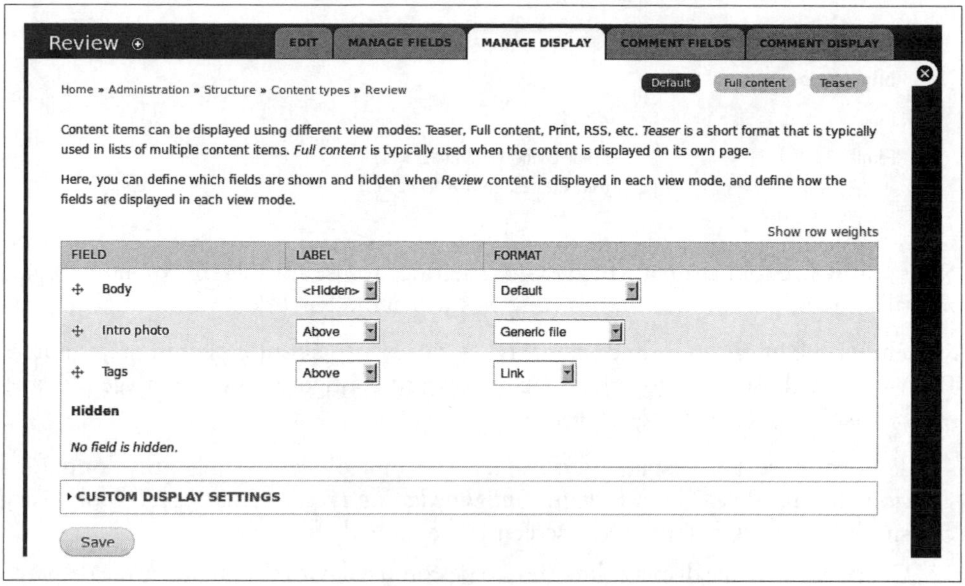

Figure 4-26. Display settings for the Review content type

icon (shown in Figure 4-27), and then select Large, as indicated in Table 4-9. Click Update, then Save, to store your changes.

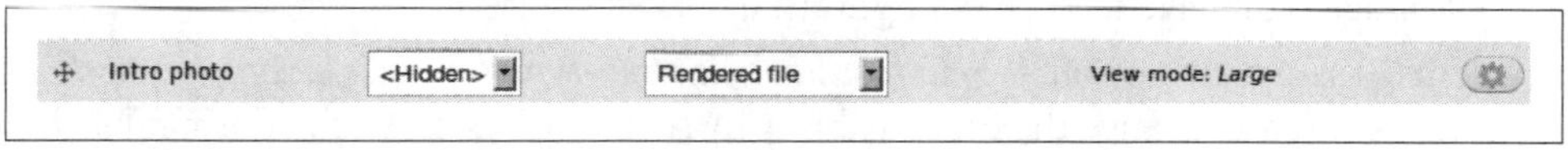

Figure 4-27. File view settings for the "Intro photo" field

Table 4-9. Full content display settings for the Review content type

Field	Value
Intro photo	
Label	\<Hidden\>
Format	Rendered file; View mode: *Large* (click the gear icon to change this)

6. Next, go to the display configuration page for the Teaser display (*admin/structure/types/manage/review/display/teaser*) to configure the display settings for review teasers. The steps are the same as with the "Full content" display configuration. Drag the "Intro photo" field from Hidden to just below the Body field. Set the intro photo's label to Hidden, as indicated in Table 4-10, and set its format to "Rendered file," and its view mode to Small, by clicking the gear icon and selecting that option. Don't forget to save the field's display settings page afterward.

Table 4-10. Teaser display settings for the Review content type

Field	Value
Intro photo	
Label	<Hidden>
Format	Rendered file; View mode: *Small* (click the gear icon to change this)

Now that we've told Drupal which display settings to use for the "Intro photo" field, we still need to configure how those displays will actually work.

Remember the image styles and the file types we learned about earlier in this chapter? This is where those come together. We're going to configure how the Image file type will be displayed, using image styles:

1. To configure the display settings for the image file type, go to Configuration→Media→File Types (*admin/config/media/file-types*). This screen looks very similar to the "Content types" screen you're already familiar with.

2. Click the "manage display" link (not to be confused with the "manage file display" link) for the Image file type (*admin/config/media/file-types/manage/image/display*). You'll see a series of buttons in the top-right corner of the overlay, similar to the ones you saw when configuring field display settings on the Review content type. These buttons allow us to configure the display of the file types: every view mode of images can have its own configuration.

3. Click the Small button (*admin/config/media/file-types/manage/image/display/media_small*) and change the file's visibility by selecting Visible in the Format list and saving the page. This will ensure that the image file will be visible in the Small view mode (which we've chosen for the "Intro photo" field in our content type's teaser display). Save the form.

4. Next, return to the file types overview screen and click the "manage file display" link next to Image (*admin/config/media/file-types/manage/image/file-display*). This is where you configure the display of the file itself for the Small view mode. Check the box next to Image to enable and configure image display settings, and set its image style to "thumbnail" at the bottom of the page, as indicated in Table 4-11 and shown in Figure 4-28.

Table 4-11. Small display settings for the Image file type

Field	Value
Enabled displays	
Image	Checked
Display settings	
Image	Image style: *thumbnail*

Figure 4-28. File display settings for the Image file type

5. For the Large file view mode, the Media module provides us with good default settings, so we'll leave those alone.

Sweet! We've set up our content type, added a file field for intro photos, and configured everything to display correctly. Go ahead and add some reviews (*node/add/review*) and see the power of the Media module, the media browser, and image styles in action. In particular, you should notice that when you're viewing a review on its main review page, the image is large, but on the front page it's much smaller.

Furthermore, if you add one or more tags to your reviews using the Tags field on the node form, you'll see the tags appear on the node page after you submit the form. Clicking one of those tags will take you to the page listing all the nodes that have that tag attached. Tagging is explained in detail in Chapter 7.

Spotlight: Content Editing and Image Handling

We now have a site with most of the basic functionality the Band Wagon project needs to start. However, one important piece remains: streamlining the content editing process, and allowing easy image and video integration in posts.

Content Editing

By default, Drupal's content entry is done with HTML. Like most Earthlings, the majority of John and Lisa's music fan friends aren't fluent in code, so it's important that they are able to format their content and add images without seeing any spooky HTML. Not surprisingly, a number of community solutions to this issue have cropped up over the years:

Toolbars

> Some users can use HTML fine if they're given a toolbar that inserts the tags on their behalf. The BUEditor module (*http://drupal.org/project/bueditor*), pictured in Figure 4-29, is an example of a module that provides such a toolbar.

Figure 4-29. The BUEditor module provides a toolbar to assist with HTML

Text-to-HTML translators

> Modules such as Markdown Filter (*http://drupal.org/project/markdown*) or Textile (*http://drupal.org/project/textile*) provide the ability to take simple text such as **bold** and transform it into its HTML equivalent (`<strong>bold</strong>`). This syntax, once learned, is much easier and faster to type in than raw HTML.

What You See Is What You Get (WYSIWYG) editors

> WYSIWYG editors not only provide a toolbar, but also display the formatting directly in the text area, which looks similar to a word processor, as pictured in Figure 4-30. There are two ways of adding a WYSIWYG editor to a Drupal site. You can either add a module that supports a specific editor, like CKeditor (*http://drupal.org/project/ckeditor*), or you can use the WYSIWYG module (*http://drupal.org/project/wysiwyg*), which integrates a large number of existing WYSIWYG editors with Drupal. For the Band Wagon site, we'll be using the WYSIWYG module option to ease the content editing process.

Figure 4-30. The WYSIWYG module, with the CKeditor enabled

The further away from raw HTML entry you go, the greater chance there is that the "smart" WYSIWYG editing plug-in will get confused and choke on complex formatting. Subtle differences between web browsers, incompatibilities with the CSS that you're using to customize your site, and other problems are all possible—if not common. Many times, the trade-off is still worth it, because the users of your site aren't interested in learning the subtleties of HTML to make something bold or italic. But due to the pitfalls, it's often best to ask, "Does my site *really* need this?" before dropping in a "pretty" HTML editor module.

Integrating Media in Content

In the past, one of the biggest criticisms of Drupal, apart from the fact that it didn't (and unfortunately, still doesn't) come with a WYSIWYG editor built in, was that it had no built-in image handling. Users had to either manually insert images in their posts, or choose one of the many available contributed modules to support images (and other media) on their site.

As we've seen earlier in this chapter, Drupal 7 has changed this. Out of the box, Drupal core now comes with an image field that allows users to upload images. For a lot of sites, this is exactly what they need: a way to add images to nodes and display them in a predefined size and position. An example might be an Album content type, which always has an Album Cover image on each individual node, placed in exactly the same place every time.

However, the Band Wagon site needs something more advanced. John and Lisa want to allow their friends to be able to freely mix photos and videos with their written content. This requires the ability to insert images in a text area, rather then in a fixed position on the node page. Luckily, the Media module that we use for photo and video support provides integration with the WYSIWYG module. We'll learn more about this when we set up the WYSIWYG editor later in this chapter.

Spotlight: Text Formats and Filters

You may have noticed a funny fieldset on node and block body fields that we keep ignoring, called "Text format," pictured in Figure 4-31. The *text format* you select for the content will affect how that content is displayed on the site. Text formats are an important security feature of Drupal, so it pays to understand them. A text format will "scan" your content and make HTML formatting changes to it before sending it to the browser for display. Each piece of content will be associated with a text format so that Drupal always knows what it is looking for and modifying, on a case-by-case basis.

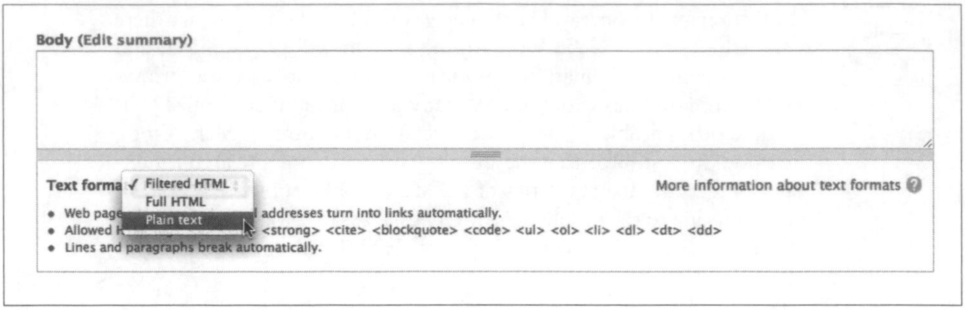

Figure 4-31. *Text formats attached to a node body*

The Text format select list in Figure 4-31 provides three choices, Filtered HTML, Full HTML, and "Plain text." These are the default text formats that come with Drupal core. Sites can have several text formats to choose from; some can be provided by modules, like Drupal core's PHP filter module, and you can also create custom formats. Text formats are restricted by roles so that you can allow everyone to use one text format, like Filtered HTML, but also make a more permissive text format, like Full HTML, available only to your most trusted users (e.g., the "site administrator" role).

> If a user reports a node's edit tab as mysteriously missing when she should otherwise have access to it, check its text format. Drupal will disallow editing on content if the user's role does not have access to the text format of the content. This behavior can be used to your advantage if you want to protect certain pages from editing by users who would otherwise have access to do so.

Text formats are composed of *filters*. Figure 4-32 shows the list of filters that are used in the Filtered HTML text format. The filters are doing the real work; the text format is simply a group of filters. A filter modifies content and outputs the proper HTML for display. Filters can transform new lines (carriage returns) into `<br />` and `<p>` tags; transform a text URL such as *http://www.example.com* into a clickable link, like `<a href="http://www.example.com">http://www.example.com</a>`; and a whole lot more. The Media module uses its own filter to allow users to securely add media assets directly in text fields.

Filters are really important for security on your site. People can do all kinds of malicious things when given a text entry box in a web browser. Using the filters that are specifically designed to help strip out malicious content, like the "Limit allowed HTML tags" filter, can save your site from being compromised.

The most important filter of all is "Limit allowed HTML tags." It strips out dangerous HTML tags such as `<script>` and `<object>` and protects your site from various sneaky attacks that could trick a browser into embedding malicious JavaScript or other executable code. This filter is enabled by default only on the Filtered HTML and "Plain text" formats. Make sure that you implicitly trust anyone who has access to a format without this filter included, such as Full HTML.

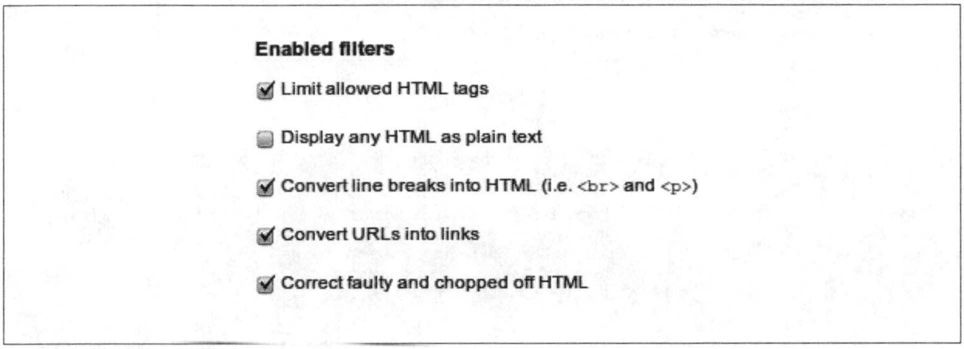

Enabled filters

☑ Limit allowed HTML tags

☐ Display any HTML as plain text

☑ Convert line breaks into HTML (i.e.
 and <p>)

☑ Convert URLs into links

☑ Correct faulty and chopped off HTML

Figure 4-32. Filters for the Filtered HTML text format

You order filters within text formats by assigning them "weights," and the filter modifications happen in that sequence. You can see the default order for the Filtered HTML format in Figure 4-33. Many contributed modules let you add more filters to your site, and you can mix and match them as you like, either adding them to the existing text formats or making your own.

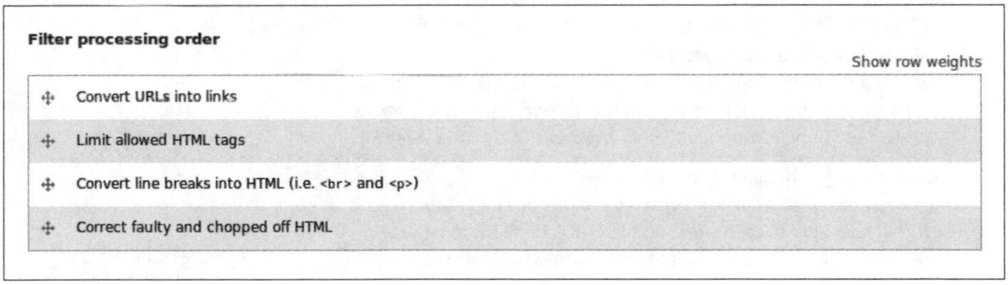

Filter processing order

Show row weights

⊹ Convert URLs into links

⊹ Limit allowed HTML tags

⊹ Convert line breaks into HTML (i.e.
 and <p>)

⊹ Correct faulty and chopped off HTML

Figure 4-33. Reordering filters for the Filtered HTML text format

A very important point to understand about text formats is that they are applied only when the content is leaving the database and about to be displayed on the page. When a user enters content into a form and saves it, that content is stored in the database exactly the way it was written. When someone visits the page to view it, Drupal retrieves the raw information from the database; applies the text format that is associated with it, running through each filter in turn; and then displays the final result to the browser, as shown in Figure 4-34.

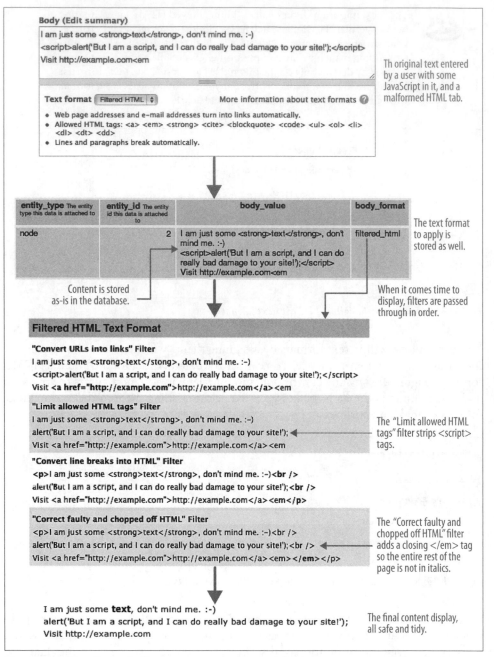

Figure 4-34. How Drupal's filter system removes potentially dangerous content before displaying it

The order of the filters is extremely important. If your text doesn't seem to be outputting properly, always check that the filters are in a logical sequence.

You should note that each filter is applying its own rules, in turn, to get to the finished display. If we had set this particular piece of content to use the Full HTML text format, instead of Filtered HTML, then the end result would be a bit different. With Filtered HTML, the text "alert('But I am a script, and I can do really bad damage to your site!');" is printed out to the screen because the `<script>` tags are removed prior to display. With Full HTML, these tags would not be stripped and the script in the text would be *executed* rather than displayed as plain text. In this example, that script would cause a harmless JavaScript window to pop up that has some text in it, but it could just as easily be a malicious script that could wreak havoc.

 Because Drupal strips only on output, if you are using something in your content that is not allowed, you will still see it there when you go to edit it; it is just stripped on display. If you notice this happening and think you are going crazy, you should check the text format for the content and make sure it is not set to one that is designed to strip what you want to display. The most common instance of this behavior is when you're trying to display an image using the Filtered HTML text format.

Hands-On: Setting Up WYSIWYG

Let's set up the WYSYWIG editor for the Band Wagon website, using the WYSIWYG module (*http://drupal.org/project/wysiwyg*) and CKEditor (*http://ckeditor.com/*). Note that if you prefer a different WYSIWYG editor, such as TinyMCE or Aloha, the installation instructions are very similar.

Set Up and Configuration

1. In the administrative toolbar, click Modules (*admin/modules*), and enable the following modules:
   - User interface
     — WYSIWYG

 Users with the administrative role have access to the WYSIWYG configuration page. Permission for the actual WYSIWYG editor on node forms is regulated by the user's permission to use the text format for which the editor is configured.

2. In the administrative toolbar, click Configuration→"Content authoring"→"Wysiwyg profiles" (*admin/config/content/wysiwyg*).

3. You'll be presented with a screen that prompts you to download an editor for use in the WYSIWYG module, as pictured in Figure 4-35. The WYSIWYG module actually supports a number of different editors, as well as the ability to use many of them at a time and mix and match editors per text format. However, for our site, we're going to keep things simple and just use one editor everywhere. Click the Download link next to CKEditor.

Figure 4-35. When first visiting the WYSIWYG module configuration page, you are prompted to download an editor

4. You'll now be on the CKEditor website's download page. Download the plain CKEditor library, *not* the "CKEditor for Drupal" version (which is a standalone module + plug-in package), pictured in Figure 4-36.

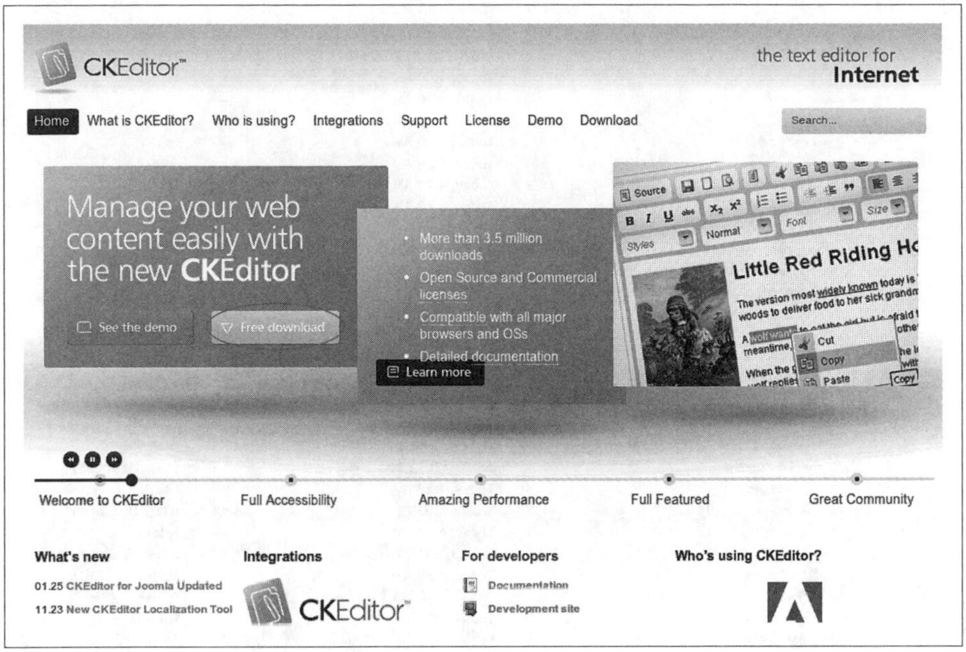

Figure 4-36. The CKEditor download page

> In "real life," you may actually want to use the bundled module and editor plug-in that CKEditor itself provides. It has a few additional features and deeper integration with the editor, so is worth evaluating for your needs. Sticking with the WYSIWYG module, however, gives you the flexibility to switch editors if you discover in testing that your users prefer a different one, and also helps ensure that the instructions in this book will work for readers with other editor interests as well.

5. In your root Drupal directory, navigate to the *sites/all* directory. Create a new folder called libraries within that directory. Inside the new *sites/all/libraries* directory, extract the *.zip* file you just downloaded within the folder to create a *sites/all/libraries/ckeditor* directory, with a *ckeditor.js* inside. When you're finished with this process, your *sites* directory should now look as pictured in Figure 4-37.

>
>
> Using the *sites/all/libraries* directory for third-party dependencies is a common pattern used in many contributed modules.

robots.txt	Feb 1, 2012 2:03 PM	4 KB	Plain Text
▶ scripts	Feb 6, 2012 12:18 AM	--	Folder
▼ sites	Today, 4:30 AM	--	Folder
▼ all	Today, 4:30 AM	--	Folder
▼ libraries	Today, 4:20 AM	--	Folder
▼ ckeditor	Today, 4:20 AM	--	Folder
▶ _samples	Today, 4:20 AM	--	Folder
▶ _source	Today, 4:20 AM	--	Folder
▶ adapters	Today, 4:20 AM	--	Folder
CHANGES.html	Sep 13, 2011 10:23 PM	160 KB	HTML Document
ckeditor_basic_source.js	Sep 13, 2011 10:23 PM	4 KB	JSON File
ckeditor_basic.js	Sep 13, 2011 10:23 PM	8 KB	JSON File
ckeditor_php4.php	Sep 13, 2011 10:23 PM	16 KB	PHP script
ckeditor_php5.php	Sep 13, 2011 10:23 PM	16 KB	PHP script
ckeditor_source.js	Sep 13, 2011 10:23 PM	4 KB	JSON File
ckeditor.asp	Sep 13, 2011 10:23 PM	33 KB	Unix Executable File
ckeditor.js	Sep 13, 2011 10:23 PM	369 KB	JSON File
ckeditor.pack	Sep 13, 2011 10:23 PM	8 KB	Unix Executable File
ckeditor.php	Sep 13, 2011 10:23 PM	4 KB	PHP script
config.js	Sep 13, 2011 10:23 PM	4 KB	JSON File
contents.css	Sep 13, 2011 10:23 PM	4 KB	CSS style sheet
▶ images	Today, 4:20 AM	--	Folder
INSTALL.html	Sep 13, 2011 10:23 PM	4 KB	HTML Document
▶ lang	Today, 4:20 AM	--	Folder
LICENSE.html	Sep 13, 2011 10:23 PM	74 KB	HTML Document
▶ plugins	Today, 4:20 AM	--	Folder
▶ skins	Today, 4:20 AM	--	Folder
▶ themes	Today, 4:20 AM	--	Folder
▶ modules	Feb 25, 2012 12:43 AM	--	Folder
README.txt	Oct 27, 2011 12:20 AM	4 KB	Plain Text
▶ themes	Jan 22, 2012 3:06 PM	--	Folder
▶ default	Today, 2:09 AM	--	Folder

Figure 4-37. Drupal's new directory structure after you extract the CKEditor script to sites/all/libraries

6. If these steps were completed correctly, when you return to the WYSIWYG settings page in Drupal at Configuration→""Content authoring"→"Wysiwig profiles" (*admin/config/content/wysiwyg*), you should now see a table with a selection of text formats instead of the screen you saw before. If you expand the "Installation instructions" fieldset below, you should see CKEditor at the top of the list in green.

7. The WYSIWYG module allows us to create a separate profile for each of those formats. If we want to, we could even use a different editor per text format. For the Band Wagon site, we'll create a profile for the Filtered HTML text format, using the CKEditor. Next to the Filtered HTML text format, select CKEditor, as pictured in Figure 4-38, and click Save. Next, click Edit under Operations to configure the profile.

8. The next screen provides oodles of configuration options for your editor to customize its look and behavior. The default settings that the profile provides us with are pretty good for what the Band Wagon website needs. The only thing we need to configure are the buttons the users will be able to use when editing content. Click "Buttons and plugins" to open the fieldset, and enable the buttons shown in Table 4-12 and pictured in Figure 4-39.

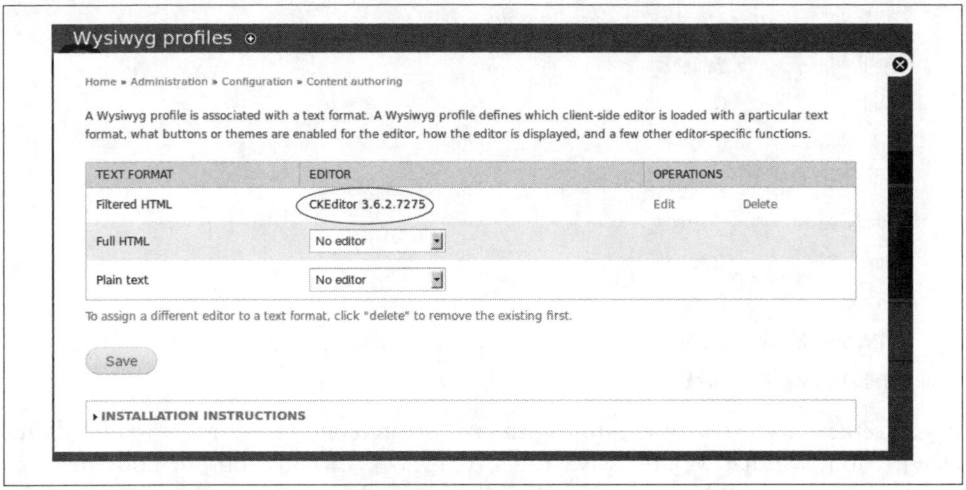

Figure 4-38. If CKEditor is successfully installed, when returning to the WYSIWYG module configuration form, a table will appear with text formats and editor options

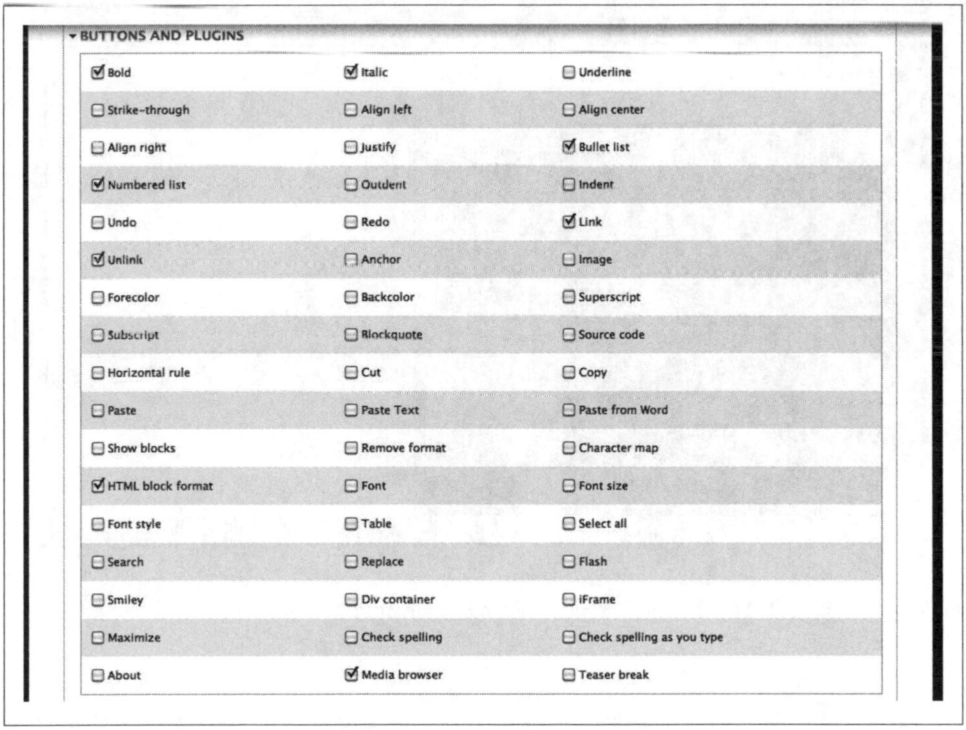

Figure 4-39. The WYSIWYG module allows you to easily enable editor buttons by checking the relevant boxes

Table 4-12. Buttons for the CKeditor profile

Field	Value
Bold	Checked
Italic	Checked
Bullet list	Checked
Numbered list	Checked
Link	Checked
Unlink	Checked
HTML block format	Checked
Media browser	Checked

If you return to the review creation form at "Create content"→Review (*node/add/re-view*), you'll see that we now have a nice WYSIWYG toolbar on our body field, as shown in Figure 4-40. Awesome! You can click the "Add media" button on the far right, select a picture from your desktop, and see it drop right in, in all its image-y glory.

Figure 4-40. WYSIWYG editor, including the Media browser button

Enabling the Media Filter

Hooray! We're all done now, right? Right? BZZT. Wrong! Try saving the form. What the? If your review looks full of gibberish like [{"type":"media","view_mode":"media_large","fid":"2","attributes":{"alt":"","class":"media-image","height":"402","typeof":"foaf:Image","width":"314"}}]] instead of like what the supposedly WYSIWYG editor showed you, you might understandably be confused. Perhaps even upset. Worry not! We're just missing one last configuration detail.

What's being shown here is the actual raw output provided by the "Add media" button. The Media module can read the gibberish strings and turn them into its own smart, sanitized creation of potentially dangerous tags, which the "Limit allowed HTML tags" filter normally strips out. But in order for this magic to work, we need to add Media's filter to the Filtered HTML text format.

1. In the administrative toolbar, click Configuration→"Content authoring"→"Text formats" (*admin/config/content/formats*). You will see the available text formats listed.

2. Click the configure link for the Filtered HTML format (*admin/config/content/formats/filtered_html*).

3. Under "Enabled filters," check the box for "Converts Media tags to Markup" and save the text format's configuration. Media filter tags will now work properly.

 This same page is also how you expand the list of allowed tags that Filtered HTML will let through its clutches. Underneath "Filter settings," click the "Limit allowed HTML tags" vertical tab to add more white-listed tags. Once again, though, since this filter represents a major component of the security of your site, be *very* cautious about which tags you allow here.

If you navigate back to the review you created earlier, you'll see your picture now shows up as expected. Awesome!

Spotlight: Media Internet Sources

The Media module for Drupal 7 not only supports adding and managing media that is uploaded from a user's computer into Drupal, but it also comes with a submodule, called Media Internet Sources, that allows using media assets from various Internet locations. Media Internet Sources provides the interface and the central piece of functionality that other contributed modules can leverage to allow usage of media files in specific places.

For example, the Media: YouTube (*http://drupal.org/project/media_youtube*) module allows users to post YouTube videos on a Drupal site by using the video's URL or embed code. While Media: YouTube makes sure that Drupal can talk to YouTube, in order to fetch the correct video, Media Internet Sources provides the interface to add the video in Drupal.

There are several "provider modules" available. Media: Flickr (*http://drupal.org/project/media_flickr*) allows users to post photos that are hosted on Flickr in Drupal, and Media: Vimeo (*http://drupal.org/project/media_vimeo*) allows the same for videos on Vimeo. The full list of provider modules can be found at *http://groups.drupal.org/node/168009*, under "Provider projects." Check back regularly; developers continue to add support for various sites and services.

Stream Wrappers: Enabling a File Browser for the Internet

The Media Internet Sources module uses so-called *stream wrappers* to do its magic. Stream wrappers, a feature of PHP and supported in Drupal 7, make it possible to access external files as if they were stored on the local server, the server where Drupal is installed. Drupal identifies stream wrappers (and individual files) by their URI scheme (the first part of a file's URL, like *http://*). Public files in Drupal are known by *public://*, private files by *private://*. YouTube videos that are added using the Media: YouTube module are identified in Drupal by their *youtube://* scheme. Because it handles remote files as if they were on your own server, the Media module is sometimes dubbed "a file browser for the Internet."

If you have a provider module enabled, like the Media: YouTube module, adding a video from YouTube (or whichever external service the module supports) is child's play. In the Media Browser, there is a tab called Web, as shown in Figure 4-41. If you click it, you'll see a simple form where you can paste the media asset's external URL or its embed code (the code typically used to add external videos or photos to a site). The provider module will find the remote media asset and display it on your site. Since you added the external asset using Internet Media Sources, the asset will also be available to other users on the Drupal site.

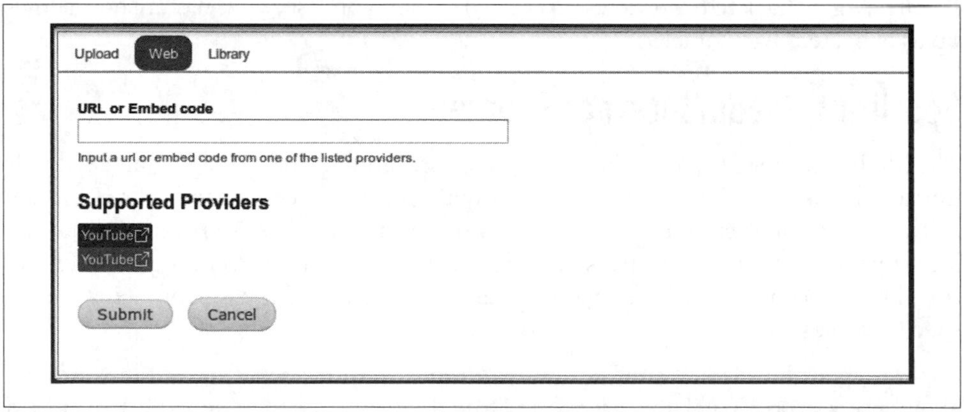

Figure 4-41. The Media Internet Sources module allows you to add external media assets as if they existed on the local server

If you configure a file field to add media using the media browser, that field's settings let you limit the remote media types to allow in the field. For example, you might only want to allow remote image files for a field that should only handle photos, or remote video files for a field where you want users to add a video from a third-party site. On top of that, you can control which providers a user can add remote media from by configuring the "Allowed URI schemes," as shown in Figure 4-42.

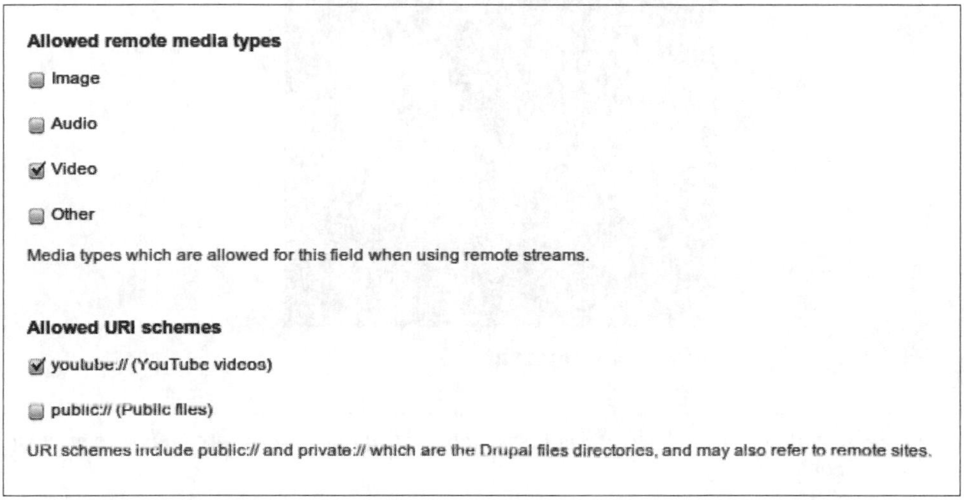

Allowed remote media types

☐ Image

☐ Audio

☑ Video

☐ Other

Media types which are allowed for this field when using remote streams.

Allowed URI schemes

☑ youtube:// (YouTube videos)

☐ public:// (Public files)

URI schemes include public:// and private:// which are the Drupal files directories, and may also refer to remote sites.

Figure 4-42. File field settings allow you to control which media types and sources users are allowed to use

Hands-On: Posting Videos

Because we already installed the Media module, it's really easy to enable support to post videos from YouTube on the Band Wagon site.

In the administrative toolbar, click Modules (*admin/modules*), and enable the following modules:

- Media
    - Media Internet Sources
    - Media: YouTube

Go ahead and add a new review (*node/add/review*), and click the Media button in the WYSIWYG toolbar. Click the Web tab, paste the URL of your favorite YouTube video in the "URL or Embed code" field, and click Submit. When you save the new node, the YouTube video should appear, as pictured in Figure 4-43.

Figure 4-43. With the Media Internet Sources module, adding third party video and other media to your site is a breeze

You can configure the display of remote video files in the file display settings that we learned about in "Displaying Media Files" on page 174. The Media: YouTube module allows you to configure the size of the video player for each display, and specify whether to automatically start the video when the content page loads.

Great! We have included support for adding remote media files, so users can post YouTube videos of their favorite bands. Note that you can mix and match text, videos, and photos, all by using the Media button in the WYSIWYG editor. This is a great way to create the attractive, multimedia-rich review pages that John and Lisa wanted.

Taking It Further

If you've completed the Band Wagon site to this point, you've built a solid foundation for a Drupal-based music fan site! However, there's no need to stop here. One of the great things about building a site with Drupal is that you can continuously refine it, adding new features to any part of your site. This section details a few additional pieces of functionality that are common in photo- and video-sharing websites. Also make sure to keep an eye on the list of modules that extend the Media module on *http://groups .drupal.org/node/168009*.

Views Slideshow (http://drupal.org/project/views_slideshow)

   Views Slideshow, a plug-in for the Views module, allows you to build fancy slide-shows using any content you can display in a view. The module supports a lot of transition effects, options to set slide timing and to use different control widgets. Once the Media 7.x-2-x branch is released (which provides Views integration), combining it with Views Slideshow will open up a lot of possibilities.

Fivestar (http://drupal.org/project/fivestar)

   The Fivestar module allows users to vote on content using a star-voting widget. Several widget designs are available out of the box, with the ability to add your own. The Band Wagon could use this to allow visitors to vote on reviews and individual photos. Fortunately, this module is covered in the very next chapter, Chapter 5.

Service Links (http://drupal.org/project/service_links)

   Adding social network integration is a breeze with the Service Links module: it adds links or buttons to node pages to share content in Drupal on social network sites (Twitter, Facebook, Google+, etc.). There is support available for just about every existing social network, and with some PHP skills, you can add support for other services if necessary.

Summary

In this chapter, we introduced the Media and WYSIWYG modules to build a music fan site that allows users with limited technical knowledge to publish music reviews. We also used the image styles functionality of Drupal core's Image module to crop and scale our photos so they look nice on our site. We discussed the option to enrich our community site with voting, slideshows, and social network integration.

Here are the modules that we referenced in this chapter:

- Fivestar: *http://drupal.org/project/fivestar*
- Image (core)
- ImageCache Actions module: *http://drupal.org/project/imagecache_actions*
- Media: *http://drupal.org/project/media*
- Media: Flickr: *http://drupal.org/project/media_flickr*
- Media: YouTube: *http://drupal.org/project/media_youtube*
- Service Links: *http://drupal.org/project/service_links*
- Views Slideshow: *http://drupal.org/project/views_slideshow*
- WYSIWYG: *http://drupal.org/project/wysiwyg*

CHAPTER 5

Product Reviews

With more and more options for shoppers arriving on the Internet every day, finding the right products can be a challenge. Special interest websites that feature specific kinds of products and reviews by dedicated hobbyists are a popular way to help consumers sort through all of the options and find the right stuff. In this chapter, we're going to use a handful of Drupal modules to build a product review website that lets community members give their opinions on every featured product.

This chapter introduces the following modules:

Field Group (http://drupal.org/project/field_group)
  Allows fields to be grouped into fieldsets

Amazon (http://drupal.org/project/amazon)
  Gathers product information from Amazon.com (*http://www.amazon.com*)

Voting API (http://drupal.org/project/votingapi)
  Provides a framework for standardizing voting data

Fivestar (http://drupal.org/project/fivestar)
  Allows rating of content

Search (core)
  Indexes content and allows searching within a site

CSS Injector (http://drupal.org/project/css_injector)
  Allows administrators to easily add CSS styling to the site

If you would like to participate in the hands-on exercises in this chapter, install Drupal using the *Reviews* installation profile from the book's sample code. This will create the example website on your web server. The completed website will look as pictured in Figure 5-1 and found at *http://reviews.usingdrupal.com*. For more information on using the book's sample code, see the Preface.

Figure 5-1. The completed Super Duper Chefs website

Case Study

Bob and Sarah are coworkers and food lovers who've both built up impressive kitchens full of gadgets, pots and pans, and other cooking tools. Supporting a culinary habit can be expensive, though, and they usually turn to fellow foodies for advice before purchasing new gear. They've decided to set up Super Duper Chefs, a website where they and their friends can write recommendations about the cooking equipment they use, share tips, and brag about their latest culinary achievements. They'd like it to be the kind of site they wanted when they were getting started: a fun place that highlights the most useful products and advice.

After talking things over with their friends, Bob and Sarah think they have a handle on what the site should offer. The most important feature is that kitchen products reviewed by the site's official contributors should be listed with ratings and quick summaries of their best and worst features. Each review should also provide up-to-date pricing information. In addition to the official reviews, visitors to the site should be able to offer their opinions on the products and compare the official ratings with the opinions of other visitors who've read the reviews. Everyone who uses the site should also be able to search for reviews that match certain criteria. For example, it should be easy to find reviews of products by a particular manufacturer, or products that mention waffles.

Implementation Notes

The next step is figuring out how to translate that set of features into a shopping list of Drupal functionality. Bob and Sarah are fortunate: the core Drupal software can provide most of what they're looking for without any additions. We'll use Drupal's administrative tools to create a custom "Product review" content type, and set up special permissions for contributors. Those product reviews will be the meat of the site's content. Core also provides a way to add custom fields to the "Product review" content type for the various bits of information we want to record, with the Field module. We'll use the Views module to build a listing page of products for quick scanning.

Three requirements for Bob and Sarah's website, though, will require functionality that we haven't seen yet: importing product information from another website, allowing users to rate and review content, and building a custom search page.

Product information

First, the site will need to display information about the product that is being reviewed. Who manufactured it? How much does it cost? Where can a visitor to the website purchase it? Although it's possible to set up custom fields for each of these pieces of information with the core Field module, it's a real hassle for the site's editors to fill out all of them for every review. In addition, keeping the pricing information up-to-date can be a chore as the site grows older.

The easiest solution is to let someone else do the work! Amazon.com provides access to its full database of product information, including kitchen gadgets (shown in Figure 5-2), using the Amazon Product Advertising API. The Amazon module (*http://drupal.org/project/amazon*) lets sites access that product information. That means that writers on the site can fill out one field about the product, and the rest will be handled behind the scenes.

In addition to saving time and energy spent entering in the product details, using the Amazon API means that Bob and Sarah can get referral fees whenever someone clicks from their website and purchases an item on Amazon.com. It's a simple way of earning revenue, and for high-traffic sites, the commissions can add up quickly.

Product ratings

The second challenge is product ratings. The site will need every product to have an official review by an editor, but visitors reading the site need to be able to rate the products as well. Displaying the official rating and the users' ratings separately will give a more trustworthy representation of how the products perform, reassuring new visitors that the site's ratings aren't dominated by a one-sided editor.

The Drupal community has built dozens of plug-in modules that add rating and voting capabilities to sites. A full list is available at *http://drupal.org/project/modules?filters= tid:60*. Modules such as the Plus1 module (*http://drupal.org/project/plus1*) add the

Figure 5-2. The Amazon.com website, displaying kitchen products

ability to vote items up in a queue, like the popular sites Reddit (*http://www.reddit
.com*) and Digg (*http://digg.com*). Others allow each reader to rate content on a scale,
then display the average to new visitors. Because it is this average rating capability that
we're interested in, we're going to use the Fivestar module (*http://drupal.org/project/
fivestar*).

In addition to letting users vote on content, Fivestar provides a Field to separate "official
ratings" by a site editor from the normal ratings given by visitors. We can use the Views
module to list the two kinds of ratings side by side for comparison. The Fivestar module,
like most rating and evaluation modules, is based on Voting API (*http://drupal.org/
project/votingapi*), another Drupal module that handles storage and presentation of
voting and rating information for content. We'll need to install it to use Fivestar.

Custom searching

The third piece of the puzzle is the custom search page that will let visitors to the site
find the product reviews they're looking for. Drupal's built-in Search module can index
the contents of each post, and give visitors a general search page to find posts that
contain specific keywords. However, it's difficult to customize how search results are
presented to users, and difficult to control exactly what kinds of content are searched.
For example, finding reviews of kitchen appliances written by Bob and sorting them
by price would be tricky. Fortunately, the Views module allows us to tie into that search
index as well, giving full control over how the results are displayed. We'll use it to build
our custom product search page.

Hands-On: Basic Product Reviews

Before we get started, log into the site with the *admin* account. We'll begin with a few things that we are going to need.

The first is a new content type for the product reviews. Based on the Super Duper Chefs requirements, we'll need the following for each review:

- A Pros field and a Cons field to list quick summaries of each product's strengths and weaknesses
- An Amazon Product field to hold detailed product information
- A Rating field, so that visitors can quickly find the cream of the crop
- A Field Group that combines the rating with the pros and cons for a more attractive presentation
- Comments so that visitors can weigh in with their own opinions

Creating the Product Review Content Type

We'll start by creating the base content type and adding the simplest pieces: the basic text fields needed for the Pros and Cons, grouping those fields together, and allowing comments:

1. First, in the administrative toolbar, click Modules (*admin/modules*) and enable the following modules:
   - Chaos Tools Suite package
     - Chaos tools
   - Fields package
     - Fieldgroup
2. Next, in the administrative toolbar, click Structure→"Content types" (*admin/structure/types*) and add a new content type called "Product review," using the settings indicated in Table 5-1.

Table 5-1. Settings for the "Product review" content type

Setting	Value
Name	Product review
Description	A featured Product review by a contributing editor.
Submission form settings	
Title field label	Headline
Comment settings	
Allow comment title	Unchecked

3. Save the changes you've made by clicking the "Save and add fields" button, and you'll be taken to the "Product review fields" screen to begin setting up the rest of our fields.

4. First, let's change the label on the Body field to something that makes more sense for our editors. Click the "edit" link for the Body field and change the Label to Review. Click the "Save settings" button, and we'll be returned to the fields listing.

5. Because we want to group several of the fields in this content type together (the Pros and Cons, ratings, and so on), we'll first create a Field group to organize them. Under "Add new group," create a new group with a label of Summary and a group name of "summary"; leave the widget at the default, Fieldset; and then save the form.

6. Next, create a new field using the settings indicated in Table 5-2 and click the Save button.

Table 5-2. Settings for the Pros field

Setting	Value
Label	Pros
Field name	pros
Field type	Long text
Widget type	Text area (multiple rows)

7. On the following screen, click the "Save field settings" button to move on to the full field settings screen. All of the additional settings for the new field can be left at their default values; click the "Save settings" button. Next, repeat the process to create a second field using the same settings, but using the label Cons and the field name "cons."

8. We have added the fields and a group to the content type. Now let's group the Pros and Cons together in the Summary group and move them to the top of the form. Drag the fields into the following order (make sure to drag Pros and Cons to the right in order to indent them):

   • Headline
   • Summary
       — Pros
       — Cons
   • Review

When you're finished, click the Save button. Your screen should look as pictured in Figure 5-3.

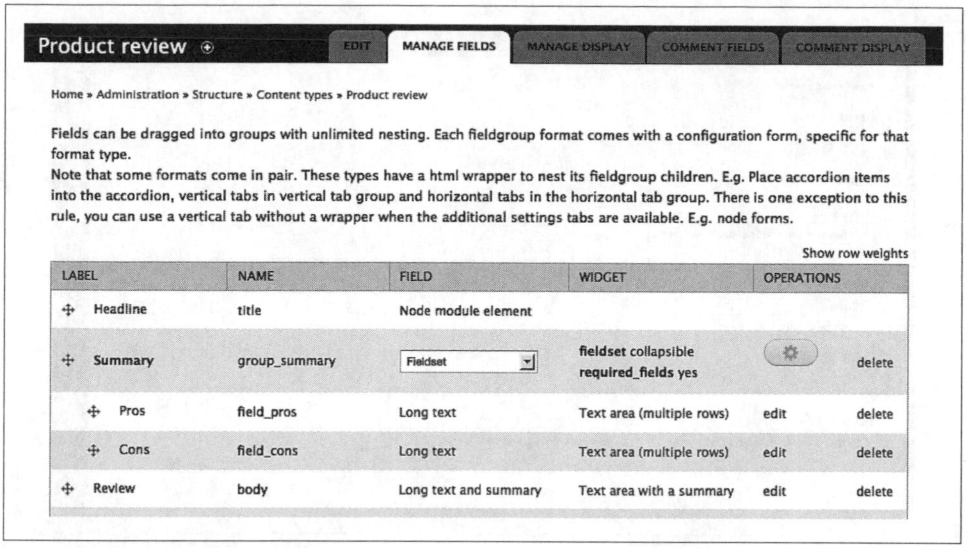

Product review ⊕   EDIT   **MANAGE FIELDS**   MANAGE DISPLAY   COMMENT FIELDS   COMMENT DISPLAY

Home » Administration » Structure » Content types » Product review

Fields can be dragged into groups with unlimited nesting. Each fieldgroup format comes with a configuration form, specific for that format type.
Note that some formats come in pair. These types have a html wrapper to nest its fieldgroup children. E.g. Place accordion items into the accordion, vertical tabs in vertical tab group and horizontal tabs in the horizontal tab group. There is one exception to this rule, you can use a vertical tab without a wrapper when the additional settings tabs are available. E.g. node forms.

Show row weights

LABEL	NAME	FIELD	WIDGET	OPERATIONS	
✛ Headline	title	Node module element			
✛ Summary	group_summary	Fieldset ▾	**fieldset** collapsible **required_fields** yes	⚙	delete
✛ Pros	field_pros	Long text	Text area (multiple rows)	edit	delete
✛ Cons	field_cons	Long text	Text area (multiple rows)	edit	delete
✛ Review	body	Long text and summary	Text area with a summary	edit	delete

Figure 5-3. The Fieldgroup module allows grouping multiple fields together

Now that we have the "Product review" content type started, we need to add permissions to allow the right people to create them. Bob and Sarah's friends will each have their own account and be able to post and edit their own reviews as editors of the site. Bob and Sarah themselves will be the administrators of the site and will therefore be able to edit or delete anyone's posts so that they can keep the site tidy, if needed. In the administrative toolbar, click People, then the Permissions tab (*admin/people/permissions*), and fill in the values shown in Table 5-3. Click "Save permissions" when you are done.

Table 5-3. Permissions for the "Product review" content type

Permission	anonymous user	authenticated user	editor	administrator
Node				
Product review: Create new content			Checked	Checked
Product review: Edit own content			Checked	Checked
Product review: Edit any content				Checked
Product review: Delete own content			Checked	Checked
Product review: Delete any content				Checked

Once you have everything set up, go to Create Content→"Product review" (*node/add/review*) and enter a simple review. Your new review creation form should look like Figure 5-4.

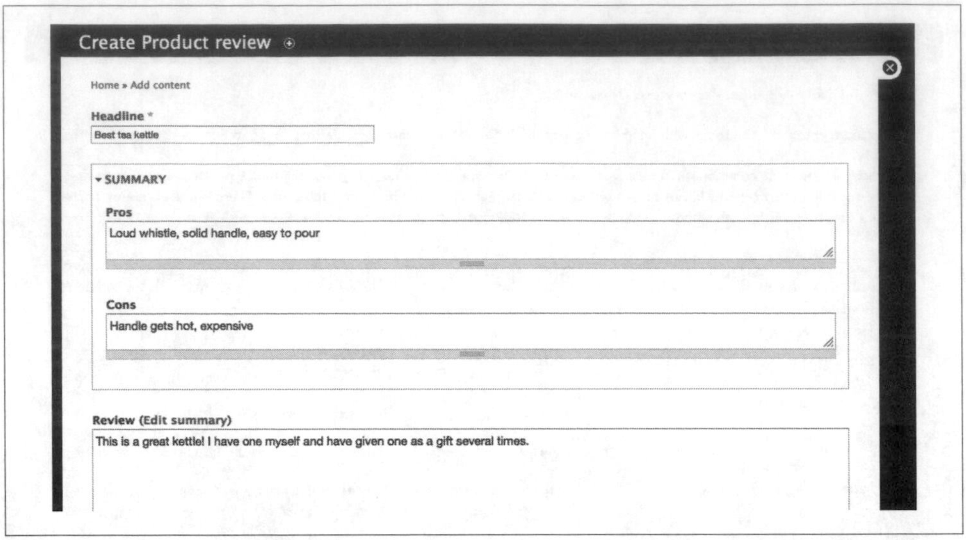

Figure 5-4. Creating a product review

The "Product review" content type is well on its way—it's now possible to create a new review, fill out the pros and cons, and display the results on the front page of the site. The finished review should look something like Figure 5-5. In the next section, we'll be adding more complete product information, straight from Amazon.com.

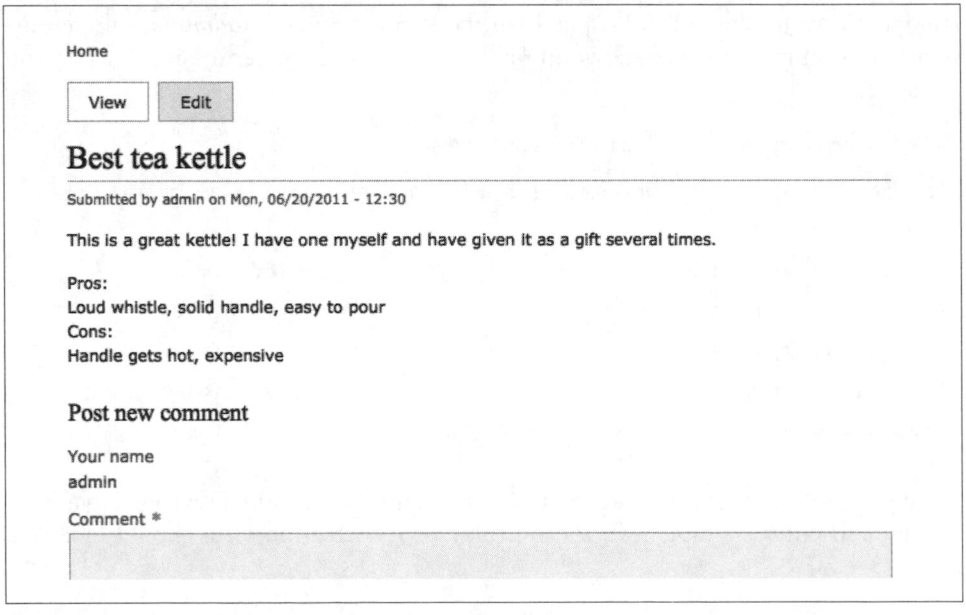

Figure 5-5. A completed review with basic information

Spotlight: Amazon Module

Amazon.com is one of a large number of web-based businesses that have opened up their product information databases for other sites to access. In the case of Super Duper Chefs, we want to retrieve useful data like product photos, pricing, and manufacturer information for display on our own website. The Amazon module for Drupal allows us to do just that.

What's Included?

The Amazon module is actually a collection of modules, each with its own purpose:

- The core Amazon API module handles communication with the Amazon.com website and ensures that pricing information on products stays up-to-date. All of the other modules included in the package require this one.

- The Amazon Field module allows administrators to add a field to any content type that stores an Amazon product ID, and displays a photo of the product straight from Amazon.com. This module is the one that we'll be using to enhance our "Product review" content type.

- The Amazon Filter module allows writers to insert product images and information into the text of any piece of content using the [amazon] tag. It's useful for bloggers or writers who want to link to products occasionally but don't need the structure of an explicit field just for product links.

- The Amazon Media module stores extra information about certain types of products. For example, it's responsible for storing and displaying the MPAA rating for movies and the console that video games run on.

- The Amazon Search module adds the ability to search for Amazon.com products from Drupal's default Search page.

Additionally, the Amazon module's configuration page exposes a number of settings. Next, we'll provide an overview of a few of them before we dive into the hands-on steps.

Web Service Tools

The Amazon module is what's known as an *API* module—it uses an *application programming interface* to give Drupal developers access to another website's data or another program's functionality. Similar modules allow Drupal sites to retrieve maps from the Google Maps web service, post messages to the Twitter microblogging service, log in with Facebook Connect, and more.

Hundreds of these API modules are available in the "Third-party integration" category (*http://drupal.org/project/modules?filters=tid%3A52*) of the Downloads section. If you'd like to connect your Drupal site to a popular website, it's worth checking that page out.

Locale

Because each country that Amazon operates in has a separate database of products, prices, and availability information, you'll want to choose the locale where your website's users reside in the Amazon module's configuration settings. This setting will determine which Amazon website (*http://www.amazon.com*, *http://www.amazon.jp*, and so on) will be used to look up the information for a given product. In addition, whenever links from your site to Amazon.com are generated, they'll point to the local Amazon site for the locale you've chosen. If you don't choose a specific locale, the Amazon module will assume that your site is operating in the United States.

Referral Settings

Although it's not required, setting up an Associate ID at *http://affiliate-program.amazon .com/gp/associates/join* allows Amazon to credit your site when your visitors click on an Amazon.com link and purchase a product. If you're feeling generous, the Amazon module also allows you to use the Drupal Association's ID, automatically donating any commissions from purchases to support the Drupal project.

Amazon Keys

To have our Drupal site communicate with Amazon's API, we will need to get an Amazon AWS account. This is a free account and service provided by Amazon. Once you create an account, Amazon will provide you with the keys you need to enter into these fields on the configuration page. You can find more information on getting an AWS account at *http://aws.amazon.com*.

Hands-On: Adding an Amazon Field

In the previous section of this chapter, we set up a content type for our product reviews. Now, we're ready to add a field to store a link to the product on Amazon.com. We need to do a few things to get set up before we add the field to our content type:

1. First, in the administrative toolbar, click Modules (*admin/modules*) and enable the following modules:
   - Amazon package
     - —Amazon API
     - —Amazon Field

2. Next, in the administrative toolbar, click Configuration→Amazon Settings→Amazon API (*admin/config/amazon_settings/amazon*), pictured in Figure 5-6. Select your locale and set the Amazon Associate ID to the one you wish to use. If you are in the United States and do not have an Amazon Associate ID, you can use the default settings for the first two settings on the page. This gives the Drupal Association, the nonprofit organization that supports the Drupal community, a tiny financial kickback.

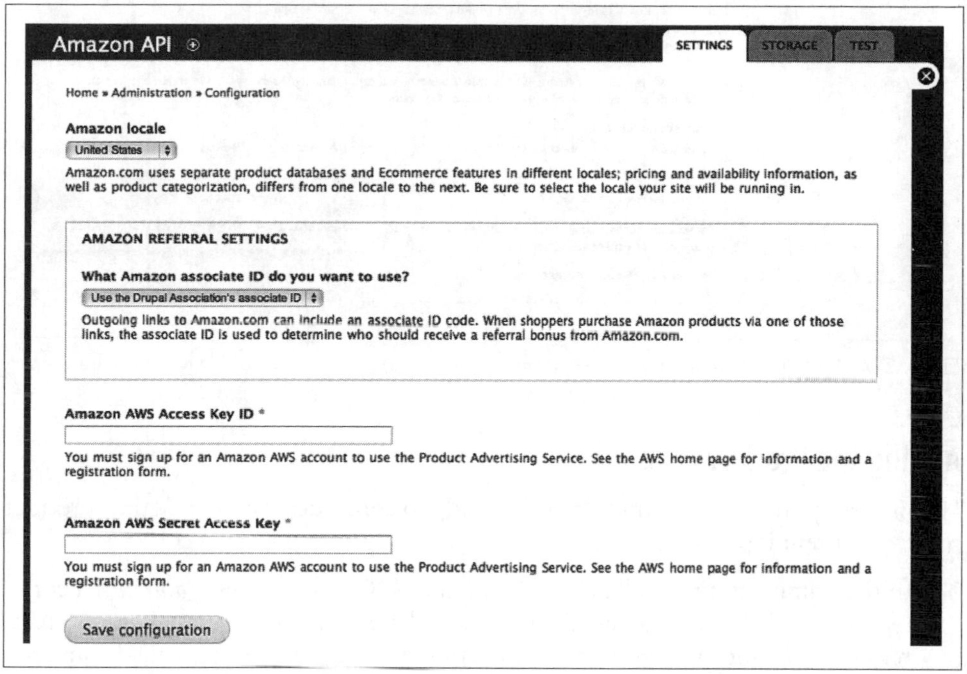

Figure 5-6. The Amazon module's settings page

3. Log into (or create) your Amazon AWS account at *http://aws.amazon.com* and navigate to the Security Credentials section (there is also a direct link to this page in the key field descriptions on the Amazon module's configuration page). In the Access Credentials area of the page, there is a tab for Access Keys, which will provide you with the keys you need to copy into the Drupal site, as shown in Figure 5-7. Copy these into the appropriate fields back in Drupal, and click the "Save configuration" button.

4. To test that the Amazon module is working properly, click the Test tab (*admin/config/amazon_settings/amazon/test*) and enter a valid Amazon Product ID such as "9781449390525" to ensure that a result comes back without errors.

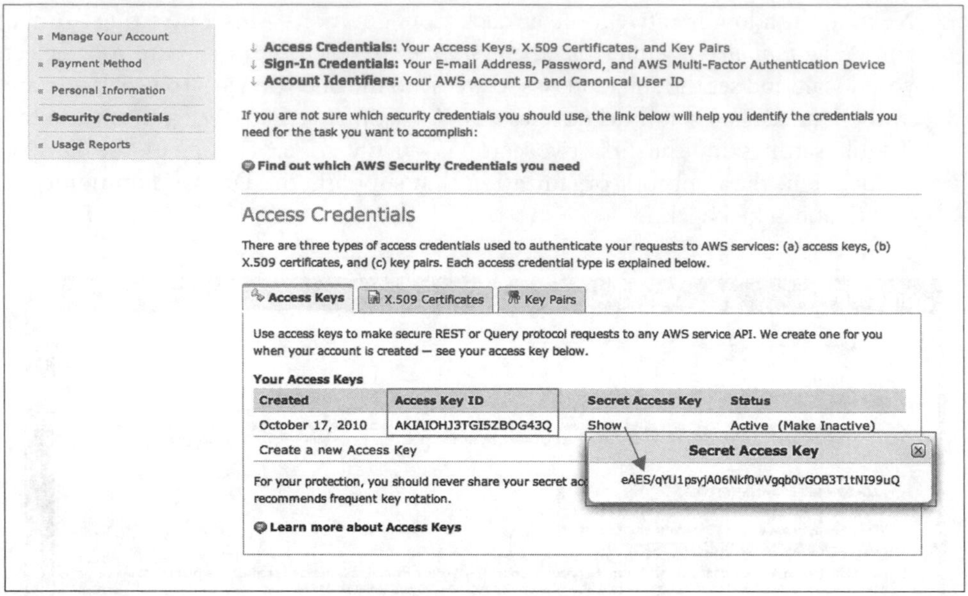

Figure 5-7. AWS access credential information

Adding the Product Field

Having set up the Amazon module, we're ready to continue customizing the "Product review" content type:

1. In the administrative toolbar, click Structure→"Content types" (*admin/structure/types*) and click the "manage fields" link (*admin/structure/types/manage/product-review/fields*) for the "Product review" content type. Create a new field using the settings indicated in Table 5-4.

Table 5-4. Creating the Product ID field

Setting	Value
Label	Amazon Product ID
Name	product_id
Field type	Amazon item
Widget	Amazon ASIN text field

2. Click the Save button to create the field and then click the "Save field settings" button to proceed. You'll be taken to the next screen to fill out the product review field settings. Add some Help text, like "Enter the Amazon product ID of the item you're reviewing. Often indicated by an ASIN, ISBN, or other field in the product details of an Amazon product page."

Finding Product IDs

Our Amazon field will automatically load product photos and pricing information whenever we enter a product ID. That's great—but how will the site's reviewers find those product IDs in the first place?

The simplest way is to find the product on the Amazon.com website using its own search function. Each product has its own page on Amazon.com, and the product ID usually appears there in two locations: the URL of the page itself, and the "Product details" section of the page, listed as the ASIN (short for Amazon Standard Identification Number). See Figures 5-8 and 5-9 for examples.

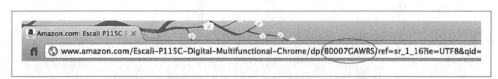

Figure 5-8. An Amazon product page's URL, with the product ID highlighted

Figure 5-9. An Amazon product page's details section

3. Click the "Save settings" button to complete the process, and you'll be returned to the "Manage fields" page for the "Product review" content type.

4. On the "Manage fields" page (*admin/structure/types/manage/product-review/fields*), rearrange the new Amazon field so that it is listed just above the Review field, like so:

   - Headline
   - Summary
     —Pros
     —Cons

- Amazon product ID
- Review

5. Click the Save button to save your ordering. In the administrative toolbar, click "Add content"→"Product review" (*node/add/product-review*) and add a new review. This time, fill out the Amazon Product field as well as the normal Headline, Pros and Cons, and Review fields. Your new review should look something like Figure 5-10 (showing Amazon product ID B0007GAWRS).

Figure 5-10. A review with Amazon.com product details

Later, we'll use the field display settings to control what information is output by Amazon on these nodes, as well as the order in which it is displayed with the other review information.

For even more fine-grained control over the display of Amazon product data, particularly on more standard "media" products such as books and software, the Amazon Media module we touched on in "Spotlight: Amazon Module" on page 203 includes a series of template files that can be customized to grab the specific fields you want for your site.

Our product reviews now contain fields for product pros and cons, and a link to Amazon.com for each product. What's left? We need some way to capture the editorial rating for each product that's reviewed, and a way for visitors to the site to add their own ratings as well. For that, we'll take a look at the Voting API and Fivestar modules.

Spotlight: Voting API and Fivestar

Giving visitors a chance to evaluate and rate content is an extremely common pattern on content-rich websites. In addition to giving visitors a way to jump to the best content, it can give you—the site's administrator—a way to determine what content on your site is most effective.

Almost all rating and evaluation modules for Drupal rely on a shared module called Voting API. Though it offers no features for your site on its own, it gives developers a set of tools for building rating systems and provides a common format for storing votes and calculating the results. This allows developers to focus on what makes their work unique (presenting vote results in a novel way, for example) while Voting API handles the grunt work.

The Fivestar module offers numerous configuration options, from the style and color of stars that it uses to display ratings to how results are presented when visitors look at a new piece of content. Figure 5-11 shows the Fivestar module's selection of rating widgets. The widget visitors use to rate each post can be displayed in the post itself, in a floating sidebar block, or even in the commenting form when visitors submit a reply.

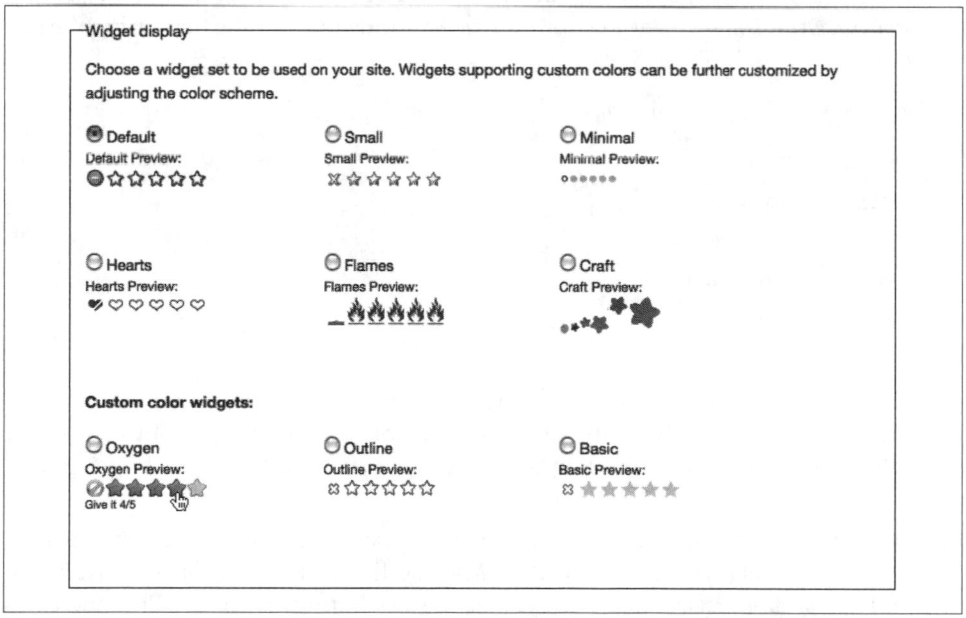

Figure 5-11. The Fivestar module's selection of rating widgets, available on its configuration screen

Despite what its name suggests, Fivestar can display any number of stars: 10 stars, 3 stars—even 1-star scales can be used. In addition, it provides a custom field type: a simple numeric field on any piece of content can be displayed using Fivestar's custom widget, separate from the ratings cast with Voting API.

Hands-On: Adding Ratings

For the Super Duper Chefs site, we'll be using both of the Fivestar module's unique features: adding a static Rating field to the "Product review" content type for the editors to use, and attaching a voting widget to the comment form on each review for the site readers to use. That approach will keep the official rating on each review separate from the reader ratings.

First, in the administrative toolbar, click Modules (*admin/modules*) and enable the following modules:

- Voting package
  - —Fivestar
  - —Voting API

Adding the Product Rating Field

1. In the administrative toolbar, click Structure→"Content types" (*admin/structure/types*), click the "manage fields" link for the "Product review" content type (*admin/structure/types/manage/product-review/fields*), and create a new field using the settings indicated in Table 5-5.

   Table 5-5. Creating the Rating field

Setting	Value
Label	Editor Rating
Name	editor_rating
Field type	Fivestar Rating
Widget	Stars

2. Click the Save button to create the field, and you'll be taken to the field settings page. Leave the default settings and click the "Save field settings" button. On the following screen, check the Required checkbox and click "Save settings" to add the field.

3. We'll also add this field to the Summary group so that it's displayed with the pros and cons. When you return to the "Manage fields" tab (*admin/structure/types/manage/product-review/fields*), rearrange the new Rating field above Pros and Cons in the Summary group. After you click the Save button, the list should look like this:

- Headline
- Summary
  - —Editor rating
  - —Pros
  - —Cons
- Amazon product ID
- Review

Adding the Reader Rating Field

As we've pointed out elsewhere in the book, fields can be added to anything in Drupal that is exposed as an entity. Now we will make use of this in practice, by adding a Rating field to the comments, so visitors can comment and rate the products as well.

1. In the administrative toolbar, click Structure→"Content types" (*admin/structure/types*), click the "edit" link for the "Product review" content type (*admin/structure/types/manage/product-review*), and then click the Comment Fields tab (*admin/structure/types/manage/product-review/comment/fields*). Add a new field using the settings in Table 5-6.

Table 5-6. Creating the Rating field for comments

Setting	Value
Label	Reader Rating
Name	reader_rating
Field type	Fivestar Rating
Widget	Stars

2. Click the Save button. On the field settings screen, it is important to set the "Voting target" to "Parent node," so that these votes will add ratings to the node; then, click the "Save field settings" button. We'll use the defaults on the "Product review" comment settings page, so just click "Save settings" to finish.

3. When you return to the Comment Fields screen, reorder the fields so that the "Reader rating" field is at the top and then click Save.

 Remember that you can play with the settings by going to the administrative toolbar, then Configuration→Fivestar (*admin/config/content/fivestar*), to choose fun icons such as hearts or flames that readers can use to rate content. If you choose a widget listed under "Custom color widgets," you can even choose a color scheme that matches your site.

4. With the ratings in place, we need to allow the site users to actually rate things. In the administrative toolbar, click People, then the Permissions tab (*admin/people/permissions*), and set the permissions shown in Table 5-7. Click the "Save permissions" button to finish up.

Table 5-7. Permissions for Fivestar ratings

Permission	anonymous user	authenticated user	editor	administrator
Fivestar				
Rate content		Checked	Checked	Checked
Use PHP for Fivestar target				Checked

 Recall from "Hands-On: Configuring Permissions" on page 62 that any permission name with "PHP" in it should only be given to *extremely* trusted users.

All of the essentials for the reviews are now in place. Editors on the site can write reviews that include pros and cons about the product, rate the product using an intuitive five-star scale, and pull in product information from Amazon.com. In addition, visitors can post their own comments about the product and rate it themselves. Figure 5-12 shows our new Fivestar ratings in action.

Spotlight: CSS Injector

Drupal's theming system gives designers complete control over how a site's content is rendered for a web browser, and custom themes (like the Tarski theme that we're using for the Super Duper Chefs site) can give any site a distinctive look. But sometimes it's useful to make minor tweaks to a site's appearance using nothing but CSS rules. They allow designers to tweak font sizes, colors, and so on without altering the underlying HTML that defines the site's structure.

The CSS Injector module (*http://drupal.org/project/css_injector*) gives administrators the ability to add those snippets in an administration screen within your site, without having to make changes to the current theme's files. This feature can be useful when a new version of your site's theme is released on Drupal.org—if you change the theme to add your own CSS, it's easy to lose those modifications when you download the new version. Keeping them in CSS Injector will preserve them even if you change themes.

CSS Injector offers a number of advanced options, including the ability to add the CSS rules conditionally on certain pages. If your CSS tweaks only apply to the front page, for example, you can ensure that it won't add the unnecessary rules to the entire site. You can also specify a media type for your CSS, which makes it possible to add styling information that applies only when a page is being printed. Finally, each rule can use the Preprocess CSS checkbox to control whether Drupal should merge its rules with

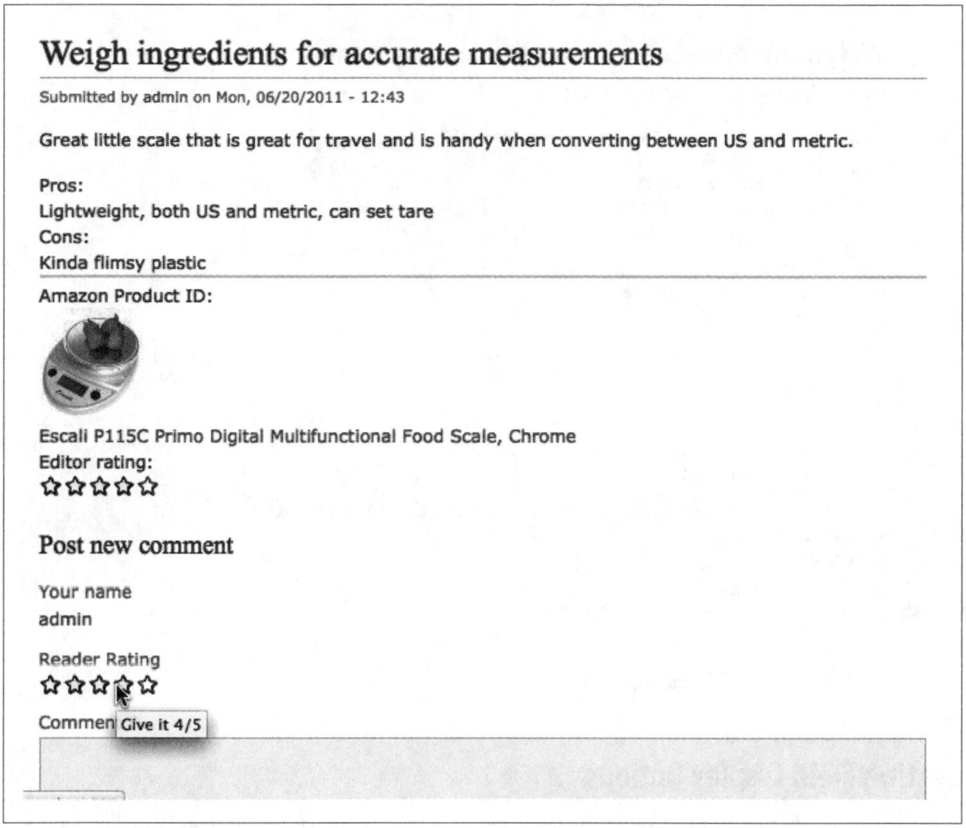

Weigh ingredients for accurate measurements

Submitted by admin on Mon, 06/20/2011 - 12:43

Great little scale that is great for travel and is handy when converting between US and metric.

Pros:
Lightweight, both US and metric, can set tare
Cons:
Kinda flimsy plastic

Amazon Product ID:

Escali P115C Primo Digital Multifunctional Food Scale, Chrome
Editor rating:
☆☆☆☆☆

Post new comment

Your name
admin

Reader Rating
☆☆☆☆☆
Commen Give it 4/5

Figure 5-12. A product with an editorial rating, along with a user review in progress

the current theme's CSS. In most cases, this step saves time, because a visitor's web browser makes only a single trip to your site's web server to download all the stylesheets. If you're adding extremely large amounts of CSS code that only apply to one or two pages, it can be more efficient to keep that code separate by turning preprocessing off. Otherwise, leave it enabled.

> If you're mystified by CSS, the Mozilla Developer Network documentation (*https://developer.mozilla.org/en-US/docs*) provides information and tutorials for learning all types of web technologies, including CSS. It's a great resource to keep bookmarked.

Hands-On: Polishing the Presentation

In this section, we'll do some final tweaking to make the review display look nice and tidy, as pictured in Figure 5-13.

Weigh ingredients for accurate measurements

Submitted by admin on Mon, 06/20/2011 - 12:43

Escali P115C Primo Digital Multifunctional
Food Scale, Chrome
Manufacturer: Escali
Part Number: P115C
Price: $29.95

Editor rating:
☆☆☆☆☆
Pros:
Lightweight, both US and metric, can set tare
Cons:
Kinda flimsy plastic

Great little scale that is great for travel and is handy
when converting between US and metric.

Add new comment

1 comment

I have the same scale and it
by admin on Mon, 06/27/2011 - 10:22

I have the same scale and it really is flimsy, so you need to be bit careful with it.
Reader Rating:
☆☆☆☆☆

Delete   Edit   Reply

Figure 5-13. Completed review display

Setting Field Display Options

Although our "Product review" content type has all of the data we need, and our product listing pages are looking great, the individual reviews still look a bit untidy. Fortunately, we can use the Field module's display settings to tweak how each type of field is displayed in the reviews.

1. In the administrative toolbar, click Structure→"Content types" (*admin/structure/types*) and click the "manage display" link for the "Product review" content type (*admin/structure/types/manage/product-review/display*).

2. The first thing we want to do is to add a field group to the display for our Editor Rating, Pros, and Cons fields, just like we did for the form input fields. This time, we'll make the HTML element a `<div>` for tidy markup. Fill out the "Add new group" settings as shown in Table 5-8. Save the settings.

Table 5-8. Settings for the Summary fieldset

Field	Setting
Label	Summary
Group name	summary
Format	Div

3. Click the gear icon next to the Summary format information and change the "Fieldgroup settings" to Open. Click the Update button and then the Save button to save the settings.

4. Drag the fields into the proper order so that they look like this:

   - Summary
     - —Editor rating
     - —Pros
     - —Cons
   - Amazon Product ID
   - Review

5. Click the Teaser subtab (*admin/structure/types/manage/product-review/display/ teaser*) and repeat the preceding steps to create a Summary div (set to "open") on the teaser display as well. Then drag the fields so that you have the following fields displayed in this order (note that the Review field should be moved down to the Hidden part of the form):

   - Summary
     - —Editor rating
     - —Pros
     - —Cons
   - Amazon Product ID
   - Review

6. Finally, fill out the settings as shown in Table 5-9 for the default and teaser displays, respectively. Figure 5-14 shows the default display settings after we've made these changes; the teaser display will look very similar. Click the Save button when you are done.

Table 5-9. Display settings for the "Product review" content type

Field	Label	Format
Default		
Editor Rating	Inline	As Stars (default)
Pros	Inline	Default (default)
Cons	Inline	Default (default)
Amazon Product ID	<Hidden>	Thumbnail with details
Review	<Hidden> (default)	Default (default)
Teaser		
Editor Rating	Inline	As Stars
Pros	Inline	Default

Field	Label	Format
Cons	Inline	Default
Amazon Product ID	\<Hidden\>	Thumbnail with title
Review	\<Hidden\>	\<Hidden\>

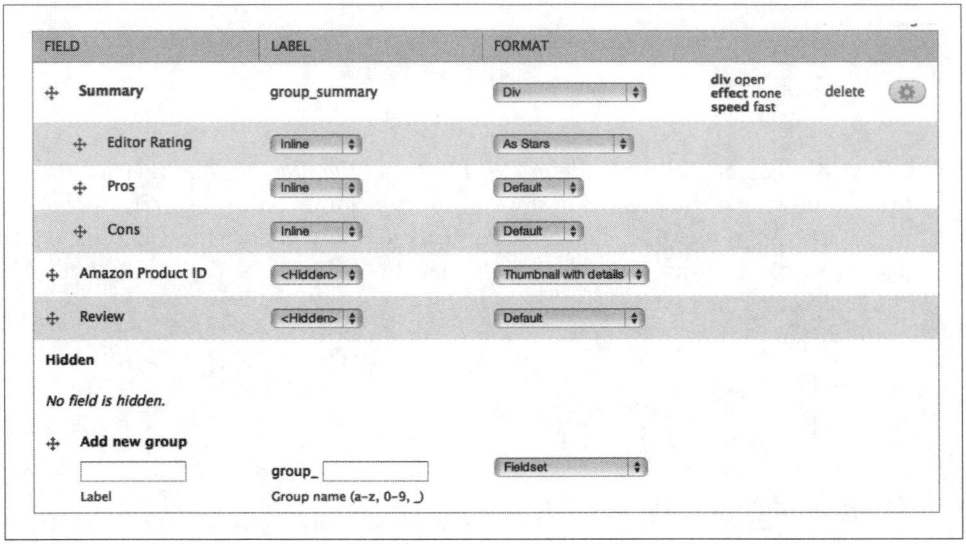

FIELD	LABEL	FORMAT	
⊹ **Summary**	group_summary	Div ⬍	div open effect none speed fast delete ⚙
⊹ **Editor Rating**	Inline ⬍	As Stars ⬍	
⊹ **Pros**	Inline ⬍	Default ⬍	
⊹ **Cons**	Inline ⬍	Default ⬍	
⊹ **Amazon Product ID**	\<Hidden\> ⬍	Thumbnail with details ⬍	
⊹ **Review**	\<Hidden\> ⬍	Default ⬍	

Hidden

No field is hidden.

⊹ **Add new group**

[ ]	group_ [ ]	Fieldset ⬍
Label	Group name (a–z, 0–9, _)	

Figure 5-14. Settings for the default product review display; the teaser display will look very similar

If you navigate back to one of your reviews, the node view will look essentially the same at this point. In the next section, though, we'll add some fanciness!

Configuring CSS Injector

Changing the display settings for our reviews cleans things up quite a bit, but the Summary information still seems awkward. We can significantly improve things by adding some CSS rules using CSS Injector. We'll use it to reduce the width of the Summary box and float it to the side of each review, turning it into a floating sidebar rather than a header at the top of each review. Here's how:

1. In the administrative toolbar, click Modules (*admin/modules*) and enable the Other: CSS Injector module.

2. In the administrative toolbar, click Configuration→Development→CSS Injector (*admin/config/development/css_injector*) and click the "Create a new rule" link to add a new CSS rule.

3. Name the rule "Floating Summary fields," and enter the following text into the CSS code field. You can see the completed form in Figure 5-15:

```
div.group_summary {
    border: 1px solid lightgrey;
    float: right;
    padding: 10px;
    width: 250px;
    font-size: .9em;
}

div.group_summary div.field-label {
    font-weight: bold;
}

div.field-type-asin {
    clear: none;
    width: 400px;
    margin-bottom: 10px;
    border: none;
}

div.field-type-asin img {
    float: left;
    padding-right: 10px;
}
```

 Not a fan of typing? Not to worry. This code is also available in the *assets/ch05-reviews/amazon.css* file in the book's source code for easy copying and pasting.

4. Click the Save button to add the new rule.

Depending on your web browser's settings, you may need to clear the browser's cache to see the changes to the stylesheet. Once you've done that, return to one of the product reviews added earlier. It should look quite a bit more attractive, as shown earlier in Figure 5-13. What a difference a dash of CSS makes!

Hands-On: Building a Product List

Now that we have a few products, we really ought to add a listing page that lets visitors look over all of the products that have been reviewed, comparing official ratings with visitor ratings and sorting by various criteria, as pictured in Figure 5-16. This page will be simple to build with the Views module.

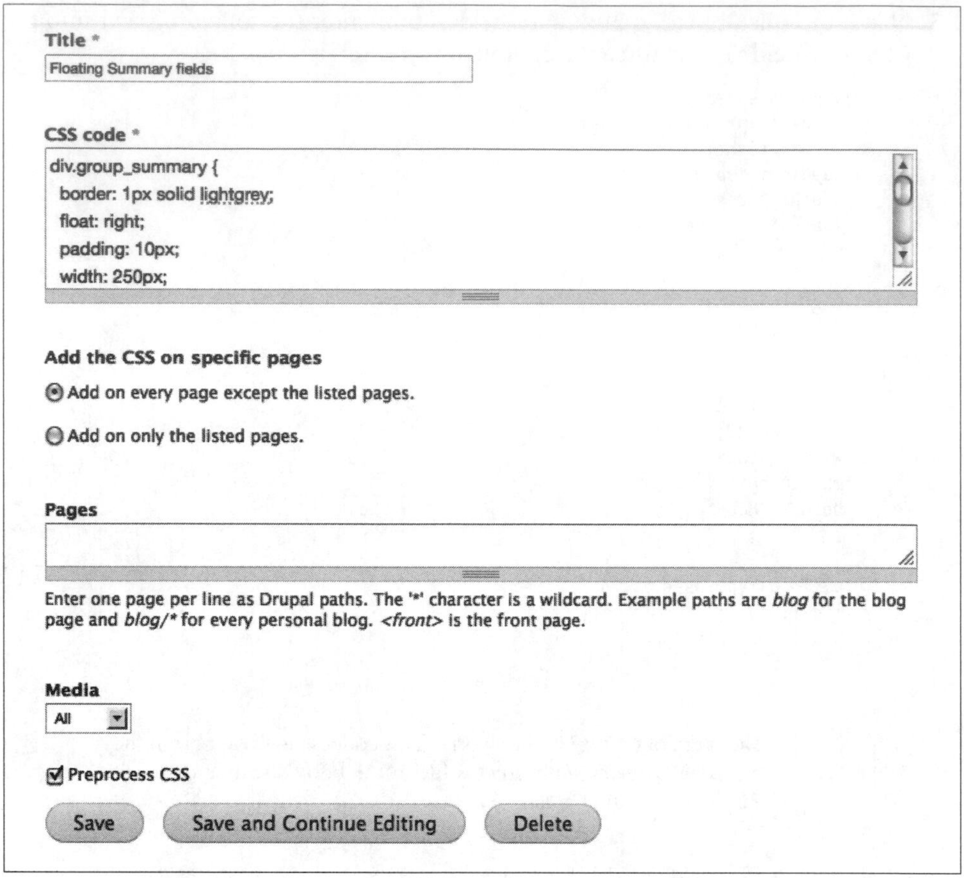

Figure 5-15. Adding a new CSS Injector rule

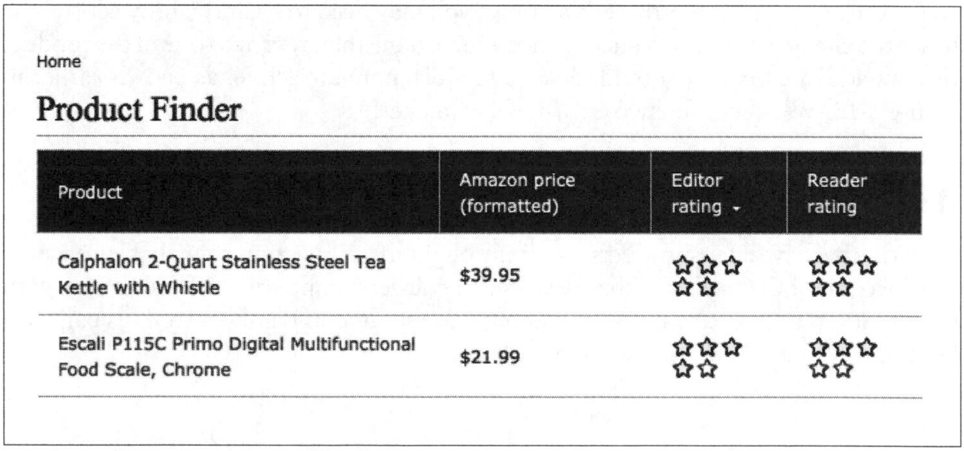

Figure 5-16. Product Finder view

1. In the administrative toolbar, click "Site building"→Modules (*admin/build/modules*) and enable the following modules:
   - Other package
     — Advanced help
   - Views package
     — Views
     — Views UI

2. In the administrative toolbar, click Structure→Views (*admin/structure/views*), click on the "Add new view" link (*admin/structure/views/add*), and fill in the new view settings using Table 5-10.

Table 5-10. Settings for creating the Product Finder view

View setting	Value
View name	Product Finder
View description	Checked: List of reviewed products
Show	*Content* of type *Product review* sorted by *Newest first*
Display format	*Table* of fields
Items to display	10 (default)
Use a pager	Checked (default)
Create a menu link	Checked
	Menu: Navigation
	Link text: Product finder (default)
Include an RSS feed	Unchecked (default)
Create a block	Unchecked (default)

3. After clicking the "Continue & edit" button, we want to add some more fields to our view. We are going to go ahead and do that in a minute, but first we need to create a relationship for our fields so that we can use Amazon-specific fields in the view and display the average rating given to each product by visitors to the site.

   Open the Advanced fieldset and click the "add" button in the Relationships section. Check both the "Content: Amazon Product ID (field_product_id)" and "Content: Vote results" relationships. Click the "Apply (all displays)" button to add the relationships and then fill out the settings in Table 5-11 when prompted. Click the "Apply (all displays)" button after each form is presented.

Table 5-11. *"Vote results" relationship settings for the Product Finder view*

Defaults: Relationships	Value
Content: Amazon Product ID (field_product_id)	Identifier: Product ID
Content: Vote results	Value type: Percent
	Vote tag: vote
	Aggregate function: Average vote

4. In the Fields section of the View, click the "add" button, check the following fields, and click "Add and configure fields." This will give us the product title, price, official rating, and reader rating:

   - Amazon: Amazon price (formatted)
   - Amazon: Title
   - Content: Editor rating
   - Vote results: Value

5. Configure the settings for each new field as shown in Table 5-12. Click "Apply (all displays)" when you're finished configuring each field's settings.

Table 5-12. *Field configuration settings for the Product Finder view*

Defaults: Field configure setting	Value
Amazon: Amazon price (formatted)	Relationship: Product ID (default) Label: List price
Amazon: Title	Relationship: Product ID (default)
	Label: Product
	Link behavior: A link to the product's Amazon page (default)
Content: Editor rating	Keep all defaults
Vote results: Value	Relationship: Vote results
	Label: Reader rating
	Appearance: Fivestar Stars (display only)

6. Let's rearrange the fields into a different order and remove the review title from the list. In the Fields section, click the drop-down next to the "add" button, and select "rearrange." Drag the "(Product ID) Amazon: Title Product" field to the top of the list so that the product title is listed first. Then click "remove" for the "Content: Title" field. Click Apply to save your changes.

7. Now that we have the fields, under Format, ensure the format is set to Table, then click the Settings link next to it. Use the values listed in Table 5-13 for a sortable table. Click Apply when finished.

Table 5-13. Table style options for the Product Finder view

Defaults: Table style option	Value
Sortable	All checked
Default sort	Editor rating
Editor rating: Default order	Descending

When all those steps have been completed, save the view, which should look like Figure 5-17.

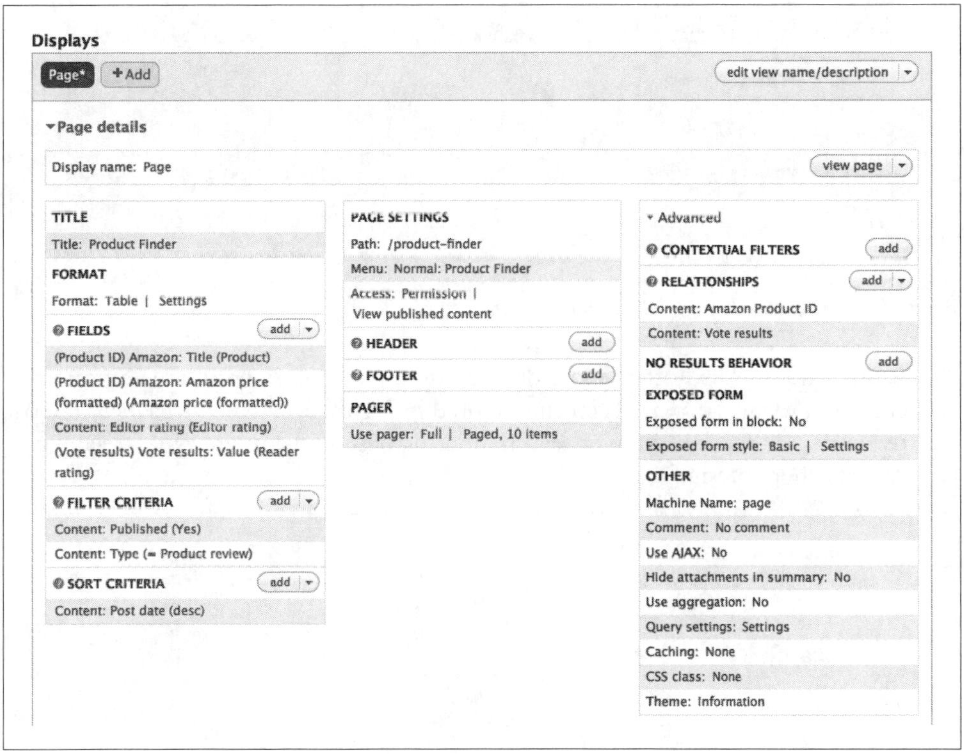

Figure 5-17. Completed Product Finder view settings

With the settings we've used, you should now see a "Product finder" link (*product-finder*) in the site's Navigation menu. Upon clicking it, you should see a tidy listing of all the reviews on the site, with official and reader ratings compared side by side, as shown earlier in Figure 5-16.

Only one feature remains from our to-do list: build searching capabilities into our product list so visitors can easily filter it down to find products that interest them.

Spotlight: The Search Module

Drupal's built-in Search module offers powerful, flexible searching features and intelligent ranking of results. Behind the scenes, it's silently building an index of all the words used in the site's content. When users search for a phrase on the site, content is ranked using customizable rules and displayed in order of relevance. On any Drupal site, you can refine these rules by going to the administrative toolbar and clicking Configuration→"Search and Metadata"→Search Settings (*admin/config/search/settings*) and changing the Content Ranking weights, pictured in Figure 5-18.

Figure 5-18. The Search module's content ranking settings

The Search module also offers more detailed options for sites with large amounts of content. The Advanced Search screen, pictured in Figure 5-19, allows users to choose exactly what content they want to search, filtering based on content type, free tagging terms, and other criteria.

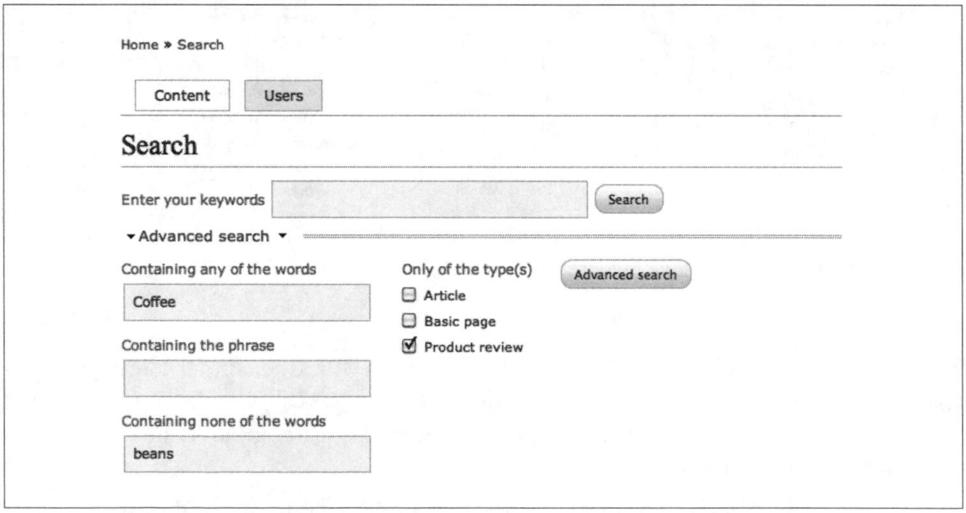

Figure 5-19. The Advanced Search page in action

The Importance of Cron

The indexing process used by Drupal's Search module only works when the "cron" utility has been properly configured. cron is a utility used to run various commands at scheduled intervals on your web server. It is responsible for performing maintenance tasks on a Drupal site like clearing old log entries, as well as scheduling bulk email and other tasks that happen with regular frequency.

Drupal 7 comes with a built-in cron process, which passes along the task of checking to see whether scheduled events need to happen to your website's visitors, transparently (the same functionality is offered by a module called Poormanscron in Drupal 6 and previous versions). Each time a visitor hits the website, core will check to see if the allotted time has passed since the last time cron ran. If enough time has passed, core will then see whether it needs to do anything new since the last time it ran and, if so, will perform the cron actions. This check triggers events after the page is loaded, so the visitor doesn't know the difference. You can configure how often cron will run by going to the administrative toolbar and clicking Configuration→System→Cron (*admin/config/ system/cron*). Of course, this works only if your site gets regular traffic. But then again, if it isn't getting traffic, it probably doesn't matter how often your search index is updated.

While this automated "lazy" cron functionality is great for making sure that basic clean-up tasks are performed, and is sometimes the only option available to you in some hosting environments, it is recommended that you set up a cron task on your site's server, as this will be much more regular and reliable than site traffic for making sure the tasks are completed. For more information on setting up cron for your site, see *http: //drupal.org/cron*.

Each time cron runs, Drupal will catalog some of the site's content; by default, it indexes 200 posts each time. If your site has a large number of posts already, the speed of the indexing will depend on how frequently cron is configured to run on your server.

You can tell Drupal to perform its cron tasks manually by going to the administrative toolbar, clicking Configuration→System→Cron (*admin/config/system/cron*), and then clicking the "Run cron" button. This is particularly handy when you are working and testing on your local site and want to see the results of a cron process immediately.

Searching with Views

Although the Advanced Search form allows quite a bit of control for users, it's very difficult to change how that page appears and how the results are displayed. It also can present a daunting array of options, especially when a site has lots of taxonomy terms.

The Views module is one way to exercise more control over searching: its filters can narrow down lists of content based on words indexed by the search system. A view might list only blog posts mentioning kittens, for example. For the Super Duper Chefs site, we'll be using this module to add custom filtering to our Product Finder page.

Hands-On: Make the Product List Searchable

To transform the Product Finder page into a searchable index, we'll be adding two new filters to the view: one that restricts the results by manufacturer and another that restricts results to reviews that mention specific words.

Normally, these filters are locked in place and can't be modified except by the site's administrator. We need users to enter their own criteria, however. Fortunately, Views allows us to "expose" any of its normal filters. Doing so adds a small form to the heading of the view's display page. Visitors to the site can use it to change how Views filters its results, turning any view into a simple search tool, as pictured in Figure 5-20.

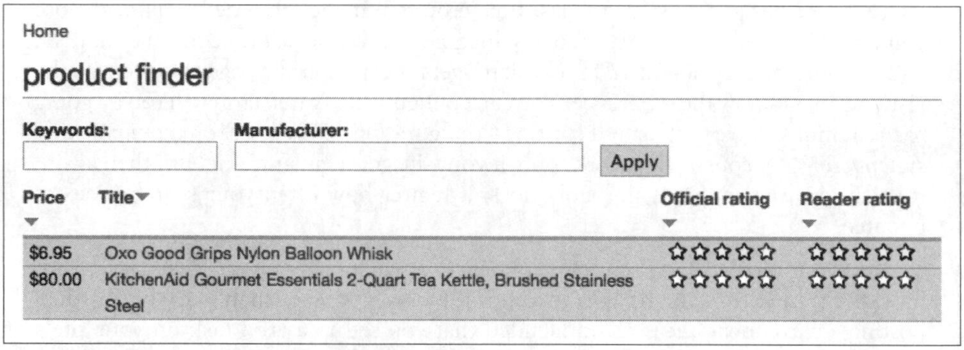

Figure 5-20. Searchable Product Finder view

Here are the steps to get your searchable list:

1. In the administrative toolbar, click Structure→Views (*admin/structure/views*) and click the "edit" button for our Product Finder view (*admin/structure/views/view/product_finder/edit*).

2. Click the "add" button in the "Filter criteria" section to check the "Amazon: Manufacturer" and "Search: Search Terms" filters, and click the "Apply (all displays)" button.

3. On the settings form for each of the filters, click the "Expose this filter to visitors, to allow them to change it" checkbox, which will present the filter as a form field that a site visitor can interact with. Configure the exposed filter settings for each filter using the values in Table 5-14. As usual, click "Apply (all displays)" to move between the configuration forms.

Table 5-14. Settings for the search filters

Defaults: Configure filter setting	Value
Amazon: Manufacturer	Operator: Contains
Search: Search Terms	Label: Keywords
	On Empty Input: Show All (default)

4. Click the drop-down next to the "add" button in the "Filter criteria" section and select "and/or, rearrange." Move "Search: Search Terms" above "Amazon: Manufacturer" so that its box will appear first.

 By creating filter groups here, we can do very complex conditions, like "Product has this search keyword OR this manufacturer AND this price." For the purpose of our search form, though, a straight-up "AND" between all filter criteria will work fine.

5. Save the view, which should now look like Figure 5-21.

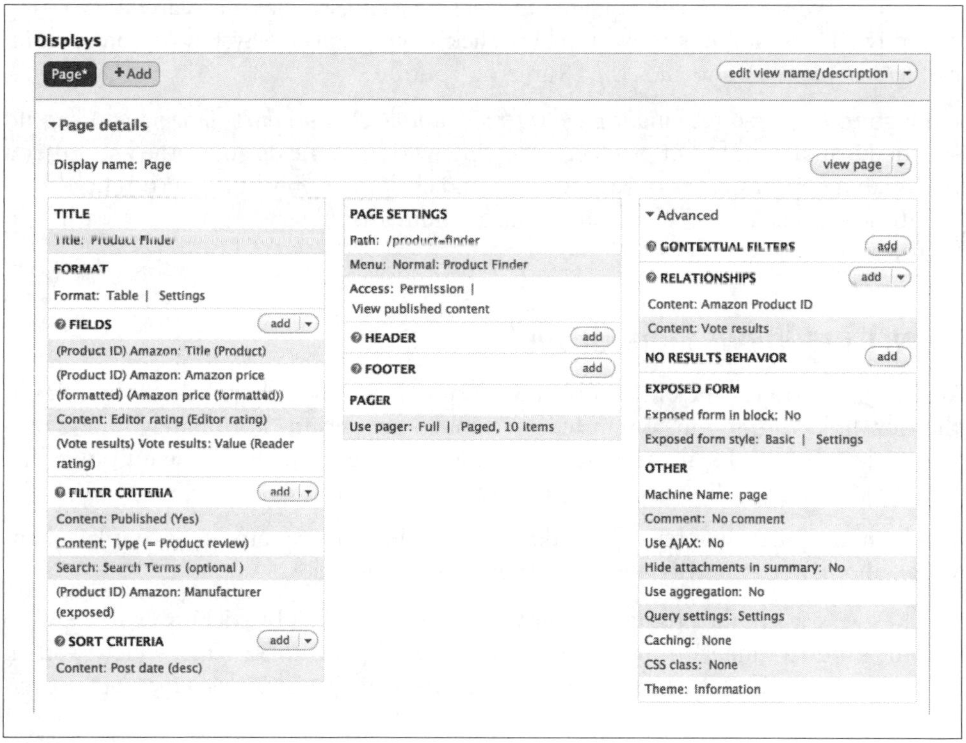

Displays

Page* | + Add   edit view name/description ▾

▾ **Page details**

Display name: Page   view page ▾

TITLE
Title: Product Finder

FORMAT
Format: Table | Settings

⊘ FIELDS   add ▾
(Product ID) Amazon: Title (Product)
(Product ID) Amazon: Amazon price
(formatted) (Amazon price (formatted))
Content: Editor rating (Editor rating)
(Vote results) Vote results: Value (Reader rating)

⊘ FILTER CRITERIA   add ▾
Content: Published (Yes)
Content: Type (= Product review)
Search: Search Terms (optional)
(Product ID) Amazon: Manufacturer (exposed)

⊘ SORT CRITERIA   add ▾
Content: Post date (desc)

PAGE SETTINGS
Path: /product-finder
Menu: Normal: Product Finder
Access: Permission |
View published content

⊘ HEADER   add
⊘ FOOTER   add

PAGER
Use pager: Full | Paged, 10 items

▾ Advanced

⊘ CONTEXTUAL FILTERS   add
⊘ RELATIONSHIPS   add ▾
Content: Amazon Product ID
Content: Vote results

NO RESULTS BEHAVIOR   add

EXPOSED FORM
Exposed form in block: No
Exposed form style: Basic | Settings

OTHER
Machine Name: page
Comment: No comment
Use AJAX: No
Hide attachments in summary: No
Use aggregation: No
Query settings: Settings
Caching: None
CSS class: None
Theme: Information

Figure 5-21. Completed Product Finder view settings

Before we test our new search feature, we need to make sure that we give search permissions to the users. We want everyone who visits the site to be able to search. In the administrative toolbar, click People, then the Permissions tab (*admin/people/permissions*), and set the permissions as indicated in Table 5-15, which will give the option to all users, both logged in and anonymous. Save the permissions.

Table 5-15. Permissions for searching

Permission	anonymous user	authenticated user	editor	administrator
Search				
Administer search				Checked
Use search	Checked	Checked	Checked	Checked
Use advanced search			Checked	Checked

If you search for a keyword like "whistle" that ought to be returning results but find that it is not, fear not! The last thing we need to do is make sure that our site has been indexed, so that when we do a search the keywords will be accessible. While testing things out, we will manually update our site so we can see that our search is working properly. In the administrative toolbar, click Configuration→System→Cron (*admin/config/system/cron*), and click the "Run cron" button.

Now go to our Product Finder page (*http://example.com/product-finder*). You should see the normal page full of products, this time with filter fields above the list. Enter a phrase that appears in one of your reviews, and click the Apply button. You should see an attractive list of the top results that contain the phrase, as we saw earlier in Figure 5-20.

Rewriting Views Field Output

We're almost done! The only problem with our view now is that clicking the titles in the view links to Amazon.com instead of to our own website. Fortunately, Views provides a handy trick for just this sort of situation; we can "rewrite" the output of the Title field to create a link back to its referring node instead.

Doing this requires two steps: first, adding the field(s) you want to use as a replacement value, and then configuring the output settings for the field:

1. Return back to the Product Finder view settings—either by clicking "edit view" in the Product Finder's contextual links, or by navigating to Structure→Views—then click "edit" next to Product Finder (*admin/structure/views/view/product_finder/edit*).

2. Under Fields, click "add" and add the "Content: Nid" field. Check the "Exclude from display" checkbox on the field's settings screen, which will ensure the output of this field is hidden from view. We don't actually want "1" and "63" showing up in the table; we merely need that value to create the URL *node/NODE_ID*. Click "Apply (all values)" to save.

3. Next, click the drop-down next to the "add" button in the Fields section, and click "rearrange." Move the new "Content: Nid" field to the top and click Apply. This field needs to precede the "Amazon: Title Product" field so that we can use the node ID as a replacement value. Click "Apply (all values)" to save.

4. Next, click on the "(Product ID) Amazon: Title (Product)" field to change its settings. Change "Link behavior" to "No link" to remove the automatic linking to Amazon.com. Expand the "Rewrite results" fieldset and check the "Output this field as a link" checkbox. Checking this box will expose a new field, "Link path," for the link destination.

5. Scroll down to the "Replacement patterns" collapsed fieldset below, and expand it to see a list of possible dynamic tokens you can choose from, including [nid] for the node ID, and [title_1] for the Amazon product title. Scroll back up to the "Link path" field and enter "node/[nid]" as the value, as shown in Figure 5-22. Click "Apply (all displays)" to save changes.

6. Finally, save the view when finished. Now, when you click on the titles in the view, you should be taken to the product review, not the Amazon.com product page.

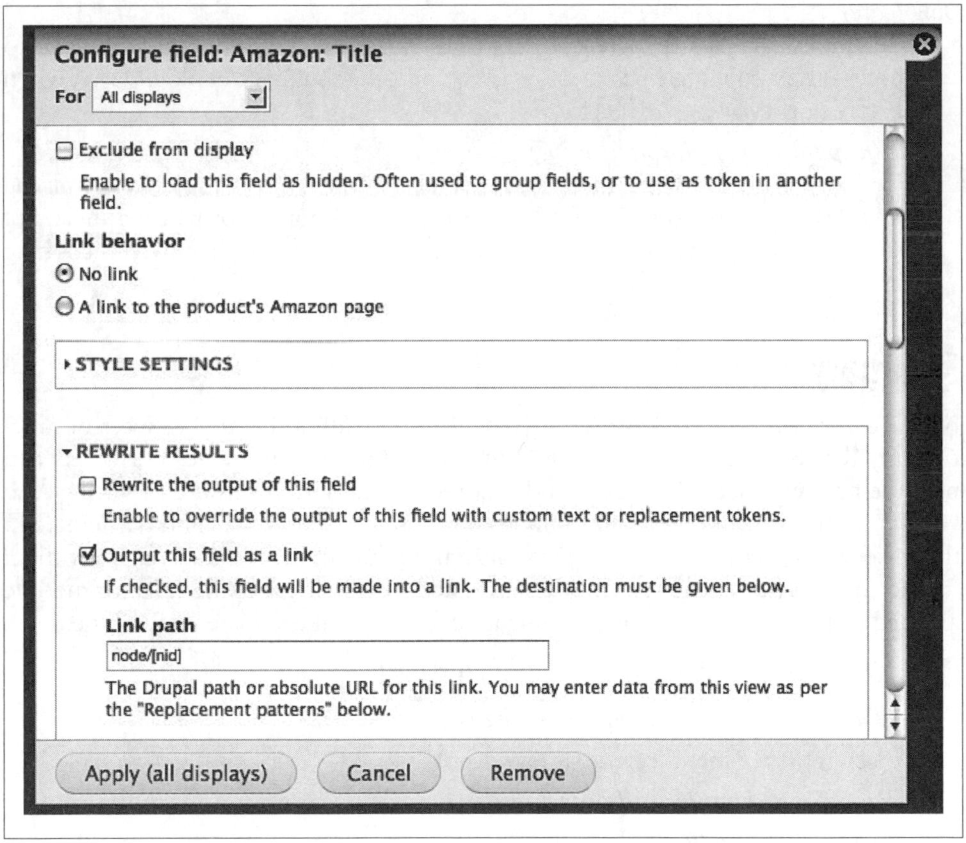

Figure 5-22. *The Views module allows you to rewrite field output using dynamic values*

Taking It Further

Congratulations! All of the major features for the site are in place. If you're interested in experimenting further, there are quite a few opportunities for additional enhancements using other Drupal modules:

AdSense (http://drupal.org/project/adsense)
> This module allows Bob and Sarah to place ads in the sidebar to offset the costs of hosting the site.

Display Suite (http://drupal.org/project/ds)
> For even more control over the layout of a content body than CSS Injector provides, check out the Display Suite module, which provides regions within content that fields can be moved around within.

Blog (core)
> This module allows the site's writers to each have their own blogs on which to discuss their cooking tips, latest recipes, and other culinary exploits, even when they're not reviewing products.

Recipe (http://drupal.org/project/recipe)
> For taking our cooking site further, the Recipe module—one of the longest-running modules on Drupal.org—might be a welcome addition. It provides a means of adding detailed ingredient information and can show details like overall cooking time.

Summary

After all that work, where have we arrived? We've hit all of the major pieces of functionality that Bob and Sarah wanted. Using Field, Amazon, and Fivestar, writers can post their reviews of cool kitchen products to the site. With Fivestar and Voting API, visitors to the site can offer their opinions on those same products and participate in the reviewing process. And with Views' Search module integration, it's easy for them to find the exact products that they're interested in. Finally, the CSS Injector module allowed us to sprinkle on those finishing touches that make the site really shine.

Here are the modules that we referenced in this chapter:

- AdSense (*http://drupal.org/project/adsense*)
- Amazon (*http://drupal.org/project/amazon*)
- Chaos Tools (*http://drupal.org/project/ctools*)
- CSS Injector (*http://drupal.org/project/css_injector*)
- Field Group (*http://drupal.org/project/field_group*)
- Fivestar (*http://drupal.org/project/fivestar*)

- Views (*http://drupal.org/project/views*)
- Voting API (*http://drupal.org/project/votingapi*)

Here are some other resources we referenced:

- Amazon Associates program (*http://affiliate-program.amazon.com/*)
- Amazon Web Services (*http://aws.amazon.com/*)
- Configuring cron jobs (*http://drupal.org/cron*)
- Evaluation and rating modules (*http://drupal.org/project/modules?filters=tid:60*)
- Third-party integration modules (*http://drupal.org/project/modules?filters=tid:52*)
- Voting Systems Drupal group (*http://groups.drupal.org/voting-systems*)
- Mozilla Developer Network documentation (*https://developer.mozilla.org/en-US/docs*)

CHAPTER 6

Event Management

Managing online calendars and event registration can present a huge challenge. Without a dynamic system, the task is nearly impossible. Generating the HTML required to display a calendar and all the various presentation options (day, week, month views, and so on) is unreasonable; and worse, because the events are time-sensitive, remembering to update "next" or "upcoming" event lists can be onerous. Nothing looks worse than having last week's meeting listed first on your Upcoming Events page.

Even with dynamic systems, you tend to be constrained to certain parameters with fixed options. However, by taking advantage of the flexibility of Drupal and building on the powerful base of Views, you can accommodate nearly any variation on event listings for your site.

This chapter introduces the following modules:

Date (http://drupal.org/project/date)
> Provides a field for entering date and time information, as well as libraries to handle operations like date math and time zone conversion

Calendar (http://drupal.org/project/calendar)
> A view style for displaying a list of site content in a rich calendar display

Flag (http://drupal.org/project/flag)
> A flexible utility module that enables administrators to add on/off toggle switches to entities such as nodes and comments

To follow along with the hands-on example in this chapter, you should install Drupal using the *Events* installation profile. The completed website will look as pictured in Figure 6-1 and at *http://events7.usingdrupal.com*. For more information on using the book's sample code, see the Preface.

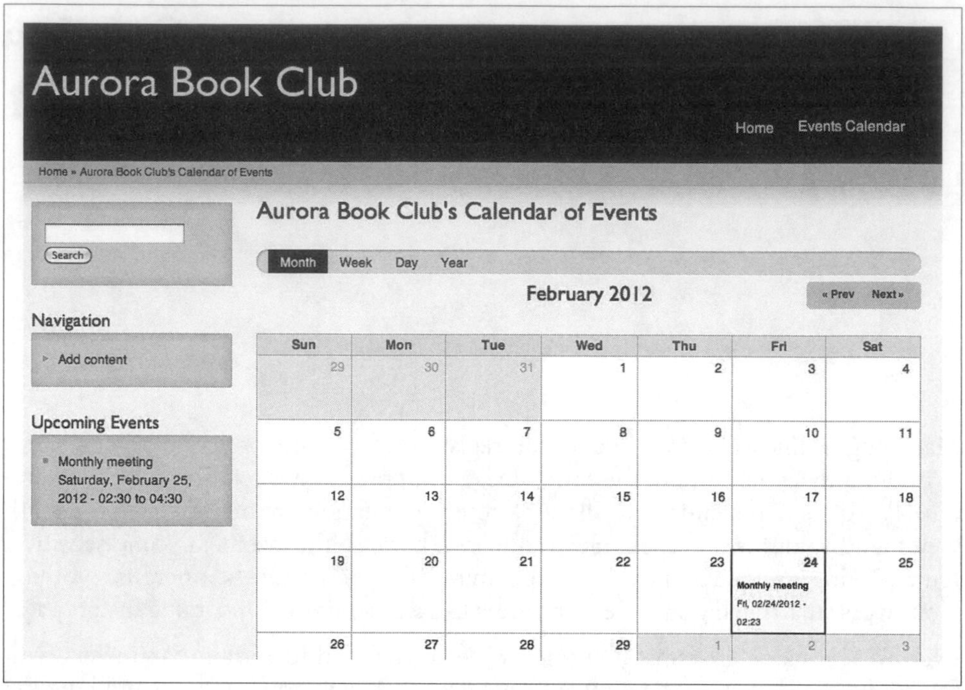

Figure 6-1. The completed Aurora Book Club site

Case Study

The Aurora Book Club is a rather social group of local book enthusiasts. They hold semiregular monthly meetings and events for both current and prospective members. Members want to be able to see when and where the next meeting is happening. Additionally, members should be allowed to post their own events to the site. Events should have start and end times and dates, as well as information about the event and where it will take place. To make it easy for members to see what is happening soon, there should be a short list of upcoming events in addition to the full calendar. The calendar needs to offer day, month, and annual views, and a way for members to subscribe to the club's calendar using Microsoft Outlook or Apple's iCal. Finally, since the club members would like to know how many cookies to bring and how many chairs to have on hand, the club president has asked that we include a way to track who plans to attend each event.

Implementation Notes

In order to build Aurora Book Club's site, we need to investigate two main features: event management and attendance tracking.

Event Management

At one time, doing event management in Drupal meant the choice between a module called Event (*http://drupal.org/project/event*), which provided an out-of-the-box event handling solution with some assumptions about how that handling should work, or a combination of the Date (*http://drupal.org/project/date*), Calendar (*http://drupal.org/project/calendar*), and Views modules, a more flexible but also a more "elbow grease required" solution to accomplish the same thing. Nowadays, however, the choice is pretty much made for you. While the Event module was popular during the days of Drupal 5 and earlier, in later years the Drupal community has clearly clustered around the flexibility that the Field and Views modules offer, which enables site builders to tailor features to their sites' exact needs. Too bad that those old, historical modules that no one uses anymore have claimed such great namespaces!

With the "building block" approach, the Date module will provide a date/time entry field on our events, and the Views module will provide us with event listings. And with the Calendar module layered on top of these views, we can deploy a feature-rich and filterable calendar display in a few clicks.

Attendance Tracking

The Signup module (*http://drupal.org/project/signup*) is designed specifically for the purpose of tracking event attendance, and has some nice features such as the ability to email reminders to attendees prior to an event. However, this module was unavailable for Drupal 7 and was undergoing development at the time of this writing.

Instead, we will use this opportunity to highlight a helpful general-purpose module called Flag (*http://drupal.org/project/flag*). Flag allows users to mark or "flag" a piece of content. This functionality can be used for a myriad of useful purposes, including marking content as offensive, allowing users to bookmark interesting stories, and even letting users mark events as "attending" or "not attending."

Hands-On: First Steps

First, we'll set up a few basics for our site just using Drupal core. The main thing that we need to start is a content type to handle our events. Log into the Aurora Book Club site with the username *admin*, password *oreilly*, if you are using the installation profile.

Creating an Event Content Type

We'll start by creating a new, basic content type just for events. We just need the event name and description along with an easy way to add the event location. We won't promote it to the front page, as we want more control over the display of events in our forthcoming calendar. We will, however, leave comments enabled, for more of a "social" vibe for the site.

1. In the administrative toolbar, go to Structure→"Content types" (*admin/structure/types*) and select "Add content type" (*admin/structure/types/add*) to create a new content type called Event, using the settings from Table 6-1.

Table 6-1. Settings for the Event content type

Field	Value
Name	Event
Description	A book club meeting or social event
Submission form settings	
Title field label	Name
Publishing options	
Default options	Uncheck "Promoted to front page"

2. When finished, click the "Save and add fields" button.
3. Now, add a text field to store the location of the event (that is, where the event takes place). At the event field listing page (*admin/structure/types/manage/event/fields*), complete the "Add new field" form using the values from Table 6-2.

Table 6-2. Settings for adding a location field to the Event content type

Field	Value
Label	Location
Field name	location
Type of data	Text
Form element	Text field

4. Click Save. This will take us to the configuration settings page for the Location field. We will just use the default settings here, so click the "Save field settings" button, and then "Save settings" on the following form, to finish.

Access Control

Now that we've got the content type created and configured properly, we need to grant permissions to our members to allow them to create events.

In the administrative toolbar, go to People→Permissions (*admin/people/permissions*) and set the permissions as shown in Table 6-3. Click the "Save permissions" button when you are done.

Table 6-3. Permissions for the store

Permission	anonymous user	authenticated user	editor
Node			
Event Create new content		Checked	
Event Edit own content		Checked	
Event Edit any content			Checked
Event Delete own content			Checked
Event Delete any content			Checked

Spotlight: Date Module

The main building block for the site is our new Event content type. The information that we need it to provide us with is "where" and "when." We have taken care of the "where" part in our initial setup. The Date module helps us effectively answer the "when" question, in an incredibly flexible manner.

As mentioned previously, our real interest in the Date module is the ability to add a field to our Event content type to indicate date and time. However, looking at the Date module more closely, there are a few extra pieces worth noting.

Date Submodules

A core requirement of all modules in the Date package is the Date API module. The Date API module provides a set of underlying functionality for date handling. These functions consist of things like utility functions for generating month and day names, converting between date formats, and even generating date input select boxes. Though covering the full extent of the API is outside the scope of this chapter, it is worth noting that any module in Drupal that performs any sort of date handling or manipulation could take advantage of this module.

The Date module also ships with modules to extend a basic date field functionality, like Date All Day, which lets you specify that an event happens for an entire day, or Date Repeat, which offers support for repeating dates, so you can schedule recurring events (weekly, every third Monday, etc.).

Date Tools is a utility module in the package. It sports a Date Wizard, which can autocreate a content type, date field, view, and calendar from a form you fill out. Once you've read this chapter and understand how the underlying mechanics work, this feature can be useful for shortcutting future site buildouts. The Date Tools module also provides conversion tools that can change your data from one type of date field to another, and import tools that can help migrate data from the legacy Event module to date fields.

Finally, the Date module offers integration with other contributed modules through the Date Context, Date Migration, and Date Views modules, which expose date field data to the Context (*http://drupal.org/project/context*), Migrate (*http://drupal.org/project/migrate*), and Views modules (*http://drupal.org/project/views*), respectively.

Date Field Types

At its most basic level, the Date module itself defines three field types for adding date fields to content types, depending on how you care to represent them. The differences among these fields are summarized in Table 6-4.

Table 6-4. Fields offered by the Date module

Name	Description	Example	Database storage
Date	Date field types are stored using the database system's internal "datetime" format for date handling. It has the advantage of being able to use database-specific functions for date handling, including ease of extracting a single part of the date, but with the caveat of inconsistent support across database systems.	2012-02-24 01:28:00	datetime
Date (ISO format)	Store a date in the database as an ISO8601 date, used for historical (pre-1000 A.D.) or partial dates (for example, only a year and no day or month). This field type should be avoided otherwise, as it's extremely expensive to sort and perform conversions on this style of date.	2012-02-24T01:28:00	varchar(20)
Date (Unix timestamp)	Datestamp field types are stored using the common Unix timestamp format containing the number of seconds since January 1, 1970. As such, these have a limited date range available (1901 A.D.–2038 A.D. on most systems) but are quick to calculate time zone offsets and sort in listings. A legacy format that is supported across all database systems.	1330075725	int(11)

 For much, much more than you ever wanted to know about the pros and cons of various date storage formats, there's an interesting discussion on the Events working group at *http://groups.drupal.org/node/731*.

Because the Aurora Book Club has no intention of moving from MySQL, and all dates will be well within "normal" ranges, we will be using the standard Date field type for our site.

Date Form Elements

In addition to the base field types, the Date module also defines three form elements for entering date information, which are pictured in Figure 6-2:

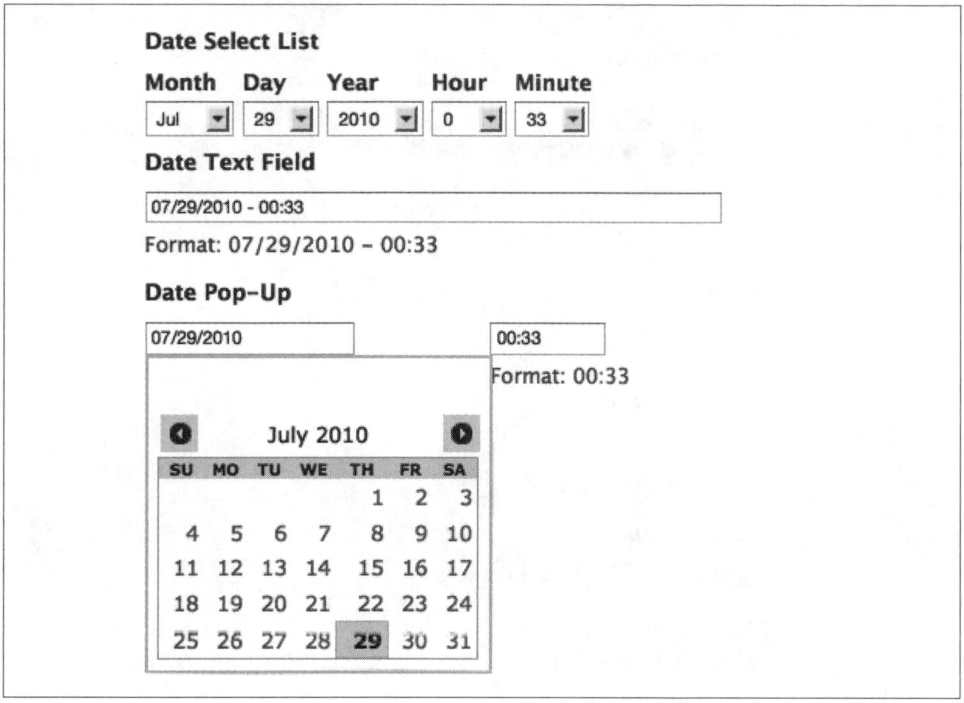

Figure 6-2. Date form elements

Select list
> Presents a series of drop-down lists for each of year, month, day, hour, minute, and second, based on the configured granularity for the date field defined by the data settings.

Text field
> Provides a simple text field for date entry that will then be converted to the appropriate storage format. The advantage of this widget is that it lets advanced users enter dates much faster. However, for the uninitiated, it can be frustrating if your natural date entry format is not properly recognized.

Pop-up calendar
> Adds an elegant, user-friendly option for date value entry. This widget uses Java-Script to present a calendar pop up when a user clicks in the date text field. The user can then click the date on the calendar to select the date that he wants.

If the Date Repeat Field module is enabled, you will also see an extra option for each element to add it with "Repeat options." This will add another fieldset below the form element, where you may configure it as a recurring event, as shown in Figure 6-3.

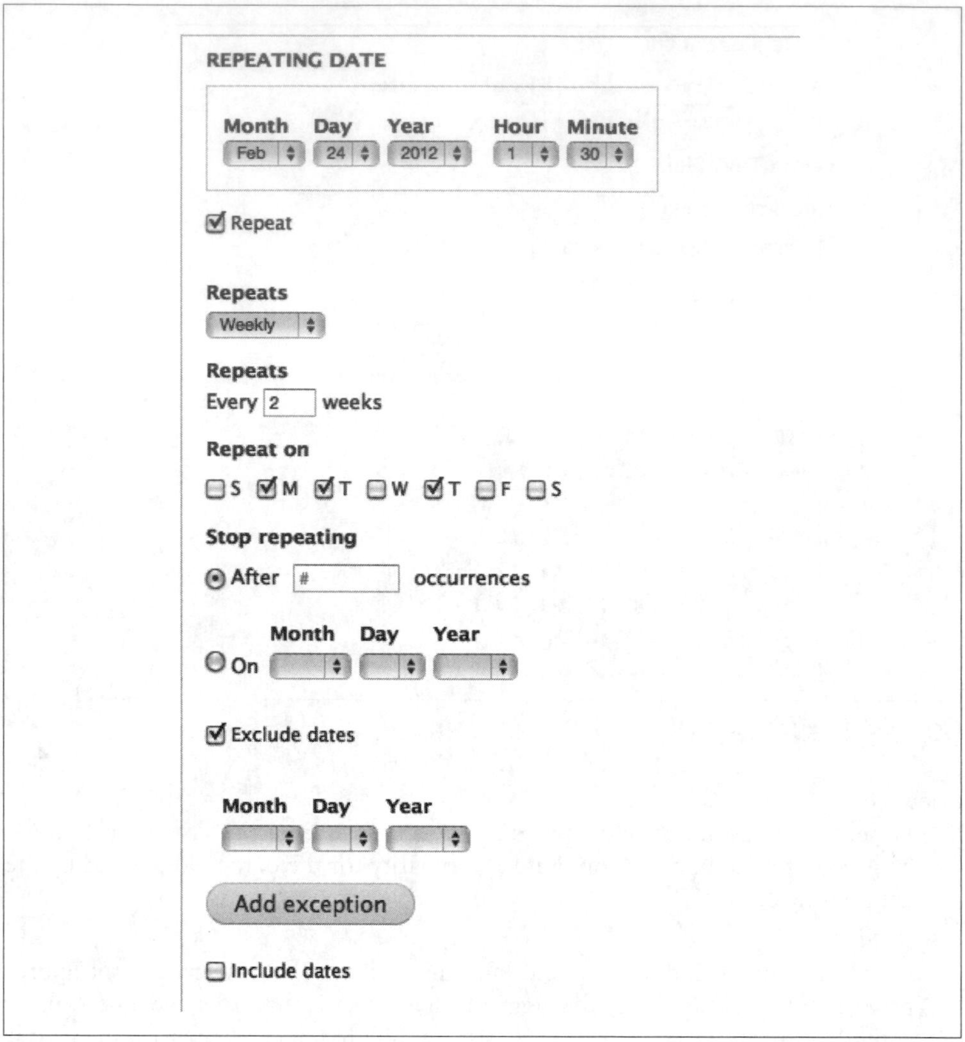

Figure 6-3. Date repeat options

Here, you may specify the frequency with which an event should recur: for example, every week, the first Monday of the month, or daily except for statutory holidays. Rather than making a separate Event node for each repetition of the event, which would get costly in terms of data storage (not to mention annoying to update if a title or description needed changing), Date Repeat Field stores the repetition patterns in a format called RRULE from the iCalendar specification (*http://www.ietf.org/rfc/rfc2445.txt*). The Calendar module can then read these rules and display the events as intended, as well as generate feeds for easy import into other calendar applications such as iCal or Outlook.

For Aurora Book Club's purposes, meetings aren't predictable enough to make them repeating events. However, the "Pop-up calendar" form element offers improved usability for date selection, so we will incorporate it into our site.

Date Field Settings

There are quite a few settings available specific to date fields and different from other field types, as shown in Figures 6-4 and 6-5.

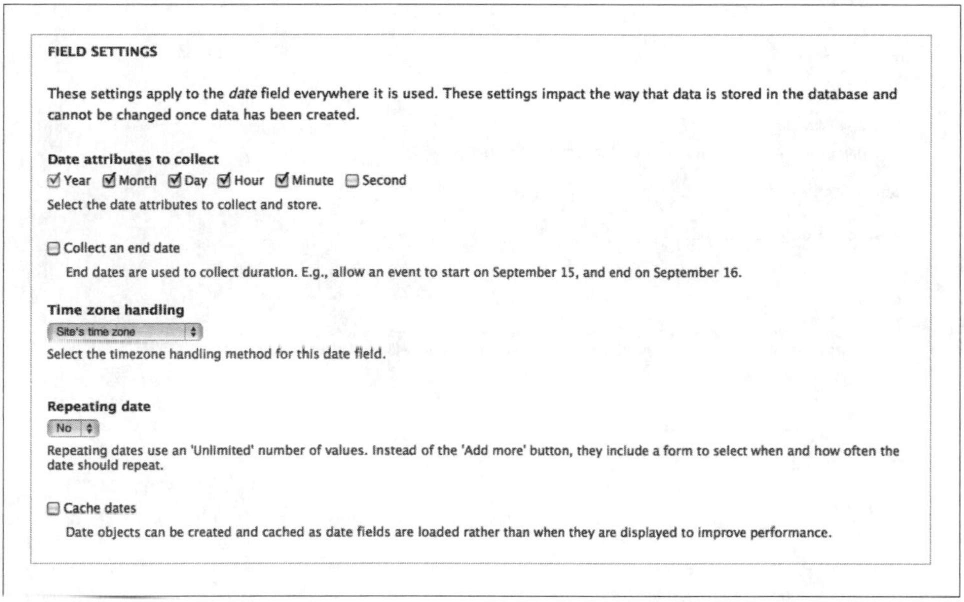

FIELD SETTINGS

These settings apply to the *date* field everywhere it is used. These settings impact the way that data is stored in the database and cannot be changed once data has been created.

Date attributes to collect
☑ Year ☑ Month ☑ Day ☑ Hour ☑ Minute ☐ Second
Select the date attributes to collect and store.

☐ Collect an end date
End dates are used to collect duration. E.g., allow an event to start on September 15, and end on September 16.

Time zone handling
Site's time zone ⬍
Select the timezone handling method for this date field.

Repeating date
No ⬍
Repeating dates use an 'Unlimited' number of values. Instead of the 'Add more' button, they include a form to select when and how often the date should repeat.

☐ Cache dates
Date objects can be created and cached as date fields are loaded rather than when they are displayed to improve performance.

Figure 6-4. Date field settings

Date attributes to collect

This setting dictates how much information will be retained about the dates supplied. The check boxes for Year, Month, Day, Hour, Minute, and Second can be selected independently to provide extreme flexibility. For instance, if we wanted someone's birthday (but not a full birth date), we could select only Month and Day like "July 10." For the purpose of event management, the default selection of Year, Month, Day, Hour, Minute is suitable, which allows us to display the date like July 10, 2008 - 7:30.

Note that this setting will impact the date entry widget, in that only the appropriate options will be displayed.

Collect an end date

Optionally, you can specify an end date for a given date, which we'll want to do for Aurora Book Club since we're tracking events and when they begin and end. However, for fields such as birthday, this setting would remain off.

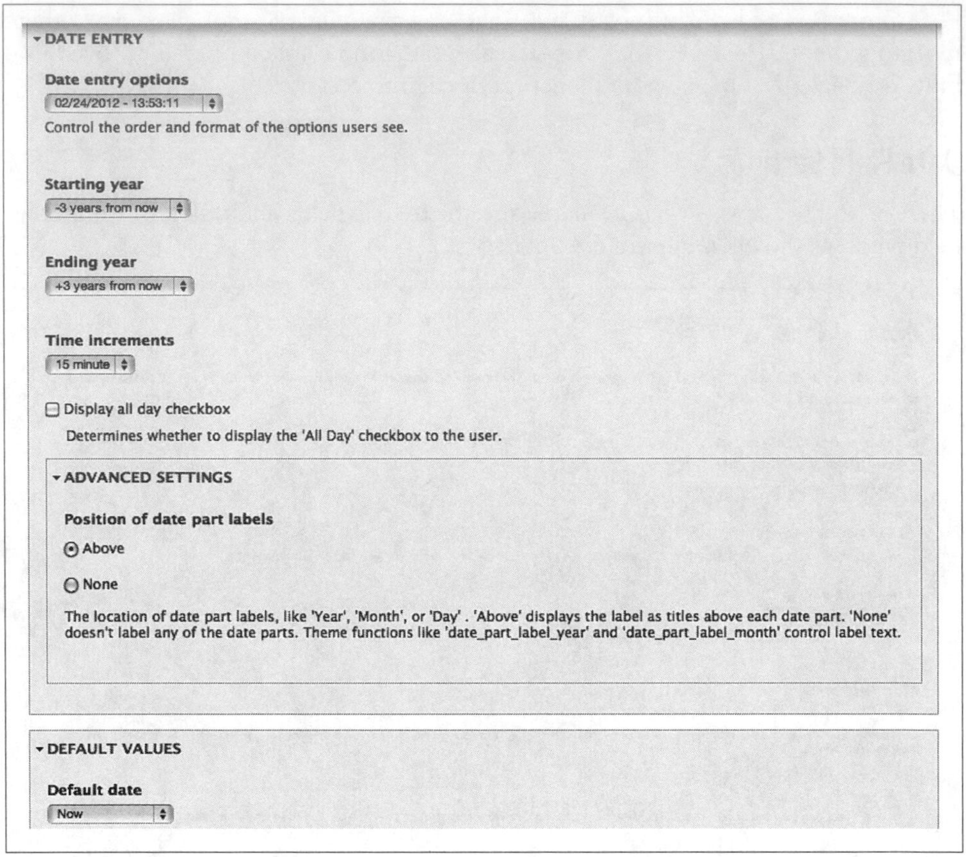

Figure 6-5. Date field instance settings

Time zone handling

The time zone handling settings allow us to configure how time zones should affect the stored date values and whether conversions should be performed. The options are described in Table 6-5.

Table 6-5. Date field time zone options

Option	Description
Site's time zone	The time zone specified for the entire site, specified in the administrative toolbar at Configuration→"Regional and language"→Regional Settings (*admin/config/regional/settings*). Useful for making sure each date field shares a consistent time throughout the site, even if users are from different time zones.
Date's time zone	Adds a "Time zone" drop-down next to the date widget to specify the time zone for the date. Useful for sites where many users from many different time zones will be creating events across the globe.

Option	Description
User's time zone	The time zone specified in each user's account settings (if the "Users may set their own time zone" option is enabled under Configuration→"Regional and language"→Regional Settings (*admin/config/regional/settings*). This option is useful if you mainly have events in one time zone, but users from many different places, and want to ensure the start time always appears correct for your visitors.
UTC	Coordinated Universal Time (UTC), which is informally equivalent to GMT. This is a standard time zone that is the same across all systems.
No time zone conversion	For events with dates only, rather than dates and times, or for sites with both local events and users. This option performs no time zone conversions on the date.

For the book club, we will not have to worry about doing time zone conversions, as all members will be local.

 You should set this time zone handling value with care, especially when dealing with international events posted to an international audience. The last thing you want is for your band's rock concert to show up on the wrong day of the week if it's viewed by a reader a few time zones away from you!

Repeating date

With the optional Date Repeat Field module enabled, you can specify a particular date field to allow repeating events.

Cache dates

If you're using date fields that can accept multiple or repeating values, this advanced setting can speed things up by precaching them for quicker retrieval. For single date values, it has no effect. If you're not actively experiencing date-related performance problems—such as with the Full Calendar module (*http://drupal.org/project/fullcalendar*)—leave this unchecked.

Date entry options

The "Date entry options" setting allows us to configure the format that will be used when displaying the date value. A variety of international formats are supported. There is also a "Custom format" option for the "Select list" and "Text field" widgets, which allows an arbitrary date format to be used for ultimate flexibility. The custom format is set using PHP's date() formatting syntax (*http://php.net/date*).

Starting year/Ending year

This setting gives us control over how many years will be listed in the widget for a user to select from. If the current year is 2012, you can allow people to choose between 2009 (–3 years) and 2015 (+3). For our event site, there is probably little point in using a wide range here, particularly to allow support for events in the distant past. However, for something like a birthday field, this can be handy to ensure validity of values.

Time increments

The "Time increments" setting allows us to constrain the granularity of minutes stored in a date field. By default, minutes may be entered in 15-minute increments, which only exposes minute selections of 00, 15, 30, and 45.

Display all day

If you're using the Date All Day module, this checkbox will appear, which lets you expose an "All day" selection on the date widget.

Position of date part labels

With this advanced setting, you can customize where you would like to display the label in relation to its field: above the field, within the field (either as an option in a select list or inserted inside a text field), or not at all.

The "Select list" widget has a few more options. Despite its name, we can actually have text field entry for certain values in the date, mixing drop-downs and text fields. For instance, rather than having a select list of 31 days, we could set Day to be a text field input, in which case Drupal will render the input as select lists for year and month with a small text field for day. This option again allows us full control over the widget and a chance to select the interface that's easiest to use for our target audience.

Default values

The "Default values" setting specifies what value the field starts with when presented to the user. The "No default value" and Now settings are pretty straightforward. Relative will let you set the default to a date that is relative to the current time, such as two days from now. To set up a relative default, you must enter a value in Customize Default Value that uses PHP's `strtotime()` syntax, such as +2 days. You can find out more about `strtotime()` at *http://www.php.net/manual/en/function.strtotime.php*.

As you can see, the Date module offers options for nearly any date entry use case that you can imagine!

Hands-On: Adding Dates

In this section, we will enhance our basic Event content type by adding a date field, so that members may schedule meetings.

Add the Date Field

1. In the administrative toolbar, click on Modules (*admin/modules*) and enable the following modules:

    • Date/Time package

        — Date

        — Date API

—Date Popup

2. Next, go to Structure→"Content types" (*admin/structure/types*) and click the "manage fields" link for the Event content type (*admin/structure/types/manage/event/fields*). Complete the "New field" form with the values in Table 6-6. As noted earlier, the Date field type is most appropriate for our site, since it is more performant than ISO dates, and our date values will remain within "normal" ranges.

Table 6-6. Settings for adding a time field to the Event content type

Field	Value
Label	Time
Field name	time
Select a field type	Date
Select a widget	Pop-up calendar

3. Click Save. This brings us first to the field settings page for our new Time field. It's worth taking a moment to discuss the available options and why we're choosing the ones that we are:

- The "Date attributes to collect" setting dictates which fields will appear in the form. Because it's pretty unusual to schedule events down to the second, we will go for just Year, Month, Day, Hour, and Minute granularity (the default).

- Most meetings will happen over a range of time; for example, 12pm to 2pm on August 29. As a result, we want to check the "Collect an end date" option to add a second field to any date field for exactly this purpose. However, for the odd day-long event, such as April 16, National Librarian Day, we want to make specifying the "to date" optional.

- For "Time zone handling," because the Aurora Book Club is a local book club with all members in the same region, there is no reason to factor time zones into the meeting events. Therefore, we will set this value to "No timezone conversion."

Enter the values in Table 6-7, and click the "Save field settings" button to complete adding the configuration.

Table 6-7. Time field settings

Field	Value
Date attributes to collect	(all selected except "Second") (default)
Collect an end date	Checked
	Required: Unchecked
Time zone handling	No timezone conversion
Cache dates	Unchecked

4. Click "Save field settings" to be directed to the second settings form. We can use most of the defaults here. Change the field values as shown in Table 6-8.

Table 6-8. Event Time field settings

Field	Value
Event settings	
Required field	Checked
More settings and values	
Date entry options	(select a format such as Feb 24 2012 - 02:19:39am)
Starting year	−1 year from now
Ending year	+3 years from now

5. Click "Save settings," to return to the "Manage fields" tab (*admin/structure/types/manage/event/fields*). Reorder the fields as follows and click Save:
   - Name
   - Time
   - Location
   - Body

With the content type fully created, our members can now post events to the site! To try it out, go to "Add content"→Event (*node/add/event*) and complete the form with the settings in Table 6-9, then click Save. If all has gone well, you should see something like the page in Figure 6-6. Go ahead and create a few more events for the Aurora Book Club.

Table 6-9. Initial example event

Field	Value
Name	Monthly meeting
Time	
From date	(choose tomorrow's date and the current time)
To date	(choose tomorrow's date and a later time)
Location	The Book Nook on Main Street
Body	Andrew and Camryn are bringing cookies.

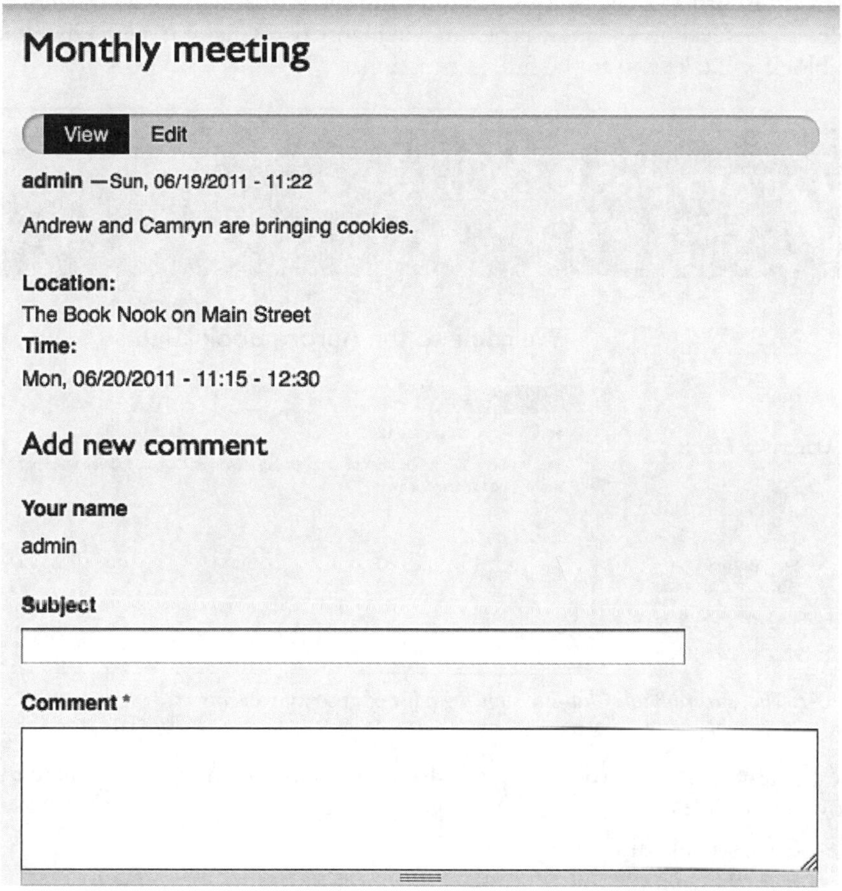

Monthly meeting

View   Edit

admin —Sun, 06/19/2011 - 11:22

Andrew and Camryn are bringing cookies.

Location:
The Book Nook on Main Street
Time:
Mon, 06/20/2011 - 11:15 - 12:30

Add new comment

Your name
admin

Subject

Comment *

Figure 6-6. Our initial event

Hands-On: Upcoming Events View

Now that we've created our Event content type and started populating some content, it's clear that we need to add in a way to access all our event data. For part of the book club's requirements, we need an Upcoming Events listing that will allow members to quickly see the meetings happening in the coming days or weeks. To achieve this, we will use the Views module to create our block. Keep in mind that when building views of event data, we generally want to do our sorting or our limiting on the new date field we added, not the content's created or updated time, as we normally do.

We will create a simple block view of published events where the event's time field is in the future. In terms of the views configuration, having a date value "greater than now" represents dates "in the future." Finally, the view will be sorted in chronological (or ascending) order of the event's date (not the event posting's created date). When completed, this section will look as pictured in Figure 6-7. Clicking the event name link in the block will take you to the full information.

Figure 6-7. The Aurora Book Club site showing a list of upcoming events

1. In the administrative toolbar, click Modules (*admin/modules*) and enable the following modules:
   - Chaos Tool Suite package
     — Chaos tools
   - Date/Time package
     — Date Views
   - Other package
     — Advanced help
   - Views package
     — Views
     — Views UI
2. Once the modules are enabled, go to Structure→Views (*admin/structure/views*) and click "Add new view" (*admin/structure/views/add*).
3. Fill out the view form using the values in Table 6-10.

Table 6-10. The Upcoming Events view configuration values

View setting	Value
View name	Upcoming Events
Description	Checked; "A block list of upcoming events"
Show	*Content* of type *Event* sorted by *Newest first*
Create a page	Unchecked
Create a block	Checked
Block settings	
Block title	Upcoming Events (default)
Display format	*HTML list* of titles (linked)
Items per page	5 (default)

4. Clicking the "Continue & edit" button places us in the full Views interface with our basic view built. From here, we can customize our view.

5. First, we will add our time field to our view. In the Fields section, click the "add" button, and select the "Content: Time" field. Click the "Apply (all displays)" button, then uncheck the "Create a label" box to remove an unnecessary "Time." label on each entry. Click the "Apply (all displays)" button to save the field.

6. Next, we'll use our time field to only show future events. Date handles this slightly oddly compared to other modules, with a single filter for all date fields that can then be more specifically configured. In the Filter criteria section, click the "add" button, and select "Date: Date (node)." Click the "Apply (all displays)" button to save, and then choose the "Content: Time (field_time)" field as the "Date fields" value on the next screen.

7. Click "Apply and continue" to configure the filter. Under "Operator," choose "Is greater than or equal to," and change the "Select a date" field to "Enter a relative date," and type **now**. This is a relative value that will be constantly updated so our site will never show stale events in the Upcoming Events sidebar. Cool! When you're finished, click the "Apply (all displays)" button.

8. Now we will sort our events by the event date (not the date the content was created). In the "Sort criteria" section, click the "add" button, select "Content: Time - start date (field_time)" and click the "Apply (all displays)" button to save. On the next screen, make sure the "Sort ascending" setting is selected and click the "Apply (all displays)" button again.

9. We should also remove the old post date sort, which is no longer needed. Under "Sort criteria," click the "Content: Post date (desc)" link and click the Remove button.

10. Save the view, which should now look like Figure 6-8.

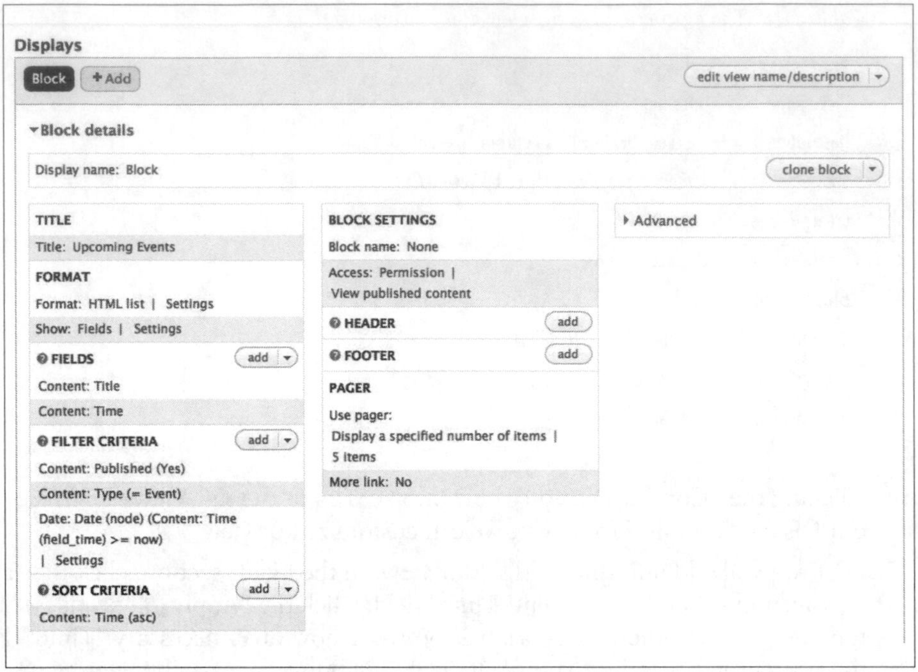

Figure 6-8. Upcoming Events block view

11. Because we created a block view, we should see no change to our site until we enable the block that we've created. To do this, go to Structure→Blocks (*admin/structure/block*). Drag the "View: Upcoming Events" row to the "Left sidebar" region (or simply change the region value in the drop-down) and click "Save blocks."

If you close the Overlay, you should now see a sidebar block on the left side of the page with your new Upcoming Events block, as pictured back in Figure 6-7!

Spotlight: Calendar Module

Although a simple list of upcoming events is very useful (particularly in a sidebar block), the book club has additional requirements for the display of the event data. As is extremely common for event management websites, this site needs an interactive calendar for browsing through past and future events. We will implement this feature using the Calendar module in conjunction with Views.

Calendar View Type

The Calendar module provides a new view type that shows the results of a view in a calendar rather than a list or table as with the default view types. Figure 6-9 shows the list of Drupal community events from *http://groups.drupal.org/events*, which also uses the Calendar module. Because Calendar builds on top of Views, all the standard Views tricks work to enhance a calendar, such as exposing filters for "Event type" as groups.drupal.org does.

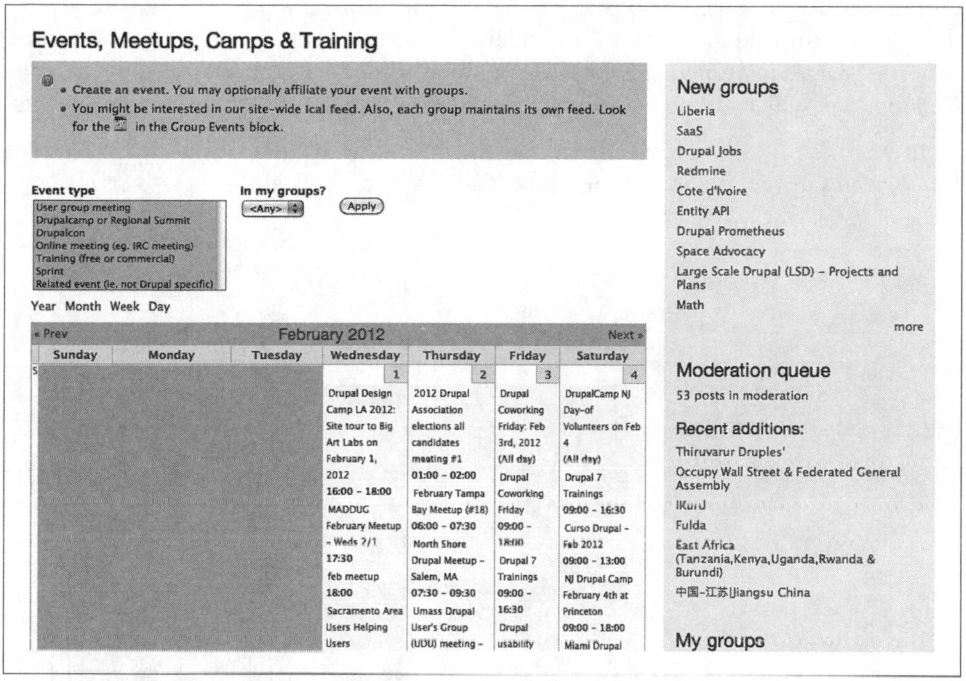

Figure 6-9. Event calendar at groups.drupal.org, using the Calendar module

The Calendar view type is one of the more complicated ones available. It provides full day, week, month, and year views of the event data on our site, with lots of links between views and paging through days, months, and years. To achieve this rich functionality, Calendar requires certain views arguments to exist, and to be ordered and configured in a certain way.

The Calendar view type then determines which view the user would like to see based on the arguments that exist. For example, if our view URL is *calendar*, the Calendar view will handle the paths described in Table 6-11.

Table 6-11. Calendar path-based display

Path	Calendar display
calendar	Month view, defaulting to the current month
calendar/1970	Year view, for the year 1970
calendar/1970-1	Month view for January 1970
calendar/1970-1-1	Day view for January 1, 1970

iCal Integration

In addition to creating a nice online calendar, the Calendar module can handle the need for book club members to be able to update their desktop calendars (in Microsoft Outlook or Apple's iCal) with the event information from the book club site. To do this, the desktop applications use a standardized format known as iCalendar (*http://en .wikipedia.org/wiki/iCalendar*), or iCal for short. Calendar comes with the Calendar iCal module, which allows us to easily provide this format for the interested members.

Figure 6-10 shows the groups.drupal.org events calendar after being imported from *http://groups.drupal.org/ical* to the Apple iCal desktop application.

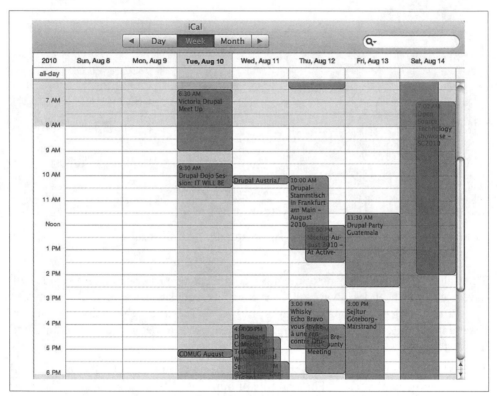

Figure 6-10. Event calendar iCal feed in the Apple iCal desktop application

Hands-On: Calendar View

In this section, we'll be enabling the Calendar view of book club events. Although this is potentially a daunting task, the Calendar module conveniently comes with a default view that handles most of the difficult bits for us. In this section, we'll alter that default calendar view to fit our requirements.

Figure 6-11 shows the finished Aurora Book Club calendar. Note the small iCal icon in the bottom-right corner. Clicking this link will download the calendar to an appropriate desktop application.

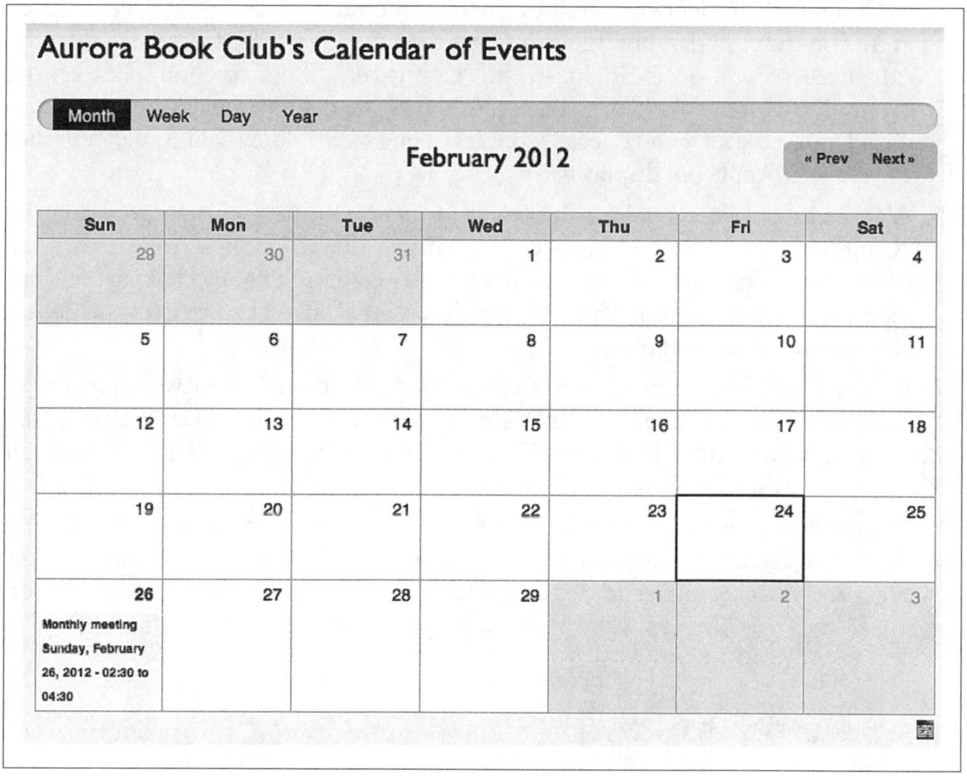

Figure 6-11. Completed event calendar, with iCal link

1. In the administrative toolbar, click Modules (*admin/modules*) and enable the following modules:
   - Date/Time package
     — Calendar
     — Calendar iCal
2. Go to Structure→Views (*admin/structure/views*). You should now see "calendar" listed and enabled by default.
3. Click the arrow next to the "edit" button in the Operations column next to the view, and choose "clone" in order to make your own version of it (*admin/structure/views/view/calendar/clone*). Give it a name of Aurora Calendar.

4. First, let's tell it to only show Event content in the calendar. Do this by clicking the "add" button in the Filters section, and selecting "Content: Type." Click "Apply (all displays)," then check the box under "Content types for Event," and click "Apply (all displays)" once more.

5. By default, the Calendar view uses the date the node was last changed to place events on the calendar, but we want to use the time of the event instead. Under the Advanced section on the right, in the "Contextual filters" section, click on the "Date: Date (node)" link. Scroll down to the "Date field(s)" field, uncheck "Content: Updated date," and check "Content: Time - start date (field_time)" instead. Then click "Apply (all displays)."

6. We need to make a similar adjustment for fields. In the Fields section, add the "Content: Time" field and uncheck the "Create a Label" box, as we did with the event block. Then, remove the "Content: Updated date" field by clicking on it and then the Remove button. This will show our event's date, rather than the node's last updated date, in the view.

7. As a minor cosmetic item, note that the current title of the view in preview is "calendar." Let's change that to "Aurora Book Club's Calendar of Events" by clicking on the "title" link in the Title section and changing it. Click "Apply (all displays)" when finished.

8. Finally, we should add an entry to the main menu so visitors can find the calendar page. The default view already provides us with a path of "calendar," which makes sense for us to keep. To add this to the menu link, edit the "Page settings" section according to Table 6-12. Click Apply after you enter the menu settings.

Table 6-12. The Calendar view's Page settings

Calendar Page: Page settings	Value
Menu	Type: Normal menu entry
	Title: Events Calendar
	Menu: Main menu
	Weight: 1 (so it appears after "Home")

9. Save the view, which should look like Figure 6-12.

Now we have a working events calendar that users can reach by clicking on the "Events calendar" link in the main menu navigation. Next, we need a way for club members to sign up for these events.

Spotlight: Flag Module

The Flag module is an incredibly flexible module that allows you to create relationships between users and content on your site. After you create a flag, an item can be marked with it a few different ways, including links displayed below content, as shown in Figure 6-13, or checkboxes displayed on the edit form, as shown in Figure 6-14.

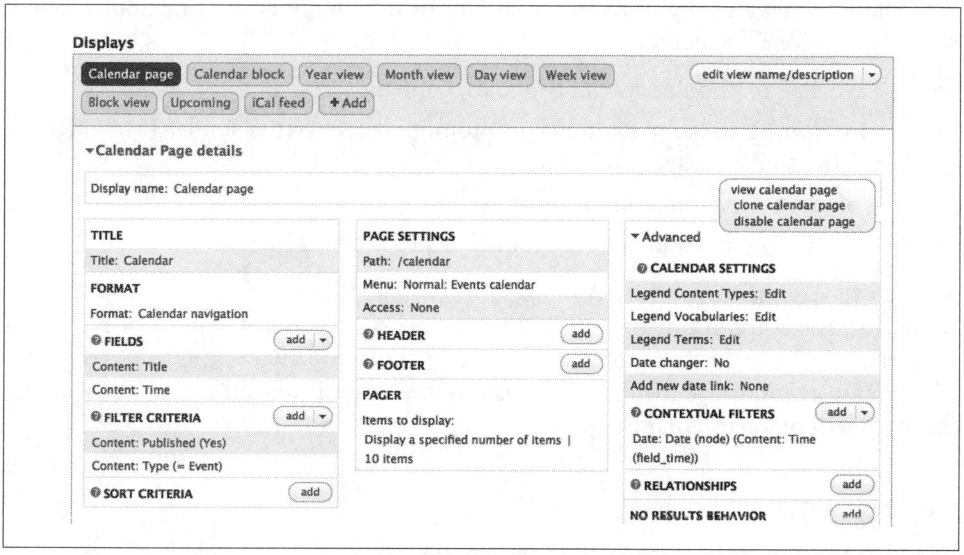

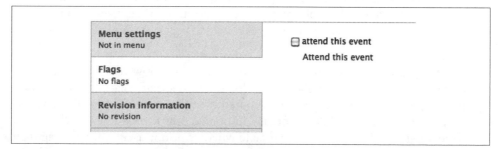

Figure 6-12. *Upcoming Events calendar view settings*

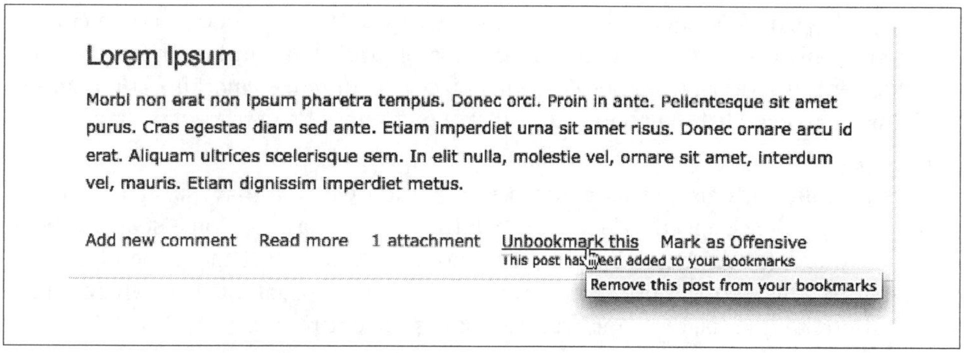

Lorem Ipsum

Morbi non erat non ipsum pharetra tempus. Donec orci. Proin in ante. Pellentesque sit amet purus. Cras egestas diam sed ante. Etiam imperdiet urna sit amet risus. Donec ornare arcu id erat. Aliquam ultrices scelerisque sem. In elit nulla, molestie vel, ornare sit amet, interdum vel, mauris. Etiam dignissim imperdiet metus.

Add new comment   Read more   1 attachment   Unbookmark this   Mark as Offensive
This post has been added to your bookmarks
Remove this post from your bookmarks

Figure 6-13. *Flags as links shown on content*

Menu settings
Not in menu

Flags
No flags

Revision information
No revision

☐ attend this event
Attend this event

Figure 6-14. *Flags as checkboxes shown on the node edit form*

Upon installation, the Flag module defines a "bookmark" relationship, allowing users to maintain a list of bookmarks (or posts they find interesting) on the site. However, this default behavior only touches the surface of the Flag module's flexibility. Some possible uses for Flag include:

- A "favorite" or "bookmark" flag to mark content
- A "promote" flag (or many different promote flags) that is similar to the default "Promote to Frontpage" checkbox
- An "offensive" flag for comments or nodes
- A "friend" flag that allows users to mark other users as friends

As you can see, there are a variety of uses for flagging content. After creating a flag for some purpose, you can construct views that create lists of content that has been flagged by users. We'll use this functionality to let users indicate whether they plan to attend a book club event. Once the flag relationships are created, we can create a view to list the attendees of a particular event.

Flag Settings

The Flag module offers an incredible array of flexible options, detailed as follows:

Flag type
Each flag can be associated with a particular type of entity: nodes, comments, or users. This makes the Flag module a versatile tool that can be applied to many different situations, from bookmarking pieces of content to marking comments as abusive to establishing relationships between users.

Global flag
By default, flags are per user; for example, each user can have a separate list of items that she's flagged as her favorite. If the "Global flag" option is selected, however, the flag becomes a binary yes or no, associated with the piece of content directly. This setting is useful for setting up a "Featured content" flag, where a piece of content either is, or is not, featured across the entire site.

Messages settings
The Flag messages settings, shown in Figure 6-15, allow fine-grained control over all text related to the flag: the link text and description for flagging and unflagging content, and the confirmation messages shown to users who interact with the flag.

Flag access
The Flag access settings, as illustrated in Figure 6-16, allow you to set which role or roles may set or unset a flag. This allows you to specify that only editors may mark a piece of content as "Featured content," or that normal authenticated users may Like, but not Un-Like, content. Additional restrictions follow, which vary depending on the type of flag, to dictate whether or not users can only flag their own content (or themselves, in the case of a user flag). For example, it probably

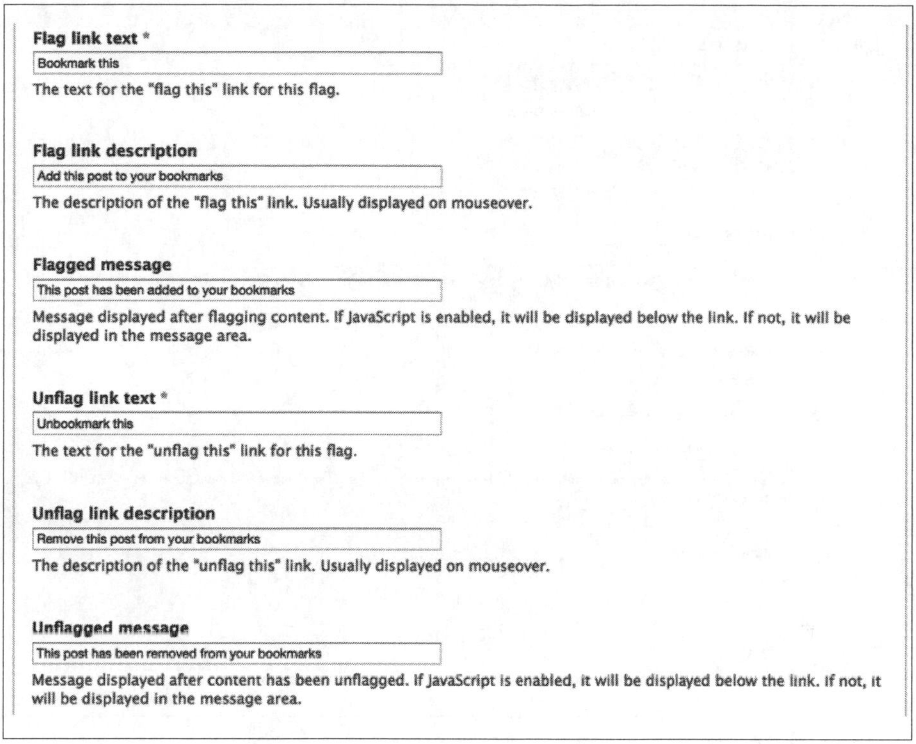

Flag link text *

`Bookmark this`

The text for the "flag this" link for this flag.

Flag link description

`Add this post to your bookmarks`

The description of the "flag this" link. Usually displayed on mouseover.

Flagged message

`This post has been added to your bookmarks`

Message displayed after flagging content. If JavaScript is enabled, it will be displayed below the link. If not, it will be displayed in the message area.

Unflag link text *

`Unbookmark this`

The text for the "unflag this" link for this flag.

Unflag link description

`Remove this post from your bookmarks`

The description of the "unflag this" link. Usually displayed on mouseover.

Unflagged message

`This post has been removed from your bookmarks`

Message displayed after content has been unflagged. If JavaScript is enabled, it will be displayed below the link. If not, it will be displayed in the message area.

Figure 6-15. Flag messages settings

doesn't make sense for users to be able to flag their own content as "Best of site." Finally, for comment and node flags, in this section you can choose which content types are flaggable.

Display options

Finally, you can choose how the flag should be displayed in the UI, as shown in Figure 6-17. Choose any combination of options for how flags should appear: a checkbox on the content edit form, links shown in the teaser view or full page of a node, or on a user profile. The Flag module even allows you to choose *how* the link represents itself when output, for ultimate control over your site's user experience. Select from a JavaScript toggle that can turn the flag on and off without a page refresh, a standard link, or even a confirmation form (which, naturally, has configurable confirmation and unconfirmation text settings).

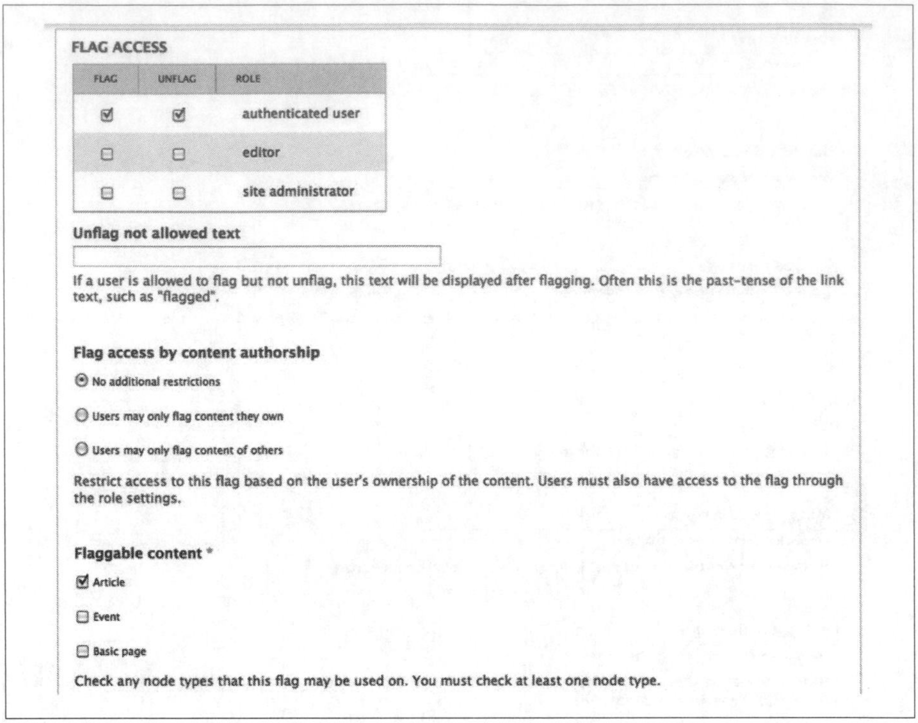

Figure 6-16. Flag access settings

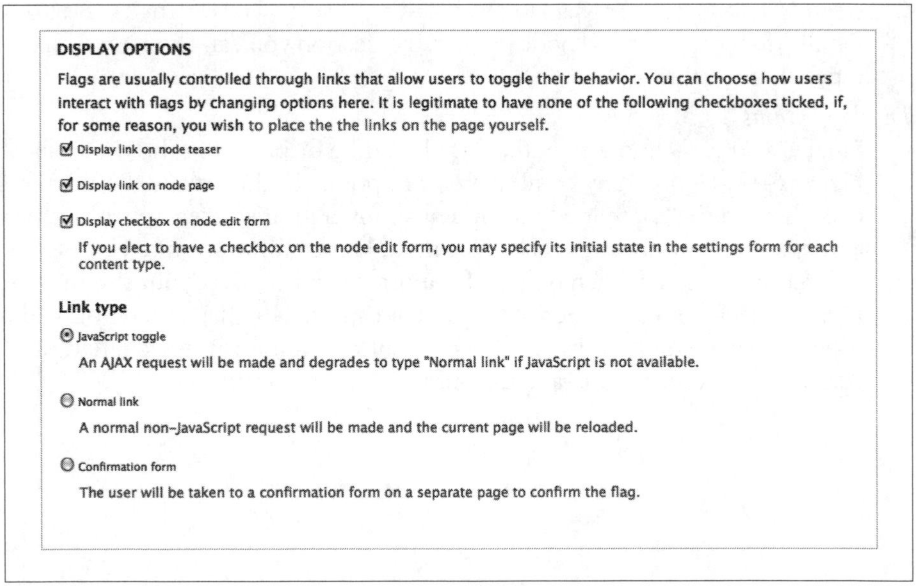

Figure 6-17. Flag display settings

Flag Actions Module

The Flag module also ships with the Flag Actions module, which allows you to associate one or more system tasks (publish or unpublish content, send an email, and so on) to take place when a flag is used. Flexible options exist for performing actions only after a flag has hit a certain threshold (for example, once five users have flagged something as "abusive"), and also to repeat the action every *n* times that this threshold is reached.

Figure 6-18 shows the Flag Actions module in action. Here, we've added a custom action to the Bookmarks flag so that once 10 or more people have flagged it as a favorite, the content will automatically get promoted to the front page. This is a useful way to involve your community in deciding what content is interesting and relevant on your website.

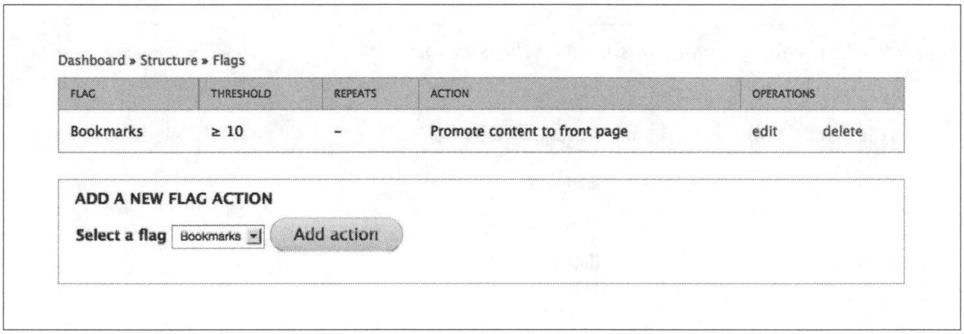

Figure 6-18. Flag actions settings

Hands-On: Flag Configuration

In this section, we will configure the Flag module to allow our users to indicate that they are attending our events, as pictured in Figure 6-19:

1. In the administrative toolbar, go to Modules (*admin/modules*) and enable the "Flags package: Flag" module.

2. Now go to Structure→Flags (*admin/structure/flags*) to manage the defined flags. By default, the Flag module defines a Bookmarks flag when installed. We can either add a new flag or edit the default one to suit our purpose. As we won't be using Bookmarks on this site, we're going to edit the default. Click the "edit" link next to the bookmark flag (*admin/structure/flags/edit/bookmarks*). Fill out the form according to Table 6-13.

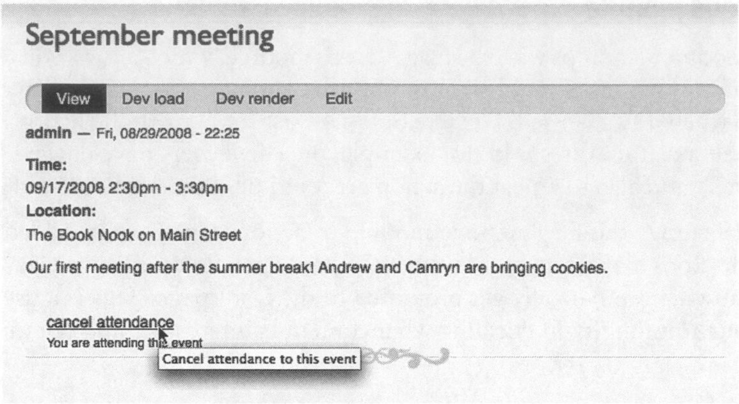

Figure 6-19. Attendance indicator shown on the node form

Table 6-13. Attendance flag configuration

Field	Value
Name	attendance
Title	Attendance
Global flag	Unchecked (default)
Messages	
Flag link text	attend this event
Flag link description	Attend this event
Flagged message	You are attending this event
Unflag link text	cancel attendance
Unflag link description	Cancel attendance to this event
Unflagged message	You are no longer attending this event
Flag access	
Flag access	Flag and Unflag both checked for authenticated user (default)
Unflag not allowed text	(leave blank - default)
Flag access by content authorship	No additional restrictions (default)
Flaggable content	Article: Unchecked, Event: Checked
Display options	
Display link on node teaser	Unchecked
Display link on node page	Checked (default)
Display check box on node edit form	Unchecked
Link type	JavaScript toggle

3. Clicking Submit will create our attendance flag. We can now go to any events that we previously created and click the "attend this event" link.

Hands-On: Attendee View

The book club would like users to see a list of who will be attending each event. For this, we will need to create a new view, pictured in Figure 6-20.

Figure 6-20. Event attendees list view

1. In the administrative toolbar, go to Structure→Views and click on the "Add new view" link (*admin/structure/views/add*).

2. Complete the form according to Table 6-14 and then click the "Continue & edit" button.

Table 6-14. Attendees view settings

Setting	Value
View name	attendees
Description	Checked; "Attendees for a given event"
Show	*Users* sorted by *Newest first*
Page: Display format	*HTML list* of *Fields*

3. The first thing we need is a relationship to give us access to the flag information related to our users in our view. Open the Advanced section, and click the "add" button in the Relationships section. Check the "Flags: User's flagged content" relationship and click "Apply (all displays)." Complete the relationship settings based on Table 6-15 and click "Apply (all displays)" once more.

Table 6-15. Settings for the Flags relationship

Advanced: Relationship	Value
Flags: User's flagged content	Include only users who have flagged content: Checked
	Flagged: Attendance

4. We want our view to show the users who have flagged a given Event node; therefore, we need to add a contextual filter for the Node ID that was flagged. To do this, we click the "add" button for "Contextual filters." Check the "Flags: Content ID" argument and click "Apply (all displays)." We only want this list to appear for Event nodes, so we need to limit when this contextual filter is used. Configure the filter as shown in Table 6-16, then click Apply.

Table 6-16. Settings for the Flags contextual filter

Advanced: Contextual filter	Value
When the filter value IS *NOT* in the URL	Display contents of "No results found"
When the filter value IS in the URL or a default is provided	Specify validation criteria : Checked
	Validator: Content
	Content Types: Event: Checked

5. Let's add the aforementioned "no results found" text by clicking the "add" button in the No Results Behavior section on the right. Check "Global: Text area" and click "Apply (all displays)." Give it a label of "No attendees" and fill out the text field with "No attendees for this event yet." Then, click "Apply (all displays)." Now when we click on an event with no signups yet, it will show this text instead of a blank page.

6. It would be helpful if the attendees were listed in an ordered list so that we could quickly glance at the total number of people attending. To add this functionality, we need to change the style of the view. Click the Settings link for "Format: HTML list" and set the "List type" field to "Ordered list." Click "Apply (all displays)" to save the change.

7. To complete the view, we need to add the display as a tab on the event node. Complete the View Page settings according to Table 6-17.

Table 6-17. The Attendees view Page settings

Page settings	Value
Path	node/%/attendees
Menu	Type: Menu Tab
	Title: Attendees
	Weight: 5 (to put it as the last tab)

8. Save the view, which should look like Figure 6-21.

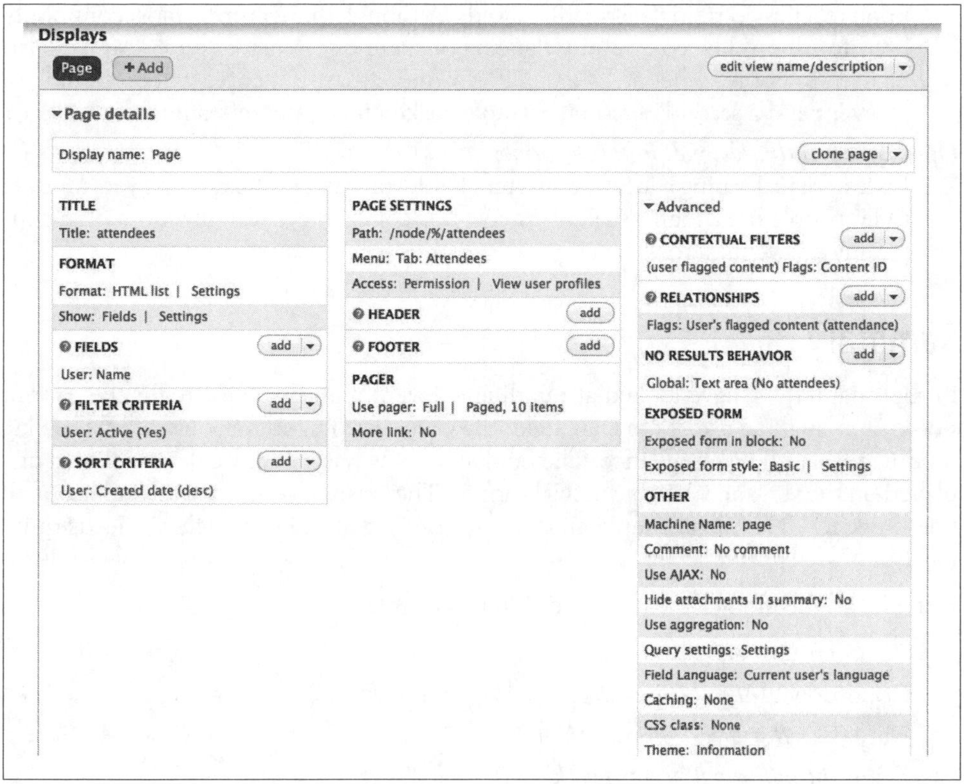

Figure 6-21. Event attendees list view settings

Now, when you visit an Event post, you should see an Attendees tab. Clicking on that tab will display a list of all of the users who have said they will attend the event.

Taking It Further

The site we have built covers all of the needs for the club. Down the road, the members may want to spruce things up a bit. Here are a few modules that could round out the site even more:

Full Calendar (http://drupal.org/project/fullcalendar)
> An alternative to the Calendar module that provides a JavaScript-based drag-and-drop calendar through an alternate Views format.

Countdown (http://drupal.org/project/countdown)
> This module adds a block that shows the time left until an event. This is a nice way to let people quickly know that the next meeting is in four days or four hours.

Flag Actions (part of the Flag module)
> The Flag module can be set up to send emails, and to unpublish or delete nodes upon reaching certain flagging thresholds. Although this feature is most commonly used for things like community flagging of spam or offensive content, it can also be used to notify someone by email if, say, more than 10 people will be coming to an event and a second person needs to be asked to supply refreshments.

OpenLayers (http://drupal.org/project/openlayers)
> Instead of just typing a location in a text field, you can use the OpenLayers module to let people use a map to select the location for each event, and view a map containing all events across the city.

Summary

In this chapter, we have looked at building an event management site for the Aurora Book Club, making use of the Date field, the Calendar plug-in for Views, and the Flag module for handling attendance. The book club now has a handy calendar that is displayed on the site and available in iCal format. They also have an easy-to-find list of all the attendees. The site is simple and easy to use, yet fits all of the club's needs quite nicely.

Here are all the modules we referenced in this chapter:

- Calendar (*http://drupal.org/project/calendar*)
- Countdown (*http://drupal.org/project/countdown*)
- Date (*http://drupal.org/project/date*)
- Event (*http://drupal.org/project/event*)
- Flag (*http://drupal.org/project/flag*)
- GMap (*http://drupal.org/project/gmap*)
- Location (*http://drupal.org/project/location*)
- Signup (*http://drupal.org/project/signup*)
- Views (*http://drupal.org/project/views*)

Additional resources:

- Date module handbook (*http://drupal.org/node/262062*)
- Event-related modules (*http://drupal.org/project/modules?filters=tid:61*)
- iCalendar (*http://en.wikipedia.org/wiki/ICalendar*)
- PHP date formatting (*http://php.net/date*)
- PHP strtotime (*http://www.php.net/manual/en/function.strtotime.php*)

CHAPTER 7

Managing Publishing Workflows

For large, content-driven web projects, building the initial site structure and getting the design "just so" is only the beginning of the work. If more than a handful of people are writing content for the site, the process of reviewing, editing, and publishing articles can be a Herculean task. Newspapers, online magazines, and even many large blogs with multiple contributors need tools to ensure that editors can effectively manage the review process. In this chapter, we'll be using Workbench, a series of modules that improve content management in Drupal, to build an editorial workflow for a news site. We'll also look at some other modules that can help us achieve this goal.

This chapter introduces the following modules:

Workbench (http://drupal.org/project/workbench)
> Improves the content management on a Drupal site. Workbench is the central part of the Workbench module suite.

Workbench Moderation (http://drupal.org/project/workbench_moderation)
> Part of the Workbench module suite. Allows administrators to define custom publishing states for content, like "In review" and "Ready for publication."

Workbench Access (http://drupal.org/project/workbench_access)
> Part of the Workbench module suite. Makes it possible to give editors access to content based on the category or menu item that is assigned to the content.

Taxonomy (core)
> Allows administrators to create and manage sets of categories or tags that can be used to organize content.

Pathauto (http://drupal.org/project/pathauto)
> Automatically creates path aliases for content, categories, and user profile pages.

If you would like to participate in the hands-on exercises in this chapter, you should install Drupal using the *Chapter 7: News website* installation profile from the book's sample code, which creates the example website on your web server. The completed website will look like the image pictured in Figure 7-1 and found at *http://workflow .usingdrupal.com*. For more information on using the book's sample code, see the Preface.

Figure 7-1. Our News website

Case Study

Our Media is a Vancouver-based independent news website. The content is mainly produced by volunteers, while a small staff of paid editors manages the website. They make sure the volunteers know where the next press conference is taking place, and actually review, edit, and publish the content that the volunteer reporters post.

In recent months, the site has grown more popular. More and more volunteers have signed up to write articles and make video reports—so many that the staff can hardly keep up with all the work. They've decided they need to delegate some of the editorial work in order to keep things feasible. This means that their site's editorial process needs to be changed.

After some meetings with a group of volunteers, they have come up with a new editorial process, which would be based on the editorial groups that already work together for Our Media. The groups are mostly topic centered: there is a group that works on international news, a group that covers politics, another that reports on cultural events, and so on. The team figures that if they could distribute the editorial work among those groups, rather than managing all the content centrally themselves, their workload would decrease significantly. Every group would be responsible for the content within its own section.

For this organizational change to be possible, however, the website needs some work. It needs to be set up in such a way that certain volunteer editors are only able to access content within certain categories. The editors also need an easy way to find the content they are responsible for. They should not have to look around in Drupal's administrative interface to find the content that they need: everything should be nicely grouped together in one place.

In the editorial interface, the volunteer editors should be able to easily find new content that reporters sent in for review. The editors should be able to review their content, send it back to the reporter if it needs work, and communicate with the reporters about changes they propose. If the editors make a change to the content themselves, a new version of the content should be saved, so the reporter's original is preserved. When dealing with a hot news story, editors should be able to publish a temporary, quick version of the article on the site, while editing and refining a final version behind the scenes.

Implementation Notes

Drupal core allows administrators to change the default publishing settings for each content type, and by deselecting the Published flag on content types, the editors can ensure that stories posted by contributors won't show up until they are published manually. However, the grunt work of checking for new unpublished posts, reviewing them, editing them, publishing them, and then saving the changes is cumbersome for sites with a lot of activity. We'll be using Workbench, a series of modules that was developed precisely to improve content management in Drupal.

Content management tools

On busy sites with a lot of content, Drupal core's built-in content management tools might not be adequate. In the case of Our Media, the staff wants to delegate the management of content to several editors, which means the site's editorial interface should be very easy to use. The Workbench module suite was developed to solve this problem, and solve it well.

First, Workbench provides editors with an easy-to-use landing page where they can find the site's content and work with it. It tries to get in the way as little as possible, while allowing editors to focus on their task, rather than on learning Drupal.

Workbench integrates very well with Drupal core. In fact, we'll combine Workbench with one of Drupal core's most powerful features, the Taxonomy module, which allows administrators to set up categories to organize a site's content.

Content access control

Recall that the staff of Our Media wants to empower volunteers with access to editorial tools, but only within their own designated sections. Once we've set up categories for each area, we'll use Workbench Access, part of the Workbench suite, to define an access control model for our content management, based on those categories. By doing this, we'll make sure that editors can only edit content in sections that are assigned to them.

Editorial workflow

Out of the box, Drupal allows any piece of content to be marked as "published" or "unpublished." The Our Media site needs something more advanced: it must be able to track the difference between an article that's an in-progress draft, one that's submitted to the editors for review, and one that's been approved and published.

Workbench Moderation, another part of the Workbench family of modules, comes in very handy here. We'll use it to set up custom "workflow states" for our articles and to control who has permission to move them from one state to another. When an article is posted on the site, it will need to move through those workflow states before it gets published.

Spotlight: Taxonomy

While this chapter focuses primarily on the Workbench module suite, we need to do some basic setup of our Drupal site in order to benefit from Workbench's full potential. One of those things we need to do beforehand is set up categories to organize our content, using the Taxonomy module.

If you're new to Drupal, you've probably wondered what *taxonomy* is—the word pops up all over the place, and it can sound a bit mysterious. Don't worry, it's just a technical term for a way of organizing and classifying things, like content on a website. If you've sorted your family photo album, filed your email in folders, or argued with a friend about whether a band is punk or ska, you've already worked with taxonomies!

If a site has a lot of content, editors need a way to group it into categories. By doing so, they make it possible for users to easily navigate the website and find the content they're looking for. Additionally, assigning content to categories, whether by using a predefined set of sections or a free-for-all tagging system, opens up all sorts of interesting possibilities. For instance, site builders can expose content with similar tags on article pages. Or they can turn the category pages into rich landing pages, pulling in all kinds of different content that has the same categories assigned to it.

Vocabularies and Terms

Creating a taxonomy for your site starts when you identify what kinds of content you'll have, and how it can be described. News articles, for example, might be classified by their subject matter or by the geographical area they cover. In Drupal, these groups of categories are called *vocabularies* (like Section). Each vocabulary contains specific *terms* (like "International affairs," "National news," or "Culture") that can be used to describe content. Whenever you post an article, a photograph, or a blog entry, you can select the terms that match it.

Drupal supports three kinds of vocabularies: simple lists of terms, organized hierarchies of terms, and "free tagging" vocabularies that allow you to define new terms as you post new content. Drupal's "Term reference" field type provides widgets that allow you to expose a vocabulary's terms as checkboxes, radio buttons, select lists, or auto-complete fields. Each is useful in different situations. Figure 7-2 shows an example of how each type of vocabulary might be used on a hypothetical news article content type.

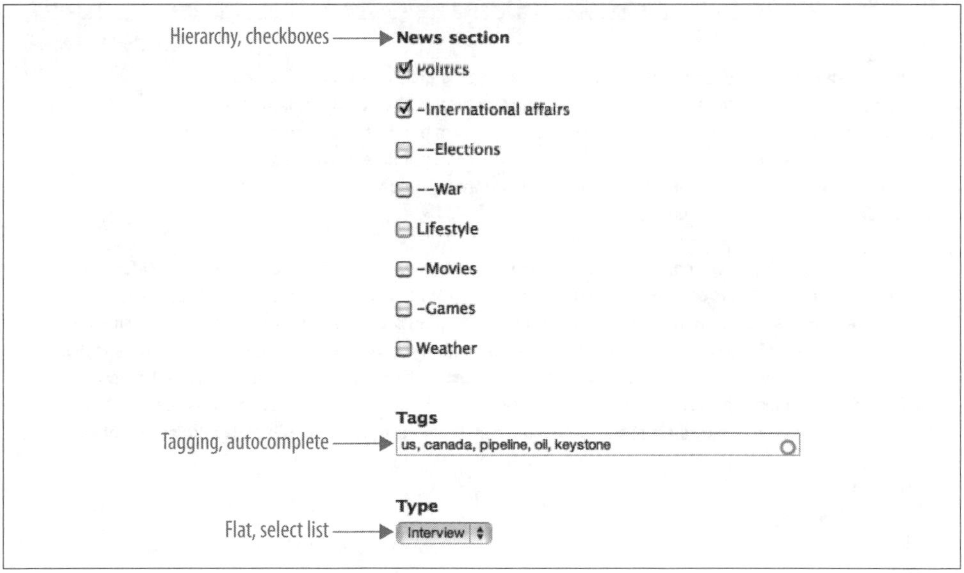

Figure 7-2. Examples of taxonomy types and widgets

Like other entities in Drupal (nodes, users, files), taxonomy terms can be extended with fields. The default fields for a term are Name and Description, but you can add whatever field you want. For example, it may be handy to provide a "Term image" field in order to add a picture for every term, which you can then show on the term overview page. And because term reference fields can be placed on taxonomy term entities, you can even tag your tags. Whoa.

The taxonomy system is incredibly powerful, and is one of Drupal's greatest assets as a content management system. In addition to the features provided out of the box, several contributed modules also make use of taxonomy in interesting ways, the Taxonomy Menu module (*http://drupal.org/project/taxonomy_menu*), which turns a vocabulary into a Drupal menu that can be placed in Primary or Secondary links.

Taxonomy Term Links

After you submit a piece of content, any terms it has attached will appear as links on the node page, as displayed in Figure 7-3. Each of these links displays a page listing all content to which that term has been applied, along with an RSS feed that visitors can subscribe to in order to receive notifications whenever new content with that term attached is posted.

Figure 7-3. Taxonomy terms are listed as links on the node page

Hands-On: Categorizing Content

The Taxonomy module is included in core and is enabled by default when you install Drupal, along with a Tags vocabulary, which you can use to allow users to freely tag their content. Let's use Drupal core's Taxonomy module to set up a "News section" vocabulary with predefined terms, in order to organize the articles that are posted on our news site:

1. In the administrative toolbar, click on Structure→Taxonomy (*admin/structure/taxonomy*). Click "Add vocabulary," enter the settings from Table 7-1 as shown in Figure 7-4, and click the Save button. After clicking Save, you will be redirected to the Taxonomy administration page. A message at the top of the overlay will confirm that you've successfully created a new vocabulary, called "News sections."

Table 7-1. "News sections" vocabulary settings

Setting	Value
Name	News sections
Description	Leave blank (default)

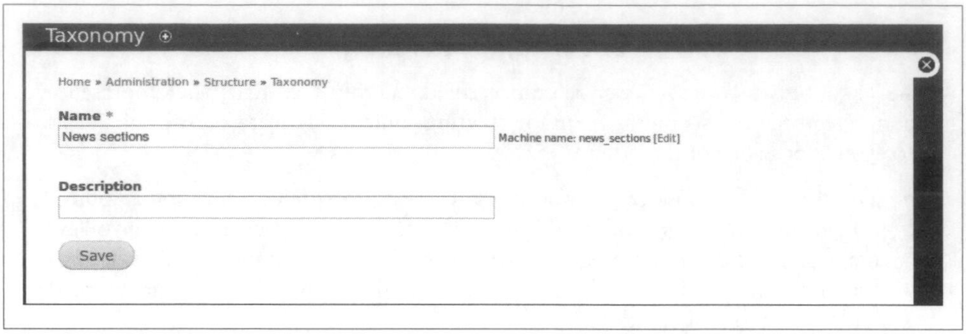

Figure 7-4. Taxonomy settings for the "News sections" vocabulary

2. Now that we have a vocabulary set up, it's time to create some terms. On the Taxonomy page, next to the "News sections" vocabulary, click "add terms" in the Operations column (*admin/structure/taxonomy/news_sections/add*). Enter the settings from Table 7-2, as shown in Figure 7-5, and click Save. Do the same for a few other terms—for example, "National news," "Culture," and "Politics"—so we have a number of terms available later in the chapter when we get to configure the editorial workflow for the site, using the Workbench modules.

Table 7-2. Term settings

Setting	Value
Name	International affairs
Description	Leave blank (default)

On the term creation page, there are some other options available as well, which we won't configure right now:

URL alias

As we've seen in "Spotlight: Taxonomy" on page 266, the Taxonomy module automatically creates links to pages that list content with the same term. The "URL alias" field allows us to define a more human-readable URL for the term, like *news/international*. The field gets added by the Path module, which we learned about in "Creating a Basic Page" on page 36. We'll get back to it later in this chapter, when we set up automatic aliasing using the Pathauto module.

Relations

In the Relations fieldset, you can define parent terms for the term you are creating, so it becomes part of a hierarchy. Additionally, you can determine the place where the term appears in the hierarchy by giving it a weight. However, an easier way to create hierarchical terms and move them around is to navigate to a vocabulary's "list terms" page and use the drag-and-drop arrows to do so.

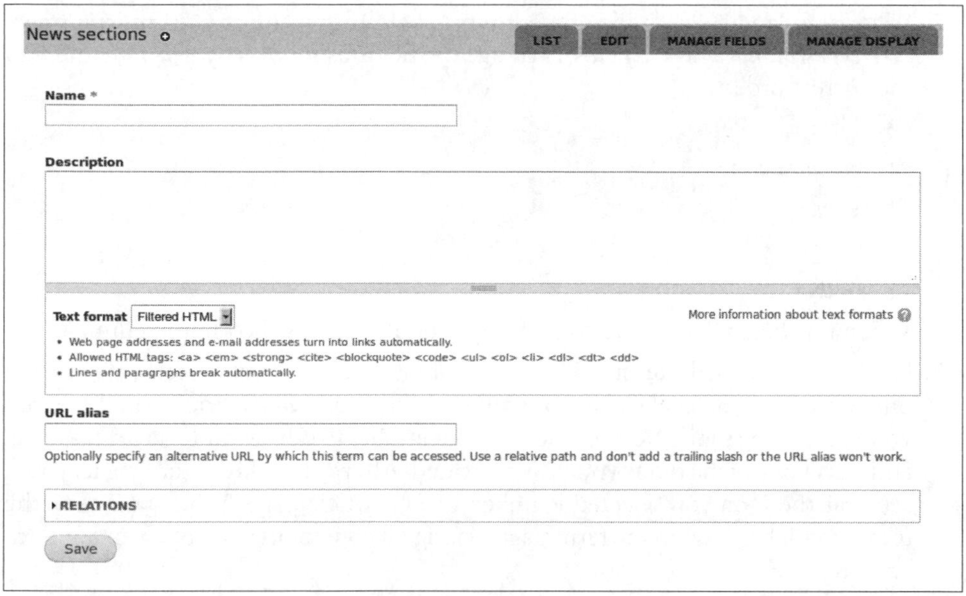

Figure 7-5. Term settings for the "International affairs" taxonomy term

To use the terms we've just created with nodes, we need to add a term reference field to the content type we want to categorize. In the administrative toolbar, click Structure→"Content types" (*admin/structure/types*). We'll add a term field to the Article content type.

1. Next to Article, click the "manage fields" link (*admin/structure/types/manage/article/fields*) to bring up the field management page for the Article content type. Under "Add new field," enter the settings from Table 7-3 and click Save.

Table 7-3. Term field settings

Setting	Value
Label	News section
Field name	field_news_section
Type of data to store	Term reference
Form element to edit the data	Select list

2. After you click Save, the "Field settings" page appears. When configuring a term reference field for a content type, this page allows you to determine which vocabulary to use for the field. In the Vocabulary select list, make sure the "News sections" vocabulary is selected, and click "Save field settings."

3. On the next page, we'll stick to the default settings, so just click "Save settings."

4. When you land back on the content type's field management page (*admin/struc-ture/types/manage/article/fields*), arrange the fields as follows by dragging them in the correct order:

- Title
- News section
- Tags
- Image
- Body

When finished, your Article content type should look as shown in Figure 7-6.

5. Now we have added a term field to our content type, we're set to start categorizing our content! If you click "Add content"→Article (*node/add/article*), you'll see that you're able to assign a News section to your article. Go ahead and create an article, and select one of the terms you've just created. After you've saved the article, you'll see that the term you selected is linked on the article page. When you click the term, you'll be taken to the term page, listing all content items that have that term attached.

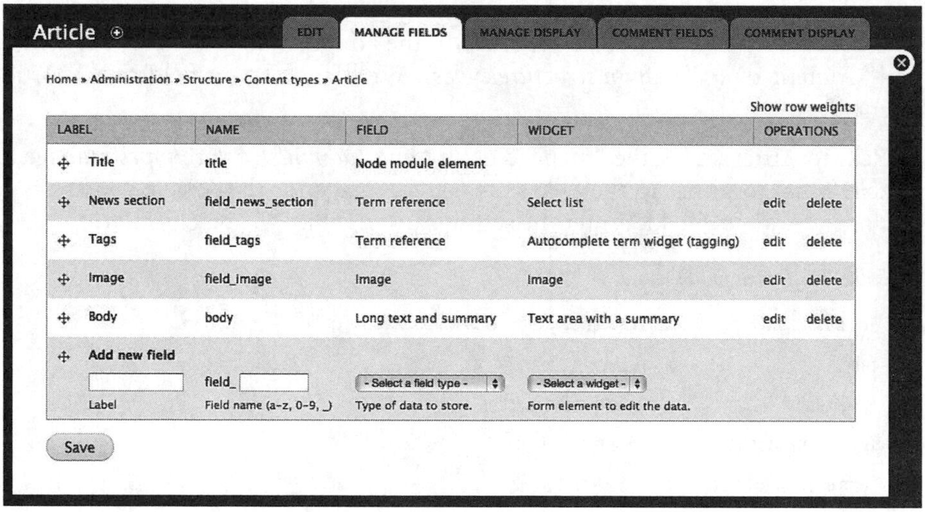

Figure 7-6. Adding a term reference field to the Article content type

Nice! You've learned how to organize the content on your Drupal site, using core's Taxonomy module. We're almost ready to build our distributed workflow with Workbench, but first we'll do a little bit more preparation work.

Spotlight: Pathauto

In "Creating a Basic Page" on page 36, you learned about Drupal paths and how to use clean URLs. One reason to use clean URLs is so that they don't look so ugly. (To review, clean URLs remove the *?q=* from the URL.) That helps, but still leaves the URLs lacking a bit. Having a URL with *node/123* in it doesn't really tell either humans or search engines much about the page itself. Isn't it much better to have a URL with something like *article/the-article-title* in it? That will be much more memorable, and the addition of pertinent keywords in the URL makes for better search engine optimization. So, even without clean URLs, you can still benefit from good pathnames.

Path Aliases

We'll quickly review the core Path module that we mentioned in Chapter 2. When enabled, it will add a new vertical tab to the node creation/editing form called "URL path settings," as shown in Figure 7-7. When you click that vertical tab, you will have a field in which to enter an alternative name for that node's path (called a URL/path alias). The name that you enter here will be used in place of the Drupal path, the part of the URL that comes after *http:// example.com/* (or *http://example.com/?q=* if you don't have clean URLs enabled).

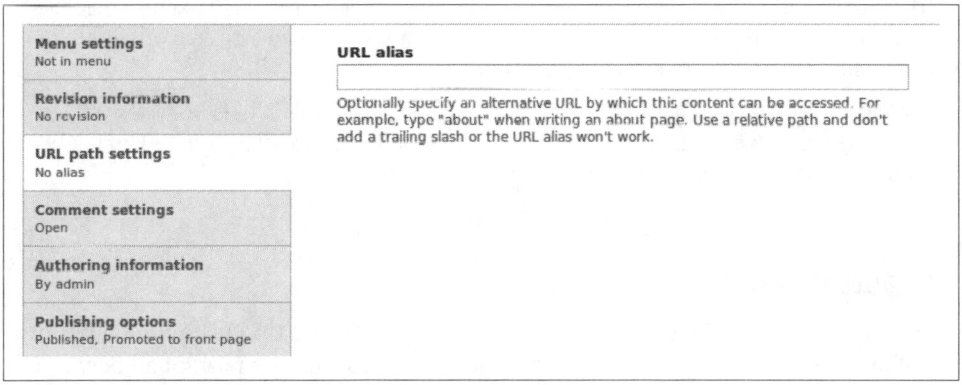

Figure 7-7. Configuring a URL alias for a node

This field is a huge help, but it can be somewhat tedious to enter all of those names by hand if you are creating a lot of content. Also, if you have many users creating content, you need to make sure that they all understand this and use consistent naming throughout the site, which can be an administrative headache.

As often occurs in Drupal, contributed projects provide us with a module that deals with this issue. Enter the Pathauto module (*http://drupal.org/project/pathauto*). As its name implies, it creates automatic path aliases for nodes, taxonomy, and user paths. Pathauto is dependent upon the core Path module and another module called Token, discussed in the sidebar below.

What Is a Token?

Tokens are placeholders that get swapped out dynamically for real values later on. For example, [yyyy] represents a four-digit year, and [author-name] represents the username of a node author. These are very similar to what we saw in Views when switching the Amazon link destination in "Rewriting Views Field Output" on page 226.

Drupal core exposes a number of default tokens, but by default there is no user interface to browse or input them. So unless you're extremely PHP-savvy, tokens can be difficult to use out of the box. Additionally, there are some tokens that Drupal core does not provide, such as field-related tokens. Enter the Token module (*http://drupal.org/project/token*), which provides a UI to any token-enabled text field in Drupal to get at the central repository of token placeholders, as well as a bundle of extra tokens that haven't yet made their way into Drupal core.

Modules that have data (like the core Node module, which knows the date a node was created), can let the token system know they have something to share. You can think of these as "suppliers." Modules that want to use that data, like Pathauto, can tap into the list of what is available. These are more like "consumers." Drupal's token system acts like a storefront that can sell various things that the suppliers bring in to the customers who want to consume them.

Contributed modules can become "suppliers" as well by providing new placeholders that represent data that they know about. They just need to speak Token's language and say "Hey, I have this *xyz* bit of data in the database, and you can tell others about it by telling them to use the [xyz] placeholder."

Tokens in Drupal 7 are also chainable; for example, the "node" token exposes an "author" element, which gets you the user properties for the author of the node. This allows you to use tokens such as [node:author:email]. Handy!

Pathauto Patterns

Pathauto uses a combination of plain text and tokens to set up URL naming patterns to follow. For instance, you can set up a pattern for naming the path of all new article pages to be [node:content-type]/[node:title] so that you automatically get something like *article/my-first-article*, as shown in Figure 7-8.

The bits of text in square brackets are placeholders for the Token module mentioned earlier. You can use different patterns for each unique content type or vocabulary if you choose. For example, basic pages could use a pattern of [node:title], since they're generally things like About Us and there's no need to specify "page/" in front of it. Pathauto also has configurable default patterns that will be applied if you don't make specific choices. You can decide things like how long your alias is allowed to be, what kind of separator you would like to use in the place of spaces or punctuation, and which common, short words you want to remove (e.g., *a*, *and*, *in*, etc.) from the path. In addition to making these automatic aliases upon creation of new content, Pathauto can

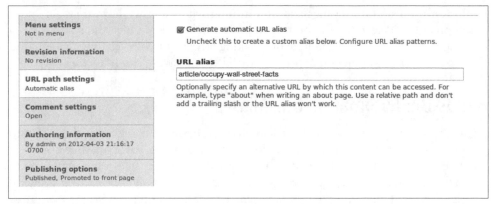

Figure 7-8. Pathauto's version of the path settings on a node edit form with a path automatically prefilled

also update all of your existing content so that your entire site uses the same pattern, even if that content was created prior to your turning on the Pathauto module.

One important thing to consider when using Pathauto is how you want to manage changing your aliases in case of a typo or similar problem. Because the alias is created based on information that Pathauto is getting about that content, if you update the content you can change your alias. You can decide what you want to do when you make updates. You can:

- Do nothing. Leave the old alias intact.
- Create a new alias. Leave the existing alias functioning.
- Create a new alias. Delete the old alias. (This is the default.)

Different sites may have different reasons for choosing which option they want to use. The default is to make a new one and delete the old so that your aliases always match your content. This option can be problematic in that it can cause a condition called *link rot*. If you have a certain URL on your site, such as *http://example.com/about*, other sites on the Web may create links pointing to that URL. If you change that URL to *http:// example.com/about-us* and delete the old one, all of those outside links will stop working. That's link rot, and it's generally frowned upon since it's bad for the Internet when URLs break.

The second option, making a new alias and keeping the old one, may sound ideal, because you can then access the content from either path and the problem of link rot is eliminated. But, while this option addresses the issue of link rot, its disadvantage is that some search engines will penalize you for having many paths that point to the same page, because they think you may be trying to game the search results. One way to get around this issue is to use the Redirect module (*http://drupal.org/project/redirect*) with Pathauto, which can be configured to automatically create redirects for changed URLs so that content coming in via duplicate paths is sent instead to the one canonical path in the system.

Look over the Pathauto settings and play around with them while your site is under development to determine the best fit for your site's needs. Once the site has been launched and people are using it, avoid making any major changes to your Pathauto settings, as users may come to depend on the URLs behaving in a particular way.

Hands-On: Automating URL Aliases

To get those handy human-readable URLs on our site, we are going to use the Pathauto module. As you saw in the previous section, this relies on the Token module as well as the core Path module. The Pathauto settings are divided over two pages: one page to set up the actual replacement patterns, and another one to configure Pathauto's general settings. These configuration pages can seem a bit intimidating at first. Luckily, most of the defaults are what most sites will want to use anyway, so that makes our job with configuration a lot simpler than it may first appear.

1. In the administrative toolbar, click Modules (*admin/modules*) and enable the following modules:

    • Other
        — Pathauto
        — Token

2. In the administrative toolbar, click Configuration→"Search and metadata"→"URL aliases," and then the Patterns tab (*admin/config/search/path/patterns*). This is the page where we'll set up the URL patterns for our site. Add the settings from Table 7-4, as shown in Figure 7-9, and click Save configuration.

Table 7-4. Pattern settings in the Pathauto module

Setting	Value
Content paths	
Pattern for all Article paths	[node:content-type]/[node:title]
Taxonomy term paths	
Pattern for all "News sections" paths	news/[term:name]

These settings will now take care of the paths of all future articles and taxonomy terms that we create. However, we already created a few articles in the previous section. How do you account for content that's already created? To do this, we'll have Pathauto bulk-update the existing URLs, as shown in Figure 7-10:

1. Click the "Bulk update" tab.
2. Check the "Content paths" and "Taxonomy term paths" checkboxes.
3. Click "Update."

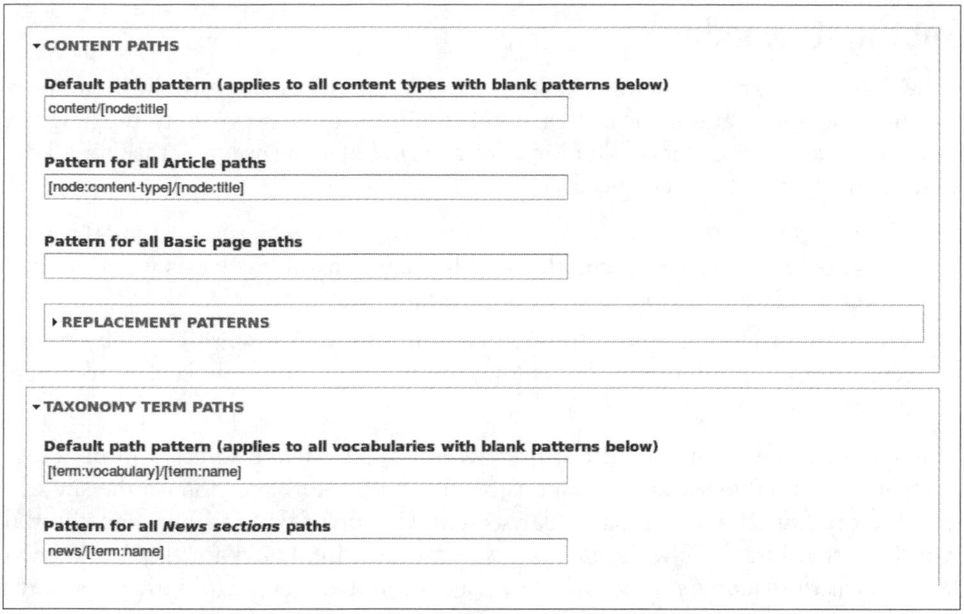

Figure 7-9. Configuring Pathauto's URL patterns

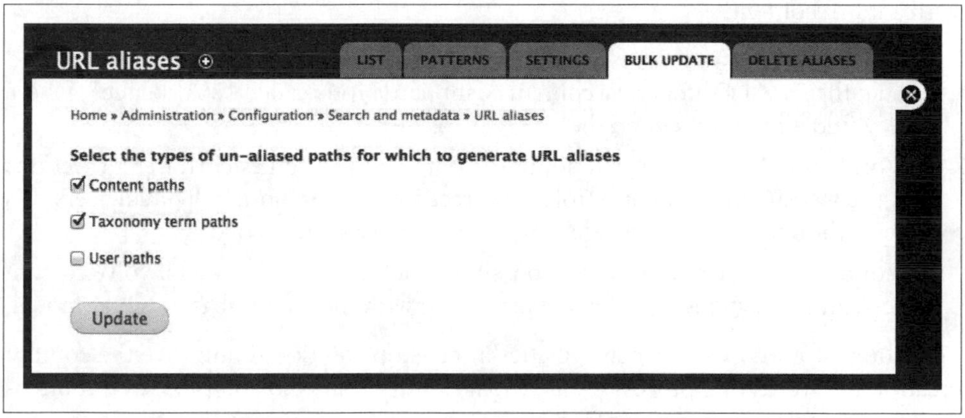

Figure 7-10. Updating URL aliases using Pathauto's bulk-update function

Once Pathauto's bulk update has run, you'll see that all our existing taxonomy terms (and articles, if you created some already) have a pretty human-readable URL like *news/ culture*, and our article URLs look something like *article/occupy-wall-street-facts*.

Spotlight: Workbench

Now that we have created a way to categorize content on our site with the Taxonomy module, and added automatic aliases with Pathauto, we can move on to building the editorial system needed for the Our Media site. As noted in the use case, the Our Media staff members have two main needs:

1. They need to be able to delegate content management to existing editorial teams. Those teams are subject-focused, so we'll use the taxonomy terms we've created earlier in this chapter to grant access to certain editors.

2. The content needs to move through an editorial workflow, so that editors can review articles, and publish them if they are ready, or send them back to reporters if they need more work.

This use case can seem complex at first. We need to provide some form of access control, so that editors who are responsible for the "culture" section on the site can only see draft articles in that particular section. On top of that, we need an editorial workflow that integrates with that access control feature. Lucky for us, Workbench (*http://www.drupal.org/project/workbench*), a contributed module (or rather, a suite of modules), provides exactly what we need.

Workbench was developed to solve a number of important needs of websites that deal with a lot of content:

- Workbench makes it easy for editorial users who only deal with content to find what they need. Editors get a content dashboard (aptly called "workbench") where they find all the content on the site.

- Workbench Access allows site administrators to assign content in different sections of the website to certain user roles or directly to one or more individual users. It's up to the site builder to decide what to base those sections on.

- Workbench Moderation makes it possible to define workflows that involve custom steps and transitions, and that are integrated with the section-based access model.

For administrators, Workbench provides a one-stop solution to improve the content creation and reviewing process on a Drupal site. Its goal is to combine several often-requested content management features into one module suite, so that administrators can easily implement complex editorial workflows by simply installing Workbench.

For users, Workbench provides a consistent and unified way to deal with content. Users (like our editors) who primarily work with content only need to find their way to the Workbench page, and can take it from there. They don't need to learn all the ins and outs of Drupal, but can focus on what they like doing: working with content.

The Workbench suite was developed in a modular way, making it possible for users to only install the modules that are needed for a certain site. If you don't need the section-based access control, but only the content moderation states, simply leave Workbench Access disabled.

Apart from the aforementioned Workbench modules, there is also Workbench Files, which provides an interface to efficiently manage files that are uploaded, and Workbench Media, which integrates with the Media module. Both Workbench Files and Workbench Media extend the initial Workbench interface, meaning that editors can access everything from the same place in the Drupal administrative interface.

My Workbench

When Workbench is installed on a Drupal site, it provides an overview page, called My Workbench. Editors will use this page, which groups all of Workbench's editorial functionality together, to find content that was published on the site, review it, and manage it. The My Workbench page is easily accessed through the administrative toolbar, as shown in Figure 7-11.

Figure 7-11. My Workbench is always accessible through the administrative toolbar

Without any of Workbench's add-ons, the My Workbench page, pictured in Figure 7-12, contains the following:

My profile
> The My Workbench page shows a picture of the user who is currently logged in, along with a link to the user's profile, to provide easy access to the user's profile page.

My edits
> A convenient overview of the content that the currently logged-in user has worked on, ordered according to the time the content was last updated. By default, this list displays five items. To see all content items that he has edited, the user can click "View all."

All recent content
> A listing of all the content on the site, ordered according to the time the content was last updated. This list will contain up to 25 items. Just like with the "My edits" list, users can click "View all" to see more content.

The My Workbench page also displays a tab that links to the "Create content" page, so users can easily navigate to that page, right from the main Workbench page.

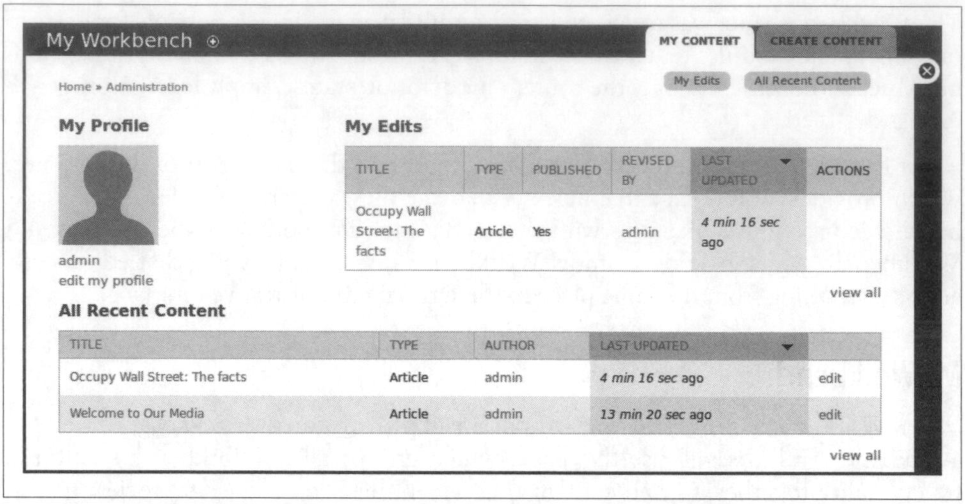

Figure 7-12. *My Workbench serves as the central point for content management in Drupal*

> The content listings you see on the My Workbench page are created with the Views module (*http://www.drupal.org/project/views*), which means you can change them as you see fit. For example, you might want to display more than five items under My Edits, or remove the username under the "My profile" picture. Using what we learned in Chapter 3, making simple and more complex changes to the default Workbench page is possible.

Hands-On: Creating Editorial Work Spaces

Since implementing Workbench can seem complex if you're doing it for the first time, we'll break it down into smaller steps. In this section, we'll focus on configuring the basic Workbench environment. Once that's done, we'll look at setting up more advanced features like access control and editorial workflows.

1. In the administrative toolbar, click Modules (*admin/modules*) and enable the following modules:
   - Chaos Tools Suite package
     - Chaos tools
   - Views package
     - Views
     - Views UI
   - Workbench package
     - Workbench

In the Workbench fieldset, you'll also see two other Workbench-related modules, Workbench Access and Workbench Moderation. We'll leave them disabled for now, and come back to those later in the chapter.

2. We can determine who will get access to Workbench's functionality by configuring the relevant permissions. In the administrative toolbar, click People, then Permissions (*admin/people/permissions*), and scroll down until you see the Workbench permissions. Enter the permissions as shown in Table 7-5.

Since the Workbench module is intended for editors, we won't grant anonymous and authenticated users any of the Workbench permissions. Users with the "editor" user role will get access to My Workbench, and only administrators will be able to administer the Workbench settings.

Table 7-5. Permissions for Workbench

Permission	anonymous user	authenticated user	editor	administrator
Workbench				
Administer Workbench Settings				Checked
Access My Workbench			Checked	Checked

After you've configured the Workbench permissions, click My Workbench (*admin/workbench*) in the administrative toolbar: this will be the main content management page from now on.

Hands-On: Generating Sample Content

Since we haven't been creating much content on our site, the My Workbench page is rather empty. This can make it hard to understand what's going on and to grasp the module's possibilities. This is a situation that you'll encounter often when developing a site: at a certain point, you need content to test a certain feature, or to verify what a certain section on your site will look like.

The Devel Generate module, which comes with the Devel module (*http://www.drupal.org/project/devel*) allows us to quickly generate sample content, users, taxonomy vocabularies/terms, and menu items, so testing functionality on our new site becomes a lot easier, since it will more closely resemble its actual functioning.

1. In the administrative toolbar, click Modules (*admin/modules*), and enable the following modules:
   - Devel package
     — Devel
     — Devel generate

2. Click Configuration (*admin/config*) in the administrative toolbar and scroll down until you see the Development section of the Configuration page, as shown in Figure 7-13.

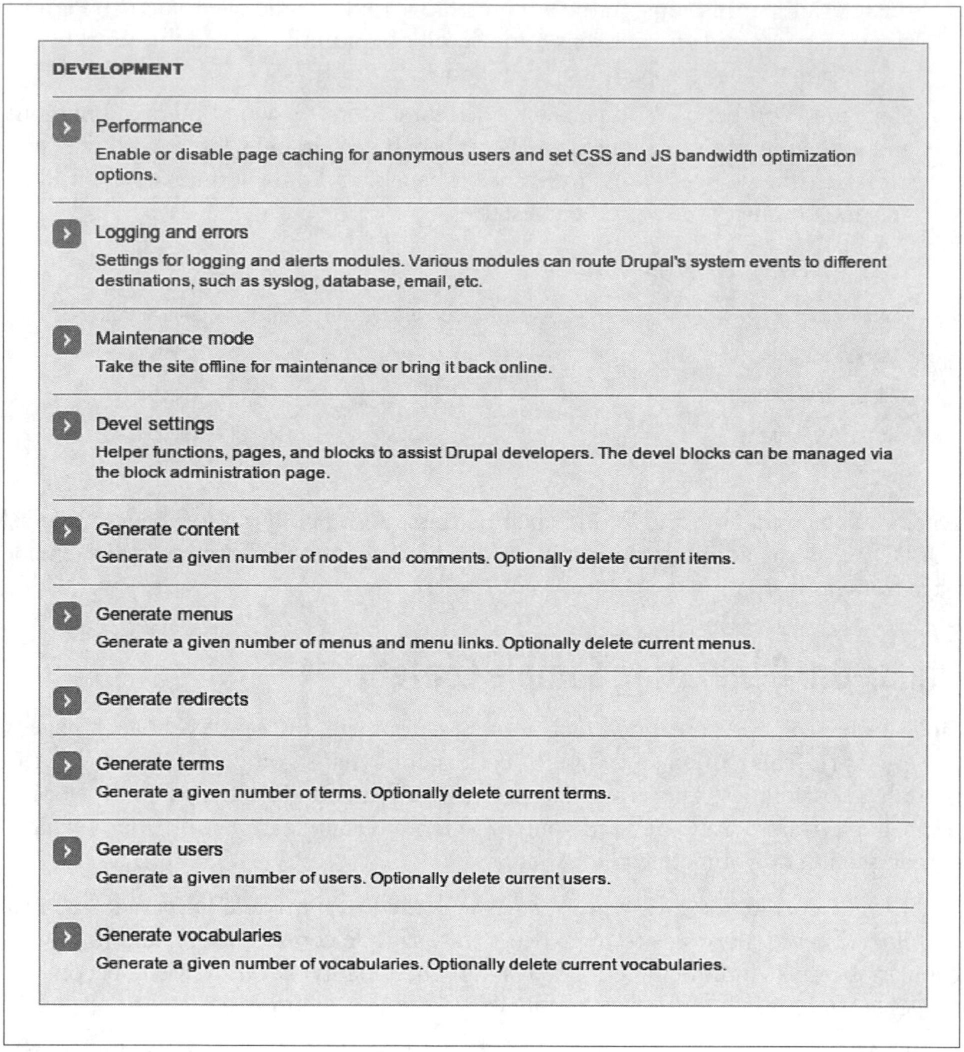

DEVELOPMENT

Performance
Enable or disable page caching for anonymous users and set CSS and JS bandwidth optimization options.

Logging and errors
Settings for logging and alerts modules. Various modules can route Drupal's system events to different destinations, such as syslog, database, email, etc.

Maintenance mode
Take the site offline for maintenance or bring it back online.

Devel settings
Helper functions, pages, and blocks to assist Drupal developers. The devel blocks can be managed via the block administration page.

Generate content
Generate a given number of nodes and comments. Optionally delete current items.

Generate menus
Generate a given number of menus and menu links. Optionally delete current menus.

Generate redirects

Generate terms
Generate a given number of terms. Optionally delete current terms.

Generate users
Generate a given number of users. Optionally delete current users.

Generate vocabularies
Generate a given number of vocabularies. Optionally delete current vocabularies.

Figure 7-13. Devel Generate allows you to quickly generate sample content

We'll generate some sample articles in order to populate the My Workbench page. Click "Generate content" (*admin/config/development/generate/content*), enter the settings from Table 7-6, as shown in Figure 7-14), and click Generate.

Table 7-6. "Generate content" settings

Setting	Value
Content types	Article
Delete all content	Unchecked (default)
How many nodes would you like to generate?	70
How far back in time should the nodes be dated?	1 week ago (default)
Maximum number of comments per node.	0 (default)
Max word length of titles	4 (default)
Add an url alias for each node.	Checked
Set language on nodes	Language neutral (default)

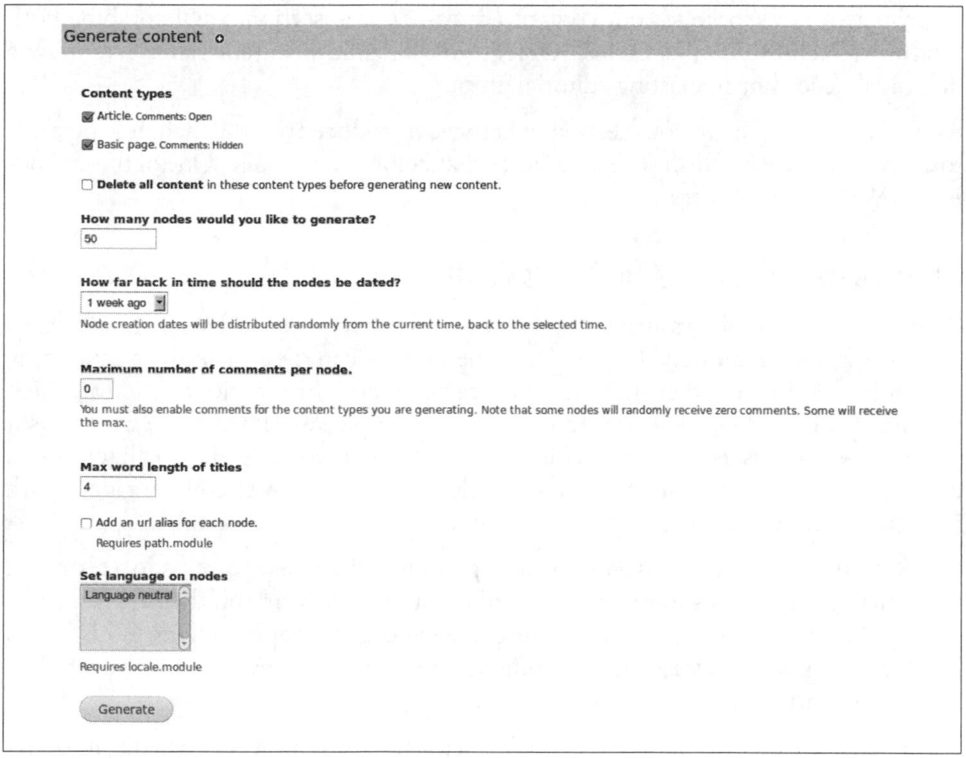

Figure 7-14. Generate sample content for your site

Once the sample content has been generated, return to the My Workbench page. Despite the content being far from realistic, the Workbench will look much more like what you would expect to see on a working site. This makes it easier for us to further explore Workbench features, which we'll do in the following sections.

It's definitely worth sitting down and exploring the Devel module as you get deeper into Drupal site development. Devel contains several useful utilities that support site builders and developers during site creation, such as the ability to easily switch back and forth between users on the site in order to test permissions. If you ever run into code-related problems, Devel also has several handy tricks to assist with debugging, including "pretty" output functions such as `dpm()`, an object inspector, and more.

Spotlight: Workbench Access

In the previous sections of this chapter, we've created a taxonomy vocabulary and terms to organize the content on our site, and we've configured the main Workbench module to provide a workspace for our content editors. In this section, we'll combine both modules to achieve another of this chapter's goals: to allow content management to be delegated according to existing editorial groups.

As we've seen in the previous section, where we introduced Workbench, it is possible to extend Workbench using other modules that belong to the suite. One of those modules is Workbench Access.

Using Hierarchies to Define Access Control

Workbench Access allows an administrator to create access control mechanisms based on existing hierarchies on the site. Such hierarchies can be a menu or a taxonomy vocabulary. With Workbench Access, you can use those hierarchies to control which user has editorial access to certain content. For example, Workbench Access makes it possible to grant users of one role editorial access to content tagged with all terms of a certain vocabulary, while users of another role have access only to content tagged with one specific term within the same vocabulary.

In addition to per-role access, you can also grant individual users access to a term or a vocabulary. This makes it easy to allow different users to work on their own specific part of the site's content, without getting in each other's way. In Figure 7-15, which displays Workbench Access's main configuration page, the "News section" vocabulary is used to control editorial access to articles.

Workbench Access also supports Drupal's menu system as an access scheme, meaning you can grant editorial access to content based on a content item's place in the site's menu structure.

While Workbench Access supports the Taxonomy module and the menu system out of the box, module developers can expose their own access schemes to Workbench Access, so administrators can use them to build access control systems for their editors. The module is designed to be extensible.

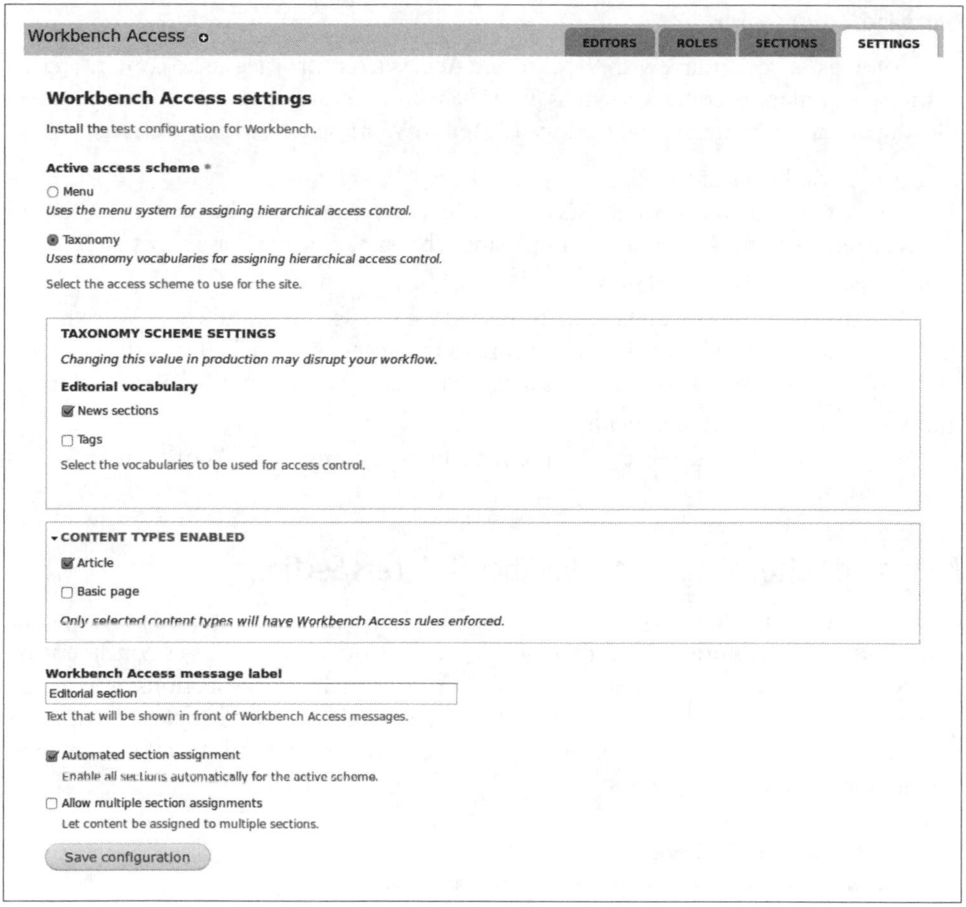

Workbench Access ⊙

| EDITORS | ROLES | SECTIONS | **SETTINGS** |

Workbench Access settings

Install the test configuration for Workbench.

Active access scheme *

○ Menu
Uses the menu system for assigning hierarchical access control.

● Taxonomy
Uses taxonomy vocabularies for assigning hierarchical access control.

Select the access scheme to use for the site.

TAXONOMY SCHEME SETTINGS

Changing this value in production may disrupt your workflow.

Editorial vocabulary

☑ News sections

☐ Tags

Select the vocabularies to be used for access control.

▾ CONTENT TYPES ENABLED

☑ Article

☐ Basic page

Only selected content types will have Workbench Access rules enforced.

Workbench Access message label

Editorial section

Text that will be shown in front of Workbench Access messages.

☑ Automated section assignment
Enable all sections automatically for the active scheme.

☐ Allow multiple section assignments
Let content be assigned to multiple sections.

(Save configuration)

Figure 7-15. Configuring Workbench Access settings

It's important to note here that Workbench Access only works on an editorial level: it does not interfere with permissions to *view* content on a site. Other modules, such as Taxonomy Access (*http://drupal.org/ project/taxonomy_access*) and Content Access (*http://drupal.org/project/ content_access*) are examples of *node access modules*, and can provide fine-grained control over who can see content on the site, and in what contexts. See a full list of all available Content Access control modules on Drupal.org at *http://drupal.org/project/modules?filters=tid %3A13434*.

Workbench Access sections

When you use a vocabulary with Workbench Access to control access to content, terms in that vocabulary become known as *Workbench Access sections*. Workbench Access allows you to configure several options related to Workbench Access sections:

Workbench Access message label
> How to refer to Workbench Access sections on node forms. In this case, they are referred to as an "Editorial section," since that makes sense for a news site.

Automated section assignment
> Whether to automatically use all terms within the used vocabulary as Workbench Access sections (when using taxonomy as the access scheme). If you disable this, you'll have to manually enable individual terms as Workbench Access sections.

Allow multiple section assignments
> Whether to allow a piece of content to belong to multiple Workbench Access sections.

Assigning Editorial Access to Workbench Access Sections

Once you've set up access control with Workbench Access, you still need to determine which users have editorial access to which content. Workbench Access's configuration is very fine grained: you can enable individual Workbench Access sections, and assign editorial access to complete user roles or only to certain users. In Figure 7-16, users with the role "national editor" have editorial access to content that has the term "National news" attached.

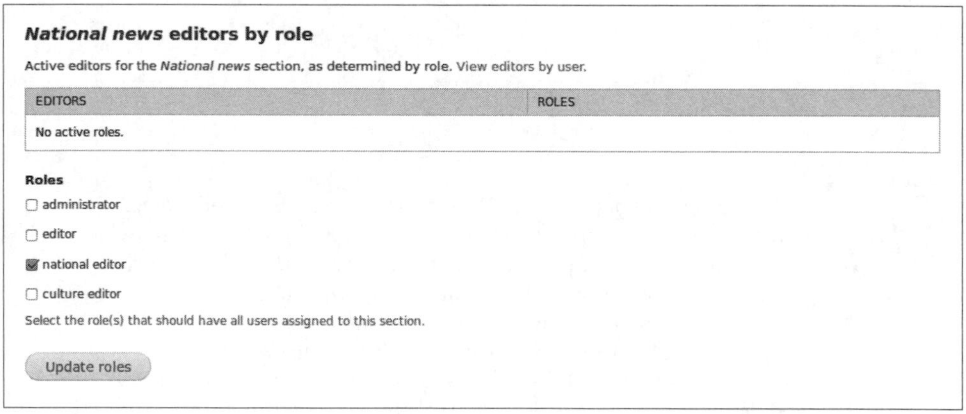

Figure 7-16. Configuring Workbench Access role settings

You assign content to a Workbench section on the node form. Once you've configured Workbench Access, users will be able to put content into sections using a select list, as shown in Figure 7-17. Once the content belongs to a certain section, users with editorial access to that section will be able to edit it.

Editorial section *

- National news

Select the proper editorial group for this content.

Figure 7-17. Assigning a node to a Workbench section on the node's edit page

Also note that Workbench Access extends the My Workbench page by adding a tab called My Sections, as shown in Figure 7-18. By clicking on the tab, an editor can verify which Workbench Access sections she can access.

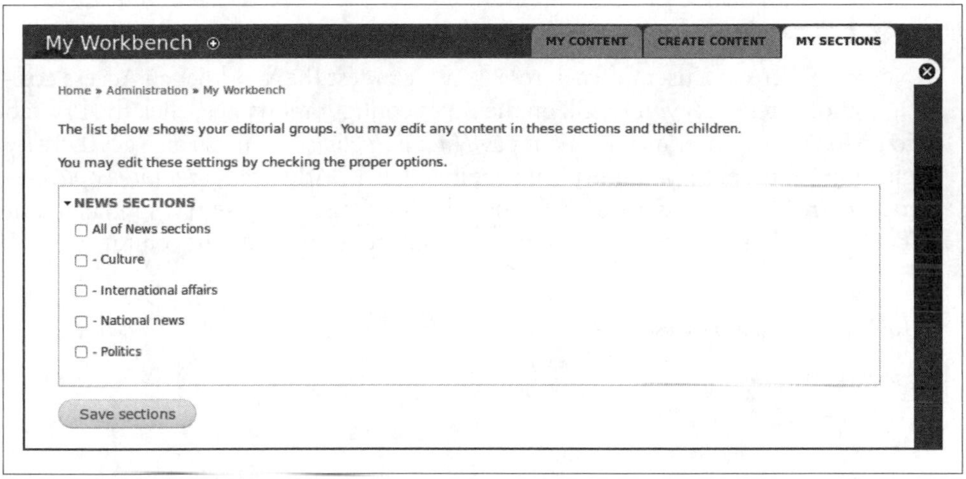

Figure 7-18. The My Sections tab shows the sections a user can access

Hands-On: Workbench Access

Let's extend our Workbench implementation with one of the more advanced features our client has asked for. We'll build upon the structure we've created with the Taxonomy module (the "News sections" vocabulary), and use that to grant users within specific roles access to content tagged with one of the "News sections" terms. We'll start with a little preparation work: creating two new user roles and adding a user for each role.

1. In the administrative toolbar, click People→Permissions, then click the Roles subtab in the top-right corner (*admin/people/permissions/roles*).
2. Add two new roles, one called "national editor" and another called "culture editor." Since they will have fewer permissions than the general "editor" role, reorder them to be just before "editor" in the list, as pictured in Figure 7-19.

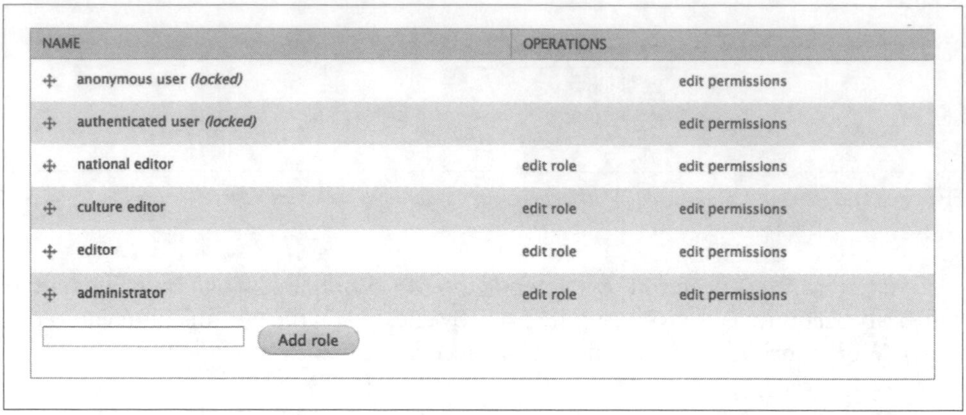

NAME		OPERATIONS
⊹ anonymous user *(locked)*		edit permissions
⊹ authenticated user *(locked)*		edit permissions
⊹ national editor	edit role	edit permissions
⊹ culture editor	edit role	edit permissions
⊹ editor	edit role	edit permissions
⊹ administrator	edit role	edit permissions

[_____] (Add role)

Figure 7-19. Extra roles to use with Workbench Access

3. Next, we'll create a user for each role, so we can test the Workbench Access configuration later on. If you're still on the Roles configuration page, click the List tab to go to Drupal's user management page (*admin/people*). You can also get there by clicking People in the administrative toolbar. Click "Add user" (*admin/people/create*) to create a new user called "national editor" using the settings indicated in Table 7-7. Afterward, create another user, "culture editor" with the "culture editor" role.

Table 7-7. Creating new users

Setting	Value
Username	national editor
E-mail address	(Choose an e-mail address)
Password	(Choose a password)
Roles	national editor

4. We also need to set up some permissions for our user roles. Only users with the general "editor" role (staff members) should be able to edit all content. We'll also grant the three "editor" roles—national, culture, and general—permission to view the administration theme and to access the administrative overlay and toolbar, to present the Workbench pages in a more user-friendly way. In the administrative toolbar, click People→Permissions (*admin/people/permissions*), and assign the permissions as indicated in Table 7-8.

Table 7-8. Permissions before configuring Workbench Access

Permission	anonymous user	authenticated user	culture editor	national editor	editor	administrator
Node						
Bypass content access control					Checked	Checked
Administer content					Checked	Checked
Access the content overview page					Checked	Checked
Article: Create new content			Checked	Checked	Checked	Checked
Article: Edit any content			Checked	Checked	Checked	Checked
Overlay						
Access the administrative overlay			Checked	Checked	Checked	Checked
System						
View the administration theme			Checked	Checked	Checked	Checked
Toolbar						
Use the administration toolbar			Checked	Checked	Checked	Checked
Workbench						
Access My Workbench			Checked	Checked	Checked	Checked

 It's important to note here that Workbench Access's permissions are applied *on top of*, not *instead of*, Drupal's own editorial permissions. That's why we grant our "national editor" and "culture editor" user roles permission to edit article content. Workbench Access will then refine those permissions, using its Workbench Access sections.

As you've probably guessed by now, we'll create an access control mechanism that grants users with the "national editor" role editorial access to content tagged with the term "national news." Users that have the role "cultural editor" will eventually get editorial access to content that has the term "culture" attached. Before that can happen, we need to enable and configure Workbench Access. After this configuration, the taxonomy terms we created earlier will become Workbench Access sections, which will be used to enforce access control on our site's content.

Setting Up Access Control with Workbench Access

In the administrative toolbar, click Modules (*admin/modules*) and enable the following modules:

- Workbench
  — Workbench Access

After enabling Workbench Access, we'll go ahead and configure it.

 If you were to go to the My Workbench page (*admin/workbench*) as the "national editor" user, you'd notice that it doesn't list any content yet. That's because Workbench Access is enabled, but hasn't been configured. The My Workbench page will remain empty until content has been assigned to Workbench Access sections. Administrative users or users with the "editor" role, however, can still edit all content on the site by going to Drupal's content configuration page (*admin/content*).

1. Click the "configure Workbench Access settings" link in the message, or navigate to Configuration→Workbench→Workbench Access, then click the Settings tab (*admin/config/workbench/access/settings*).

2. When you land on the Workbench Access settings page, you'll see that the default configuration for Workbench Access is to use Taxonomy as its access scheme. For the Our Media site, we'll use our newly created "News sections" vocabulary to control editorial access to content. On the Workbench Access settings page, enter the settings in Table 7-9 and click "Save configuration."

Table 7-9. Workbench Access settings

Setting	Value
Active access scheme	Taxonomy (default)
Taxonomy scheme settings	News sections
Content types enabled	Article
Workbench Access message label	Editorial section
Automated section assignment	Checked (default)
Allow multiple section assignments	Unchecked (default)

We have the most basic configuration for Workbench Access set up: taxonomy terms within our "News section" vocabulary will be used as Workbench Access sections to determine access control. Now it's time to decide who gets access to which terms. Remember the new roles we just created? We'll use those to grant users access to content that's tagged with terms in the "News sections" vocabulary.

If you want to prevent some of the vocabulary's terms from becoming Workbench Access sections (so they're not used for access control), you should leave "Automated section assignment" unchecked. If automated section assignment is disabled, you can click the Sections tab (*admin/config/workbench/access/sections*), and leave the terms you don't want to use for content access disabled.

1. First, we need to allow users of our new roles to be assigned to Workbench Access sections. Go to the Permissions page by clicking People→Permissions (*admin/people/permissions*). Configure the permissions as indicated in Table 7-10:

Administer Workbench Access settings
> Allows users to configure Workbench Access. This permission is intended for users who administer the site.

Assign users to Workbench Access sections
> Users with this permission can assign users and roles to Workbench Access sections. Meant for "super editors," like the Our Media staff members.

Allow all members of this role to be assigned to Workbench Access sections
> Users of these roles will be able to edit content in certain Workbench Access sections (whichever sections they are assigned to).

Batch update section assignments for content
> Allows users to assign content to Workbench Access, using the batch-update options on Drupal's content management page (*admin/content*). We'll explain how this works later in this section. A user needs to be assigned to a Workbench Access section to batch-assign content to a section.

View Workbench Access information
> Allows users to see messages concerning content assignment to Workbench Access sections.

View taxonomy term pages for Workbench Access vocabulary
> Workbench Access can create its own vocabularies for testing purposes. This permission has nothing to do with the normal vocabularies and terms on a site, and we won't be using it for editors on our site.

Table 7-10. Workbench Access permissions for the "national editor" and "culture editor" user roles

Permission	anonymous user	authenticated user	culture editor	national editor	editor	administrator
Workbench Access						
Administer Workbench Access settings						Checked

Permission	anonymous user	authenticated user	culture editor	national editor	editor	administrator
Assign users to Workbench Access sections					Checked	Checked
Allow all members of this role to be assigned to Workbench Access sections			Checked	Checked	Checked	Checked
Batch update section assignments for content					Checked	Checked
View Workbench Access information			Checked	Checked	Checked	Checked
View taxonomy term pages for Workbench Access vocabulary						Checked

2. Next, go to the Workbench Access roles page by navigating to Configuration→Workbench→Workbench Access, then the Roles tab (*admin/config/workbench/access/roles*). This is the page where you can assign user roles to Workbench Access sections.

You'll see a listing of the taxonomy terms within the "News sections" vocabulary that are currently actively used as Workbench Access sections. Right now, all the terms within our vocabulary are being used as Workbench Access sections, because we checked the "Automated section assignment" checkbox on the Workbench Access settings page. Later in this section, we'll see how you can control which terms are used as Workbench Access sections.

One of the two new roles we created is called "national editor": users within this role should have access to content tagged with the term "national news." To set this up, click the "National news" link in the list of active Workbench Access sections. On that page, check the "national editor" role and click the "Update roles" button.

Now do the same for users with the "culture editor" role in order to give those users access to content tagged with the "culture" term. Go back to the Workbench Roles overview page by clicking the Roles tab (*admin/config/workbench/access/roles*), and click Culture in the list of active Workbench Access sections. Check "culture editor" under Roles and click "Update roles."

Note that users with the "administrator" and "editor" roles also need to be assigned to Workbench Access sections in order to be able to assign content to sections. We'll assign both user roles to all sections. Click the "News sections" link at the top of the hierarchy in the Workbench Access sections list and check the boxes for both the "administrator" and "editor" roles. They will automatically inherit permissions to all subterms.

Congratulations! Our new user roles now have access to content that's relevant to them, as shown in Figure 7-20.

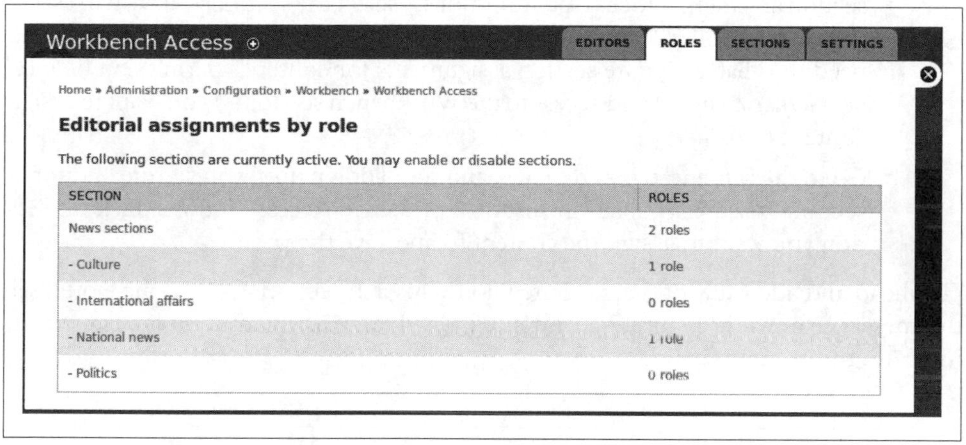

Workbench Access ⊕

| EDITORS | **ROLES** | SECTIONS | SETTINGS |

Home » Administration » Configuration » Workbench » Workbench Access

Editorial assignments by role

The following sections are currently active. You may enable or disable sections.

SECTION	ROLES
News sections	2 roles
- Culture	1 role
- International affairs	0 roles
- National news	1 role
- Politics	0 roles

Figure 7-20. The assigned Workbench Access sections for each role

> If your use case requires you to assign certain Workbench Access sections to individual users rather than user roles, you're in luck, since Workbench Access allows for that as well, via the Editors tab. This page works the same way as Workbench Access's Roles page, but for individual users instead of roles: click "0 editors" next to the Workbench section you want to assign to an individual user, and simply add the user(s) on the next page.

Now that you've configured which roles or users have editorial access to content in certain Workbench Access sections, it's time to assign some of our content to a section, so our editors can access it. Normally, content is assigned to a Workbench section when an author creates the content and attaches a taxonomy term to it; the node is assigned to the section that corresponds to the taxonomy term. The content will then appear on the My Workbench page. Since we didn't assign any Workbench Access sections to any of our content items yet, however, the My Workbench page is still empty at this point.

1. Click the "Find content" shortcut in the administrative toolbar (*admin/content*). Since you're an administrator and thus have the "Administer content" and "View content overview page" permissions, you can administer content through this page as well. Editors don't have these permissions won't be able to access this page and will use the My Workbench page for managing content, seeing only the content that is relevant for them.

2. You can assign a Workbench section in two different ways:

   a. Check the box in front of the content item you wish to assign to a Workbench section and then, under "Update options," select the section you wish to assign the item to under "Set editorial section." Note that in order to do this, you need the "Batch update section assignments for content" permission (*admin/people/permissions*) and access to the Workbench section(s) you want to assign content to.

   b. Go to the content items edit page, and scroll down until you see the "Editorial section" select list; this is the list of Workbench Access sections. Pick the section you want to assign the content to and save the page.

Go ahead and add a few of the generated nodes to each section. Once done, you'll see the message shown in Figure 7-21 on any individual piece of content's page, which indicates the section it's in.

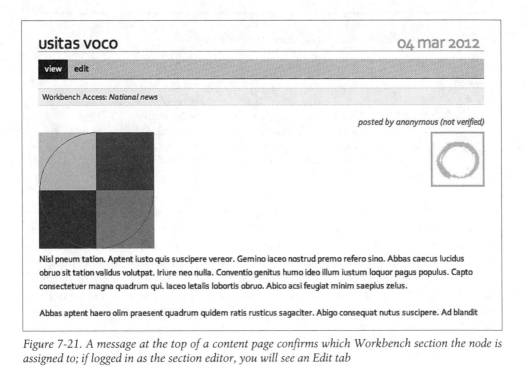

Figure 7-21. A message at the top of a content page confirms which Workbench section the node is assigned to; if logged in as the section editor, you will see an Edit tab

That is the final step we need for this part of the site's functionality: editors with access to the "National news" Workbench section will be able to edit this node, either via the My Workbench page, or by clicking Edit on the node page. However, editors with only "culture" access will not. If you navigate to the My Workbench page as one of the specialty editors, you'll notice the list of content there is now filtered to show only things in their section.

Spotlight: Workbench Moderation

In the previous section, we completed an important feature of the Our Media site. Existing editorial groups can now edit content they are responsible for, and only that content. However, to enable editors to effectively manage the flow of articles coming in, we need something else: an editorial workflow system that allows them to easily determine when an article is ready for review, and to either send it back to the reporter when it needs more work, or to publish it on the site when it's good to go.

Out of the box, Drupal allows a piece of content to be either published or unpublished. When the "published" checkbox is unchecked on the node editing form, only users with the "administer nodes" permission are allowed to view the content. That's enough for some sites, but it doesn't give our reporters and editors as much control as they need. For example, there's no way for a reporter to mark an article as an in-progress draft and come back to it later. In addition, there's no easy way for an editor to tell a reporter that an article needs more work—the editor must contact the author manually.

This problem is exactly what Workbench Moderation (*http://drupal.org/project/work bench_moderation*), another part of the Workbench suite, was designed to solve. It allows site administrators to set up predefined steps, called *states*, through which every piece of content must pass before publication. A news site might need "Draft," "Needs review," and "Published" states, where a software development company might need "New," "Verified," "Needs review," "Needs work," "Passes QA," and "Fixed" states. You can set up access control around who is allowed to move things from one state to another (and back), ensuring that the right people give the content their stamp of approval before content goes live.

Editorial Workflow Management with Workbench Moderation

Using Workbench Moderation, administrators can define workflow states that suit their site's needs. As shown in Figure 7-22, they can decide how the states are called, determining the order of the states a piece of content has to move through. As we will see when we configure Workbench Moderation later in this chapter, administrators can also configure the transitions between workflow states to allow only those state changes they need or want to allow.

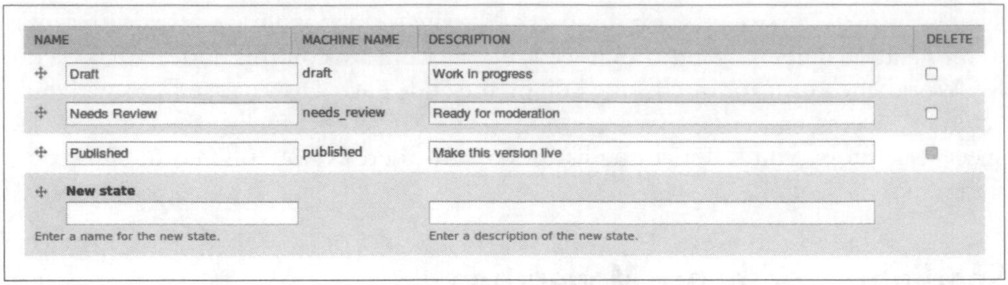

NAME		MACHINE NAME	DESCRIPTION	DELETE
⊹	Draft	draft	Work in progress	☐
⊹	Needs Review	needs_review	Ready for moderation	☐
⊹	Published	published	Make this version live	☑
⊹	**New state**			
	Enter a name for the new state.		Enter a description of the new state.	

Figure 7-22. Configuring Workbench Moderation states settings

Since Workbench Moderation is part of the Workbench series of modules, it tightly integrates with the central Workbench page that users get as their content management "home base." When Workbench Moderation is enabled, the "My Workbench" page (*admin/workbench*) displays a tab for every moderation state, as shown in Figure 7-23. This makes it very easy for editors to find content that is currently being worked on by reporters (drafts), content that needs review, and content that is published on the site.

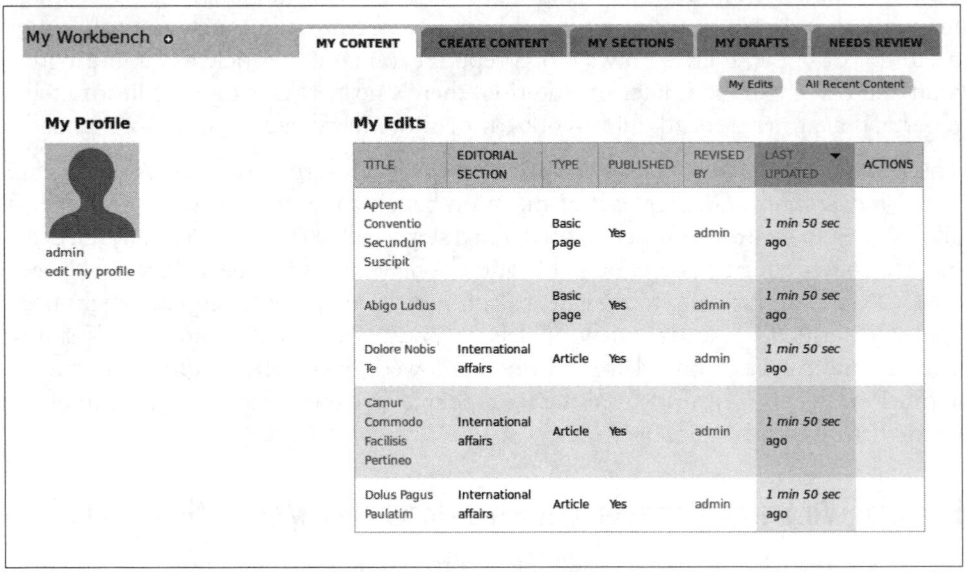

Figure 7-23. Workbench Moderation tabs

Remember that all of the pages displayed by these tabs are powered by the Views module, so they can be modified and extended to fit your own site's needs.

My Drafts
> This page lists content created by the currently logged-in user and that hasn't been published yet.

Needs Review
This page lists content that has the state "Needs review" assigned to it.

These pages offer editors an overview of what's going on with the content on the site, and editors can moderate content directly from them, by clicking the desired moderation state. More often than not, though, an editor will want to go into a piece of content, make changes, and update the content's moderation state accordingly. Not to worry—Workbench Moderation provides several features on individual node pages.

1. When you go to one of the node pages, Workbench Moderation provides a block that displays the node's moderation state, or rather, the revision's current moderation state (since Workbench Moderation acts on revisions). An editor can also change the moderation state directly from this block, as shown in Figure 7-24.

    Workbench Moderation automatically creates a new revision each time a user changes a node's moderation state. This means it is very easy to roll back changes and to revert to an earlier version of the node, if the changes are unwanted or not relevant. It also makes it possible to compare versions with each other, to see exactly what has changed.

Figure 7-24. Workbench Moderation state transitions

2. One of Workbench Moderation's great strengths is the ability to work on a new revision of a node (called a *draft*), while another revision is published. For example, when a reporter posts a story that has very high news value, an editor can decide to publish it, even though it could use some work. The editor can create a new draft by clicking on the "new draft" tab (shown when a node has the Published moderation state), and then give that new draft a moderation state and leave a note explaining the changes (as shown in Figure 7-25) to send it through the editorial process or publish it on the site.

    Note that Workbench Moderation's states take over Drupal's Published option: when a node has the moderation state Draft and no Published revision, the content will not be published on the site.

3. Another very handy feature that Workbench Moderation provides for us on node pages is the moderation history. When on the node page, click the Moderate tab; you'll see the list of recent moderation state changes, along with the changes' details, as shown in Figure 7-26. Again, Workbench Moderation allows us to change the moderation state right from that page.

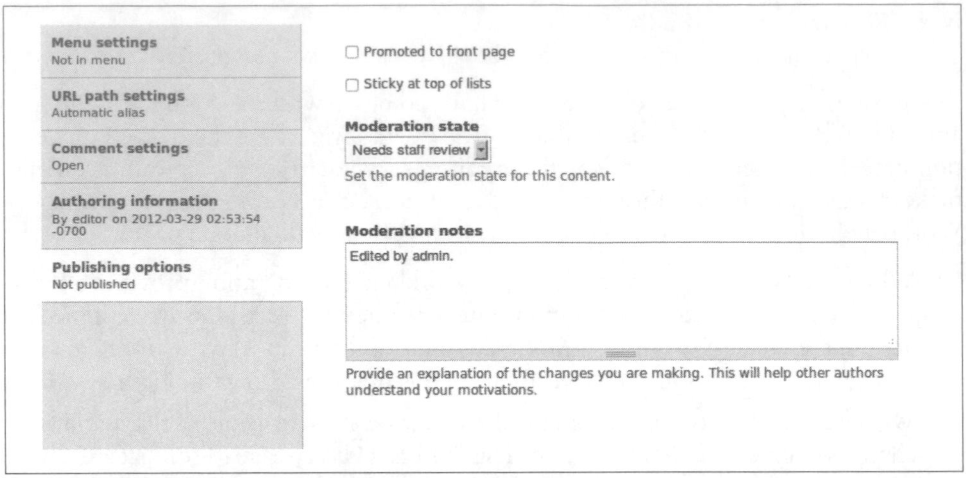

Figure 7-25. Changing the moderation state on a newly created draft

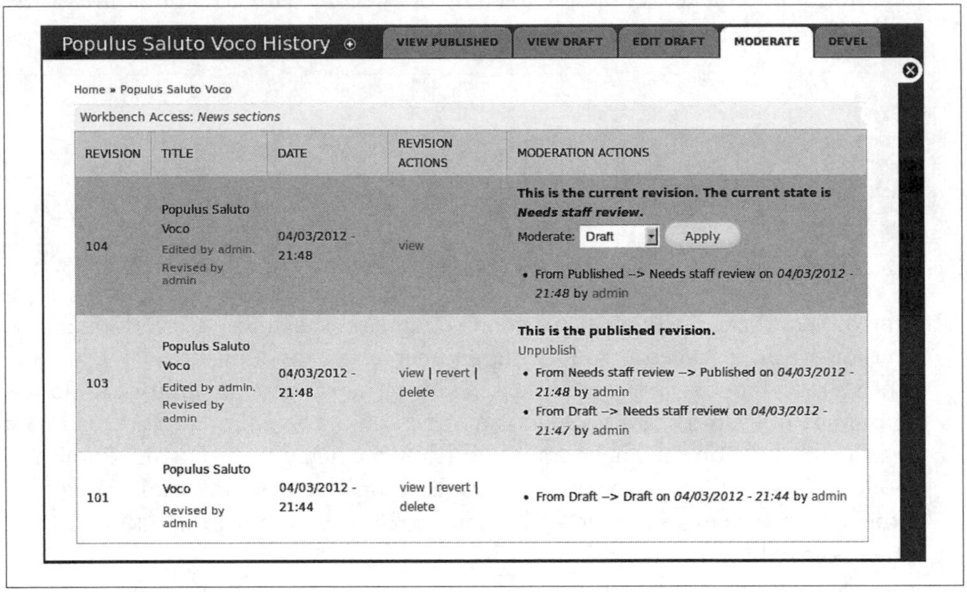

Figure 7-26. Workbench Moderation history of a node

Hands-On: Workbench Moderation

In the administrative toolbar, click Modules (*admin/modules*), and enable the following modules:

- Workbench
  —Workbench Moderation

Remember that you can use Workbench's modules independently of each other. If you only need an editorial workflow on your site without access control like we set up in the previous section, you can disable Workbench Access. For the purpose of this section, it doesn't matter if you have Workbench Access or not.

After enabling the module, you need to activate content moderation for each content type you want to use it with:

1. Navigate to Structure→"Content types" (*admin/structure/types*). Next to Article, click "edit" (*admin/structure/types/manage/article*) and go to the "Publishing options" vertical tab. Enter the settings from Table 7-11, as shown in Figure 7-27, and save the content type. Note that "Default moderation state" will be the state of the node's first revision right after it is created.

Table 7-11. Workbench Moderation content type settings

Setting	Value
Published	Unchecked
Create new revision	Checked
Enable moderation of revisions	Checked
Enforce Workbench Access control	Checked (default)
Default moderation state	Draft (default)

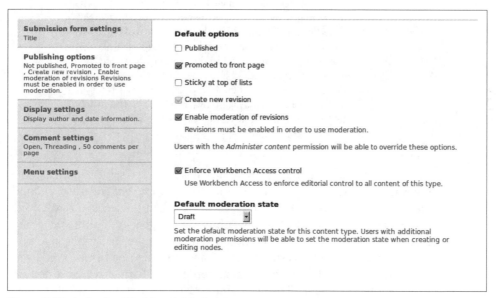

Figure 7-27. Activating Workbench Moderation on a content type

2. Once you've saved your changes, head over to see Workbench Moderation's configuration options at Configuration→Workbench→Workbench Moderation (*admin/config/workbench/moderation*):

a. On the States tab, you can configure the states you want content to pass through between its creation and publishing. Workbench Moderation's default states ("Draft," "Needs review," and "Published") fit pretty well with a news site like the one we're building, but we want to add one more state. If one of the editors feels unsure about an article, there has to be a way to flag that to the Our Media staff, so we'll create a custom state, "Needs staff review," between "Needs review" and "Published." Enter the values from Table 7-12; drag the new state between "Needs review" and "Published," as pictured in Figure 7-28; and click Save.

Table 7-12. Workbench Moderation state settings

Setting	Value
State name	Needs staff review
State description	Questionable content; needs sanity checking from staff member

After you save the new Workbench Moderation state, a message will ask you to "reconfigure Views that leverage Workbench Moderation." This message is referring to My Workbench and related pages. As we have seen earlier in this chapter, these pages are built with the Views module, which we learned about in Chapter 3. By default, Workbench Moderation comes with a page for each of its default moderation states to make it easy for users to find the content they need. If you create custom moderation states, you can also add an extra view display to the "workbench_moderation" view by cloning one of the existing displays and overriding its "Page settings," "Filter criteria," and "No results behavior" values to match the new workflow state.

b. Now that you've configured the moderation states, let's set up the transitions between each state. Click the Transitions tab (*admin/config/workbench/moderation/transitions*) to see the existing transitions: Draft→Needs Review, Needs Review→Draft, and Needs Review→Published. To give our editors the ability to flag content for staff review, we need to add two more transitions: one from "Needs review" to "Needs staff review," and another one from "Needs staff review" to "Published," which staff members can use to push reviewed content live. Select the From and To states under "New transitions" and click Save. The list of transitions is shown in Figure 7-29.

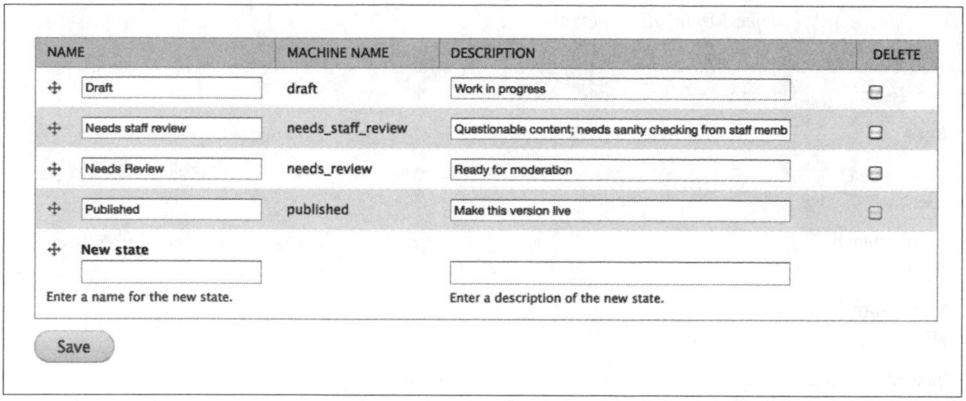

NAME		MACHINE NAME	DESCRIPTION		DELETE
⊹	Draft	draft	Work in progress		☐
⊹	Needs staff review	needs_staff_review	Questionable content; needs sanity checking from staff memb		☐
⊹	Needs Review	needs_review	Ready for moderation		☐
⊹	Published	published	Make this version live		☐
⊹	**New state**				
		Enter a name for the new state.		Enter a description of the new state.	

Save

Figure 7-28. Workbench Moderation allows site builders to create custom workflow states

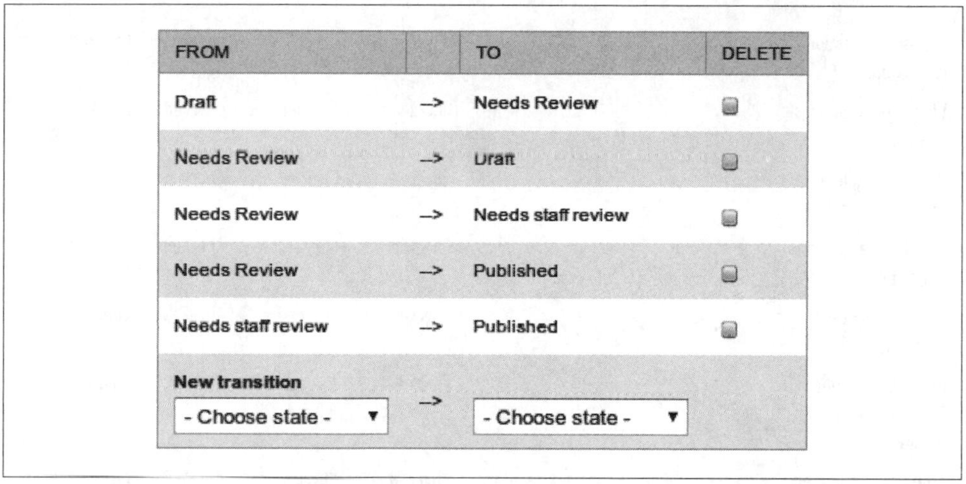

FROM		TO	DELETE
Draft	—>	Needs Review	☐
Needs Review	—>	Draft	☐
Needs Review	—>	Needs staff review	☐
Needs Review	—>	Published	☐
Needs staff review	—>	Published	☐
New transition	—>		
- Choose state - ▾		- Choose state - ▾	

Figure 7-29. Configuring Workbench Moderation transitions

To decide which role is allowed to move content from one state to another, return to the Permissions page by heading back to People→Permissions (*admin/ people/permissions*). Scroll down to the Workbench Moderation permissions and configure them for the "editor" user role (the Our Media staff editors) and the "national editor" and "culture editor" user roles (the volunteer editors), as indicated in Table 7-13. Note that we configure permissions for content revisions as well, since Workbench Moderation uses revisions to create new drafts, as we will see later in the chapter.

Table 7-13. Workbench Moderation permissions

Permission	anonymous user	authenticated user	culture editor	national editor	editor	administrator
Node						
View content revisions			Checked	Checked	Checked	Checked
Revert content revisions			Checked	Checked	Checked	Checked
Workbench Moderation						
View all unpublished content			Checked	Checked	Checked	Checked
Administer Workbench Moderation						Checked
Bypass moderation restrictions					Checked	Checked
View moderation history			Checked	Checked	Checked	Checked
View the moderation messages on a node			Checked	Checked	Checked	Checked
Use "My Drafts" workbench tab			Checked	Checked	Checked	Checked
Use "Needs Review" workbench tab			Checked	Checked	Checked	Checked
Moderate all content from Draft to Needs Review			Checked	Checked	Checked	Checked
Moderate all content from Needs Review to Draft			Checked	Checked	Checked	Checked
Moderate all content from Needs Review to Needs staff review			Checked	Checked	Checked	Checked
Moderate all content from Needs Review to Published			Checked	Checked	Checked	Checked

Setting up these permissions can seem complex. To help avoid accidental inappropriate moderation settings, Workbench Moderation provides a tool for verifying the permissions configuration. Click the "Check permissions" tab from the Workbench Moderation settings page at Configuration→Workbench→Workbench Moderation (*admin/config/workbench/moderation/check-permissions*); select the user role, the moderation task, and the content type you want to verify permissions for; and click Check.

Now that we've configured our Workbench Moderation states, transitions, and permissions, let's see how all of this looks to our editors. When you go back to the My Workbench page (*admin/workbench*), you'll see the tabs that Workbench Moderation exposes. Go ahead and edit a piece of content, and create a new draft to publish on the site.

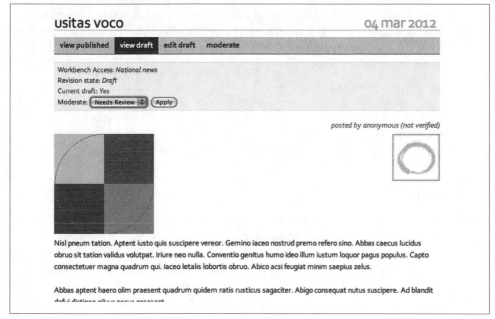

Figure 7-30. Possible state transitions for the logged-in user are now visible on draft of node

Great! Having set up Workbench Moderation to manage the content workflow, we have completed the needed restructuring of the Our Media site, enabling editors to work with the content that is relevant to them, in an easy-to-navigate administrative interface.

Taking It Further

We now have our new editorial system in place. We've met the needs of our client, but there are some other modules that are also worth checking out:

Workbench Files (http://drupal.org/project/workbench_files)
> Part of the Workbench suite, Workbench Files provides file management from within the Workbench framework, making it easy for editors to see which files have been uploaded to the site and where on the site they are being used.

Workbench Media (http://drupal.org/project/workbench_media)
> Also part of the Workbench family of modules, Workbench Media provides integration between Workbench and the Media module, which we covered extensively in Chapter 4. Workbench Media simplifies the management of media assets by allowing editors to work with assets right on Workbench's page (My Workbench).

Views Bulk Operations (VBO) (http://drupal.org/project/views_bulk_operations)
> This is a wonderful little utility module that provides checkboxes and action buttons to views, allowing you to extend the default Workbench screens with the ability to move content to various states en masse, without giving nonstaff members access to the full content overview page.

Nodequeue (http://drupal.org/project/nodequeue)
> This module is often used on online news sites, as it allows for displaying arbitrary articles in a list with a user-specified order, such as an Editor's Picks list of articles. Nodequeue also has actions integration, which allows you to do things like automatically add new articles to queues on a per-topic basis.

Summary

Congratulations! The Our Media website now includes all the major features that the staff wanted. We've used the Workflow Access module to create a distributed system for content management, preventing collisions when editors review content they are responsible for. We've also provided the team with an editorial workflow, which makes it easy for them to track changes to content as it moves through the editorial process. On top of that, all of this is done in a consistent, easy-to-use interface, so editors quickly find the content they need.

Here are the modules that we referenced in this chapter:

- Devel Generate (*http://drupal.org/project/devel*)
- Nodequeue (*http://drupal.org/project/nodequeue*)
- Pathauto (*http://drupal.org/project/pathauto*)
- Taxonomy: Part of the Drupal core
- Token (*http://drupal.org/project/token*)
- Workbench (*http://drupal.org/project/workbench*)

- Workbench Access (*http://drupal.org/project/workbench_moderation*)
- Workbench Files (*http://drupal.org/project/workbench_files*)
- Workbench Media (*http://drupal.org/project/workbench_media*)
- Workbench Moderation (*http://drupal.org/project/workbench_moderation*)

CHAPTER 8

Multilingual Sites

Creating a website with community content is great, but what if some or all of your community doesn't read or write English? It's a big world, and only about 6% of it speaks English as a native language. Multilingual sites allow you to reach out to your community members and let them feel comfortable contributing. Having multiple languages is not as simple as having users post content in whichever language they like. There are other things to consider, like navigation, date formatting, and help text. And what about having the same post available in multiple languages, and easily navigating between them? Once you start thinking about it in detail, there is a lot of ground to cover. Luckily, Drupal core and a few contributed modules have done a lot of that hard work for us so we can concentrate on building our community and content.

The two main concepts for multilingual sites are internationalization, often abbreviated i18n, and localization, often abbreviated l10n. *Internationalization* is the underlying structure that allows software to be adapted to different languages, and *localization* is the process of actually translating the software for use by a specific locale. Localization is not necessarily limited to just translating text, but also encompasses changing things like date formats and currency.

Drupal has made great strides toward building a better internationalization system inside Drupal core that makes localization much easier. Core does not quite provide us with all of the tools we need to completely localize a site, but there are contributed modules ready to fill the gaps.

This chapter introduces the following modules:

Locale (core)
> Provides interface for translating and importing translations for user interface text

Content Translation (core)
> Handles translation of user-generated content

Localization update (http://drupal.org/project/l10n_update)
> Checks for translation updates from the Drupal translation site and provides an interface to update translations from within your site.

Localization client (http://drupal.org/project/l10n_client)
>   An easy-to-use frontend for the Locale module

Internationalization (http://drupal.org/project/i18n)
>   Allows other elements to be translated, such as menus, blocks, and taxonomy terms

Variable (http://drupal.org/project/variable)
>   Provides an API for registering data for variables (required by Internationalization)

Book (core)
>   A module that allows multiple users to collaborate on documentation

Forum (core)
>   A simple discussion system, grouped by topic

If you would like to participate in the hands-on exercises in this chapter, install Drupal using the *Chapter 8: Multilingual* installation profile from the book's sample code. This will create the example website on your web server. The completed website will look as pictured in Figure 8-1 and at *http://multilingual.usingdrupal.com*. For more information on using the book's sample code, see the Preface.

Figure 8-1. The finished Blue Peak Fanatics website, displaying in Danish

Case Study

Our client, Blue Peak Fanatics, is an international group that loves to climb mountains. They need a website that will allow everyone to have forums to discuss their shared passion as well as keep a repository of shared knowledge. They would like the site to provide language-specific forums for discussion, and allow members to navigate the site in their preferred language. They will also need an online knowledge base where members can share useful information, and a way to post news about the site. Additionally, they want to allow nonforum content to be translated by group members who know more than one language, so they can all share the accumulated knowledge. They currently have members who speak three different languages—English, Danish, and French—but they would like the ability to add more languages later as the group grows.

Implementation Notes

Though Drupal core's default Article content type can easily be used to post news to the front page, other features that the client requires warrant some further discussion.

Forum Discussions

There are contributed modules available that add integration between Drupal and other forum systems, such as phpBB, but Drupal itself comes with its own simple forum using the built-in Forum module. The Forum module uses regular Drupal core concepts such as taxonomy (for forum containers and forums themselves), nodes (for posts inside a forum), and comments (for replies), which makes it integrate seamlessly with the rest of the website, including Drupal's translation features.

Knowledge Base

Another core Drupal module, the Book module enables multiple users to collaborate together in order to create a collection of documentation. Book pages are structured into one or more hierarchies, with previous, next, and up links generated automatically on each page. Each page also provides a "printer-friendly version," which will create an unformatted page consisting of the content of the current page and any subpages for easy printing or downloading for offline reading.

Translating User Interface Text

User interface is the text that is provided by Drupal, both in core and contributed modules. This includes things like form labels, help text, and navigation. Drupal core's Locale module provides the framework that allows user interface translations. To get the bulk of our localization, we will download translation projects that will supply us with translations of the core user interface. To easily download translations, as well as keep them up-to-date, we'll use the "Localization update" module. As we add contributed modules, we'll need to check whether they supply a module-specific translation. The "Localization update" module will help us with this as well. If there are no module translations for our language yet, we are not out of luck, because core also gives us the framework to add and update our own translations as needed within our site. The "Localization client" module uses this framework to add a nice, user-friendly frontend to make translating interface text a breeze.

Locale does not cover every single aspect of user interface text, though, so we will be using the excellent Internationalization (i18n) module to fill in the gaps. The Internationalization module provides us the tools to translate taxonomy, blocks, and certain site variables like the site name and mission statement. In addition to providing extra translation, it also helps us manage our multilingual content.

Translating User-Generated Content

The final missing piece is translation for all of the user-generated content on the site: forum posts, pages, and so on. Core provides the "Content translation" module to do the heavy lifting. This will allow us to decide which content is translatable, and lets us create multiple versions of each node, each in a different language. It also provides a simple way for users to switch between languages. Again, the Internationalization module will fill out some of the content features.

Spotlight: Interface Translation

Drupal core comes with the Locale module, which works with the user interface text and gives you a nice set of tools that let you import existing translations, create or edit your own, or export your site's translations for use on other sites.

Another really nice feature in Drupal core is support for right-to-left (RTL) languages, such as Arabic or Hebrew. If a language is set as an RTL language, Drupal will automatically flip all of the text so that it reads in the proper direction, as seen with Arabic in Figure 8-2.

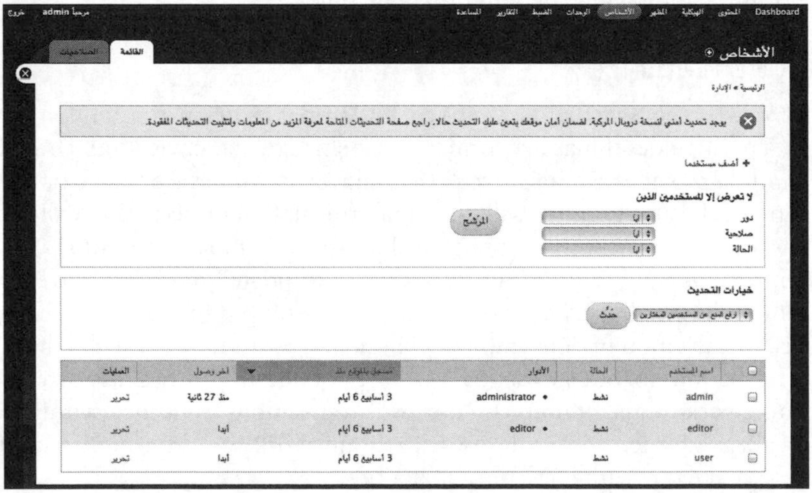

Figure 8-2. A right-to-left language page

Locale

Locale handles the translation files and language switching options on the site. Let's break it down and look at what that means.

Translations

A *translation* is simply a file or collection of files that follows a standardized format. Translation files that follow this format have a special file extension, *.po*, which stands for "portable object." A *.po* file is a simple text file that identifies strings of text and a particular language's translation of the strings. In Drupal, translations contain a list of all user interface strings in Drupal, along with their translated versions.

Drupal translation *.po* files are downloaded from *http://localize.drupal.org*. Here you will find core Drupal translations, along with any contributed module translations that have been created. An important thing to note about the translation projects is that they may be in various states of completion, coverage for contributed modules can be spotty, and sometimes you may not agree with the way something was translated. Not to worry; we'll show you how to deal with that, too.

While you can manually download the *.po* files you need and add them to your site, it can quickly become tedious, especially as you add contributed modules to your site. The Localization update module (*http://drupal.org/project/l10n_update*) will do this tedious chore for you. It will find the correct files from the Drupal translations server, download them to your site, and install a language, all in one process. You can also use it to check for and download updates to your translations.

Interface translation

Many volunteers have worked hard to translate the Drupal interface into as many languages as possible. You may find that you need to add to or modify the translation you are using. If this happens, Drupal has tools built in to assist you.

When you visit the interface translation page at Administer→"Site building"→"Translate interface" (*admin/build/translate*), you will see that there is a list of the languages you have enabled, along with a count and percentage of the number of strings that have already been translated, as shown in Figure 8-3. As you move through your site, Drupal will keep track of all the interface strings that you encounter. It can do this because translatable strings are identified in the code itself whenever a developer uses a translation function (the t() function). Once you visit a page, all of the translatable strings will be available for searching and translation. Visiting the page is an important step that is easy to forget. If you start searching for words that you know exist on the site, but you haven't actually visited the page where they are, your interface search will come back empty. We'll look more into translating in "Hands-On: Translating the Interface" on page 321.

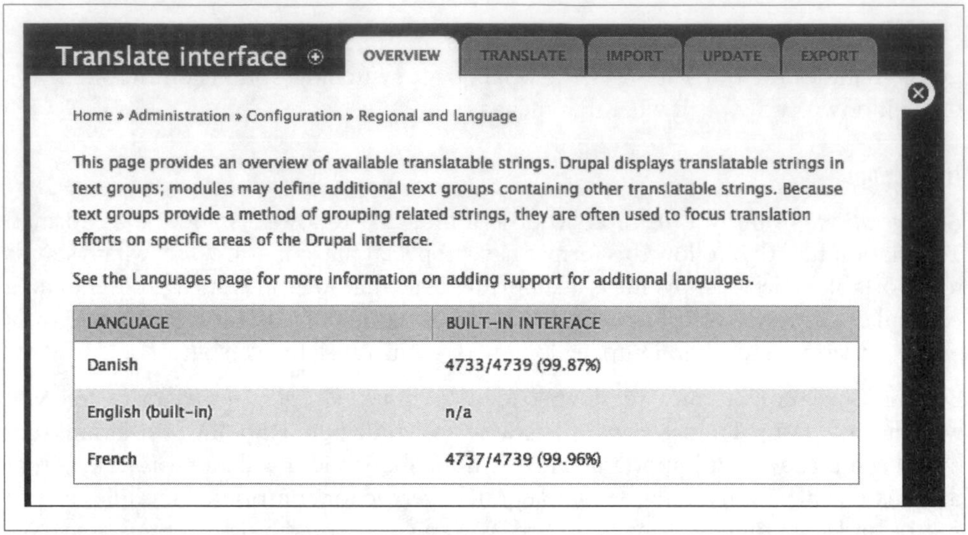

Translate interface ⊕   OVERVIEW   TRANSLATE   IMPORT   UPDATE   EXPORT   ⊗

Home » Administration » Configuration » Regional and language

This page provides an overview of available translatable strings. Drupal displays translatable strings in text groups; modules may define additional text groups containing other translatable strings. Because text groups provide a method of grouping related strings, they are often used to focus translation efforts on specific areas of the Drupal interface.

See the Languages page for more information on adding support for additional languages.

LANGUAGE	BUILT-IN INTERFACE
Danish	4733/4739 (99.87%)
English (built-in)	n/a
French	4737/4739 (99.96%)

Figure 8-3. String count with percentage translated

One thing to understand is that any translations you make through the Drupal interface, rather than by importing a *.po* file, will be stored in the database, not in a file. Drupal has an export feature that will put your translations back into a file format that you can then import into other sites.

> If you do translation work on your site, you should definitely consider giving your work back to the community. By giving translations back, you not only help the larger Drupal community, but also yourself, as you will have a larger number of people to test your work and help maintain it.

Language switching

Every site must have a default language, but how do we get the other languages to display? There are two main core mechanisms for this: the language detection and selection setting, and the language switcher block. After you have installed and enabled at least one other language, the first thing you should do is tell Drupal how to automatically handle multilingual display by configuring the language detection and selection. By default, Drupal will do nothing, and users will need to manually choose their language. You can select from several options, seen in Figure 8-4, which will automatically choose the language based on a variety of available information.

With the URL detection method, Drupal can set the language based on the domain name of the site or by a path prefix. You can choose this in the Configure screen for URL. If you choose to use a separate domain name for each language you will offer, you can assign the domain name to a language in the language settings. For example,

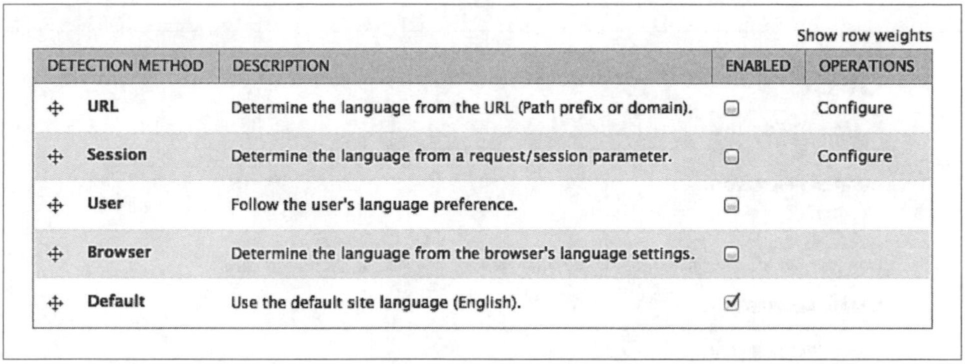

	DETECTION METHOD	DESCRIPTION	ENABLED	OPERATIONS
			Show row weights	
⊹	URL	Determine the language from the URL (Path prefix or domain).	☐	Configure
⊹	Session	Determine the language from a request/session parameter.	☐	Configure
⊹	User	Follow the user's language preference.	☐	
⊹	Browser	Determine the language from the browser's language settings.	☐	
⊹	Default	Use the default site language (English).	☑	

Figure 8-4. Automatic language switching options

you can configure the Danish language to use the domain name *http://dk.example.com* or even *http://foo.example.com*. Whenever someone accesses the site using one of these domain names, the language you have set will always be used.

The more common negotiation method is using the path prefix. Again, you can configure the prefix you wish to use. By default, a translation that you install will set its language code as the path prefix identifier. With this setting, Drupal will check the path for a language code directly after the domain name—for example, *http://example.com/dk/forum*. If Drupal finds a valid code, it will display the language associated with it. You don't need a prefix for your default language, so that language will be used for all of your "plain" paths, as in *http://example.com/forum*.

Your users can also set a language preference for themselves, if you enable the User method. The Locale module provides users with a "Language settings" section on their account page, which lets them choose the language for system emails. Once you enable the User detection method, you will see that those settings will then indicate they are also being used for site presentation, as you can see in Figure 8-5. However, this allows only authorized users to pick a language. To give all users a choice, including anonymous users, you can enable a core language switcher block that lists the available languages and will switch the site language as needed.

You can enable as many or as few detection methods as you wish. You can determine the priority for the different methods by reordering them in the table. The method at the top will be used first, and if that one does not provide adequate information to determine the language, Drupal will continue down the list until it finds a method that does. At that point, it will set the language and stop checking.

Localized installer

You can add new translations at any time, but if you wish to use a translation during the installation process as well, you will need to get a translation prior to going through the installer. By default, after you have selected an installation profile, the installer presents the default option to install Drupal in English along with a link to "Learn how

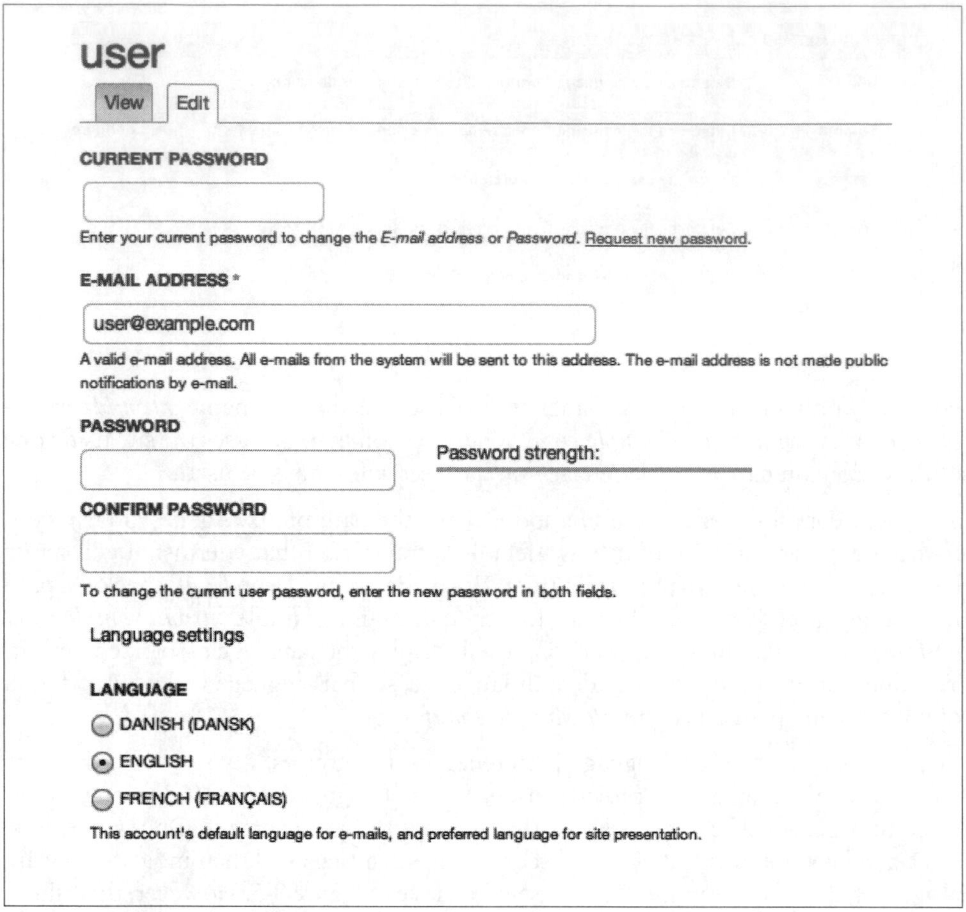

Figure 8-5. Personal language settings under the My Account page

to install Drupal in other languages." That link explains where you can download a translation file, and where you need to place that in your Drupal file structure: in the *profiles/standard/translations* folder. A much, much easier way to do this is to use the Localized Drupal Distribution (*http://drupal.org/project/l10n_install*) to install Drupal. This is a normal version of Drupal that is packaged with the "Localization update" and "Localization client" modules. This will let you choose a new Localized Drupal profile for installation, as shown in Figure 8-6, and then it will present you with a list of languages.

You can then choose which language to use, and the rest of the installation screens will be displayed in that language, as pictured in Figure 8-7. Once you complete the installation of Drupal, the language you selected will be set as the default language for your site.

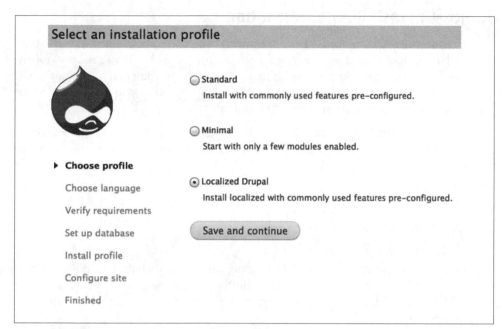

Figure 8-6. Selecting the Localized Drupal profile during installation

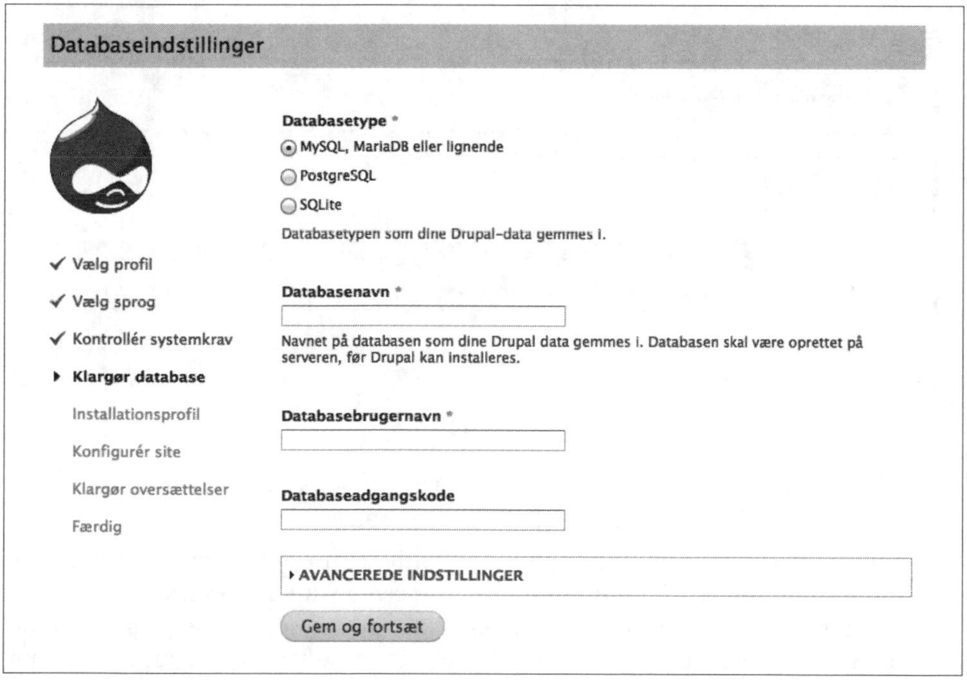

Databaseindstillinger

Databasetype *
- MySQL, MariaDB eller lignende
- PostgreSQL
- SQLite

Databasetypen som dine Drupal-data gemmes i.

✓ Vælg profil

✓ Vælg sprog

✓ Kontrollér systemkrav

▶ **Klargør database**

Installationsprofil

Konfigurér site

Klargør oversættelser

Færdig

Databasenavn *

Navnet på databasen som dine Drupal data gemmes i. Databasen skal være oprettet på serveren, før Drupal kan installeres.

Databasebrugernavn *

Databaseadgangskode

▶ AVANCEREDE INDSTILLINGER

Gem og fortsæt

Figure 8-7. The installation screen displaying with Danish

Hands-On: Installing a Translation

The first step to using any of Drupal's multilingual features is installing a translation, so that Drupal has more than one language to choose from. As mentioned previously, you can use a localized distribution so that you install your language during the site installation process. Alternatively, you can add a language after you have installed the site by using the "Localization update" module.

1. First, in the administrative toolbar, click Modules (*admin/modules*) and enable the following modules (note that if you installed Drupal with the localization distribution, these will already be enabled):

   • Core
     — Locale
   • Multilingual package
     — Localization update

2. In the administrative toolbar, click Configuration→Languages (*admin/config/regional/language*) under the "Regional and languages" section. Then click the "+ Add language" link, as shown in Figure 8-8, to be taken to the screen shown in Figure 8-9.

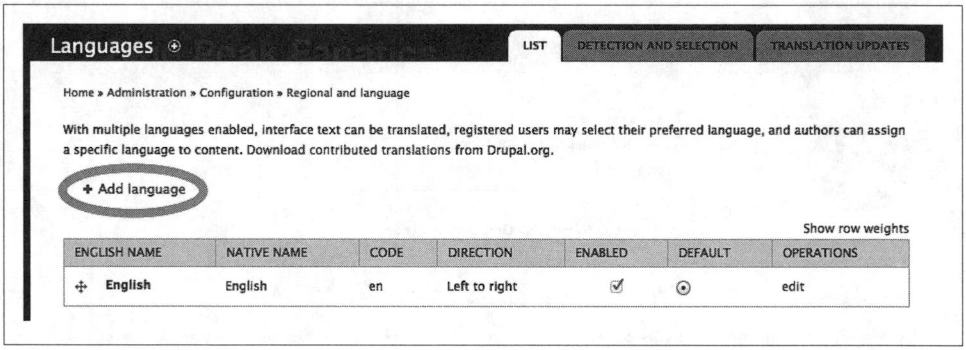

Figure 8-8. The "Add language" link

3. Select your language from the "Language name" select list (in this case, we are adding Danish) and click the "Add language" button.

4. The translation files will be imported from the Drupal.org server into your site, and you will see an "Updating translation" screen with a progress bar, as shown in Figure 8-10. Once the import is completed, you will see a message that outlines all of the updates you have imported and indicates that the site successfully imported the translation.

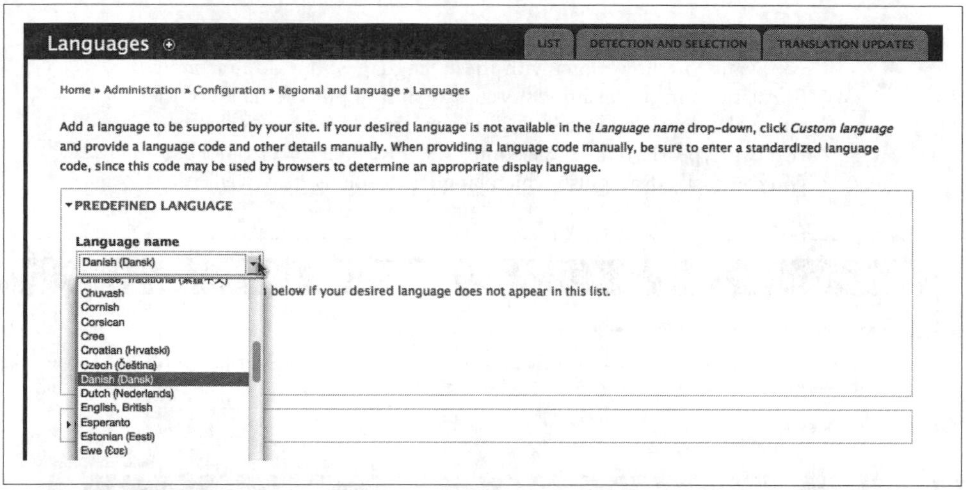

Figure 8-9. The "Add language" screen with a drop-down select list

Figure 8-10. The "Updating translation" page showing progress

You can repeat the language selection for each language that you wish to have available on your site. In our examples throughout the chapter, we have also installed French, using the same process as we did to install Danish. When done, the Languages settings page will list all of the site languages in a table that lets you take various actions, such as disabling a language, changing the site default language, affecting the order in which the languages are displayed in lists, and deleting them altogether. Figure 8-11 shows this table with our site's three languages: Danish, English, and French. English is marked as the default language, which means it will be used as the fallback language when there is no language specified either through the language negotiation settings or a logged-in user's personal settings under his "My account" page, as we saw in the section "Language switching" on page 312. The crosshair icon at the beginning of each line in the table will let you drag and drop the languages into a particular order; this is the order in which the languages will appear when listed together—in form select lists, for example.

Our examples in this chapter are using English, Danish, and French. If you want to follow along with these languages, but do not know the translations in our examples, you can simply put the name of the intended language in place (e.g., if you are translating the Welcome post, you can type "DANISH Welcome" or "FRENCH Welcome") so that you can easily distinguish which language is being displayed.

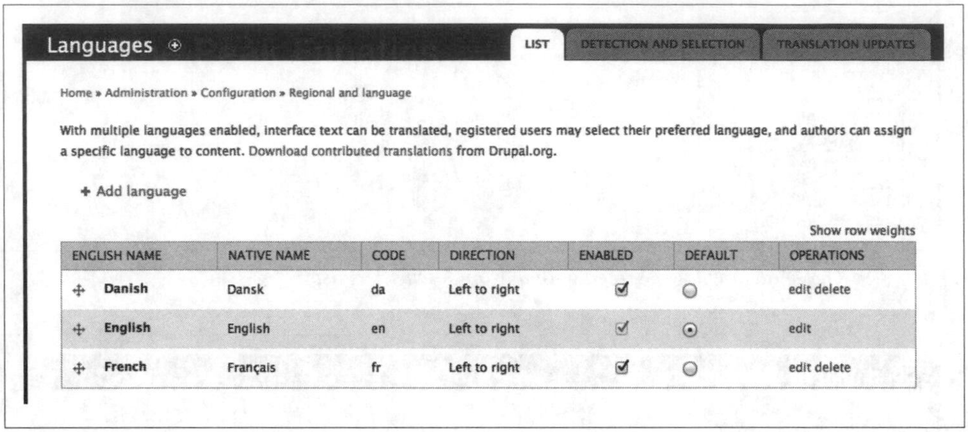

ENGLISH NAME	NATIVE NAME	CODE	DIRECTION	ENABLED	DEFAULT	OPERATIONS
Danish	Dansk	da	Left to right	☑	◯	edit delete
English	English	en	Left to right	☑	⦿	edit
French	Français	fr	Left to right	☑	◯	edit delete

Figure 8-11. The installed languages table

You can also choose to edit the language name, negotiation identifiers, and direction, as seen in Figure 8-12, by clicking the "edit" link. Normally, you won't want to change these settings unless you have a very good reason, so we are going to leave all of our settings at their comfortable defaults.

Hands-On: Configuring Locale Features

Now we need to make a choice about how and when Drupal will use our new languages. To make it easy for users to see our site in different languages and allow them to pick as they like, we will also add a simple language switcher to the site.

Language Detection and Selection

As discussed earlier in "Language switching" on page 312, we have several options to choose from. Our client does not have separate domains for the languages, so they are just going to use Drupal's path prefix. We also want to make sure that we honor the user's preference, if she has set a preference in her account settings. We are going to use the URL and User detection methods, so that the site will first check the URL, and if that is not valid information, it will fall back to the user's preference, if she's selected

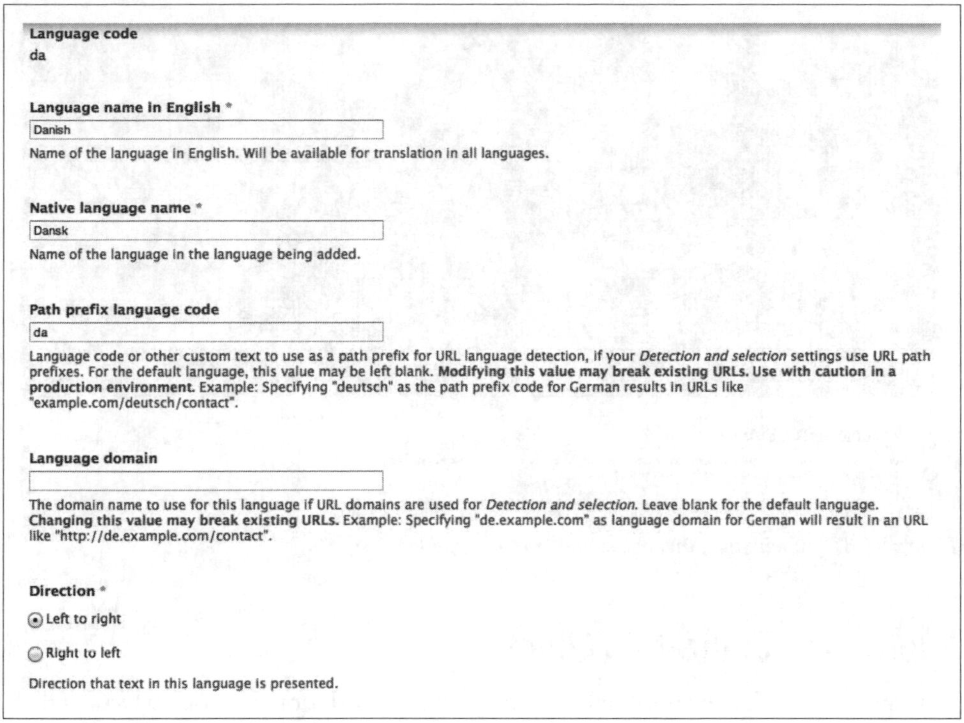

Language code
da

Language name in English *
Danish

Name of the language in English. Will be available for translation in all languages.

Native language name *
Dansk

Name of the language in the language being added.

Path prefix language code
da

Language code or other custom text to use as a path prefix for URL language detection, if your *Detection and selection* settings use URL path prefixes. For the default language, this value may be left blank. **Modifying this value may break existing URLs. Use with caution in a production environment.** Example: Specifying "deutsch" as the path prefix code for German results in URLs like "example.com/deutsch/contact".

Language domain

The domain name to use for this language if URL domains are used for *Detection and selection.* Leave blank for the default language. **Changing this value may break existing URLs.** Example: Specifying "de.example.com" as language domain for German will result in an URL like "http://de.example.com/contact".

Direction *
⦿ Left to right
◯ Right to left

Direction that text in this language is presented.

Figure 8-12. Screen for editing an installed language

one. If neither of those are applicable, then the site will fall back to using the default language, which in this instance is English.

1. Return to the Languages page by going to the administrative toolbar and clicking Configuration→Languages, then click the "Detection and Selection" tab (*admin/config/regional/language/configure*).

2. Check the boxes for URL and User and click "Save settings."

Language Switcher

The Locale module provides a block to switch languages, which can be configured just like any other block to have a different (or no) title, and have various display options set.

1. In the administrative toolbar, click Structure→Blocks (*admin/structure/block*) and find the "Language switcher" block in the list under the Disabled section.

2. Set the block to appear in the "First sidebar" region, drag it to the top of the block list for that region, and then click the "Save blocks" button.

3. You should now see a new block called Languages, which contains a list of each installed language on the site, as shown in Figure 8-13.

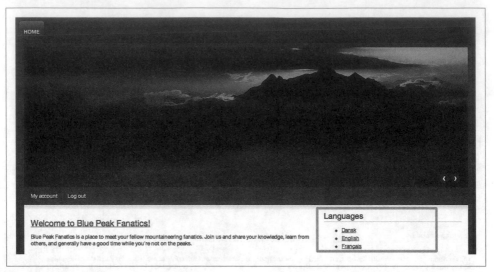

Figure 8-13. Site with the language switcher block enabled

Spotlight: Localization Client

You may notice that even though you are using a translation that you have installed, there might still be some untranslated text peeking out here and there. This will become more likely as you add contributed modules. Almost no site will have absolutely 100% language coverage out of the box, so you will probably need to translate a few items yourself. Drupal has a built-in system to do this with the Locale module, but using it can be clunky and tedious. This is where the contributed "Localization client" module really shines. It makes quick text fixes easy and intuitive.

The "Localization client" module adds a translation editor right on the bottom of your screen that stays with you as you move through the site. You can minimize it when you don't need it and then expand it when you do. Figure 8-14 shows the editor expanded on a page. It provides a nice, easy-to-use interface to see which strings on the page have been translated and, more importantly, which have not. It allows you to browse or search through the list; you can simply select the string you wish and add the translation right there on the screen.

There are some important caveats to keep in mind, however. The "Localization client" module is a great tool but it does depend on JavaScript and, at the time of this writing, it does not assist with translating strings that are added by the Internationalization module (which we'll discuss later). Additionally, it can only translate text that can be seen by the person running "Localization client"; for example, if the text is visible only under certain conditions, it may not be translatable with the "Localization client" module.

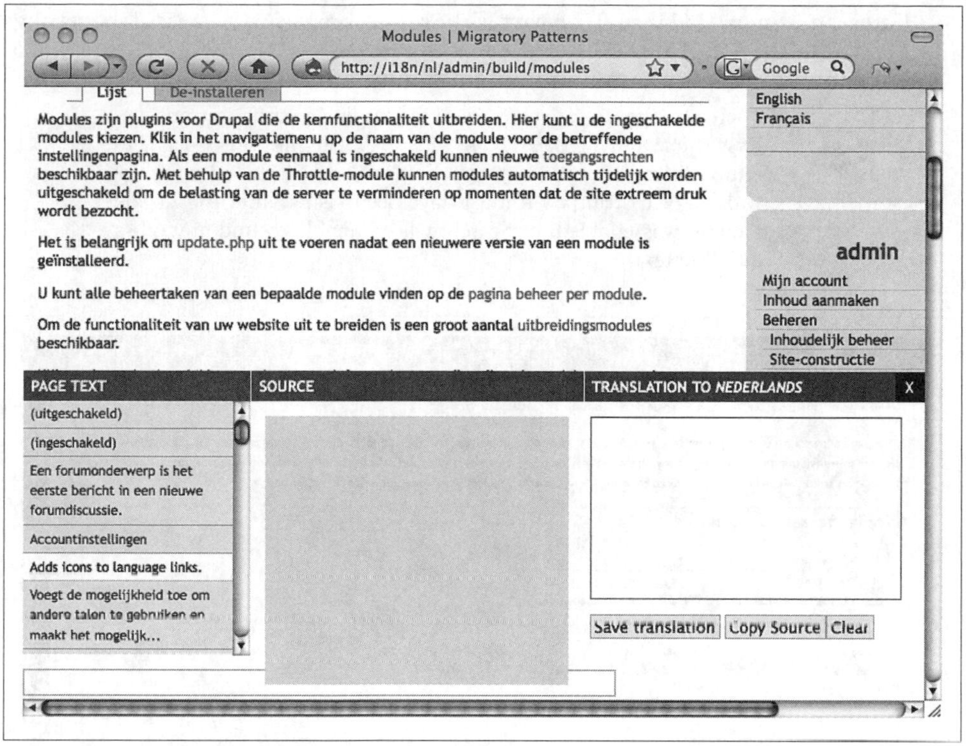

Figure 8-14. The "Localization client" interface

Hands-On: Translating the Interface

Not everyone wants or needs to install yet another module, and due to the caveats we mentioned about "Localization client", it is still a good idea to be familiar with how core translation works, so let's start there.

Using the Locale Module

Interface translation depends on the Locale module, which should already be enabled on your site once you have installed a translation.

1. In the administrative toolbar, click Configuration→"Translate interface" in the "Regional and language" section (*admin/config/regional/translate*) to get started.

2. You will be presented with a table of your languages and the percentage of strings that have been translated so far. Click on the Translate tab (*admin/config/regional/translate/translate*).

3. The "String contains" search box, pictured in Figure 8-15, allows you to search for a specific piece of text somewhere in Drupal's interface and then translate it.

Enter the string **multilingual support** in the search box, leave the rest of the settings at their defaults, and click Filter.

 There are two caveats to successfully finding a string to translate. First, the search interface is case-sensitive. Searching for "User" will return different results than searching for "user." Second, the page with a given string on it must have been visited after the Locale module was enabled, or Search will be unable to find any of its interface text.

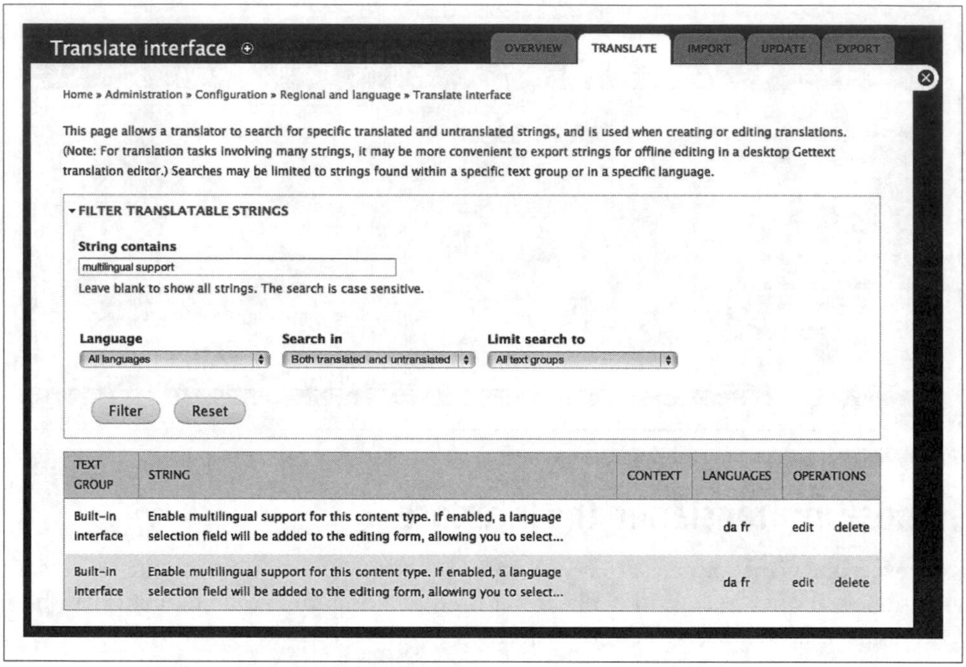

Translate interface ⊕   OVERVIEW   **TRANSLATE**   IMPORT   UPDATE   EXPORT ⊗

Home » Administration » Configuration » Regional and language » Translate interface

This page allows a translator to search for specific translated and untranslated strings, and is used when creating or editing translations. (Note: For translation tasks involving many strings, it may be more convenient to export strings for offline editing in a desktop Gettext translation editor.) Searches may be limited to strings found within a specific text group or in a specific language.

▾ FILTER TRANSLATABLE STRINGS

String contains

multilingual support

Leave blank to show all strings. The search is case sensitive.

Language   **Search in**   **Limit search to**
All languages   ▲▼   Both translated and untranslated ▲▼   All text groups ▲▼

[Filter]   [Reset]

TEXT GROUP	STRING	CONTEXT	LANGUAGES	OPERATIONS	
Built-in interface	Enable multilingual support for this content type. If enabled, a language selection field will be added to the editing form, allowing you to select...		da fr	edit	delete
Built-in interface	Enable multilingual support for this content type. If enabled, a language selection field will be added to the editing form, allowing you to select...		da fr	edit	delete

Figure 8-15. Search results for the string "multilingual support"

4. On the search results page, pictured in Figure 8-15, you will see a list of all the places on the site where that string is seen. The translation status is in the Languages column, which lists the language codes. A strike through a language code means it is not translated yet. Here, searching returned several results, which are all translated.

5. Click the "edit" link next to one of the strings, which will bring you to the translation page, as shown in Figure 8-16. You will be presented with a text area for each language, where you can add or edit the text as appropriate. When you click the "Save translations" button, the strings will be updated.

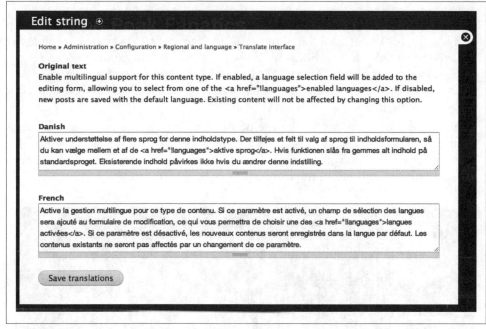

Figure 8-16. The string translation page showing the original string and translations for each language

Using the Localization Client

As you can tell from the previous section, it is hard to see the strings that need to be translated on your site, remember them, go to the Translate interface, search for them, and only then actually be able to translate. It is a cumbersome, tedious process. Luckily, there's an easier way: the "Localization client" module.

1. In the administrative toolbar, click Modules (*admin/modules*) and enable:
   - Multilingual package
     — Localization client
2. In the administrative toolbar, click People→Permissions (*admin/people/permissions*), configure the permissions shown in Table 8-1, and then click "Save permissions."

Table 8-1. "Localization client" module permissions

Permission	anonymous user	authenticated user	administrator	editor
Localization client: use on-page translation			Checked	Checked

3. One very important thing you need to understand is that the "Localization client" module will not work with text that is located in the administrative overlay. To make it work correctly in the administrative interface, we are going to disable the Overlay module temporarily as we work through our translations. When we are done, we can re-enable Overlay. So, head back to the administrative toolbar and click Modules (*admin/modules*). Disable the "Core: Overlay" module and click "Save configuration."

4. Now you can go to the home page of your site, where the Languages block is displayed, and switch your site into a language other than English by clicking a language name. You will see a small blue bar appear at the bottom of your screen with a black Translate Text button on the right side (Figure 8-17).

Figure 8-17. The "Localization client" module's Translate Text button

5. Click the Translate Text box, and a translation area will open up at the bottom of your browser window, as shown in Figure 8-18. All of the highlighted green items listed under Page Text have already been translated. Ones in white still need work.

6. You can limit the list by searching in the text box at the bottom of it. In the administrative toolbar, click Modules (*admin/modules*) and type **Translate** into the search box (note the capital "T"). The list will update as you type, and it should bring up the string "Translate field properties," which is provided by Internationalization's "Field translation" module. as its description. Unless someone has provided a translation file for the module in your language, the English should show up as white (untranslated) in the search results.

Figure 8-18. The "Localization client" module's translation interface, showing both translated and untranslated strings

7. When you click an item in the Page Text list, it will be placed in the Source box so that you know which text you are working with. If it already has a translation, that text will appear in the "Translation to language" box.

8. You can add or edit the translation as needed and click the "Save translation" button. For example, "Oversæt feltegenskaber" is the translation of this string into Danish. Figure 8-19 shows the "Localization client" screen with the English string selected and the Danish translation ready to be saved.

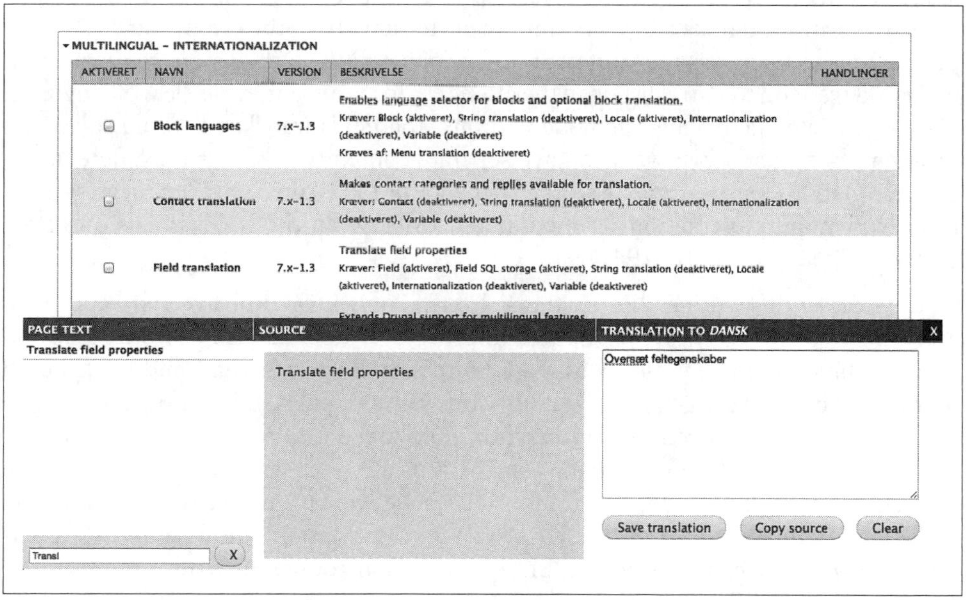

Figure 8-19. Using the "Localization client" module to translate a string to Danish

9. When finished, click the black X in the top bar of the translation area to close the client.

10. When you reload the page, you will see the changes you made, if any.

11. Once our translations are done, we can re-enable the Overlay module and click "Save configuration." You can also switch the site back to English by going to the home page and selecting English from the Languages block.

Spotlight: Content Translation

When it comes to translating your site's content in Drupal 7, we have two possibilities. There is the core "Content translation" module and the contributed "Entity translation" module (*http://drupal.org/project/entity_translation*). They have quite different approaches to translation. The major difference is that "Content translation" lets you create multiple versions of the same content in different languages and associates the translated versions together as a set. Each translation is an individual node, so for each piece of content on your site, you will have as many nodes as you have translations. For example, an English node with three other language translations (say, Danish, French, and Spanish) will be a set of four full nodes on your site. With "Entity translation," you only have one node (an entity), and each field on the node will have multiple values, one for each translation.

Both systems have pros and cons, and you could mix and match both of them on your site for different content. Having multiple nodes can cause problems when you have associated metadata that you don't want spread out over several nodes. For example, if you have an event node and you want people to sign up for the event, you don't want people to sign up across four different nodes, depending on the language they read it in. You'd want one, central list of all the attendees for the event, regardless of language. On the other hand, having one node with just the fields translated would solve that problem, but what if you want to have separate content workflows for different languages? Gábor Hojtsy, who has worked on a lot of the Drupal core language system, has a very good presentation on the differences between the two systems on *http://groups.drupal.org/node/165194*.

At the time of this writing, "Entity translation" is only in an alpha version, and there are plans to make significant changes to improve it by updating the user interface and by providing more integration with core (with search in particular) and contributed modules. The ultimate goal is to get this work into Drupal 8. It is simply too early to use it for a real site since it is very much in flux. Once it settles down and there is a stable release in the future, though, "Entity translation" is very likely to become the standard way to provide content translation. Since we have to use what is available, we'll stick with the tried-and-true core "Content translation" module here, but it is definitely worth keeping an eye on "Entity translation" down the road.

So, let's look at the core method for identifying and creating multilingual content. The Locale module will give you the option to enable multilingual support for your content types. Enabling multilingual support will give you a drop-down select box, shown in Figure 8-20, to choose the language that each post is written in. All this will do is identify the language being used for that content.

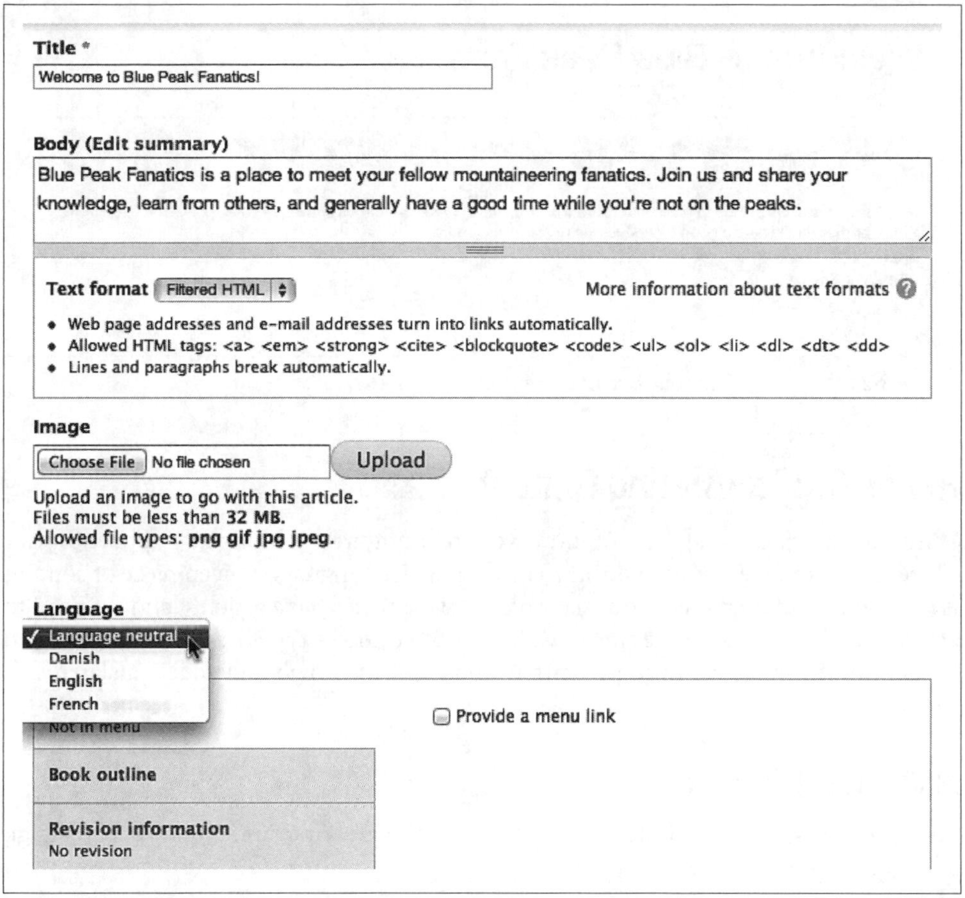

Title *

> Welcome to Blue Peak Fanatics!

Body (Edit summary)

> Blue Peak Fanatics is a place to meet your fellow mountaineering fanatics. Join us and share your knowledge, learn from others, and generally have a good time while you're not on the peaks.

Text format [Filtered HTML ◆]   More information about text formats ❓

- Web page addresses and e-mail addresses turn into links automatically.
- Allowed HTML tags: `<a> <em> <strong> <cite> <blockquote> <code> <ul> <ol> <li> <dl> <dt> <dd>`
- Lines and paragraphs break automatically.

Image

[Choose File] No file chosen   [Upload]

Upload an image to go with this article.
Files must be less than **32 MB**.
Allowed file types: **png gif jpg jpeg.**

Language

| ✓ Language neutral |
| Danish |
| English |
| French |
| Not in menu |

☐ Provide a menu link

Book outline

Revision information
No revision

Figure 8-20. Selecting a language for a piece of content

When you use the "Content translation" module, you get an additional option under multilingual support: "Enabled, with translation." Using this setting not only identifies the language for the post as written, but also allows you to associate other nodes as translated versions of the same content. For example, you may want to have an About page on the site that has the same content translated into French and Danish. With translations enabled, you would create the original About page and then, from that, create a brand-new node each for the French and Danish versions. Drupal will keep track of these three nodes and know that they are related, each one simply a version of the same page. On each page, there will be a link for the other translations at the bottom of the post, as indicated in Figure 8-21.

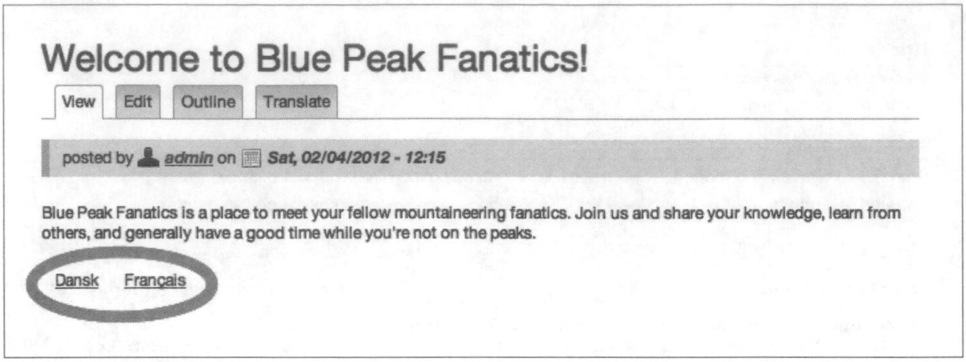

Figure 8-21. Language links on content to view other translations

Hands-On: Translating Content

With our interface taken care of, now we can configure multilingual support for our content. That is, we need to be able to identify which language a given piece of content is written in and then create translations. So, we already have articles, and we need to add a knowledge base to the site as well. For both of these types of content, we'll need to identify the language they are written in, as well as provide related, translated versions.

Multilingual Content

First, we will set up our content types with multilingual options so that we can assign a language to each piece of content:

1. In the administrative toolbar, click Modules (*admin/modules*) and enable the following modules:
   - Core
     - Book
     - Content translation
2. Then, in the administrative toolbar, click Structure→"Content types" (*admin/structure/types*) and click the "edit" link for the "Book page" type.
3. Scroll down the screen and click on the "Publishing options" tab. You will see several options for "Multilingual support." Select the "Enabled, with translation" radio button, as seen in Figure 8-22, and click the "Save content type" button. This lets us identify the language for each piece of content, and in addition, lets us create translated versions of the content that will be linked together automatically.

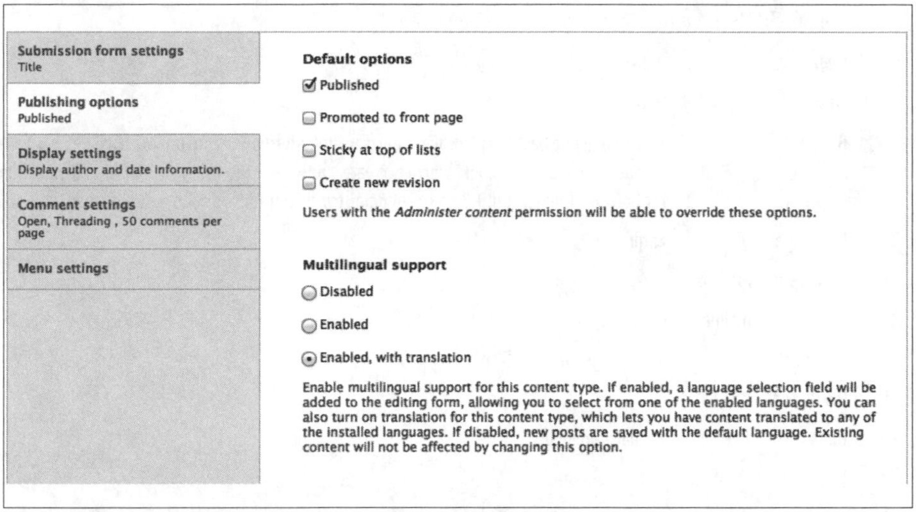

Submission form settings	**Default options**
Title	☑ Published
Publishing options	☐ Promoted to front page
Published	
Display settings	☐ Sticky at top of lists
Display author and date information.	☐ Create new revision
Comment settings	Users with the *Administer content* permission will be able to override these options.
Open, Threading , 50 comments per page	
Menu settings	**Multilingual support**
	○ Disabled
	○ Enabled
	⦿ Enabled, with translation

Enable multilingual support for this content type. If enabled, a language selection field will be added to the editing form, allowing you to select from one of the enabled languages. You can also turn on translation for this content type, which lets you have content translated to any of the installed languages. If disabled, new posts are saved with the default language. Existing content will not be affected by changing this option.

Figure 8-22. Multilingual support options for content types

4. Repeat for the Article content type.

5. Now we can edit our front page article and set the language for it. (If you are not using the installation profile that provides a front page article, go ahead and create one.) Go to the front page of the site, click the title for the article there, and then click the Edit tab. Scroll down to the Language setting and select English. Save the content.

6. We want all users to be able to translate content for us, so we need to make sure we set the permissions for everyone but anonymous users. Because all users are authenticated, we can do this by enabling the permission for all authenticated users. In the administrative toolbar, click People→Permissions (*admin/people/permissions*), configure the permissions shown in Table 8-2, and click "Save permissions."

Table 8-2. "Content translation" module permissions

Permission	anonymous user	authenticated user	administrator	editor
Content translation: translate content		Checked	Checked	Checked

Translation

We now have a way to assign a language to content, and we've done this for our existing front page article. Now we need to look at creating translations and set up the Knowledge Base section of our site:

1. Make the Introduction to the Knowledge Base in English. From either the toolbar's shortcuts bar, or the Navigation block, click "Add content"→"Book page," fill in the fields as shown in Table 8-3, and click Save.

Table 8-3. "Book page" content

Field	Value
Title	Introduction
Body	This knowledge base is a place to organize useful information. Anyone with a Blue Peak Fanatics account can add to this book! You may create a new page by clicking the "Add child page" link at the bottom of any existing KB page or by going to Add content→Book page in your navigation block.
Language	English
Menu settings tab	
Provide a menu link	checked
Menu link	Knowledge Base
Book outline tab	
Book	<create a new book>

2. After you save the content, you will see that there is a Translate tab next to the normal View, Edit, and Outline (for book content) tabs. Click the Translate tab, and you will be presented with a table listing all of your site's enabled languages, which you can see in Figure 8-23.

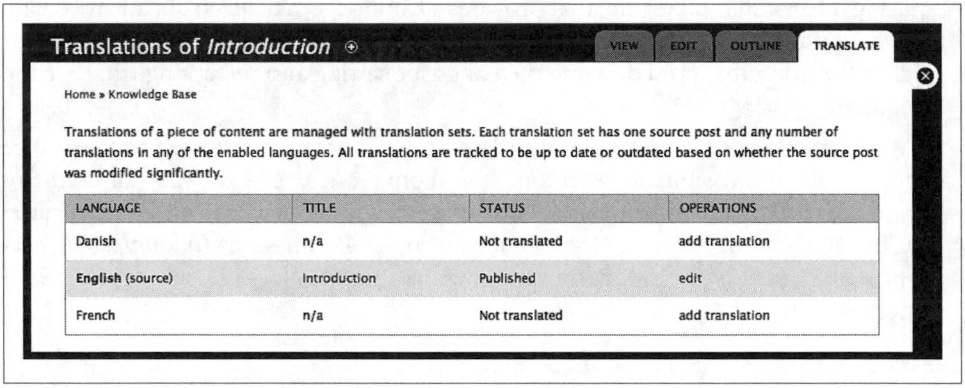

Figure 8-23. The Translate tab on a book page, showing available languages and translation status

3. Click "Add translation" for a language, and you will be presented with a screen containing the form values that were previously submitted. You may now edit the text for the Title and Body. Notice the language is already selected for you. Translate the text into the selected language, and remember to again create a menu item, give it a title, and choose "<create a new book>" in the "Book outline" tab as well, so that this translated introduction page will also be a top-level book entry for those viewing the site in this language.

4. When you click Save for this new translation page, you will see that there is now a link at the bottom that will take you to the other language's version of the page. You can also see that our Languages block indicates which languages this page is available in. The translated pages have active links, but the untranslated language (French, in this case) is not an active link and has a strikethrough, as seen in Figure 8-24.

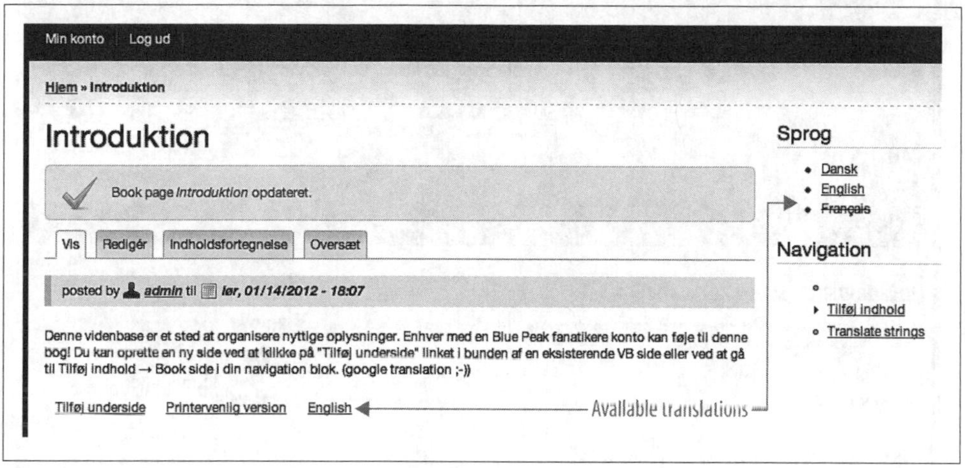

Figure 8-24. Translations available for the Introduction page

You should do the same for the Welcome post on the front page or any other content that was created prior to enabling content translation. Just edit the existing post to select the language and use the Translate tab to add versions for other languages, as we did previously.

> Keep in mind that the default language setting for all content is "Language neutral." You must identify the content with a language in order to see the Translate tab and proceed with creating translations. If you do not set a language when initially creating the content or if you have enabled the "Content translation" module after already creating content, that content will be set to "Language neutral."

When you create a translation for any content that is on the front page of the site (like the Welcome post in the profile), you will notice that each translation appears. The same thing is happening for our Knowledge Base menu items, as you can see in Figure 8-25. We're going to address that issue in the next section.

Figure 8-25. Duplicate items—one for each language

Spotlight: Internationalization

So far we've got a nice start with getting our site translated, but everything is not quite smooth yet. We have translations for some of our content and menu items, but they all appear at the same time. There are multiple posts on the front page, and all the language menu items are shown regardless of which language we are viewing the site in. You will also see some stray text still in English. For example, under the "Create content" menu item, our content type names and descriptions are not translated, nor is the Home menu tab. To take our multilingual site further and really make it shine, we are going to turn to a package of modules called Internationalization (i18n). There is a central Internationalization module, which comes packaged with a handful of other modules designed to work together to extend core's multilingual features.

One important thing that these modules do is help us get various strings of text into core's translation interface that are otherwise not available. Drupal's core interface tools can detect only strings that are hardcoded directly into the code (using Drupal's t() function)—that is to say, that are code-generated. All of the user-generated strings are not accessible. It is important to realize that these strings that are added by the

Internationalization modules will *not* be available to you through the "Localization client" module's "Translate Text" interface. To translate these, you must use the core interface, covered earlier in "Hands-On: Translating the Interface" on page 321.

A second feature that many of these modules add is a way to select a language for an item, such as for menus, blocks, or taxonomy terms, like the one we saw in our "add content" forms earlier with the "Content translation" module. Being able to discretely identify the language being used for an item allows the Internationalization module to filter the display based on the languages we want to see, leading to less duplication and confusion.

The Internationalization package of modules provides a lot of tools; we will not need all of them for the Blue Peak Fanatics site. We will discuss what these tools are and then see some of them in action as we proceed with building our site.

Multilingual Content Selection

One of the first things you probably noted after making your first piece of translated content was that all of the translations were showing on the front page, regardless of the language in which you were viewing the site. Internationalization's "Multilingual select" module helps us get this under control. It adds a new tab called "Multilingual settings," seen in Figure 8-26 , where you can determine if the site will filter the content based on language. You can enable it site-wide in the "Content to filter by language" section, but you can also exclude certain items from the Internationalization filtering. The best example of this is provided as a default setting by the module: Views. Since Views provides its own ways of filtering the content, you don't necessarily need or want Internationalization to get involved. You can also disable the language filtering for certain pages on the site. The default setting excludes the administrative pages from language filtering. This makes all administrative pages display in the site default language.

Strings

The Strings module is required for most of the Internationalization modules. It doesn't do anything on its own, but when used in conjunction with other Internationalization modules, it turns various pieces of text on the site into translatable strings that are added to the core translation interface.

Site-Wide Language-Dependent Variables

A Drupal site can have many bits and pieces of text that are not associated with any particular node. These site-wide settings are stored in the database and referred to as *variables*. Some examples are the site name and slogan, found on the Site Information screen, or the registration email templates found under "User settings." There is no

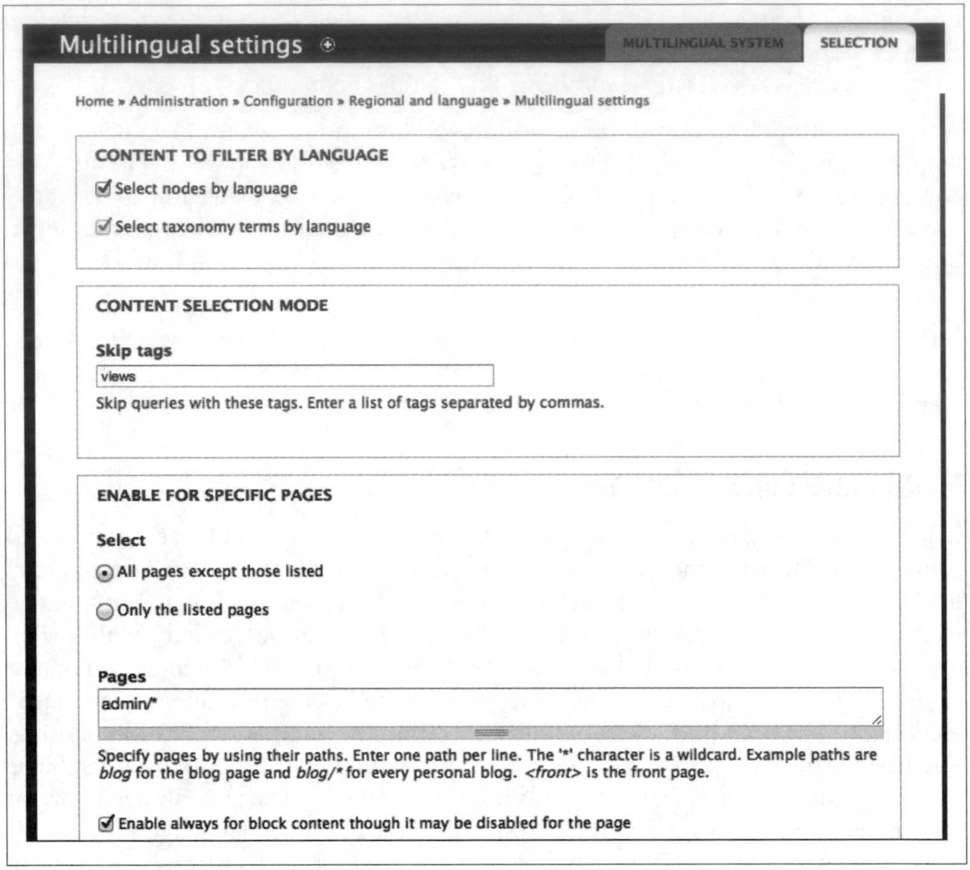

Figure 8-26. The Internationalization module's content selection options

simple way to get these particular kinds of text into the regular translatable string interface. The Internationalization "Variable translation" module, which is dependent on the Variable module, adds the ability to tell Drupal specifically that you wish to provide translations for these variables.

Module Helpers

The Internationalization module also works with a number of core modules to aid with translations:

Menu translation

The Multilingual Menu module adds any custom menu items you create to the translate interface string list. You can also specify which language a particular menu item is for, and its display will follow the rule you selected for content display. You should note that, independently of this module, you can create a menu item in a language for each node, which will also follow the display rules. So if you are only creating menu items based on nodes, you do not need to enable this module. If you wish to have menu items that don't point to specific nodes, then this module will let you create the translations you need.

Taxonomy translation

Multilingual taxonomy gives you a few options for keeping track of your taxonomy translations. When creating a new vocabulary, you can choose whether you want to localize the terms using the regular translate interface method, set up independent terms per language, or set one language for the entire vocabulary. When you choose to create terms per language, you will be able to select a language for each term. Once you have created the terms and assigned a language for each, you can then create associations between them. For example, the terms "cat" (assigned to English) and "le chat" (assigned to French) can be marked as equivalent terms.

Block languages

The Multilingual Blocks module will let you pick a language for each block. Assigning a language to a block will determine when it is displayed according to the main content display settings. For custom blocks that you create, you can also decide whether you wish the block text to be translatable by adding the strings to the translation interface.

Multilingual content

This module provides some extended settings for nodes to give you more control over the translations and workflow for content. For example, you can set a default language per content type, require certain languages, as well as use this to provide translations for the configuration text (e.g., the content type names).

Field translation

While this may seem like it will allow you to translate individual field *content*, this is actually a module that lets you translate the text for a field's *settings*, including things like the help text.

The "Contact translation" and Multilingual Forum modules simply allow for those two core modules to work well with Internationalization.

Paths

The "Path translation" module allows you to map together existing paths that are translations of each other. Most paths are linked for you through regular translation modules like "Content translation" and "Taxonomy translation." This module will let you link arbitrary paths, such as when you are using the Panels or Views modules.

Synchronization

One last Internationalization module in the package is Translation Synchronization. This module will keep your taxonomy and node fields synchronized between several translations of a node. For instance, if you have a piece of content like a blog post that is in three languages and has a term selected, this module will make sure that the term changes on the other two nodes when you change it on one.

Hands-On: Internationalization Features

Now that we have these great tools available to us, let's enable a few of them and start to really round out our site.

Content Selection

Translated content is all shown by default. The main Internationalization module will let you display only content that is relevant to the language currently in use:

1. In the administrative toolbar, click Modules (*admin/modules*) and enable the following modules:
   - Multilingual – Internationalization package
     — Internationalization
     — Multilingual select
   - Other package
     — Variable

2. In the administrative toolbar, click Configuration→Multilingual system, under the "Regional and language" section (*admin/config/regional/i18n*), where you will see the options for "Languages for content." By default, it is set to "Enabled languages only," which what we want, so we can leave it be.

3. Click the Selection tab (*admin/config/regional/i18n/select*). This is where we determine how we would like our translated content to appear. The default settings are good for us, so we can leave this alone as well. Close the Overlay screen and you will be returned to the site.

If you go to the front page of the site, you will see that we now only get one Welcome post and one Knowledge Base menu item. If you choose Dansk from the "Language switcher" block, you will see that the Danish "Velkommen" post appears, and the menu items change to the Danish versions.

Now the content we see is more streamlined, as shown in Figure 8-27. Let's move on to translating other items in the site that are being stubborn, such as the site name, Blue Peak Fanatics.

Site-Wide Variables

Before we can translate the various site-wide variables, we need to let Drupal know which ones we want to make translatable. To do this, we'll need to use the "Variable translation" module.

Figure 8-27. With content selection mode enabled, we no longer see duplicate items

1. In the administrative toolbar, click Modules (*admin/modules*) and enable:
   - Multilingual package
     —Variable translation
   - Other package
     —Variable realm
     —Variable store

2. Before we can begin translation, we'll need to identify which variables we would like to be made translatable. In the administrative toolbar, click Configuration→"Multilingual settings," and click the Variables tab (*admin/config/regional/ i18n/variable*). You will be presented with a list of variables that are available to be translated.

3. You can select as many variables here as you would like, but all we need for this task is to check the box for "Site name" and click the "Save configuration" button.

4. Now we can begin translating. In the administrative toolbar, click Configuration→"Site information" (*admin/config/system/site-information*). At the top of the

page, you will see a box indicating that there are multilingual variables on the page, as well as providing language switcher links. As shown in Figure 8-28, each variable that is translatable will also have underneath it the text "This is a multilingual variable."

Site information ⊕

ⓧ

Home » Administration » Configuration » System

THERE ARE MULTILINGUAL VARIABLES IN THIS FORM.
Check you are editing the variables for the right language or select the desired one. To enable more multilingual variables visit multilingual variables configuration.

Select language
Danish | **English** | French ◄——————Language switcher

SITE DETAILS

Site name *
~~Blue Peak Fanatics~~
This is a multilingual variable.

Slogan

How this is used depends on your site's theme.

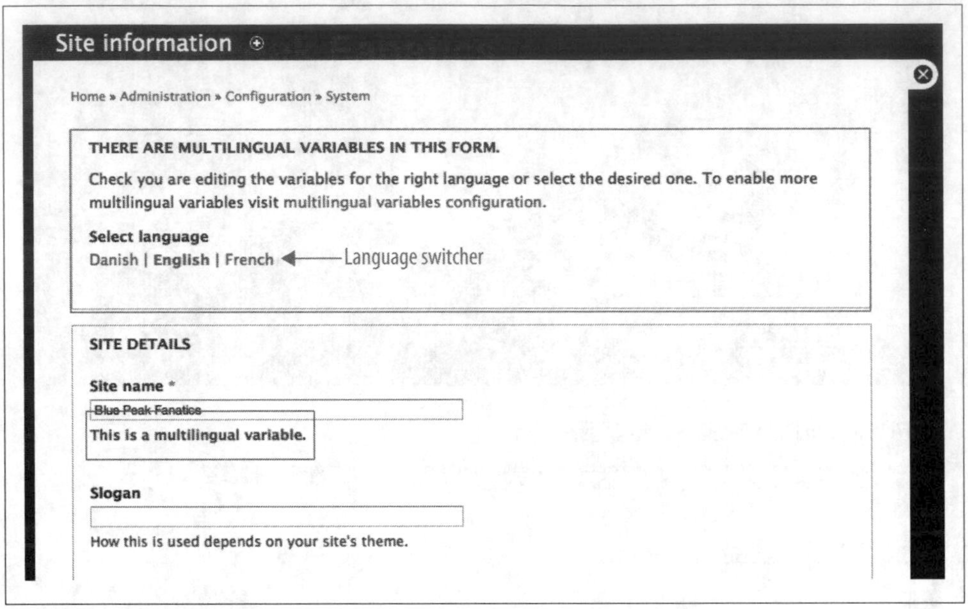

Figure 8-28. The "Site name" field is now indicating that it is a multilingual variable

5. Switch to another language by clicking a link under "Select language."

6. Change the text in the "Site name" field, and click the "Save configuration" button. Notice that you are returned to the page with the language set back to the default language (in our case, English).

> The language selection links provided by the "Variable translation" module don't change the language of the entire site or page. They only change the language for the fields that can be translated. The language you are currently looking at is indicated by that language's link displaying as bold text. It is a subtle difference, so make sure you look closely to ensure you are working with the correct language.

After you have translated the languages you wish, return to the home page and select a non-English language. You will now see that the site name has changed to what we entered. If you switch back to English or another language, you will see that the site name changes with the language.

Content Types

We've changed the site name variable, but we still have other stubborn text on the site that wasn't listed on the "Variable translation" page to select. Our content types for the site are still using English for the content type name on the "Create content" page, and for field names when making new content.

1. In the administrative toolbar, click Modules (*admin/modules*) and enable:

   - Multilingual package
     - Field translation
     - Multilingual content
     - String translation

   You should now see a message at the top of the module list that indicates a number of strings were refreshed.

2. In the administrative toolbar, click Configuration→"Translate interface" (*admin/config/regional/translate*), and you will see two new columns, "Fields" and "Node types" added to the Language table. It shows the number of new translatable strings that the Internationalization module has created for each of them. You can see the new column in Figure 8-29 and compare that to the table shown in Figure 8-3 earlier in the chapter. The percent translated should still be 0, because we haven't translated any content types yet.

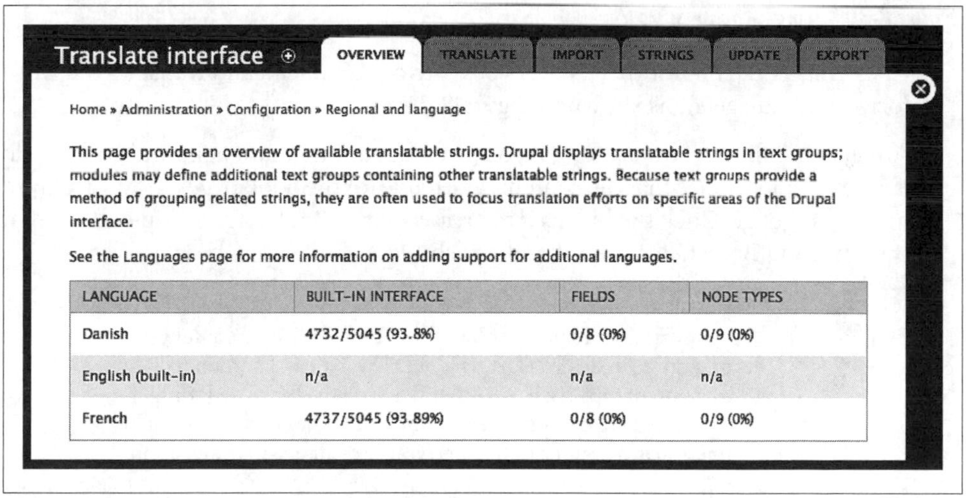

LANGUAGE	BUILT-IN INTERFACE	FIELDS	NODE TYPES
Danish	4732/5045 (93.8%)	0/8 (0%)	0/9 (0%)
English (built-in)	n/a	n/a	n/a
French	4737/5045 (93.89%)	0/8 (0%)	0/9 (0%)

Figure 8-29. "Fields" and "Node types" columns have been added to the Translate interface table

3. Click the Translate tab and search for "Book page" (note the capital "B"). You should see three results, just like Figure 8-30: two that are already translated from the "Built-in" interface group and another, not translated, in the "Node types" group.

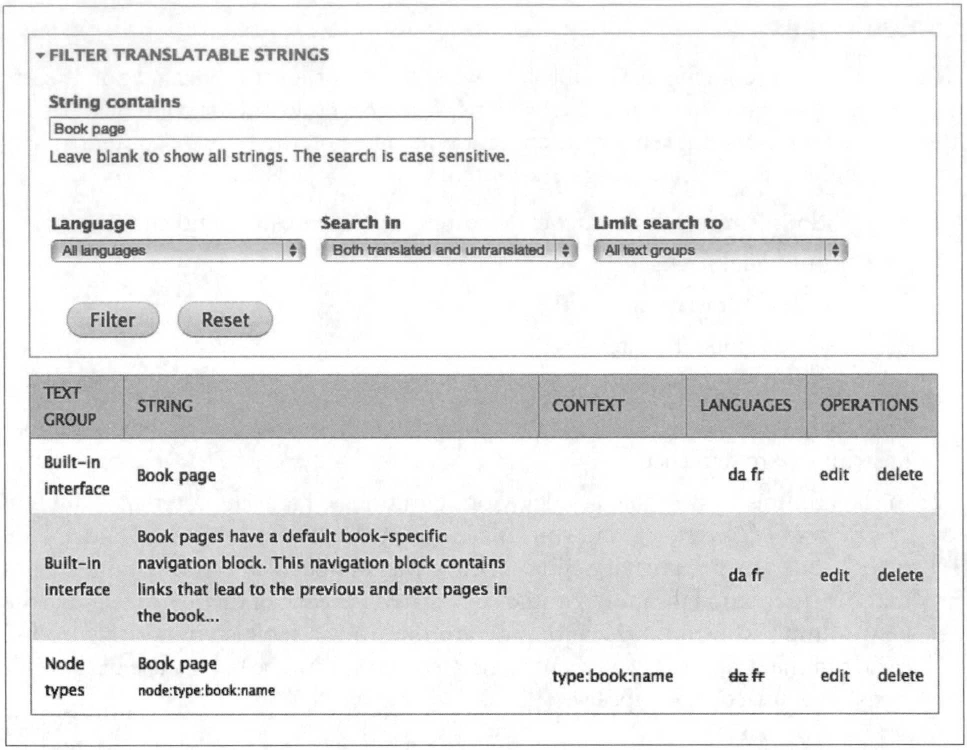

FILTER TRANSLATABLE STRINGS

String contains

Book page

Leave blank to show all strings. The search is case sensitive.

Language	Search in	Limit search to
All languages	Both translated and untranslated	All text groups

Filter   Reset

TEXT GROUP	STRING	CONTEXT	LANGUAGES	OPERATIONS
Built-in interface	Book page		da fr	edit delete
Built-in interface	Book pages have a default book-specific navigation block. This navigation block contains links that lead to the previous and next pages in the book...		da fr	edit delete
Node types	Book page node:type:book:name	type:book:name	~~da fr~~	edit delete

Figure 8-30. String search results for "Book page"

4. Click the "edit" link for the "Node types" string. Go ahead and translate the word for your language(s), as shown in Figure 8-31.

5. After saving the new translation, if you switch to another language and go to "Add content," you will see that the content type name for the book page is now displayed in that language. Click the link as if to create a new "Book page." You will see that the Title and Body fields are still in English.

> It is important to remember that the Title "field" on a content type form is not technically a Drupal field. The Title is a hardcoded part of the content type itself. All other fields on the form, including the Body field, are real Drupal fields, *attached to* the content type. This distinction is very important when you're dealing with translations.

6. Let's switch back to English and go back to our translation administration. In the administrative toolbar, click Configuration→"Translate interface" (*admin/config/ regional/translate*) and click the Translate tab.

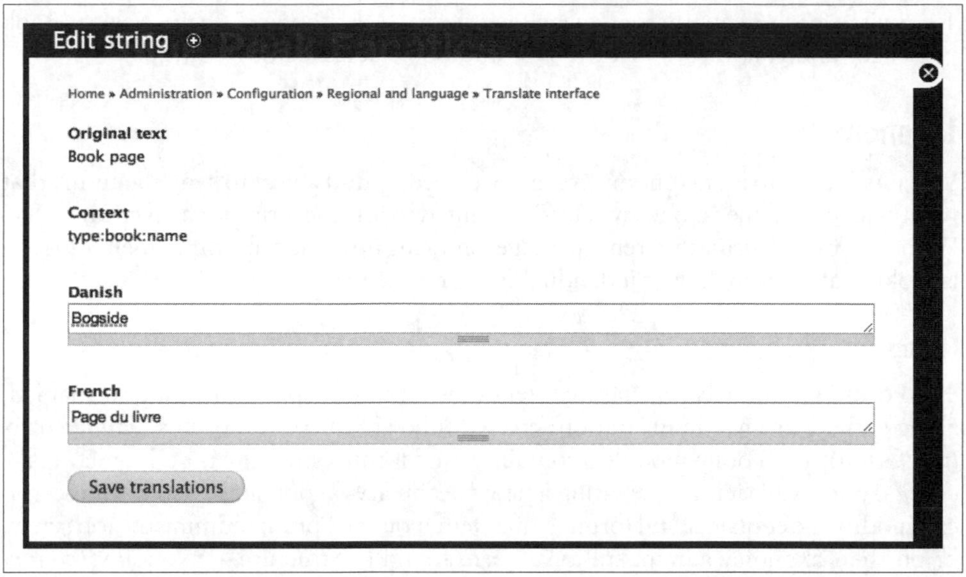

Figure 8-31. "Book page" string editing screen showing two translations

7. Enter the word **Title**. We also know that we are looking for this word in the context of node types right now, so select the "Node types" item under the "Limit search to:" section of the search form as shown in Figure 8-32. Then click Filter.

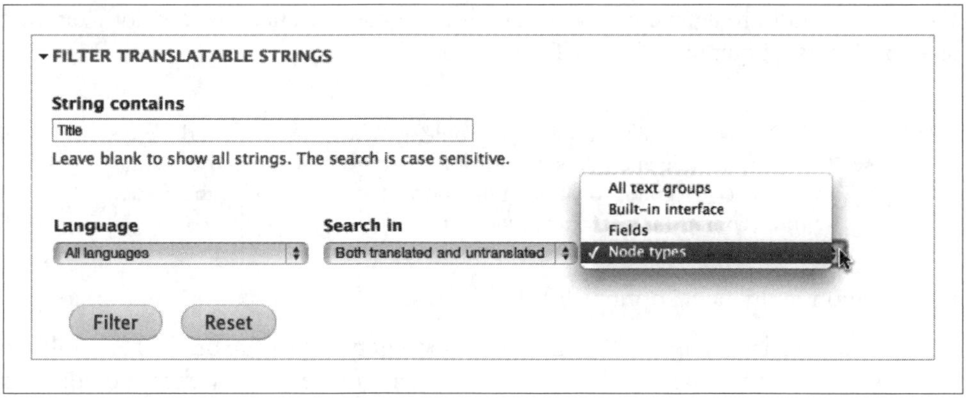

Figure 8-32. Limiting a string search by content type

8. We get three results for this, one for each of the content types we have on the site (Article, Basic page, and Book page). Click the "edit" link for the one that is listed with a Context of "type:book:title_label," translate it, and save.

9. We can do the same thing for the Body field, but we will want to limit the search to "Fields" this time.

10. Switch back to another language, and go to "Add content" again. Select "Book page" and you will see that the Title and Body labels are now translated.

Taxonomy

When using Drupal's taxonomy system, we need to find a way to sync the terms that we create to keep the taxonomy selection limited to just the terms for a given language. We don't want all of the different languages showing up at the same time when someone is looking at a vocabulary or individual terms on the site.

Forums

The Forum module creates a new content type ("Forum topic") when it gets enabled, along with a Forums administration screen, found at Structure→Forums (*admin/structure/forum*). The Forum module's containers and forums structure is built on Drupal's core taxonomy, so it is also creating a new vocabulary on our site, titled Forums. You can modify the container and forum names either on the Forums administration screen or on the Taxonomy administration screen, found at Structure→Taxonomy (*admin/structure/taxonomy*).The forums on our client's site need to display the threads that follow the same content selection rule as the rest of the content on the site. That is, we'll only show the forum posts for the selected language. The site will have preset containers and forums, and then users may post to them using whichever language they choose.

Using the install profile, we have the default container, "General discussion," as well as two forums, "Equipment" and "Travel advice."

 If you have not used the install profile, go ahead and enable the core Forum module and add some forums under the "General discussion" container by going to the administrative toolbar and clicking Structure→Forums (*admin/structure/forum*).

Let's turn on multilingual options for the forums:

1. First we need to set up the "Forum topic" content type so it can be used for multiple languages. Unlike the "Book page" and "Article" content types, these do not need to be translatable. We just want a user to identify the language of the post so it appears in the proper language forum. In the administrative toolbar, click Structure→"Content types" (*admin/structure/types*), and then click the "edit" link for the "Forum topic" content type.

2. Under the "Publishing options" tab, select the Enabled radio button for "Multilingual support." (Note, we are *not* using "Enabled, with translation.") Click "Save content type."

---

3. Now let's see about making the forum container and forum names translatable. In the administrative toolbar, click Modules (*admin/modules*) and enable:

- Multilingual package
  - Multilingual Forum
  - Taxonomy translation
  - Translation sets

4. In the administrative toolbar, click Structure→Taxonomy (*admin/structure/taxonomy*) and click the "edit vocabulary" link for Forums. You will see in Figure 8-33 that we now have a "Multilingual options" section on the page.

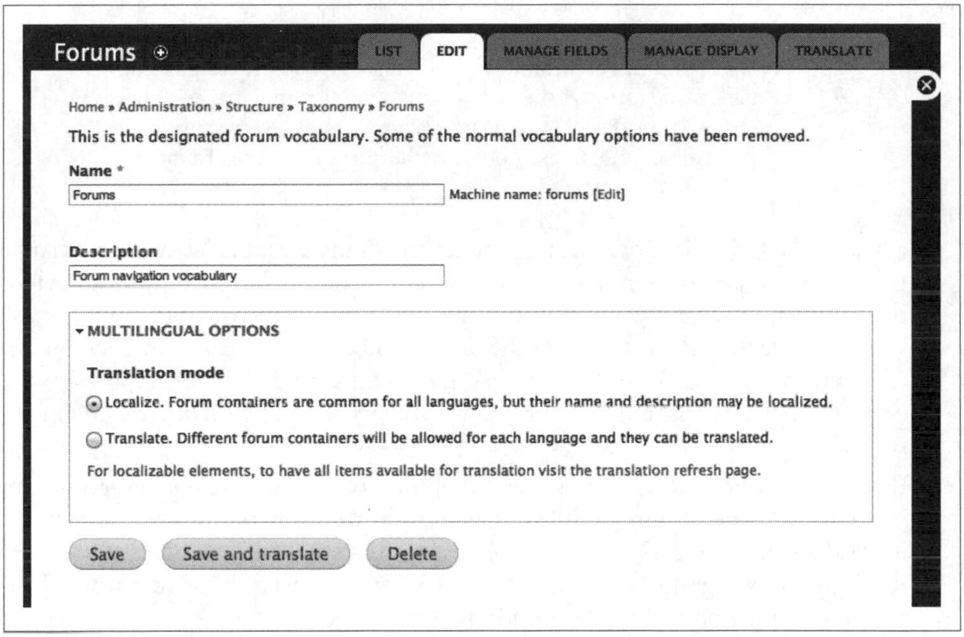

Figure 8-33. Taxonomy multilingual options

5. Select the radio button for Localize and then click the "Save and translate" button to save your changes and move directly to translation. You will see a table listing the languages available for translation, along with the translation status, as shown in Figure 8-34.

6. Click the "translate" link for a language, enter the translated text for Forums, and save your changes.

7. When you are done with these translations, click the List tab for the Forums vocabulary (*admin/structure/taxonomy/forums*). We still need to translate the containers and forums now, which are simply nested terms in our Forums vocabulary.

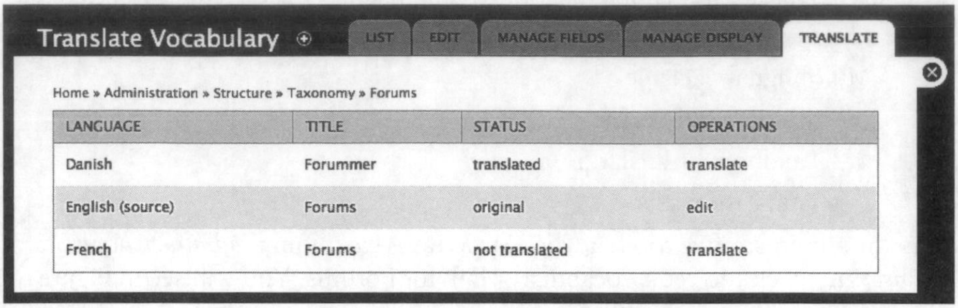

Translate Vocabulary ⊕ | LIST | EDIT | MANAGE FIELDS | MANAGE DISPLAY | TRANSLATE

Home » Administration » Structure » Taxonomy » Forums

LANGUAGE	TITLE	STATUS	OPERATIONS
Danish	Forummer	translated	translate
English (source)	Forums	original	edit
French	Forums	not translated	translate

Figure 8-34. Taxonomy translation table for the Forums vocabulary

 While you can control the default language and ordering of containers and forums using the Forums administration page—found at Structure→Forums (*admin/structure/forum*)—you must complete all of the translations for the forums in the Taxonomy administration pages.

8. Click on the "edit" link for a term, then click the Translate tab. Here you can change the name and description, just as you did for the vocabulary. Do this for each of the Forum terms. After you edit a term, you will notice that you don't have an easy way to get back to the list of all of the terms. You can either use your back button on your browser, or go to the administrative toolbar and click Structure→Taxonomy, then "list terms" for the Forums vocabulary (*admin/structure/taxonomy/forums*).

9. Last, we want to add a Forums menu item into our Main menu so everyone can easily find it. The Forum module has already created a menu item for us, but it is located in the Navigation menu. (Remember that modules will add new menu items to the Navigation menu by default.) So we just need to move it from Navigation into the Main menu. In the administrative toolbar, click on Structure→Menus (*admin/structure/menu*), then click the "list links" link for the Navigation menu. Find the Forums menu item and click the "edit" link. Select "<Main menu>" from the "Parent link" select list and save your changes. You can drag it into a better location if you'd like.

When you close the administrative overlay, you will see a Forums menu item in the Main menu. If you change the language using the language switcher, you will see the menu item change names with the language selected. When you go to the Forums page, the forum names are also translated. Finally, if you click the link to "Add a new Forum topic" from within the forums, you will see that the node creation form includes a select list to pick the language for the post.

Menu Translation

The last little thing we need to do to clean up our site is to get our Home tab in the Main menu translated as well:

1. In the administrative toolbar, click Modules (*admin/modules*) and enable:
   - Multilingual package
     — Block languages
     — Menu translation

2. Now, in the administrative toolbar go to Structure→Menus (*admin/structure/menu*), and click the "edit menu" link for the Main menu. There is a new "Multilingual options" section here. Select "Translate and Localize." Menu items with language will allow translations. Menu items without language will be localized." Then save your changes.

3. You will be returned to the list of items in the Main menu. Click the "edit" link for the Home menu item. Scroll down, select English for the language, and save your changes.

4. Now when you click the "edit" link again for the Home menu item, you will see there is a Translate tab. Click on that tab, enter in your translations, and save them.

5. When you are done, go back to the Main menu list of menu items; in the administrative toolbar, go to Structure→Menus (*admin/structure/menu*); and click the "list links" link for the Main menu. Drag and drop the menu items so all of them are in the correct order, especially your translated items.

6. Return to the home page on the site and switch to another language. You will have a fully translated menu now.

Taking It Further

We've covered quite a bit of ground for setting up a site with multiple languages. There are a lot of tools available, and therefore there is a lot of flexibility when it comes to handling languages. We have delivered a site to our clients that has the community features they need and allows their users to both participate and manage the site in the language of their choice. They can easily add new languages to the mix in the future, and everyone can help with translating their knowledge base. Here are some additional modules that can add some nice touches to your site:

Language icons (http://drupal.org/project/languageicons)
   This module will add a default set of flag icons to the language switching links on the site (in the "Language switcher" block and language links on the content). You can replace the included icons with ones of your choosing.

Language switcher dropdown (http://drupal.org/project/lang_dropdown)
> This gives you language switcher that provides a drop-down select list, instead of a list of links. This integrates with the Language Icons module as well.

Transliteration (http://drupal.org/project/transliteration)
> This important module will transliterate Unicode characters into ASCII. This is very important to avoid creating URLs and filename paths that are unreadable in some circumstances due to non-ASCII characters.

Translation overview (http://drupal.org/project/translation_overview)
> This module creates a page with a table that tracks the translation status of all the content on your site. It supplies basic information like the title and a link to the content, content type, and creation date. Then, for each piece of content, it uses a legend so you can see the translation status (original language, current translation, out-of-date translation, or untranslated) at a glance.

Translation table (http://drupal.org/project/translation_table)
> This module provides a nice table interface to make it easier to change the text for menus, taxonomy, and other strings.

Summary

We built a nice, simple, easy-to-use site for our clients that gave them the tools they needed for discussions and a knowledge base. We set up a forum that displays only posts that are in the user's language and a knowledge base book where all of the site members can create translations for the pages. The major need for this community was being able to use multiple languages and easily extend those languages in the future. Using Drupal's core internationalization features with a handful of contributed modules, we have given them a very flexible multilingual solution.

For more information and discussion about internationalization in Drupal, see the Internationalization group (*http://groups.drupal.org/i18n*). To get more information about core Drupal translations and how you can help, check out the Translations group (*http://groups.drupal.org/translations*). If you'd like to help the project by providing your own translations for Drupal core or contributed modules, the Drupal.org translator's guide (*http://drupal.org/contribute/translations*) has all the information you need.

Here are the modules that we referenced in this chapter:

- Book: Part of the Drupal core
- Content Translation: Part of the Drupal core
- Entity translation (*http://drupal.org/project/entity_translation*)
- Forum: Part of the Drupal core
- Internationalization (*http://drupal.org/project/i18n*)
- Language icons (*http://drupal.org/project/languageicons*)

- Language switcher dropdown (*http://drupal.org/project/lang_dropdown*)
- Locale: Part of the Drupal core
- Localization client (*http://drupal.org/project/l10n_client*)
- Localization update (*http://drupal.org/project/l10n_update*)
- Translation overview (*http://drupal.org/project/translation_overview*)
- Translation table (*http://drupal.org/project/translation_table*)
- Transliteration (*http://drupal.org/project/transliteration*)
- Variable (*http://drupal.org/project/variable*)

These are some other resources that we referenced and community resources for learning more about the new concepts introduced in this chapter:

- Drupal translations (*http://localize.drupal.org/*)
- Localized Drupal Distribution (*http://drupal.org/project/l10n_install*)
- Internationalization group (*http://groups.drupal.org/i18n*)
- Multilingual modules (*http://drupal.org/project/modules?filters=tid:97*)
- Translations working group (*http://groups.drupal.org/translations*)
- Translator's guide (*http://drupal.org/contribute/translations*)

CHAPTER 9

Online Store

Many businesses, both large and small, would like to take better advantage of their web presence by selling their products or services directly online. Setting up ecommerce, however, can be a very daunting task. There are several options with varying complexity. Many hosting providers offer ecommerce or "shopping cart" packages that may be either included with your web hosting plan or available for purchase. With other services, such as PayPal, you can enable online purchases by using an HTML form that submits to their processing system. There are still more options for using dedicated ecommerce packages, both open source and proprietary, that you host and configure. The biggest issue with all of these methods tends to be the lack of integration with the rest of the website—all shopping cart and checkout functions take place within the other, external system.

This chapter will introduce the following modules:

Drupal Commerce (http://drupal.org/project/commerce)
    Provides a full ecommerce package for running an online store

Feeds (http://drupal.org/project/feeds)
    Provides data import capabilities for Drupal

Rules (http://drupal.org/project/rules)
    Provides a means of clicking together custom programming logic

To follow along with the hands-on examples in this chapter, install Drupal using the *Online Store* installation profile, which installs Drupal with a few sample users and basic settings, as shown in Figure 9-1 and found at *http://store.usingdrupal.com*. For more information on using the book's sample code, see the Preface.

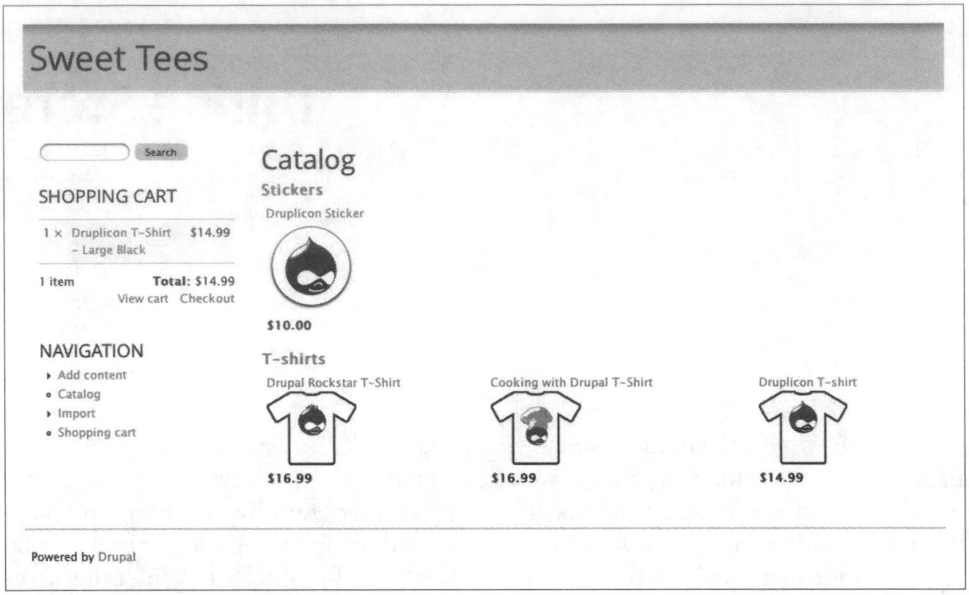

Figure 9-1. Sweet Tees' completed website

There are two highly useful resources to have nearby as you're learning your way through Drupal Commerce. The first is the official Drupal Commerce website at *http://www.drupalcommerce.org/*, which contains documentation, a list of add-on modules, and other great stuff. The second is *http://www.commerceguys.com/*, which contains a series of screencast tutorials on how to do various tasks in Drupal Commerce that fall outside the scope of this chapter.

Case Study

Sweet Tees is a local T-shirt store that sells wildly popular, custom-printed T-shirts. It has a physical storefront, and the owners enjoy running a small store and love their current location. However, they get frequent mail-order requests for their shirts and stickers, and would like to grow that end of the business. Taking orders on the phone and tracking sales has proven to be inefficient and time-consuming for both them and their customers.

In order to increase sales, we will equip the Sweet Tees website with an online store that has integrated shopping cart functionality, where visitors to the site can add items to their cart without the hassle of having to create an account first. A shopping cart should be visible on all pages with a link to "check out" at any time. The store needs to flow seamlessly with the existing website so that customers have a consistent experience. Sweet Tees would like to make the checkout process as simple as possible, so we will also need to make sure we provide them with a single-page checkout, without requiring customers to create a user account. Finally, they wish to accept credit cards on their orders, so we will need to set up a payment gateway for this purpose.

Implementation Notes

Sweet Tees has several options to manage their online store; however, they really want to provide a seamless, user-friendly experience for their customers. They are looking for a solution that is simple and elegant, yet also comprehensive.

For Drupal, there are two primary ecommerce solutions, both of which consist of several modules, to implement the various features required.

Ubercart (*http://drupal.org/project/ubercart*), the premier ecommerce solution in Drupal 6, aims to provide a simplified installation, configuration, and management process. Ubercart also has some features that make it attractive for our implementation: a single-page checkout process, anonymous user purchases, and a nice administration interface.

Drupal Commerce (*http://drupal.org/project/commerce*) is a highly customizable ecommerce framework that was developed by Ubercart's former lead developer, and is a ground-up rewrite of Ubercart that makes use of modern Drupal 7 constructs such as entities and fields, views, and rules. Drupal Commerce takes a "framework" approach to building out an ecommerce site, allowing the ultimate in customizability and flexibility to support everything from standard product-based stores to subscription websites.

For Sweet Tees, we will be using Drupal Commerce due to its native support of Drupal 7, and its inherent flexibility, which will help them handle any future requirements.

> Thanks to its five-year head start, Ubercart generally has more add-on modules available than Drupal Commerce, a fact that may make our choice a bit puzzling. However, the broader Drupal developer community effort is much more focused on Drupal Commerce, making it the more future-proof choice for Drupal 7 sites.

Spotlight: Drupal Commerce

Drupal Commerce is a complete package for running an online store. As such, it actually contains numerous submodules that each implement features of an online store, and can be turned on or off depending on the precise functionality required. In this section, we'll look at each module in turn, and outline its purpose and where it fits.

If you'd like to play with a quick demonstration of the Drupal Commerce module, try installing the Commerce Kickstart installation profile at *http://drupal.org/project/commerce_kickstart*.

Commerce and Commerce UI

Commerce is a required module that provides the underlying APIs and functionality for the Drupal Commerce suite as a whole, and doesn't provide much in the way of configurability. The Commerce UI module provides the main Store (*admin/commerce*) configuration panel, pictured in Figure 9-2.

Nearly all modules in the Drupal Commerce package are split into both a "functional" module and a "UI" module. This is to allow other contributed or custom modules to potentially replace the default user interface with one more streamlined to a particular use case.

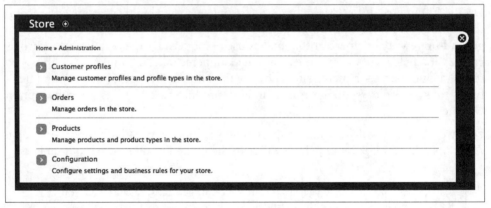

Figure 9-2. Commerce UI provides the default Store management screens

Cart

Cart handles the shopping cart, pictured in Figure 9-3, and provides features such as a handy sidebar block showing cart contents on all pages, and the ability for customers to add or remove cart contents. Both the block and checkout page are views, so you can customize the precise fields and order they're displayed in, just like any other listing built in the Views module.

The Cart module also exposes a number of events and actions that can trigger system behavior through the Rules module. For example, for a site selling multiple subscription levels, it might make sense to remove the old subscription level from the cart when adding a different subscription.

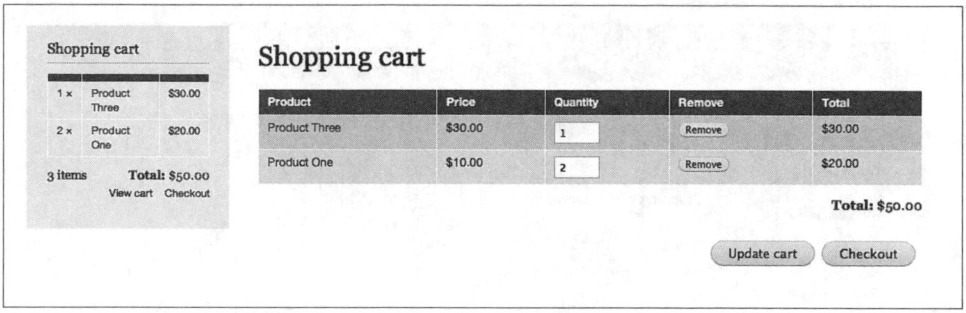

Figure 9-3. The shopping cart page and sidebar block provided by the Cart module

Checkout

The Checkout module, pictured in Figure 9-4, handles the display of the checkout screens, as well as the overall checkout process. There are four stages to the checkout process: "Checkout" (where billing information and payment details are typically gathered), "Review order" (which allows the customer to check over her order one last time before being charged), "Payment" (where the actual charging takes place), and "Checkout complete" (where final notifications and next steps are explained). The information displayed on each page (e.g., cart contents, billing information) is encapsulated in "checkout panes," the visibility and order of which are configurable in the store settings, as pictured in Figure 9-5. One example of where this flexibility could come in handy is in a site selling memberships; since these aren't "products" in the traditional sense, it may not make sense to show the cart contents on the checkout page.

One other very nice feature of the Checkout module, thanks to the Address Field module it lists as a dependency, is its ability to autopopulate proper address fields based on country selection—for example, "State" and "Zip code" for United States addresses, but "Province" and "Postal Code" for Canadian addresses.

Customer and Customer UI

The Customer module exposes an entity type called Customer Profile, which can be used to store information a customer must fill out during the checkout process. By default, Drupal Commerce ships with a profile type called "Billing information," pictured in Figure 9-4. However, other modules—such as Commerce Shipping, which exposes a profile type called "Shipping information"—may offer additional types as well. Because customer profiles are entities, they may have other fields added to them, such as phone number or Tax ID.

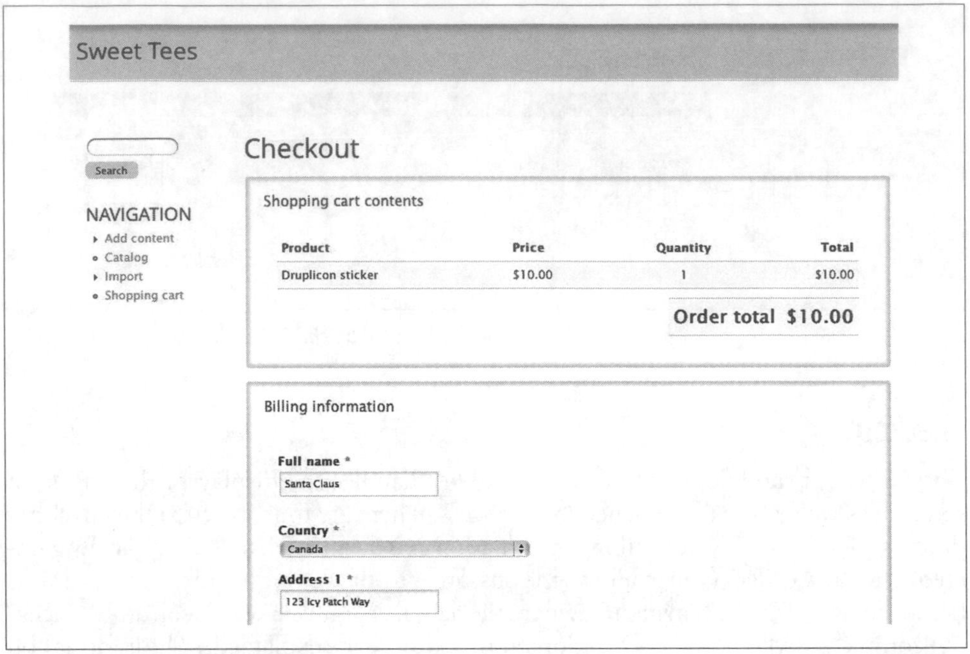

Figure 9-4. Checkout panes are provided by the Checkout module

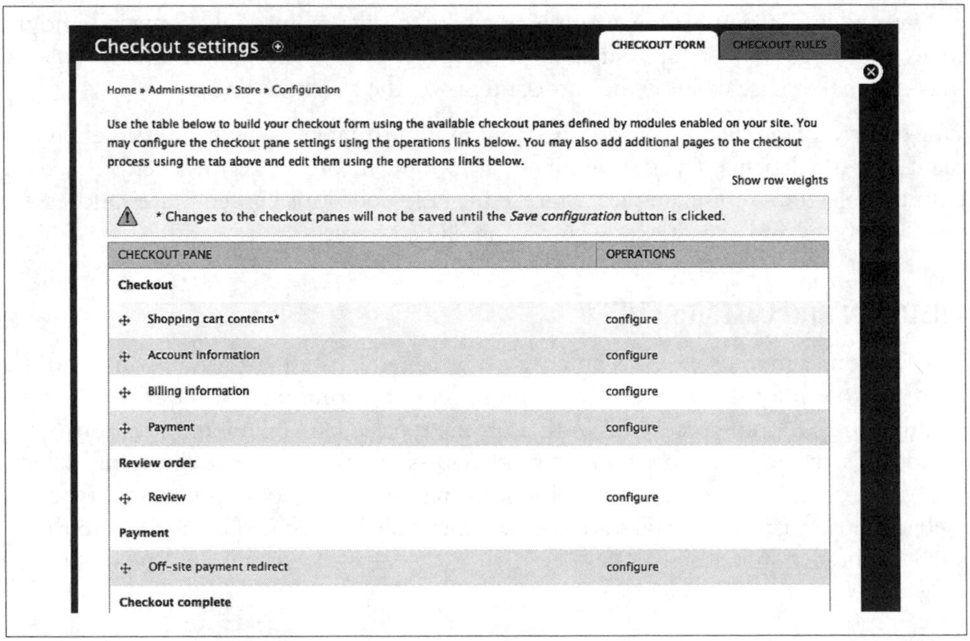

Figure 9-5. The page elements ("checkout panes") to show during the checkout process, as well as their order, are configurable in the Checkout module settings

Order, Order UI, Line Item, and Line Item UI

The Order and Line Item modules are responsible for recording, tracking, and managing individual orders to the store. Figures 9-6 and 9-7 show the default user interface for managing orders, provided by the Order UI and Line Item UI modules. You can view orders that are completed as well as those still in the shopping cart phase, and you can also create and edit orders manually—for example, to accept orders over the phone.

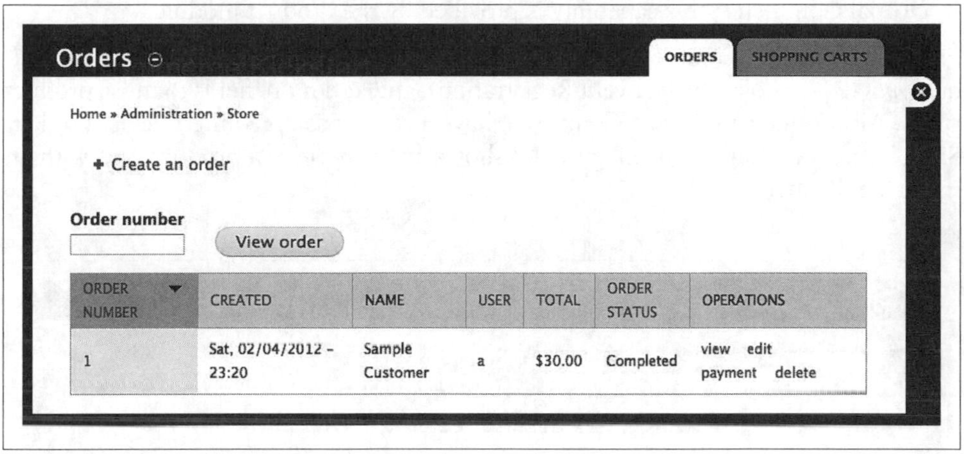

Figure 9-6. Orders overview listing page

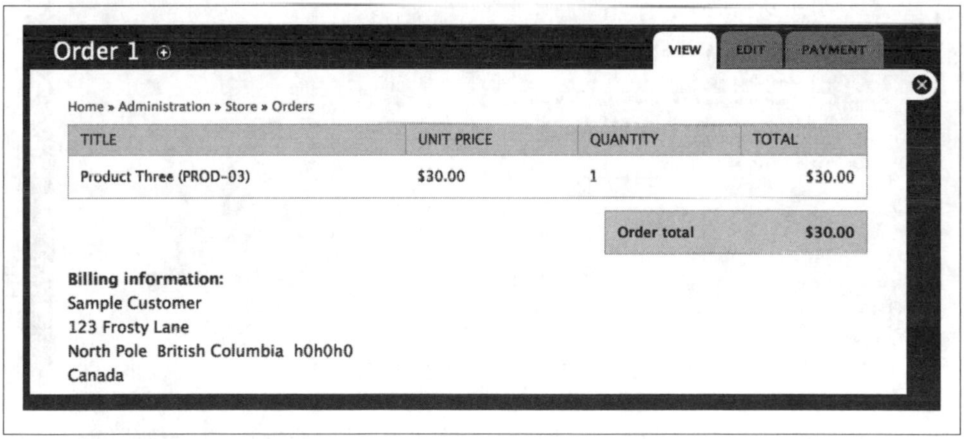

Figure 9-7. A sample order

Payment and Payment UI

There are a number of add-on modules that expose different sorts of payment types to Drupal Commerce, including PayPal, Authorize.Net, and CyberSource. Check *http://www.drupalcommerce.org/faq/payment-methods* for a full listing.

Payments are configured with the Rules module, covered in "Spotlight: Rules Module" on page 383, which provides nearly limitless customizability over specific business logic requirements.

Product and Product UI

Something that's pretty essential to any store is cataloguing all of the products it sells. In Drupal Commerce, this capability is provided by the Product module.

Products in Drupal Commerce are entities, which means you can create different *product types* (e.g., Book, Music, Event Registration), and add more fields to those product types. All products in Drupal Commerce have a set of basic, required fields: Product SKU, Title, Price, and Status. Figure 9-8 shows an example of a product type with an image field added to it.

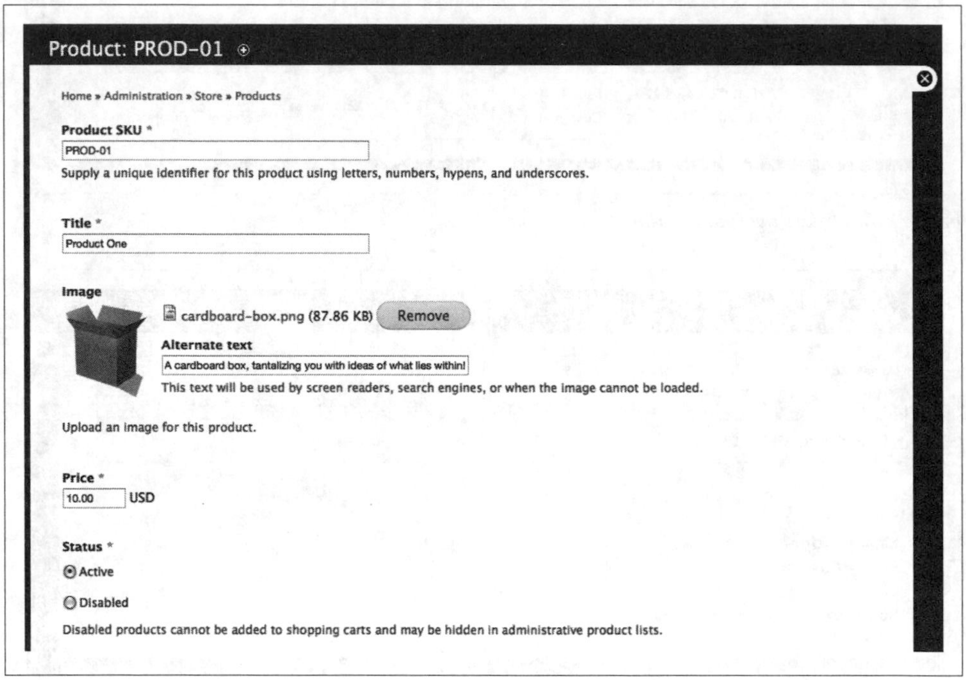

Figure 9-8. A sample product form including both the standard, required fields as well as an extra image field

Like elsewhere in Drupal Commerce, the default product view exposed by the optional Product UI module, pictured in Figure 9-9, can be customized with the Views module. This allows you to add extra fields, expose filters for product type or keyword search, or whatever else you can envision doing with Views.

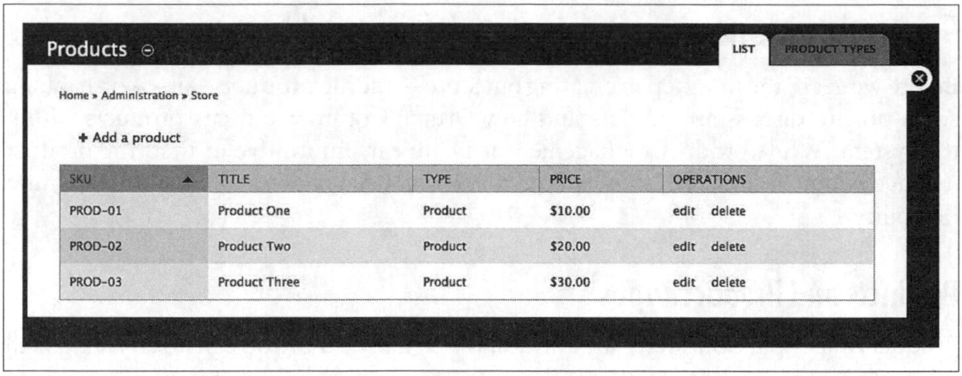

Figure 9-9. The default view from the Product UI module

Product Reference

The Product Reference module exposes a field that can be placed on content types. A content type with a product reference field is called a *product display*, and it handles output of the raw product data to customers, as well as the display of the "Add to Cart" button. We'll go into more detail about products and product displays in the next Spotlight section, "Spotlight: Managing Products with Drupal Commerce" on page 358.

Price, Product Pricing, and Product Pricing UI

This set of modules enables a store site owner to establish how much things cost—a rather important functionality in an online store! These modules provide Rules elements, such as the ability to react when the price of goods is being calculated. Most of the rest of the Commerce suite relies on these modules.

Tax and Tax UI

Drupal Commerce supports both Sales and VAT tax calculations, using the Rules module to allow for special cases, such as different sales taxes in different states, or a higher tax for certain types of items.

Additional Drupal Commerce Add-Ons

If the modules that come with Drupal Commerce aren't quite enough for your needs, there is also a rich library of contributed add-ons at *http://www.drupalcommerce.org/contrib*. Here you'll find payment processor modules for services such as Authorize.Net and PayPal, modules to facilitate shipping and stock keeping, and modules that provide new features such as the ability to purchase and spend points or keep wishlists.

Spotlight: Managing Products with Drupal Commerce

Before we get to the first step in creating our store—adding products—it's worth taking some time to discuss and understand how Drupal Commerce treats products within the system. While product management may appear unintuitive at first, the product management features in Drupal Commerce are designed to allow for maximum flexibility.

Products and Product Types

Products in Drupal Commerce are entities, which means that you can do anything with products that we've done with entities in the rest of this book, such as add fields to hold additional properties, display products in listings with the Views module, and so on. This seamless integration of store products with the rest of the content that Drupal can manage is a killer feature of Drupal Commerce.

All product types share a common set of required fields, which are:

Product SKU
> A unique identifier for a product. Some stores might choose to make this the same as the UPC code, in the case of a physical product, but others may create their own naming convention, such as BOOK-123456789-A.

Title
> The title describes the unique product configuration in human-readable terms, and is used in content listings to identify the product to store administrators.

Price
> The product base price, which defaults to the site's default currency.

Status
> Either Active or Disabled. If a product is marked as Disabled, it cannot be added to the shopping cart (the "Add to Cart" button is replaced with a "Product not available" message). Product status can also be used as a filter in Views to remove disabled products from listing pages.

By default, Drupal Commerce provides a sample product type called Product. This is sufficient if you are only selling one style of product in your store, such as a club membership. Many online stores are more complex, however. Amazon.com sells books, movies, and, as we saw in Chapter 5, kitchen utensils (among other things). Books have properties like "author" and "ISBN," and movies might have properties like "rating" and "movie studio." Can you imagine how long the product form would be if it needed to provide a field for every single one of these properties for all possible types of products? No, thanks.

Luckily, the Drupal Commerce developers have a solution to this predicament: you can create as many product types as you'd like, and uniquely customize the fields on each of those product types. Other examples of product types might be Book, Music, Event Ticket, or Donation. A Book product type might have fields like Author and Publisher, whereas a Music product type could have Artist and Label. And the two product types might share an image field to facilitate showing them together in product listings.

Note that you must create a unique product with a unique SKU for each configuration of each product. Let's say your store is selling movies. If each movie comes in VHS, DVD, or Blu-Ray format, that's three different products with three different SKUs per individual movie title. If each format also comes in English, Spanish, or French, that's *nine* different products with nine different SKUs. And if your store sells 3,000 movies, all in all that's 27,000 products with 27,000 SKUs. Egads! As you can well imagine, it can become tedious to enter that much data by hand. We'll cover bulk-importing product data in "Hands-On: Bulk-Importing Product Data" on page 366.

Hands-On: Products and Product Types

The first step in setting up our online T-shirt store is to turn on a formidable array of modules to enable the Drupal Commerce module, and then set up product types for the merchandise that Sweet Tees sells: T-shirts and stickers.

Initial Setup Tasks

1. Log into the Sweet Tees site as the "admin" user if you have not done so already.
2. Go to the Modules (*admin/modules*) page and enable the Product UI module. Choose Continue at the prompt to enable the large number of dependent modules (Commerce, Entity API, Rules, Entity tokens, Commerce UI, Product, Price, Views, and Chaos tools).

Configuring Product Types

1. Go to Store→Products (*admin/commerce/products*), the main product admin panel, and click the Product Types tab. By default, you'll see a single product type listed there called Product. That's a bit too generic for our tastes, so click the Delete link to remove it.
2. Click "Add product type" and give it a Name of "T-shirt" and Description of "Our award-winning T-shirts." Then click "Save and add fields." At the Managed Fields screen for T-shirt (*admin/commerce/products/types/t-shirt/fields*), pictured in Figure 9-10, you'll see we already have a few fields predefined: Product SKU, Title, Price, and Status.

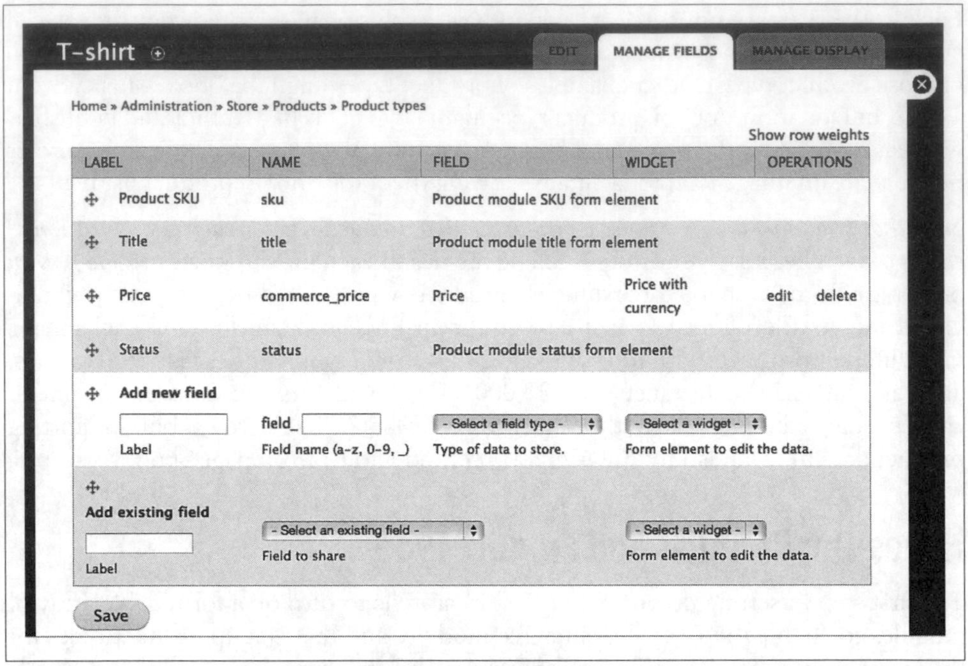

Figure 9-10. Default fields available to product types

3. Add two new fields—Size and Color—to the T-shirt product type, using the values in Tables 9-1 and 9-2, respectively.

Table 9-1. Settings for the T-shirt product type's Size field

Field	Value
Label	Size
Machine name	size
Field type	List (text)
Widget	Select list
Allowed values list	S
	M
	L
	XL
Required field	Checked

Table 9-2. Settings for the T-shirt product type's Color field

Field	Value
Label	Color
Machine name	color

Field	Value
Field type	List (text)
Widget	Select list
Allowed values list	White
	Black
Required field	Checked

4. We also want to add an image field, but thanks to the default Article content type, we already have one we can use. Under "Add existing field," choose "Image: field_image (Image)" as the field to share, then provide a Label of "Image" and click Save. Leave the default settings.

5. Finally, reorder the fields as indicated in Figure 9-11 (Product SKU, Title, Price, Image, Size, Color, and Status), and click Save.

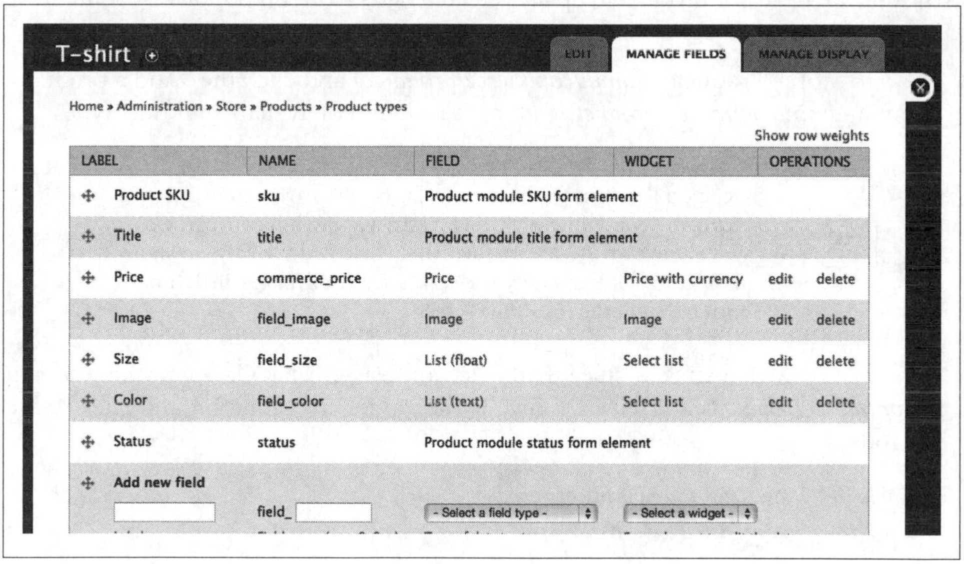

Figure 9-11. The completed T-shirt product type with reordered fields

6. Return to the main Product Types screen and create a second product type at "Add product type" (*admin/commerce/products/types/add*) for Sticker. Give it a Name of "Sticker" and Description of "A sticker with a witty phrase." We can just keep the default fields here, so simply click "Save product type."

7. As you did with T-shirt, add the existing image field to Sticker, leave the default settings, and drag it just above Status in the list of fields.

8. When finished, your product types screen (*admin/commerce/products/types*) should look as pictured in Figure 9-12.

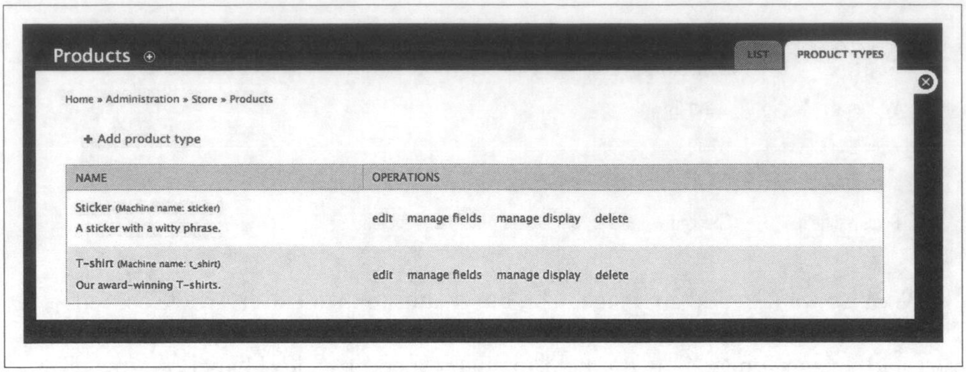

Figure 9-12. Product types for the Sweet Tees store

Creating Sample Products

Now that we have our product templates created, let's work on populating some store content!

1. Go to Store→Products (*admin/commerce/products*) and click the "Add a product" link (*admin/commerce/products/add*) to see a menu of available product types.

> Since you'll return to this screen fairly often over the course of managing your online store, you might want to hover over the plus sign (+) next to "Add a product" and click "Add to *Default* short-cuts" so the link is easily accessible from all pages in Drupal's Shortcut bar at the top of the screen.

2. Let's start with a sticker, since that's nice and easy. Click Create Sticker (*admin/commerce/products/add/sticker*). Give it the values in Table 9-3 and click "Save product."

Table 9-3. Values for a sample Sticker product

Field	Value
Product SKU	STICKER-001
Title	Druplicon sticker
Price	10.00
Image	(Upload the *drupal-sticker.png* file from the *assets/ch09-store* folder.)
Status	Active (default)

In almost all cases, you'll leave the Status field as Active. The Disabled status is useful in the case of items that are discontinued. You wouldn't want to *delete* the product, as that could destroy customer order data. Setting the product as Disabled will ensure it can't be added to anyone's shopping cart and will hide it from view.

3. Now let's add a T-shirt by clicking "Add a product" and then Create T-shirt (*admin/commerce/products/add/t-shirt*). Give it the values in Table 9-4 and click "Save product."

Table 9-4. *Values for a sample T-shirt product*

Field	Value
Product SKU	TSHIRT-001-M-WH
Title	Druplicon T-Shirt - Medium White
Price	1.99 (Note: this is a deliberate typo that we will fix in the next section!)
Image	(Upload the *druplicon-tshirt-white.png* file from the *assets/ch09-store* folder.)
Size	M
Color	White
Status	Active (default)

As mentioned in "Spotlight: Drupal Commerce" on page 351, Drupal Commerce needs one product with a unique SKU per product configuration. Our T-shirt store sells both multiple sizes (S, M, L, XL) and multiple colors (White, Black) of each of the three T-shirt designs. As a result, if we keep going along with this example, we would have to enter in a whopping 24 products by hand. Yowza! Let's hope Sweet Tees doesn't think about adding any new T-shirt designs or, heaven forbid, decide to offer women's and children's styles of each design as well!

Luckily, there's a way to bulk-import lots of products at once, which will be the focus of the next section of this chapter.

4. Now that we've entered a couple of products, our product administration screen at Store→Products (*admin/commerce/products*) should look as pictured in Figure 9-13.

Remember: nearly all listing pages in Drupal Commerce are Views, including the product overview page. You can easily customize this page to add extra columns for the Image, Size, and Color fields; add an exposed filter or two to restrict the list by certain product types or provide a keyword search; or anything else you do with Views module. Be creative!

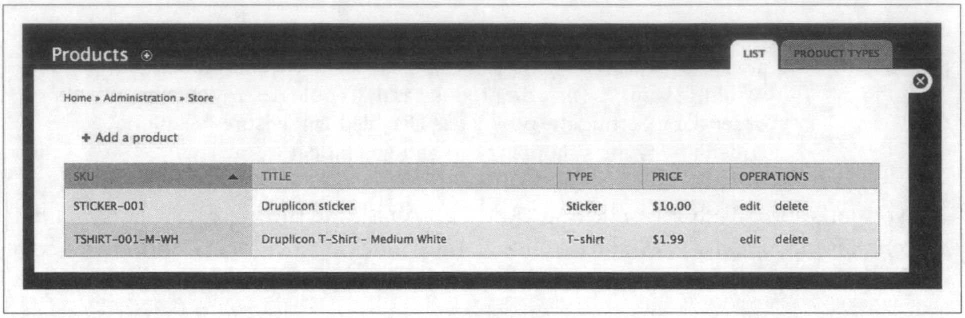

Figure 9-13. Sample products for the Sweet Tees store

Of course, a company like Sweet Tees has many more products than just a single sticker and T-shirt they'd like to sell. However, entering their entire inventory by hand will quickly become tedious and carpal tunnel–inducing. Luckily, using standard Drupal data import tools, we have a solution to this problem.

Spotlight: Feeds Module

The Feeds module provides the capability to ingest data from any number of different sources and transform it into native Drupal constructs. It's a versatile tool that can be used for things such as large-scale data migration, automatically populating a block of recent content from external sites, or synchronizing content posted among multiple sites.

Among its features are the ability to scan incoming data for already existing content and decide whether to ignore it or merge in the defaults. Content ingestion can be scheduled and queued, even for large jobs.

The Feeds module works by creating one or more "importers" to do the data ingestion. Importers have three basic components: the Fetcher, the Parser, and the Processor.

Fetcher
> This component defines how the Feeds module should bring in the feed data. The default options are either "File upload," which provides a field to upload a file from the computer's hard drive (perfect for things like comma-separated values [CSV] files or XML), or "HTTP fetcher," which provides a field to enter a URL of a remote data feed, such as *http://drupal.org/node/feed*.

Parser
> When provided the format of the feed, the parser reads it into logical chunks. The default options are: "Common syndication parser" (handles RSS and Atom), "CSV parser" (for files stored with comma-separated values), "OPML" (Outline Processor Markup Language, a common format for sharing hierarchical lists), and "Sitemap" (which can read feeds stored in the *http://www.xml-sitemaps.com/* format).

Processor

The processor turns data coming in from a feed parser into native Drupal structures. By default, processors are included for Nodes, Taxonomy Terms, and Users.

Figure 9-14 shows the default feed importer settings. This configuration creates an importer that fetches an RSS or Atom feed from a URL every 30 minutes, then imports the contents into Drupal as nodes. The fetcher, parser, and processor settings can then be customized to allow for other behaviors.

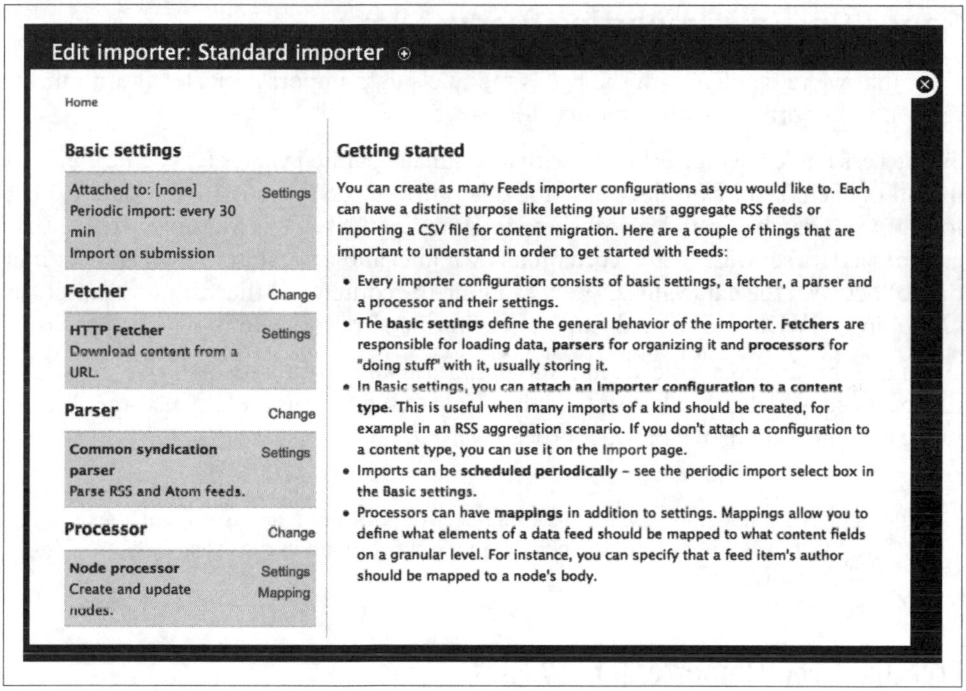

Figure 9-14. A feed importer showing default options

There are also several contributed modules that can extend the Feeds module's capabilities. For example, the "Feeds YouTube parser" module (*http://drupal.org/project/ feeds_youtubehttp://drupal.org/project/feeds_comment_processor*) provides the capability to read feeds of videos from YouTube; the "Feeds Comment Processor" module (*http://drupal.org/project/feeds_comment_processor*) allows importing feed content as comments; and the "Feeds Directory Fetcher" module (*http://drupal.org/project/feeds _fetcher_directory*) can monitor a directory for new files and turn them into a feed for parsing.

Another option for data imports is using the Migrate module (*http://drupal.org/project/migrate*), and the Commerce Migrate module (*http://drupal.org/project/commerce_migrate*), which adds support for Drupal Commerce and Ubercart data migrations. These are particularly useful for larger-scale data migrations from legacy systems, and for situations where a lot of data needs to be transformed in order to be suitable for Drupal.

Hands-On: Bulk-Importing Product Data

Now that we're familiar with the Feeds module's data import tools, let's turn our attention to importing T-shirt products for Sweet Tees.

Sweet Tees has kindly furnished us with a comma-separated values (CSV) file containing all of their T-shirt product data for this purpose. CSV is a common data export format from databases and spreadsheet programs. A CSV file is a simple text file that encodes a data set with each record on its own line, and a separator (such as a comma or tab) between the data values. We'll examine the contents of this file more closely in "Mapping CSV Data to Drupal Commerce Products" on page 368.

We'll use the Commerce Feeds module (*http://drupal.org/project/commerce_feeds*) for this purpose, which provides two new Feeds processors: Commerce Customer Profile processor and Commerce Product processor.

 To follow along with this example, you will need the *using_drupal_tshirts.csv* file from the book's source code, found in the *assets/ch09-store* folder.

Creating a Feed Importer for CSV Files

1. Go to the Modules page and enable the following modules:
   - Commerce (contrib) package
     — Commerce Feeds
   - Feeds package
     — Feeds
     — Feeds Admin UI
   - Other package
     — Job Scheduler
2. Go to Structure→Feeds Importers (*admin/structure/feeds*) and click the "New importer" tab (*admin/structure/feeds/create*).
3. Fill out the form with the values in Table 9-5 and click the Create button.

Table 9-5. Settings for the Product importer

Field	Value
Name	T-shirt importer
Description	Import the Sweet Tees T-shirt catalog from CSV file.

4. At the next screen, there is a table with many settings, most of which can be ignored. "Basic settings" allows you to configure things like how often to import from a feed and whether the process should happen in the background or immediately upon form submission. Then the Fetcher, Processor, and Parser sections affect the settings for each of those components.

5. Under Fetcher, click Change, choose "File upload" instead of "HTTP fetcher," and click Save. While the "HTTP fetcher" option would be useful for reading in feed data from a remote URL, the Sweet Tees product list is in a CSV file sitting on your computer's hard drive, so it makes sense to show a file upload field instead of a URL field. If you wish, you can click Settings for the file upload fetcher to configure additional settings such as what file extensions are allowed, but that's unnecessary for this example.

6. Under Parser, click Change, choose "CSV parser," and click Save. Once again, you can click Settings for the CSV parser to change options such as what delimiter is used in the file, but we don't need to do that here.

7. Under Processor, click Change, choose "Commerce Product Parser," and click Save. The CSV items will now be imported as Drupal Commerce products, not nodes.

8. Click the Settings link next to "Commerce Product processor," enter the values found in Table 9-6, and click Save.

Table 9-6. Settings for the Commerce Product processor

Field	Value
Update existing commerce products	Update existing products
Text format	Plain text (default)
Product type	T-shirt
Author	admin

 The one value worth mentioning here is "Update existing commerce products." This value means that if incoming product data from the feed matches existing data within Drupal, the values coming in from the feed will "win" and override the site's data. In this case, we want that, since it's an initial import of the CSV data. In future imports, however, we'd probably want to leave that at "Do not update existing products" so only new products are added.

9. When completed, the settings along the left side should look as shown in Figure 9-15.

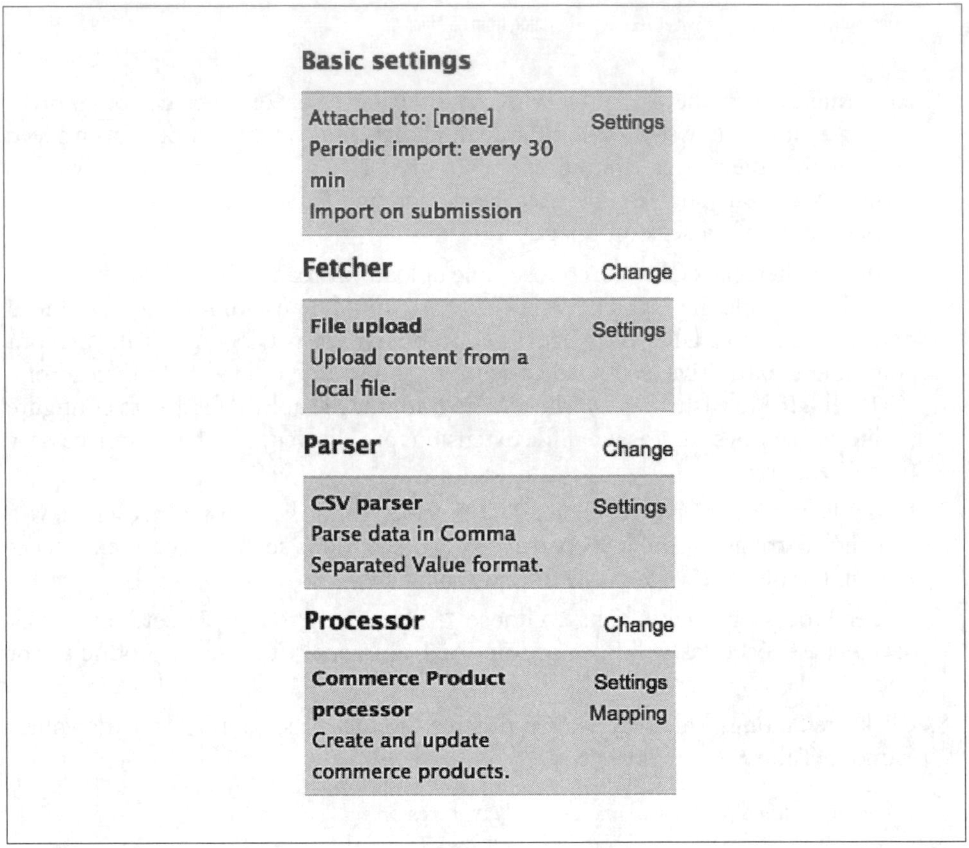

Basic settings

Attached to: [none] Periodic import: every 30 min Import on submission	Settings

Fetcher   Change

File upload Upload content from a local file.	Settings

Parser   Change

CSV parser Parse data in Comma Separated Value format.	Settings

Processor   Change

Commerce Product processor Create and update commerce products.	Settings Mapping

Figure 9-15. Settings for the product feed importer

Mapping CSV Data to Drupal Commerce Products

Now for the fun part: telling the Feeds module how to take incoming CSV data and turn it into Drupal products!

1. Click the Mapping link next to the Commerce Product processor on the T-shirt importer edit page to view the "Mapping for Commerce Product processor" page (*admin/structure/feeds/edit/t_shirt_importer/mapping*).

2. Take a peek inside the *using_drupal_tshirts.csv* file and examine its contents. Of particular note is the first row of the file, which lists the columns of the incoming data: SKU, Title, Price, Size, Color, and Image. These are the "source fields" we need to map. Here is an excerpt:

```
SKU,Title,Price,Size,Color,Image
TSHIRT-001-S-WH,Druplicon T-Shirt - Small White,1699,S,White,
    http://usingdrupal.com/sites/default/files/v7/ch09-store/druplicon-tshirt...
TSHIRT-001-M-WH,Druplicon T-Shirt - Medium White,1499,M,White,
    http://usingdrupal.com/sites/default/files/v7/ch09-store/druplicon-tshirt...
TSHIRT-001-L-WH,Druplicon T-Shirt - Large White,1499,L,White,
    http://usingdrupal.com/sites/default/files/v7/ch09-store/druplicon-tshirt...
```

Note that the data intentionally charges more for Small shirts—both to show that it can be done, and also because skinny people have it way too easy in life.

 The first question you might reasonably ask is, "What's up with those weird prices?" Because Drupal Commerce supports multiple currencies, and different currencies have different rules on how they're formatted, the developers made the decision to store all pricing data in the "minor unit" of the amount (so the price in cents, in the case of US or Canadian Dollars). If your incoming data stores price information in the more predictable "16.99"-style format, try the Feeds Tamper module (*http://drupal.org/project/feeds_tamper*) for manipulating the source data before it hits the Feed parser.

3. Back in Drupal, examine the values under the "Select a target" drop-down: Product SKU, Product Title, and so on. These are the "target fields" in products, to which the source data will be mapped.

 If you find yourself puzzled by some of the options here, such as GUID, there's a handy Legend fieldset down below that contains descriptions of each target.

4. One after another, add the source-to-target mappings indicated in Table 9-7 by typing the name of the Source field from the CSV file, selecting the name of the Target field from the drop-down box, and clicking the Add button. If you make a mistake, check Remove next to the field and click the Save button at the bottom of the form.

Table 9-7. Source-to-target mappings for product import

Source	Target
SKU	Product SKU
Title	Product title
Price	Price: Amount
Size	Size
Color	Color
Image	Image

5. Check the Unique Target checkbox next to the SKU field and click Save, to indicate that this value uniquely identifies each record.

6. When your mapping configuration is finished, your screen should look as pictured in Figure 9-16.

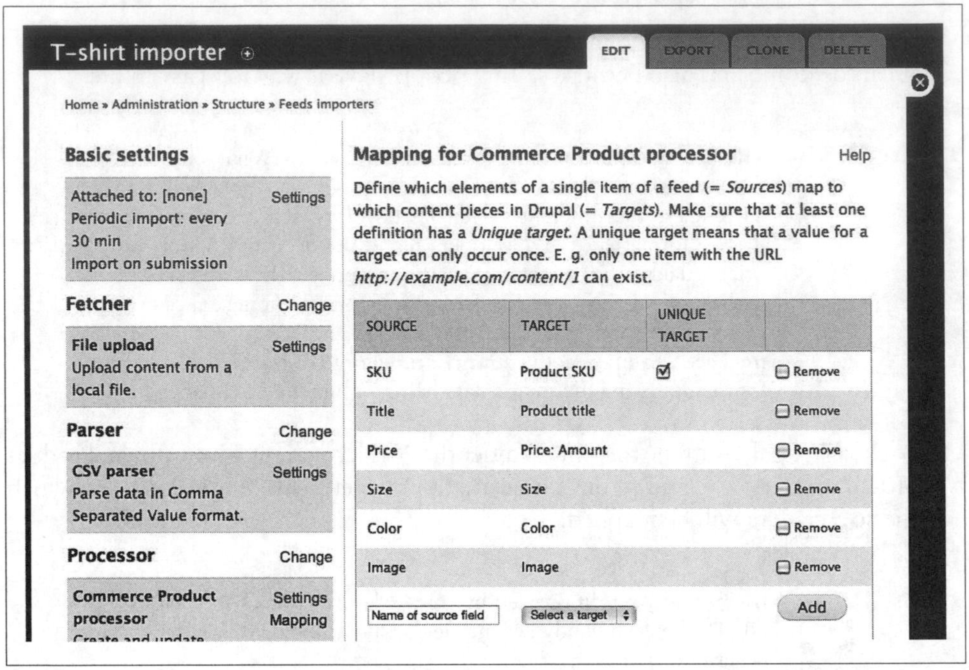

Figure 9-16. Mapping for the T-shirt feed importer

Importing CSV Product Data

And now, the moment we've all been waiting for.

1. Close out of the Feeds administration screen and go to Import (*import*) in the Navigation block, then click on "T-shirt importer" (*import/t_shirt_importer*).

2. Click "Choose file" on the File field and point it to the *using_drupal_tshirts.csv* file, then click Import.

3. A progress bar should appear for a few seconds, and then you should see a notification that Drupal created 23 commerce products, and updated 1 commerce product. Score! Let's check it out.

> If anything goes awry here, the Delete Items tab will present an option to remove all imported values and try again.

4. To confirm, head to Store→Products (*admin/commerce/products*), which should appear similar to Figure 9-17. You should see a heck of a lot more products there than before, and our previously mistyped $1.99 T-shirt from earlier should now be the correct $14.99 price. Yippee!

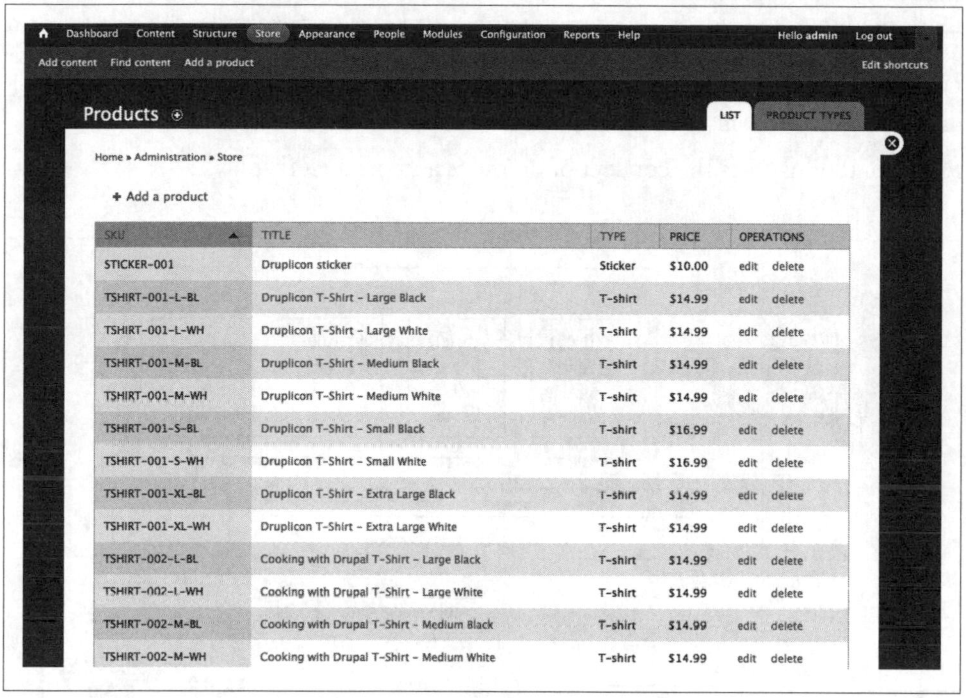

Figure 9-17. Mapping for the product feed importer

Spotlight: Building the Storefront and Shopping Cart

Now that all of this groovy product data is showing up fine in the administrative interface, there's just one problem: how do we expose these products on our public website to our customers? And further, how do we avoid displaying a product catalog with 25 entries in it, when from a customer's point of view we only sell four products (three T-shirts and a sticker)?

Drupal Commerce's "Products" concept essentially acts as your "warehouse" or "product catalog": any and all items your store sells or has sold in the past should be represented in Drupal as products. However, that only gets you part of the way there: while your products will show up great in the administrative listings, they're not visible on the site and your users can't actually purchase them yet. Additionally, in our movie store example, paging through 27,000 products with titles like "Airplane! Blu-Ray Spanish Version" and "Airplane! DVD English Version" won't make much sense to our customers. They'll simply want to search for individual movie titles, and then choose the format and language they want as they're adding the movie to their shopping cart.

The way Drupal Commerce facilitates both of these needs is through the use of one or more content types with a Product Reference field attached. The Product Reference field can group together one or more products into a single product display node, and mark the required fields in those products as *attributes* (for example, the Size field on a T-shirt) and expose them as *attribute selection fields* on the "Add to Cart" form. Updating these fields will also switch product-specific properties, such as the image attached to a product, or its price.

Figure 9-18 illustrates the concept of products and product displays.

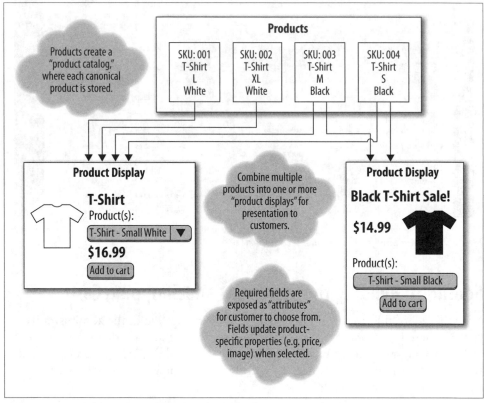

Figure 9-18. Product displays collect one or more products and expose their required fields as attributes for customers to select from

Now it's time to create the storefront our users will view, from which they can add products to their shopping cart.

Hands-On: Product Displays

Let's try putting what we just learned into action by creating a content type for product displays, and a few sample products to get the hang of how things work.

1. Go to the Modules (*admin/modules*) page, enable the Cart module, and confirm the gaggle of dependent modules that it will prompt you to enable.

2. First, we need to create a content type to hold our product displays. Go to Structure→"Content types" and click "Add content type" (*admin/structure/types/add*).

3. Give the new content type a Name of "Product display," and a Description of "A publicly visible product on the website." Click "Save and add fields."

4. Add a new field to the content type, using the settings in Table 9-8, and click Save.

Table 9-8. Product reference field properties

Field	Value
Label	Product(s)
Field name	product
Field type	Product reference
Widget	Check boxes/radio buttons

5. Click past the first settings page, then enter the settings in Table 9-9 and click "Save settings."

Table 9-9. Settings for the Product reference field

Field	Value
Required field	Checked
Render fields from the referenced products when viewing this entity.	Checked (default)
Help text	Enter one or more product SKUs.
Product types that can be referenced	(Leave unchecked for all)
Default value	(Leave blank)
Number of values	Unlimited

6. Let's test the new content type, starting with the Druplicon T-shirt. We'll create a single product display for all variations of that product (S–XL, both Black and White).

7. Go to "Add content"→"Product display" (*node/add/product-display*), and fill in the settings in Table 9-10.

As with the "Add product" form, you will probably be coming back here often. Feel free to hover over the plus sign (+) next to the title and click "Add to *Default* shortcuts" to add this page to your shortcut bar.

Table 9-10. Settings for the T-shirt product display

Field	Value
Title	Druplicon T-shirt
Description	A T-shirt starring the charming Druplicon, mascot of the Drupal project.
Product(s)	(Check off all eight products starting with "TSHIRT-001.")

8. Click Save when finished, and as shown in Figure 9-19, you should not only see the product showing up with an "Add to cart" button, but also a selector to choose which product to buy. Switching between a white and black T-shirt should switch the image, and choosing between Small and Large should switch the price, as well.

9. Repeat steps 7 and 8 for the other T-shirt SKUs as well. And for the sticker, you should only need to reference the single sticker product in its product display node.

While this manual product assignment method is fairly tedious, there are other contributed modules that can help automate the task. Check out the *http://drupal.org/project/commerce_product_display_manager* module for an alternate way of assigning and creating product displays.

Hands-On: Creating a Product Catalog

Next, let's create a nice interface for browsing products. We can categorize product displays using the Taxonomy system, and use the Views module for providing the browsing page:

1. Go to the Structure→Taxonomy (*admin/structure/taxonomy*) and click the "Add vocabulary" link (*admin/structure/taxonomy/add*).

2. Give the vocabulary a name of "Catalog" and a description of "Sweet Tees product catalog." Click the Save button.

3. Now, let's add a couple of product catalog categories. Click the "add terms" link (admin/structure/taxonomy/catalog/add).

4. Add two terms, using the values in Tables 9-11 and 9-12. The terms' descriptions will display at the top of the term listing pages at the specified URLs.

Druplicon T-shirt

Submitted by admin on Mon, 02/06/2012 – 02:29

A T–shirt starring the charming Druplicon, mascot of the Drupal project.

Product(s):

| Druplicon T-Shirt – Large White | ◆ |

Add to cart

$14.99

Image:

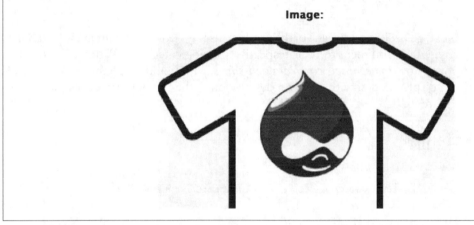

Figure 9-19. A Drupal Commerce product display node

Table 9-11. Settings for the T-shirt category

Field	Value
Name	T-shirts
Description	How Sweet Tees got its name! Check out our excellent selection of Drupal-themed T-shirts.
URL alias	catalog/t-shirts

Table 9-12. Settings for the Sticker category

Field	Value
Name	Stickers
Description	The stickiest stickers that ever got stuck.
URL alias	catalog/stickers

5. Next, we need to add our product displays to the product catalog categories. Navigate to Structure→"Content types" and click "managed fields" next to "Product display" (*admin/structure/types/manage/product-display/fields*).

6. Add a new field with the settings in Table 9-13. All other settings can be left as their defaults.

Table 9-13. Settings for the Catalog field for product displays

Field	Value
Label	Catalog
Field name	catalog
Field type	Term reference
Widget	Select list (default)

7. Next, go back and edit each of the product displays from the Content menu (*admin/content*) to add them to their respective Catalog categories. When completed, if you go to *http://example.com/catalog/t-shirts*, you should see all three T-shirt product display nodes, with the term description at the top of the page, as pictured in Figure 9-20.

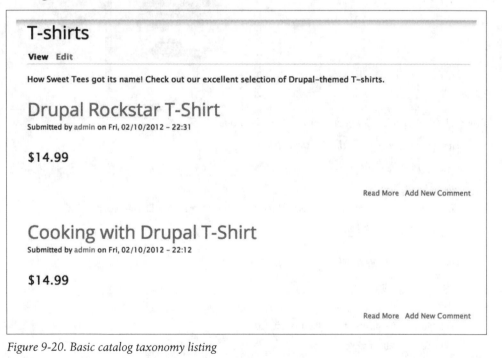

Figure 9-20. Basic catalog taxonomy listing

8. Let's see if we can clean up that display a little bit. For example, there are no images in this listing, nor is there a way to add the products to your shopping cart! Go to

Structure→"Content types" and click "manage display" next to the product display type (*admin/structure/types/manage/product-display/display*). Note that any fields here prefixed with "Product:" will inherit the settings of the parent product's configuration, so configuring the display of teasers is actually a two-step process.

9. First, let's configure the display of the product display node fields. Click the Teaser subnavigation (*admin/structure/types/manage/product-display/display/teaser*) to change the settings for the product display node when it's shown in teaser view, as it is in taxonomy listings.

10. Drag the Catalog and Product(s) fields out of the Hidden section of the form, and place them as pictured in Figure 9-21. You'll notice that when you do this, the Format column for each field will automatically change from "None" to "Add to cart form" in the case of Product(s), and to "Link" in the case of Catalog. Go ahead and leave these settings in place, but change the Label on Product(s) to <Hidden> so we don't have a nonsensical Product(s) label next to the "Add to Cart" form. Click Save when finished.

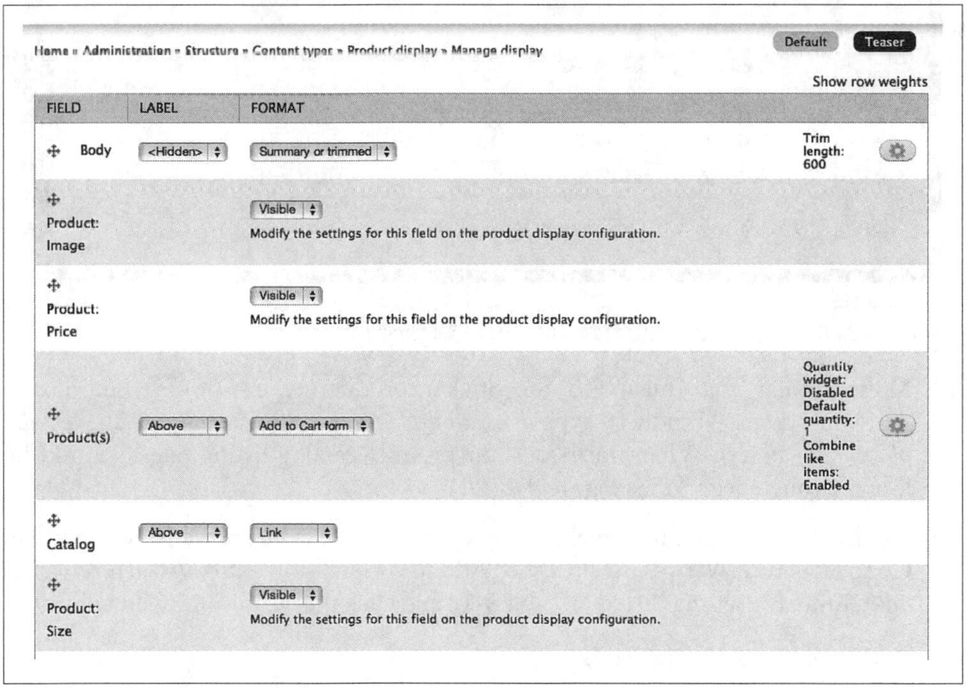

Figure 9-21. "Product display" content type's Manage Display Settings

11. If you go back and look at the T-shirt listing, you'll notice that it's looking a little bit better already; the "Add to cart" button is there. Hooray! However, the product image is still missing. Because the product image is part of the "parent" product type, we need to change its display settings over in the Store settings instead.

12. Navigate to Store→Products→"Product types" (*admin/commerce/products/types*), and click "manage display" next to the T-shirt product type (*admin/commerce/products/types/t-shirt/display*). Click on the "Node: Teaser" subnavigation, and drag the Image field just above Price.

13. Click on the Image field's configure (gear) icon, and change "Image style" to "medium," and "Link image to" to "Content." While we're at it, change Label to Hidden since there's no point in placing a label of "Image:" before an image. Click Update, then Save. Your screen should now look as pictured in Figure 9-22.

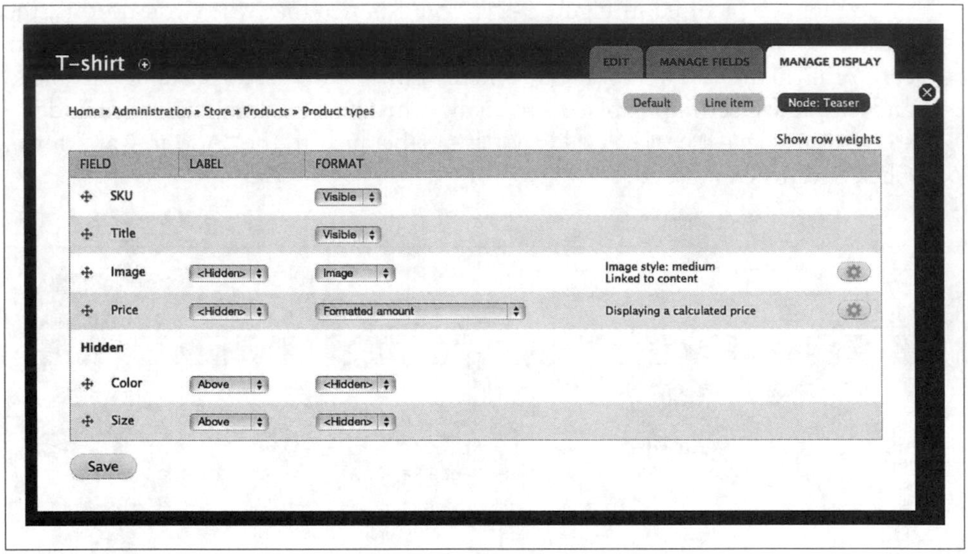

Figure 9-22. T-shirt product type's Manage Display Settings

14. Make similar adjustments to the Sticker product type's display settings at Store→Products→"Product types" (*admin/commerce/products/types/sticker/display/node_teaser*). When finished, your product catalog listing pages should be looking much better! (See Figure 9-23.)

15. Finally, let's design a top-level catalog overview screen using the Views module. Go to Structure→Views and click the "Add new view" link (*admin/structure/views/add*). Enter the settings listed in Table 9-14 and click the "Continue & edit" button.

Table 9-14. Product catalog view settings

Field	Value
View name	Catalog
Description	Checked; "Sweet Tees product catalog."
Show	*Content* of type *Product display* sorted by *Title*
Create a page	Checked

Stickers

The stickiest stickers that ever got stuck.

Druplicon Sticker

Submitted by admin on Fri, 02/10/2012 – 22:31

$10.00

Product(s):

Add to cart

Catalog:
Stickers

Figure 9-23. Catalog category listing page

Field	Value
Page title	Catalog
Path	catalog
Display format	*Grid* of *fields*
Items to display	10 (default)
Use a pager	Checked (default)
Create a menu link	Checked
Menu	Navigation
Include an RSS feed	Unchecked (default)
Create a block	Unchecked (default)

16. At the moment, only product display titles are showing up in the preview. We want to also add Image and Price. But recall that those fields are both on the referenced product *type*, not the product *display*. So first, we must add a relationship to each product display node's referenced products.

17. Expand the Advanced fieldset, then click the "add" button in the Relationships section. Choose "Content: Referenced product" and click "Apply (all displays)." On the settings page, since all product displays have referenced products, choose "Require this relationship" and click "Apply (all displays)" once more.

18. Uh oh! The Views preview is now showing multiples of the same product display nodes, as pictured in Figure 9-24. This is because each of the T-shirt product display nodes is actually referencing multiple unique products. We can fix this using a Views feature called *aggregation*, which allows you to group records together. Under the Advanced fieldset, then Other, click the No link next to "Use aggregation." Check the Aggregate checkbox and click the "Apply (all displays)" button.

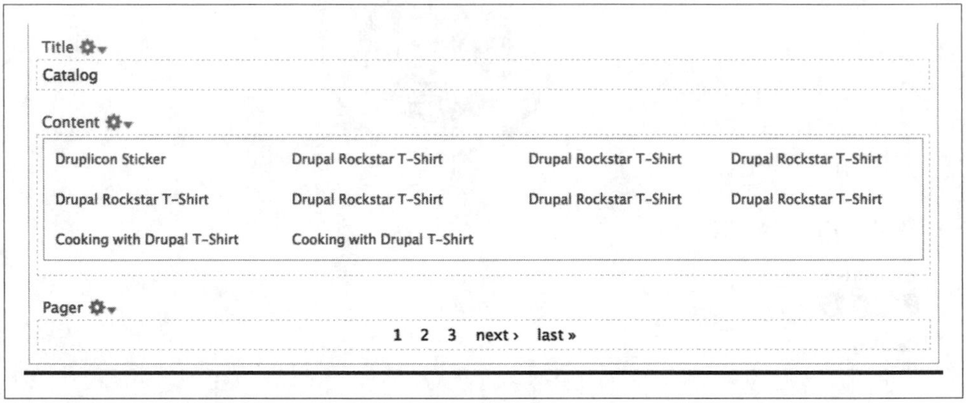

Figure 9-24. Catalog view with duplicate titles in it after adding a relationship to the referenced product

19. The setting doesn't appear to have done anything, but it will in a moment. Next, let's add the fields that we want, now that the product relationship is in place. Click the "add" button in the Field area and check the following fields, then click the "Apply (all displays)" button.

Table 9-15. Settings for the Catalog field for product displays

Fields: Add Fields	Value
Content: Path	Checked
Field: Image	Checked
Commerce Product: Price	Checked
Content: Catalog	Checked

20. After you click the "Add and configure fields" button, Views will display configuration forms for each field, one by one. The first configuration screen will prompt for aggregation settings, then the standard field settings form. Enter each of the settings values from Table 9-16. When finished, your preview should look like Figure 9-25.

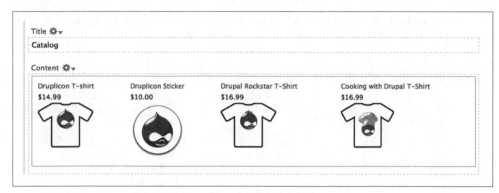

Figure 9-25. New Views preview after adding fields and aggregation

Table 9-16. Individual field configuration for the catalog view

Defaults: Configure field setting	Value
Commerce Product: Price	Aggregation type: Group results together (default)
	Group column: Entity ID (default)
	Relationship: Product (default)
	Create a label: Unchecked
	Formatter: Formatted amount, Display the original price as loaded.
Content: Catalog	Aggregation type: Group results together (default)
	Group column: Entity ID
	Create a label: Unchecked
	Exclude from display: Checked
Content: Path	Aggregation type: Group results together (default)
	Create a label: Unchecked
	Exclude from display: Checked
Field: Image	Aggregation type: Group results together (default)
	Group column: Entity ID (default)
	Relationship: Product
	Create a label: Unchecked
	Image style: thumbnail
	Rewrite Results→Output this field as a link: Checked
	Rewrite Results→Link path: [path]

21. Finally, let's make one last visual tweak. In the Format section, click Settings next to Format. Change the Grouping field "Nr.1 field" to "Content: Catalog." This will visually group like products together. Make any other visual tweaks you'd like and then save your view; its configuration should now look as shown in Figure 9-26. And when you close out of the Overlay and return to your site, clicking

on the Catalog navigation item should take you to your final, completed catalog as pictured in Figure 9-27.

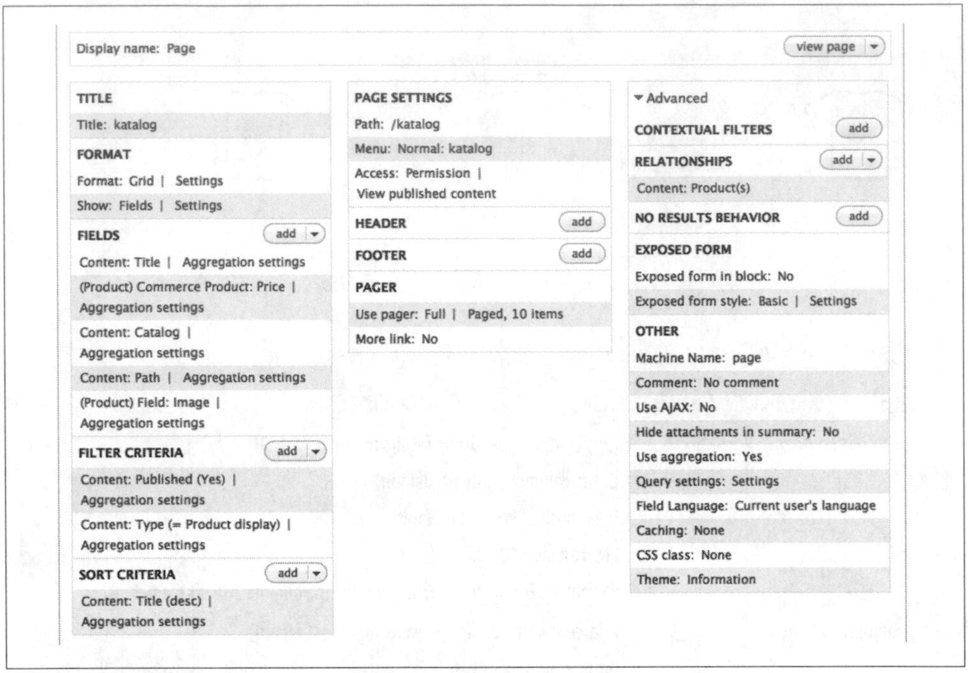

Figure 9-26. Final views configuration for the product catalog

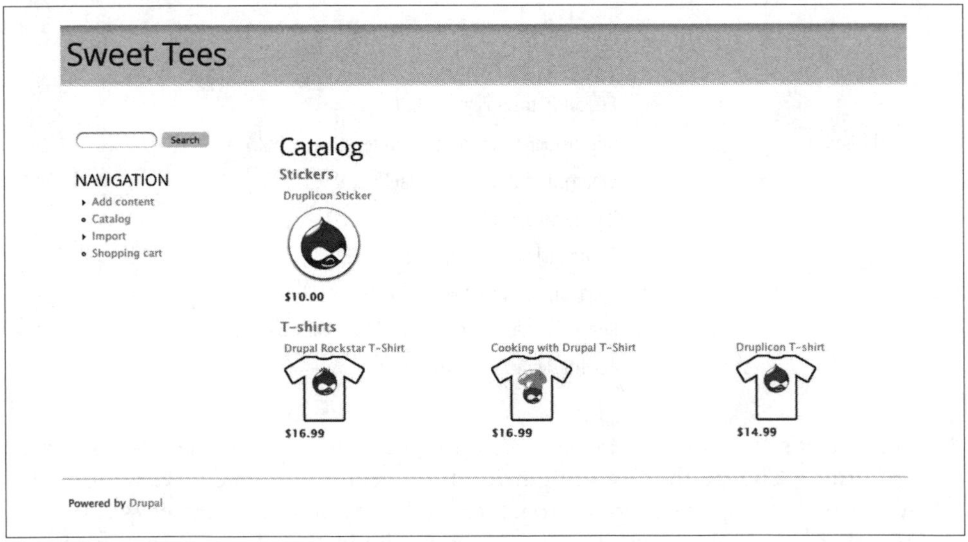

Figure 9-27. Final product catalog

Spotlight: Rules Module

It's easy to imagine that different kinds of stores might have certain things they want to have happen when various events take place throughout the purchasing process. For example, if someone adds more than 10 of an item to his cart, a store might want to provide a 10% discount. Or if someone was anonymous and then registers or logs in, a store might want to assign his old shopping cart to his newly found account.

Traditionally, this kind of custom logic would have to be done in code by a programmer. However, the Rules module exposes a user interface for clicking together custom logic in a web-based interface. This increases accessibility to nonprogrammers, and also allows for bits of business logic to be shared among multiple sites with the Rules module's import and export capabilities.

Because of the flexibility it provides, Drupal Commerce's payment system relies on the Rules module, so it's worth a quick diversion here before proceeding to setting up payments.

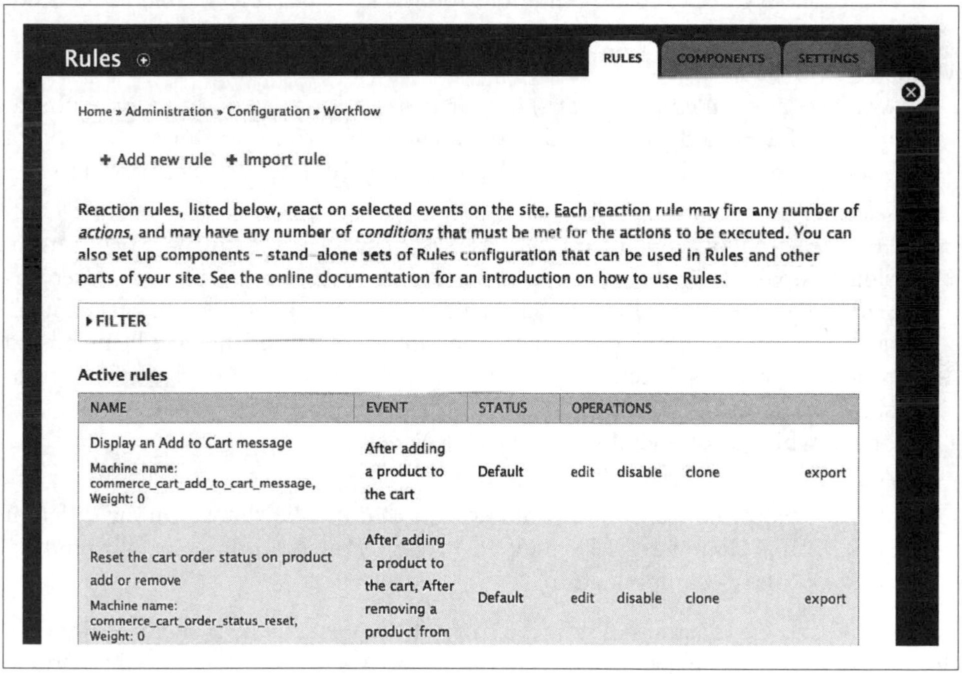

Figure 9-28. Rules module overview page

The following are the architectural blocks of Rules:

Events

> *Events* are points in the system at which something occurs, has just occurred, or is about to occur. Examples are "A comment is viewed," or "Before adding a product to the cart." In Drupal developer-speak, events are "hooks" that fire during the processing of a page and allow other modules to react with their own customizations.

Actions

> An *action* is custom programming logic for when an event fires and its associated condition(s) succeeds. Examples are "Add a product to the cart," or "Send mail to all users of a role." You can trigger multiple actions upon an event firing.

Conditions

> A *condition* is an optional way to make a decision once an event is triggered—for example, checking to see if two field values match, or whether or not the current user has a particular role. Conditions can also be combined with either "and" or "or" logic. So you can create conditions to say, "User has role(s)" *and* "User is not blocked."

Variables

> *Variables* (also called *parameters*) are often passed into a condition or action to provide additional data required to complete it. For example, for a condition of "User has role(s)," the role or roles the user has would be variables passed to it.

Data selectors

> *Data selectors* allow you to select the base system elements to pull parameters from, using Drupal's token system syntax, as shown in Figure 9-29. For "User has role(s)," you need to be able to specify *which* user to check the roles of. For example, "node:author" would reference roles of the author of a node that was being posted or viewed, whereas "site:current-user" would reference the roles of the current user. Data selectors can chain as well; "comment:node:author" is the author of the node to which a comment is being posted. Whew!

Components

> *Components* are collections of configuration that can be shared among different Rules. Drupal Commerce's Tax module takes advantage of this capability and exposes tax rules as components.

Figure 9-30 shows a diagram of how the parts of the system work together. Not only does the Rules module expose events, conditions, and actions to play with, but Drupal Commerce and many other modules do as well. Two examples covered elsewhere in the book are the Flag module and the Workbench module.

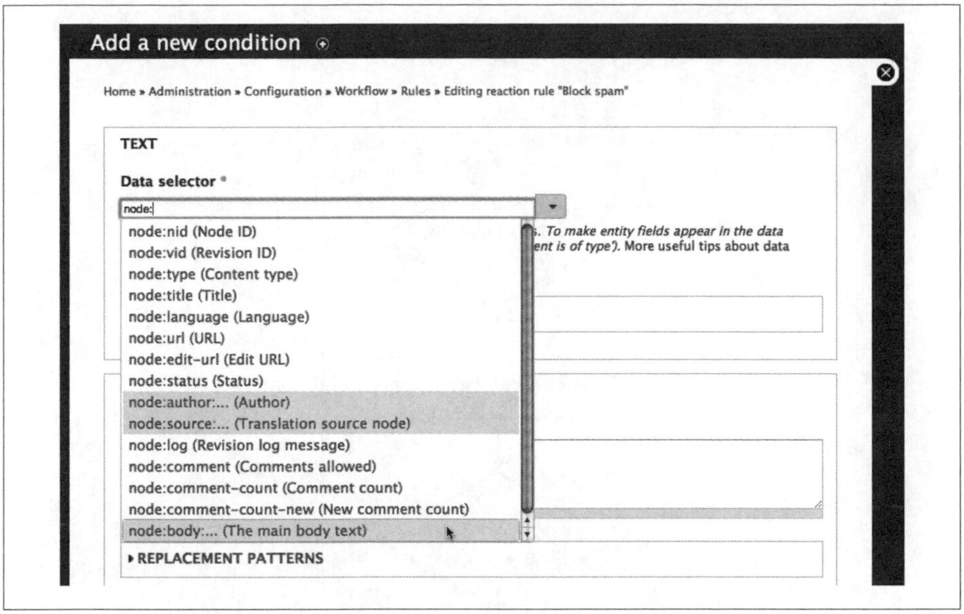

Figure 9-29. *The user interface for choosing Rules data selectors*

We won't be able to cover every detail of the Rules module in this chapter, just the basics to finish up your store. However, NodeOne offers an incredibly helpful and detailed set of online videos covering the Rules module at *http://dev.nodeone.se/en/learn-the-rules-framework*. Also see the Rules documentation from Drupal.org at *http://drupal.org/documen tation/modules/rules*.

Hands-On: Taxes

Let's try a practical example of some Rules module concepts for the Sweet Tees store. Drupal Commerce's Tax module stores its tax charging in Rules.

Before we can open up our store to the public, we need to ensure that all applicable sales taxes are being applied to our items. Because Sweet Tees is based in California, we will need to charge 7.25% sales tax on all products sold if the customer lives in the state of California.

This example is for illustrative purposes only; you must determine what types of taxes you need to charge to sell products in your own store. The Tax and Tax UI modules, part of Drupal Commerce core, allow setting all sorts of complex tax rules to calculate different rates depending on whether purchasers are from the same state or a different state, for different product types, or for international orders.

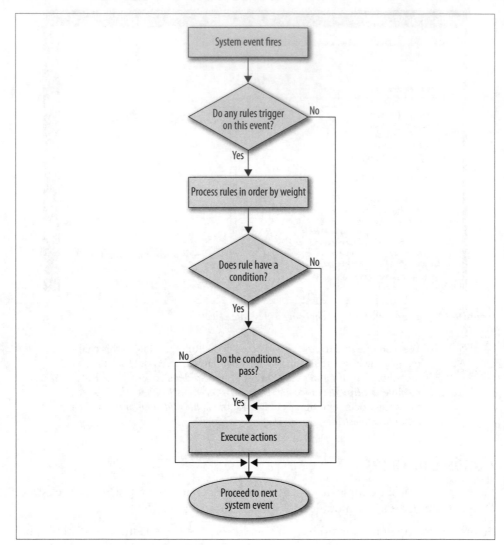

Figure 9-30. The logic for processing rules

1. Enable the following modules at the Modules (*admin/modules*) page:

    • Commerce package

        — Tax

        — Tax UI

    • Rules package

        — Rules

        — Rules UI

2. Visit Configuration→Rules (*admin/config/workflow/rules*) and you'll see two additional rules, added by the Tax module: "Calculate taxes: Sales tax," and "Calculate taxes: VAT." Both rules trigger on the "Calculating the sell price of a product" system event.

3. Go to Store→Configuration→Taxes (*admin/commerce/config/taxes*) and click the "Add a tax rate" link (*admin/commerce/config/taxes/rates/add*).

4. Complete the form using the values from Table 9-17 and click the "Save tax rate" button to save the sales tax settings.

Table 9-17. Tax form

Field	Value
Name	CA sales tax
Display title	(Leave blank)
Description	California residents must pay 7.25% sales tax.
Rate	0.725
Type	Sales tax (default)

5. Currently, a 7.25% sales tax will be added to *all* orders. To change this, we must add a condition to the rule to limit it only to California residents. Click the "configure component" link.

6. Click the "Add condition" link under Conditions. Choose "Order address component comparison" under the Commerce Order group. The form will auto-expand to a configuration form.

7. Fill out the values according to Table 9-18.

Table 9-18. Sales tax rule configuration form

Field	Value
Data selector	commerce-line-item:order
Address	Address
Address component	Administrative Area (State / Province)
Operator	equals (default)
Value	CA

8. When finished, click Save to save your changes. Your screen should look as pictured in Figure 9-31, and all orders coming from California will now receive a flat sales tax. We'll confirm this in the next section.

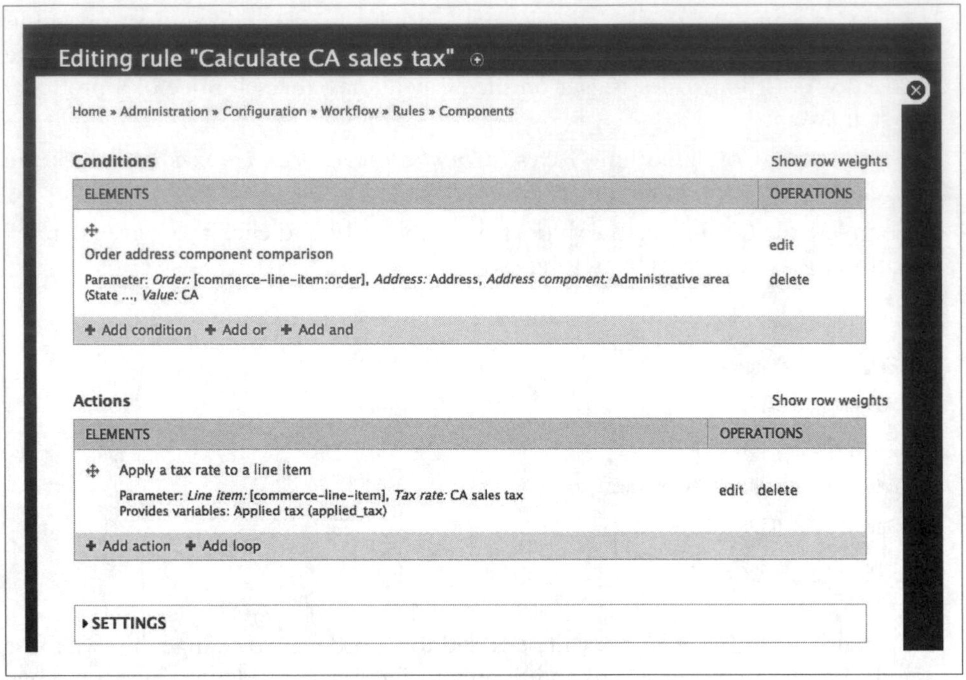

Figure 9-31. Configured Rules component for CA sales tax

Spotlight: Accepting Credit Card Payments Online

Of course, it's one thing to have a bunch of products ready for purchase. But what Sweet Tees really cares about is raking in the dough. They want to be able to accept credit card transactions on their newfangled online store.

An online retailer must have a *merchant account*: a type of bank account provided by a financial institution that allows organizations to accept credit payments. A merchant account can be provided by a merchant bank or by a third party such as PayPal or Authorize.net that authorizes payments on behalf of banks. Fees vary between services, and should be evaluated based on anticipated transaction volume and average sale price.

While customers' credit card details are entered into forms on the Drupal side, no sensitive information is ever stored by Drupal Commerce. Instead, it is passed on to the *payment gateway* for storage on their side.

Figure 9-32 outlines the process of Drupal handing off the request to the payment processor.

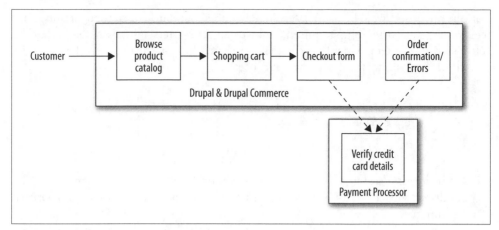

Figure 9-32. Drupal Commerce payment flow diagram

The spot where the customer's credit card details are captured depends on the payment processor, and may require additional setup on your Drupal site. For example, PayPal offers a starter, no-setup fee tier of service, called Website Payments Standard, that will redirect the customer to PayPal.com upon checkout to enter her credit card details, then return her back to your site when the transaction is verified. In this case, no additional configuration is required.

However, many shop owners would rather have a fully integrated shopping experience, and want to gather the credit card details on their own site. PayPal's Website Payments Pro offers this capability, but using it requires *secure socket layer* (SSL) encryption between your site and PayPal. Luckily, the Secure Pages module (*http://drupal.org/project/securepages*) provides this capability.

Hands-On: PayPal

PayPal is a popular payment processor, especially for new site owners. It allows credit card transactions as well as payments from within PayPal itself, which is common particularly within the eBay ecosystem. There are predominantly two "flavors" of PayPal's payment processing tools:

Website Payments Standard (WPS)
> PayPal's entry-level tier. It enables sites to process credit card transactions securely by redirecting customers to PayPal's website at checkout time in order to enter credit card details.

Website Payments Pro (WPP)
> For a monthly fee, credit card payments can happen on your own site, seamlessly. PayPal handles the credit card processing behind the scenes, provided your site meets security standards.

For our purposes, we'll be using Website Payments Standard, since there are no setup fees, no extra security setup required, and we can get started right away. Note that the setup steps for other payment processors vary depending on the provider; PayPal WPS is used in this chapter for illustrative purposes.

 PayPal's developer network at *https://www.x.com/developers/paypal* runs on Drupal, too! Nifty.

1. Go to *https://developer.paypal.com/* and sign up for a development sandbox. The sandbox will act as a "safe space" to test financial transactions from Drupal Commerce.

2. After confirming your email address, log into the sandbox, which will look similar to Figure 9-33.

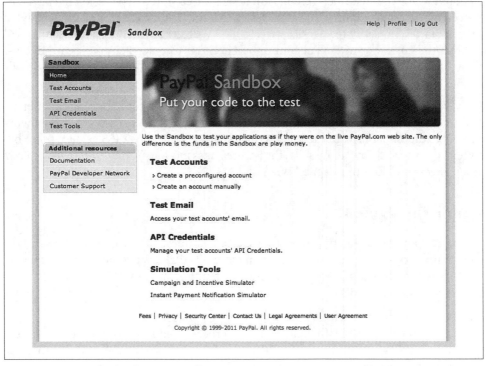

Figure 9-33. PayPal's development sandbox

3. Click "preconfigured account" under Test Accounts.

4. Fill out the values in Table 9-19 and click Create Account to create a fake "buyer" account with whom we'll test.

Table 9-19. *Settings for the PayPal test buyer account*

Field	Value
Country	(Your country)
Account Type	Buyer
First / Last name	Test Buyer
Login Email	(Your email)
Password	(Change to something memorable)
Add Credit Card	Visa (default)
Add Bank Account	Yes (default)
Account Balance	9999

5. Create another "preconfigured" account, repeating the values from Table 9-19, but this time for the seller. Enter "Sweet Tees" as the account's first and last name. When finished, your screen should look similar to Figure 9-34.

Figure 9-34. *PayPal's development sandbox*

PayPal will automatically generate nonworking email addresses based on your real email address. Don't panic! These email addresses are not real; they're simply used for testing.

6. Copy and paste the autogenerated "Business (seller)" email address into a text file for safekeeping. You will need it in a few minutes to configure PayPal on the Drupal Commerce side.

7. Let's take a look around the sandbox. Select the radio button next to the Personal account and click the Enter Sandbox Test Site button.

8. At the login screen, enter the buyer account password you created a few minutes ago (not your actual sandbox account's password!) and click "Log in." This allows you to masquerade as a buyer and see what happens through his eyes. Once logged in, you should see something like Figure 9-35, which shows the current balance of the account. Keep this window open, as we'll want to refer to it while we're testing transactions later.

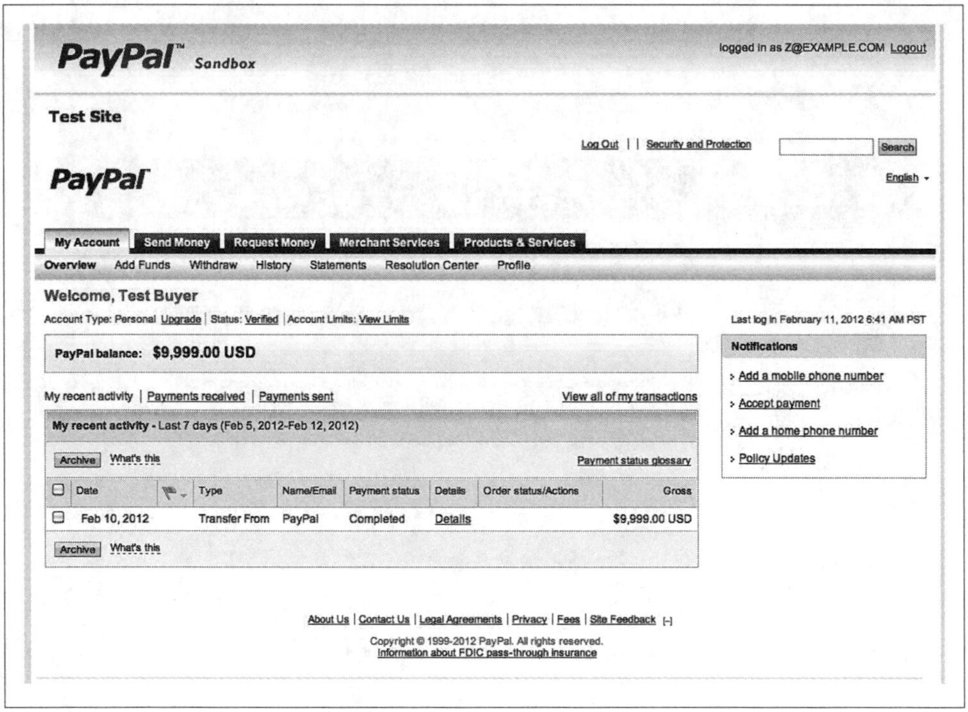

![Screenshot of PayPal Sandbox Test Site dashboard showing "logged in as Z@EXAMPLE.COM Logout" at the top. The page shows PayPal Sandbox, Test Site, navigation tabs (My Account, Send Money, Request Money, Merchant Services, Products & Services) and sub-navigation (Overview, Add Funds, Withdraw, History, Statements, Resolution Center, Profile). Welcome, Test Buyer. Account Type: Personal Upgrade | Status: Verified | Account Limits: View Limits. PayPal balance: $9,999.00 USD. My recent activity - Last 7 days (Feb 5, 2012-Feb 12, 2012). A transaction row: Feb 10, 2012, Transfer From, PayPal, Completed, Details, $9,999.00 USD.]

Figure 9-35. Dashboard for PayPal test account

Hands-On: Configuring a Payment Method

Now that we have the PayPal side of payments set up, it's time to set up the Drupal side of things. We'll do this with the Commerce PayPal module from *http://drupal.org/ project/commerce_paypal*, and Drupal Commerce's Order and Payment (UI) modules. Just as we saw with Taxes, Ubercart payment methods are Rules-enabled for maximum flexibility.

1. Enable the following modules:
    - Commerce package
        —Order
        —Order UI
        —Payment
        —Payment UI
    - Commerce (PayPal) package
        —PayPal
        —PayPal WPS

2. Navigate to Store→Configuration→"Payment methods" (*admin/commerce/config/ payment-methods*).

3. First, you must enable the PayPal WPS payment method. Click its "enable" link under the Operations column and confirm.

4. Click "edit" in the Operations column. Oh, look. Another rule. This one only defines an event ("Select available payment methods for an order") and an action ("Enable payment method: PayPal WPS"). We want to change the action so that we can point it to the PayPal sandbox. Click "edit" in the actions Operations column.

5. In the PayPal email address field, fill in the autogenerated seller email from the previous section, and make sure the PayPal server value is set to "Sandbox." Once you're finished testing, you'll want to come back and switch these settings to your real PayPal email address and "Live," respectively. The form is shown in Figure 9-36.

6. Click Save to submit the form and return to the PayPal WPS rule overview page.

 Your Drupal site *must* be accessible from the Internet in order for PayPal transactions to complete properly. Either upload your practice files to a public domain, or use a service such as *https://www.no-ip.com/* to expose your local development environment to PayPal.

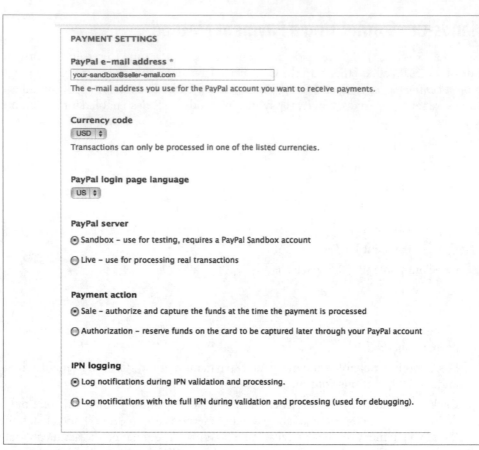

Figure 9-36. Configuring PayPal WPS payment settings

Hands-On: Processing Orders

The remaining element of our site is actually implementing the ecommerce portions: an online shopping cart and the ability to process orders, as well as reporting tools to tell us how our store is doing. We will now complete our store configuration.

To complete this section, we must first enable one final set of modules. Go to Modules (*admin/modules*) and enable the remaining UI modules in the Commerce package:

- Commerce package
    — Customer UI
    — Line Item UI
    — Order UI

Shopping Cart

Thanks to the Cart module that we enabled earlier, everything we need for a shopping cart is pretty much done. Let's make some final tweaks:

1. Drupal Commerce ships with an optional block that can display a visitor's shopping cart on all pages. Go to Structure→Blocks (*admin/structure/block*), drag the Shopping Cart block to the top of the "Sidebar first" region, and click "Save blocks."

2. Test it out by navigating to a product page and clicking the "Add to cart" button. You should see the product and total show up instantly in the left sidebar.

3. Click the "View cart" button to see the full shopping cart. It's looking a little bland. Luckily, the shopping cart (as well as the shopping cart block) is a view, which means we can make tweaks to it.

4. Let's add a product thumbnail image field as well. Hover over the larger shopping cart view, click the gear icon, and click "Edit view."

5. The view is currently showing order information. To add product information, we need to add a relationship to it. In the Relationships section, click "add," and select "Commerce Line item: Referenced product." Accept the default settings.

6. Click the "add" button in the Fields section and check "Field: Image." Uncheck "Create a label" and choose an image style of "thumbnail." Click Apply to save changes.

7. Finally, reorder the image field so it comes first in the list. In the Fields section, click the drop-down next to "add" and choose "rearrange." Use the drag-and-drop handles to move "(Product) Field: Image" to the top of the list, then click Apply.

When finished, save and close the view and return to the shopping cart page, which should now be visible in all its glory, as pictured in Figure 9-37.

Figure 9-37. Drupal Commerce shopping cart, along with a sidebar block

We now have our shopping cart ready to go. That was easy! Next, we'll talk about what happens when someone clicks the Checkout button.

Checkout Process

Drupal Commerce provides the ability to fully customize the checkout workflow to your store's specific needs. By default, the checkout process contains four distinct steps: "Checkout," "Review order," "Payment," and "Checkout complete." A variety of page elements called *panes* are provided and can be placed in any step in any order, and you can control certain cosmetic aspects of panes such as whether they appear in a fieldset.

1. Go to Store→Configuration→"Checkout settings" (*admin/commerce/config/checkout*) to view the current checkout configuration settings.

2. Because PayPal WPS forces a redirect to a third-party website when gathering payment details, it behooves us to make the checkout process as simple as possible. We can omit the "Review order" step of the process altogether by removing all of the panes within it. Drag the Payment pane to the bottom of the Checkout section, and the Review pane to the Disabled section.

3. When you're finished, your checkout settings should be as pictured in Figure 9-38. We'll see this change in action in the next section.

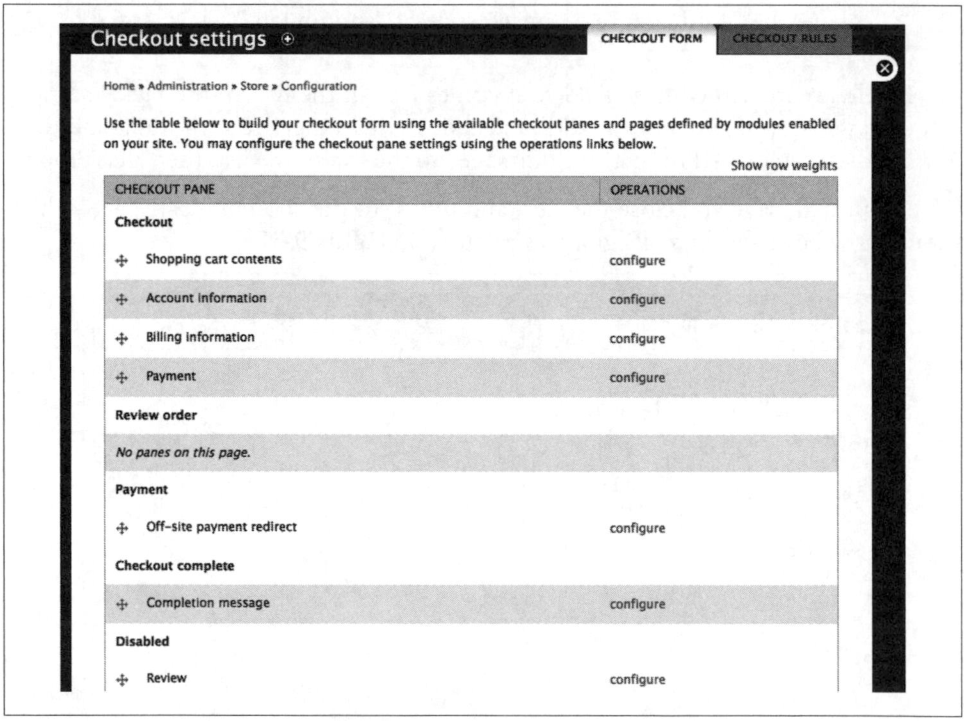

Figure 9-38. The newly customized checkout workflow

Placing a Test Order

We are now ready to make our first test order! Here's how:

1. Click Checkout from either the left sidebar block or the shopping cart page.

2. We are now on the checkout screen, pictured in Figure 9-39. By default, this page displays the contents of our shopping cart for confirmation, followed by account information, and fields to enter a billing address. Because we customized it to do this, it also contains the payment selector. Complete the billing information section with your information. Click "Continue to next step" when finished.

Sweet Tees			
Search	**Checkout**		
NAVIGATION	Shopping cart contents		
▸ Add content			
● Catalog	**Product**	**Price**	**Quantity**	**Total**
▸ Import	Druplicon sticker	$10.00	1	$10.00
● Shopping cart			**Order total**	**$10.00**

Billing information

Full name *

Santa Claus

Country *

Canada

Address 1 *

123 Icy Patch Way

Figure 9-39. The order summary and delivery details of the checkout screen

 If you wish to whittle down the exhaustive default country list to something more appropriate for your customer base, you can do so from Store→"Customer profiles"→"Profile types" (*admin/commerce/customer-profiles/types*). Click "manage fields," then edit the Address field and change the "Available countries" selection.

3. The next screen will inform you that you are being redirected to PayPal's site. Wait for a few seconds, and you should see a screen similar to Figure 9-40. To test credit card transactions, choose the "Don't have a PayPal account?" option. You'll be prompted to enter your billing information and credit card details.

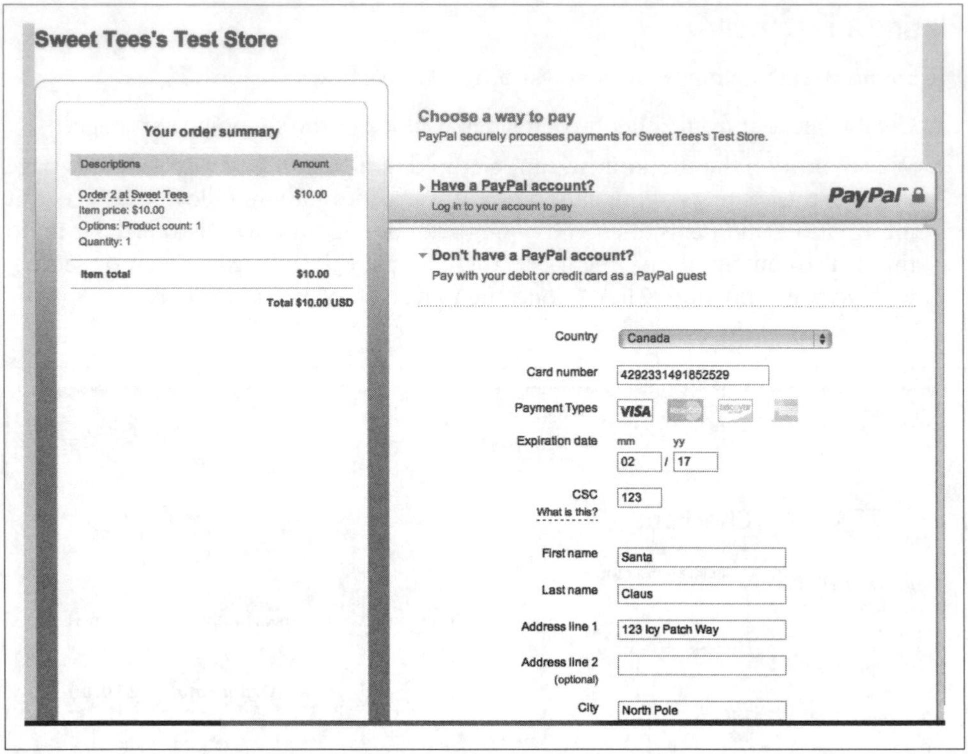

Sweet Tees's Test Store

Your order summary

Descriptions	Amount
Order 2 at Sweet Tees	$10.00
Item price: $10.00	
Options: Product count: 1	
Quantity: 1	
Item total	**$10.00**
	Total $10.00 USD

Choose a way to pay
PayPal securely processes payments for Sweet Tees's Test Store.

▸ **Have a PayPal account?**
Log in to your account to pay

PayPal 🔒

▾ **Don't have a PayPal account?**
Pay with your debit or credit card as a PayPal guest

Country	Canada
Card number	4292331491852529
Payment Types	VISA
Expiration date	mm yy 02 / 17
CSC *What is this?*	123
First name	Santa
Last name	Claus
Address line 1	123 Icy Patch Way
Address line 2 (optional)	
City	North Pole

Figure 9-40. PayPal's billing information screen

4. Before proceeding, return to your browser tab with the PayPal developer sandbox we set up earlier (or log in again). Under "Test accounts," click "View details" on the Personal account. Copy and paste the credit card number and expiration date there into the payment form. For CSC, fill in any 3-digit number.

5. Complete the rest of the form and then submit it. Because you're using a credit card number that PayPal knows about, you will be prompted to log in with your PayPal account. Choose the option to "Continue to pay as a guest and do not use my PayPal account."

6. If all goes well, you should see a PayPal confirmation page for your order. Click Pay Now. You'll be taken to a final screen showing a confirmation message, as pictured in Figure 9-41. Click "Return to Sweet Tees's Test Store" to go back to your Drupal site.

7. Back on the Sweet Tees website, you'll be presented with a short thank-you page, with a link to view the current order status from the Orders section of your user profile, shown in Figure 9-42. Click the "view your order" link, and you should see a screen similar to Figure 9-43.

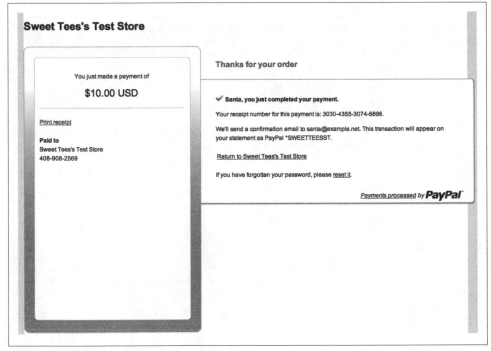

Figure 9-41. *PayPal's order confirmation screen*

Sweet Tees

Search

NAVIGATION
▸ Add content
• Catalog
▸ Import
• Shopping cart

Checkout complete

Your order is number 1. You can view your order on your account page when logged in.

Return to the front page.

Figure 9-42. *The final checkout confirmation form*

 You can customize the text on this page in the checkout configuration at Store→Configuration→"Checkout settings" (*admin/commerce/config/checkout*). Click the "configure" link next to "Completion message," and check the "Override the default checkout completion message" checkbox.

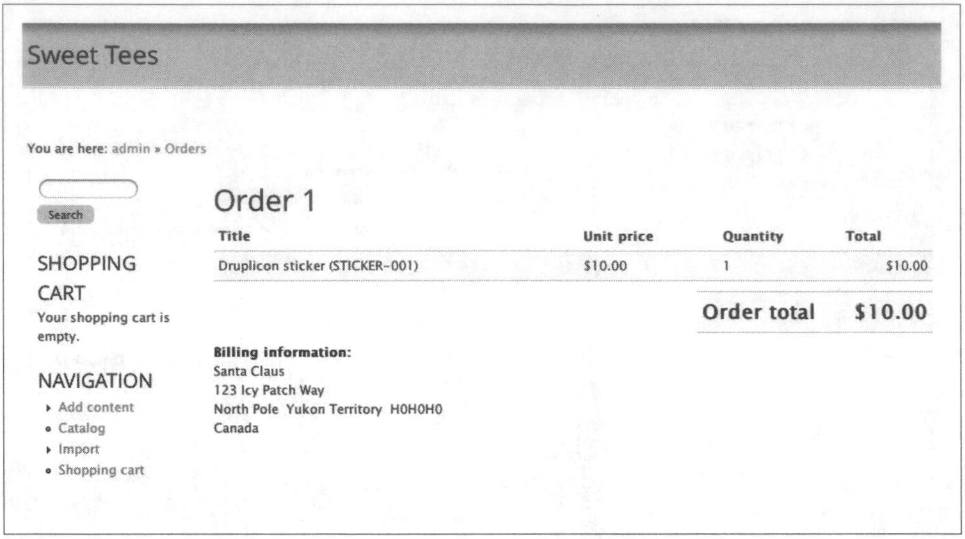

Figure 9-43. The completed order, as seen by the customer

Access Control

Finally, let's configure the permissions for the new modules that we enabled in this chapter. Go to People→Permissions (*admin/people/permissions*), set them as indicated in Table 9-20, and click "Save permissions."

Table 9-20. Permissions for Drupal Commerce modules

Permission	anonymous user	authenticated user	editor	site administrator
Checkout				
Administer checkout				Checked
Access checkout	Checked	Checked	Checked	Checked
Commerce				
Configure store settings				Checked
Customer				
Administer customer profile types				Checked
Administer customer profiles			Checked	Checked
Create customer profiles of any type			Checked	Checked
Edit own customer profiles of any type			Checked	Checked
Edit any customer profile of any type			Checked	Checked
View own customer profiles of any type			Checked	Checked
View any customer profile of any type			Checked	Checked
Create *Billing information* customer profiles				Checked

Permission	anonymous user	authenticated user	editor	site administrator
Edit own *Billing information* customer profiles				Checked
Edit any *Billing information* customer profile				Checked
View own *Billing information* customer profiles				Checked
View any *Billing information* customer profile				Checked
Line item				
Administer line item types				Checked
Administer line items			Checked	Checked
Order				
Administer orders			Checked	Checked
Create orders of any type			Checked	Checked
Edit own orders of any type			Checked	Checked
Edit any order of any type			Checked	Checked
View own orders of any type	Checked	Checked	Checked	Checked
View any order of any type			Checked	Checked
Create *Order* orders				Checked
Edit own *Order* orders				Checked
Edit any *Order* order				Checked
View own *Order* orders				Checked
View any *Order* order				Checked
Payment				
Administer payment methods				Checked
Administer payments			Checked	Checked
View payments			Checked	Checked
Create payments			Checked	Checked
Update payments			Checked	Checked
Delete payments			Checked	Checked
Product				
Administer product types				Checked
Administer products				Checked
Create products of any type			Checked	Checked
Edit own products of any type			Checked	Checked
Edit any product of any type			Checked	Checked

Permission	anonymous user	authenticated user	editor	site administrator
View own products of any type			Checked	Checked
View any product of any type			Checked	Checked
Create *Product Type* products			Checked	Checked
Edit own *Product Type* products			Checked	Checked
Edit any *Product Type* product			Checked	Checked
View own *Product Type* products			Checked	Checked
View any *Product Type* product				Checked
Product Pricing UI				
Administer product pricing			Checked	Checked
Rules				
Administer rule configurations				Checked
Bypass Rules access control				Checked
Access the Rules debug log				Checked
Tax UI				
Administer taxes			Checked	Checked

Taking It Further

In this chapter, we have covered the basics of setting up an online storefront and shopping cart using the Ubercart package for Drupal. However, there are several additional modules that you will likely want to consider before taking your online store live:

Secure Pages (http://drupal.org/project/securepages)
> When collecting sensitive, personal information online—particularly credit card information—it is highly recommended that you do it via an SSL connection. The Secure Pages module allows you to specify certain Drupal paths that should be visited only via HTTPS. The recommended paths to protect are *user/** and *cart/**.

Commerce Shipping (http://drupal.org/project/commerce_shipping)
> Since Sweet Tees is in the business of shipping physical goods, it probably makes sense to charge shipping for them. The Commerce Shipping module provides a framework for shipping calculation, and there are modules available for "Flat rate shipping," and "US Postal Service," among others.

Commerce Stock (http://drupal.org/project/commerce_stock)
> Particularly when you are selling something like T-shirts, it is a good idea to keep track of the current available stock level to avoid selling someone a product that is not available. The Commerce Stock module maintains stock levels for each product, and validates each time a purchase is made to ensure that products are never oversold.

Summary

In this chapter, we were able to set up a complete online store for our customer, Sweet Tees, using Drupal Commerce, a powerful, flexible ecommerce framework built on Drupal. We set up a payment system through PayPal's Website Payments Standard. We also delved into the topic of data imports with the Feeds module, and covered tweaking Drupal's functionality at various system points with the Rules module.

Here are the modules we referenced in this chapter:

- Drupal Commerce: *http://drupal.org/project/commerce*
- Commerce PayPal: *http://drupal.org/project/commerce_paypal*
- Feeds: *http://drupal.org/project/feeds*
- Rules: *http://drupal.org/project/rules*
- Ubercart: *http://drupal.org/project/ubercart*

Here are the additional resources that we referenced in this chapter:

- Drupal Commerce official site: *http://www.drupalcommerce.org/*
- Commerce Guys Drupal Commerce resources: *http://www.commerceguys.com/resources*
- Contributed add-ons that extend Drupal Commerce: *http://www.drupalcommerce.org/contrib*
- NodeOne's Rules learning series: *http://dev.nodeone.se/node/684*
- PayPal's developer sandbox: *https://developer.paypal.com/*

Installing and Upgrading Drupal

The first step to using Drupal, of course, is to actually get the software and install it. Drupal comes with an installation script that will walk you through a few screens to gather information and then set up your database and create your site settings file for you. We'll look at everything you need to make that process run smoothly; you'll find that installing Drupal is quick and painless once some basic requirements are in place.

Once you have Drupal up and running, it's important to keep your site up-to-date. New releases of contributed modules and Drupal core come out periodically to address critical security fixes, and it's important to stay on top of updates as they are released. We'll take a look at Drupal 7's built-in Update Status module, which will notify you of updates available for your site, and we'll talk about the steps required to update both individual modules and the Drupal core itself from one version to another.

 You will notice that many people (and even Drupal core's documentation) use the terms "updating" and "upgrading" interchangeably. They both refer to replacing existing code with newer code.

Before You Begin Installation

Prior to installing Drupal, it's important to make sure that you can actually do so, and understand a bit about how Drupal is structured. This section provides a checklist of Drupal's requirements, and also highlights important things in the Drupal file structure that are worth knowing before diving into the installation process.

Gathering Requirements

It's important to have a few things ready prior to installing Drupal. A full list of requirements is available at *http://drupal.org/requirements*. Use the following as a basic checklist prior to installing Drupal:

1. Ensure access to a web host or local development environment with the following:

    a. A *web server*, such as Apache (*http://httpd.apache.org*), which handles serving up Drupal's pages to the browser. Having access to Apache's *mod rewrite* extension also allows you to use Drupal's "Clean URLs" feature, which transforms URLs like *http://www.example.com/index.php?q=contact* to *http://www.example.com/contact*.

    b. PHP (*http://php.net*), the dynamic scripting language that powers Drupal. Drupal 7 requires at least PHP version 5.2 or higher. The requirements page at Drupal.org has more information on required and recommended PHP extensions, most of which are enabled in PHP by default.

    c. A *database server*, such as MySQL (*http://mysql.com*), where Drupal will store all of the content, data, and settings that it needs in order to function.

 This book assumes that you are using Apache and MySQL. For additional help and support with other web and database servers, see the Drupal installation guide (*http://drupal.org/ documentation/install*).

2. Write down the following information from your web host:

    a. Your (S)FTP or SSH username and password, so you can put Drupal's files into place.

    b. Your database server's details, including username, password, and database name, so that Drupal can connect to the database. Some web hosts also require additional information to access the database, such as specifying a remote hostname or a specific database port.

3. Before you start installing Drupal, you also need a database to which it can be installed; Drupal doesn't create the database for you, as this normally requires "elevated" permissions on a server. You can install Drupal either in its own separate database, or alongside other applications in a single database using table prefixes, but it's generally better if it has its own dedicated database. Check with your hosting provider or system administrator if you need information on how to create a new database, and jot down its name for later. Make sure you have the database username and password handy, too.

For development purposes, you may find it easier to have your web environment installed locally to make your changes prior to uploading them to their final locations. There are several free programs that are more or less a "drop in and go" solution, including XAMPP (*http://www.apachefriends.org/en/xampp.html*) on Windows and Linux, WampServer (*http://www.wampserver.com*) on Windows, or MAMP (*http://mamp.info/en/download.html*) on Macintosh.

Once you have checked to make sure you have everything, you're ready to begin.

Downloading Drupal

The first step before installation is to actually acquire the Drupal code. You can use the Drupal source code provided at *http://usingdrupal.com/source_code*, or you can download it directly from Drupal.org. Here are the steps to get it from Drupal.org:

1. Go to *http://drupal.org*, and you will see two links to download Drupal. They are marked in Figure A-1. Click on the "Download & Extend" link in the upper-right corner of the screen.

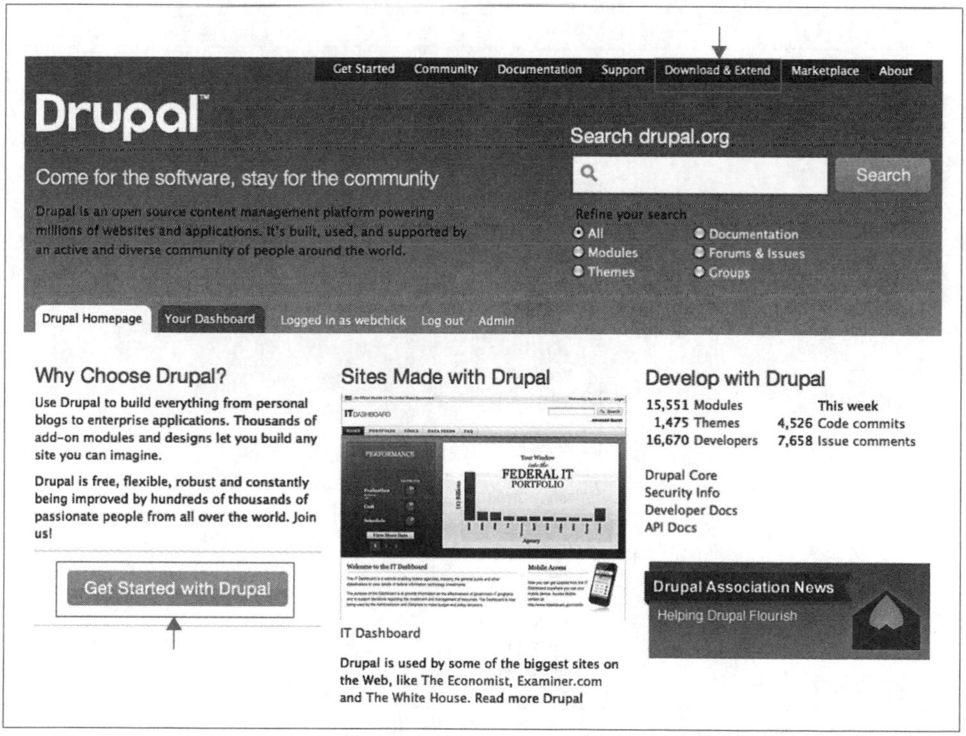

Figure A-1. Download links on the Drupal.org website

2. The following page lists all of the types of projects you can download: core, modules, themes, translations, and so on. Click the green Download Drupal 7.x button.

3. This leads to a page that has the release notes for the current version of Drupal core. Click the green Download Drupal 7.x button, and you will begin the download for the latest version.

4. Drupal files are packaged using either zip, or using the tar program and compressing with gzip. This gives the file an extension of *.zip* or *.tar.gz*, respectively. Save one of the files, whichever you prefer, and then extract the files using your favorite extraction application.

5. Place the extracted files on your web server using an (S)FTP program, or by logging in via shell access and downloading and extracting the files directly on the server.

Drupal's Files and Directories

Now that you have downloaded Drupal, you should take a few moments to open it up and take a look around. Getting familiar with the basic structure and locating important files and directories can take some of the mystery out of how all of this works. When you open up the Drupal folder, you will see the files structured as shown in Figure A-2.

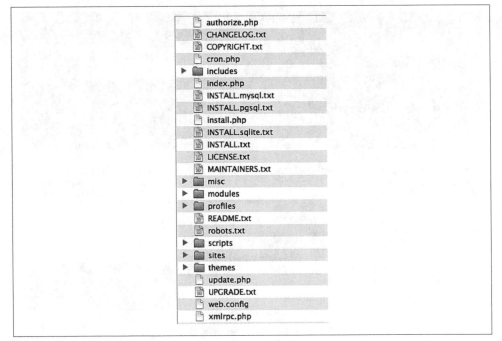

Figure A-2. Drupal's file structure

The important pieces that we'll be covering here are the installation and update files, along with the *sites* directory. The *install.php* and *update.php* files are the two scripts that actually do the work according to their respective names. Because they are located in the top-level folder, also called the Drupal *root directory*, you can access them directly in your browser's address bar by typing in something like *http://example.com/install.php*. In addition to the scripts themselves, there are also two text files, one for each operation: *INSTALL.txt* and *UPGRADE.txt*. These files contain instructions on how to use the scripts, which we'll also be covering in this appendix.

Most first-time Drupal administrators will take a look at the directories in Figure A-2 and place contributed and custom modules and themes into the *modules* and *themes* directories, respectively, in the Drupal root. That is where Drupal keeps the core modules and themes, so it only makes sense, right? Placing your files there will work, and Drupal will recognize them; however, this becomes a problem when you first attempt to update to the next security release—overwriting these directories with the new core versions will destroy any modifications that you have made. The best practice is to keep all of a site's contributed and custom code inside the *sites* directory. Unless you are running a complex multisite installation (see the sidebar "Multiple Sites from One Drupal Installation" on page 410), this means that you should create new *modules* and *themes* directories inside of the *sites/all* directory, and place your contributed and custom code there, as shown in Figure A-3. This way, all of the files that are particular to your site are in one tidy location rather than all mixed up together with the core files. This makes it *much* easier to work with when performing upgrades.

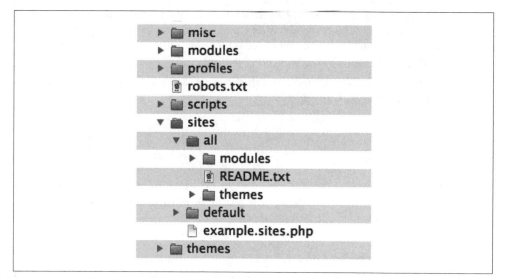

Figure A-3. Contributed modules and themes go under the sites/all directory

Multiple Sites from One Drupal Installation

For more advanced setups, one of Drupal's most powerful features is the ability to run multiple Drupal websites off of the same single set of files. This is referred to as Drupal's *multisite capability*. The example websites at *http://www.usingdrupal.com* use this feature in order to run off of the very same source code files that readers can use on their own computers.

How does it work? On the Apache side of things, a virtual host entry is set up in *httpd.conf* for each subdomain to point to the same set of Drupal files, like so:

```
<VirtualHost *>
  ServerName usingdrupal.com
  ServerAlias *.usingdrupal.com www.usingdrupal.com
  DocumentRoot /home/www/public_html
</VirtualHost>
```

Then, on the Drupal side of things, we create a new folder within the *sites* directory for each subsite, each with its own *settings.php* file and *files* directory. You end up with the settings being located at *sites/jumpstart.usingdrupal.com/settings.php*. When a browser hits a URL like *http://jumpstart.usingdrupal.com*, Drupal searches through the *sites* folder for the entry that matches best, then loads its settings file.

The multisite feature is not limited to just subsite relationships like this, however. Completely different websites can also be shared, each with modules and themes specific to it. You can even do trickier setups like sharing database tables among the various sites to have a single sign-on or searching across content on all websites.

New in Drupal 7, there is also an advanced feature that allows you to create aliases for a multisite installation's directories. This lets you map one or more arbitrary site names that would be used in a URL to a specific configuration folder. The *example.sites.php* file located in the *default* folder contains instructions.

For more information about Drupal's multisite feature, consult the documentation on Drupal.org at *http://drupal.org/node/43816*.

Installing Drupal

Once you have met all of the requirements and gathered the information you need, you can get down to the installation. These instructions assume that you have already created your database, downloaded Drupal, and placed the extracted files on your web server:

1. Navigate to *http://www.example.com* to begin the installation process.
2. The first page of the installation presents you with the choice between a Standard or Minimal installation profile, shown in Figure A-4. In most circumstances, you will want to leave the default, Standard, selected. The Minimal profile will not install core modules beyond those that are necessary for the site to function, nor

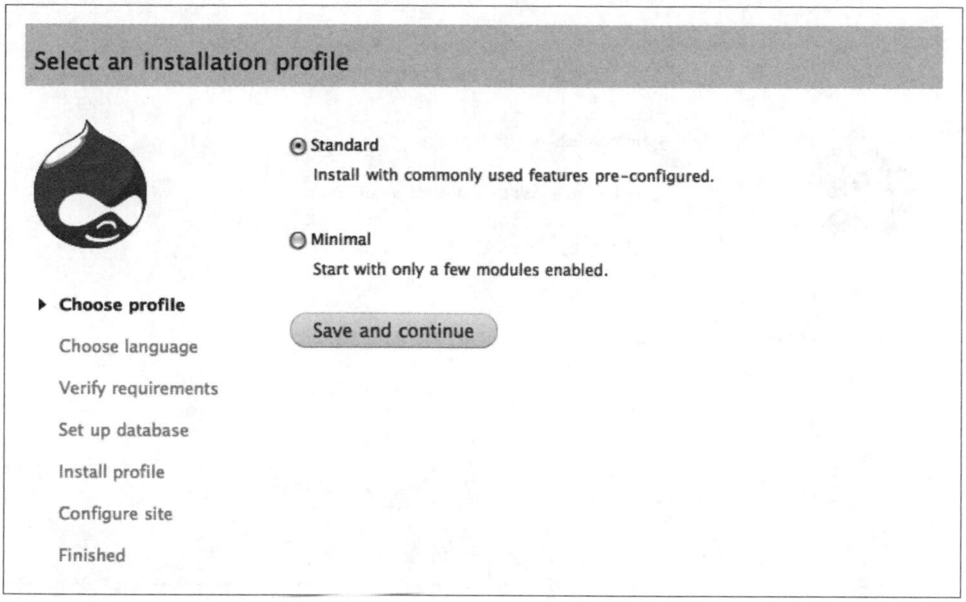

Select an installation profile

⦿ Standard
Install with commonly used features pre-configured.

◯ Minimal
Start with only a few modules enabled.

▸ **Choose profile**

Choose language

Verify requirements

Set up database

Install profile

Configure site

Finished

[Save and continue]

Figure A-4. Profile selection to begin Drupal installation

will it do any basic configuration for you. Make sure Standard is selected and click the "Save and continue" button.

3. Once you have selected your installation profile, the next screen allows you to choose a language, as shown in Figure A-5. By default, the only language available is English. However, you may also download other translations and install Drupal in your language of choice. Chapter 8 has more information on installing and configuring multilingual sites. Go ahead and click the "Save and continue" button.

 The next screen will initially check for correct permissions before letting you proceed. You may need to change permissions on the parent *sites* directory, depending on your host configuration. View the help pages referenced in the installer error messages for more details.

4. Providing all went as expected, you should see a screen asking for your database credentials, as pictured in Figure A-6.

5. Remember earlier when you wrote down the details of your database connection, including username and password? Now it's time to use them. At a minimum, you need the name of the database, the database username, and the database password. If your web host requires additional information such as hostname or database port, expand the "Advanced options" fieldset to enter these options. Once you have entered all of the database information, click the "Save and continue" button.

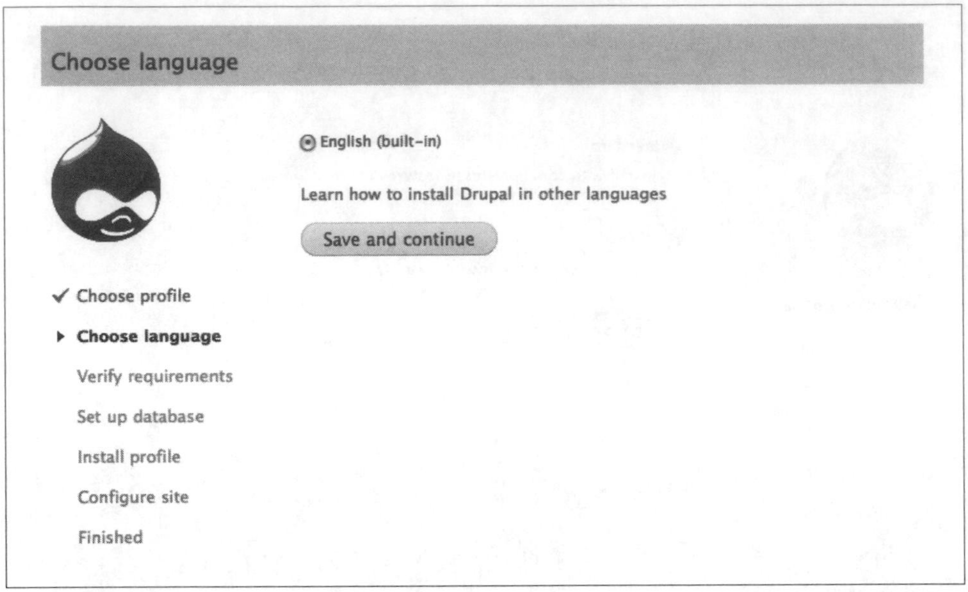

Choose language

○ English (built-in)

Learn how to install Drupal in other languages

Save and continue

✓ Choose profile

▶ **Choose language**

Verify requirements

Set up database

Install profile

Configure site

Finished

Figure A-5. Language selection for installing Drupal

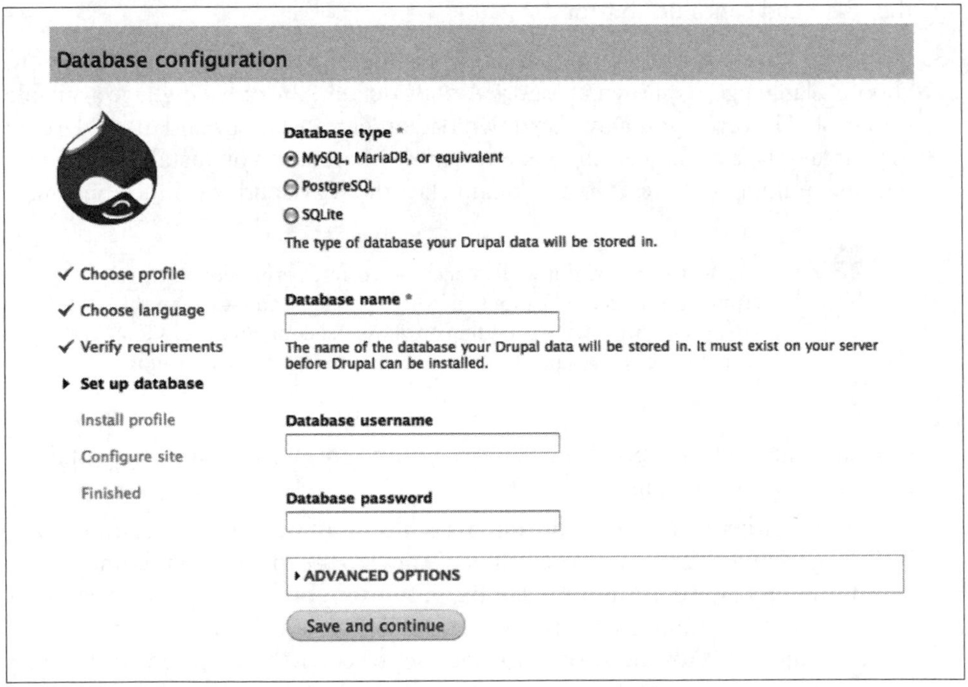

Database configuration

Database type *
○ MySQL, MariaDB, or equivalent
○ PostgreSQL
○ SQLite
The type of database your Drupal data will be stored in.

✓ Choose profile

✓ Choose language

✓ Verify requirements

▶ **Set up database**

Install profile

Configure site

Finished

Database name *

The name of the database your Drupal data will be stored in. It must exist on your server before Drupal can be installed.

Database username

Database password

▶ ADVANCED OPTIONS

Save and continue

Figure A-6. Database configuration during the Drupal installation

6. The next page, as shown in Figure A-7, contains a list of initial settings that should be configured on any site.

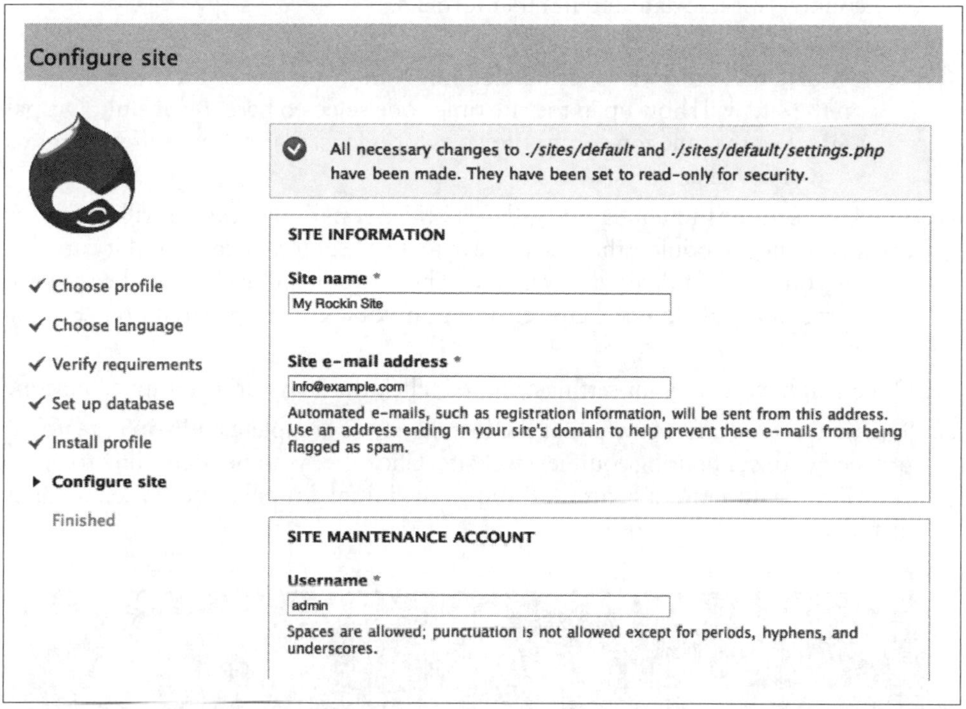

Figure A-7. Configuring settings during the Drupal installation

7. First, you should fill out the "Site information" fieldset. This deals with important global site settings:

Site name

This is the name that will be displayed in the title bar on all pages, as well as in the upper-left corner of all pages, by default.

Site e-mail address

All system emails will be sent from this address—for example, new user registration emails.

8. The next step is configuring the "Site maintenance" account. The "Site maintenance" account (also referred to as "User 1") is a "superuser" account that is exempt from all permission checking and has full powers to do everything on the site. You should therefore create a very strong password for this account (fortunately, Drupal will try to help you out by verifying the strength of the password as you type). Use this account sparingly, and only for administrative tasks. For day-to-day usage, create a second user account with fewer privileges.

9. The "Server settings" section can normally be left at the defaults selected. These options include:

Default country

> You can select the default country for your site. This allows Drupal to define country-specific date and number formats.

Default time zone

> Unless a user otherwise specifies her time zone in her account settings, all posts on the site will show up in the site time zone selected here. By default, Drupal will select the time zone of the browser during installation in an effort to guess what you'd like.

10. The last section is to configure Update notifications. This feature will check for updates of new modules, themes, and Drupal core automatically, and it can also inform you when updates are available. These options (checked by default) are *highly* recommended, as it helps ensure that your site is up-to-date on security releases.

11. Once you have all of your settings entered, click the "Save and continue" button.

12. The final screen informs you that the installation is complete and you're ready to proceed with configuring your new website. Click the "your new site" link to begin your Drupal adventure! Figure A-8 shows the initial Drupal screen when it's first installed.

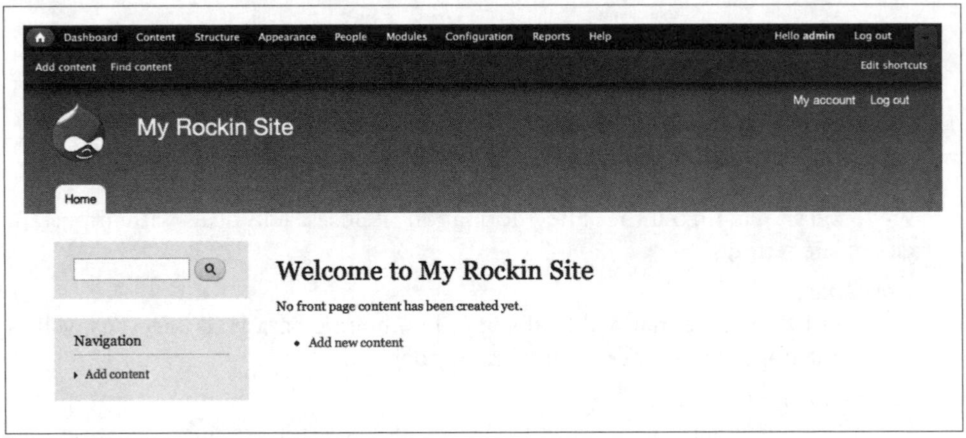

Figure A-8. A newly installed Drupal site

Keeping Drupal Up-to-Date

It's not enough to just get Drupal installed, however; you also need to make sure to keep it up-to-date. New releases of modules and Drupal core come out periodically, most of which fix problems, some of which add new whiz-bang features, and some of which address critical security problems.

Version Numbers

When discussing updates, you'll find it helps to have some background information about Drupal's version numbering system. For all the gory details, see *http://drupal.org/handbook/version-info*, summarized in Figure A-9.

Each "major" release of Drupal core gets a new number: Drupal 5, Drupal 6, Drupal 7, and so on. A new major Drupal version consists of new features, improved usability, and more flexible APIs. Throughout a major version of Drupal's release cycle, several "minor" versions of Drupal are also released, such as 7.1, 7.2, and 7.3. Minor Drupal versions fix critical security problems and important bugs as well.

Releases of projects like contributed modules, themes, and translations have a version naming scheme such as 7.x-1.3. The "7.x" indicates the major version of Drupal that it is intended to work with; in this case, Drupal 7. The "1" indicates the "major" release *of the contributed module.* And the "3" indicates that this is the third bug fix release of this major release of the module.

Some releases also have "extra" version information, such as "-beta4" or "-rc2." These indicate that the modules are still in development, but available for testing.

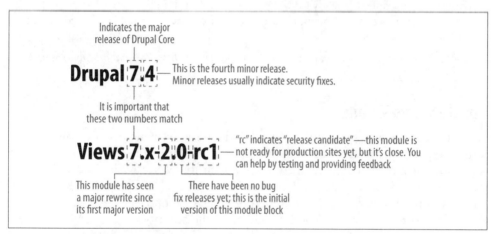

Figure A-9. Drupal version numbers explained

Updates between minor versions of Drupal core and modules, such as between Drupal 7.3 and 7.4, or Views module 7.x-3.0 and 7.x-3.1, are normally fairly painless, as long as your site is kept up-to-date. Updates between major versions, however, such as Drupal 6.3 to 7.0, or Organic Groups module 6.x-1.0 to 6.x-2.0, and especially to 7.x-1.0, will need special care because the changes are generally quite extensive.

Backward Compatibility

The Drupal project's policy on backward compatibility is that between major versions (such as Drupal 6.x to 7.x), developers are allowed to freely break the underlying *code*, but must always provide a migration path for a user's *data*. If a cleaner, faster, or better way of doing something is discovered, developers are allowed (and encouraged) to change the underlying code to work in that fashion. This allows Drupal to stay on the cutting edge of technology without the burden of legacy code that needs to be supported and maintained throughout the ages. However, the result of this policy is that contributed module authors must incorporate these code changes into their own modules between major versions in order to upgrade and stay compatible.

Additionally, the Drupal project currently has a policy of supporting only the current release and one release previous. Although Drupal 7 is the newest release of Drupal as of this writing, both Drupal 6 and Drupal 7 will continue to have bug fixes applied, security updates, and so on. But when Drupal 8 comes out, Drupal 6 will no longer be supported.

What these policies mean to you as a Drupal user is that there is often a lag time of a few months between when a new major version of Drupal is released and when key contributed modules are ready for widespread use. You should also plan on upgrading your Drupal sites to a new major release shortly after a new version is released so that you don't get left behind.

For more on Drupal's backward compatibility policy, see *http://drupal.org/node/65922*.

Update Status Module

Drupal 7 core includes a module called Update Status, which periodically checks Drupal.org for new releases of modules, themes, and Drupal itself. If one or more of these projects is out of date, or if there is a new security release available, a red warning will be displayed on all pages of the administration panel, telling you to head to the administrative toolbar, and click Reports→"Available updates" (*admin/reports/updates*) for more information. You can read all of the security announcements (*http://drupal.org/security*) on the web and/or follow the Security RSS feed (*http://drupal.org/security/rss.xml*). It is recommended that you subscribe to the Security newsletter, which you can do under your Drupal.org user profile (*http://drupal.org/user*).

 Security updates should be taken very seriously and updated as soon as possible. Read the module's release notes for more information about bug fixes or features that the update offers.

The "Available updates" screen, as shown in Figure A-10, displays an index of projects installed on your website, colored according to status.

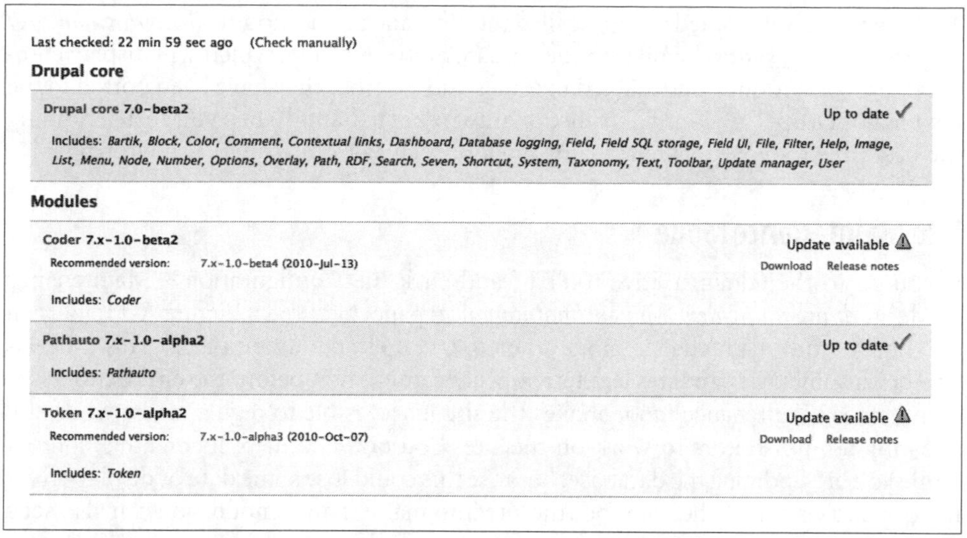

Last checked: 22 min 59 sec ago   (Check manually)

Drupal core

Drupal core 7.0-beta2	Up to date ✓

Includes: *Bartik, Block, Color, Comment, Contextual links, Dashboard, Database logging, Field, Field SQL storage, Field UI, File, Filter, Help, Image, List, Menu, Node, Number, Options, Overlay, Path, RDF, Search, Seven, Shortcut, System, Taxonomy, Text, Toolbar, Update manager, User*

Modules

Coder 7.x-1.0-beta2		Update available ⚠
Recommended version:	7.x-1.0-beta4 (2010-Jul-13)	Download Release notes

Includes: *Coder*

Pathauto 7.x-1.0-alpha2	Up to date ✓

Includes: *Pathauto*

Token 7.x-1.0-alpha2		Update available ⚠
Recommended version:	7.x-1.0-alpha3 (2010-Oct-07)	Download Release notes

Includes: *Token*

Figure A-10. Update Status showing the different project statuses

The color codes indicate the following status states:

Red

A new recommended version of this project is available, and the version on this website is out of date. Pay special attention to projects marked "Security update required!" and download the new recommended versions immediately.

Yellow

Update Status was not able to find the state of this project. This will happen on projects such as a specific site's custom, hand-built theme; on projects that were not downloaded from Drupal.org; or if there was a problem reading the status information for this project.

Green

Project is up-to-date. No further action is required.

 The Update Status module can be very noisy if you have many modules installed; over the course of a week, several modules may report that new updates are available if they're undergoing heavy development. You can adjust the notification threshold at Administer→Reports→"Available updates" on the Settings tab (*admin/reports/updates/settings*) to email only about security releases, which are mandatory, rather than regular bug fix releases.

There is also a contributed module called the Upgrade Status module (*http://drupal.org/project/upgrade_status*), similar to the Update Status module, which will display comparable information about enabled modules and whether they have been ported to the next major Drupal version. This functionality comes in handy when you're determining the best time to move to a new major version, such as from Drupal 7 to Drupal 8.

Site Maintenance Mode

If you go to the administrative toolbar, and click the Configuration→"Maintenance mode" (*admin/config/development/maintenance*) page, pictured in Figure A-11, you can set the site into maintenance mode prior to the upgrade taking place. This mode is useful, as sometimes updates can temporarily cause errors before the entire process is completed. Maintenance mode makes the site inaccessible to regular users while still allowing administrators to work on the site. You don't want users creating content while you are updating the database, because this could lose some data or display errors to your site visitors. When you put the site into maintenance mode, you can also set a message to display to your users to let them know what is going on.

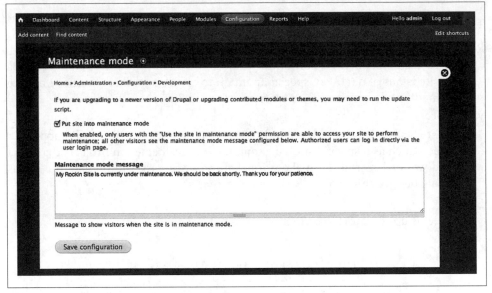

Figure A-11. Putting a Drupal site into maintenance mode

 If you wish to log into the site while it is in offline mode, your user account must be assigned to a role that has the "administer site configuration" permission. Pull up the login form by heading to *http://www.example.com/user*.

The update.php Script

The *update.php* script, pictured in Figure A-12, automatically runs through any underlying database changes that a module requires in order to move from one version to another. Whether you're updating between minor or major versions of Drupal and contributed modules, *update.php* is the piece that ensures your data ends up in the places that it should when all is said and done.

Because *update.php* performs updates against the database, it's *very* important to create a backup of your database before running this script. The Drupal handbook has instructions at *http://drupal.org/node/22281*.

The script lists all of the enabled modules on your site, and specifies whether updates are required to be run. A progress bar counts up as each module is updated. And finally, at the end, a report is generated that lists the database changes that were performed, along with any errors that occurred.

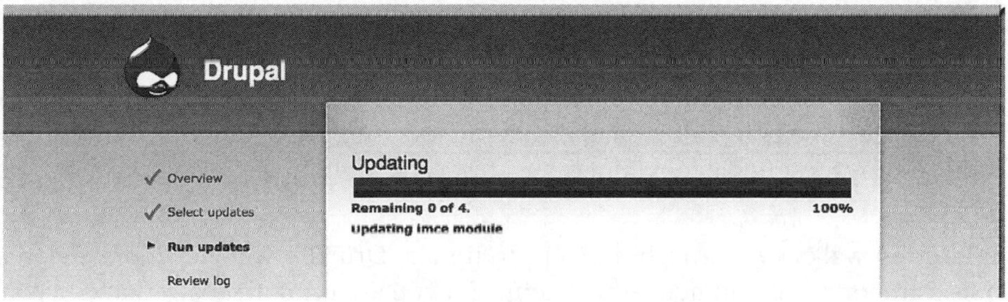

Figure A-12. The update.php script, which performs database updates between versions

The update.php script is intended to be run by User 1. If you are not using the User 1 account, you need to edit the *settings.php* file manually in order to be able to run the update script. You must change the `$update_free_access` variable in *settings.php* so that it is equal to `TRUE` rather than `FALSE`.

But be careful, if you change this value in *settings.php*, make *sure* that you change it back to `FALSE` as soon as you are done running the update script! Failure to do so means that anonymous users might be able to rerun database updates, which could cause all manner of problems.

Updating Drupal Core

Updating your site often sounds much scarier than the actual experience is. In addition to the included *UPGRADE.txt* file, the online handbook has a great deal of documentation available at *http://drupal.org/upgrade* and a helpful support forum at *http://drupal.org/forum/21*. The most important step to remember is creating and testing backups of your site.

 It cannot be stressed enough how important backups are when you are doing upgrades. This holds true for upgrading both Drupal core and contributed modules. You need to make sure you back up both essential parts of a Drupal site: the filesystem and the database. Every system can have a different way to do backups, so that won't be covered in detail here. You can ask your system administrator or refer to the backup section of the upgrade guide on Drupal.org at *http://drupal.org/upgrade/backing-up-the-db*. Make sure that you test the backups as well, so that you are sure that you can recreate your site if something goes awry.

Drupal does not automatically download updates. This is to prevent overwriting existing module code before you have a chance to test it. For example, it's possible that a module may make a change that requires a newer version of PHP than you have installed, which could result in fatal errors on your site if the files were downloaded blindly. Always test updated modules on a test server before deploying them on your "live" site.

This section walks you through the steps to update Drupal within a major version to the next minor release number—for example, if you are using Drupal 7.3 and need to upgrade to Drupal 7.4. When upgrading to a new major version of Drupal, such as Drupal 8, the steps are essentially the same, except that you must also upgrade all of your contributed and custom modules and themes at the same time:

1. Get the latest release for your version of Drupal by following the same steps as covered in "Downloading Drupal" on page 407.

2. Before you do anything else, you must make backups of both your database and files. Again, refer to your system administrator or the backup guide at *http://drupal.org/upgrade/backing-up-the-db*.

3. Once you have your backups done, log into your site as User 1.

4. In the administrative toolbar, click Configuration→"Maintenance mode" (*admin/config/development/maintenance*) and check the "Maintenance mode" checkbox. Feel free to edit the "Maintenance mode message" to whatever you choose. Click the "Save configuration" button to take the site offline.

If you set the site to maintenance mode and log out before changing it back to online mode, you can still log in by going to the user login page manually in the address bar at *http://example.com/user*.

5. For major version upgrades, it's also recommended to go to the administrative toolbar, click Appearance (*admin/appearance*), and switch the site theme to a core theme such as Bartik or Garland. This step can prevent errors if underlying things have changed that your site's normal theme depends on.

6. Extract the Drupal files from the tarball and replace all of the existing files on your server with the new files.

7. Make sure that all of your site's files are back in place. Your entire site's contributed and custom code, along with your *files* directory, should be in the *sites* folder in your backup. Grab a copy of the *sites* folder from the backup you made and add it to your Drupal files. If you have made modifications to other system files, such as *.htaccess* or *robots.txt*, restore those from backup as well.

8. Now that all of the files are in place, it is time to update the database, too. Go to *http://example.com/update.php* in your browser. You will be presented with a screen that outlines the steps you should take to update the site. Click the Continue button.

9. You are taken to the update screen. Click the Update button to run the script.

If you expand the "Select versions" fieldset, you can see which modules have registered that they have update code to be run. Modules that have updates to be run will have a schema version number, such as 7001, preselected in their drop-down select list. Drupal keeps track of this for you, so you shouldn't change this. Modules with no updates will have "No updates available" selected. Even if there are no updates marked, you should still run the *update.php* script, as it will reset your cache, making sure that Drupal recognizes all of the new files. Failing to run the script may cause some weirdness in the newly updated site until you clear the cache by going to the administrative toolbar, Configuration→Performance (*admin/config/development/performance*), and clicking the "Clear all caches" button.

10. After the script runs, you will be returned to a screen indicating that the update is complete. If you changed to a core theme for the upgrade, switch it back to your regular theme by going to the administrative toolbar and clicking Appearance (*admin/appearance*).

11. Click around your site and verify that the update was successful. Once you are convinced the site looks OK, return to the administrative toolbar, click Configuration→"Maintenance mode" (*admin/config/development/maintenance*), uncheck the "Maintenance mode" checkbox, and click "Save configuration" to take the site back online.

Updating Contributed Modules

Drupal's contributed projects tend to move more quickly than Drupal core and therefore require more updates within a Drupal version's life cycle. You can upgrade multiple modules at the same time, although it's best to do one at a time to reduce the chance of errors, and to allow you to isolate problems that might come up during an upgrade.

In Drupal 7, updating contributed modules has become quite a lot easier than in the past, due to the new update manager. To update contributed modules, follow these steps:

1. You can see which modules are ready for an update by visiting the Available Updates page: go to the administrative toolbar and click Reports→"Available updates" (*admin/reports/updates*). You should always read the release notes for each project to be sure you understand what may have changed and whether there are any specific steps you need to take to complete the upgrade beyond running Drupal's *update.php* script.

2. It is still important to make backups of your entire Drupal installation, even though you are only updating a module. If something goes wrong, you want to be able to restore the site to the state it was in before you began. So make your backups before proceeding.

3. Log into your site as User 1.

4. Go to the administrative toolbar, click Configuration→"Maintenance mode" (*admin/config/development/maintenance*) and check the "Maintenance mode" checkbox. Edit the "Maintenance mode message" to whatever you choose. Click "Save configuration" to put the site into maintenance mode.

5. Now it's time to start the update. Return to the Available Updates page by going to the administrative toolbar, and clicking Reports→"Available updates" (*admin/reports/updates*) and click the Update tab. You will be shown a concise list of all of your pending updates, as shown in Figure A-13.

6. Check the boxes for the modules you wish to update and click the "Download these updates" button.

7. You will be asked to proceed in maintenance mode. Make sure this box is checked and click Continue.

8. Once the update is complete, return to the front page of the site and make sure that everything looks OK by navigating around the site. You should especially check the functionality for the particular module or modules provided for your site and make sure that there are no errors.

9. Repeat steps 5 through 8 for each module that you wish to update.

10. To finish up, go back to the administrative toolbar, click Configuration→"Maintenance mode" (*admin/config/development/maintenance*), uncheck the "Maintenance mode" checkbox, and click "Save configuration" to take the site back online.

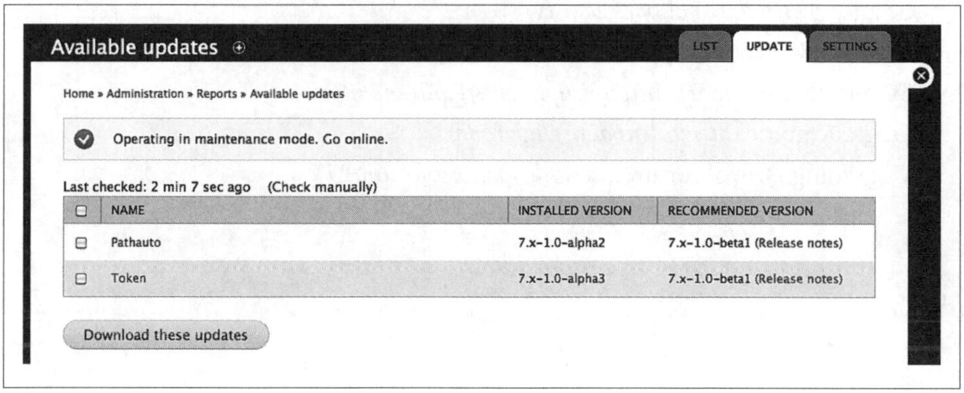

Figure A-13. Modules to be updated

References

Here is a list of modules we referenced in this appendix:

- Update status: Part of the Drupal core
- Upgrade status (*http://drupal.org/project/upgrade_status*)

Here is a list of the external references we used in this appendix:

- Apache web server (*http://httpd.apache.org*)
- MAMP (*http://mamp.info/en/download.html*)
- MySQL (*http://mysql.com*)
- PHP (*http://php.net*)
- PostGreSQL (*http://postgresql.org*)
- WampServer (*http://www.wampserver.com*)
- XAMPP (*http://www.apachefriends.org/en/xampp.html*)

Here are the Drupal.org resources we referenced:

- Drupal project (*http://drupal.org/project/drupal*)
- Backward compatibility (*http://drupal.org/node/65922*)
- Backing up the database and files (*http://drupal.org/node/22281*)
- Clean URLs (*http://drupal.org/node/15365*)
- Installation guide (*http://drupal.org/documentation/install*)
- Multisite installation (*http://drupal.org/node/43816*)
- Security (*http://drupal.org/security*)
- Security RSS feed (*http://drupal.org/security/rss.xml*)
- System requirements (*http://drupal.org/requirements*)
- Upgrade guide (*http://drupal.org/upgrade*)
- Upgrading Drupal forum (*http://drupal.org/forum/21*)

Choosing the Right Modules

With over 10,000 modules to choose from, and more added every single day, finding the contributed module you need for a given task can be a daunting process. Throughout this book, we have endeavored to highlight and identify most of the "must-have" modules, particularly architectural modules that are commonly used to build Drupal websites. We've also endeavored to cover modules that have a proven track record and are likely to continue to be used to build sites.

However, each new website project has unique requirements that may be outside the scope of what this book has covered, and the landscape of available contributed projects is a constantly shifting space. Modules that were once critical building blocks may be abandoned or deprecated by superior alternatives, and new modules may come along that completely blow away anything else that came before them.

This appendix, therefore, attempts to highlight some of the best practices used by those "in the know" for evaluating and selecting the right module for the job. It's important to keep in mind that no simple set of guidelines—these included—can tell you everything about a module. The important thing to remember is that evaluating modules carefully before you commit to them will help prevent unpleasant surprises down the road.

Finding Modules

The first step to choosing the right module for your needs is actually *finding* it. Fortunately, all Drupal modules (with only a few rare exceptions) are located directly on the main Drupal.org website, so there's only one resource for finding them. Here's how you do it.

Browse Module Listings

The main module listing page at *http://drupal.org/project/modules*, and pictured in Figure B-1, lists all of the available modules and sorts them so that the most popular modules (based on the number of active installations) are listed at the top. If the module you want to use is on the first few pages of this listing, you're in good company. You can narrow this huge list by using the variety of filters at the top of the page. You can see a list of all the categories for modules at *http://drupal.org/project/modules/categories*.

 Drupal 6.x modules are not compatible with Drupal 7.x, and vice versa. To see an accurate list for your site, make sure to change the "Filter by compatibility" filter to show only those modules that are compatible with your Drupal version.

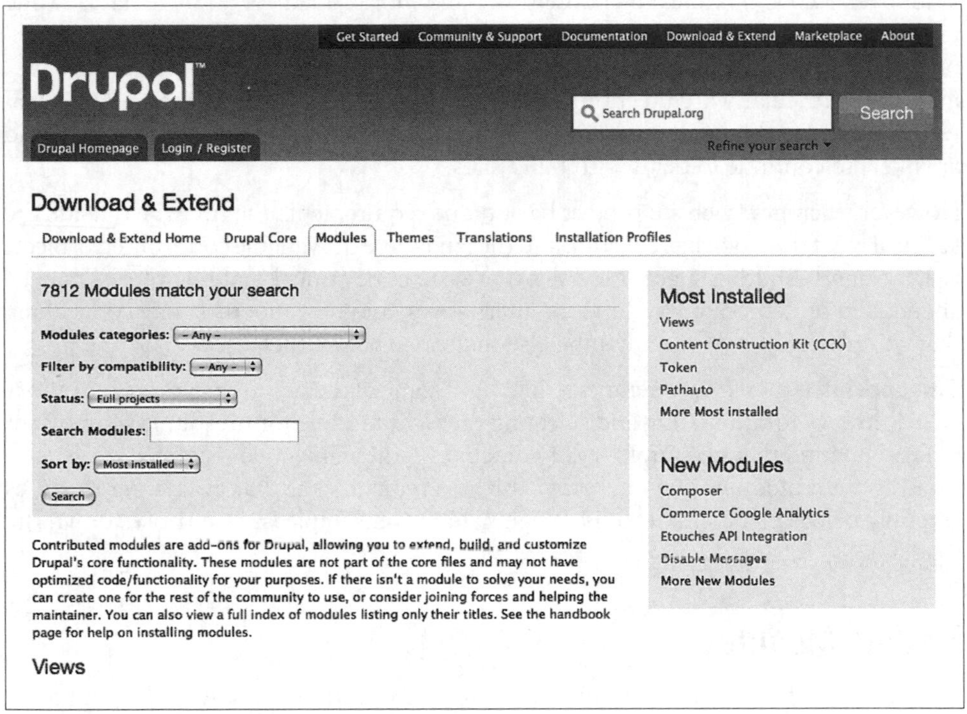

Figure B-1. Module browse pages on Drupal.org

Another nice Drupal.org "hack" is keeping an RSS reader pointed at *http://drupal.org/taxonomy/term/14/0/feed*, which is a list of all the newest modules on Drupal.org as they are created. You can see this listing in the regular module browser by changing the default sort order from "Most installed" to "Date."

Keyword Search

Drupal.org also provides several places for searching the downloads on the site, also shown in Figure B-1. There is a search box directly on the module page, and the main site search box also provides an option for you to limit your search to just modules by clicking the "Refine your search" link, then selecting modules from the options. Searching by keyword allows you to drill down to modules specific to your needs faster than browsing by the default category view.

Local User Groups

http://groups.drupal.org/ is a collaboration space for working groups, event planning groups, and geographical groups. There are over 450 local user groups worldwide listed at *http://groups.drupal.org/groups*. Many of these groups hold monthly meetups where you can meet other human beings in the "real world" who've heard of this "Drupal" thing before. Whether you're in New York City or the Philippines, attending these meetups can be a great way to learn about new modules and technologies, get help on questions you might have, brainstorm on solutions with others, or just meet friends!

Similar Module Review Group

The Similar Module Review group at *http://groups.drupal.org/similar-module-review* provides posts that perform comprehensive analysis of all modules that overlap in certain areas of functionality. If you want to know which is the best WYSIWYG module to use, or why you'd want to use one sort of voting module over another, this is a great place to look first (and, if the comparison you're looking for doesn't exist already, research and contribute your own)!

Drupal.org Forums

The Drupal.org support forums at *http://drupal.org/forum*, particularly the "Before you start" forum at *http://drupal.org/forum/20*, can provide a wealth of information in the form of questions from other users about the modules they used for their own projects. Often, you can receive some helpful advice not only about the feature you're trying to implement now, but also for future things your website will need to take into consideration. The "Drupal showcase" forum at *http://drupal.org/forum/25* is also filled with people showing off websites they built with Drupal—and they are often more than happy to share details about how they built a particular piece.

Case Studies

Chances are good that no matter how crazy the use case, someone else has had to solve the very same problem with Drupal as you have. You can cut down tremendously the time required to find modules by discovering how that person went about it. The

Drupal documentation contains a section for case studies at *http://drupal.org/cases*. These consist of detailed writeups, often about major websites using Drupal, why Drupal was chosen, and how the site was put together.

Planet Drupal

Planet Drupal (*http://drupal.org/planet*), pictured in Figure B-2, is an aggregation of Drupal contributing members' blogs and is a great way to find out what's new and hot in the module world. Module tutorials, reviews, and news are often posted there, and Planet Drupal is also a great general resource for keeping your finger on the pulse of what's happening in the larger community.

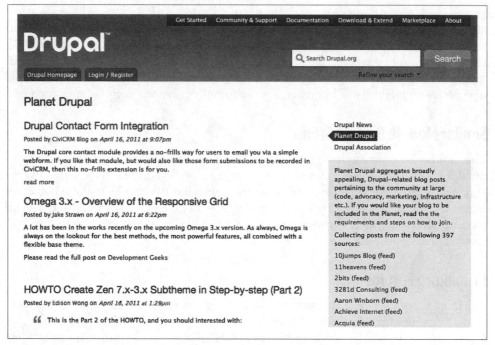

Figure B-2. Planet Drupal, which aggregates content from blogs of Drupal companies and contributors

Third-Party Websites

http://drupal.org/node/289913 provides a list of third-party websites—that is, separate from Drupal.org—that often provide useful information for evaluating modules. For example, *http://drupalmodules.com* provides user ratings and reviews of Drupal modules, and *http://www.lullabot.com* has a variety of articles, videos, and podcasts, many of which highlight popular modules and how to use them.

Assessing a Module's Health

An open source project's strength comes from the power of its base of contributors, and the Drupal project is no different. Although every line of code added or changed in Drupal core goes through rigorous peer review, contributed modules are more of a Wild West where anyone who jumps through a few basic hoops can add modules for everyone to download. Drupal strives to keep the barriers to contributing code as low as possible in order to facilitate growing Drupal's thriving development community. This approach has both pros (for almost any problem, there's a module that can get you fully or at least partway there) and cons (developers' experience levels are varied, so contributed code quality is uneven; the code can have inefficiencies and security problems; and developers can become overextended and unable to keep up with maintenance of their modules).

Whether or not a module is well maintained, its overall code quality, and how well used it is in the overall community are all important factors for you to consider when selecting modules. This section will talk about determining these factors by closely inspecting the tools Drupal.org provides, starting with the central feature of all Drupal modules: the project page.

Project Pages

Modules, themes, and even Drupal core itself are all referred to as *projects* on Drupal.org. Each project has its own page at *http://drupal.org/project/project_name*, which contains a wealth of information that you can use to evaluate a module's health.

Figure B-3 shows the first part of a module's project page. Here you can find the name of the module's *lead maintainer* (usually the original author and/or the module's primary developer), the date the project was first created, some basic project information, a description of what the module does, and sometimes a screenshot showing what the module does. The project information section gives you important information, like whether the project is being actively maintained, and shows the number of reported installations of the module. The usage statistics are helpful to gauge how widely used a module is. A module that only has 50 or 100 sites using it may (or may not) be a good module, but the community support for improvements and troubleshooting will be very limited. The original project creation date can be useful when you are looking for time-tested solutions (if the module was created in the past week, it's probably best to let it mature a bit before depending on it). But also be aware that some older modules may be legacy solutions that more modern modules deprecate.

The sidebar on the project page contains a lot of useful information as well. Here you will find a full list of up to four of the most recently active maintainers—that is, people who have permission to modify the code—and a search box to do a search within the project's issue queue. You can also see the number of currently pending issues for this project and a short list of the latest issues that have been updated. Farther down the sidebar is a list of related projects, which is very useful to investigate to make sure you are using the module that best fits your needs. The resources section is an optional list of links, including resources such as a project's external home page, a link to its documentation, or a demonstration site. The presence of these links tends to indicate a maintainer who is passionate about his module, and wants it to be as high-quality as possible.

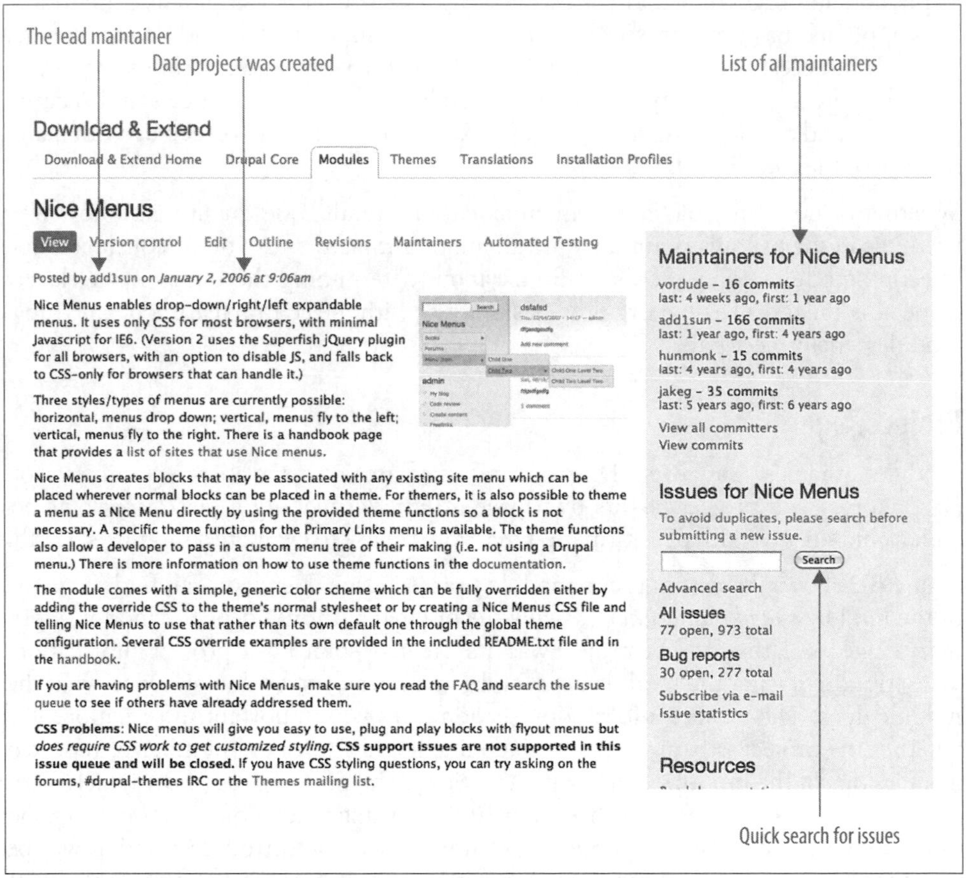

Figure B-3. The project page for the Nice Menus module

Further down, we see the module release table (pictured in Figure B-4), which we discussed briefly in Chapter 2. A plethora of useful information is available here, including the date that the code was last updated; whether the module has "Recommended releases," which indicate stable releases that the maintainer recommends for use; links to release notes for each release to tell what bugs were fixed and features were added; and a link to view all releases—even old, outdated ones.

Downloads

Recommended releases

Version	Downloads	Date	Links
7.x–1.0	tar.gz (100.61 KB) | zip (132.81 KB)	2011–Jan–05	Notes | Edit
6.x–2.1	tar.gz (277.56 KB) | zip (368.31 KB)	2010–Mar–16	Notes | Edit

Other releases

Version	Downloads	Date	Links
6.x–1.4	tar.gz (253.05 KB) | zip (346.6 KB)	2009–Sep–30	Notes | Edit

Development releases

Version	Downloads	Date	Links
7.x–1.x–dev	tar.gz (255.67 KB) | zip (297.41 KB)	2011–May–01	Notes | Edit
6.x–2.x–dev	tar.gz (86.47 KB) | zip (115.74 KB)	2011–Feb–25	Notes | Edit

View all releases

Figure B-4. The module release table for a typical module

The release table in Figure B-4, taken from the Organic Groups module on May 1, 2011, is indicative of a healthy project. The module has stable releases for both Drupal 6 and Drupal 7. The date on the module's development releases indicates that the code has been updated very recently, which means that the maintainer is actively developing on the project. Clicking on "View all releases" shows releases of this module dating back to Drupal 4.7.

Here are some signs to look for on a project page that indicate it might be worth searching elsewhere:

- If there are only development snapshots available and no recommended releases, or if there is no release table *at all*, this indicates that this module is undergoing development and should not yet be relied upon for production websites.

- If the last updated date of the latest release (or at least the development release) is more than several months in the past, this could indicate lack of maintainer activity and interest in the module. It *could* also mean that you've found an example of a completely perfect module that has no bugs and needs no new features added (it's extremely rare, but it happens), so you should investigate the module a little more to determine if this is a positive or negative indicator.

Issue Queues

Development of code in the Drupal community happens in a project's *issue queue*, such as *http://drupal.org/project/issues/3060*, pictured in Figure B-5. The issue queue is a log of bugs, feature requests, support requests, and tasks for a given project that module maintainers use as their public working space. Anyone in the community can log issues against a project, and anyone can provide solutions for them as well.

Issues for Drupal core

Create a new issue   Advanced search   Statistics   Subscribe

Search for	Status	Priority	Category	Version	Component
	– Open issues –	– Any –	– Any –	– Any –	– Any –

Search

Summary	Status	Priority	Category	Version	Component	Replies	Last updated	Assigned to
No more White Screen Of Death (graceful shutdown) new	needs review	normal	feature requests	8.x–dev	base system	4 4 new	42 min 19 sec	
Autocomplete doesn't handle Enter key well when in vertical_tabs updated	active	normal	bug reports	7.0	forms system	2 1 new	55 min 5 sec	
Warning: array_flip() Error message when switching from user account node to any other node updated	fixed	normal	bug reports	7.0	user system	8 3 new	1 hour 31 min	
When installing module through UI, get error updated	postponed (maintainer needs more info)	major	bug reports	7.0	update.module	5 5 new	1 hour 45 min	
Fatal error: Cannot access empty property in field.attach.inc updated	active	major	bug reports	7.0	node system	59 18 new	1 hour 49 min	
language_count is never decremented when removing a language updated	patch (to be ported)	normal	bug reports	6.x–dev	language system	31 24 new	2 hours 22 min	
Misleading help text for the translation support settings updated	reviewed & tested by the community	minor	bug reports	8.x–dev	translation.module	5 2 new	2 hours 24 min	

Figure B-5. The issue queue from the Drupal core, an example of a healthy project

You can find an issue queue for a project in several ways. The most common way is simply to start on the project's page. If you look in the sidebar, you will see an "Issues for *Project Name*" section, which has a quick search box and some links to the current issues. You can also look at the main list of all issues across all projects at *http://drupal .org/project/issues*, and use the Project box to select the project you're interested in.

Because issue queues provide an open window into what's happening with development of a given project, being able to "read" an issue queue is an invaluable skill in evaluating a project's health.

For example, most people might logically assume that a project with lots of issues is a poor-quality project, and one with very few issues is a high-quality project. While this certainly can be the case, it's worth pointing out that Drupal itself currently has more than 5,000 open issues, and its code is written to a very high standard of quality. More often than not, the number of issues in an issue queue indicates the *popularity* of a project, not necessarily a lack of quality.

That said, the specific details of said issues are very important. In Figure B-5, we see a number of things that indicate an overall healthy project. There is an issue that has been marked "fixed" within the past 24 hours. Several of the open issues have code associated with them in one way or another: one that is ready for larger community review, one that has been fixed in the current version and is ready to be back-ported to Drupal 6, and one that has been reviewed and is waiting to be committed to the code. This is indicative of a healthy developer community around the project. Only two of these issues are marked "active," which indicates that they are still awaiting code to fix them.

Figure B-6 shows a different story. This is the issue queue from the Flexinode module, which was the predecessor to the current Field feature of Drupal core. At first glance, it looks similar to the Drupal issue queue that we saw earlier. Sure, there are a few more "active" issues, and none that are currently marked as having been fixed, but what's the problem?

The problem is the "Last updated" column, which indicates when a reply was last posted to the issue. In the Drupal project issue queue, shown in Figure B-5, replies are typically at most an hour or two apart, with some replies as recent as eight minutes ago! This means that at almost any given hour, people from all over the world are constantly contributing to the project. However, the last time that anyone responded to Flexinode's most recent issue was over a year ago. This is a sure sign of an abandoned module whose maintainer has lost interest.

Most modules are somewhere in between these two extremes, with a mix of issues that haven't been looked at in a while and those that have more activity. Spot-check a couple of issues by clicking them and seeing who's actually responding. Is it the maintainer, specifying what she found when she looked at the problem, or is it other desperate users who are saying, "I have this problem too. Help!"

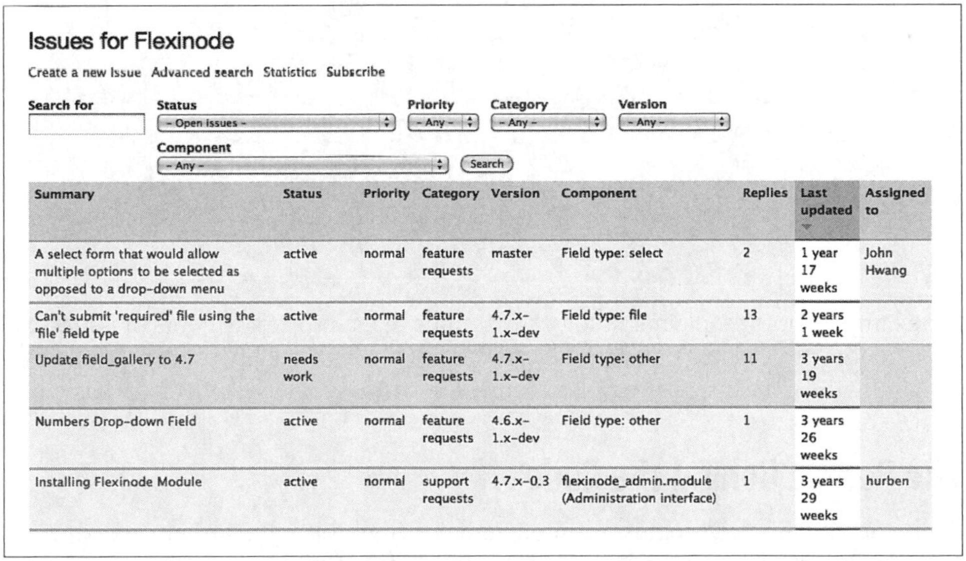

Issues for Flexinode

Create a new Issue   Advanced search   Statistics   Subscribe

Search for [ ] Status [– Open issues –] Priority [– Any –] Category [– Any –] Version [– Any –]

Component [– Any –] (Search)

Summary	Status	Priority	Category	Version	Component	Replies	Last updated	Assigned to
A select form that would allow multiple options to be selected as opposed to a drop-down menu	active	normal	feature requests	master	Field type: select	2	1 year 17 weeks	John Hwang
Can't submit 'required' file using the 'file' field type	active	normal	feature requests	4.7.x– 1.x–dev	Field type: file	13	2 years 1 week	
Update field_gallery to 4.7	needs work	normal	feature requests	4.7.x– 1.x–dev	Field type: other	11	3 years 19 weeks	
Numbers Drop–down Field	active	normal	feature requests	4.6.x– 1.x–dev	Field type: other	1	3 years 26 weeks	
Installing Flexinode Module	active	normal	support requests	4.7.x–0.3	flexinode_admin.module (Administration interface)	1	3 years 29 weeks	hurben

Figure B-6. The issue queue from Flexinode, an example of a project that has been abandoned

Code

All of Drupal's contributed modules are stored in a central code repository. You can browse a project's repository by clicking on the "Repository viewer" link on the project page, located in the bottom sidebar under the Development section. Once there, you'll see a code browser page, as pictured in Figure B-7. Scroll to the list of "heads" (the code that development releases come from) at the bottom to find the version you wish to look at, and then click the "tree" link page to see the list of files to browse for that version. Obviously, people with a PHP background are going to be able to get more out of this, but in general anyone can spot some basic best practices. Look for clearly written, documented, well-organized code that conforms to a standard coding style. Code that does not meet these criteria is harder to maintain, and harder for other developers to jump in and help with.

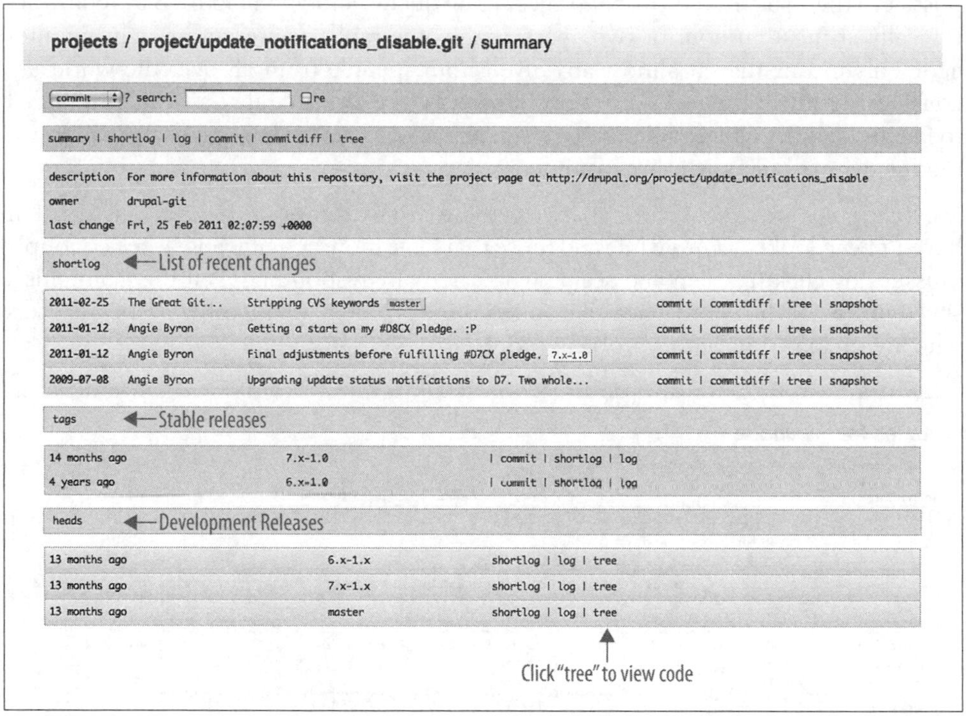

Figure B-7. Drupal.org's code browser allows inspection of a module's code, as well as its recent development activity

The People Behind the Code

Each contributor to Drupal is a unique individual who has his or her own areas of interest, expertise, background, and motivations for contributing. Some contributors are master programmers who live, breathe, sleep, and eat code. Some are backed by

Drupal development and consulting companies, and are paid to maintain their modules. Others are hobbyists who run a fan club site and maintain one or two particular modules that act as the main backbone of their community. Still others help out for the fun of it, because it feels good and they enjoy it. There are those who get code as far as they need it, toss it out there, and move on to bigger and greener pastures. And, of course, there are those who are some, all, or none of the above.

Therefore, a critical piece to evaluating a module is to also learn more about the humans behind the code. Drupal.org has a few useful tools to help.

Maintainer Activity

The first is the "View all committers" link in the project page sidebar (for example, *http://drupal.org/node/3060/committers*), which takes you to a table, shown in Figure B-8, displaying a list of the individual developers who are maintaining (or have maintained) the project. The data shown here are the *commits*, or code changes to a project, by everyone who has ever had access.

From this information, you can get a general idea of who within the project has been working on it the longest, how active each contributor is, and how much experience each has with a given project's code. A sign of a good, healthy project is lots of recent commit activity, along with numerous contributors in the list if some of the original folks are no longer around. If this list is small, and the last commit was more than several months ago—and particularly if the project's issue queue shows warning signs—it may be worth looking for alternative solutions, or perhaps offering the maintainer payment for the changes you need in order to help spark her interest again.

Committers for *Drupal core*

User	Last commit	First commit	Commits
Dries	3 hours ago	10 years ago	9944 commits
webchick	1 week ago	2 years ago	2363 commits
Gábor Hojtsy	2 weeks ago	4 years ago	1565 commits
Git Migration	9 weeks ago	9 years ago	38 commits
drumm	16 weeks ago	5 years ago	764 commits
killes@www.drop.org	3 years ago	5 years ago	506 commits
Steven	3 years ago	10 years ago	1156 commits
Kjartan	4 years ago	10 years ago	383 commits
Jeroen	9 years ago	10 years ago	101 commits

Figure B-8. A list of developers for the Drupal project, along with commit activity

User Profiles

Anytime you see a username on Drupal.org, you can click it to view the user's profile (for example, *http://drupal.org/user/35821*), as shown in Figure B-9. Although there's information here that's typical of any user profile on any site—such as first and last name, a list of interests, gender, and country—there are a few elements that are particularly useful if you're looking to find out more about the person behind the code.

The user profile begins with a brief blurb about the user's contributions to Drupal. This typically mentions modules that he has written, various initiatives that he's a part of (such as the documentation team or site administration team), and other such data. This information can help provide insight into the person's motivations and background.

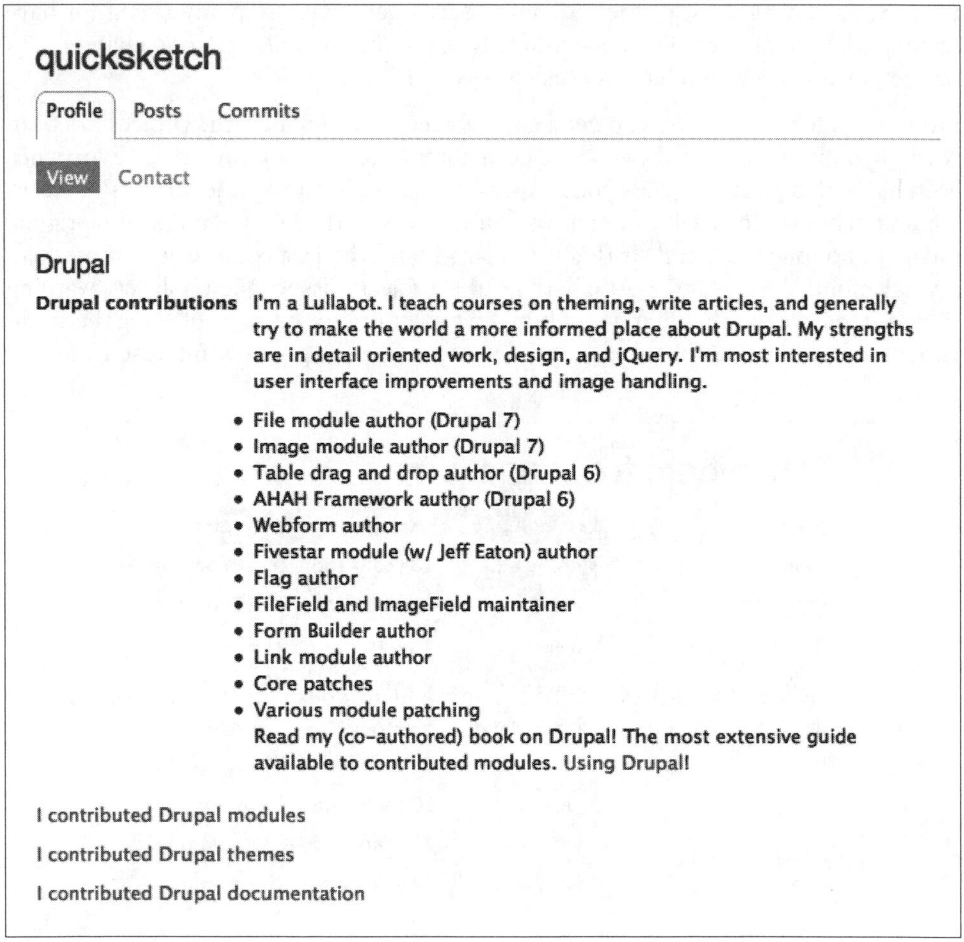

quicksketch

| Profile | Posts | Commits |

View   Contact

Drupal

Drupal contributions I'm a Lullabot. I teach courses on theming, write articles, and generally try to make the world a more informed place about Drupal. My strengths are in detail oriented work, design, and jQuery. I'm most interested in user interface improvements and image handling.

- File module author (Drupal 7)
- Image module author (Drupal 7)
- Table drag and drop author (Drupal 6)
- AHAH Framework author (Drupal 6)
- Webform author
- Fivestar module (w/ Jeff Eaton) author
- Flag author
- FileField and ImageField maintainer
- Form Builder author
- Link module author
- Core patches
- Various module patching
  Read my (co-authored) book on Drupal! The most extensive guide available to contributed modules. Using Drupal!

I contributed Drupal modules

I contributed Drupal themes

I contributed Drupal documentation

Figure B-9. User profile page on Drupal.org

This information is followed by a series of "flags" that indicate things such as whether the person helps out with documentation, user support, and module development, as well as what Drupal conferences he has attended. Each flag is a link that displays a list of other users who have that flag checked. A user with many of these links displayed is generally much more tied into the larger Drupal community than one without.

The tabs at the top of the profile are useful as well. The Posts tab shows a list of all of the posts on Drupal.org that the user has created or responded to, including forums and issue queues. This can help gauge his overall involvement in the Drupal community and how active he is, as well as his general attitude toward others. The Commits tab is a list of the person's code commits so you can quickly take a peek at the kind of code he has committed.

The Contact link, if it's enabled, can be used to contact the contributor directly via email.

 Although it can be tempting to use the Contact form to ask maintainers support questions or to report bugs about their modules directly, this is considered bad form. Time a maintainer spends answering emails is time that is *not* spent further developing the module and helping other users who might have the same problem.

Always use a module's issue queue for reporting problems, as that method allows anyone who uses the module to respond, not just the maintainer, and allows the results to be searched by others. In general, use a maintainer's contact form only for topics that are intended to be kept private, such as requests for hire.

Note that the contact form can also be used to send a general "thanks" for a job well done; most module developers hear only about problems from their users, so it can make a maintainer's day to hear from someone who has nice things to say about the code she received for free.

Further down the profile page, there's an indication of how long the user has been a member of Drupal.org, as well as a list of the projects that the user has committed code to during that time, shown in Figure B-10. Some maintainers have 1 or 2 projects listed here, and others have 50 or more. A list consisting of many projects is usually indicative of someone who's been around awhile and likely knows what he's doing. On the other hand, *because* he has been around awhile, he might also be overextended and trying to do too many things at once, and all of his modules may be suffering as a result.

Getting Involved

By far, the best way to keep up-to-date on which modules are the most useful, and to ensure that those modules do what you need, is to actually get directly involved and help. The Drupal community offers a myriad of ways for *everyone*, from the person

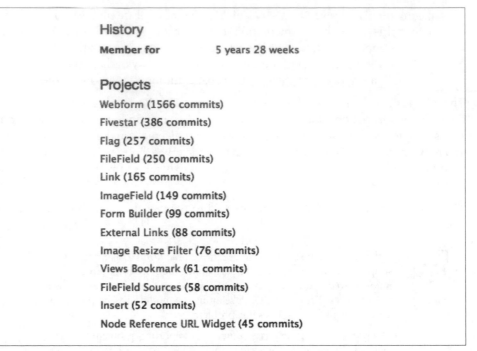

History

Member for   5 years 28 weeks

Projects

Webform (1566 commits)

Fivestar (386 commits)

Flag (257 commits)

FileField (250 commits)

Link (165 commits)

ImageField (149 commits)

Form Builder (99 commits)

External Links (88 commits)

Image Resize Filter (76 commits)

Views Bookmark (61 commits)

FileField Sources (58 commits)

Insert (52 commits)

Node Reference URL Widget (45 commits)

Figure B-10. Drupal developers have a list of projects they've committed to at the bottom of their user profiles

who just installed Drupal for the first time yesterday to the person who has been coding since she was in diapers, to give something back.

The Getting Involved handbook at *http://drupal.org/getting-involved-guide* is the main jumping-off point for ways to get involved in the Drupal project. Here are a few that are suited to nonprogrammers as well:

Issue queue cleanup

While you're evaluating modules, you'll naturally be in the issue queue anyway. Why not take a few extra minutes and look for places you might be able to clean things up? If there are two or more similar issues, mark the higher-numbered one as a "duplicate." See if a bug report is still valid, and if it's not, mark it "fixed." If you see a support request that you know the answer to, answer it. Every minute spent by someone other than the module maintainer on this type of activity is more time that she can spend improving her modules, and so this type of contribution is hugely appreciated by maintainers.

Helping with user support

If you've gotten as far as getting Drupal installed, congratulations! You now officially know enough to help someone else. Head to the Drupal forums or *#drupal-support* on *irc.freenode.net* and look for opportunities to answer other users' questions. You're guaranteed to learn a ton in the process, and might end up with a job!

Filing issues

If you come across a problem with a module, or something that you think would be really cool, file it as a detailed bug report or feature request in the module's issue queue using the guidelines at *http://drupal.org/node/317*. Remember to search using the search box and filters at the top of the issue queue first to check for an existing issue before creating one of your own.

Documentation

Did you just spend a frustrating half hour on something because there was a lack of documentation or an error in the existing documentation? Edit the page with your corrections, so that you can spare the next person the same fate. You can also join the documentation team at *http://drupal.org/contribute/documentation/join* to collaborate with others on the overall direction of Drupal's documentation.

Donations

Don't have time to contribute yourself, but have some spare change rolling around? You can donate to the Drupal Association, the legal entity that provides server infrastructure, organizes Drupal conferences, and handles fundraising for the Drupal project at *http://association.drupal.org/donate*. Many individual developers also gladly accept donations. If using someone's module has helped save you some money, give them a little back to say thanks.

Why get involved? Aside from the warm fuzzy feeling, there are a number of practical reasons, which include:

- As a general rule, more attention is paid to your support requests, bug reports, and feature requests if you are known to be a contributor to the project.

- Being an active part of the community helps forge relationships, which can lead to clients and employers.

- Being involved can help take months off of your Drupal learning curve by exposing you to discussions and individuals that you wouldn't otherwise have come across.

- You can help shape the exact direction of modules and even the Drupal core itself, so that they meet the requirements for your project.

- It's also really fun! You meet people from all over the world, and get to learn from some of the best and brightest minds out there on web design.

Looking forward to meeting you on Drupal.org!

Summary

The tips and techniques outlined in this chapter can help identify must-have modules long after this book is out of date. By assessing things such as how active a project's maintainer is, how large the user community is around a project, and how well documented and easy to read its code is, you can help make smart, future-proof choices on your module selection. And by getting involved directly in the community itself, you can meet the awesome people who make Drupal what it is, and become one of them yourself!

References

Here is a list of the resources referred to in this appendix:

- Bug report and feature request guidelines (*http://drupal.org/node/317*)
- Case studies (*http://drupal.org/cases*)
- Contribute page (*http://drupal.org/contribute*)
- Contributed module list (*http://drupal.org/project/Modules*)
- Developers list for the Drupal project (*http://drupal.org/node/3060/committers*)
- Documentation team (*http://drupal.org/contribute/documentation/join*)
- Donate money (*http://association.drupal.org/donate*)
- Drupal core project issue queue (*http://drupal.org/project/issues/drupal*)
- Drupal.org forums (*http://drupal.org/forum*)
- Drupal "Before You Start" forum (*http://drupal.org/forum/20*)
- Drupal showcase forum (*http://drupal.org/forum/25*)
- Planet Drupal (*http://drupal.org/planet*)
- Third-party resources (*http://drupal.org/node/289913*)

Modules and Themes Used in This Book

This appendix lists the modules and themes used in each project throughout the book. These are all included with the source code and are listed here for quick reference or if you would like to replicate the chapters without using the source code.

This book was written against Drupal 7.12.

Chapter 1, *Drupal Overview*

Not applicable.

Chapter 2, *Drupal Jumpstart*

Modules:

- Module Filter (*http://drupal.org/project/module_filter*)

Theme:

- Bartik (core)

Chapter 3, *Job Posting Board*

Modules:

- Advanced help (*http://drupal.org/project/advanced_help*)
- Chaos Tools (*http://drupal.org/project/ctools*)
- References (*http://drupal.org/project/references*)
- Views (*http://drupal.org/project/views*)

Theme:

- Mayo (*http://drupal.org/project/mayo*)

Chapter 4, *Media Management*

Modules:

- Media (*http://drupal.org/project/media*)
- Media: YouTube (*http://drupal.org/project/media_youtube*)
- WYSIWYG (*http://drupal.org/project/wysiwyg*)

Theme:

- Corolla (*http://drupal.org/project/corolla*)

Chapter 5, *Product Reviews*

Modules:

- Advanced help (*http://drupal.org/project/advanced_help*)
- Amazon (*http://drupal.org/project/amazon*)
- Chaos Tools (*http://drupal.org/project/ctools*)
- CSS Injector (*http://drupal.org/project/css_injector*)
- Field Group (*http://drupal.org/project/field_group*)
- Fivestar (*http://drupal.org/project/fivestar*)
- Views (*http://drupal.org/project/views*)
- Voting API (*http://drupal.org/project/votingapi*)

Theme:

- Tarski (*http://drupal.org/project/tarski*)

Chapter 6, *Event Management*

Modules:

- Advanced help (*http://drupal.org/project/advanced_help*)
- Chaos Tools (*http://drupal.org/project/ctools*)
- Calendar (*http://drupal.org/project/calendar*)
- Date (*http://drupal.org/project/date*)
- Flag (*http://drupal.org/project/flag*)
- Views (*http://drupal.org/project/views*)

Theme:

- Deco (*http://drupal.org/project/deco*)

Chapter 7, *Managing Publishing Workflows*

Modules:

- Pathauto (*http://drupal.org/project/pathauto*)
- Workbench (*http://drupal.org/project/workbench*)
- Workbench Access (*http://drupal.org/project/workbench_access*)
- Workbench Moderation (*http://drupal.org/project/workbench_moderation*)

Theme:

- Nitobe (*http://drupal.org/project/nitobe*)

Chapter 8, *Multilingual Sites*

Modules:

- Internationalization (*http://drupal.org/project/i18n*)
- Localization client (*http://drupal.org/project/l10n_client*)
- Localization update (*http://drupal.org/project/l10n_update*)
- Variable (*http://drupal.org/project/variable*)

Theme:

- Marinelli (*http://drupal.org/project/marinelli*)

Chapter 9, *Online Store*

Modules:

- Chaos Tools (*http://drupal.org/project/ctools*)
- Commerce Feeds (*http://drupal.org/project/commerce_feeds*)
- Drupal Commerce (*http://drupal.org/project/commerce*)
- Entity API (*http://drupal.org/project/entity*)
- Feeds (*http://drupal.org/project/feeds*)
- Rules (*http://drupal.org/project/rules*)
- Views (*http://drupal.org/project/ctools*)

Theme:

- AT Commerce (*http://drupal.org/project/at-commerce*)

Major Changes Between Drupal 6 and 7

A lot of basic concepts from Drupal 6 are still present in Drupal 7, but there have also been lots of changes in the new version. The Drupal 7 release cycle was the longest to date, which gave developers a lot of time to pack in a ton of new features as well as make some significant changes to existing features. For those people coming from Drupal 6, we'll take a look at some of the biggest changes and note any "gotchas" to look out for.

New Features in Drupal 7

Let's start off with things that are new in Drupal 7 core. Some of these are brand-spanking-new, while others are features that used to be in contributed modules for Drupal 6 that have now been integrated into core. These are the biggest items from a long list that you will notice right away and will have an impact on your new sites.

New Themes

The first thing that many people will be struck by with Drupal 7 is that it looks quite different when you first install it. There is a new default core theme, named Bartik, shown in Figure D-1. Bartik was written from the ground up as a new, modern design that also provides a guideline for theming best practices. Bartik offers many more regions for structuring the site than Drupal 6's old default theme, Garland. Like Garland, it also has "Color module integration," which lets you recolor sections of the theme, such as header background and links, in the appearance settings.

To help visually separate Drupal's backend and frontend, Drupal 7 also ships with a new theme called Seven, pictured in Figure D-2. Seven is a theme designed specifically for use in Drupal's administration section, to help provide a visual cue between tasks that only privileged users can perform (i.e., everything under the *admin/* URL and, optionally, the node edit forms), and the frontend of the site that all visitors will see.

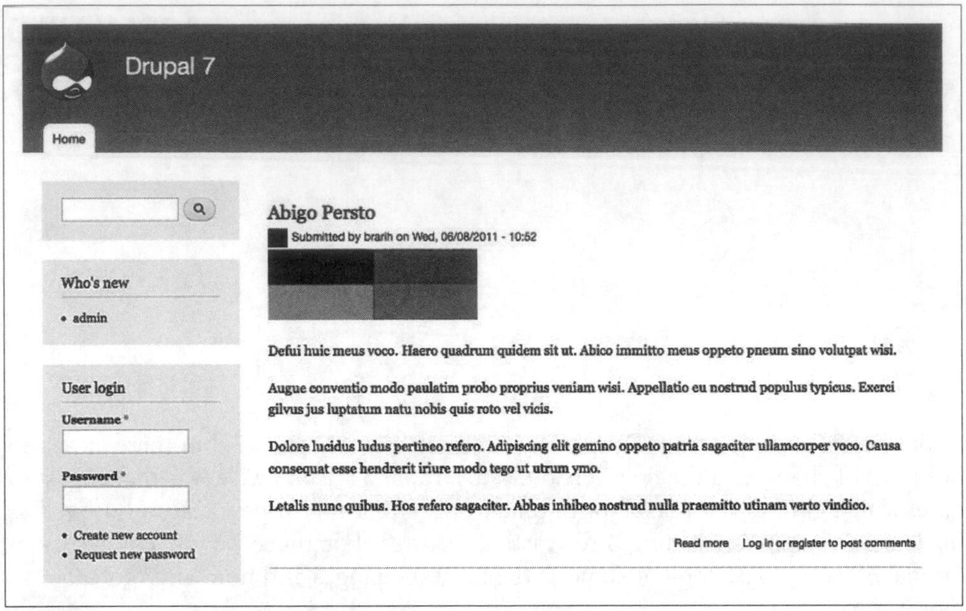

Figure D-1. Drupal 7's new default theme, Bartik

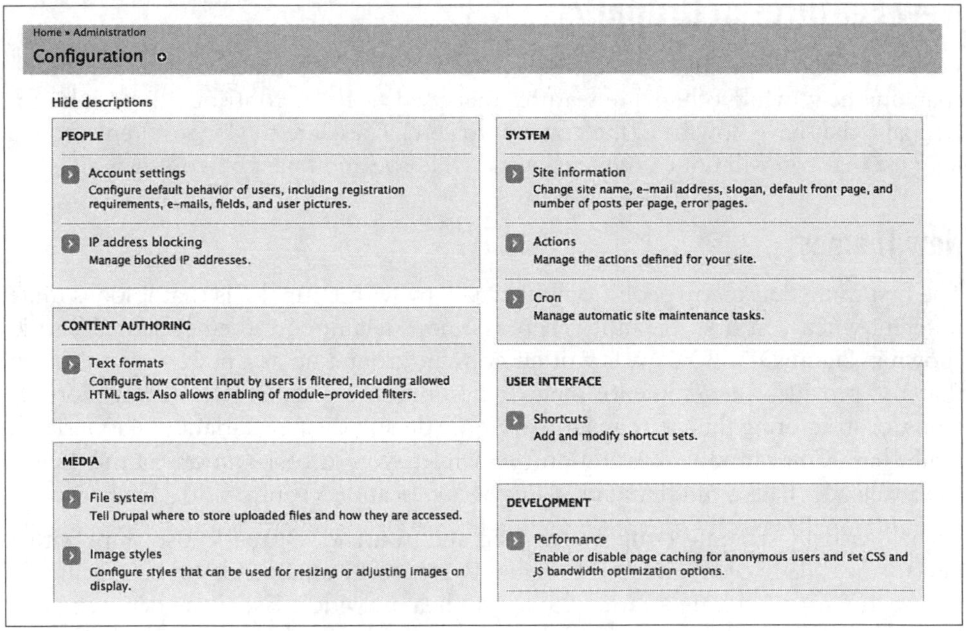

Figure D-2. Drupal 7's new default administration theme, Seven

The final new theme in Drupal 7 is called Stark. This theme isn't designed to look pretty, but rather is intended to be a tool for theme authors. When you enable Stark, you will see the bare-bones default HTML and CSS that Drupal core creates, as shown in Figure D-3. Stark provides only minimal CSS of its own—just enough to provide a basic layout so sidebars show up in the correct place. You can use Stark as a starting place for creating your own CSS-only themes. Stark shows you the raw HTML so you can dive straight into the fun of styling with CSS.

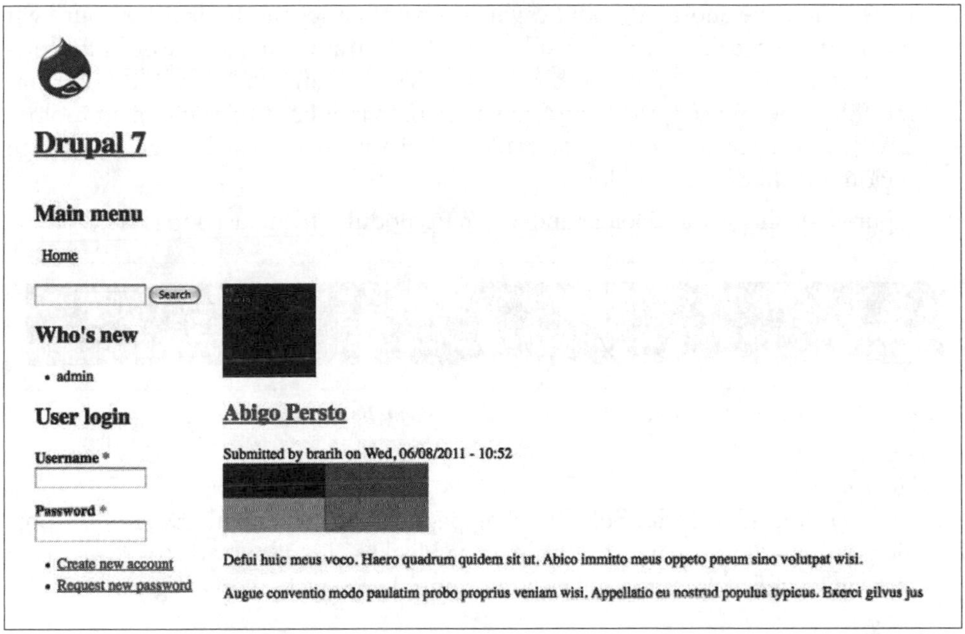

Figure D-3. Stark, a bare-bones theme for people who want to start their designs from scratch

Administration User Interface

Another thing that looks very different out of the box is the entire administrative user interface (UI) for Drupal 7. In addition to the new Seven theme, there are five new modules that have been added in order to make Drupal easier to navigate and less overwhelming. These modules are all enabled by default when you do a fresh installation of Drupal 7, but if you are upgrading from a Drupal 6 site, you'll need to enable them yourself:

Toolbar module
> This new module provides a menu of all the main administrative links across the top of the screen. It allows you to have handy access to all administrative tasks as you move around the site, without affecting the design or layout of the underlying theme.

For more advanced users and site builders, the "Administration menu" module (*http://drupal.org/project/admin_menu*) provides a more fully featured toolbar with drop-downs for subnavigation and additional helpers.

Shortcut module

While the toolbar provides links to all administrative functions, often an individual person's duties on the site will be limited to just a handful of frequently accessed links. Enter the Shortcut module, which provides a second toolbar for your own most-often-used administrative links. An administrator can provide default shortcut sets, or users with the proper permissions can create their own. If the Toolbar module is being used, the shortcuts will appear in a bar under the main toolbar navigation. There is also a Shortcuts block available, which can be placed in a page region, just like a regular block.

Figure D-4 shows the Toolbar and Shortcut modules being used together.

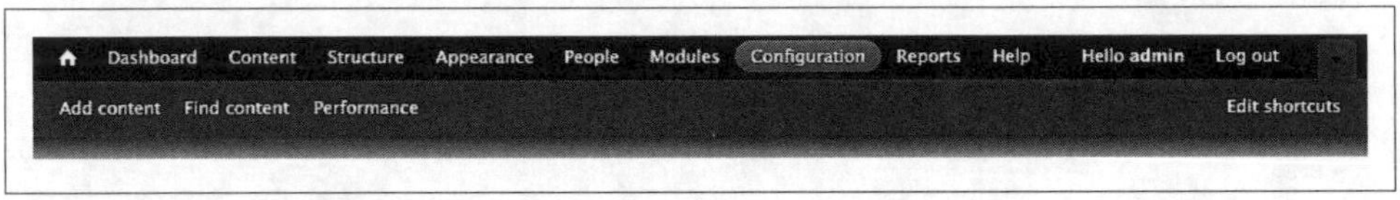

🏠	Dashboard	Content	Structure	Appearance	People	Modules	Configuration	Reports	Help	Hello admin	Log out
Add content	Find content	Performance									Edit shortcuts

Figure D-4. Drupal 7's Toolbar and Shortcut modules' menu bars

Dashboard module

This module adds a Dashboard landing page, pictured in Figure D-5, which provides a drag-and-drop interface for placing blocks. This allows you to create a nice overview page of common things you want to keep track of on a regular basis.

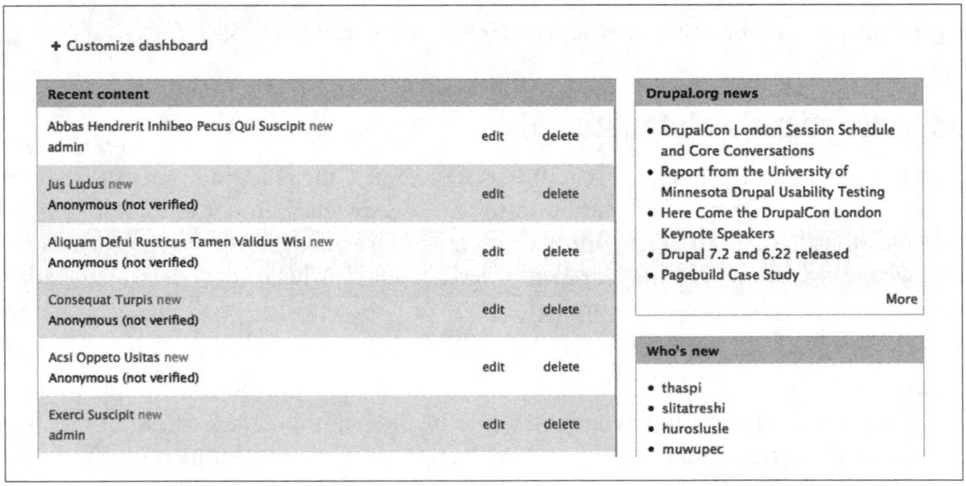

+ Customize dashboard

Recent content			Drupal.org news
Abbas Hendrerit Inhibeo Pecus Qui Suscipit new admin	edit	delete	• DrupalCon London Session Schedule and Core Conversations
Jus Ludus new Anonymous (not verified)	edit	delete	• Report from the University of Minnesota Drupal Usability Testing
Aliquam Defui Rusticus Tamen Validus Wisi new Anonymous (not verified)	edit	delete	• Here Come the DrupalCon London Keynote Speakers
Consequat Turpis new Anonymous (not verified)	edit	delete	• Drupal 7.2 and 6.22 released • Pagebuild Case Study
Acsi Oppeto Usitas new Anonymous (not verified)	edit	delete	More
Exerci Suscipit new admin	edit	delete	

Who's new
• thaspi
• slitatreshi
• huroslusle
• muwupec

Figure D-5. Blocks in the Dashboard show current site activity

Contextual Links module

If you hover over a piece of content or a block, you will see a small gear icon with a drop-down list of administrative actions you can take that pertain to that specific item, as shown in Figure D-6. This functionality is provided by the new Contextual Links module, which makes getting to the place you want to go to do work much faster since you don't have to remember or drill down to the menu in the administration panel that contains it.

Navigation
Add conten
List links
Edit menu
Configure block

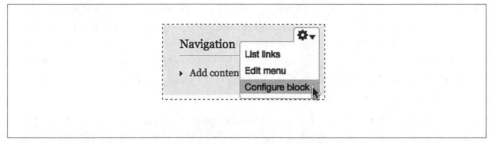

Figure D-6. Contextual links on a menu block

Overlay module

The Overlay module, pictured in Figure D-7, opens a lightbox-style pop up for performing administrative tasks, instead of taking you to a new page. This system works particularly well with contextual links, as it allows you to click a link on the frontend to be taken to the appropriate administrative section, make your changes in the overlay window, and when finished, close the window to return to the original frontend page without losing your context.

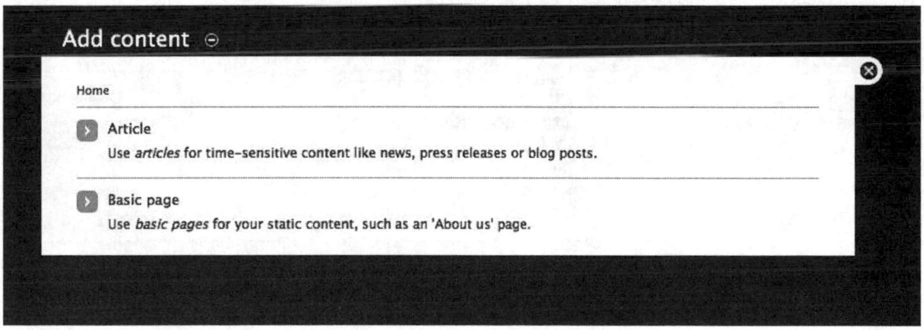

Add content
Home
Article
Use articles for time-sensitive content like news, press releases or blog posts.
Basic page
Use basic pages for your static content, such as an 'About us' page.

Figure D-7. Overlay showing the frontend of the site in the background while in administrative context

All of these features can be enabled and disabled individually, as you see fit. They do not depend on one another, but they have been designed to work well together to create a more productive administrative environment. An overview of these new modules is available in Chapter 2.

Fields

In addition to a whiz-bang new look and handy administrative tools, Drupal 7 offers some significant new site building features as well. The Content Construction Kit (CCK) was a top module in Drupal 6, used on almost all Drupal sites. Most of the functionality of CCK has now been incorporated into core as the Field module.

The field functionality in Drupal 7 also improves upon CCK in the following ways:

- Fields can not only be applied to content, but to anything in Drupal that declares itself as an "entity": users, taxonomy terms, and comments are supported out of the box, with many more options from contributed modules.

- The storage for fields is also swappable. By default, field values are stored in an SQL database like Drupal itself. However, additional modules can save field data to external services, such as Amazon S3 or Mongo DB.

Core comes bundled with a large list of field types, pictured in Figure D-8, and like CCK, ships with Text, List, Number, and Options (select lists, radios, and checkboxes) modules. Just like in Drupal 6, you can extend this list further with contributed modules.

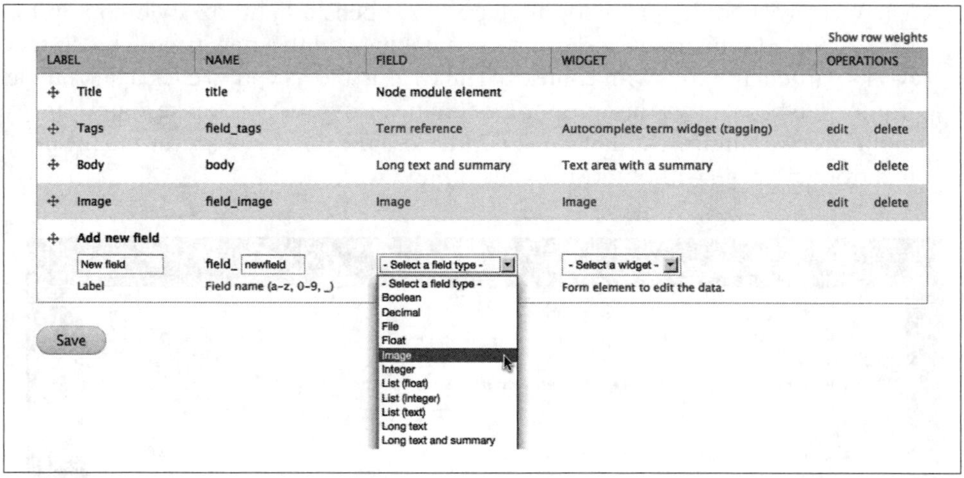

Figure D-8. The Field UI can be used to place additional data fields on any entity in the system context

You may notice that a few of the "core" CCK field types that were provided in Drupal 6 are not in this list. These are now provided by contributed modules in Drupal 7:

- The Node Reference and User Reference features are now provided by the References module (*http://drupal.org/project/references*).

- Content Permissions is now provided by the Field Permissions module (*http://drupal.org/project/field_permissions*).

- Fieldgroups are now provided by the Field Group module (*http://drupal.org/project/field_group*).
- The Content Copy module does not have a direct replacement per se, but the Features module (*http://drupal.org/project/features*) for Drupal 7 will allow you to export and import fields and content types.

There is a Drupal 7 version of the CCK module, but its main purpose is to provide an upgrade path from Drupal 6 CCK to Drupal Field. It also provides a few helper functions for special features you may have used with your Drupal 6 CCK fields, like using PHP within the field.

For an introduction to using the core Field module along with a few contributed fields, you should review Chapter 3.

Image Handling

Another group of contributed modules that has made its way into Drupal core relates to images. In Drupal 6, there was a common contributed module recipe for adding images to your content, since core did not provide any image handling. This recipe included the Filefield, Imagefield, Imagecache, and Image API modules. These are now all in Drupal 7 core itself:

- Filefield is now the core File module, which provides a "File" upload field. The File module replaces the old core Upload module.
- Imagefield is now the core Image module, and this provides an image field that can be attached to content types, users, and so on. It relies on the File module for uploading the images.
- Imagecache is now known as Image Styles in core, pictured in Figure D-9. Image Styles lets you automatically manipulate images that have been added to the site.
- Image API has been incorporated directly into the core's image handling code. It isn't visible in the UI, just as Image API was not.

You can read more about how to use the new core image handling features in Chapter 4.

Update Manager

A brand-new, exciting feature in Drupal 7 is the ability to update your modules and themes from within your Drupal administrative interface instead of having to dig into the server's filesystem. The new core Update Manager, pictured in Figure D-10, will let you know which of your modules or themes have updates available, then install the updates directly through the UI.

You can read all about the update process and using the Update Manager module in Appendix A.

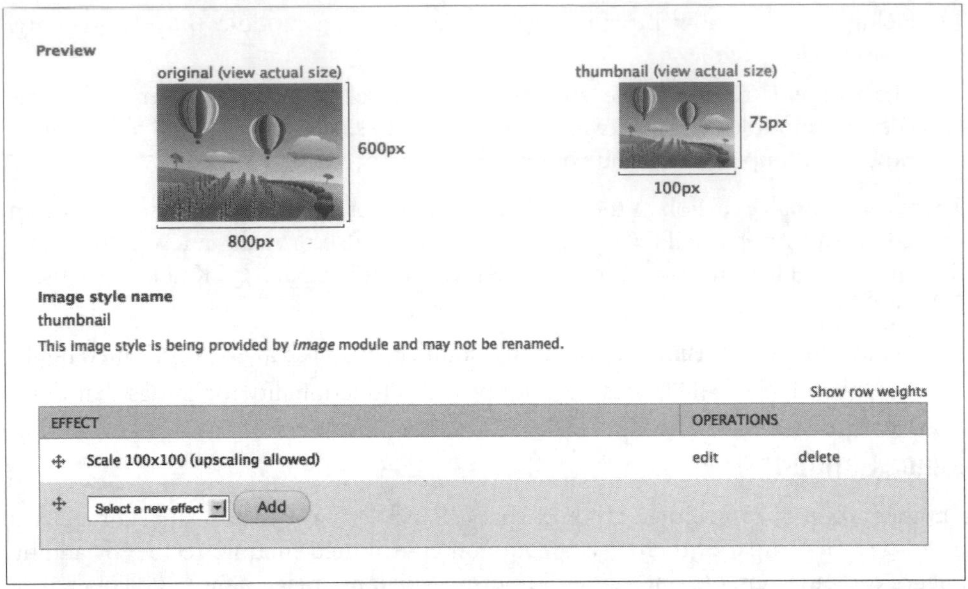

Figure D-9. Image Styles provides automatic image manipulation effects such as cropping and resizing

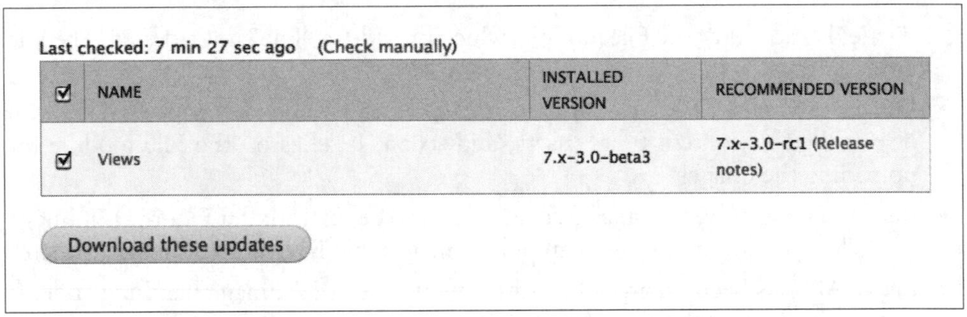

Figure D-10. Update Manager allows users to install and upgrade their modules and themes from the administrative interface

Other Nips and Tucks

There are a few other interesting things that have been added in Drupal 7, although you aren't likely to see or directly interact with them very much:

Minimal installation profile

During the installation process, you now have two profiles to choose from: Standard and Minimal. Most people will use the Standard profile, but if you want to install Drupal without any features turned on, you can use the Minimal profile instead. This way, you don't need to turn off lots of things that Drupal would normally install for you.

RDFa

Using the new Resource Description Framework (RDF) module, Drupal now outputs machine-readable metatags in site output, embedded in the HTML. Various services on the Web, such as Google, can then use this metadata to provide more context around the information, as well as tie your content to other information sources on the Web. Basic RDF is included in core now, and if your theme is using Drupal 7 theme best practices, you will have RDFa tags added to your content HTML without having to do any extra work. You can read more about RDF and Drupal at *http://drupal.org/documentation/modules/rdf*.

cron out of the box

cron is a way to run scheduled tasks on your site. This is important to keep things such as old error log entries tidy and provides functionality for things that don't necessarily happen immediately, such as content search indexing. Normally, you run cron by having your server trigger a script within Drupal, but it can be complicated to set up, and is a step often forgotten. In Drupal 7, a method fashioned after the Poor Man's Cron module (*http://drupal.org/project/poormanscron*) allows cron to be triggered in the background at set intervals when visitors load pages on your site.

Increased security

Drupal 7 includes a number of security improvements over Drupal 6, including requiring users to enter their current password in order to change it, limiting login attempts to prevent brute-force password attacks, adding a new permission for running the *update.php* script, and providing much stronger encryption to user passwords stored in the database.

Better private file handling

In Drupal 6 and below, the decision to use private or public files was a one-time choice that you had to make at the beginning of the site creation, and applied to all file uploads on the entire site. In Drupal 7, private and public files are stored in separate places, so they can be used interchangeably and you can decide on a per-file field basis whether uploads should be private (in the case of sensitive documents) or public (in the case of product thumbnails).

Changes in Drupal 7

In addition to brand-new features in Drupal 7, a few things that have been around for a while got an update.

Administration Navigation

The most notable change is obvious when you look at the administration navigation. If you go to the main administration page (*admin*), you will see that things are organized differently than they were in Drupal 6, in addition to some terms being changed. This reorganization and renaming is also apparent in the Toolbar module's list of top-level links for handling administrative tasks. There was a large user experience (UX) project for Drupal 7 called D7UX (*http://www.d7ux.org/*) that brought a fresh look to how Drupal's administrative interface is organized. The reorganization is designed to guide a new administrator intuitively by using terminology and categorization that is more accessible to the average person. For instance, you will find administration tasks for creating and managing users and permissions on the site in the People section.

While this new interface takes some getting used to, it's now much more task-oriented than before, so hopefully you'll find your way around quickly!

cron

As we mentioned previously, Drupal 7 now comes with an internal way to trigger the cron script. The preferred method to run the cron script, though, is to have a server trigger it. This is a more reliable method, and reduces the amount of work your Drupal site must do. In Drupal 6, you just needed to point the server cron to the *cron.php* file, and it would fire it off when scheduled. You could also just type the URL (*http://example.com/cron.php*) into any web browser and trigger the cron that way. In Drupal 7, more security was added to the cron URL so that not just anyone can fire the cron script on your site. When using cron in Drupal 7, you need to get a special URL for the script by going to the administrative toolbar and clicking Reports→Status Report (*admin/reports/status*), and then you will see the external link in the "Cron maintenance tasks" section of the report.

Input Formats

Input formats, renamed to "Text formats" in Drupal 7, got a major revamp in this release. You can now provide default text formats for different roles by reordering them on the administrative screen, so anonymous users can default to Filtered HTML, while editors default to Full HTML. Access to text formats is now controlled on the Permissions page, along with all other access permissions, for better consistency. And finally, a new "Plain text" format is available as a fallback for all users if no other formats are accessible.

Features Removed from Drupal 7

As things progress in the world of the Web, there are also some things that inevitably get left behind. Drupal core tries to be very focused on providing features that a majority of people would need for their sites, leaving the contributed world to add on lots of bells and whistles. This means that a few outdated features have been removed from core. Many, but not all, of these features have new modules in contrib, so you can continue using the feature it provided in core. If a feature you rely on is not fully upgraded to Drupal 7 yet, you should consider helping out in the issue queue by either supplying patches or helping to test and review the work that the developers are doing. The following modules have been removed from Drupal core:

- Blog API (*http://drupal.org/project/blogapi*) has been made into a contributed module. This module allowed desktop blogging software to post new content to, and edit existing content on, a Drupal site. The development has been slow, and so at the time of this writing the module is not fully functional in Drupal 7, nor is there an upgrade path for this feature from Drupal 6 to 7.

- The Ping module functionality, plus more, is already provided by the existing contributed Multiping (*http://drupal.org/project/multiping*) module. The work for upgrading this module to Drupal 7 has started, but at the time of this writing there is no working version available yet.

- All of the core themes were removed from Drupal 6 except for Garland. The Bluemarine theme (*http://drupal.org/project/bluemarine*), Pushbutton theme (*http://drupal.org/project/pushbutton*), and Chameleon (and Marvin) themes (*http://drupal.org/project/chameleon*) are all now contributed themes, and they all have Drupal 7 versions available.

- The Profile module has been removed from new Drupal 7 installations (the module still exists for legacy purposes), and there are two ways to achieve the same features in Drupal 7, depending on which ones you are looking for in particular. Drupal core fields can be added to any entity, not just nodes, so you can easily add fields to a user (and the user registration form) by just using core fields. The contributed Profile 2 (*http://drupal.org/project/profile2*) module provides more features, like private fields.

- The Upload module has been replaced by the core File module in Drupal 7, which provides a file upload field that can be attached to nodes, users, and so on. The Upload module has been fully deprecated.

- The Throttle module, which turned off certain site functionality in the event of a traffic spike, was deprecated due to the much better caching options that have been added to Drupal core in the last few releases. There is no contributed module to explicitly replace this feature, and it is recommended that you use Drupal's caching settings instead.

Under-the-Hood Changes

In addition to these changes in Drupal 7, there are literally hundreds of other changes under the hood. Here are some of the big ones. Although these will not affect site builders particularly, they are good to know about nonetheless:

New database abstraction layer
> Drupal 7 includes a new, object-oriented database abstraction layer, nicknamed "Database: The Next Generation" (DBTNG). This functionality provides support for many new database types in Drupal, including SQLite, Oracle, and Microsoft

SQL Server. It also provides support for advanced database features such as transactions and master/slave replication.

Automated tests

The core Testing module provides an interface for running the more than 30,000 automated tests that ship with Drupal 7. These tests are code that checks to see that Drupal's code is working, and cover functionality ranging from content creation and user registration to security filtering and more.

User interface effects

Drupal 7 ships with all kinds of new user interface enhancements for developers to use in their modules. jQuery UI now ships with Drupal core, providing drag and drop, accordions, and other visual effects. Additionally, Drupal ships with a revamped AJAX framework and new JavaScript "States" system, which allows for dependent drop-downs and other eye candy.

Improved file handling

Drupal 7's file and image API was completely revamped in Drupal 7, and is much more robust than before. Files can now be saved to and served from external services such as content delivery networks, and other modules can react when events happen to files such as saving, deleting, and downloading.

More granular theming

Thanks to the new Render API, themers now have much more control over placement of page elements, and now have access to perform cosmetic alterations without hassling a module developer.

Resources

The following resources provide more detailed information on the changes between Drupal 6 and Drupal 7:

- The *CHANGELOG.txt* file in the Drupal root directory talks about high-level changes between Drupal versions.

- Look at *http://www.unleashedmind.com/en/blog/sun/more-than-50-drupal-modules -moved-into-drupal-7* for a list of all Drupal 6 modules that are either moved to core or deprecated by functionality in Drupal 7.

- See *http://drupal.org/update/modules/6/7* for a list of all developer-facing changes between Drupal 6 and Drupal 7.

- See *http://drupal.org/update/themes/6/7* for a list of all themer-facing changes between Drupal 6 and Drupal 7.

Index

We'd like to hear your suggestions for improving our indexes. Send email to *index@oreilly.com*.

creating sample products, 362
product type configuration, 359
product type fields, 358
setup, 359
Profile module, 455
project pages, 47
published and unpublished content, 295
publishing workflow management, 263
content access control, 266
content management tools, 265
editorial workflow, 266

R

rating and voting plug-in modules, 197
Recent log entries, 24
Recipe module, 228
Redirect module, 275
reference fields, adding, 100–107
field order, 103
References module, 82, 100
reference fields, adding, 100
use in making content types, 92
regions, 34
Relation module, 100
Relations fieldset, 270
releases, 47
reports section, Administrative interface, 24
resizing images, 155
Resource Description Framework (RDF)
module, 453
Résumé file field settings, 109
Résumé title field settings, 110
Review content type, 168–177
content display settings, 175
file field settings, 169
permissions, 172
small display settings, image file type, 176
Tags field settings, 170
Teaser display settings, 175
Revisioning module, 68
right-to-left languages, support in Drupal, 310
roles, 21, 53
rotating images, 155
RSS view mode, 89
Rules module, 349, 383–387
rule processing logic, 384

S

scaling and cropping images, 156
scaling images, 156
Schrauwen, Benjamin, 66
scripts, 6
Search index view mode, 89
Search module, 195, 222–223
Search result view mode, 89
Secure Pages module, 402
security
filters, 181
Text formats and security, 179
select list, 237
Select list widget, 86
server-side includes (SSI), 6
Service Links module, 193
settings.php, 410
Seven theme, 76, 445
shopping cart, 395
Signup module, 233
Single on/off checkbox, 86
site configuration example, 25
site navigation, managing, 40
site themes, 34
site-wide language-dependent variables, 333
sites directory, 409
spam prevention, 66
SQL, 115
SSI (server-side Includes), 6
stack, 8
standard and minimum installation profiles,
452
Stark theme, 74, 447
states, 295
Status field, 358
Status reports, 24
stream wrappers, 190
Strings module, 333
Structure administration, 24
summaries, 27
Summary fieldset, 214
Support forums, 16
supporting content types, 15
Sweaver module, 78

T

t( ) function, 311
Tax and Tax UI modules, 357

About the Authors

Angela Byron is an open source evangelist, and has been called a Drupal freak by those in the know. She got her start as a Google Summer of Code student in 2005 and since then, she has immersed herself in the Drupal community. Her work includes coding and reviewing patches, creating and contributing to modules and themes, testing and providing quality assurance efforts within the project, improving documentation, and providing user support on forums and IRC. Angela is on the board of directors for the Drupal Association, and helps drive community growth by leading initiatives to help get new contributors involved. She is the Drupal 7 core co-maintainer, and leads a development team of 1,000 contributors whose efforts became Drupal 7.

Addison Berry is deeply involved with Drupal and takes part in many aspects of both the software and the community. She contributes patches to core Drupal, maintains several contributed modules, and is active in various mentoring programs such as the Drupal Dojo group and Google's Highly Open Participation (GHOP) program. Addison helps maintain the drupal.org website, and is a permanent member of the Drupal Association General Assembly. Her work focuses on improving Drupal documentation, and she has worked to provide a wide range of tutorials covering all aspects of Drupal from community involvement to code.

Bruno De Bondt has been theming and developing with Drupal since 2005, specializing in independent media sites. After stumbling upon Drupal while looking for an open source CMS to build a major Belgian citizen journalism website, he was captivated with its flexibility and the project's community. His contributions to Drupal include documentation and usability testing, with a focus on multimedia, and modules that improve editorial workflows.

Colophon

The animal on the cover of *Using Drupal* is a dormouse. Dormice are part of the *Gliridae* family and originally come from Africa and Southern Europe. There are many species of this rodent, but the most popular and common one on the pet market is the African dormouse. The other known dormice are the "common dormouse" or the "hazel mouse," and most resemble small squirrels. Their name is derived from the French word *dormir*, which means to sleep—significant because dormice hibernate for as long as six months, or longer if the weather is cool, awaking only briefly to eat food they stored nearby. During the summer months, they accumulate fat in their bodies, allowing them to hibernate for such long periods of time.

On average, dormice are about four inches long, not including the two-inch bushy tail. They have rounded ears, large eyes, and thick, soft, reddish-brown fur. Dormice have an excellent sense of hearing and use a range of different vocalizations to signal each other. They are very playful, social, and personable animals (more so if you raise them from a young age). Their playfulness consists of flips, climbing rope, and leaping and jumping; they are nocturnal, so they play mostly at night. Being left alone may cause them to become stressed and unhappy, as they thrive on interaction with others.

Dormice feed on fruit, insects, berries, flowers, seeds, and nuts, and they are especially partial to hazelnuts. They are unique among other rodents because they lack a "cecum," a pouch connected to the colon of the large intestine, which is used in fermenting vegetable matter. Dormice breed once or twice a year and produce an average litter of four young. Their average lifespan is a somewhat short five years. They are born hairless, and their eyes don't open until about 18 days after birth, rendering them helpless at birth. They become sexually mature after the end of their first hibernation.

The cover image is from an unknown source. The cover font is Adobe ITC Garamond. The text font is Linotype Birka; the heading font is Adobe Myriad Condensed; and the code font is LucasFont's TheSansMonoCondensed.

Have it your way.

O'Reilly eBooks

- Lifetime access to the book when you buy through oreilly.com
- Provided in up to four DRM-free file formats, for use on the devices of your choice: PDF, .epub, Kindle-compatible .mobi, and Android .apk
- Fully searchable, with copy-and-paste and print functionality
- Alerts when files are updated with corrections and additions

oreilly.com/ebooks/

Safari Books Online

- Access the contents and quickly search over 7000 books on technology, business, and certification guides
- Learn from expert video tutorials, and explore thousands of hours of video on technology and design topics
- Download whole books or chapters in PDF format, at no extra cost, to print or read on the go
- Get early access to books as they're being written
- Interact directly with authors of upcoming books
- Save up to 35% on O'Reilly print books

See the complete Safari Library at safari.oreilly.com

O'REILLY®

Get even more for your money.

Join the O'Reilly Community, and register the O'Reilly books you own. It's free, and you'll get:

- $4.99 ebook upgrade offer
- 40% upgrade offer on O'Reilly print books
- Membership discounts on books and events
- Free lifetime updates to ebooks and videos
- Multiple ebook formats, DRM FREE
- Participation in the O'Reilly community
- Newsletters
- Account management
- 100% Satisfaction Guarantee

Signing up is easy:

1. Go to: oreilly.com/go/register
2. Create an O'Reilly login.
3. Provide your address.
4. Register your books.

Note: English-language books only

To order books online:

oreilly.com/store

For questions about products or an order:

orders@oreilly.com

To sign up to get topic-specific email announcements and/or news about upcoming books, conferences, special offers, and new technologies:

elists@oreilly.com

For technical questions about book content:

booktech@oreilly.com

To submit new book proposals to our editors:

proposals@oreilly.com

O'Reilly books are available in multiple DRM-free ebook formats. For more information:

oreilly.com/ebooks

Spreading the knowledge of innovators   oreilly.com